THE GREENWOOD ENCYCLOPEDIA OF FOLKTALES AND FAIRY TALES

ADVISORY BOARD MEMBERS

THE GREENWOOD ENCYCLOPEDIA OF FOLKTALES AND FAIRY TALES

Volume 1: A–F

Edited by
Donald Haase

GREENWOOD PRESS
Westport, Connecticut · London

Library of Congress Cataloging-in-Publication Data

The Greenwood encyclopedia of folktales and fairy tales / edited by Donald Haase.
　　p. cm.
　　Includes bibliographical references and index.
　　ISBN-13: 978-0-313-33441-2 ((set) : alk. paper)
　　ISBN-13: 978-0-313-33442-9 ((vol. 1) : alk. paper)
　　ISBN-13: 978-0-313-33443-6 ((vol. 2) : alk. paper)
　　ISBN-13: 978-0-313-33444-3 ((vol. 3) : alk. paper)
　　1. Folklore—Encyclopedias. 2. Tales—Encyclopedias. 3. Fairy
tales—Encyclopedias. I. Haase, Donald.
　　GR74.G73 2008
　　398.203—dc22　　　2007031698

British Library Cataloguing in Publication Data is available.

Library of Congress Catalog Card Number: 2007031698

ISBN-13: 978-0-313-33441-2 (set)
　　　　978-0-313-33442-9 (vol. 1)
　　　　978-0-313-33443-6 (vol. 2)
　　　　978-0-313-33444-3 (vol. 3)

First published in 2008

Greenwood Press, 88 Post Road West, Westport, CT 06881
An imprint of Greenwood Publishing Group, Inc.
www.greenwood.com

Printed in the United States of America

The paper used in this book complies with the
Permanent Paper Standard issued by the National
Information Standards Organization (Z39.48–1984).

10　9　8　7　6　5　4　3　2　1

CONTENTS

LIST OF ENTRIES

Volume 3: Q–Z

PREFACE

The Greenwood Encyclopedia of Folktales and Fairy Tales offers English-speaking readers a unique introduction to the burgeoning field of folktale and fairy-tale studies. Interest in the subject is not new, of course. Nonetheless, despite almost two centuries of scholarly study and popular interest, and despite the dynamic growth of fairy-tale studies and the creative revitalization of the genre over the last thirty to forty years, there is to date no reference work in English that offers an encyclopedic treatment of the fairy tale's multifaceted existence around the world and the new knowledge that scholars have generated about it. In other words, there has been no central English-language resource that teachers, students, scholars, and other interested readers could consult to find reliable information about folktales and fairy tales in a global context. This encyclopedia is an effort to fill this gap. The scope of this work is accordingly broad in terms of its geographic and cultural coverage, its historical range, its disciplinary breadth, and its topical variety.

Scope and Coverage

Geographic-Cultural Scope. The encyclopedia's coverage is global and multicultural. It extends beyond Europe and North America to include information about significant individuals, titles, and traditions from regions and cultures throughout the world. While every attempt has been made to offer worldwide coverage, the finite nature of a three-volume encyclopedia makes it impossible to include every discrete tale tradition. Consequently, coverage is necessarily representative and not comprehensive or exhaustive.

Historical Scope. In terms of its historical scope, this encyclopedia ranges from antiquity to the present. Recent scholarship has produced a wealth of new, well-documented information about the relation of fairy tales not only to medieval literature but also to ancient literature and culture. Therefore, it is now possible to include historically accurate coverage of periods predating the birth of the literary fairy tale in the early modern period.

Disciplinary Scope. A wide range of disciplines is represented throughout this encyclopedia. Folklorists, anthropologists, ethnologists, children's literature specialists, film scholars, and scholars of literary and cultural studies have all contributed in different but useful ways to the study of folktales and fairy tales. It is a fundamental premise of this encyclopedia that multi- and interdisciplinary perspectives are vital to our understanding of these genres. Accordingly, the contributors who have written the entries for this encyclopedia do so from the vantage point of their individual disciplines. While the folklorist may write about a particular tale or motif from a perspective decidedly different from that of a specialist in children's literature—invoking different texts and using different terms, analytical concepts, and perspectives—each will produce useful insights and information. Juxtaposed, these diverse approaches will stimulate fresh ideas and new questions, leading the reader in different, perhaps unexpected directions. Taken together, the distinct voices speaking throughout this encyclopedia offer insights into the possibilities for fairy-tale studies and demonstrate the rich texture of this multidisciplinary field of study.

Topical Scope. Because the potential number of topics reaches into the thousands, a judicious selection was necessary. The topics covered were chosen (1) to provide representative global coverage; (2) to emphasize matters of fundamental importance in the field of fairy-tale studies; (3) to highlight important developments in the field of fairy-tale studies since roughly 1970, when the field was revitalized by cultural forces and by a thorough critical reevaluation of the fairy-tale tradition; (4) to signal emerging trends in the production and reception of fairy tales; and (5) to highlight important but otherwise neglected dimensions of fairy-tale studies. In selecting topics, I also took into account the topics and tales that are covered in contemporary courses and anthologies and that therefore may be of special interest to students.

Entries

The encyclopedia's 670 entries, many of which are illustrated, fall into the following eight categories:

1. **Cultural/National/Regional/Linguistic Groups.** Entries in this category provide succinct introductions to the narrative traditions of specific groups. In some instances, the coverage is defined by linguistic, cultural, ethnic, or national categories (e.g., French Canadian tales, Japanese tales, Slavic tales, Spanish tales); in other cases, the coverage is organized in broader geographic terms (e.g., African tales, Pacific Island tales, Scandinavian tales, South Asian tales).
2. **Genres.** This category includes not only entries elucidating how scholars have understood the principal terms "folktale" and "fairy tale" but also entries discussing many other fundamental genres and subgenres at the core of folktale and fairy-tale studies (such as animal tale, cautionary tale, didactic tale, wonder tale, etc.). Entries in this group also describe genres that play a significant role in the history of the fairy tale and in the discourse of fairy-tale studies (e.g., ballad, cante fable, epic, legend, etc.).
3. **Critical Terms, Concepts, and Approaches.** Entries in this category describe the terminology, ideas, and methods of scholars specializing in the study of folktales and fairy tales. These entries define the fundamental vocabulary of oral

narrative research and fairy-tale studies—from "adaptation," "anthropological approaches," and "authenticity" to "tale type," "urform," and "variant."

4. **Motifs, Themes, Characters, Tales, and Tale Types.** This category consists of especially important subjects selected from the very corpus of folktales and fairy tales and includes topics such as "Ali Baba," "Beauty and the Beast," "Spinning," "Violence," and "Witch."

5. **Eras, Periods, Movements, and Other Contexts.** Entries in this group address important historical, intellectual, and cultural contexts—colonialism, magical realism, and postmodernism, for example—that helped to shape both the production and reception of folktales and fairy tales.

6. **Media, Performance, and Other Cultural Forms.** This category includes entries focusing on manifestations of the fairy tale in a variety of expressive and cultural forms, from "Animation," "Art," and "Internet" to "Puppet Theater," "Storytelling," and "Tourism."

7. **Television, Film, Animation, and Video.** This category encompasses entries dealing with the fairy tale's role in visual culture, from "Bluebeard Films" to "*The Wizard of Oz*."

8. **Individual Authors, Editors, Collectors, Translators, Filmmakers, Artists/ Illustrators, Composers, Scholars, and Titles.** Entries in this category provide information about a wide range of individuals and titles that have played a role in the history of folktales, fairy tales, and the scholarship about them. In no way exhaustive, these entries were chosen to offer a global mix of historical and contemporary figures, including a selection of those who are well-known internationally for their key contributions and canonized works (e.g., Charles Perrault, Jacob and Wilhelm Grimm, Hans Christian Andersen, and Angela Carter) and those historically overlooked or emerging individuals who deserve more attention from fairy-tale scholars (e.g., Mary W. Wilkins Freeman, Neil Gaiman, Miyazaki Hayao, Luisa Valenzuela, and Tawada Yoko).

Each entry contains cross-references to related topics that may deepen the reader's understanding and provide opportunities for further exploration and discovery. Cross-references are signaled in the body of an entry by words appearing in **boldface type** and, where appropriate, by a "See also" section following the entry. Terms that occur in nearly every entry—for instance "folktale" and "fairy tale"—are marked as cross-references only in those instances where the further exploration would be especially illuminating for understanding the topic at hand.

The Further Reading list that follows the entry text provides the reader with suggestions for pursuing additional research on that topic. In some cases, "readings" include not only printed books and essays but also Internet resources and visual materials such as DVDs. Whenever possible, reliable and authoritative readings in English are included. Given the encyclopedia's global scope, of course, readings in languages other than English are also offered; and in a few instances relevant readings in English may not be available at all. Many foundational works of fairy-tale scholarship are written in languages other than English, and while such works might be linguistically inaccessible to some readers, the expert contributors to this encyclopedia have done a great service in synthesizing and summarizing the research and knowledge of scholars from around the world.

Bibliography and Resources

The encyclopedia concludes with an extensive section devoted to Bibliography and Resources reflecting the project's multicultural and multidisciplinary orientation. The primary and secondary literature related to folktales and fairy tales is enormous, and even the extensive selection offered here constitutes only a sampling and starting point for anyone interested in pursuing further research. The bibliography has four divisions. The first offers a list of useful collections, editions, anthologies, and translations of folktales, fairy tales, and related primary texts (such as fantasy, legend, and myth). The second includes a selection of scholarship devoted to the folktale, fairy tale, and related areas of study (such as children's literature, folklore, and illustration). The third division provides a list of especially important journals and serial publications. I have included the URLs for those that have Web sites, although the existence of a Web site does not necessarily indicate that the publication itself is available online. Many scholarly journals, of course, are available in electronic form online through libraries and subscription services. The fourth division offers an annotated list of selected Web sites relevant to the study of folktales and fairy tales. Internet resources pose a special challenge for the student or scholar seeking reliable texts or accurate information in digital form. In my selection, I have endeavored to list sites that have had a stable existence and in my judgment are knowledgeable, reliable, and useful.

Also included is a Guide to Tale-Type, Motif, Migratory Legend, and Ballad References Used in the Entries that describes the various classification systems used in the entries. These systems defining such things as tale types and motif and ballad numbers are well known to folklorists but will likely be unfamiliar to students and interested general users. A Guide to Related Topics groups entries by broad topical categories and allows users to more easily trace important ideas, themes, concepts, and connections across the more than 600 entries. The extensive Introduction places the current state of folktale and fairy-tale studies into useful context, especially for nonspecialist readers.

These three volumes are offered as a resource for users interested not only in looking back at the history of the folktale and fairy tale but also in looking forward to a new century of fairy-tale production and scholarship—a time in which tales can be produced and disseminated quickly in new media and as transnational phenomena. With its broad scope and wide range of topics, this encyclopedia strives to offer a rich and representative overview of an infinitely diverse worldwide phenomenon, to encourage exploration beyond each reader's individual realm of experience and expertise, and to promote thinking, reading, writing, and discussion about folktales and fairy tales across disciplinary boundaries.

ACKNOWLEDGMENTS

On the path to completing a project of this kind, an editor inevitably incurs an enormous debt to many others—every one a magic helper. I am especially indebted to my editorial assistants, Helen Callow and Juliana Wilth. Helen not only took the lead in managing the daunting and time-consuming process of tracking more than 100 contributors and nearly 700 entries, but also provided endlessly cheerful and indispensable assistance in research and editing. Juliana, in addition to serving as translator, took charge of researching illustrations and acquiring permissions, an equally demanding and indispensable responsibility. The words "I could not have done this without them" were never meant more sincerely. Diana Tomsche also provided editorial assistance in the project's earliest stages, and I am grateful to her for the valuable contributions she made. For sound advice in developing the list of topics and consulting on editorial matters, my Advisory Board deserves special thanks and recognition. I am also grateful to Laura Smith and Nancy Stair for their help during the copyediting process. The debt of gratitude I owe my editor at Greenwood Press, John Wagner, is large. His wise counsel and patience kept me and this project on track.

Special thanks are also due to: John Callow, who volunteered his time and expertise to design the contributors' Web site and provide technical assistance; Karen Bacsanyi, who facilitated our research in the Eloise Ramsey Collection of Literature for Young People in the Wayne State University Libraries; my departmental colleague Laura Kline, who provided invaluable advice concerning Slavic topics; Louise Speed, who has provided both moral support and practical assistance; and Amanda Donigian, whose expert administrative assistance in my home department enabled this project at every stage. I want to express my special appreciation to my colleague Anne E. Duggan, whose support of this project and willingness to help in extraordinary ways at every stage, even in the eleventh hour, has meant a great deal.

For financial support of the work on this encyclopedia, I am grateful to Dean Robert Thomas of the College of Liberal Arts and Sciences at Wayne State University. I am also grateful to Walter Edwards, Director of the Wayne State University Humanities Center, for the Resident Scholars Grant that provided research space and financial support for the editorial work on this project.

At the heart of this encyclopedia, of course, is the work of the international team of contributors, every one of whom deserves my profound thanks for their collaboration. Their work represents an extraordinary global effort.

Finally, I wish to thank Connie Haase, who has supported my work in countless ways and reminded me all along this journey that there will be life after the encyclopedia.

GUIDE TO TALE-TYPE, MOTIF, MIGRATORY LEGEND, AND BALLAD REFERENCES USED IN THE ENTRIES

Tale-Type Numbers and Names

Folklorists do not always refer to tales by their individual titles. Some tales told in oral tradition might not even have a fixed title in the same way that a published tale usually would. Instead, folklorists often refer to the *tale type* to which a certain narrative belongs. Folklorists have developed a system for classifying tale types using a number and name. The original classification system developed by Antti Aarne in 1910 was revised and enlarged by Stith Thompson in 1961. That revised classification was thoroughly overhauled by Hans-Jörg Uther in 2004. Additional tale-type catalogues for specific cultures have been developed, but they usually build on the Aarne-Thompson or the Aarne-Thompson-Uther classifications. The following abbreviations are used throughout this encyclopedia to refer to tale types:

ATU = Aarne-Thompson-Uther
Example: ATU 333, Little Red Riding Hood
Example: ATU 510B*, The Princess in the Chest
Source: Uther, Hans-Jörg. *The Types of International Folktales: A Classification and Bibliography Based on the System of Antti Aarne and Stith Thompson*. 3 volumes. Helsinki: Academia Scientiarum Fennica, 2004.

AT or AaTh = Aarne-Thompson
Example: AT 780A, The Cannibalistic Brothers
Source: Aarne, Antti. *The Types of the Folktale: A Classification and Bibliography*. Translated and enlarged by Stith Thompson. 2nd revision. 1961. Helsinki: Academia Scientiarum Fennica, 1987.

Motif Numbers and Names

The *motifs* out of which tales are constructed recur in many different contexts. Folklorist Stith Thompson has classified these recurring motifs with a letter-number combination and descriptive label. Motif references throughout this encyclopedia are based on Thompson's motif index and appear as follows:

Example: Motif D735, Disenchantment by Kiss
Source: Thompson, Stith. *Motif-Index of Folk-Literature: A Classification of Narrative Elements in Folktales, Ballads, Myths, Fables, Mediaeval Romances, Exempla, Fabliaux, Jest-Books, and Local Legends.* Revised and enlarged edition. 6 volumes. 1955–58. Bloomington: Indiana University Press, 1975.

Migratory Legend Numbers

Like tale types, *migratory legends* have also been classified and given numbers and names. The standard classification system is that of Reidar Thoralf Chistiansen. Occasional references to migratory legends are found throughout this encyclopedia and appear as follows:

ML = Migratory Legend
Example: ML 6035, Fairies Assist a Farmer in His Work
Source: Christiansen, Reidar Thoralf. *The Migratory Legends: A Proposed List of Types with a Systematic Catalogue of the Norwegian Variants.* 1958. Helsinki: Academia Scientiarum Fennica, 1992.

Ballad Numbers

When citing English-language ballads, scholars refer to the collection of traditional ballads published by Francis James Child. Such references occur occasionally in this encyclopedia and are given as follows:

Example: Child 2
Source: Child, Francis James. *The English and Scottish Popular Ballads.* 5 volumes. Boston: Houghton Mifflin, 1882–98.

GUIDE TO RELATED TOPICS

Critical Terms, Concepts, and Approaches

Adaptation
Anthropological Approaches
Archetype
Archives
Authenticity
Collecting, Collectors
Comparative Method
Conduit Theory
Contamination
Context
Diffusion
Editing, Editors
Ethnographic Approaches
Fakelore
Feminism
Fieldwork
Folk
Folklore
Function
Gender
Historic-Geographic Method
Hybridity, Hybridization
Informant
Intertextuality
Linguistic Approaches
Memory
Metafiction
Monogenesis
Moral
Motif
Motifeme
Mythological Approaches
Oicotype

Oral Theory
Performance
Polygenesis
Psychological Approaches
Sociohistorical Approaches
Structuralism
Tale Type
Translation
Trauma and Therapy
Urform
Variant

Cultural/National/Regional/Linguistic Groups

African American Tales
African Tales
Albanian Tales
Australian and Aotearoan/New Zealand
    Tales
Aztec Tales
Celtic Tales
Chinese Tales
Dutch Tales
Egyptian Tales
English Tales
Estonian Tales
Finnish Tales
French Canadian Tales
French Tales
German Tales
Greek Tales
Inca Tales
Indian Ocean Tales
Inuit Tales

Iranian Tales
Italian Tales
Japanese Popular Culture
Japanese Tales
Jewish Tales
Korean Tales
Latin American Tales
Maya Tales
Native American Tales
North American Tales
Pacific Island Tales
Portuguese Tales
Russian Tales
Scandinavian Tales
Slavic Tales
South Asian Tales
Spanish Tales

Eras, Periods, Movements, and Other Contexts

Anti-Semitism
Childhood and Children
Classical Antiquity
Colonialism
Faerie and Fairy Lore
Feminism
Gay and Lesbian Tales
Japanese Popular Culture
Magical Realism
Middle Ages
Nationalism
Négritude, Créolité, and Folktale
Pedagogy
Politics
Postmodernism
Race and Ethnicity
Salon

Genres

Anecdote
Animal Tale
Anti-Fairy Tale
Aphorisms
Ballad
Bawdy Tale
Beech Mountain Jack Tale
Bible, Bible Tale
La bibliothèque bleue
Broadside

Cante Fable
Cartoons and Comics
Cautionary Tale
Chain Tale
Chapbook
Conte de fées
Cumulative Tale
Didactic Tale
Epic
Erotic Tales
Etiologic Tale
Exemplum, Exempla
Fable
Fabliau, Fabliaux
Fairy Tale
Fantasy
Feminist Tales
Folktale
Frame Narrative
Ghost Story
Graphic Novel
Incantation
Jack Tales
Jātaka
Jest and Joke
Legend
Literary Fairy Tale
Märchen
Memorate
Myth
Nonsense Tale
Novel
Novella
Opera
Pantomime
Parable
Parody
Poetry
Proverbs
Puppet Theater
Religious Tale
Riddle
Saga
Saint's Legend
Simple Forms
Tall Tale
Theater
Unfinished Tale
Urban Legend
Wonder Tale
Young Adult Fiction

Individuals

Animators and Filmmakers

Avery, Frederick "Tex"
Burton, Tim
Davenport, Tom
Disney, Walt
Duvall, Shelley
Henson, Jim
Khemir, Nacer
Méliès, Georges
Miyazaki Hayao
Pasolini, Pier Paolo
Reiniger, Lotte
Trnka, Jiří
Walt Disney Company

Artists/Illustrators

Amano Yoshitaka
Anno Mitsumasa
Bachelier, Anne
Beskow, Elsa
Bilibin, Ivan
Crane, Walter
Disney, Walt
Doré, Gustave
Dulac, Edmund
Ekman, Fam
Froud, Brian
Gág, Wanda
Grimm, Ludwig Emil
Housman, Laurence
Innocenti, Roberto
Kittelsen, Theodor
Mizuno Junko
Nielsen, Kay
Nyström, Jenny
Parrish, Maxfield
Rackham, Arthur
Rego, Paula
Richter, Ludwig
S., Svend Otto
Schwind, Moritz von
Sendak, Maurice
Smith, Kiki
Spiegelman, Art
Steig, William
Ubbelohde, Otto
Ungerer, Tomi
Vess, Charles

Walt Disney Company
Windling, Terri
Zelinski, Paul O.

Authors

Aesop
Alcott, Louisa May
Alexander, Lloyd
Andersen, Hans Christian
Andersen, Hans Christian, in Biopics
Andersson, Christina
Apuleius, Lucius
Arnim, Bettina von
Arnim, Gisela von
Asturias, Miguel Angel
Atwood, Margaret
Aulnoy, Marie-Catherine d'
Auneuil, Louise de Bossigny,
    Comtesse d'
Balázs, Béla
Barrie, Sir James Matthew
Barthelme, Donald
Basile, Giambattista
Baum, L. Frank
Bechstein, Ludwig
Bécquer, Gustavo Adolfo
Benavente, Jacinto
Bernard, Catherine
Beskow, Elsa
Block, Francesca Lia
Bly, Robert
Boccaccio, Giovanni
Böhl de Faber, Cecilia
Borges, Jorge Luis
Brentano, Clemens
Brontë, Charlotte
Broumas, Olga
Browne, Anthony
Burnett, Frances Eliza Hodgson
Byatt, A. S.
Cabrera, Lydia
Calvino, Italo
Čapek, Karel
Capuana, Luigi
Carroll, Lewis
Carter, Angela
Castroviejo, Concha
Cazotte, Jacques
Chamisso, Adalbert von

Chamoiseau, Patrick
Chaucer, Geoffrey
Chukovsky, Kornei
Clarke, Susanna
Cocchiara, Giuseppe
Collodi, Carlo
Coloma, Luis
Coover, Robert
Correia, Hélia
Craik, Dinah Maria Mulock
Crowley, John
Dadié, Bernard Binlin
Dahl, Roald
Daudet, Alphonse
Dazai Osamu
De Lint, Charles
De Morgan, Mary
Dean, Pamela
Deledda, Grazia
Deulin, Charles
Dickens, Charles
Diop, Birago
Donoghue, Emma
Duffy, Carol Ann
Dumas, Philippe
Eichendorff, Joseph Freiherr von
Ekman, Fam
Ende, Michael
Erdrich, Louise
Ershov, Pyotr
Ewald, Carl
Ewing, Juliana Horatia
Fagunwa, Daniel Orowole
Ferré, Rosario
Fouqué, Friedrich de la Motte
Freeman, Mary E. Wilkins
Frost, Gregory
Gaarder, Jostein
Gaiman, Neil
Galland, Antoine
García Márquez, Gabriel
Garner, Alan
Gautier, Théophile
Goethe, Johann Wolfgang von
Gozzi, Carlo
Grace, Patricia
Grass, Günter
Grimm, Wilhelm
Gripari, Pierre
Gripe, Maria
Hamilton, Anthony
Hamilton, Virginia

Harris, Joel Chandler
Hartzenbusch, Juan Eugenio
Hauff, Wilhelm
Hau'ofa, Epeli
Hawthorne, Nathaniel
Hay, Sara Henderson
Helakisa, Kaarina
Helvig, Amalie von
Hesse, Hermann
Hoban, Russell
Hoffmann, E. T. A.
Hofmannsthal, Hugo von
Hopkinson, Nalo
Housman, Laurence
Hurston, Zora Neale
Ihimaera, Witi
Ispirescu, Petre
Ingelow, Jean
Janosch
Jansson, Tove
Jarrell, Randall
Jones, Diana Wynne
Jones, Terry
Kafka, Franz
Keller, Gottfried
Khemir, Nacer
Kreutzwald, Friedrich Reinhold
Kurahashi Yumiko
Kushner, Ellen
La Fontaine, Jean de
La Force, Charlotte-Rose de Caumont de
Laforet, Carmen
Lagerkvist, Pär
Lagerlöf, Selma
Le Guin, Ursula K.
Lee, Tanith
Leprince de Beaumont, Jeanne-Marie
Lewis, C. S.
Lhéritier de Villandon, Marie-Jeanne
Lindgren, Astrid
Lochhead, Liz
Lubert, Marie-Madeleine de
MacDonald, George
Maeterlinck, Maurice
Maguire, Gregory
Mailly, Jean, Chevalier de
Malerba, Luigi
Marie de France
Martín Gaite, Carmen
Matute, Ana María
McKillip, Patricia A.
McKinley, Robin

Metaxa-Krontera, Antigone
Mhlophe, Gcina
Miyazawa Kenji
Mizuno Junko
Molesworth, Mary Louisa
Momaday, N. Scott
Munro, Alice
Murat, Henriette-Julie de Castelnau,
    Comtesse de
Musäus, Johann Karl August
Namjoshi, Suniti
Napoli, Donna Jo
Naubert, Benedikte
Nesbit, E.
Nodier, Charles
Novalis
Nyblom, Helena
Ocampo, Silvina
Oehlenschläger, Adam
Ovid
Pérez Galdós, Benito
Perodi, Emma
Perrault, Charles
Pitzorno, Bianca
Piumini, Roberto
Pizarnik, Alejandra
Planché, James Robinson
Pogorel'sky, Antony
Pourrat, Henri
Pratchett, Terry
Prøysen, Alf
Pú Sōnglíng
Pullman, Philip
Pushkin, Aleksandr
Raud, Eno
Ritchie, Anne Thackeray
Rodari, Gianni
Rossetti, Christina Georgina
Rowling, J. K.
Rumi, Jalal al-Din
Rushdie, Salman
Ruskin, John
Sand, George
Sandburg, Carl
Sarnelli, Pompeo
Schami, Rafik
Scieszka, Jon
Ségur, Sophie, Comtesse de
Sendak, Maurice
Sexton, Anne
Shakespeare, William
Sherman, Delia

Shua, Ana María
Shvarts, Evgeny
Silko, Leslie Marmon
Singer, Isaac Bashevis
Solinas Donghi, Beatrice
Spiegelman, Art
Stahl, Caroline
Steig, William
Stevenson, Robert Louis
Storm, Theodor
Straparola, Giovan Francesco
Strindberg, August
Swan, Anni
Tawada Yōko
Tennyson, Alfred, Lord
Terayama Shūji
Thackeray, William Makepeace
Thurber, James
Tieck, Ludwig
Tolkien, J. R. R.
Tolstoy, Lev
Topelius, Zacharias
Tournier, Michel
Trnka, Jiří
Trueba, Antonio de
Tutuola, Amos
Twain, Mark
Ungerer, Tomi
Valenzuela, Luisa
Valera, Juan
Verdaguer, Jacint
Villeneuve, Gabrielle-Suzanne Barbot de
Volkov, Aleksandr
Walker, Alice
Walker, Barbara G.
Warner, Marina
Welty, Eudora
Wieland, Christoph Martin
Wilde, Oscar
Windling, Terri
Woolf, Virginia
Wú Chéng'ēn
Yeats, William Butler
Yep, Laurence
Yolen, Jane
Zur Mühlen, Hermynia

Composers

Bartók, Béla
Dvořák, Antonín
Glinka, Mikhail

Humperdinck, Engelbert
Rimsky-Korsakov, Nikolai
Tchaikovsky, Pyotr Il'ich

Editors, Collectors, Translators, and Scholars

Aarne, Antti
Afanas'ev, Aleksandr
Alcover, Antoni Maria
Amades, Joan
Anderson, Walter
Asbjørnsen, Peter Christen
Bârlea, Ovidiu
Bechstein, Ludwig
Benfey, Theodor
Bettelheim, Bruno
Bolte, Johannes
Boratav, Pertev Naili
Bošković-Stulli, Maja
Brentano, Clemens
Briggs, Katharine M.
Brothers Grimm in Biopics
Burton, Richard Francis
Busk, Rachel Harriette
Calvino, Italo
Croker, Thomas Crofton
Cruikshank, George
Dégh, Linda
Delarue, Paul
Dorson, Richard M.
Dundes, Alan
Espinosa, Aurelio M.
Franz, Marie-Louise von
Freud, Sigmund
Frobenius, Leo
Galland, Antoine
Gonzenbach, Laura
Gregory, Lady Isabella Augusta Persse
Grimm, Jacob
Grimm, Wilhelm
Grundtvig, Svend
Hamilton, Virginia
Harris, Joel Chandler
Holbek, Bengt
Honko, Lauri
Hurston, Zora Neale
Ihimaera, Witi
Imbriani, Vittorio
Ispirescu, Petre
Jacobs, Joseph
Jung, Carl Gustav

Karadžić, Vuk Stefanović
Köhler, Reinhold
Lane, Edward W.
Lang, Andrew
Loorits, Oskar
Lüthi, Max
Machado y Alvarez, Antonio
Mardrus, Joseph Charles
Matičetov, Milko
Mayer, Charles-Joseph, Chevalier de
Megas, Georgios A.
Metaxa-Krontera, Antigone
Moe, Jørgen
Müller, Friedrich Max
Opie, Iona, and Opie, Peter
Pitré, Guiseppe
Polívka, Jiří
Pourrat, Henri
Propp, Vladimir
Ranke, Kurt
Róheim, Géza
Röhrich, Lutz
Salmelainen, Eero
Salomone-Marino, Salvatore
Schenda, Rudolf
Seki Keigo
Tang Kristensen, Evald
Taylor, Edgar
Tenèze, Marie-Louise
Thompson, Stith
Verdaguer, Jacint
Wossidlo, Richard
Yanagita Kunio
Zipes, Jack

Media, Performance, and Other Cultural Forms

Advertising
Animation
Aphorisms
Art
Bible, Bible Tale
La bibliothèque bleue
Broadside
Cartoons and Comics
Chapbook
Children's Literature
Dance
DEFA Fairy-Tale Films
Film and Video
Graphic Novel

Illustration
Internet
Music
Novel
Opera
Oral Tradition
Pantomime
Parody
Pedagogy
Performance
Poetry
Politics
Proverbs
Puppet Theater
Silent Films and Fairy Tales
Stamps
Storytelling
Television
Theater
Tourism
Walt Disney Company
Young Adult Fiction

Motifs, Themes, Characters, Tales, and Tale Types

Age
Aladdin
Ali Baba
Anansi
Animal Bride, Animal Groom
Anti-Semitism
Baba Yaga
Bear's Son
Beauty and the Beast
Beech Mountain Jack Tale
Birth
Blood
Bluebeard
Brothers
Cannibalism
Cat
Changeling
Childhood and Children
Cinderella
Clergy
Clothing
Colors
Coyote
Cross-Dressing
Cupid and Psyche
Death

Devil
Disability
Dragon
Dwarf, Dwarves
El Dorado
Elf, Elves
Faerie and Fairy Lore
Fairy, Fairies
False Bride
Family
Father
Fisherman and His Wife
Food
Forbidden Room
Frog King
Gilgamesh
Hair
Hansel and Gretel
Harun al-Rashid
Incest
Infertility
Initiation
The Kind and the Unkind Girls
King
La Llorona
Little Red Riding Hood
Magic Helper
Magic Object
Marriage
Men
Mermaid
Mirror
Mother
Mother Goose
Mother Holle
Music and Musical Instruments
Nasreddin
Numbers
Ogre, Ogress
Peasant
Pig
Prince
Princess
Proverbs
Puck
Punishment and Reward
Puss in Boots
Queen
Race and Ethnicity
Reynard the Fox
Sex, Sexuality
Sheherazade

Freeway and *Freeway II*
Gesta Romanorum
Into the Woods
Kalevala
Kathasaritsagara
Kinder- und Hausmärchen
Kirikou et la sorcière
The Lord of the Rings Trilogy
The NeverEnding Story
Once upon a Mattress
Panchatantra
Pear ta ma 'on maf (*The Land Has Eyes*)
Peau d'âne
The Piano

Popeye the Sailor
Pretty Woman
The Princess Bride
The Red Shoes
Le roi et l'oiseau (*The King and Mister Bird*)
The Secret of Roan Inish
Shrek and *Shrek II*
Snow White: A Tale of Terror
Splash
Sukasaptati
Taketori monogatari
Willow
The Wizard of Oz

INTRODUCTION

Since the 1960s, folktales and fairy tales have been a veritable growth industry. To be sure, interest in the fairy tale is hardly breaking news, and historical surveys reveal a long lineage and international presence. However, this history is also characterized by periods of profound interest and prolific production. For instance, the so-called French fairy-tale vogue of the late seventeenth and early eighteenth centuries generated a corpus of tales that was so extraordinary and influential that it even gave a special name to the genre—"*conte de fées*"—which later gave birth to the English term "fairy tale." Germany during the late eighteenth and the early nineteenth centuries provides another case in point. The period was characterized on the one hand by the German Romantics' creative experimentation with the literary fairy tale and on the other by the cultural reverence and scholarly enthusiasm for folktales that produced Jacob and Wilhelm Grimm's landmark collection, the *Kinder- und Hausmärchen* (*Children's and Household Tales,* 1812–15). These two manifestations of what Jack Zipes has called the "German obsession with fairy tales" were the catalysts for the further spread of the literary fairy tale, the widespread collecting and editing of folktales, and the birth of folktale scholarship. By 1878, when the Folk-Lore Society was established in London, the study of folktales and fairy tales had developed into a recognizable discipline, and the way had been paved for the "golden age of folklore discovery," that fruitful period in the nineteenth and early twentieth centuries characterized by the collection and publication in English of folktales from around the word (Jacobs, ii). Such "vogues," "obsessions," and "golden ages" map for us both the persistence of the folktale and fairy tale and those periods in which there has been intense activity around them.

Whether we label the production and reception of the fairy tale in the last four decades of the twentieth century a "vogue," an "obsession," a "golden age," or a "growth industry," one thing remains certain: an enormous amount of cultural energy and creative, intellectual, and economic capital have been invested internationally in the folktale and fairy tale—and this continues to be the case during this first decade of the twenty-first century. It is significant that these years have seen in particular the international institutionalization of folktale and fairy-tale studies. Two signal events set the stage for this. In 1959, the

International Society for Folk Narrative Research (ISFNR) was established under the leadership of German folklorist Kurt Ranke, an event that followed by just two years Ranke's founding of *Fabula*—a pioneering international *Journal of Folktale Studies,* as its subtitle announces in German, English, and French. This formation of a professional organization and scholarly journal signaled that the study of folktales and fairy tales had emerged as an internationally recognized discipline with a future.

As scholarly activity around the subject grew, so did the number of forums for research and publication. Given the iconic status of the Brothers Grimm and the canonical role of their fairy-tale collection, important initiatives focusing on their work followed one upon the other during the last decades of the twentieth century. In 1963, the hundredth anniversary of Jacob Grimm's death, German Grimm scholar Ludwig Denecke published the *Brüder Grimm-Gedenken*—a compendium dedicated to the work of the Brothers Grimm and the first volume of what was to become a serial publication. In 1979, the Brüder Grimm-Gesellschaft (Brothers Grimm Society) inaugurated its monograph series, Schriften der Brüder Grimm-Gesellschaft, which over the years has devoted a number of significant volumes to Grimms' fairy tales. Then, in 1991, as interest in the Grimms and their work continued to grow, the Society began publishing the *Jahrbuch der Brüder Grimm-Gesellschaft* (*Yearbook of the Brothers Grimm Society*), a scholarly forum replete with contributions documenting the genesis and reception of Grimms' fairy tales, as well as a copious annual bibliography (through the year 2000) documenting the worldwide scholarly interest in the Grimms.

This latest fairy-tale vogue, however, has not been only about the Grimms. In 1963—the same year that Denecke established the *Brüder Grimm-Gedenken*—American folklorist Robert M. Dorson launched Folktales of the World, an influential series of folktale collections, in English translation, edited by leading experts and published by the University of Chicago Press. In 1980, the Europäische Märchengesellschaft (European Fairy-Tale Society), an organization of storytellers and scholars established in 1956, published the first of its annual volumes, which are typically based on papers from its yearly conferences. The series—Veröffentlichungen der Europäischen Märchengesellschaft (Publications of the European Fairy-Tale Society)—includes thirty-one volumes to date.

The international scope of the steadily growing work on folktales and fairy tales is evident in the *Enzyklopädie des Märchens* (*EM*), which was established by Kurt Ranke at the University of Göttingen and began publication with its first fascicle in 1975. With eleven of its projected fourteen volumes currently in print, the *EM* aims to cover approximately 3,600 entries emphasizing the comparative study of folktales in sociohistorical context and the relation between oral and literary traditions. If Ranke had set the stage for the institutionalization of folktale and fairy-tale studies in the late 1950s by establishing both a professional organization (the ISFNR) and a journal (*Fabula*), with the *EM* he gave the field its most comprehensive reference work. The *EM* was the first in a string of complementary reference volumes that appeared over the next three decades, including Walter Scherf's *Lexikon der Zaubermärchen* (*Lexicon of the Magic Tale*) in 1982 and *Märchenlexikon* (*Fairy-Tale Lexicon,* 1995; CD-ROM

2003), Ulf Diederich's *Who's Who im Märchen* (*Who's Who in the Fairy Tale*) in 1995, Jack Zipes's *Oxford Companion to Fairy Tales* in 2002, and Ulrich Marzolph and Richard van Leeuwen's *The Arabian Nights Encyclopedia* in 2004. Also in 2004, Hans-Jörg Uther, a member of the *EM*'s editorial team, published *The Types of International Folktales,* a comprehensive revision of the Aarne-Thompson tale-type index, thus internationalizing and revitalizing that foundational taxonomy of folktales for the new era of global folktale studies. Moreover, by involving scholars around the world in decades of encyclopedic research, the *EM* has generated additional interest and new research, which in turn has encouraged the creation of new scholarly forums devoted to folktales and fairy tales.

Taking his lead from *Fabula,* Jacques Barchilon—a scholar of French literature at the University of Colorado, Boulder—founded in 1987 the international journal *Merveilles et contes.* Its inaugural issue presented scholarship from France, Sweden, and the United States on topics ranging from the classical Herodotus to Victorian-era children's book author E. Nesbit. Devoted not only to disseminating scholarship from around the world and from different disciplines but also to publishing primary texts, *Merveilles et contes* was an effective response to the burgeoning interest in fairy tales. When it moved to Wayne State University Press in 1997 as *Marvels & Tales: Journal of Fairy-Tale Studies,* it soon spawned a book series—the Series in Fairy-Tale Studies (2004-)—and further contributed to the institutionalization of fairy-tale studies, especially as a transdisciplinary phenomenon.

More specialist journals followed. In 1990, the Märchen-Stiftung Walter Kahn (Walter Kahn Fairy-Tale Foundation), which had been established in Germany in 1985, began publishing the journal *Märchenspiegel* (*Fairy-Tale Mirror*). Directed at both scholars and a broader range of readers, *Märchenspiegel* is dedicated to fairy-tale studies and the cultivation of storytelling, which has also undergone a worldwide revival sparking additional interest in fairy tales (see, e.g., Calame-Griaule; Sobol; Stone, 8–9). In 2003, the French journal *Féeries* appeared under the editorship of Jean-François Perrin of the University of Grenoble. A scholarly journal focusing on the French fairy tale from the seventeenth to the nineteenth centuries, *Féeries* has published special issues on such vital topics as fairy-tale collections, the Orientalist tale, and the politics of the fairy tale. *Fairy Tale Review,* the most recent of the new professional journals, debuted in 2006. Edited by author Kate Bernheimer of the University of Alabama, *Fairy Tale Review* is an annual literary journal that demonstrates the thriving interest of creative writers and artists in the genre by publishing their original fiction, poetry, and art.

The texts of folktales and fairy tales themselves have also been issued and reissued in great numbers during this period, recreating and redefining the corpus of texts available to scholars, students, and other avid consumers. Academic presses and trade publishers issued and continue to issue scholarly and popular editions, translations, anthologies, and textbooks to meet the demand created by new fairy-tale courses being offered at universities. These include on the one hand important new editions and translations of canonical tale collections based on advances in fairy-tale scholarship. For example, since the 1970s, there have been numerous new editions and translations of major fairy-tale works by

Hans Christian Andersen, Giambattista Basile, the Brothers Grimm, and Charles Perrault (see this encyclopedia's Bibliography and Resources section), as well as an important edition of the Arabic text of the *Arabian Nights* (Mahdi) and new English translations of the *Nights* (Haddawy). On the other hand there are volumes offering tales that have been historically ignored, neglected, suppressed, or overshadowed. In this category, collections of tales by or about women have been especially common—such as Kathleen Ragan's *Fearless Girls, Wise Women, and Beloved Sisters: Heroines in Folktales from Around the World*; Hasan M. El-Shamy's *Tales Arab Women Tell;* Jack Zipes's *Beautiful Angiola: The Lost Sicilian Folk and Fairy Tales of Laura Gonzenbach;* Nadine Jasmin's edition of the tales of Marie-Catherine d'Aulnoy; and Shawn C. Jarvis and Jeannine Blackwell's anthology, *The Queen's Mirror: Fairy Tales by German Women, 1780–1900*. The possibilities of using electronic media to reissue folktales and fairy tales in ways that make them easily accessible to a wide range of readers eager to consume them is demonstrated by two digital projects on CD-ROM edited by Hans-Jörg Uther in 2003 and 2004: *Deutsche Märchen und Sagen* (*German Folktales and Legends*) and *Europäische Märchen und Sagen* (*European Folktales and Legends*). The latter alone includes more than 7,000 tales and legends from some of the most important European collections representing some fifty linguistic regions. These few examples represent just a small fraction of the many texts that have been made available in recent years. If there is any doubt that the term "growth industry" truly applies to the steady ascent of the folktale and fairy tale, then consider that in 1999 even the *Wall Street Journal* took note of this fairy-tale publishing phenomenon (Praeger).

This steady stream of professional journals, book series, reference volumes, and primary texts attests both to the continuing institutionalization of fairy-tale studies and to the unrelenting escalation of both scholarly and popular interest in folktales and fairy tales, especially since the 1970s. It is no mere coincidence that this remarkably rapid expansion parallels other scholarly developments and cultural trends. The simultaneous surge in the study of children's literature during this period reinforced the rise of critical interest in the fairy tale. In the same vein, sociohistorical and political approaches to literature—which were influenced by Marxism, critical theory, and the sociopolitical dissent of the 1960s and 1970s—focused a critical light on classical fairy tales, which were thought to have been co-opted by a conservative bourgeois ideology and enlisted in the repressive cultural indoctrination of children. The feminist critique of fairy tales, which emerged explosively in the 1970s, also fueled public debate in the West about the social value and historical role of fairy tales (Haase, "Feminist Fairy-Tale Scholarship"). The influence of feminism on fairy-tale studies has persisted and continues to prompt study of the relationship between folktale and gender in narrative traditions worldwide (e.g., Apo, Nenola, and Stark-Arola; Appadurai, Korom, and Mills). The interest generated by feminism and gender studies in women's roles in the production and reception of fairy tales also led to the rediscovery of those women who actually created the vogue for fairy tales in late seventeenth-century France and to the recovery of neglected fairy-tale writings by women, as noted earlier.

Grimm scholarship in particular gave a significant impetus to the critical reevaluation of fairy tales. Beginning in 1975, Heinz Rölleke's numerous editions of Grimms' tales and his study of the brothers' informants and editorial practices shed new light on the genesis and nature of the *Kinder- und Hausmärchen*. The findings of Rölleke and others revealed the extent to which the Grimms themselves had shaped the content and ideology of their tales through their methods of collecting, selecting, and editing. This not only raised important questions about the sociohistorical roots of the Grimms' tales, it also challenged conventional wisdom about the tales' relationship to oral tradition. Research on these topics was propelled by the attention lavished on the Grimms worldwide in 1985 and 1986—the bicentennial years of their births (Haase, "Reviewing"). This work, however, had implications that transcended the Grimms and has had far-reaching and long-lasting consequences for folktale and fairy-tale studies in general. Questions about the Grimms' sources, informants, and editorial interventions have since been translated into questions about the very nature of collecting and editing. Leela Prasad and Sadhana Naithani, for example, have critically examined the work of collectors and editors in the intercultural context of colonial India. Naithani's work has challenged in particular the "system of binary oppositions" (57) that we typically use to understand the production of folktale collections by colonial folklorists. Similarly, questions about the authenticity of the Grimms' tales and their relation to oral tradition have prompted reassessment of "authenticity" itself (Bendix) and destabilized the oral-literary opposition that has long defined and constrained the discourse of folktale and fairy-tale studies.

To be sure, fairy-tale studies have been spurred over the last forty years by the extraordinary production of *literary* fairy tales, and the default position has frequently been to consider these literary works as belonging on one side of the conventional oral-literary divide. Responding to the same cultural trends that have motivated scholars to critically reexamine the fairy-tale tradition, creative writers for both children and adults have produced an enormous corpus of new tales that question, challenge, subvert, revise, and otherwise adapt classical tales. Authors such as Margaret Atwood, Angela Carter, Robert Coover, Michael Ende, Alejandra Pizarnik, Salman Rushdie, Lusia Valenzuela, Tawada Yoko, and countless others have returned repeatedly to the folktale and fairy tale to engage both sociocultural themes and issues of narrative and storytelling. At the same time, numerous authors have drawn on oral storytelling traditions to revalidate the history, values, and narrative traditions of peoples whose cultures are threatened by the spread of Western, Anglo-European cultures. Patrick Chamoiseau, Bernard Binlin Dadié, Birago Diop, Louise Erdrich, Nalo Hopkinson, N. Scott Momaday, and others have created innovative works that frequently mediate between oral tradition and Western literary forms, as well as between (or among) several cultures. Such texts—which have emerged in a postmodern, postcolonial era and are not easily squeezed into the nineteenth-century category of "literary fairy tale"—exist in an intercultural space. They challenge our conventional terminology, our habit of ascribing to tales a singular cultural identity, and our dichotomous (and politically charged) thinking about orality and literacy (see Bacchilega; Seifert).

That the oral and the literary need not exist in an oppositional relationship or be the defining terms of fairy-tale studies should be self-evident, especially in the twenty-first century. Folktales and fairy tales have manifested themselves in extraordinarily diverse ways, not just in oral and literary narratives but also in theater, puppet plays, pantomime, music, dance, opera, art, illustration, advertising, theme parks, cartoons and comics, graphic novels, television, live-action film and video, animation, and hypertextually on the Internet. In some forms, they may appear as full-fledged narratives, especially in oral and written storytelling, but frequently they appear as fragments, motifs, allusions, inter-texts—fairy-tale synecdoches. The terms "folktale" and "fairy tale" may initially suggest principally narrative forms and the media-based polarity of "oral vs. written"; or they may suggest the generic variety signaled by the term "märchen," which—as the Grimms used it—encompasses not only the wonder (or magic) tale but also "etiologies, fables, animal tales, moralistic stories, jests, exempla, religious and other legends, and mixed forms, such as humorous religious tales and humorous magic tales" (Uther, *Types,* 1: 9). In the title and conception of this encyclopedia, the terms are intended to be inclusive rather than exclusive, flexible rather than fixed, embracing a wide range of genres, media, texts, and intertextualities—a "fairy-tale web," in the words of Cristina Bacchilega (209).

To be freed from our fixation on the oral-literary dichotomy and to make sense of the latest fairy-tale vogue that has accompanied globalization and the digital age, it is necessary not only to acknowledge the flexibility and adaptability of folktales and fairy tales but also to understand their dynamic intertextuality and intermedial potential (Haase, "Hypertextual Gutenberg"). It is also necessary to understand fairy-tale studies as an interdisciplinary effort. Folklorists and literary scholars, who have learned a great deal from each other over the last forty to fifty years, need to continue listening and talking to each other—as do all who work on these topics using the perspectives and methods of different disciplines and specialties. The institutionalization of fairy-tale studies has not resulted in a monolithic discourse, universally recognized canon, or dominant methodology, which actually attests to the vitality of the field. The challenge for fairy-tale studies is to cultivate a constructive transnational inter-disciplinary conversation that can promote approaches that are appropriate both for rethinking the past and for coming to grips with new forms of production and reception during this dynamic era of fairy-tale proliferation and change.

References

Apo, Satu, Aili Nenola, and Laura Stark-Arola, eds. *Gender and Folklore: Perspectives on Finnish and Karelian Culture.* Helsinki: Finnish Literature Society, 1998.

Appadurai, Arjun, Frank J. Korom, and Margaret A. Mills, eds. *Gender, Genre and Power in South Asian Expressive Traditions.* Philadelphia: University of Pennsylvania Press, 1991.

Bacchilega, Cristina. "Reflections on Recent English-Language Fairy-Tale Fiction by Women." *Fabula* 47 (2006): 201–10.

Bendix, Regina. *In Search of Authenticity: The Formation of Folklore Studies.* Madison: University of Wisconsin Press, 1997.

Calame-Griaule, Geneviève. *Le renouveau du conte.* Paris: Centre National de la Recherche Scientifique, 1991.

Diederichs, Ulf. *Who's Who im Märchen*. Munich: Deutscher Taschenbuch Verlag, 1995.

El-Shamy, Hasan M., ed. and trans. *Tales Arab Women Tell and the Behavioral Patterns They Portray*. Bloomington: Indiana University Press, 1999.

Haase, Donald. "Feminist Fairy Tale Scholarship." *Fairy Tales and Feminism: New Approaches*. Edited by Donald Haase. Detroit: Wayne State University Press, 2004. 1–36.

———. "Hypertextual Gutenberg: The Textual and Hypertextual Life of Folktales and Fairy Tales in English-Language Popular Print Editions." *Fabula* 47 (2006): 222–30.

———. "Re-Viewing the Grimm Corpus: Grimm Scholarship in an Era of Celebration." *Monatshefte* 91.1 (1999): 121–31.

Haddawy, Husain, trans. *The Arabian Nights*. 1990. New York: Norton, 1995.

———, trans. *The Arabian Nights II*. 1995. New York: Norton, 1996.

Jacobs, Joseph. *English Fairy Tales and More English Fairy Tales*. Edited by Donald Haase. Santa Barbara, CA: ABC-CLIO, 2002.

Jarvis, Shawn C., and Jeannine Blackwell, eds. and trans. *The Queen's Mirror: Fairy Tales by German Women, 1780–1900*. Lincoln: University of Nebraska Press, 2001.

Jasmin, Nadine, ed. *Madame d'Aulnoy: Contes des fées, suivis des Contes nouveaux ou Les fées à la mode*. Paris: Champion, 2004.

Mahdi, Muhsin, ed. *The Thousand and One Nights* (Alf Layla wa-Layla) *from the Earliest Known Sources*. 3 vols. Leiden: Brill, 1984–94.

Marzolph, Ulrich, and Richard van Leeuwen, eds. *The Arabian Nights Encyclopedia*. 2 volumes. Santa Barbara, CA: ABC-CLIO, 2004.

Naithani, Sadhana. *In Quest of Indian Folktales: Pandit Ram Gharib Chaube and William Crooke*. Bloomington: Indiana University Press, 2006.

Praeger, Josh Harris. "Everyone's Porridge: Small Publishers, Illustrators and Authors Use the Popularity of Fairy Tales without the Expense of Licensing Fees." *Wall Street Journal* (Eastern ed.), September 27, 1999, 13.

Prasad, Leela. "The Authorial Other in Folktale Collections in Colonial India: Tracing Narration and its Dis/Continuities." *Cultural Dynamics* 15.1 (2003): 5–39.

Ragan, Kathleen, ed. *Fearless Girls, Wise Women, and Beloved Sisters: Heroines in Folktales from Around the World*. New York: Norton, 1998.

Scherf, Walter. *Lexikon der Zaubermärchen*. Stuttgart: Kröner, 1982.

———. *Das Märchenlexikon*. 2 volumes. Munich: Beck, 1995.

———. *Das Märchenlexikon*. Digitale Bibliothek 90. CD-ROM. Berlin: Directmedia Publishing, 2003.

Seifert, Lewis C. "Orality, History, and 'Creoleness' in Patrick Chamoiseau's *Creole Folktales*." *Marvels & Tales* 16 (2002): 214–30.

Sobol, Joseph Daniel. *The Storytellers' Journey: An American Revival*. Urbana: University of Illinois Press, 1999.

Stone, Kay. *Burning Brightly: New Light on Old Tales Today*. Peterborough: Broadview, 1998.

Uther, Hans-Jörg, ed. *Deutsche Märchen und Sagen*. Digitale Bibliothek 80. CD-ROM. Berlin: Directmedia Publishing, 2003.

———. *Europäische Märchen und Sagen*. Digitale Bibliothek 110. CD-ROM. Berlin: Directmedia Publishing, 2004.

———. *The Types of International Folktales: A Classification and Bibliography*. 3 volumes. Helsinki: Academia Scientiarum Fennica, 2004.

Zipes, Jack. "The German Obsession with Fairy Tales." *The Brothers Grimm: From Enchanted Forests to the Modern World*. 2nd edition. New York: Palgrave MacMillan, 2002. 106–33.

———, ed. *The Oxford Companion to Fairy Tales*. Oxford: Oxford University Press, 2002.

A

Aarne, Antti (1867–1925)

The Finnish scholar Antti Aarne created a system for classifying **folktale**s and a widely used index of folktale plots. Aarne's tale typology—which first appeared in 1910 in *Verzeichnis der Märchentypen* (*Index of the Types of the Folktale*) and has been revised three times since—continues to be used by researchers in many countries. Archivists the world over have organized their folktale collections according to Aarne's eminently practical system of classification. Folktale scholars have published dozens of type indices of folktales collected from specific countries or language areas.

Aarne was first introduced to the research, collection, and publication of folktales under the tutelage of Kaarle Krohn at the University of Helsinki. Aarne later pursued his study of the folktale in Russia, Germany, Denmark, and Sweden. He earned his doctoral degree in 1907 and went on to become a professor of **folklore** in 1922.

When Aarne was writing his doctoral dissertation, *Vergleichende Märchenforschungen* (*Comparative Studies of Folktales*, 1908), he was struck by the difficulty of acquiring research materials from other countries. He began preparing a catalogue classifying folktales that were represented in the **oral tradition** of several European countries. As his base material, he used Finnish folktales (more than 25,000 texts), the Danish folktale collections of Svend **Grundtvig** (about 850 texts), and **Grimm**s' *Kinder- und Hausmärchen* (210 texts).

Aarne divided folktales—which he designated with term "**märchen**"—into three sub-genres: (1) **animal tale**s (*Tiermärchen*), (2) ordinary folktales (*eigentliche Märchen*), and (3) **joke**s and **anecdote**s (*Schwänke*). He also distinguished each type of folktale plot with a name, number, and a brief description of its contents. For example, the ordinary folktale about the strange little man (Tom Tit Tot, Rumpelstiltskin) who helps a girl spin gold from straw was called The Name of the Supernatural Helper and given the tale-type number 500 (which would be known in the standard practice of folklorists as Aa 500, later as AaTh or AT 500, and most recently as ATU 500). The story is a typical representation of the subcategory that Aarne called "tales of magic" (*Zaubermärchen*). The other subcategories of ordinary folktales identified by Aarne are (as rendered into English by Stith **Thompson**): **religious tale**s (*legendenartige Märchen*), **novella**s or romantic tales (*novellenartige Märchen*), and tales of the stupid **ogre** (*Märchen vom dummen Teufel* [*Riesen*]). In 1911, Aarne published his index of Finnish folktales, *Finnische Märchenvarianten* (*The Finnish Folktale Variants*).

Aarne based his investigations of the folktale on the **historic-geographic method**. He published numerous monographs in which he analyzed and outlined the distribution, variation, and history of individual folktales. His studies often led him to conclude that a given folktale's starting point was in India, thus lending credence to Theodor **Benfey**'s vision of the genre's primal home. Aarne outlined his research methodology in his handbook *Leitfaden der vergleichenden Märchenforschung* (*Guide for the Comparative Investigation of Folktales*, 1913).

Aarne's most enduring achievement, however, is his folktale index. The international tale-type index proved to be so useful that there are now three expanded editions. Stith Thompson compiled the first two in 1928 and 1961. The latest, *The Types of International Folktales: A Classification and Bibliography* (2004), is a three-volume edition by Hans-Jörg Uther. *See also* Seki Keigo; Tale Type; Wonder Tale.

Further Readings: Hautala, Jouko. *Finnish Folklore Research, 1828–1919*. Helsinki: Societas Scientarum Fennica, 1969; Jason, Heda. *Motif, Type and Genre: A Manual for Compilation of Indices and a Bibliography of Indices and Indexing*. Helsinki: Academia Scientiarum Fennica, 2000; Rausmaa, Pirkko-Liisa. "Aarne, Antti Amatus." *Enzyklopädie des Märchens*. Edited by Kurt Ranke et al. Volume 1. Berlin: Walter de Gruyter, 1975. 1–4.

Satu Apo

Adaptation

The concept of "adaptation" refers to the process that occurs when folktales and fairy tales are changed into new versions, or **variant**s, in the course of their transmission. Adaptations can occur when a text or **tale type** is retold orally or rewritten and when it is transferred into a different generic form (for example, into a **novel**) or into a different medium (such as, orality to print, print to orality, print to film, and so on).

Jack **Zipes** makes the important distinction between duplication and revision as forms of adaptation (Zipes, 8–11). Duplication is the process of making copies of originals, which tends to perpetuate canonical tales in spite of changes brought about by adaptation. Easily recognizable, they merely mimic a primordial matrix, the "hypotext," to use Gérard Genette's taxonomy. While adaptations based on duplication may take the major colors of their new cultural environment and reflect specific customs, they still reinforce well-known models and repeat predictable moral lessons. For example, although many new versions and adaptations of tales by Charles **Perrault** and the Brothers **Grimm** continue to appear, they constitute essentially faithful retellings of these canonical tales and leave their core ideologies unchanged.

Revision, on the other hand, is a process of critical adaptation in which the new version implicitly questions, challenges, or subverts the story on which it is based by incorporating new values and perspectives. Perrault and the Brothers Grimm were themselves in many cases adaptors of preexisting tales, and the tales as they published them did not always duplicate their sources. Instead, in rewriting or **editing** the tales, they revised their meaning and in turn presented their readers with a new set of values. Addressing educated, literate classes, those revisions reflected new concerns and different tastes to accomplish new goals.

Many twentieth- and twenty-first-century fairy-tale adaptations are revisionist tales that critically engage the classical fairy-tale tradition established by Perrault, Grimm, Hans

Christian **Andersen**, and others. Reflecting the cultural criticism that characterized Anglo-European societies during the 1960s and 1970s, including the critique of fairy tales by **feminism**, writers such as Margaret **Atwood**, Angela **Carter**, Philippe **Dumas**, **Janosch**, Tanith **Lee**, and many others produced fairy-tale adaptations that call into question the values and aesthetic of traditional tales. The challenge posed by such revisionist rewritings is signaled by the title of Dumas's *Contes à l'envers* (*Upside Down Tales*, 1977), a book in which recycled red riding hoods terrorize the **wolf** and drive him out of town.

Folktales and fairy tales have been adapted for a variety of genres and media, including **theater**, **cartoons and comics**, **illustration**s, **animation**, **film and video**, **poetry**, **television**, the **graphic novel**, and so on. Adapting tales for each of these genres or media involves different formal or technological considerations, in addition to matters of content and theme. Walt **Disney** is certainly the most famous adaptor of classic fairy tales for the cinema. One may say that he appropriated tales such as *Pinocchio*, *Cinderella*, and "**Snow White**" to "freeze" them in a sanitized form. However, media adaptations can also be critical and revisionist, as seen in such films as Neil Jordan's *The Company of Wolves* (1984) or *Shrek and Shrek II* (2001 and 2004). *See also* Diffusion; Intertextuality; Translation; Variant.

Further Readings: Beckett, Sandra. L. *Recycling Red Riding Hood.* New York: Routledge, 2002; Zipes, Jack. *Fairy Tale as Myth/Myth as Fairy Tale.* Lexington: University Press of Kentucky, 1994.

Claire L. Malarte-Feldman

Advertising

Folklore has long been used to attract attention in advertising slogans and texts. While **proverbs**, folk songs, and nursery rhymes are particularly prevalent, folktales have also been used to lure people into a purchasing choice. In fact, the "Pied Piper of Hamelin" can well be considered as a symbol of the world of advertising, with the pied piper playing his pipe ever so sweetly and the consumers following him without resisting his charming and manipulative music. Little wonder that the city of Hamelin in Germany uses the pied piper to attract tourists and that "The Pied Piper" toy shop in St. Armands Key, Florida, used a pied piper figure with children following him as a sign and as an illustration on its shopping bags.

Fairy tales, however, are especially suitable to create a perfect world of desire and wish fulfillment in the mind of consumers. Any merchant would want to describe a product in such a miraculous fashion that a purchaser would not be able to resist buying it. And since fairy tales appeal to people's **wish** for a happy and contented life, the tales' **motif**s become perfect tools in their original or adapted wording to promote consumerism in a society informed by the drive toward instantaneous gratification. Advertising copywriters are only too aware of the fact that traditionally or innovatively employed fairy-tale motifs are ideal for spreading irresistible messages to consumers.

When the phenomenon of advertising took hold at the beginning of the twentieth century, titles or poetic verses of fairy tales or short allusions to well-known stories began to be used as effective bait. The readers or viewers of an advertisement would immediately be reminded of the happy ending of the underlying fairy tale, leading them more or less subconsciously to the conclusion that the product must be equally wonderful. Color printing and, since the latter half of the twentieth century, **television** spots added important visual

CARRERAS CIGARETTES

Bluebeard.

Portrayal of Bluebeard on a Carreras Cigarettes card. [Lake County Museum/Corbis]

aspects to the verbal message, making such advertisements even more appealing. Again and again, beautiful women such as **Snow White** or **Sleeping Beauty** are illustrated in front of a **mirror** or gently sleeping to advertise a cosmetic product or a piece of fine **clothing**. After all, who does not want to be beautiful, and who could resist that famous fairy-tale question, "Mirror, mirror on the wall, who is the fairest of them all?" The message is always that perfection and satisfaction are attainable, and fairy-tale formulas and allusions together with explanatory if not manipulative texts and exquisite **illustration**s create an enchanted world of irresistible consumerism. Like it or not, many consumers have little choice but to accept such advertisements as convincing signs of the wish fulfillment that also underlies the basic idea of traditional fairy tales.

To assure meaningful communication with their readers and viewers, advertisers choose primarily those motifs of fairy tales that are commonly known. Fairy-tale titles such as "Rapunzel" or "**Cinderella**" have been used to advertise beautiful **hair** or a piece of clothing that has transformed a woman from rags to riches. A German champagne company called its product "Rotkäppchen" (**Little Red Riding Hood**) and quite appropriately every bottle has a red cap on top of the cork. The name and the cap conjured up positive memories of Little Red Riding Hood—or Little Red Cap—bringing a special beverage to her beloved grandmother. The message was clearly that a bottle of Rotkäppchen champagne will help to bring some joy and bliss into the everyday world. It is exactly this promise of making wishes come true that makes such advertisements so appealing, with some of them also simply using such slogans as "Fairy tales can come true" or "Three secret wishes."

Cosmetic firms in particular have found fairy-tale allusions useful to sell their products. Revlon used the slogan "Cinderella—nails and the Magic Wand," claiming that its cosmetics make all the difference between homeliness and beauty. The U.S. Forest Service asked provocatively, "Where would **Hansel and Gretel** be without a forest?" The car manufacturer Subaru used the catchphrase "Don't let your coach turn into a pumpkin," with the illustration making the allusion to the "Cinderella" fairy tale perfectly clear. The Lindt chocolate company used illustrations from the Walt **Disney**'s animated version of "Snow White" on its wrappers to sell its milk chocolate as heavenly sweets. And an antismoking advertisement carried the message "Kiss Me—I Don't Smoke," with the illustration showing that the frog to be kissed is the nonsmoking prince from "The **Frog King**" fairy tale. In any case, such advertisements suggest a better world where wishes can become true, and the slogans, texts, and illustrations make this look as easy as fairy-tale magic.

Some companies have built entire advertising campaigns on fairy-tale motifs. For example, the Waterford Crystal Company frequently uses fairy-tale allusions for its marvelous glass creations. With cultural literacy being high regarding the most popular fairy tales, people will have no difficulty recognizing the fairy tale behind the slogan "One of her glass slippers fell off." The same is true for the slogan "Oh, what lovely ears you have" above the image of several pitchers whose handles brought about this variation of Little Red Riding Hood's questions to her grandmother. Such wordplay presupposes that the reader and consumer will also recall the traditional tale, thus creating a world where magic and reality can meet in harmony. Perhaps the most elaborate use of fairy tales for advertising purposes was AT&T's special issue of *Time* (spring 1995) entitled "Welcome to Cyberspace." In numerous two-page spreads AT&T illustrated the fairy-tale-like inventions of modern electronic technology. Fairy-tale motifs of "The Frog King," "Little Red Riding Hood," "Hansel and Gretel," "Cinderella," and "Rumpelstiltskin" appear. The fairy-tale heroes and heroines are, of course, transformed to fit the age of cyberspace. The same is true for their modern fairy-tale-like messages, as for example: "Bread crumbs are for the birds. We'll get home in no time with this.—Hansel and Gretel have one very smart dad. He uses AT&T PersonaLink Services, a new messaging and information network." No matter what new products and wishes emerge in the future, advertisers will continue sell their wares to consumers by relying on traditional fairy tales as symbolic expressions of wish fulfillment. *See also* Tourism.

Further Readings: Dégh, Linda, and Andrew Vázsonyi. "Magic for Sale: Märchen and Legend in TV Advertising." *Fabula* 20 (1979): 47–68; Dundes, Alan. "Advertising and Folklore." *New York Folklore Quarterly* 19 (1963): 143–51; Herles, Helmut. "Sprichwort und Märchenmotiv in der Werbung." *Zeitschrift für Volkskunde* 62 (1966): 67–80; Horn, Katalin. "Grimmsche Märchen als Quellen für Metaphern und Vergleiche in der Sprache der Werbung, des Journalismus und der Literatur." *Muttersprache* 91 (1981): 106–15; Mieder, Wolfgang. *Tradition and Innovation in Folk Literature.* Hanover, NH: University Press of New England, 1987; Odber de Baubeta, Patricia Anne. "Fairy Tale Motifs in Advertising." *Estudos de Literatura Oral* 3 (1997): 35–60; 4 (1999): 23–53; Preston, Cathy Lynn. "Disrupting the Boundaries of Genre and Gender: Postmodernism and the Fairy Tale." *Fairy Tales and Feminism: New Approaches.* Edited by Donald Haase. Detroit: Wayne State University Press, 2004. 197–212; Röhrich, Lutz. "Folklore and Advertising." *Folklore Studies in the Twentieth Century: Proceedings of the Centenary Conference of the Folklore Society.* Edited by Venetia J. Newall. Totowa, NJ: Rowman and Littlefield, 1980. 114–15.

Wolfgang Mieder

Aesop (sixth century BCE)

Aesop is one of the most famous authors of **fable**s. Because information about him is sparse and uncertain, some believe that he was not a historical figure. The best sources to reconstruct his life and work are provided by the historians Herodotus and Euagon (or Eugeon) from the fifth century BCE and by the *Vita Aesopi*, a popular written text from the first century CE. According to these sources, Aesop lived in Greece in the sixth century

BCE and was from Thrace. He was reportedly very ugly but had charismatic skills to tell stories for didactic purposes or entertainment. Sold as a slave on the Greek island Samos, Aesop exhibited a cleverness greater than that of his master, probably the philosopher Xanthos, who later set him free because Aesop was able to interpret an important augury to Xanthos's benefit. Aesop's death, apparently by execution in Delphi, remains shrouded in myth. By the fifth century the talented and intelligent Aesop had apparently taken on legendary dimensions.

From antiquity Aesop's name has been synonymous with fables. Based on **oral tradition,** Aesop's fables were stories with mostly animals as main protagonists (the tricky fox, the powerful lion, etc.). There are also fables that describe relationships between humans and animals and fables that have protagonists who are humans or even plants. The fables have a simple structure: the description of the situation at the beginning is followed generally by a short dialogical part and then by the concluding statement containing the **moral**. The fables function metaphorically and have an ironic character similar to wellerisms.

Although Aesop has been perceived since antiquity as the creator of the fable, many attempted to write fables before him, in particular Homer, Hesiod, Archilochos, Semonides, Stesichoros, Herodotus, Sophocles, Aristophanes, and Plato, among others. The first collection of Aesop's fables in written form was made by the philosopher Demetrius of Phaleron in about 300 BCE. Since then—during the Roman period, through the **Middle Ages**, and up to the present day—Aesop's fables have circulated widely as part of the fable tradition. The fable was established as an autonomous literary genre in Roman poetry in 40 CE by Phaedrus, whose five-volume work with fables in Latin verse survives only in fragments. In the second century CE, the Roman Babrius distributed 143 of Aesop's fables in verse, as they played an important role in Roman and Byzantine education. During the Middle Ages fables were integrated into Christian literature and sermons. Aesop's influence continued in Renaissance and Baroque fable books, and in seventeenth-century France Aesop's reception is especially evident in the stories of Jean de **La Fontaine,** who gave his fables a more humorous and satirical tone. Translated into almost all languages, Aesop's fables are often encountered allusively in popular culture and over time have also become an indispensable part of **children's literature**.

Further Readings: Blackham, H. J. *The Fable as Literature.* London: Athlone Press, 1985; Holzberg, Niklas. *The Ancient Fable: An Introduction.* Translated by Christine Jackson-Holzberg. Bloomington: Indiana University Press, 2002; Patterson, Annabel M. *Fables of Power: Aesopian Writing and Political History.* Durham, NC: Duke University Press, 1991.

Maria Kaliambou

Afanas'ev, Aleksandr (1826–1871)

In Russia, Aleksandr Afanas'ev holds the same position as the Brothers **Grimm** in western Europe. The son of a lawyer, born in the small town of Boguchar, in the province of Voronezh, Afanas'ev left for law studies at Moscow University when he was eighteen. During his four years of academic life, Afanas'ev published his first article, "The National Economy under the Reign of Peter I." The article was praised by the leading literary critic Vissarion Belinsky, who especially stressed the scholarly level of the work. However, success was followed by distress. Having given a lecture on the influence of the criminal code during the sixteenth and seventeenth centuries in Russia, Afanas'ev provoked the disapproval of the Minister of Education, Sergei Uvarov. Afanas'ev's career as professor of history was over. Afanas'ev nevertheless received an assignment at the Moscow Archives of the Ministry of Foreign Affairs, where he remained until 1862. By then he had turned to journalism and published articles on several literary personalities of the previous century. He was also the main editor of *Bibliograficheskie zapiski* (*Bibliographical Notes*), a position he left to devote himself to folklore studies.

After initially writing articles on sorcery in ancient Russia and pagan **legend**s about the island of Buyan, Afanas'ev published a collection of Russian fairy tales in eight fascicles. A keystone in fairy-tale history, *Russkie narodnye skazki* (*Russian Folktales,* 1855–63; often translated as *Russian Fairy Tales*) contains 640 stories and is probably the largest collection of folktales by one individual. Inspired by the collection of the Brothers Grimm, Afanas'ev outfitted his tales with philological annotations. Furthermore, he considered it necessary to comment upon the tales' mythological heritage, which he thought would enable a comparison of the **Russian tales** to fairy tales from other countries. About 150 tales of the entire collection, including **variant**s, were contributed by the linguist and author Vladimir Dal (from whom Afanas'ev received roughly 1,000 texts to from which to choose); others were taken from the **archives** of the Russian Geographical Society. A dozen of these tales were recorded by Afanas'ev himself, in his native region, Voronezh. The extent to which Afanas'ev's edited the texts of the tales that had been collected is difficult to ascertain, although some editorial intervention is likely. He grouped all the texts according to specific categories: **animal tale**s, **wonder tale**s, and tales of everyday life. The tales of everyday life seem to be the most complex, due not least to their depiction of Russian community. Afanas'ev, however, had an exclusively mythological approach to the tales and therefore showed little or no interest in the storytellers themselves; and since he regarded the texts as inviolable, he more or less ignored their geographical background as well.

In the 1860s, Russia found itself in a state of social and economic change. Afanas'ev was once again in for trouble since his folktales were considered to be coarse and abusive towards the clergy and nobility. Furthermore, they hailed the peasants' wit, which was not in accord with the authorities' approach to the social upheavals taking place. After police raided the printing works and a printing of the tales was burned, Afanas'ev applied for permission to go abroad. Shortly after his return to Russia, the police searched Afanas'ev's house, and he was summoned to appear before an investigative committee. This might have been due to his contact abroad with Aleksandr Herzen, the exiled leader of the opposition. Although no evidence of subversive activity was ever found, Afanas'ev was nonetheless dismissed from his job at the Foreign Ministry in 1862 and deprived of his house. To survive, he was forced to sell his outstanding library. In 1865, after several years without work, Afanas'ev was eventually employed as an assistant clerk in a Moscow court, and after two years he was promoted to Clerk to the Congress of Commune Judges in the Second Parish of the City of Moscow. The hardships had ruined his health; nevertheless, in his spare time he continued his scholarly work, and between 1865 and 1869 Afanas'ev published the monumental three-volume *Poeticheskie vozzreniya slavyan na prirodu* (*The Poetic Interpretations of Nature by the Slavs*). In more than 2,500 pages, he elaborates his theories of folk mythology and its various manifestations in the tales. Since press censorship had been reformed in 1865, Afanas'ev succeeded in publishing his work, and he even received an award from the Russian Academy of Science. Five years later, he realized a longtime dream of his by publishing *Russkie detskie skazki* (*Russian Children's Tales*) in two volumes, which was to become his last work. Even now tsarist censorship interfered, which eventually lead to a fierce debate about fairy tales as **children's literature**.

Afanas'ev died of tuberculosis at only forty-five years of age. One interesting posthumous publication is a collection called *Russkie zavetnye skazki* (*Russian Forbidden Tales*), which was published in 1872 in Geneva, Switzerland. This first edition of seventy-seven bawdy and obscene stories—which included motifs such as homosexuality, bestiality, and **incest**—gives no information about the editor, publishing house, or date. Censorship had prevented the volume's publication in Russia during Afanas'ev's lifetime, and it is notable that these highly satirical tales were officially published in Russia only in 1992. However, unofficial copies are known to have been circulating in the late nineteenth century.

The significance of Afanas'ev's contribution to the study of Russian folklore and Slavic mythology has been praised and admired but also debated and criticized. Nevertheless, his influence on Russian literature as such remains indisputable. Not only did he reveal the prodigious richness of Russian tales, his collections also became an inexhaustible well of inspiration for authors like Lev **Tolstoy**, Maksim Gorky, Ivan Bunin, and others. *See also* Bawdy Tale; Collecting, Collectors; Editing, Editors; Erotic Tales; Gay and Lesbian Tales.

Further Readings: Afanas'ev, Aleksandr. *Russian Fairy Tales.* Translated by Norbert Guterman. 1943. New York: Pantheon, 1975; ———. *Russian Secret Tales: Bawdy Folktales of Old Russia.* Introduced by G. Legman. Baltimore: Genealogical Publishing Co., 1998; Riordan, James. "Russian Fairy Tales and Their Collectors." *A Companion to the Fairy Tale.* Edited by Hilda Ellis Davidson and Anna Chaudhri. Cambridge: Brewer, 2003. 217–25.

Janina Orlov

African American Tales

African American folktales provide some of the strongest evidence for African cultural continuities in the New World. The majority of tales on both sides of the Black Atlantic are animal **trickster** tales, which focus of the breaking of friendship or **family** norms by an asocial comic figure. The percentage of such tales in the total repertoire is further dramatized by the relative scarcity of those that feature the small animal or the little boy as hero. The centrality of a figure who is more clever than those who otherwise appear to be superior has been interpreted by many to mean that the stories are responses to enslavement and the need to live by one's wits. This may be so, though there is little evidence that this was the dominant message as the tales were performed within African American communities. They are primarily stories about how *not* to act when around other people.

These trickster tales came to popular notice through the publications of the **Uncle Remus** tales by Joel Chandler **Harris** beginning in 1882. The books were read to children in middle-class homes throughout North America. Their content is strongly affected by the need to make the stories acceptable to adults who read the stories to children. More commonly in live **storytelling** situations among African Americans in villages and towns, the trickster is portrayed as unrelentingly selfish and more malicious. He has a number of ingenious ways of stealing **food** or committing outrageous physical acts that bring physical harm and even **death** to trickster's targets. He is not clever enough to evade capture; but he does escape in many stories, thus demonstrating how quick his wits are. In some of his adventures, the upset he causes leads to death or banishment.

The Br'er Rabbit trickster figure of Harris's books is perhaps most widely identified with his adventure with the Tar Baby. Caught by his enemies when he gets physically stuck while trying to fight the figure they have constructed (ATU 175, The Tarbaby and the Rabbit), Br'er Rabbit manages to escape by cleverly getting thrown into the briar patch. While the details of this tale vary from one community to another, this is indeed one of the stories most often found in African American communities. Ironically, unlike most of the other common trickster stories, it is not uniquely African in origin, for it occurs in other places as well.

Many stories depict the trickster's mastery of larger and more powerful creatures through the operation of his wits. He engineers this with elaborate fictions or by pulling off a seemingly magical task. For instance, making a bet that he can teach the lion to be his riding horse, he shams sickness and persuades Lion to carry him into town (ATU 4, Sick Animal Carries the Healthy One; Motif K1241, Trickster rides dupe horseback). In allowing trickster to ride on his back, Lion was committing an act of basic friendship. Equally widely found is the trick of making the stone smoke (ATU 1060, Squeezing the [Supposed] Stone).

In turning that act into an awareness by the other animals that the trickster had subdued his larger and more powerful friend, the trickster breaks one of the paramount rules of community understanding, for work was carried out as a common enterprise which relied on friendship contracts. Having a best friend on whom one can rely is central to male life throughout the region. The friends often farm together or carry out some other set of tasks in everyday life.

The betrayal of community norms goes even deeper, for the trickster also consumes and contaminates everything that he sees as being valuable. His eating is voracious, and so are his sexual appetites. He even consumes his own children and those of his friends. These stories, then, are **cautionary tale**s, fascinating in their focus on this protean figure but surely not to be emulated. As the storytellers say, "When the people don't do what they're told to do, they always get in trouble."

Somewhat less widely found on both sides of the Atlantic are stories concerned with the courtship and **marriage** of the unnamed "**King**'s Beautiful Daughter" who has been hidden or kept in a glass box. The courtship calls for candidates to pass tests of ingenuity. The victor in this contest is actually an animal who has assumed human form (Motif D314, Transformation: ungulate animal [wild] to person). After the wedding, however, the winner carries the **princess** into the bush and transforms himself into an animal or a supernatural creature. He is revealed by a clever little boy who uses this discovery not only to kill the creature, but to better his own lot in life (ATU 300, The Dragon-Slayer). More commonly, however, the boy (old witch boy or chiggerfoot boy) enjoys no benefit from the recovery. His sole reward seems to reside in the demonstration of his cleverness.

The boy in this tale is the king's son, though he has no status in the king's household and lives under a bed or in the ash heap and sneaks around the yard spying on everybody. He has witching powers and thus is able to recognize the character of his sister's suitor; however, when he tries to warn their father, no one listens. He stealthily follows his sister and her lover into the bush and discovers the magical formula the animal uses to take on his human disguise. When the spy says the magical formula, the animal returns to his natural form and is killed.

As with other trickster tales, the moral center of the story lies in the careful maintenance of the household. One's business should be kept to oneself if possible. The story reveals the king's foolishness in letting his affairs get out of hand and be discovered by the lowest member of the family, who is a gossip, likes to stir up others, and seems content in his status as troublemaker. Whatever motives may be disclosed on the part of the boy, and no matter how clever he is, his status is not altered. As with animal tricksters, his powers reside in his ability to transform himself, which seems to intensify his outsider status. In the Anglophonic Caribbean, he is sometimes called the Old Witch Boy and is endowed with the power of witchcraft of a sort. He has the power of disruption but not of reconciliation.

These actions are understood as taking place in the world before now, and just in case that is not obvious, the storytellers remark that they are "lies above suspicion," from the time when animals talked like humans, and humans acted like animals. As with trickster tales, they are the source of great humor. In fact, in the United States they are commonly told in the context of a joking-contest along with other narratives of community disruption. Such tales are framed by a real world of social rules ("doing what you're told to do"), which the trickster violates.

As the cultural productions of an enslaved and culturally heterogeneous population, the folktales of African Americans testify to the resilience and inventiveness of millions of the slaves' descendants. While they came from a great many different nations and spoke a wide range of languages, those enslaved shared certain principles of worship, healing, and **performance** styles. With regard to patterns of performance, they and their descendants maintained a set of practices in dances, songs, religious rituals, and festival enactments, as well as most of the stories passed on from one slave generation to the next. The stories especially could be performed in the relative privacy of the slave yard. Commonly performed at funeral wakes, they seem to have thrived even under the most repressive plantation regimes.

Folktales as well as songs, dances, orations, sermons, and rhyming are all animated by the same impulses of creative opposition between voices. Even the much-discussed call-and-response pattern common on both sides of the Black Atlantic occurs not only in games, songs, and dances, but also as a core element of storytelling. In fact, storytelling is often found within display events in which song, dance, riddling, and playfully competitive speechmaking take place. This competition is performed not so much to produce winners and losers as it is in the spirit of enabling each virtuoso performance to be matched by the one that follows it. In many African American communities, voice overlap is central to all play, including storytelling. The good storytellers will have a second performer with them to introduce an alternative answering and commenting voice. Moreover, when told in the deepest Creole languages, and fast paced, the stories bewilder outsiders.

Silence is expected only during the occasional activities in which older members of the community communicate with younger listeners, and the stories tend to have either an absurd comic flavor or a moral ending. Because the Br'er Rabbit tales first popularized by Harris were presented as children's entertainment, the view of reading audiences has underscored this dimension of such storytelling. Although there have been many collections of African American folktales from North America and the West Indies, few of them come from actual **fieldwork**. This has skewed the view of the repertoire of the slave and the ex-slave populations as being primarily made up of tales about a clever trickster, Br'er Rabbit. As Harris presented them, the stories were told to white children on the plantation by an aged family retainer. The recasting of the Uncle Remus tales in the Walt **Disney** movie of that name has simply reinforced this attitude.

Harris and many others since who grew up with house-slaves thought the stories reflected slaves' lowly status, even after Emancipation. This impression arose from the ways in which the stories were put into the mouths of those superannuated slaves, those Uncle and Aunt characters who told tales of how to get by via wit in the face of those who were larger and more powerful. In this dimension the tales work not unlike **märchen**, in that the smaller, cleverer figure appears to obtain a prize or some other source of power that he then uses to gain his rewards. In the case of Br'er Rabbit, however, the prize commonly involves slipping out of harm's way rather than any golden goose.

This is not to say that the Br'er Rabbit or Daddy Jake stories reported by Harris did not tell the common stories of the African American repertoire. The 138 tales that Harris printed in his lifetime were predominately from an African substrate of storylore. However, he did not collect them from black storytellers himself but accumulated them from correspondence with whites raised on the plantation. In this, Harris operated no differently than most nineteenth-century collectors. But he made claims for the authenticity of the stories "as told by slaves" that can't be proven from his correspondence.

Despite the fact that Harris and other southern Americans wrote down these stories in remarkably accurate Creole speech, they were actually several times removed from the tellers. Harris's papers make it clear that he did not take the tales directly from ex-slaves but rather from the recitation of whites who had grown up on plantations and developed similarly close relationships with one or another slave nurturer. It is also significant that these stories are presented as typical of the entire repertoire but are written as if they were told to children and were thus used as tales with important messages. Black folklorists who collected tales directly from ex-slaves found a different repertoire, one that included in fact a number of the Uncle Remus tales, which were told as jokes, often at the expense of the planter Old Master or his overseer.

In an attempt to present the full range of African American folktales, the faculty at the Hampton Institute in Virginia initiated a project of **collecting** both tales and songs of ex-slaves. Their efforts were aimed not just at Harris's work but at the blackface minstrel shows, which purported to portray real plantation scenes and sketches. They presented the results of this collection at their meetings before publishing them in their journal *Southern Workman and Hampton School Record* beginning in the early 1890s.

Readers had to wait until the mid-1930s, with the publications of the Floridian Afro-American ethnographer, novelist, and collector Zora Neale **Hurston** before a reasonable sample of continental African American tales were published by a trade publisher. Even then her classic *Mules and Men* (1935) did not have many readers until it was reissued during the 1960s. During that period of rising awareness of civil rights, more contemporary stories were reported, first from prisons and ghettos. Public attention grew as these stories achieved some prominence. Many of them were tales of tricksters not unlike those reported earlier, but they were performed as "toasts"—narrative poems with subjects reflecting the growing sense of resistance in urban areas. One of these, "The Signifying Monkey," became emblematic of the concerns of young men in African American street-corner groups. This toast concerned "signifying," a term for brazen trickery not unlike that pulled off by Br'er Rabbit and Compe Nansi; but now the trickster was openly identified with young black men, and the butts of his hijinks were whites in command. Even more openly critical of the white power structure is another toast dealing with Shine, an African American sailor on the Titanic who outswims all of those whites left behind, signifying at them as he swims away. *See also* African Tales; Anansi; Hamilton, Virginia; Négritude, Créolité, and Folktale; North American Tales.

Further Readings: Abrahams, Roger D., ed. *African American Folktales: Stories from the Black Traditions of the New World.* New York: Pantheon, 1999. Reprint of *Afro-American Folktales,* 1985; Baer, Florence E. *Sources and Analogues of the Uncle Remus Tales.* Helsinki: Academia Scientiarum Fennica, 1980; Bontemps, Arna, and Langston Hughes, eds. *The Book of Negro Folklore.* New York: Dodd, Mead, 1958; Dance, Daryl Cumber. *Shuckin' and Jivin': Folklore from Contemporary Black Americans.* Bloomington: Indiana University Press, 1978; Harris, Joel Chandler. *Uncle Remus: His Songs and His Sayings; The Folk-Lore of the Old Plantation.* New York: D. Appleton, 1880; Waters, Donald, ed. *Strange Ways and Sweet Dreams: Afro-American Folklore from the Hampton Institute.* Boston: G. K. Hall, 1983.

Roger D. Abrahams

African Tales

The African continent is home to thousands of different groups distinguished by language, lifestyle, and culture. As the self-proclaimed continent of orality, it is also home to vibrant and still-active traditions of oral performance and narrative, although the march of modernization is imperiling these traditional forms. Despite the enormous opportunities presented by this wealth of variety, the collection and study of African folktales has lagged behind other parts of the world, in part because of the very challenges of the material. The diversity of local languages in which stories are told, the effort required to transpose these stories from an oral medium to writing, usually with a translation into a European language, and the diverse languages in which scholarship is published make the task of study daunting. Thousands of folktales have been collected from all parts of the continent in the past two centuries, but the collections are not fully supported by tools such as **tale-type** or **motif** indexes, or the study of individual narrators' repertoires and life histories. Much work remains to be done.

Early Collections

The systematic collection of African folktales began in the nineteenth century, as Christian missionaries, and later colonial administrators and travelers, began to penetrate African societies, to learn the languages, and to record their observations of the cultures they encountered. (Traders, whose contacts go much further back, rarely wrote of what they experienced; an exception would be the eighteenth-century Danish trader Ludewig Rømer, who offered the first **Anansi** stories on record in 1760). To this period, until roughly 1940, we owe a number of influential collections from which tales have been widely anthologized. Many of these collections offer the original language versions of their stories, but few provide reliable information on the **informant** or the circumstances of collection; in a number of cases they clearly demonstrate the beliefs of the collector (an example being Ruth Fisher's *Twilight Tales of the Black Baganda,* 1911). But time and widespread reproduction have made some individual tales from these collections into something like classics.

In southern Africa, Wilhelm Bleek's work with San-speaking informants (often convicts assigned to serve with him) led to his collections, first *Reynard the Fox in South Africa* (1864), and later, in collaboration with Lucy Lloyd, *Specimens of Bushman Folklore* (1911), a bilingual collection of texts, in which the English is an unreadable literal **translation** of the original. Stories from this collection, rewritten, were later popularized by Bleek's daughter Dorothea in *Mantis and his Friends* (1923). Around the same time, the Reverend Henry

Callaway published his *Nursery Tales, Traditions, and Histories of the Zulus* (1868), which is also a bilingual edition.

In West Africa, R. S. Rattray published *Akan-Ashanti Folktales* (1930), collected in the British Gold Coast Colony (later the Republic of Ghana). This introduced the popular spider-trickster Ananse (that is, Anansi). His collection is supplemented for neighboring groups by A. S. Cardinall's *Tales Told in Togoland* (1931). Togoland at the time was a former German colony placed under British mandate following World War I, and at independence in 1958, the enclave chose to remain with Ghana.

For French West Africa, Laurent Jean Baptiste Bérenger-Feraud published an anthology, *Recueil de contes populaires de la Sénégambie* (*Collection of Popular Tales from Senegambia*, 1885), followed later by the administrator François-Victor Equilbecq, who in 1913 published an extensive three-volume collection of tales from different regions, preceding them with an extensive descriptive essay (*Essai sur la littérature merveilleuse des noirs, suivi de contes indigènes de l'Ouest africain français* [*Essay on the Marvelous Literature of the Blacks, Followed by Native Tales of French West Africa*]). One should also mention the influential anthology of Blaise Cendrars, *Anthologie nègre* (1927), which contributed to the Paris-based **Négritude** movement. For North Africa, René Basset published large collections of Berber and Arabic folktales, including *Contes populaires berbères* (*Popular Berber Tales*, 1887), *Nouveaux contes berbères* (*New Berber Tales*, 1897), and *Mille et un contes, legendes et récits arabes* (*A Thousand and One Arabic Tales, Legends, and Stories*, 1925–27). From central Africa (the Congo basin) there are a number of collections in French from missionaries: H. Trilles, *Contes et légendes pygmées* (*Pygmy Tales and Legends*, 1931); Joseph van Wing and Clément Scholler, *Légendes des Bakongo-Orientaux* (*Legends of the Eastern Bakongo*, 1940); and A. de Rop, *Versions et fragments de l'épopée móngo* (*Versions and Fragments of the Mongo Epic*, 1978). Some of the scholarship, however, is in Flemish, reflecting the Belgian origins of the **collectors**.

German story-collecting activity in their colonies of East and West Africa more or less ceased following World War I, when their territories were handed over to other powers. Before the war, however, the Germans had been very active in linguistic and ethnographic research, and the *Zeitschrift für Kolonialsprachen* (*Journal of Colonial Languages*), later renamed *Afrika und Übersee* (*Africa and Overseas*), and other similar journals contain numerous collections of tales from southern and eastern Africa, in the original language with a German translation. Karl Meinhof made a good anthology of stories entitled *Afrikanische Märchen* (*African Tales*, 1921), but it is eclipsed by the monumental, twelve-volume collection of Leo **Frobenius**: *Atlantis: Volksmärchen und Volksdichtungen Afrikas* (*Atlantis: Folktales and Folk Literature of Africa*, 1921–28). Each volume represented a different region of the continent, the stories having been collected during a series of expeditions Frobenius made in the early years of the century. The collection offers volumes 1–3: Tales of the Kabyles (Algeria/North Africa); volume 4: Tales from Kordofan (Ethiopia-Sudan); volume 5: Traditions of the western Sudan (a descriptive essay, and stories of the Nupe, Mossi, and Mande peoples); volume 6: Epic traditions of the western Sudan (Soninke, Fulani, Baman, and Dogon); volume 7: Spirits of the western Sudan (Mande, Bozo/Sorko, Jukun, and Hausa); volume 8: Tales of the western Sudan (Malinke, Mossi and others); volume 9: Central Sudan (Nupe, Hausa, and others); volume 10: the Yoruba; volume 11: Upper Guinea (Togo: Bassari, Tim, Munchi); volume 12: Kasai (modern Congo) (n.b. in these titles, Sudan means not the modern republic along the Nile, but the old Arabic Bilad es-Sudan, the land of the Blacks, or Africa south of the Sahara and especially the Sahel). Another book, *Eryth-räia* (1931), offers description and stories from the region of modern Zimbabwe.

Americans working in Africa have contributed to the effort. Heli Chatelain, working as a missionary in Angola, published *Folktales of Angola* in 1894. Melville and Frances Herskovits, visiting the French colony of Dahomey in the 1930s, collected materials published in 1958 as *Dahomean Narrative*, which was at the time an exemplary work; their interest in Dahomey was guided by Melville Herskovits's curiosity about the trans-Atlantic continuities of African cultures. It should be stressed that the titles mentioned above are only some of the many publications from this period that offer African tales to a wider audience outside the continent.

Later Collections

The task of collecting folktales has continued wherever there have been literate listeners who desired to preserve what they heard. Publication opportunities have perhaps not been so common. In the period since 1960, the era of independence for many African nations, the enterprise was renewed, under somewhat different premises: the collections were no longer intended to assist administrators in understanding their colonial subjects or to allow missionaries to learn the local languages, but were intended to preserve and to present the national heritages of oral literature and the collective wisdom and worldview of given peoples. A few notable series deserve mention. In the 1960s and 1970s, Oxford University Press published a series, the OLAL (Oxford Library of African Literature), devoted to scholarly editions of transcribed **oral tradition**s from a variety of peoples. Many of their texts were devoted to poetic forms, but some collections of folktales also appeared: Ruth Finnegan's *Limba Stories and Story-Telling* (1967), John Mbiti's *Akamba Stories* (1966), Harold Scheub's *The Xhosa Ntsomi* (1975), and E. E. Evans-Pritchard's collection, *The Zande Trickster* (1967). In France, the Classiques Africains offered a similar series of scholarly, bilingual editions of oral traditions, often with accompanying sound recordings. Again, some of the volumes were devoted to folktales. The French government has also subsidized the publication (in the name of Francophonie) of a series of thinner and more affordable collections of stories, usually presented in bilingual formats. From the Congo, the Centre d'études ethnographiques du Bandundu (CEEBA: Bandundu Center for Ethnographic Studies) has published over a dozen substantial collections of tales of peoples in the region: *Le père qui ne voulait pas de fille* (*The Father Who Wanted No Daughters*, 1974); *Pourquoi le coq ne chante plus?* (*Why Doesn't the Rooster Crow Any More?* 1973); *Tu es méchant, personne ne te mangera* (*You Are Naughty, No-One Will Eat You*, 1975); and *Ma femme n'est pas ton gibier* (*My Wife Is Not Your Game*, 1977).

A significant difficulty with all collections of African folktales is that of availability and access; many works have been published in limited distribution. There are also certainly countless tales, transcribed and often translated, but unpublished, in the collections of the generations of researchers who have worked in Africa.

Content and Themes

For centuries, **Aesop** was the first African storyteller of record (until earlier Egyptian folktales were discovered and translated), and since his time the realm of animal fable has seemed peculiarly African. It is true that much of the early material collected, especially from southern Africa, was in the form of **animal tale**s and that animal heroes (especially tricksters) are found across the continent. But these stories are almost never moral **fable**s; instead, the animal world mirrors the human world in most regards (such as behavior, social relations, and other problems). As an example of the differences, one might look to the classic story of the race between the hare and the tortoise, which in folktales the tortoise wins by guile: he lines up his kinsmen along the course, so that each time the hare calls out, a tortoise answers from somewhere ahead of him, and of course, one is waiting at the finish line to greet the frantic and exhausted hare (ATU 1074; variants of the story pit any one of a number of small and slow animals against larger and faster competitors). Other widespread animal tales include the hare's tug-of-war, in which the hare (or another small animal) pits the elephant and the hippopotamus against each other, each pulling a rope but unable to see who is pulling at the other end, or the story of how the hare ate the lioness' cubs and escaped. The animal world presents an array of stock characters (large or small, strong or weak, meat-eaters or prey, aquatic or terrestrial) rather than an accurate reflection of the local fauna.

Stories of human action are equally common, often involving the ordinary tensions of social existence: questions of **marriage** partners, rivalry of co-wives, and the position of children. One of the most widespread types uses the structure of ATU 480, **The Kind and the Unkind Girls**: a first actor is sent on a quest and returns with riches, whereas the second, sent in imitation, muddles the tasks and is rewarded with **death** or disgrace. The protagonists may be of either **gender** and almost any condition or status. Young **women** refuse all eligible suitors and finally go off with a man who proves to be a monster; some escape, but more, perhaps, are devoured. Suitors understand the riddling messages sent by the maiden they are courting, and so they succeed in winning her hand. Hunters are seduced by women who prove to be beasts; in some cases these hunters marry maidens whom they know to be transformed antelopes, as the hunter has hidden her skin while she bathed. Wives are cast off because they are barren, and a child is born who eventually restores them to prosperity and esteem (see **Birth**; **Infertility**). Also frequent are adventure stories in which clever humans escape monsters; often the protagonists are a group of **brothers** who are saved by the preternatural ingenuity (or magic) of the youngest sibling. A frequent **motif** in this last series is the monster's attempt to eat the children during the night, which is foiled by the hero who switches the identifying markers with the monster's own children, so that they are the ones eaten instead.

In many cases, the action involves hunger and **food**: disorder comes from the desire to avoid sharing food or from attempts to conceal a supply. The trickster traps the elephant between two trees and trims off meat to allow the larger animal to get free. While working a field with a partner, the trickster goes off to "see a friend" but really eats all the supplies they have brought for the day; he answers inquiries with punning names: "I saw my friend 'Still-some-left'" and later "It's-all-gone." A greedy husband ends up being buried because he did not wish to share food with his **family**.

Cycles of trickster stories are found across the continent. The trickster is usually animal in shape: Ananse of the Ashanti or Ture of the Zande are spiders; Leuck of the Wolof is a hare, as are Kalulu of the Bemba and Sungura of the Swahili; Ajapa of the Yoruba is a tortoise, and there are other tortoises in tales from central Africa. The trickster's guile is employed to escape traps set by larger animals, to make off with the prize (food or other desirable objects), or to make a fool of a larger foil; the hyena is the frequent butt of the trickster's schemes. One tale type occurring across the continent is that of The Profitable Exchange (ATU 1655), in which the hero starts with an object of small worth and by a combination of persuasiveness and chicanery trades up to something of great value: from honey to grain to a chicken, ending with the chiefdom; or from a corncob to a chicken to a sheep and ending with a hundred slaves; or from a cockroach to a wife. Ananse (or Anansi) is the best known of the tricksters, and his actions often have a mythological dimension; he is the companion of the sky-god. Other tricksters such as Ture may not function in an overtly mythological framework, but their actions nevertheless may benefit humanity, such as by releasing hoarded waters or discovering fire. In some areas the trickster is a terrible child of a fairly specific type (often known as the *enfant terrible*), one who does the opposite of all normal actions, often with destructive effect. The series of adventures leads to confrontation with a chief and conclude in varying ways: the child finally dies, having chosen to kill a bird who is carrying it to safety, or the child may replace the chief on the throne.

Many folktales are mythological or etiological in content, describing consequences ranging from the trivial (the color of a bird's feathers) to the cosmic (the origin of the sun and moon). The most widespread narrative on the origin of death is that of the perverted message, in which a slower animal is sent first to announce that humans will not die, or will revive after death, and a faster animal sent later; the second messenger arrives first, or the message may be misunderstood. Individual cultural heroes also give rise to story cycles, for instance, Lianja of the Mongo/Nkundo peoples of the Congo or Jeki la Nzambe of the Duala in Cameroon; often episodes of the cycles occur as stand-alone folktales. A favorite theme is a past in which current conditions were inverted: smiths worked on rooftops, the leopard played with the goat, and women had power (although in some cases women do retain their authority). Sexual themes are frequent: body parts at first may have been inconveniently placed (in the armpit for example), and their use may not have been known. **Men** cannot understand what women are (the corollary rarely occurs). Relations between husband and wife continue to be a topic of amusement and interest. Hero stories featuring hunters and warriors are frequent. One very widespread narrative is a variation on the Perseus/monster-slayer legend, in which a hero comes to a town, finds it suffering under the rule of some monstrous creature (which usually restricts access to water), and kills the beast. The story can be found from Ethiopia (part of the legend of the Queen of Sheba) through to Senegal. One variant appears in the myth of origin of the town of Abuja, the new capital of Nigeria. Serious myths (in a given culture) are not generally the subject of popular narration; they are recounted in ritual or ceremonial contexts, not as entertainment but to enlist the power they embody.

Islam spread very quickly over North Africa in the seventh century and then filtered down across the Sahara, following trade and later pilgrimage routes. In eastern Africa Islam spread somewhat later and remained a coastal phenomenon. Christianity, although present from its start in Egypt and Ethiopia, was slower to spread into the continent and is largely associated with the arrival of European traders and later **colonialism**. Both faiths brought stories (often the same ones, from slightly different perspectives), but their general impact before the modern era is difficult to assess. As an example, one might look at a motif that is found frequently in southeastern Africa (Zimbabwe and its neighbors): that of the tower built to allow contact with heaven. It falls down, causing disasters. The story resembles that of the tower of Babel, but it generally stands alone without other etiological elements out of Genesis that might argue for influence and contact. The Herskovitses, working in the old kingdom of Dahomey (modern Benin) encountered a story of creation involving Adam and Eve that is explicitly set in opposition to the account given by missionaries.

One favorite genre, not so widespread elsewhere, is the dilemma tale, a story that ends with a question put to the audience. For example, three brothers help rescue a princess; which of them should marry her? Three women help save the life of a man; which should be the principal wife? William Bascom (1975) assembled an anthology of such texts, which reflect the original and very communal **context** for **performance**—the family fireside. Such stories also serve a pedagogic purpose, in that the reasoning used to justify answers following the question is an exploration of cultural norms and expectations.

Performance Contexts

The classic African performance context, described by many nineteenth-century observers, is of course the family fireside at night, when an older adult may relate a series of tales, or the different members of the audience may make their own contributions. The audience would extend beyond a nuclear family. A given compound might house several adult siblings and their families, or several co-wives and their offspring, as well as other relatives and friends. Frequently, restrictions apply to the telling of tales. In some areas, they may not be told during the farming season, and often they are not to be told during the daytime (both forbidden periods should be devoted to work). Ordinary social norms will apply: the audience will defer to the older members present, and younger members will require explicit permission to raise their voice. A session typically involves a series of shorter tales (which may be thematically related) rather than an extended narrative. Many tales involve songs or dramatic action, in which the audience may participate; the chantefable (**cante fable**) is a staple. Stories are frequently introduced by formulas that define the subsequent content as something set apart from ordinary discourse, and often invite the audience's attention and participation.

The narration of a tale involves much more than just the story. The teller will often provide different voices for the characters; idiophones to suggest action are common; and the teller will often mime some of the action. None of these features translates readily or easily into the printed medium. The verbal element of African tales, no matter how accurately reproduced, is almost always only a shadow of the original event.

The professional storyteller appears to be rare. While a few individuals may earn some income from their performances, these are usually more specialized professionals whose output is not entirely comparable to the ordinary folktale: the initiate of *mvett*-performances in Cameroon/Gabon, the hunter's bard of the Mande world, or the *karisi*-spirit initiate who recites the Mwindo **epic**. The stories they tell, in stylized and extensive performances, often embody the plots of well-known tales, and there is a clear continuity; however, the delivery and reception are quite distinct from ordinary **storytelling**. Such a performance is more formal, often involving an ensemble, music, and special occasions. The griot of West Africa (also known as *jeli, gewel, gesere,* or *gawlo*; local names vary, as do the social expectations) is more of a praise-singer and genealogist than a storyteller, despite the current image prevalent in America (probably since the time of the popular novel *Roots*, 1976). The association of griots and folktales is due more to literary invention than to actual practice. A good anthology illustrating the difference in content and style of ordinary narrators and griots in the Gambia area is by Katrin Pfeiffer, *Mandinka Spoken Art* (1997). In this region, the social category of "griot" is defined by lineage and includes members who may not actually be performers. The idealized vision of the older male storyteller, lore-master of the group (and so recalling bards and sages of other cultures), is an imaginary construct; the typical African storyteller is an older woman.

Within a culture defined by oral tradition, however, tales have a place beyond that of fireside narration; they are part of the common heritage of the group, and so they can be used, often elliptically or allusively, in the course of ordinary conversation. In some regions, part of the art of public speaking involves the appropriate and apposite use of tales and **proverbs** in the course of making an argument.

This point raises the question of generic boundaries, which in Africa are far more fluid than the theory of folklore genre classification might wish. Folktales coexist with innumerable other forms of local narrative, from the individual **memorate** to collective histories, cult stories, and imported religious materials, and particularly what might be called the "high art" of the African oral tradition: allusive praise poetry and more expansive epic recitations. Epics are not found everywhere on the continent, and they represent a distinctive performance genre that is not identical to Eurasian forms (the use of meter and music, for instance, render them far less "textual" than European literary examples). But epics, in their considerable variety, do employ the standard techniques and building blocks of folktale materials: pattern and repletion and hero-centered plots. There are of course significant differences in tone, reference, and sophistication, but the commonalities deserve recognition. Motifs migrate very freely among these various genres, especially in the historical material that can be considered the common, secular property of the culture (specific cult myths are more restricted in their distribution). So a story of rivalry between stepbrothers (sons of different co-wives), which is part of the epic of Sunjata in the Mande world (Mali-Guinea), becomes an **etiologic tale** about social relations among the Kuranko (Guinea-Sierra Leone); and the story of the ring found in the fish's belly (ATU 736A, The Ring of Polycrates) appears as part of the history of the kingdom of Segou.

Literary Tales

Certain literary versions of folktales may be better known and more influential than the original materials. Working in Senegal, the veterinarian Birago **Diop** produced three volumes of stories that have become widely known: *Les contes d'Amadou Koumba* (*The Tales of Amadou Koumba*, 1947), *Les nouveaux contes d'Amadou Koumba* (*The New Tales of Amadou Koumba*, 1958), and *Contes et lavanes* (*Tales and Enigmas*, 1963). In Francophone Africa, Diop's protagonists, Leuck the Hare and Bouki the Hyena, are as familiar as Br'er Rabbit and Br'er Fox (to whom they are almost certainly related). Diop does not really attempt to reproduce an oral style; his stories are written in an elegant, witty, and literary French, and as such are very effective images of the culture. In Côte d'Ivoire, Bernard **Dadié** also retold folktales in *Le pagne noir: Contes africains* (1955; translated as *The Black Cloth: A Collection of African Folktales*, 1987), although with less verve than Diop. Amos **Tutuola** also made use of Yoruba folktales in constructing his first novel, *The Palm-Wine Drinkard and His Dead Palm-Wine Tapster in the Deads' Town* (1952).

Form and Analysis

Scholars such as Melville and Frances Herskovits, Ruth Finnegan, and Isidore Okpewho have critiqued the application of Eurocentric models of interpretation to African **folklore** and folktales, but the critiques have rarely been accompanied by more positive methodologies. The notion of orality, now widespread, has not proved a very effective heuristic tool, although considerations of orality remain an essential starting point in approaching the material. In France, various projects at the Centre National de Recherche Scientifique (National Center for Scientific Research) led by Denise Paulme, Geneviève Calame-Griaule, Veronika Görög-Karady, and others such as Jean Dérive, have published collective works on such topics as the theme of the tree, the family universe, and *enfants terribles*. Their focus has been to interpret tales in terms of the local sociology and perception. The French approach is more oriented to the structural/morphological approaches of Claude Levi-Strauss and Vladimir **Propp** than to the taxonomic methods of Germanic and Anglophone scholarship. Michael Jackson (*Allegories of the Wilderness*, 1982) does attempt a similar task for the Kuranko of Sierra Leone, discussing a corpus of tales from the perspective of various social issues. Harold Scheub is one of the few American scholars to approach folktales formalistically. Working principally with materials from southern Africa, where he has done extensive **fieldwork**, he identifies a doubled structure in tales, in which the elements of the initial problem are duplicated, and often transformed, in the resolution to the tale. Scheub has also given us one of the few performer-centered studies, dedicated to a Xhosa narrator, Nongenile Masithathu Zenani (*The World and the Word*, 1992). American studies of African folktales were at first oriented to tracing connections between African folktales and their continuities in the New World (the Br'er Rabbit stories, among others), but in recent years have turned more to questions of performance context, following the methods of Richard Baumann (*Verbal Art as Performance*, 1977) and Dan Ben-Amos, who applied the principles to African folklore.

Classification of African tales is an unfinished enterprise. African tales are not as well represented as they might be in indexes of motifs and tale types. Over the years, a number of dissertations have attempted to provide tools for specific regions, but their value and availability are limited. As a further complication, while many African tales do show some resemblance to foreign analogues, they are also very thoroughly acculturated in the local context so that the resemblances sometimes need to be teased out. African folktales in general seem closer to **Native American tales** in their themes and content than to the bourgeois examples collected by the Brothers **Grimm**, which served as armature for the original indexes of tale types and motifs. Many of the trickster stories are very similar: one animal visits another and is fed magically; when the animal tries to reproduce the methods, it dies or is maimed; the trickster is taken for a ride by a bird, but is dropped. This line of inquiry has not been well explored. Adding to the question of acculturation is a tendency (in the newly independent countries) to define folktales in nationalist terms as the part of a specific heritage; such chauvinism is hardly unique to the field but does discourage comparative work.

African folktales are still being be told, often with new twists and modern settings, and new collections continue to appear. The focus is very much upon individual cultures and language groups. African scholars face great difficulties in their work (a lack of support for research, poor library resources for reference work, and almost no publication outlets), but there are a growing number of studies from within cultures. Outside Africa, the value of folktales for understanding the cultural dynamics of the continents' many peoples is not appreciated, and the problem is compounded by generalized visions that efface all the specific traits of groups and social contexts. ***See also*** African American Tales; *Kirikou et la sorcière*; Ogre, Ogress.

Further Readings: Abrahams, Roger D. *African Folktales: Traditional Stories of the Black World*. New York: Pantheon Books, 1983; Bascom, William. *African Dilemma Tales*. The Hague: Mouton, 1975; Finnegan, Ruth. *Oral Literature in Africa*. London: Oxford University Press, 1970; Görög-Karady, Veronika. *Littérature orale d'Afrique noire: Bibliographie analytique*. Paris: Maisonneuve, 1981; Klipple, May Augusta. *African Folktales with Foreign Analogues*. New York: Garland Press, 1992; Scheub, Harold, ed. *The African Storyteller: Stories from African Oral Traditions*. Dubuque: Kendall Hunt Publishing, 1990; ———, ed. *The World and the Word: Tales and Observations from the Xhosa Oral Tradition*. Madison: University of Wisconsin Press, 1992.

Stephen Belcher

Age

All cultures divide life into stages. The famous **riddle** of the sphinx solved by Oedipus depicts three such phases: infancy, adulthood, and old age; whereas William **Shakespeare** puts seven "ages of life" into Jacques' famous soliloquy in *As You Like It* (1599).

The **fable** "Die Lebenszeit" ("The Life Span"; ATU 173, Human and Animal Life Spans Are Readjusted), recorded by Jacob and Wilhelm **Grimm**, but also found in collections attributed to **Aesop,** and elsewhere, depicts these phases with humor. In a typical version, man and various animals bargain with God concerning their respective life spans. Different animals relinquish some of their allocated years to man, giving him a longer life. But his final years are beastly: from the age of thirty onward he is treated respectively like a donkey (working for others), a dog (growling in a corner), and finally a monkey (a laughingstock for children).

The admonition "Honor your **father** and **mother**," however formulated, is a moral cornerstone of most cultures, and one supported by folktales everywhere. Especially relevant are tales of type ATU 980, The Ungrateful Son. An exemplary story from this group is the **Jātaka** tale describing how a middle-aged man plans to kill his elderly father and bury him. The old man's seven-year-old grandson watches as the father digs a grave, then snatches the spade and begins to dig nearby. Asked what he is doing, the boy tells his father, "When you are old I will treat you as you are now treating your father." Repentant, the man takes his old father back home and restores him to a position of respect. Tales of type ATU 980 reflect a morality based on enlightened self interest, with middle-aged people belatedly supporting a tradition that will benefit them when they themselves grow old.

Other tales depict threatened or neglected old people gaining care through deception and trickery. In "The Pretended Inheritance" (ATU 982) by J. Hinton Knowles (*Folk-Tales of Kashmir*, 2nd ed., 1893), an old man distributes his wealth to his sons before he dies, expecting to be supported by them; but, now possessing their inheritance, they neglect him. He regains their attention by having a friend deliver to him four bags filled with gravel, while loudly announcing that he is repaying a loan. Thinking that their father is again wealthy, the sons give him the best possible care until finally he dies, and they discover that the inheritance supplement is worthless.

Another tale of care gained through trickery is the fable of type ATU 101, The Old Dog as Rescuer of the Child. Here a husband and wife plan to do away with a dog deemed too old to protect the household. A **wolf** learns of the threat to his cousin, and together they conspire to help the latter. As planned, the wolf steals the couple's child, but then allows the dog to overtake him and "rescue" the baby. The grateful parents vow to care for the old dog as long as he lives.

The best-known fable about animals threatened because of their age is "Die Bremer Stadmusikanten" ("Bremen Town Musicians"; ATU 130, The Animals in Night Quarters) as recorded by the Grimm brothers. Five old animals, rather than submitting to abandonment or slaughter as threatened by their owners, set off for Bremen, where they intend to support themselves as musicians. Underway they find shelter in a house in the woods. It is inhabited by robbers, who are so frightened by the intruders that they flee, abandoning the house to its new occupants. Thus these old animals, deemed unfit by their human masters, find protection and support through their own resourcefulness, plus a generous portion of good luck.

Numerous **legend**s from around the world tell of a time in the distant past when old people were put to **death** as a matter of custom and law. Various explanations are advanced as to why this practice was stopped, typically because of one old person's demonstration of unusual wisdom. "Warum heutzutage die alten Leute ihren eigenen Tod sterben" ("Why Today Old People Die Their Own Death," ATU 981, Wisdom of Hidden Old Man Saves Kingdom), as recorded by Bohdan Mykytiuk in *Ukrainische Märchen* (*Ukrainian Folktales*, 1979), is exemplary. Here a kind-hearted son hides his old father instead of putting him to death as dictated by custom. A famine comes, and no one has seed for the next crop, until the elderly father suggests dismantling their thatched roof and rethreshing the straw, thus gaining sufficient seed for a new planting. Impressed with the old man's wisdom, people resolve henceforth to allow everyone to die their own death.

Old people in folktales can also be targets of derision, especially regarding their **sexuality**. The compilers of medieval and Renaissance **jest** books and their literary successors, preeminently Giovanni **Boccaccio** and Geoffrey **Chaucer**, made ample use of such material, taking special delight in ridiculing old men married to young **women**. Such stories are told worldwide and are found in some of the oldest collections still extant. For example, "The Old Man with the Young Wife" from the *Panchatantra* (book 3) tells of an old man married to a young woman who cannot bear to look at him. One night, while she is asleep with her back toward him, a **thief** enters the house. Terrified, she embraces her husband, thus thrilling his every limb. He is so grateful to the intruder for this stimulation that he thanks the thief profusely, inviting him to take whatever he wants.

Similarly, but with an added ironic twist, "The Farmer's Wife" (*Panchatantra*, book 4) depicts a woman married to a man "so old that he cannot stir," so she takes his money and absconds with a youthful lover. Arriving at a river, the young man asks himself, "What am I to do with this middle-aged female?" He tells her that he will carry the money and her clothing across the river, and then return for her, but instead he escapes with everything, abandoning her naked at the river's edge.

Further Reading: Ashliman, D. L. "Aging and Death in Folklore." 2006. http://www.pitt.edu/~dash/aging.html.

D. L. Ashliman

Aladdin

Aladdin is the title character of "Aladdin and the Wonderful Lamp," one of the best known and most often adapted tales of the *Arabian Nights*. Like "**Ali Baba** and the Forty Thieves," "Aladdin" is an orphan tale that does not derive directly from Arabic manuscripts of the *Arabian Nights*. It first appeared in France when the Syrian monk Hanna told it,

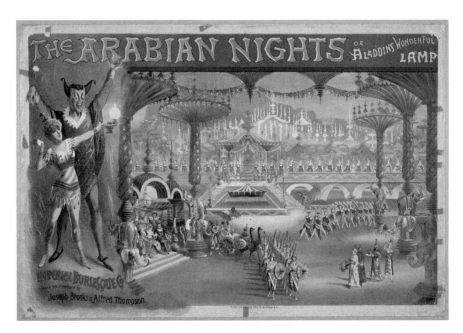

Illustration from *The Arabian Nights* titled *Aladdin's Wonderful Lamp*, by the Imperial Burlesque Co. [Library of Congress]

along with several other stories, to Antoine **Galland** in 1709. Galland then included it in his French version of the *Thousand and One Nights* in 1712. In other words, "Aladdin," like "Ali Baba," is actually a French-Syrian creation from the beginning of the eighteenth century. In contrast to "Ali Baba," there is no written version of "Aladdin" as Hanna told it to Galland, so we cannot compare the French adaptation to its source.

Because Galland's version founds its way into many **oral tradition**s, "Aladdin" has come to constitute its own **tale type**—ATU 561—in the classification system used by folklorists (although a simpler form is represented by tale type ATU 560, The Magic Ring, which provides the basic intrigue). The tale's basic structure is very close to a fairy tale: a poor young man, with the aid of a **magic object**, builds a palace more beautiful than that of the **king** and marries a **princess**; when he loses them, thanks to a second magic object, he manages to recover everything he has lost. The hero Aladdin is described as a bad sort—undisciplined, lazy, and responsible for the death of his **father** and the misery of his **mother**. At the beginning, he does no good deed that would qualify him to obtain a magic object or to marry a princess. But he is without hypocrisy; he succeeds, and in the end he becomes good and wise.

The **transformation** of the bad lot into a good boy seems to take place, as in an initiatory account, in an underground realm, during a symbolic **death** and rebirth. Initially, when Aladdin is locked up in the darkness—thirsty, famished, and ready to die—he thinks for the first time of God. When he joins his hands to pray, he unwittingly rubs the magic ring, which reveals a genie who will save him and bring him back to the light. Later in the story, in a symmetrical way, after having lost everything—full of despair and threatened by the king with death—Aladdin wants to pray to God one last time. Again he involuntarily rubs the magic ring, and the genie appears and takes him to the place where the palace and the princess have been transported. The hero, despite all of his flaws, is saved because he is able to find the right way—to act in accord with what is good. This makes him particularly human and appealing.

The international popularity of "Aladdin and the Wonderful Lamp" is evident in the tale's broad reception and in the way its motifs—especially the genie, the magic lamp, and the magic ring—have become part of popular culture. "Aladdin and the Wonderful Lamp" is frequently reprinted in children's picture-book format, and the story, characters, and individual motifs have been repeatedly adapted for the **theater**, **opera**, **television**, and **film and video**. *See also* Animation; *Arabian Nights* Films; Pantomime; Reiniger, Lotte; Thief of Bagdad Films; Walt Disney Company.

Further Reading: Cooperson, Michael. "The Monstrous Births of 'Aladdin.'" *Harvard Middle Eastern and Islamic Review* 1 (1994): 67–86. Reprinted in *The* Arabian Nights *Reader*. Edited by Ulrich Marzolph. Detroit: Wayne State University Press, 2006. 265–82.

Aboubakr Chraïbi

Albanian Tales

The Albanians are an Indo-European people inhabiting the southwestern Balkans. They live primarily in the Republic of Albania and in Kosova, where they form the absolute majority of the population, and in the western part of the Republic of Macedonia, where they form about one-quarter of the total population. There are also Albanian minorities in the neighboring countries of Montenegro and Serbia, as well as old settlements in southern Italy and Greece. Albanian territories in the Balkans formed part of the Ottoman Empire for five centuries, during which writing and publishing in Albanian was forbidden. Accordingly, written literature was late to develop. Oral literature, handed down from generation to generation, was thus of greater significance to the Albanians than to many neighboring peoples. It was in oral form that the wealth of their traditional culture was preserved, without the need for books.

The Albanians are a small population. At the declaration of independence in 1912, there were less than one million people in the country. Empires and foreign occupants have come and gone, and the Albanians have been subjected to many external influences over the centuries. Their oral literature, in particular their folktales and oral verse, reflect this heterogeneous background.

Though a historical stratification of Albanian tales has not yet been undertaken, it is evident that certain elements of **classical antiquity** have survived, in particular in figures of mythology. The *zana*, for instance, the courageous and often formidable mountain fairy of Albanian oral literature, derives its name from the Roman goddess of the hunt Diana, as does the Romanian *zînă* (forest nymph).

Evident to any knowledgeable observers, too, are many old Balkan elements common to the neighboring Balkan cultures of the southern Slavs, the Romanians, and the Greeks. It is difficult, especially in the case of Albania, to evaluate just how old these common Balkan elements are. One example is a Balkan motif of immurement in the grim tale of Rozafat Castle in Shkodra. The story of a woman being walled in during the construction of a bridge or castle to stabilize the foundations is widespread in oral literature in Albania, the Balkans, and elsewhere.

Albania's centuries as part of the Ottoman Empire and the Islamization of the majority of the population created strong links to the folk cultures of Turkey and the Middle East.

Albanian and Turkish tales have many parallels. Pashas and dervishes abound in an otherwise European context. Figures of Oriental legendry, such as **Nasreddin** Hodja and Sari Salltëk, from Turkish Sarı Saltuk, are well known in Albania, as are figures of fairy tales and mythology such as the *div* from Turkish *dev, div* (**ogre,** giant); the *qose* from Turkish *köse* (barefaced man); the *xhind* from Turkish *cin* (jinn); the werewolflike *karanxholl* from Turkish *karakoncolos* (black bogey, black **werewolf**); the *perria* from Turkish *peri* (**fairy,** good jinn); and the dwarflike *xhuxh* or *xhuxhmaxhuxh* from Turkish *cüce* (**dwarf**).

Other figures of mythology that occur regularly in Albanian fairy tales are the *kulshedra* (**dragon**), the *shtriga* (**witch**), the *lugat* (vampire), and the *katalla* (cyclops). Among the forces usually representing the power of good are the *ora*, a female fairy who can serve as a protective fairy godmother; the *drangue*, a semihuman figure who combats the dragonlike *kulshedra,* and in particular the *Bukura e Dheut* (Earthly Beauty), a fair maiden with magic powers who lives in the underworld.

Albanian fairy tales, often centered on the struggle between good and evil, typically have a young, male protagonist. Female figures are usually secondary and passive, reflecting Albania's traditional patriarchal culture. The hero will often use a ruse to get the earthly beauty or some animal to assist him. Snakes are particularly common and are uniformly good in Albanian tales and mythology. Among other animal figures familiar in folktales are owls, nightingales, and the *gjysmagjel* (half rooster), a one-legged bird who has many an adventure in the course of its travels, carrying its weary companions on its back or in its belly. Rams and stags also occur, which have magic powers in their horns.

Albanian folktales were first recorded in the middle of the nineteenth century by European scholars such as Johann Georg von Hahn (1854), Karl H. Reinhold (1855), and Giuseppe **Pitrè** (1875). The next generation of scholars to take an interest in the collection of Albanian folktales were primarily philologists, among them well-known Indo-European linguists concerned with recording and analyzing a hitherto little-known European language: Auguste Dozon (1879, 1881), Jan Jarnik (1883), Gustav Meyer (1884, 1888), Holger Pedersen (1895), Gustav Weigand (1913), and August Leskien (1915).

The nationalist movement in Albania in the second half of the nineteenth century, the so-called Rilindja period, gave rise to native collections of folklore such as: *Albanikê melissa/ Bêlietta sskiypêtare* (*The Albanian Bee,* 1878) by Thimi Mitko, *Albanikon alfavêtarion/Avabatar arbëror* (*Albanian Spelling Book*, 1882) by the Greco-Albanian Anastas Kullurioti, and *Valët e Detit* (*The Waves of the Sea*, 1908) by Spiro Dine. In the last fifty years, much fieldwork has been done by the Institute of Folk Culture in Tirana and by the Institute of Albanian Studies in Prishtina, which have published numerous collections of fairy tales and legends. Unfortunately, very little of this substantial material has been translated into other languages.

The only substantial collections of Albanian folktales to have appeared in English up to the present are: *Tricks of Women and Other Albanian Tales* by Paul Fenimore Cooper, which was translated from the collections of Dozon and Pedersen; *Albanian Wonder Tales* by Post Wheeler; *Albanian Folktales and Legends* by Robert Elsie; and *Faith and Fairies* by Mustafa Tukaj. A large and significant manuscript of Albanian fairy tales translated into English by the Scottish anthropologist Margaret Hasluck and located in Oxford remains unpublished for the moment.

Further Readings: Cooper, James Fenimore, trans. *Tricks of Women and Other Albanian Tales.* New York: W. Morrow, 1928; Elsie, Robert, trans. *Albanian Folktales and Legends.* 2nd edition. Peja: Dukagjini, 2001; Elsie, Robert. *A Dictionary of Albanian Religion, Mythology, and Folk Culture.* New

York: New York University Press, 2001; Tukaj, Mustafa. *Faith and Fairies: Tales Based on Albanian Legends and Ballads.* Edited by Joanne M. Ayers. Shkodra: Skodrinon, 2002; Wheeler, Post. *Albanian Wonder Tales.* London: Lovat Dickson, 1936.

Robert Elsie

Alcott, Louisa May (1832–1888)

Well before her major success with *Little Women* (1868), the Massachusetts writer Louisa May Alcott had tried to market tales set in Fairyland. Her collected *Flower Fables* (1854) included stories she wrote at the age of sixteen. But it was her updating of Charles **Perrault**'s "Cendrillon" in "A Modern Cinderella, or the Little Old Shoe" (1860) that significantly anticipates *Little Women*. Here, it is Nan, the oldest rather than the youngest of three sisters, who is rewarded for her drudgery. John Lord, a princely suitor, much prefers the domestic virtues of a forerunner of Meg and Beth March to the artistic ambitions of Diana and Laura, the archetypes for Jo and Amy.

In *Little Women*, Alcott seems to depreciate such literary efforts. We are told that a burned manuscript contained "only half a dozen little fairy tales" that Jo had hoped to convert into "something good enough to print." Still, direct and oblique allusions to fairy tales steadily enrich the novel. These can function ironically when, for instance, Meg is assured by the friend who has overdressed her that they will look "like Cinderella and her godmother going to the ball." But they also broaden a plot that reworks Jeanne-Marie **Leprince de Beaumont**'s "**Beauty and the Beast**," which is itself related to the **Cinderella** type of tale. Just as Charlotte **Brontë** had done in *Jane Eyre* (1847), Alcott rewards a heroine who is no "beauty" with an older suitor who retains his resemblance to an ursine "beast." *See also* Intertextuality; North American Tales.

Further Readings: Knoepflmacher, U. C. "Introduction: Literary Fairy Tales and the Value of Impurity." *Marvels & Tales* 17 (2003): 15–36; Shealy, Daniel, ed. *Louisa May Alcott's Fairy Tales and Fantasy Stories.* Knoxville: University of Tennessee Press, 1992.

U. C. Knoepflmacher

Alcover, Antoni Maria (1862–1932)

Antoni Maria Alcover was a Catalan clergyman, linguist, and folklorist. Influenced by Tomàs Fortesa, Marià Aguiló, and other Romantic writers, he took an interest from a very young age in Catalan language and literature and in the **collecting** of traditional songs and **folktales**. As a linguist, he was responsible for producing the *Diccionari català-valencià-balear* (*Catalan-Valencian-Balearic Dictionary,* 1926–62) in conjunction with Francesc de Borja Moll.

Alcover's work as a collector of folktales began among his close circle of family and friends and then continued in other places on the island of Majorca. Between 1880 and 1931, he published his folktales in the contemporary Majorcan press (*L'Ignorància, El Isleño, El Eco del Santuario*) and in Barcelona (*La Tradició Catalana*). His tales appeared under the pseudonym Jordi des Racó, which is the name he always went by as a writer of folktales. In 1885, under that pseudonym, he published a book of five tales from the oral tradition, *Contarelles d'En Jordi des Racó*. In 1896, the first volume of the *Aplec de rondaies mallorquines d'en Jordi d'es Racó* (*Jordi d'es Racó's Collection of Majorcan Folktales*) was published, with a prologue by the author explaining how the folktales were collected, who the story-tellers were, and how the tales were redrafted and with what intent. Between 1896 and 1931, twelve volumes of the *Aplec* were published, and it subsequently went through several editions. In 1914, for the second edition of the first volume of the *Aplec*, Alcover penned an additional prologue in which he indicated how well his folktales had been received not only by readers in Majorca but also by folklorists from other countries.

Encouraged by Leo Spitzer, in 1931 Alcover wrote the article "Com he fet mon Aplech de Rondayes Mallorquines" ("How I Did My Collection of Majorcan Folktales"), in which he explained the criteria he had used in selecting, editing, and rewriting them. Between 1936 and 1972, the "popular edition" of the *Rondaies mallorquines d'en Jordi des Racó* (24 volumes) was published, containing 431 folktales. In 1996, Josep Antoni Grimalt and Jaume Guiscafrè began publishing their critical edition of the *Aplec de rondaies mallorquines d'en Jordi d'es Racó*, of which four volumes have been published through 2006. This edition catalogues the folktales according to the international index of **tale type**s and reproduces not only the folktales written by Alcover but also the texts and fragments of folktales that he had jotted down in his notebooks during the collection process. Alcover's folktales, written in a popular style of language that is extremely rich and expressive, have undergone numerous reeditions and have been translated into Spanish, French, English, and German for inclusion in anthologies of folktales all over the world.

Further Readings: Alcover, Antoni Maria. "Com he fet mon Aplech de Rondayes Mallorquines." *Zeitschrift für romanische Philologie* 51 (1931): 94–111; ———. *Folk Tales of Mallorca: A Selection from "L'aplec de rondaies mallorquines."* Translated by David Huelin. Palma de Mallorca: Editorial Moll, 1999; ———. *Tales from Majorca.* Translated by John Lynch-Cummins. Palma de Mallorca: Clumba, 1968; Guiscafrè, Jaume. "Una bibliografia de les edicions i les traduccions de les rondalles de mossèn Alcover." *Randa* 38 (1996): 151–221.

Carme Oriol

Alexander, Lloyd (1924–2007)

A prolific and award-winning American writer of children's **fantasy** and folkloric adventure tales, Lloyd Alexander, although probably best known for his Prydain series based on Welsh **myth,** demonstrated across his writing a fondness for the mythology and **folklore**s of many cultures. His novels and tales are characterized by subversion, questioning, and the undercutting of narrative expectation. Themes of personal development, insight, justice, initiation, and the testing of character are strong and recurring elements in his writing, and he had a fondness for repetition, pattern, **trickster archetype**s, and **magic object**s. He was particularly good at writing strong young women, who often have the practicality and common sense that male heroes lack, and many of his novels feature the deliberate deconstruction of heroic archetypes, particularly those relating to **violence** and warrior ideals.

Alexander's five-book fantasy series, The Chronicles of Prydain (1964–68), is loosely based on the *Mabinogion*, a collection of medieval Welsh tales. Their hero, Taran, is the traditional lowborn underdog figure of fairy tales, who rises through adventure and testing to become King. His adventures introduce him to a slightly decontextualized selection of the figures and magical artifacts of Welsh folklore, including the oracular **pig** Hen Wen, talking harps and swords and Arawn, lord of the dead. A more explicitly fairy-tale feel is evident in *The Foundling* (1970), a collection of short tales set in Prydain. As with much of his work, Alexander used the folkloric **motif**s to lend strength and resonance to his storytelling, rather than attempting to reproduce the *Mabinogion* with any fidelity.

Alexander's other novel series include the Westmark trilogy (1981–84), which are non-magical and surprisingly political adventure tales, whose at times gritty and disturbing events explore notions of justice and the loss of innocence. The five Vesper Holly adventures (1986–90) are less serious, being more tongue-in-cheek alternative Victorian romps. Earlier novels also include *The Wizard in the Tree* (1974), its Merlin figure the center of Alexander's characteristic insistence on human initiative and effort. It most explicitly rejects the easy, heal-all aspect of magic. *The Marvelous Misadventures of Sebastian* (1970) employs the classic fairy-tale archetypes of a runaway **princess** and a talking fiddle.

Alexander's later fantasy adventure novels drew on the folklore of many cultures: notable among them are *The Remarkable Journey of **Prince** Jen* (1991), based on Chinese folklore, and *The Iron Ring* (1997), based on Indian tales. Both are adventure stories in which magical objects and wise companions initiate young princes into the realities of their kingdom and the importance of justice. The traditional fairy-tale quest for wisdom is overlaid with an exploration of war, power, and politics that is surprisingly adult. A similar quest motivates *The Arcadians* (1995), a loose and often amusing rehash of Greek mythology. The whimsical origin myth of *How the Cat Swallowed Thunder* (2000) returns to classic Western fairy tale with its Mother Holly **witch** figure.

Alexander's books for younger readers, with a variety of illustrators, offer simple, direct stories that function as amusing moral **fable**s. Again, in works such as *The House Gobbaleen* (1995), the comic fools of *Four Donkeys* (1972), and the colorful, African-flavored *The Fortune Tellers* (1992), an element of the unexpected undercuts the predictable, familiar path of the folkloric narrative. ***See also*** Celtic Tales; Children's Literature; Mother Holle; Young Adult Fiction.

Further Readings: Bagnall, Norma. "An American Hero in Welsh Fantasy: The Mabinogion, Alan Garner and Lloyd Alexander." *New Welsh Review* 2.4 (1990): 26–29; May, Jill P. *Lloyd Alexander*. Boston: Twayne, 1991.

Jessica Tiffin

Alf layla wa-laylah. See Arabian Nights

Ali Baba

Ali Baba is the hero of "Ali Baba and the Forty Thieves," one of the most famous and most frequently adapted tales in the ***Arabian Nights***. However, like the story of ***Aladdin***, it is an orphan tale and is not directly related to Arabic versions of the *Arabian Nights*. The story of Ali Baba arrived in France thanks to a Syrian monk named Hanna, who told it and several other stories to Antoine **Galland** in 1709. It was Galland who transformed the six-page account from his **informant** into a text of thirty-six pages and added "Ali Baba" for the first time to the *Thousand and One Nights* in 1717. In other words, "Ali Baba," like "Aladdin," is a French-Syrian creation from the beginning of the eighteenth century.

Illustration from an early nineteenth-century English version of *Ali Baba: Or The Forty Thieves, a Tale for the Nursery; With Three Copperplates* (London: Tabart, 1805). [Courtesy of the Eloise Ramsey Collection of Literature for Young People, University Libraries, Wayne State University]

Galland's version was so successful that it was taken up by storytellers in many countries. However, **variant**s independent of Galland's version are still identifiable in Syria and in the Maghreb because they include a detail that is absent in Galland's rewriting: the presence of **food** in the treasure cave. Although the **motif** of a table set with sumptuous dishes appeared in the summary provided by Hanna, Galland removed it when he rewrote the tale for publication, thereby turning the cave—which in Hanna's version served as a home where the forty **thieves** regularly had their meals—into a neutral location. Galland's transformation of the thieves' home into a treasury full of riches that was accessible to anyone knowing the magic words was a stroke of genius that facilitated the tale's widespread success and gave a special significance to the command "Open, Sesame."

However, the aesthetic improvement made by Galland was accompanied by a degradation on the anthropological level. In the versions where the sumptuous dishes laid out inside the cave appear, the food serves to test each figure's moral character, as is often the case in fairy tales. When the hero enters the cave, he controls his desire, does not touch food, and takes only gold; but, when the malicious character enters, he yields to temptation, is delayed by the act of eating—which allows him to be discovered—and is subsequently killed.

Galland's version is usually classified as belonging to **tale type** ATU 954, The Forty Thieves; but other tale types, with older subject matter, help explain the structure of "Ali Baba." The tale is composed of two parts of unequal sizes, with two successive heroes. In the first part, Ali Baba, who is poor but good, is opposed to Cassim, who is rich and malicious. The moderate behavior of the first enriches him while the greed of the second causes his death. This first part of the story constitutes 22 percent of the text and is derived from type ATU 613, The Two Travelers, especially as one finds it in the East. In the second part of the tale, the slave Morgiane, an intelligent young woman, is opposed to the robbers, whom she is able to kill. This second part makes up 78 percent of the text and is related to tale type ATU 950, Rhampsinitus. The moral aspect, which is present at the beginning (good rewarded and malice punished) and is characteristic of fairy tales, disappears in the second and most original part, where the narrative goes against the established order and depicts a woman as intellectually superior to men. *See also* Arabian Nights Films; Thief of Bagdad Films; Women.

Further Reading: Chraïbi, Aboubakr. "Galland's 'Ali Baba' and Other Arabic Versions." *Marvels & Tales* 18 (2004): 159–69.

Aboubakr Chraïbi

Amades, Joan (1890–1959)

The self-taught Catalan folklorist Joan Amades spent practically all his life collecting and studying **folklore**. In 1905, and as part of the hiking movement (which was very popular in Catalonia at the end of the nineteenth and beginning of the twentieth centuries), he started going on excursions organized by the Ateneu Enciclopèdic Popular de Barcelona (People's Encyclopedic Association of Barcelona), the aim of which was to collect samples of traditional Catalan culture in various towns in Catalonia. Between 1915 and 1926, he came into contact with the most important Catalan folklorists of the age and he took part in group projects to collect folkloric materials such as the ones organized by the Arxiu d'Etnografia i Folklore de Catalunya (Archive of Ethnography and Folkore of Catalonia) (1915–23) and the Obra del Cançoner Popular de Catalunya (Popular Song Project of Catalonia) (1922–35).

Between 1926 and 1939, he consolidated his position as one of the leading Catalan folklorists, directed institutions that studied folklore, gave lectures, took part in radio programs, and published such important works as the *Biblioteca de tradicions populars* (*Library of Popular Traditions*, 1933–39). At this time, the central topics of his activity as a folklorist were **dance**, **music**, song, and customs. After 1939 he published his most voluminous works: the five-volume *Costumari Català* (*Catalan Customs*, 1950–56) and the three-volume *Folklore de Catalunya* (*Folklore of Catalonia*, 1950–69). The volume *Folklore de Catalunya: I Rondallística* (1950) was very well received internationally, particularly because of the numerous narratives that it contained. Its 2,215 narratives were comprised of 662 **folktale**s, 727 traditions, and 826 **legend**s. Walter **Anderson** used the international index *Types of the Folktale* (1928) to catalogue these folktales and in 1954 published the results of his work under the title "Eine katalanische Märchensammlung" ("A Catalan Tale Collection") in the journal *Schweizerisches Archiv für Volkskunde*. Subsequently, Stith Thompson, in his second revision of *The Types of the Folktale* (1961), made changes that reflect his having taken this classification into account.

Amades published articles in such international journals as *Folklore* (London), *Folklore Americas*, *Revue de Traditions Populaires*, and *Fabula*. In 1957, he published *Contes catalans* (*Catalan Folktales*) as part of the series Contes des cinq continets (Folktales from Five Continents), edited by Paul Delarue. In the last years of his life, Amades began his project of classifying the folktales published in all the areas in which Catalan is spoken. His death in 1959 prevented him from finishing. Some years ago, Carme Oriol and Josep M. Pujol took up the project where he had left off, classified the folktales, and published *Índex tipològic de la rondalla catalana* (*Index of Catalan Folktales*, 2003). In 1990, on the occasion of the centenary of Amades's birth, the book *El món de Joan Amades* (*The World of Joan Amades*) was published. This volume contains an extensive biography of the author and a bibliographic catalogue of his work, which consists of 162 books, 103 articles, thirty-nine journalistic contributions to the press and radio, and 104 unpublished works.

Further Reading: Oriol, Carme. "Revision of Amades' Classification of the Catalan Folktales." *Fabula* 31 (1990): 304–12.

Carme Oriol

Amano Yoshitaka (1952–)

Amano Yoshitaka is a Japanese artist and illustrator. Influenced strongly by the art nouveau movement and traditional Japanese woodcuts, Amano has worked in numerous media, including painting with watercolors and oils, lithographs, computer animation, ceramics, and stained glass. He has designed characters for video games and for animated **television** shows as well as painting for books, comic books, and museum exhibitions. Over the course of his career, Amano has produced a number of works based on material from folktales and fairy tales. These have appeared in exhibitions, collaborative publications, and published collections.

Amano's first major work based on **folklore** was his book *Budouhime* (*Princess Budou*, 1996), which was inspired by the eponymous Princess of China from the tale "The Adventures of Prince Camaralzaman and the Princess Badoura," included in Andrew **Lang**'s 1898 collection of the ***Arabian Nights***. In collaboration with the director of the Los Angeles Philharmonic Orchestra, Esa-Pekka Salonen, the material from this book was adapted into a twenty-minute computer animated film shown at the Sundance Film Festival in 1999. Additionally, Amano expanded his original work into *1001 Nights*, a full series of paintings and lithographs inspired by the *Arabian Nights*. First exhibited in Los Angeles in 1998, these paintings grant a dreamlike, ethereal quality to the tales, with characters floating languidly through empty space.

In 1996, Amano also published *Yousei* (*Fairies*), a book that takes its subject matter from British **legend**s on **fairy** creatures, including an **adaptation** of William **Shakespeare**'s *A Midsummer Night's Dream*. While the book does not deal with explicit folktales, it does use Victorian and Edwardian folklore on the existence of fairy creatures, such as the connection between fairies and gardens evidenced in the Cottingley fairy photographs of 1917. Amano's fairies are small creatures with distinct resemblances to plant life.

Amano's next prominent work involving folktale material was *The Dream Hunters* (1999), a collaborative project with Neil **Gaiman**. This book, an extension of Gaiman's popular *Sandman* series, is told in the style of a Japanese folktale, featuring a fox and a tanuki (raccoon dog) engaging in a contest of trickery. While the plot of this story is not a direct adaptation of a specific folktale, Gaiman and Amano both draw heavily on folkloric sources for this work. And although much of *Sandman* series is in **graphic novel** format, for this book Amano worked with large paintings and lithographs, creating something closer to an illustrated storybook than a comic book.

In 2000, Amano released *Märchen*, in which he included works inspired by several folktales. *Märchen* featured Amano's renditions of both European and Japanese fairy tales, including "**Little Red Riding Hood**," "**Sleeping Beauty**," "**Snow White**," and "Kaguyahime" ("Princess Kaguya"). Amano illustrates each of the traditional tales in his distinctive art nouveau style. *See also* Art; Illustration; Japanese Popular Culture; Japanese Tales.

Further Reading: *Amano's World.* http://www.amanosworld.com/.

B. Grantham Aldred

Anansi

Anansi is one of the best-known figures from West African folktales. As a folktale **trickster** hero, Anansi is also known variously as Ananse, Kweku Ananse, Anansi-tori, Ananse-sem, and somewhat euphemistically as Aunt Nancy. Generally associated with spiders, Anansi is one of the most prominent figures from West African folklore, appearing in the folktales of all Akan-speaking tribes as well as those of diasporic groups in the United States and the Caribbean.

One of the complicated aspects of Anansi tales is the differentiation between **myth** and **folktale**. While many prominent tricksters are considered by their cultures to be gods, Anansi rarely receives such a distinction and instead serves as an intermediary between Nyame, Anansi's father the sky god, and the world. Anansi's status as a mortal culture hero rather than a god has led to debates over the status of Anansi tales as myths, a category in which many trickster tales are placed. Due to Anansi's mortal status, the Anansi tales are more frequently classified as folktales rather than myths.

Anansi's association with the spider is complicated but is typical among trickster figures. Within many of his tales, Anansi interacts with archetypal animals such as Lion, Tiger, Turtle, and Canary. Within these tales, Anansi is represented as the archetypal Spider. However, in other folktales, Anansi is represented as more humanoid, especially when interacting with people. This is typical of trickster figures, including the Native American **Coyote** and Iktomi, and reveals the variety of tales attributed to Anansi.

In folktales, Anansi has a number of different deeds attributed to him. He is said to have taught the people to sow grain. He is described as sculpting man, to whom Nyame then gave life. He married a **princess**, he won a singing contest, and he found a magic stone whose name, if mentioned, would kill the speaker. All of these deeds Anansi accomplished through trickery, his hallmark. While Anansi is successful in many of these stories, like other trickster figures, he also falls victim to chicanery himself.

One characteristic Anansi tale is that of Anansi and the Lion and Tiger. In response to an attempt to enslave him, Anansi was able to trick the Lion into killing the Tiger and then drinking poisoned water, thus allowing Anansi to escape enslavement.

Anansi is among the most adapted figures in folktales. Many of his tales have been adapted to other folktale characters. One of the best examples of this is the story of Anansi and the Tar Baby, which in Joel Chandler **Harris**'s **Uncle Remus** collections was attributed to Br'er Rabbit. This story, adapted into Walt **Disney**'s *Song of the South* (1946), achieved popularity in this form.

Anansi has also appeared in a number of modern adaptations. In **graphic novel**s, authors have used Anansi, most prominently in issues of *Spiderman* and *Hellblazer*, both times appearing as a god. He also appears in a number of **fantasy** novels including Neil **Gaiman**'s books *American Gods* (2001) and *Anansi Boys* (2005), Charles **De Lint**'s *Forests of the Heart* (2000), and China Mieville's *King Rat* (1998). *See also* African American Tales.

Further Reading: Gyesi-Appiah, L. *Ananse Stories Retold: Some Common Traditional Tales.* Portsmouth, NH: Heinemann, 1997.

B. Grantham Aldred

Andersen, Hans Christian (1805–1875)

Hans Christian Andersen is the Danish author of 156 fairy tales and stories, ranging from retellings of **folktales**, **legend**s, and old wives' tales in the early authorship to self-invented **literary fairy tale**s. In developing his corpus of fairy tales, Andersen, in his time, catered to an emerging audience of children while modernizing Danish literature. Though today primarily famous for his fairy tales, many of which have become international children's classics, Andersen experimented with several modern literary forms and was a prolific writer in genres such as **poetry**, drama, the **novel**, travelogue, vaudeville, and autobiography.

Written in the Romantic-realist period of Biedermeier, when the breakdown of the prestige of genres encouraged greater diversity in writing, the fairy tales were conceived as miniature spaces of modern literature, frequently cross-writing genres, artistic modes, and notions of addressees. Thus the early poem "Det døende Barn" ("The Dying Child," 1827), one of the first literary evocations of the child's perspective, shows a keen awareness of the importance of point of view, and by identifying with the dying child, creates a melodramatic emotional effect in the adult reader. Fairy tales such as "Den lille Idas Blomster" ("Little Ida's Flowers," 1835) and "Sneedronningen" ("The Snow Queen," 1844) further explore and establish the child's perspective as a mental space of its own in literature. Upon reading the fairy tales, Vincent van Gogh was convinced that Andersen must also be a visual artist, for his tales are indeed interartistic forms that incorporate visual, dramatic, and even musical and dancelike elements, as in "Elverhøi" ("The Hill of the **Elves**," 1845), where, in the description of the young elfins' dance, "they twirled and twisted. One could hardly make out which were legs and where were arms, or which end was up and which down." Andersen was a great admirer of the **theater**, and often his tales read like miniature theatrical pieces that cultivate a scenic, dramatic, and dialogic style foregrounding the magic and subtlety of language. In Andersen's own opinion, the first *Eventyr fortalte for børn* (*Fairy Tales Told for Children*, 1835) were inferior works but apparently also functioned as a relief from the pressures of the emerging vernacular literary canon, in which structure and idealism were deemed important, as in the Bildungsroman (novel of development).

As a reflection of the democratization of the reading audience from Russia in the East

Hans Christian Andersen. [Library of Congress]

to America in the West, Andersen's literary reputation was initially built on the novel. In Danish literary history, Andersen pioneered the development of the novel as a genre discussing contemporary issues for a wider readership with works such as *Improvisatoren* (*The Improvisatore*, 1835) and *Kun en spillemand* (*Only a Fiddler*, 1837). In the 1830s, Andersen was, in fact, one of only a handful of writers who took the novel seriously as a literary form, and the turn from the novel to the fairy tale was partly triggered by Søren Kierkegaard's devastating criticism of *Only a Fiddler*. In *Af en endnu levendes papirer* (*Early Polemic Writings: One Still Living*, 1838), Kierkegaard argued that Andersen was better at writing journalistic travelogues than reading the "ideas" of characters in the light of the German philosophical outlook influential at the time, and that the narrator was unable to distinguish between personal and public modes of writing but included biography as so-called amputations in the novel. Andersen took this criticism very seriously, which was one reason he moved his literary ambitions from the grand structure of the novel to the miniature form of the fairy tale, a genre that was considered a high-canonical form by writers such as **Novalis**, though still accessible to children.

The fairy tales and stories take a special position in Andersen's work, not only in terms of originality but also as the genre best able to express his complex experiences of class, **gender**, and the role of the modern writer. From the beginning the tales were intended for a non-bifurcated audience, and in a letter to B. S. Ingemann, a contemporary poet and friend, Andersen emphasized the dual address and oral qualities: "I seize an idea for older people—and tell it to the young ones, while remembering that father and mother are listening and must have something to think about." The first volume of his fairy tales, published in 1835, consisted of retellings of folktales that Andersen had heard as a child in Odense. Thse tales included "Fyrtøiet" ("The Tinderbox"), "Lille Claus og store Claus" ("Little Claus and Big Claus"), "Prindsessen paa ærten" ("The Princess on the Pea"), and the self-invented tale "Little Ida's Flowers." Despite Adam **Oehlenschläger**'s and Kierkegaard's defense of fairy tales as suitable reading matter for children, critics complained at the apparently amoral attitude in "The Tinderbox," whose plot is governed by chance and luck, and whose protagonist does not go through a process of *Bildung*—or personal and cultural development. In addition, critics opined that the deliberately colloquial style, reflecting Andersen's ingenious aesthetic of storytelling, and the theme of adultery hinted at in "Little Claus and Big Claus," were unsuitable for children. More tales followed, generally published as "Christmas gifts," and in the 1840s Andersen's mastery of the fairy tale was generally accepted.

Although it constitutes a fantastic mode, Andersen frequently alluded to the fairy tale as a realistic and subjective form: "Most of what I have written is a reflection of myself. Every character is from life." From 1842 on the subtitle "fortalte for børn" ("told for children") was omitted, and from 1852 forward the tales were interchangeably designated as "fairy tales" and "stories." This reflected the development from Romanticism to realism and a keen awareness of the consequences, in terms of literary prestige, of being conflated with a child audience; but from the beginning the stories rested on a solid foundation of reality. There are many autobiographical elements and self-portraits discussing the schism between life and art and other modern writing dilemmas, the experience of which was radicalized by Andersen's proletarian background. Thus in "Nissen hos spekhøkeren" ("The Pixy and the Grocer," 1853), the pixy's attraction to true poetry is counterbalanced by an equally strong urge to materialism. The fortune-hunting **soldier** in "The Tinderbox," also intertextually close to Oehlenshläger's *Aladdin* (1857), replaces a Romantic view of art as ennobling and elevating by a pragmatic alliance between the parvenu soldier and the round-eyed dogs—perhaps an image of the powerful new reading audience to whom this kind of story would appeal. Andersen's affairs of the heart can likewise be followed in several tales: in "Den lille havfrue" ("The Little Mermaid," 1837), the triangle formed by the **mermaid**, the **prince**, and the **princess** traces the trajectory of modern desire, and the bittersweet "Kjærestefolkene" ("The Sweethearts," 1843) describes a meeting with Riborg Voigt, Andersen's first love, thirteen years after the unsuccessful courtship. "Nattergalen" ("The Nightingale," 1843), in its contrast of the real and the artificial, is a tribute to the Swedish soprano Jenny Lind, who rejected Andersen's advances.

The fairy tales are filled with images of writing, often referred to as miniature forms, such as the tinderbox, the paper cut in "Little Ida's Flowers," the flea circus in "Loppen og Professoren" ("The Flea and the Professor," 1872), or the pea in "The Princess on the Pea." Andersen reclassified the fairy tale as a generically hybrid, interartistic form. In terms of literary ancestry the tales are related to the literary fairy tales of the German Romantics Ludwig **Tieck**, E. T. A. **Hoffmann,** and Adalbert von **Chamisso**, but also to Walter Scott and the elfin world in William **Shakespeare**'s *A Midsummer Night's Dream*. Parallel to Franz **Kafka**'s **parable**s, striving for a certain impenetrability to criticism, there is a marked uncertainty in Andersen's fairy tales, which aspire to be both autobiographical and fictional, colloquial and literary. This opacity to criticism not only reflects an attempt to invent a style suitable to avoid censorship but is also the result of a certain subjective intrusion or osmosis between Andersen the man and Andersen the storyteller, as in "Dyndkongens datter" ("The Bog-King's Daughter," 1858), a remarkable and deeply original work. The many storks and swans in the tales that lend material or biographical traces of their author's identity are reminiscent of Andersen himself when he was most awkward and "birdlike." As if modern creativity is also a question of the dislocation or shattering of selves, Andersen created a world of animation consisting of living objects and talking animals. It is a reality in which imagination and a frequently cruel poetry animate animals, flowers, and objects to become creatures that speak and act on a little scene that stands in for the great stage of life that could not be fully described in terms of class, gender, and psychology in the contemporary Danish novel. Andersen was highly aware that it is difficult to do the tales justice in **translation** since language and style are integral to their meaning. Humor, satire, irony, wordplay, shades, and undertones are important features, as are the narrator's poised, idiomatic sentences viewing a tiny section of the world through a magnifying glass, as in "Vanddraaben" ("A Drop of Water," 1847), or turning the world upside down in one sentence, as in Andersen's carnivalesque puns.

As small novels, the tales make up a catalogue of different registers. Thus "The Little Mermaid" employs a high-strung emotional style, whereas the carnivalesque tales of "The Tinderbox," "Little Claus and Big Claus," or "Klods-Hans" ("Clod-Hans," 1855) are packed with action. Among the most prevailing registers that should be mentioned is **storytelling**, with the narrator usually addressing a dual audience of children and adults, and the Romantic-pathetic, psychological style, often setting up a duality of life and **death**, as in the power of goodness of heart over cold reason in "The Snow Queen." An example of a highly analytical tale is "Skyggen" ("The Shadow," 1847), in which materialism and nihilism conquer spirituality and goodness in an almost Nietzschean analysis of the broken middle caused by a schism between idealism and the ways of the world. "De vises sten" ("The Philosopher's Stone," 1861) and "The Bog-King's Daughter" are complex philosophical-symbolic tales, and further registers are the musiclike fugues in "Vinden fortæller om Valdemar Daae og hans døtre" ("What the Wind Told About Valdemar Daae and His Daughters," 1859) and "Bispen paa Børglum og hans frænde" ("The Bishop of Børglum Cloister and His Kinsmen," 1865), the mixture of realism and symbolism in "En historie fra klitterne" ("A Story from the Dunes," 1859), experimental, almost modernist texts, such as "Hjertesorg" ("Grief," 1853), and the late grotesques of "Tante Tandpine" ("Auntie Toothache," 1872) or "The Professor and the Flea." The catalogue nature of Andersen's writing also appears in the duality between optimism and pessimism. From the beginning, elevating tales were accompanied by darker visions in the very same volume, and the fairy tales as a whole make up a texture negotiating different positions to existential dilemmas. On a similar note, animals function as a catalogue of positions, sometimes referring to autobiographical elements or psychological features. The **motif** of dogs, often signifying rebellious, libidinal, or connecting extensions of the self, as in "The Tinderbox," in "Den grimme ælling" ("The Ugly Duckling," 1843) renders the text *unheimlich*—uncanny—in the Freudian sense, inasmuch as the reader remembers the duckling's fear of the dog and its choice between the life of the wild geese and the artistic sublimation of the swan. In the ironic tale "Grief," dogs are no longer rebellious but appear in the shape of a "fat and flat-nosed" bachelor lap dog, which "hasn't got a tooth left in its mouth." It dies, and if the reader does not understand the importance of this information, he "can buy stock in the widow's tannery," in which dead animals are processed into hides, skins, and perhaps paper.

Literary as well as **folk** culture influenced the style of the tales, whose multiple ancestry is highlighted in "The Tinderbox," in which the soldier takes on a feminine complement and integrates popular elements to create stories that are sufficiently appealing to the powerful new audience, whose eyes are, like listening children's, as big as teacups. As a parallel to the contemporary novel, the phenomenon of writing is often discussed in conflicting terms. For instance, there is a double focus on the artistic contours of literature, as in "Psyken" ("Psyche," 1861) and the immortality of "The Little Mermaid," on the one hand and an emphasis on writing as carnival and play on the other.

Addressing children is seen as a feature that keeps language fresh and alive, as it appears in Clod-Hans's alternative eloquence based on an aesthetic inherited from popular culture and its more uncensored types of oral fluency. The literary reinvention of storytelling and addressing the listening child became a laboratory that experimented with calling forth the reader's response to writing. Andersen's storyteller is the director of a miniature theatrical piece, directing attention partly to the plot characters, partly to the audience's response. Using colloquial language and a childish measure of values, the mode of storytelling creates a narrative play with the audience, which in early translations was often modified into less-dialogic focalizations of the story's characters. In the Danish originals the style tends to foreground a certain causal indeterminacy, as metaphorically expressed in "Den standhaftige tinsoldat" ("The Steadfast Tin Soldier," 1838), in which it is uncertain whether "it was the troll or just the wind" moving the plot. Often specific statements could either refer to mental states within the acting figure or constitute an intrusion by the jesting storyteller, eager to relate to the audience. The strong emotions, pertinent to the characters in action, are laid out to the audience to contemplate in the same moment they are there for the characters to feel and act on. This enables the storyteller to lay bare and anticipate the expected reader response as a projection on two levels simultaneously: the fictional and the actual, making the intra- and extrafictional levels communicating vessels. Addressing the child typically invites fissures and displacements, which destabilize language, as in "Hyrdinden og skorstensfeieren" ("The Shepherdess and the Chimney Sweep," 1845), whose "childish" adventure story is, on a closer look, an analysis of adult concealment and psychological repression. The child-oriented elements are frequently among the most sophisticated features in the tales, pointing forward to modernist views of language.

In Denmark Andersen's fairy tales have primarily been considered literary art, and in an attempt to capture the experimental approach in the tales, his voice has been characterized as both young and old, primitive and refined, feminine and masculine, autobiographically embedded and, in a less common configuration, able to lay out cultural problems in aesthetic form. Some of the tales incorporate images of dramatic, even violent, shaping of subjectivity, as in "The Little Mermaid" or "De røde skoe" ("The Red Shoes," 1845). On the other hand, the tales frequently highlight the playful side of language, revolutionizing the seeming logic of the symbolic, as it appears in Clod-Hans's ingenuity.

Though an influence on Astrid **Lindgren**'s novels and Oscar **Wilde**'s "The Happy Prince" (1888), Andersen's style has rarely been imitated successfully, whether in Denmark or internationally. Numerous writers and artists have been inspired by the fairy tales, including Kafka, van Gogh, Asger Jorn, and Günther **Grass**. Innumerable artists have illustrated the tales, which have—like Andersen's life itself—also been the source of film **adaptation**s. *See also* Andersen, Hans Christian, in Biopics; Childhood and Children; Children's Literature; Film and Video; Illustration; *The Red Shoes; Le roi et l'oiseau;* Scandinavian Tales.
Further Readings: Andersen, Hans Christian. *Fairy Tales.* Translated by Tiina Nunnally. Edited by
  Jackie Wullschlager. New York: Viking, 2004; Andersen, Jens. *Hans Christian Andersen: A New Life.*
  Translated by Tiina Nunnally. Woodstock, NY: Overlook Press, 2005; Bredsdorff, Elias. *Hans Christian Andersen: The Story of His Life and Work, 1805–75.* New York: Farrar, Straus and Giroux, 1994;
  Rossel, Sven Hakon, ed. *A History of Danish Literature.* Lincoln: University of Nebraska Press, 1992;
  ———. *Hans Christian Andersen: Danish Writer and Citizen of the World.* Amsterdam: Rodopi,
  1996; Wullschlager, Jackie. *Hans Christian Andersen: The Life of a Storyteller.* New York: Knopf,
  2001.

Helene Høyrup

Andersen, Hans Christian, in Biopics

Hans Christian **Andersen** wrote several different autobiographies and would surely therefore not be surprised to find his life the subject of a growing number of very different films. Apart from his name, all they have in common is a trope found in many biopics based on artists: they interweave art and life so that the one appears to comment on, or derive from, the other.

Outside of Denmark, for more than seventy years after his death, Hans Christian Andersen was generally known only as the name associated with certain bedtime stories. But suddenly in 1952 he had a face, a voice, and a personality—that of Danny Kaye in the film *Hans Christian Andersen* (directed by Charles Vidor). So catchy were his songs that millions worldwide soon knew his version of the stories of "The Ugly Duckling," "The Emperor's New Clothes," and "Thumbelina," among many others.

Andersen's life too was tailored to suit Danny Kaye, with the film disclaiming accuracy and announcing itself as "a fairytale about that great spinner of fairytales." Guileless cobbler Hans, urged to leave Odense because his **storytelling** is keeping children from school, makes the long journey to Copenhagen, where he meets a little match girl and a chimneysweep before getting a job making shoes for the Danish State Ballet's prima ballerina, Doro. Overhearing her arguing bitterly with her husband, Hans falls in love with her and writes "The Little Mermaid" to express his (mistaken) perception that Doro and her husband come from two different worlds. She does not see his meaning, but loves the story, and has it turned it into a ballet, which then becomes the film's visual centrepiece. Hans returns to Odense.

It was forty-six years before Danish animator Jannik Hastrup combined Andersen's life and work in *H. C. Andersen og den skæve skygge* (*Hans Christian Andersen and the Long Shadow,* 1998) by taking as his starting point the central idea of the story "The Shadow." To this was added Andersen's own interpretation of his experiences, taken from his diaries. Using this material, and photographs from various parts of his life as the basis for the animated images, the film presents a complex view of the storyteller's hardships and successes.

Even before he has left Odense, the Andersen/storyteller character discovers his shadow has a life of its own, which enters into a Faustian pact with the **devil**: his soul in exchange for fame. But the shadow has no soul, so the storyteller has to give up his own. In Copenhagen, when Andersen and his shadow fall for the same girl—a singer named Jenny—it is the shadow that wins her, despite her preference for Andersen. Then Andersen decides to visit Italy, and the shadow goes too. From this tension Andersen creates not only the high-profile tales but also lesser-known ones such as "A Mother" and "Clod-Han," all of which are woven into the film's fabric. In this film the Andersen character seems to represents the lonely, private, repressed half of the author, while his shadow is the ambitious public man, hungry for fame and success.

With the two-hundredth anniversary of Andersen's birth in 2005, two more Andersen biopics soon appeared. The American-British-German coproduction *Hans Christian Andersen: My Life as a Fairy Tale* (directed by Philip Saville, 2001) was a two-part 160-minute **television** series aimed at a family audience. It covers much the same ground as *The Long Shadow,* but in a totally different way: simple and straightforward.

Andersen's life is presented as dominated by two relationships, both unsatisfactory. One is with Jenny Lind, the celebrated singer known as the "Swedish Nightingale," for whom Andersen yearns though she remains unattainable, as she thinks of him as a brother rather than a lover. In Andersen's mythopoeic mind, she is the Snow Queen and he is the boy Kai, finally released from her spell by Gerda, who represents the other woman in his life, Henriette. Henriette Collin, who has a hunched back, has been a friend since their teens. Though longing to love and be loved like other people, she sees herself as the voiceless Little Mermaid, with Andersen as the prince she rescues, and Jenny Lind as the princess for whom she is spurned. This triangle is not resolved until Jenny gets engaged to her manager, and Henriette dies alone in a fire on a ship bound for America. With this, Andersen finally gains some self-knowledge, admitting that even his life is not always a fairy tale.

Another portrayal of Henriette (as Henriette Wulff, her real name) is part of the Danish *Unge Andersen,* or *Young Andersen* (directed by Rumle Hammerich, 2005). When the rest of Copenhagen dismisses the seventeen-year-old Andersen as an untalented turnip-picker, she sticks by him, but he nonetheless publicly calls her "nasty and ugly and hunchbacked." This is part of the film's presentation of young Andersen as unformed, undisciplined, with no identity except a desire for fame. The action takes place mainly at the school in Slagelse, where Andersen is sent by means of a royal grant; there he battles the principal, Dr. Meisling, who is determined to squash his "dark and ugly" imagination (expressed by his writing of poetry) and replace it with Latin verbs. This conflict takes place through Tuk, an invented character: an orphan boy, adopted by Meisling. Even on his deathbed at the age of seventy, Andersen is in anguish as he remembers Tuk, because Tuk became his whipping boy. When Meisling was angry at Andersen's impudence or lack of academic progress, he punished Tuk, slapping him, beating him, and giving him back-breaking tasks such as picking countless turnips. To cheer up Tuk, Hans makes up his first-ever fairy tale—and Tuk laughs for the first time. Later, when Andersen returns from a brief visit to Odense, Tuk is on his deathbed; he asks for a last tale but Andersen is speechless. Tuk dies, saying, "The words will come."

Tuk's death brings Andersen and Meisling together in grief, and Andersen writes a poem that became famous across Europe—"The Dying Child"—but Meisling dismisses it as calculated and sentimental. As the film sees it, Meisling is right; and only when Andersen recognizes that, can Tuk's prediction come true, and an ugly teenage duckling turns into a beautiful literary swan. *See also* Brothers Grimm in Biopics; Film and Video.

Further Readings: Andersen, Jens. *Hans Christian Andersen: A New Life.* Translated by Tiina Nunnally. Woodstock, NY: Overlook Press, 2005; Wullschlager, Jackie. *Hans Christian Andersen: The Life of a Storyteller.* New York: Knopf, 2001.

Terry Staples

Anderson, Walter (1885–1962)

Folklorist Walter Anderson is known in particular for having formulated the Law of Stability, or the Law of Self-Correction. Developed in his monograph *Kaiser und Abt* (*The Emperor and the Abbot*, 1923), which is a study of ATU 922, the Law of Self-Correction asserts that the basic form of a tale remains the same because the narrator has generally heard the tale from many different narrators or from the same narrator on multiple occasions, and therefore random fluctuations in the story are suppressed.

After living and studying in Kazan, Russia, Anderson, who was an Estonian on his father's side, went to the University of Tartu in 1920 to work as a professor in the newly established Chair of Estonian and Comparative Folklore. In his scholarship Anderson followed the **historic-geographic method,** and it was in this context that he developed the Law of Self-Correction, pursued the search for the **urform** (or, as he later called it, the "Urtext"), and coined the concept of the "Normalform" ("normal form")—the form that was important in the dissemination of the tale. His work along these lines is evident not only in his influential monograph on ATU 922 but also in *Der Schwank vom alten Hildebrand* (1931), his thorough treatment of ATU 1360C (Old Hildebrand).

In addition to folktales, Anderson was interested in a broad spectrum of folkloric genres. For example, in 1926 he published an investigation of a rumor that had recently circulated in Estonia about Mars exploding and colliding with the earth. A polyglot, Anderson also published three volumes of folktales from San Marino (*Novelline popolari sammarinesi,* 1927–33). His experiments conducted among university students, in which he tried to find out how folktales spread, were published as *Ein volkskundliches Experiment* (*A Folkloristic Experiment,* 1951), and are also of great interest.

Anderson left Estonia in 1939 to work in Königsberg and later in Germany. In 1945, he was appointed a professor at the University of Kiel. There his large-scale manuscript on tale type ATU 408, The Three Oranges, remained unfinished at his death.

Further Reading: Seljamaa, Elo-Hanna. "Walter Anderson: A Scientist beyond Historic and Geographic Borders." *Studies in Estonian Folkloristics and Ethnology: A Reader and Reflexive History.* Edited by Kristin Kuutma and Tiiu Jaago. Tartu: Tartu University Press, 2005. 153–68.

Risto Järv

Andersson, Christina (1936–)

Christina Andersson is a Finland-Swedish author and illustrator of **children's literature** who writes humorous **adaptation**s of traditional **folktale**s. She changes the stories in unexpected ways by altering the characters, adding modern language, or changing the setting to an urban location. Her breakthrough novel was *Jakob Dunderskägg Sitter Barnvakt* (*The Babysitter Jacob Rumble Beard,* 1969), a story about a former pirate who entertains three children by telling them incredible stories from his journeys around the world.

Andersson's humorous style also characterizes the reworkings of well-known folktales in her collections: *Sagoblunten* (*Fairy Bumble,* 1974), *Sagoluvern* (*Fairy Ruffle,* 1979) and *Glada Korven Eller Inget Har en Ände ...* (*The Happy Sausage or Nothing Has an Ending ...,* 1980). The familiar tale of **Little Red Riding Hood** is transformed into a story where the Wolf is a hero who struggles against a prejudiced Woodsman. Andersson's rewriting of "**Hansel and Gretel**" depicts two children who lure their mean **father** and their stepmother into the forest. Narrative transformations and reversal of **gender** roles are also used in a reworking of "Sleeping Beauty," where an ordinary girl rescues the **prince**. The familiar tales are retold with a twist, not simply for comic effect but to revaluate the relationship between the children and their parents or to criticize the norms and morals of the adult world. Morals and the struggle between good and evil are prominent also in the fairy tale *Pojken Blå* (*The Boy Blue,* 1998), which exhibits influences from Indian mythology.

Further Reading: Huhtala, Liisi, ed. *Pieni suuri maailma: Suomalaisen lasten- ja nuortenkirjallisuuden historia.* Helsinki: Tammi, 2003.

Elina Druker

Anecdote

The term "anecdote" is used for the first time by Procopius in his *Unpublished Memoirs of Emperor Justinian* (527–65 CE), which are essentially stories of private life at the court. It is commonly used to describe a short narrative about a striking or significant event. In the plural it is used in the sense of secret or private narratives.

In the **Middle Ages**, specific anecdotes, such as the **parable**s of the gospels, circulated as **exempla**, which were used principally to illustrate sermons. Many exemplum collections containing anecdotes are found both in Latin and in various vernaculars. These were usually intended to illustrate, explain, or emphasize some moral argument. Such was the case with *Disciplina Clericalis*, a compilation of instructive tales put together by Petrus Alphonsus early in the twelfth century.

The boundaries between the genres of anecdote, exemplum, and **fabliau** were frequently blurred. Thus, the same anecdote or tale might occur in many different collections in various languages. For example, one of the exempla in the fifteenth-century Portuguese *Orto do*

Esposo, the story of the young man outwitted by his unfaithful wife, appears in at least twenty-three collections, including the *Disciplina Clericalis* and Giovanni **Boccaccio**'s *Decameron* (1349–50), while the pious tale *Dame Sirith* was reworked as the satirical fabliau *Dame Sirith and the Weeping Bitch*.

Although anecdotes are often associated with written form, many circulated orally among families and friends before becoming incorporated in memoirs, journalistic articles, biographies, and the like. Moreover, humorous personal anecdotes are still found in **oral tradition** worldwide. The anecdote resembles the **folktale**, has a simple plot, and may have animal characters. It is typically used to embellish speech, illustrate an argument, and convey a **moral**. In African Igbo culture, for example, the anecdote exists as a distinct genre of verbal art. In many of the stories the tortoise appears as the central animal character. There are also numerous amusing anecdotes in American oral tales, as is the case with the "Me All Face" story, a comic Native American anecdote that promotes a reflection on the conditions of colonial settlement.

Further Readings: Bremond, Claude, Jacques Le Goff, and Jean-Claude Schmitt. *L'exemplum*. Turnhout: Brepols, 1982; Emenanjo, E. 'Nolue. "The Anecdote as an Oral Genre: The Case in Igbo." *Folklore* 95.2 (1984): 171–76; Hancock, Cecily. "The 'Me All Face' Story: European Literary Background of an American Comic Indian Anecdote." *Journal of American Folklore* 76 (1963): 340–42; Tubach, Frederic C. *Index Exemplorum: A Handbook of Medieval Religious Tales*. Helsinki: Suomalainen Tiedeakatemia, 1969.

Ana Raquel Fernandes

Animal Bride, Animal Groom

The **marriage** or love between a human being and a person in the form of an animal—albeit an enchanted or magical one—is a **motif** found in **folklore** all over the world. Some commentators argue that tales of marriage between humans and animals differ from tales of animal lovers. Marriage tales are often **märchen**, complete with happy endings in which the animal metamorphoses into a desirable human being, often of high status. "The **Frog King**" is a classic example of this type. Animal-lover tales are sometimes etiological or moralistic, ending with the destruction of the animal lover or the desertion of the human partner. The two categories frequently merge or blur. There are some tales of animal paramours who become conventional human mates and numerous accounts of **mermaid**, seal, or swan brides, who, when they recover the means of freedom, leave their mortal partners.

Animal brides are usually viewed as victims of abduction, forcibly married and domesticated until they either find what they need to depart (caps, sealskins, or feather cloaks) or until their spouses strike them or otherwise break a taboo. Prohibited actions may include questioning the **women**, calling their names, or looking at them at a specific time or place. The bride then vanishes, sometimes forever as in the "Porpoise Girl" of Micronesia or in several of the Irish tales of the Merrow or mermaid.

Among the most popular and widespread versions of the animal bride motif is the "**Swan Maiden**" tale, elements of which are found in the ancient Indian *Rig Veda*. In some versions of this tale, the husband's quest for his wife ends in their reunion. The outcome is different in the case of Melusine, the famous *lamia* of medieval French **legend**, who reverts to her serpent form one day a week and is trapped in her reptilian shape when her husband enters her bath chamber. Her fate is tempered by her genealogical importance as the **mother** of the Counts of Lusignan. The same is true of the Welsh Lady of the Van, a mermaid thought to be the mother of three great medieval physicians.

Tales of animal brides are similar to each other, despite local coloration. When the bride is not a bird or fish, she is often a small animal—a frog in Burma, Russia, Austria, and Italy; a dog in India, Germany, and among many Native American tribes; a mouse in Sri Lanka; and a tortoise in an account from the *Arabian Nights*. She is a turtle in the ancient Japanese tale and a blue monkey in a southern African one. Among tribal groups of the North Pacific coast and Siberia, she is frequently a fox woman. And, as a seal maiden or selkie, she is a popular figure in the folklore of Scotland and Ireland.

That women could be half human and half animal, that they had mysterious ties to nature, and that could call up forces lost to civilized people made them threatening and dangerous. Significantly, while animal grooms are usually revealed as handsome **prince**s, brides, masked in human beauty, are sometimes exposed as monsters. In all, tales of animal brides serve numerous functions. They may embody women's desires for autonomy and equality in marriage; they may reflect male fantasies of domesticating and subduing female power; and they may reflect male anxiety about desertion by females.

Animal grooms have their own set of attributes and tales. They are present even in accounts that precede Lucius **Apuleius**'s "**Cupid and Psyche**." In this **tale type**, best known through the canonical tale of "**Beauty and the Beast**," a girl goes to live with a frightening or ugly male animal who is actually an enchanted prince or, in **myth**, a supernatural figure. As in animal-bride tales, the mortal partner violates a prohibition, resulting in the groom's departure and the bride's either questing for him or performing arduous tasks to regain his love.

One of most popular tales of southern Africa, where the animal groom is often a serpent or crocodil,e is "The Snake With Five Heads." As in "Cupid and Psyche," a beautiful maiden goes alone to wed or be sacrificed to a monstrous serpent; when she breaks the spell that has enchanted him, he is revealed as a noble chief. "The Queen of the Pigeons," also southern African, is similar to Celtic mermaid tales; a maiden forcibly wed to the Pigeon King bears him three sons, tricks him, and flees with her children. Stith **Thompson** describes numerous tales of Eskimo maidens wedding eagle husbands. In these cases, the maidens initially desire animal spouses but are unhappy when married to them; their **brothers** ultimately rescue them. Tales of dog husbands are frequent among Native Americans. In these, the **birth** of dog children leads to the wife's disgrace and banishment from the tribe. In most instances, she disenchants the children by destroying their dog skins, and all ends happily. In other cases, when the dog is a lover rather than a legitimate husband, the clandestine relations lead to the **punishment** of those perceived as adulterous. The same motif, including punishment for extramarital relations is found in Marie de **France**'s lay "Yonec" and Marie-Catherine d'**Aulnoy**'s "The Blue Bird."

In many cultures, the animal-groom is depicted as an exceptionally disgusting or frightening beast, as in Giovan Francesco **Straparola**'s "Pig King," Giambattista **Basile**'s "The Serpent" (both from Italy), or in the Russian "Snotty Goat." The grooms in arranged marriages may well have been perceived as noxious by their young brides, who, full of anxieties about marrying, are taught their culture's lessons about the sacrifice of female desire and/or the transforming power of love. Older versions of these tales stress female acceptance of male **sexuality** and the civilizing effect of female virtues on brute desire. More recent versions, like the stories in Angela **Carter**'s *Bloody Chamber* (1979), stress the virtues of the beast and their opposition to the evils of civilization. *See also* Transformation.

Further Readings: Bettelheim, Bruno. *The Uses of Enchantment: The Meaning and Importance of Fairy Tales.* New York: Knopf, 1976; Leach, Maria, and Jerome Fried, ed. *Funk and Wagnalls Standard Dictionary of Folklore, Mythology and Legend.* 2 volumes. New York: Funk and Wagnalls, 1949; Silver, Carole G. *Strange and Secret Peoples: Fairies and Victorian Consciousness.* New York: Oxford University Press, 1999; Tatar, Maria. "Taming the Beast: Bluebeard and Other Monsters." *The Hard Facts of the Grimms' Fairy Tales.* 2nd edition. Princeton, NJ: Princeton University Press, 2003. 156–78; Thompson, Stith. *The Folktale.* 1946. Berkeley: University of California Press, 1977; Warner, Marina. *From the Beast to the Blonde: On Fairy Tales and Their Tellers.* New York: Farrar, Straus and Giroux, 1994.

Carole G. Silver

Animal Tale

An animal tale is an entertaining story in which roles are given to animals, which makes the narrative attractive and interesting but always fanciful. Animal tales are easily distinguished from ordinary zoological lore and from superstitious beliefs about animals. Their purpose is to entertain and, although the animals may at times play roles related to their images or to their observable traits, the general drift of these stories is unrealistic and often comical. Although animal tales are not anthropomorphic, the animals that populate them may speak to each other or otherwise behave in ways more to be expected of humans.

Such stories are found worldwide and are usually short and pithy. About 300 international plots that occur in them are listed by Antti **Aarne** and Stith **Thompson** in *The Types of the Folktale* (updated in 2004 by Hans-Jörg Uther). These plots concern various kinds of quadrupeds, birds, fish, flies, reptiles, and some inanimate objects that are invested with character. Some stories tell of purported interactions between wild creatures, others tell of wild animals interacting with domesticated ones, and still other stories tell of dealings of creatures with humans.

The most frequent actor is the clever fox, the animal most noted in the natural world for its ingenuity. The ruses of the fox, by which he steals from humans and escapes from capture, were very popular, as were the tricks he plays on other animals, especially the wolf or bear, who are portrayed as stupid counterparts to his cleverness. Also popular are stories of how the fox tries, in some cases successfully and in others unsuccessfully, to trick a fowl or other animal into capture so that he can eat it. He is famously outdone by the domestic **cat,** to whom he boasts that he knows and can perform many tricks. The cat knows but one trick, climbing, and when a savage dog comes on the scene, he uses it to go up a tree, while the fox is unable to do so and is devoured (ATU 105, The Cat's Only Trick).

Some animal tales are allegorical, such as that of a rodent parliament that assembles and decides to put a bell on the prowling cat, only to be brought to their senses by an old wise rat who asks, "Who will bell the cat?" (ATU 110, Belling the Cat). The birds also convene a parliament, which decides on the functions and habitats of each (ATU 220, The Council of Birds). A related story tells of how the wren became king of the birds by flying higher than any other—a feat it was able to achieve through the trick of hiding in the eagle's feathers and by jumping out when the great bird tired and could go no higher (ATU 221, The Election of King of Birds). Another story (ATU 222, War between Birds [Insects] and Quadrupeds) tells of a dispute between the wren and the mouse, which causes a great battle between the birds and the quadrupeds. The fox acts as an umpire for the battle but is stung on the backside by a bee. The fox lowers his tail, which the quadrupeds take as a signal that they are being defeated. The heartened birds then rout their opponents off the field and forever have jurisdiction of the air and on the ground.

Several of these animal tales have an etiological theme (see **etiologic tale**), but this is rather of a humorous than of a serious nature. For instance, the cat and dog decide to settle, by a race between them, which of the two shall reside in the master's house. The dog is winning the race but stops to attack a beggar, which allows the cat to gain the advantage and the privilege of shelter ever after (ATU 200D*, Why Cat Is Indoors and Dog Outside in Cold). According to **tale type** ATU 250A (The Flounder's Crooked Mouth), the flounder cries out in jealousy of other fish or in insult to a holy man, and ever after has a crooked mouth.

Further Readings: Thompson, Stith. *The Folktale.* 1946. Berkeley: University of California Press, 1977. 217–28; Uther, Hans-Jörg. *The Types of International Folktales.* Volume 1. Helsinki: Academia Scientiarum Fennica, 2004. 16–173.

Dáithí Ó hÓgáin

Animation

Animated film, whether the popular hand-drawn or computer-generated cartoon, claymation, or puppet animation, has a long history of association with folkloric and fairy-tale forms. This may in part be attributed to the domination of Walt **Disney** and the **Walt Disney Company** over animated film and their recurring reliance on fairy-tale narrative; despite the existence of earlier films from Argentina and Germany, it is generally accepted that the first feature-length animated film to be released was Disney's *Snow White and the Seven Dwarfs* (1937). The effect of Disney's dominance and its recurring use of fairy tales has been to reconfigure the fairy tale in the twentieth century as exclusively, or at least preferably, a

An image from the 2001 Japanese animation *Spirited Away*. From left to right: Chihiro's mouse, Chihiro/ Sen (Japanese voice: Rumi Hiiragi; American voice: Daveigh Chase), and Kaonashi/ No-Face (American voice: Bob Bergen). [Studio Ghibli/Disney/Photofest]

Disney product. This equation, however, is more than circumstantial. It is also rooted in more general parallels between the medium of animation and the fairy tale—Disney, while dominant, is certainly not the only producer of animated fairy-tale films. While the popular narrative film of any sort has structural parallels with the shape and pattern of the fairy tale, particularly in its utopian impulse, aspects of animation's self-conscious constructedness and, in particular, its simplicity and stripped-down texture provide a visual echo of the classic sparseness and essentialism of folkloric forms. At the same time, animation as a medium relies on action rather than dialogue and visual trickery far more than sound; this roughly parallels the folkloric tendency to rely on action rather than words and to externalize meaning in plot. More broadly, however, the infinite, magical possibilities and metamorphoses of animation's unrealistic surface seem to predispose it intrinsically to magical narratives.

The relationship between animation and fairy tale is also interesting in that animation shadows the fairy tale's problematic association with children. The generally childlike concerns of many animated works, together with the influence of Disney's clean-cut family values, echo the Victorian tendency to relegate folkloric, magical narratives to the nursery. While marketing constraints dictate that most recent animated fairy tales operate on multiple levels, with sophisticated elements appealing to adults as well as children, as seen most recently in the **Shrek** films (*Shrek,* 2001; *Shrek 2,* 2004), a certain unease exists around the duality. This is heightened by the rise in popularity of adult animated entertainment, particularly the Japanese anime tradition and its adult sexuality and violence; like Western animation, however, anime offers children's texts such as Pokemon as well as extremely adult content. The potential difference in audiences is strongest in the categorization differences between full-length animated features and children's afternoon cartoons, which form a definite subset of commercial animation.

By and large, the fairy-tale influence on animation is most felt in feature films, since the extended series format of television animation requires somewhat different tale-telling structures. Despite this, perhaps the most common overlap between folkloric and animated forms in the serial television context is in their common interest in beast fable, as in the adventures of anthropomorphized animals who frequently conform to **trickster** archetypes. These powerful personalities are enabled by the essential lack of realism in animated forms, in their ability to warp animal characteristics into human ones. The classics of animated film are characters such as Felix the Cat, Mickey Mouse, Bugs Bunny, or Tweety and Sylvester; their adventures tend to feature the imaginative outwitting of larger opponents in the approved fairy-tale manner that celebrates the triumph of the weak. Their serialized adventures represent folklore's simplified quest or challenge motif, based on a notion of animal interaction which is archetypal and universalized, and which occasionally incorporates fragments of fairy-tale and folkloric narratives. This tendency runs right across American animated television shorts, encompassing studios such as Warner Bros. and UPA (United Productions of America) as well as Disney's dominant presence. It can also be traced in the characteristic animal-companion motif in many animated features by Disney or other studios. The beast-fable motif has been updated recently in feature-length examples that focus on dinosaur (*The Land Before Time,* 1988; *Ice Age,* 2002) or insect fables (*Antz,* 1998; *A Bug's Life,* 1999.)

Despite folkloric elements within the operation of many animated narratives, the strongest presence of such elements is explicit: from its earliest days the animated film has repeatedly made versions of familiar fairy tales. The earliest roots of animation in Europe, in the praxinoscope of Emile Reynaud in 1890s France, included works such as *Pauvre Pierrot (Poor*

Pierrot, 1892), which made use of the cultural commonality of the harlequinade, itself rooted in folklore. In Germany and later in England, Lotte **Reiniger**'s silhouette films featured **Cinderella** and Papageno. Reiniger's *Die Abenteuer des Prinzen Achmed* (*The Adventures of Prince Achmed*, 1926) was an early feature film based on the *Arabian Nights*. Czechoslovakia's Jiří **Trnka** not only made use of the folk medium of puppetry but also made stop-motion films with fairy-tale and folkloric themes, such as *Císařův slavík* (*The Emperor's Nightingale*, 1949) and *Staré pověsti české* (*Old Czech Legends,* 1953). His early drawn cartoons were also based on Czech fairy tales. Other examples abound across Europe, including a strong tradition of puppet films in early twentieth-century Britain and a recurring interest in animating children's toys via puppetry or stop-motion, allowing a literalization of children's fantasies about living playthings. The earliest experimental animation came to rely in many cases on the simple narratives and magical possibilities of fairy tales. Interestingly, this cuts across cultures: an early Japanese animated work was Seitaro Kitayama's *Momotaro* (*The Peach Boy*, 1918), based on a Japanese folktale, and anime produces folkloric tales as intrinsically and frequently as does the more experimental European work with puppetry and claymation or the American animation giants.

A similar trend is seen in the first American works, which, while tending toward drawn animation rather than puppetry or other experimental forms, also strengthen their sense of story with familiar fairy tales. Walt Disney's earliest experiments were fairy tales, such as the Laugh-O-Gram series made before 1923 for a local Kansas theater, including **Little Red Riding Hood** (1922) and *The Four Musicians of Bremen* (1922). It could be argued that the success of Disney's output in fact depended on its recurring use of the fairy tale, which gave the animated narrative a form and coherence lacking in the extended gag sequences of rival producers. Certainly other classic animated shorts of the time seemed better for their occasional use of fairy-tale themes; examples include Max Fleischer's Betty Boop character, whose adventures featured adult, sexy versions of the fairy tale in *Snow White* (1933) and *Poor Cinderella* (1934). These works underline the fact that the deliberately childlike world of Disney, while dominant over American animation throughout the twentieth century, was not a monopoly, and the strong thread of adult animated entertainment dates back to animation's earliest days. Another good example of this is in the anarchic, subversive work of Frederick "Tex" **Avery**, who was responsible for unruly fairy-tale works, which denied both the totalitarian order of the fairy-tale universe and Disney's particularly saccharine version of it, as well as cartoons that used motifs from "Goldilocks" and "The Three Little Pigs." His versions of "Cinderella" and "Little Red Riding Hood," among other fairy tales, relied on a madcap world of humor, earthiness, and sexual innuendo, but also provided a self-conscious and ironic version of the tales.

The success of Disney's *Snow White and the Seven Dwarfs* marked the transition of animation from shorts into the full-length feature film. While other studios attempted to mimic Disney's success, few achieved it: Disney both dominated the American animated feature in the twentieth century and largely cornered the market in fairy-tale adaptations. Further successes with *Cinderella* (1950) and *Sleeping Beauty* (1959) reached their apogee in the late 1980s and 1990s with the commercial and technological successes of *The Little **Mermaid*** (1989), *Aladdin* (1991), *Beauty and the Beast* (1992), and the beast fable of *The Lion King* (1994). Habitually, Disney has been most successful with Western or Westernized fairy tales, relying on familiarity and a sense of nostalgia and ownership to encourage audience identification with the film; *Mulan* (1998) was a significant departure from this tendency.

Disney's unvarying use of the musical format at this time is another important technique that highlights the innocence, stylization, and narrative unreality of the animated fairy tale, particularly in the company's version. Subsequent Disney works in the early twenty-first century have been less successful, and it is tempting to see some correlation between the company's departure from fairy tales and its slipping grasp on the market.

While Disney was certainly not the only company producing drawn animated features in America during the twentieth century, it comprehensively dominated competitors. Animated fairy-tale features such as Don Bluth's *Thumbelina* (1994) or Nest Family Entertainment's *The Swan Princess* (1994) were released on a far smaller scale, without marketing fanfare, and largely, the strength of rival companies lies in **television** shows and video releases rather than full-length films. Any real challenge to Disney's supremacy in the American animated feature has come recently from more innovative companies such as Dreamworks and Pixar, who are less set in their ways and more able to embrace new computerized techniques as well as a more flexible, less family-oriented worldview. Pixar's *Toy Story* (1995), while a joint release with Disney, represents a very different animation technique, its 3-D semirealism perhaps more related to the European fondness for puppet-animated children's toys. A more important textual tradition is that offered by animators such as Ralph Bakshi, whose feature films such as *Wizards* (1977) and *Fire and Ice* (1983) represent the subgenre of animated fantasy, itself a romance genre with strong folkloric and fairy-tale elements that adapt well to the flexible magic of animated films. The true challenge to Disney's fairy-tale supremacy, however, has been Dreamworks's *Shrek* and *Shrek 2*, which, apart from pioneering new animation techniques, demonstrate a more irreverent, flexible attitude to fairy tales that does not hesitate to satirize either itself or the Disney corpus.

The domination of the Disney monolith has created a focus on drawn animation in America, where the tradition of stop-motion animation is far weaker, represented mainly by a few giants in the field. Ray Harryhausen's films offer a mixture of live action and stop-motion animation, exploring strong fairy tale and mythological themes in movies such as *The Seventh Voyage of Sinbad* (1958) and, famously, *Clash of the Titans* (1981). In recent years it is represented most powerfully by the manic gothic fables of Tim **Burton**, whose work is aimed at a slightly different market. While the colorful and childlike Muppets of Jim **Henson**'s film and television works are an exercise in fantastic beast fable, their creation relies on live-action puppeteering and is thus not a form of animation; the same applies to fantasy films such as *The Dark Crystal* (1982) and *Labyrinth* (1986).

European animation later in the twentieth century is less homogenous than the American output; its reliance on puppet animation and claymation has links to a strong tradition of art films and interest in the surreal. It could be argued that American dominance of drawn animation has possibly influenced the European tendency to try alternative styles, resulting in a more subversive, playful, and technically innovative approach. A good example is Jan Svankmaer, whose animated works are based in the Czech surrealist movement: early films feature clowns and magicians, but a strong folkloric theme is seen in *Otesánek* (*Little Otik,* 2000), the somewhat terrifying **fable** of the couple who adopt a wooden child. Other strong European traditions include the Zagreb School of Animation—associated with the Zagreb Film Studio founded in 1953—which generally moves away from structure and coherence into technically experimental territory; the studio's diverse output tends more toward satire and political parable than toward folkloric themes. Possibly the most successful contemporary European animation is Aardman Animations, creators of the claymation Wallace &

Gromit films; these movies, including the Oscar-winning *Curse of the Were-Rabbit* (2005), are gently fantastic and feature a faithful animal companion, although their humor relies on ironic references to modern genres as well as folklore.

Generally, animation outside the United States tends to reflect far smaller budgets, resulting in innovation and experiment. Other animation loci include Australia and Canada, and in the latter case, the development of the animated film has largely been dominated by the presence of the National Film Board of Canada, which fosters experimental rather than commercial animation. Generally, the high cost of animated movies means that countries with smaller film industries are less likely to produce animated works; nonetheless, interesting and imaginative films have been made. A particularly good example is Zimbabwe's *The Legend of the Sky Kingdom* (directed by Roger Hawkins, 2004), a fantasy adventure made by amateurs and featuring animation of found objects and trash.

Animation is an increasingly important form in the East, with developing industries in countries such as China and Korea. However, it is Japan's anime industry that is dominant. Arising from manga, the Japanese comic-book tradition, anime has a strong tendency toward fantastic genres that exploit the unreal possibilities of the animated medium. A good proportion of anime follows science-fiction formats, but a powerful thread of folkloric and magical awareness runs throughout the genre, creating a high proportion of medieval sword-and-sorcery or samurai films, and romance elements such as sword fighting or legendary artifacts often occur in otherwise futuristic stories. The anime narrative tends to follow a different format than that of Western film, with a slightly scattered and diffuse storyline which accesses a somewhat different sense of folklore, but it is clear that Japanese folklore is an integral part of the anime genre. In parallel with Western development, early Japanese productions such as *Momotaro* directly utilize folklore.

Anime films have proliferated enormously from the late twentieth century onward, and are finding a vastly increased market in the United States. Perhaps the best current examples are from the vivid, gentle productions of **Miyazaki** Hayao's Studio Ghibli, whose highly successful films (some distributed in the United States by Disney) use recurring folkloric motifs. Natural spirits and monsters feature in *Tonari no Totoro* (*My Neighbor Totoro*, 1988), *Mononoke-hime* (*Princess Mononoke*, 1997), and *Sen to Chihiro no kamikakushi* (*Spirited Away*, 2001). The last of these explores a magical otherworld in which a trapped human child must complete ritualistic tasks to escape. Japanese anime artists also demonstrate a fascination with Western magical forms, and versions of classic texts such as the tales of Hans Christian **Andersen** are not uncommon. Both in Japan and in new markets the genre responds directly to an enormous contemporary appetite for the marvelous.

The recent tendency in animation studios to abandon hand-drawn animation in favor of three-dimensional computer animation is potentially significant for the animated fairy tale, since computer simulation has considerable power to model reality accurately and hence to focus attention away from the fantastic and impossible as a textual motif. *See also* Film and Video; Graphic Novel; Japanese Popular Culture; *Kirikou et la sorcière; Popeye the Sailor; Le roi et l'oiseau.*

Further Readings: Solomon, Charles. *Enchanted Drawings: The History of Animation.* Revised edition. New York: Wings Books, 1994; Wells, Paul. *Understanding Animation.* New York: Routledge, 1998; Zipes, Jack. *Happily Ever After: Fairy Tales, Children, and the Culture Industry.* New York: Routledge, 1997.

Jessica Tiffin

Anno Mitsumasa (1926–)

Anno Mitsumasa is an innovative Japanese creator of eponymous picture books for young people, whose subject is **fable**, history, and mathematical puzzles. Born in Tsuwano, Japan, he was educated at a teachers college and taught elementary math in his native country for a decade. He works in a variety of styles, from formal woodcuts to loose but highly detailed watercolor sketches, reminiscent of M. C. Escher or Pieter Brueghel. Wordless picture books emphasize the graphic elements of the story and encourage the reader to "solve" the puzzles of the narration. His first books appeared in Japan in the late 1960s and were translated into other languages, including English, in the 1970s. *Anno's Alphabet: An Adventure in Imagination* (1974) presents each letter as a visual puzzle. He often works with his son Anno Masaichiro, for example, on *Anno's Magical ABC: An Anamorphic Alphabet* (1980) and *Anno's Mysterious Multiplying Jar* (1983). These are based upon the reader's deciphering of mathematical relationships.

A number of books that use journeys as subject matter allow the artist to evoke history, fictional characters, and **folklore**. For example, *Anno's USA* (1983) shows a trip across America from west to east, through time and geography, with many famous sites and characters, ending with the landing of the Mayflower at Plymouth, Massachusetts. *Anno's Aesop* (1990) presents the fables in a way that spoofs the conventions of picture-book folktales. *See also* Children's Literature; Illustration.

Further Reading: Anno Mitsumasa. *The Unique World of Mitsumasa Anno: Selected Works, 1968–1977.* New York: Philomel, 1980.

George Bodmer

Anthropological Approaches

In general, anthropologists approach the traditional tale as a source of cultural information. Thus Franz Boas, the father of American anthropology, could produce a 150-page ethnography of the Tsimshian of British Columbia, including food-gathering, marriage, social organization, religion, and other topics, based entirely on the data in a group of sixty-nine tales. The result is on display in Boas's classic *Tsimshian Mythology* (1916). Recent anthropologists, if similarly motivated, have focused more narrowly. In his *Enchanted Maidens: Gender Relations in Spanish Folktales of Courtship and Marriage* (1990), James Taggart offers a commentary on newly collected versions of **Beauty and the Beast**, **Snow White**, and other tales as told by men and women, whose differing points of view shed light on marriage customs and **gender** roles. In between these two milestones, various anthropologists, ranging from Bronislaw Malinowski to Ruth Benedict, have rung changes on the theme of **folklore** as a key to understanding culture.

However, the term "anthropological school" as it pertains to folklore refers not to this mainstream but to a pre-Boas movement, largely British, culminating in the work of James G. Frazer and Andrew **Lang**. Much later in the nonetheless short, 150-year-old history of the discipline of anthropology we find two other engaging movements, the largely European **structuralism**, advanced by Claude Lévi-Strauss, and the American movement known as ethnopoetics, both very much concerned with folktales but only tangentially related to the usual concerns of social anthropology.

Those who represented the anthropological school, mentioned above, were reacting against a "philological" movement of the mid- and late nineteenth century, which treated folktales as broken-down remnants of an ancient lore belonging to the Aryan cultures of India and the Middle East. Friedrich Max **Müller**, chief spokesman for the philological camp, saw in modern folktales the vestiges of old allegories drawn from nature. Detected especially were hidden references to the diurnal rising and setting of the sun. In contrast, Frazer and Lang saw folklore as built up (not broken down) from the lore of "primitive" cultures still alive in the non-European world. Members of both camps relied on a **comparative method** that took for granted what was sometimes spoken of as the psychic unity of the human species.

It should be noted that the ritual theory of myth, by which all myths are traced to ancient rituals, derives from Frazer's masterwork, *The Golden Bough* (1890–1915), still regarded as a monument of anthropology. Among the many works inspired by Frazer was Jessie L. Weston's *From Ritual to Romance* (1920), in which she traced the medieval legend of the Grail—the dish used by Christ at the Last Supper—to a pre-Christian fertility cult.

In the 1920s, turning away from these concerns, Bronislaw Malinowski and other "functionalists" used traditional tales to help explain how culture works. Based on field researches among the Trobriand Islanders of the western Pacific, Malinowski's contribution to folklore study was the concept of myth as "charter." That is, the purpose of the story is not merely to entertain but to legitimize the values of an entire society. In some cases the myth may be sufficiently detailed to serve as a practical guide to the activities with which it is concerned (*Myth in Primitive Psychology*, 1926).

Meanwhile, an important German school, including Paul Ehrenreich, Eduard Seler, and Konrad T. Preuss, had been making solid contributions to cultural studies while still operating within the long shadow of Max Müller. At a surprisingly late date, Preuss could bring out a collection of tales from the Witoto of Colombia, explaining that the fictional characters represented the moon in its monthly phases (*Religion und Mythologie der Uitoto*, 1921–23). Against this background the British anthropologist A. R. Radcliffe-Brown proposed that the doings of human characters identified with the moon, the sun, or wind in traditional stories should be regarded as allegories not of natural phenomena but of social experience (*The Andaman Islanders*, 1922), thereby standing nature mythology on its head.

Like Malinowski and Radcliffe-Brown, Ruth Benedict in her influential *Patterns of Culture* (1934) brushed aside the quest for universals that had occupied Lang and Frazer as well as Müller. For her, each culture created its own pattern, or personality. With regard to stories in particular, the point was elaborated in Benedict's *Zuni Mythology* (1935): Folktales are never generic, she declared; rather, they express the values and practices of one culture (compare the earlier work of Joseph **Jacobs**). Like many anthropologists (though not Malinowski), Benedict used the term **myth** interchangeably with **folktale**, especially in non-Western contexts.

Striking out in new directions, the twin approaches of structuralism and ethnopoetics, which gained currency in the 1960s, de-emphasized the manifest content of folktales. Structuralists found a hidden geometry in verbal art, detecting binary oppositions such as male and female, old and young, or raw and cooked, while practitioners of ethnopoetics concentrated on style, discovering couplets, stanzas, pauses, and other features that revealed the narrative as a kind of poetry. Two Americanists took the lead in developing ethnopoetics:

Dennis Tedlock, who studied live **performance** (*Finding the Center: Narrative Poetry of the Zuni Indians,* 1972), and Dell Hymes, who specialized in textual analysis ("*In Vain I Tried to Tell You": Essays in Native American Ethnopoetics,* 1981).

Anthropological approaches to folklore that have most easily crossed the divide between science and art are those that may be deemed the least anthropological. Ethnopoetics has inspired such poets as W. S. Merwin and Gary Snyder, not to mention numerous linguists, whose work has been showcased in volumes edited by the poet and literary historian Brian Swann. In the field of criticism, Lévi-Strauss himself has used structuralism to illuminate Baudelaire's sonnet "Les Chats" ("The Cats"). As for the work of Frazer and Weston, which inspired T. S. Eliot's master poem *The Waste Land,* though grounded in anthropology, it would eventually be associated with literary approaches to folklore. *See also* Colonialism; Ethnographic Approaches.

Further Readings: Edmonson, Munro S. *Lore: An Introduction to the Science of Folklore and Literature.* New York: Holt, Rinehart and Winston, 1971; Segal, Robert Allan, ed. *Anthropology, Folklore, and Myth.* New York: Garland, 1996; Swann, Brian, ed. *Voices from Four Directions: Contemporary Translations of the Native Literatures of North America.* Lincoln: University of Nebraska Press, 2004.

John Bierhorst

Anti-Fairy Tale

The term "anti-fairy tale" was first used in German as *Antimärchen* by André Jolles in 1929 as a designation for fairy tales that have a tragic rather than the normal happy ending, as for example in "The Fisherman and His Wife." Even the most positive fairy tales have aspects of an anti-fairy tale if one applies the concept to the negative hero or antihero in such tales. The story of the stepmother in "Snow White," for example, would be an anti-fairy tale of sorts, since she is shown to be an utterly evil person who finds her cruel and final punishment in the end. Seen in this light, one could consider such **literary fairy tale**s as Ludwig **Tieck**'s "Der blonde Eckbert" ("Eckbert the Blond," 1797) or some of Franz **Kafka**'s short stories or **fables** as approximating the idea of an anti-fairy tale. However, the term has also been used to refer to modern literary reworkings of fairy tales that stress the more negative scenes or **motif**s, since they appear to be more realistic reflections of the problems of modern society.

Such negative, cynical, or satirical reactions to traditional fairy tales in the form of poems, prose texts, **aphorisms**, caricatures, and **cartoons and comics**, for example, are interpreted as anti-fairy tales, as contradictions to the miraculous and positive messages of the original tales. Some of these texts and illustrations are indeed "grim" reactions to the traditional **Grimm** fairy tales, contrasting the perfect world of the fairy tale with sociopolitical issues, marital problems, and economic worries. And yet, fairy tales and anti-fairy tales complement each other as traditional and innovative signs of the human condition.

Further Readings: Jolles, André. *Einfache Formen.* 1929. Tübingen: Max Niemeyer, 1965. 242; Mieder, Wolfgang. "Grim Variations: From Fairy Tales to Modern Anti-Fairy Tales." *Tradition and Innovation in Folk Literature.* Hanover, NH: University Press of New England, 1985. 1–44; Röhrich, Lutz. *Folktales and Reality.* Translated by Peter Tokofsky. Bloomington: Indiana University Press, 1991. 44–47.

Wolfgang Mieder

Anti-Semitism

There is a long tradition of anti-Semitism in European folklore. To understand it, one must look first to the **legend** rather than to the **folktale** or **fairy tale**, though anti-Semitism certainly makes its appearance even here, as folk beliefs permeate every aspect of so-called folk wisdom. Two main legendary traditions depicted Jews in an extremely negative light: the **blood** libel legend (Motif V361) and the legend of the Wandering Jew, Ahasver (ATU 777; Motif Q502.1). In the first, the belief was promulgated that Jews committed the ritual murder of a Christian, usually a boy, in the week before Easter to collect his blood for religious purposes, usually to be baked in the unleavened bread (matzo) eaten at Passover. The first occurrence of this accusation followed the unsolved murder of a boy named William in Norwich in 1144. In the years following his death, a cult gradually grew around him, and eventually he was canonized as St. William of Norwich. A rash of similar tales spread throughout Europe, first in England but soon also in France, Spain, Germany, and eventually also in Poland and beyond. The last widely publicized case was in Massena, New York, in 1928. The legend of the Wandering Jew tells that a Jewish man was punished for unkindness to Christ on the way to Calgary by being damned to wander the earth until Judgment Day.

It is important to note that a legend is a tale that is or has been believed to be true by at least some people. Because of this, the nature of these two tales is far from harmless. Both depict Jews as cast out by (the Christian) God and worthy of the cruelest **punishment**, for this tradition ascribes to all Jews, even those living much later, the guilt for the crucifixion of Jesus Christ. They disseminate stereotypes about Jews that have been extremely difficult to eradicate: that they are malignant, avaricious, and deceitful, that they are little better than vermin, that they are a diseased and somehow "unmanly" race, and that they deserve to be killed. Accusations of blood libel almost always led to loss of property and loss of life: nineteen people were executed in the case of St. or Sir Hugh of Lincoln, in 1255, for example, and the king confiscated the property even of those Jews whom he in the end chose not to kill. Pogroms continued until the twentieth century, incited by the ideas found in these and other similar tales.

Here one can see the great power of folklore by way of a negative example. Belief in blood libel confounded the most reasoned attempts to disprove it. Sometimes a pogrom took place even when there was no body found: an entirely empty accusation was enough to spark a riot. Evidence that not a single blood libel case can be proved, and that the Jewish religion prohibits the ingestion of even animal blood, has not prevented even some recent writers on the topic from asserting there must be a basis in the actions of at least some Jews.

A larger view shows that accusations of this nature have always been made of a minority group that is feared, perhaps because, paradoxically, the ruling culture knows subconsciously that it is oppressing this group. For example, early Christians themselves were accused of similar crimes in Roman times. If the oppressed group can be shown to be guilty of heinous vices, then the oppression can continue as justified. Or, in the case of the Wandering Jew, a folklore **motif** with a very wide dispersal—the figure of one who wanders the earth until the end of time—is used in a new context to justify and confirm attitudes already held. The Wanderer was once the great Nordic god Odin or Wotan and later became the Wild Huntsman. In later Christian times he becomes the outcast Jew and this "truth" is used to condone the refusal to let Jews settle in European cities. Interestingly, if the blood libel tradition started in Catholic times, the Wandering Jew tale had its heyday in a Protestant context. In 1602, a concerted effort seems to have been made to propagate this legend quickly with the simultaneous publication of pamphlets throughout Europe. This occurred at a time when Jews were beginning to settle again in Europe after a long period of absence, earlier Jewish communities having been exterminated in the Crusades from the eleventh through the thirteenth centuries. Furthermore, it has been argued that the various waves of anti-Semitic fervor tended to occur in times when the Christian church was unsure of maintaining its power: one group in power can consolidate its position by scapegoating another. The Jews were all too suitable for this role. As Christianity had grown out of Judaic traditions, the Jews could continue to be seen as the enemy, the "Other," those who were by definition different.

One fairy-tale example of anti-Semitism occurs in Jacob and Wilhelm **Grimm**'s tale "Der Jude im Dorn" ("The Jew in the Thornbush"). It is telling that the Grimms felt this tale to be suitable even for their *Kleine Ausgabe* (Small Edition, 1825) for children, despite their efforts otherwise to clean the tales up for a young audience. The misuse of folklore against the Jews culminated in the events in Germany of the 1930s and 1940s, when the Grimms' tales, Germanic mythology, and even **proverbs** were interpreted by pedagogues and folklorists in ways that underlined and reinforced the racism and anti-Semitism of Adolf Hitler's Third Reich. Of course, anti-Semitism is by no means a solely German phenomenon. Though largely a Christian phenomenon, it has also spread to Islamic cultures. Both legends mentioned here form the subject of countless local legends, **saints' legend**s, chapbooks, and **ballad**s, and anti-Semitism echoed through the "high" literary tradition as well (in Geoffrey **Chaucer** and William **Shakespeare**, for example.) The stereotyped figure of the avaricious Jew occurs in miracle plays and proverbs, and stories abound throughout the ages about Jews who poison wells and desecrate the Host, for example. Examples of relevant motifs can be found in Stith Thompson's *Motif-Index of Folk-Literature* (Motifs V360–V364).

Further Readings: Dundes, Alan, ed. *The Blood Libel Legend: A Casebook in Anti-Semitic Folklore.* Madison: University of Wisconsin Press, 1991; Felsenstein, Frank. *Anti-Semitic Stereotypes: A Paradigm of Otherness in English Popular Culture, 1660–1830.* Baltimore: Johns Hopkins University Press, 1995; Hasan-Rokem, Gakit, and Alan Dundes. *The Wandering Jew: Essays in the Interpretation of a Christian Legend.* Bloomington: Indiana University Press, 1986; Mieder, Wolfgang. "Proverbs in Nazi Germany: The Promulgation of Anti-Semitism and Stereotypes Through Folklore." *Journal of American Folklore* 95 (1982): 435–64.

Laura Martin

Aphorisms

While fairy tales and folktales have long been adapted into longer prose works, plays, and **poetry**, at times they have also been reduced to short aphorisms of just a few lines. Such short prose texts allude to the world of fairy tales in general, or they play off fairy-tale titles or well-known individual **motif**s. Literary authors have repeatedly used traditional tales to add expressiveness to their intellectual thoughts, but one can also find anonymous one-liners in the form of slogans or graffiti. These short and poignant texts are remnants of the original tales and can be considered as a special subgenre of the large corpus of aphorisms appropriately called fairy-tale aphorisms.

One of the earliest and most telling aphorisms of this type is Johann Wolfgang von **Goethe**'s definitional text "Fairy tale: indicating to us the possibility of impossible occurrences under possible or impossible conditions." Later reactions by other authors to fairy tales in general or to specific motifs repeat this apparent ambiguity between the wishful world of the magic tale (or **wonder tale**) and the reality of normal life. The utopian hopes and dreams of fairy tales seem to be unreachable in an imperfect world, but by seeing modern problems and concerns in relation to the possible solutions expressed in fairy tales, aphorisms can become a way to deal with otherwise depressing conditions.

The relevance of the universal nature of fairy tales to people of the modern age was symbolically expressed by Elias Canetti in an aphorism from 1943: "A closer study of fairy tales would teach us what we can still expect from the world." Similarly, one also finds the aphorism "Don't believe the fairy tales. They were true" by Stanisław Jerzy Lec from Poland, perhaps the most important modern aphoristic writer. As has been noted by fairy-tale scholars, folk narratives contain many harsh aspects of the social reality of former ages that can easily be related to the cruelties and anxieties of the modern age. This means that Lec can in fact claim that, "Some fairy tales are so bloody that they actually cannot be regarded as such." Such aphorisms are clear indications that intellectuals do occupy themselves with fairy-tale matters, and it should therefore come as no surprise that even philosophers such as Theodor Adorno, Walter Benjamin, and Ernst Bloch frequently return to fairy tales in their philosophical thoughts and maxims.

The seemingly insurmountable challenges and problems of modern life have led aphoristic writers to question the hope for any fairy-tale future for humanity. For example, the Austrian author Žarko Petan changed the standard introductory formula of fairy tales into the future tense to state his view that "All socialist fairy tales begin with: 'Once upon a time there will be ...'" Aphoristic writers with sociopolitical concerns also utilize the traditional closing formula of the fairy tale. For those who are tired of listening to empty promises from their leaders and waiting for improvements, the following anonymous poster parody is the perfect cynical comment: "And if they haven't died, then they are still waiting today." Numerous modern fairy-tale aphorisms are based on such a pessimistic worldview. For example: "Statistics is the fairy tale of rationality" (Martin Kessel); "Our newest longing for fairy tales is dangerous. Have we forgotten that the frog does not turn into a beautiful **prince** every time?" (Nikolaus Cybinski); "It is the old story of Brier Rose: Hundreds of knights had to croak miserably, but in front of the last one the gate finally opened itself and he got the **king**'s daughter, and that was no justice" (Franz Fühmann); "**Feminism**. Better blood in the **shoe** than a prince around the neck" (Werner Mitsch, referring to "**Cinderella**"); "Love and fashion make fairy tales possible" (Werner Schröter); and "Rumpelstiltskin: The personified principle of envy prevention" (Gerhard Uhlenbruck).

As expected, there are many aphorisms based on individual fairy tales and their motifs, with most of the short texts being grounded on an ironic or satirical reinterpretation of a well-known original text. At times the authors of these parodies are unknown, as for example in the new American formulation, "You have to kiss a lot of toads [frogs] before you meet your handsome prince," which clearly refers to "The **Frog King**," and which has become proverbial not only in the United States but also as loan translations in Europe. An anonymous graffito alludes more openly to the sexual implications of this fairy tale: "Better one night with a prince than a whole life with a frog." A number of anonymous slogans based on "**Snow White**" also enter the sexual sphere: "Better once with Snow White than seven times with the dwarfs" or "Did you know that Snow White had no rest on any day of the week?" And there is also Mae West's erotic twist, "I used to be Snow White—but I drifted," which was sold in 1999 as a quip on a postcard. On the more serious level of sexual politics, there are Edith Summerskill's "The housewife is the Cinderella of the affluent state" and Lee Miller's "I'm not Cinderella. I can't force my foot into the glass slipper." Related to all of this is, of course, also Colette Dowling's "Here it was—the Cinderella Complex," from her best-selling book *The Cinderella Complex* (1981), which echoes Septima Palm and Ingrid Brewer's somewhat earlier book, *The Cinderella Syndrome* (1979).

There is also a special subgroup of fairy-tale aphorisms that is based on the triadic structure of so-called wellerisms, that is, humorous sayings with an introductory statement, a speaker, and a situational twist. A few examples of this modern tradition are: "'I continue to be for the relaxation of tension,' said Snow White, after the evil stepmother had attempted to poison her" (Hans Weigel); "'All good things come by threes,' said the **wolf** and had the huntsman for dessert" (Werner Mitsch); and the anonymous "'Whoever sleeps does not commit sins,' said the prince and let **Sleeping Beauty** continue to slumber in the brier hedge." Such fairy-tale wellerisms are meant to be funny, although they too can take on rather macabre meanings.

Offering yet another form of fairy-tale **intertextuality**, fairy-tale aphorisms usually question the positive nature of the traditional texts. Power, crime, **violence**, selfishness, greed, materialism, and **sex**, for example, belong to the multifaceted topics of these aphorisms. It is not that these matters were not present in the fairy tales as well, but the aphorisms that express social criticism usually do not include the element of hope that is part and parcel of the fairy tale. When modern aphoristic and slogan writers present concise arguments against them, they often do so with the intention of changing life to a more fairy-tale-like existence. There is no doubt that every fairy-tale aphorism with its humor, irony, or satire calls into memory the traditional fairy-tale with its positive and hopeful outlook, and by the juxtaposition of both a balance between human misery and bliss just might be found.

Further Readings: Jones, Steven Swann. "Joking Transformations of Popular Fairy Tales: A Comparative Analysis of Five Jokes and Their Fairy Tale Sources." *Western Folklore* 44 (1985): 97–114; Mieder, Wolfgang. "Aphoristische Schwundstufen des Märchens." *Dona Folcloristica: Festgabe für Lutz Röhrich.* Edited by Leander Petzoldt and Stefaan Top. Frankfurt a.M.: Peter Lang, 1990. 159–71; ———. "Fairy-Tale Allusions in Modern German Aphorisms." *The Reception of Grimms' Fairy Tales: Responses, Reactions, Revisions.* Edited by Donald Haase. Detroit: Wayne State University Press, 1993. 149–66; ———. "Sprichwörtliche Schwundstufen des Märchens." *Proverbium* 3 (1986): 257–71; Röhrich, Lutz. *Der Witz: Figuren, Formen, Funktionen.* Stuttgart: Metzler, 1977.

Wolfgang Mieder

Apuleius, Lucius (c. 124–c. 170 CE)

Lucius Apuleius was a rhetorician, satirist, and author of the only Roman **novel** to have been preserved in complete form. His surviving works include the *Apologia* (*The Apology* or *On Magic*), a treatise he wrote to defend himself against a charge of using magic to entrance a wealthy widow into marriage, a collection of his works under the title *Florida*, and some philosophical treatises. He is principally known, however, for his prose narrative, *The Golden Ass* or *Metamorphoses*. The **frame narrative** of *The Golden Ass* relates the story of Lucius of Corinth, who is transformed into an ass and experiences many adventures before he is restored to human form after the intervention of the goddess Isis. The underlying cause of Lucius' **transformation**, and one of the central themes of the whole work, is *curiositas* (meddlesome curiosity). Curious about magic, Lucius is taken by his lover, Fotis, to spy on her mistress in the act of transforming herself into an owl. Eager to share the experience, he prevails upon Fotis to bring him the magic ointment that causes the transformation, but she carelessly brings the wrong ointment. There is a simple antidote, to eat some roses, but before Lucius can do this, he is taken by **thieves**. His restoration is continually deferred as he passes in captivity from one situation to another, and until he is ready to subordinate his appetites and desires to the principles of rationality and order. Although he has an ass's body, Lucius retains human knowledge and understanding and hence is able to absorb the myriad stories that he overhears or in which he plays a part.

The Golden Ass retells tales of many familiar types, including stories about magic, robber tales, and revenge and adultery. The best known is the allegorical story of "Cupid and Psyche," which Lucius overhears as "a pleasant old wives' tale," and which is commonly interpreted as an analogy for Lucius's own trials and eventual redemption. When Venus sends Cupid to make her human rival, Psyche, fall in love with something low and abject, he instead falls in love with her himself and keeps her in a rich palace but under the interdiction that she must never see him. "Cupid and Psyche" is the earliest fully articulated version of an animal groom tale. It anticipates the plot and motifs of later tales such as "**Beauty and the Beast**" and "East of the Sun, West of the Moon": the beast as lover instead of destroyer, jealous sisters, the invisible servants in an enchanted castle, and the female quest to recuperate a broken interdiction. The theme of curiositas reappears here when Psyche loses her lover after lighting a candle to look at him while he sleeps. She eventually wins him back after a series of hostile trials set by Venus. However, this time she is helped through the final trial by Cupid after she nearly loses her life by once more yielding to curiositas. As in the frame story, divine intervention proves efficacious when human weakness cannot prevail. *See also* Animal Bride, Animal Groom;   Classical Antiquity;   Greek Tales;   Middle Ages.

Further Readings: Apuleius. *The Golden Ass*. Translated by P. G. Walsh. New York: Oxford University Press, 1994; Birberick, Anne L. "Rewriting Curiosity: The Psyche Myth in Apuleius, La Fontaine, and d'Aulnoy." *Strategic Rewriting*. Edited by David Lee Rubin. Charlottesville, VA: Rookwood, 2002. 134–48; Leinweber, David Walter. "Witchcraft and Lamiae in 'The Golden Ass.'" *Folklore* 105 (1994): 77–82.

John Stephens

Arabian Nights

The Thousand and One Nights, in English commonly known as *The Arabian Nights' Entertainments* or, in short, the *Arabian Nights* or simply the *Nights*, was originally an Arabic collection of stories that has become an integral part of world literature ever since its French **translation** (1704–17) by Antoine **Galland**. Rather than denoting a specific book, the *Arabian Nights* imply a phenomenon, since the work is both anonymous and authored by many contributors over an extended period of time, and since its character as a shape-shifter has led to numerous differing versions in Arabic manuscripts and printed texts, as well as in European translations.

Textual History

The History of the *Arabian Nights* before Galland. European Orientalist research has brought forth various arguments for an Indian and/or Iranian origin of the collection that later materialized as the *Arabian Nights*. An Indian origin is suggested by the fact that

An 1874 illustration from *The Arabian Nights* by French artist Gustave Doré. Sindbad is shown trapped in the Pit of the Dead among dozens of stacked corpses. [Time & Life Pictures/Getty Images]

Indian versions of the tales given in the collection's **frame narrative**, including the stratagem of telling tales to prevent **death**, predate the *Arabian Nights*. An Iranian origin may be surmised from the Persian background of the main characters in the frame tale (King Shahriyar and his brother Shahzaman, **Sheherazade** and her sister Dunyazade) and from the fact that the earliest-known references to the *Arabian Nights* explicitly mention a Persian-language predecessor. These references have been preserved in the works of Arab historian al-Mas'ûdî (died 956) and Baghdad bookseller Ibn al-Nadîm (died 995). Both authors state that the Arabic book *Alf layla* (*A Thousand Nights*) derives from an earlier Persian book named *Hezâr afsân* (*A Thousand Stories*). Ibn al-Nadîm also mentions details of the work's frame tale in that a **king** used to marry a young woman every day only to kill her the next morning, and that Sheherazade by telling him stories for a period of a thousand consecutive nights reformed him and finally convinced him to quit this bloody habit by showing him their child. The references do not, however, mention the actual content of those tales. This content is, albeit summarily, intimated by a paper fragment dating from the ninth century and preserving the first pages of *The Book of the Tale of the Thousand Nights*. Here, a certain Dinazad asks Shirazad (for Sheherazade) if she is not asleep, to tell her a story and give "examples of the excellencies and shortcomings, the cunning and stupidity, the generosity and avarice, and the courage and cowardice that are in man, instinctive or acquired, or pertain to his distinctive characteristics or to courtly manners, Syrian or Bedouin." While none of the actual tales are quoted in the fragment, the description, only to some extent, matches the content documented in later Arabic manuscripts. Evidence for the physical existence of the *Arabian Nights* is found in the notebook of a Jewish physician who also sold, bought, and lent out books in mid-twelfth-century Cairo. The notice pertains to a book called *The Thousand and One Nights* and thus bears testimony to the fact that the collection's elaborate title as known today had come into use. The oldest preserved text of the *Arabian Nights* is contained in a three-volume Arabic manuscript that most probably dates from the middle of the fifteenth century. The manuscript, which was acquired and used by Galland for the first part of his translation, is fragmentary and contains the beginning of the *Arabian Nights* up to night 282, breaking off at some point in the "Tale of Qamar al-Zamân and Budûr." Besides this manuscript, fewer than a dozen Arabic manuscripts predating Galland are known. In addition to these, early Turkish translations of the work were available in the Royal Library in Paris when Galland prepared his translation.

Galland's Translation and Its Consequences. Galland in his *Les mille et une nuits* not only translated but to a certain extent created the *Arabian Nights*. When the tales of the old Arabic manuscript he used were exhausted, readers' enthusiasm demanded that he complete the work. At first, Galland's publisher without his consent published a volume containing tales translated by both Galland and his Orientalist colleague François Pétis de la Croix. Galland himself then took recourse to various other sources, including material from other manuscripts, some of which has not been identified. Even before, he had already integrated the tales of **Sindbad**. For some of the tales most popular in later European tradition, particularly those of **Ali Baba** and **Aladdin**, he is indebted to the performance of gifted Syrian storyteller Hanna Diyab. Galland's creative and enlarged **adaptation** of the Arabic text was a tremendous success in Europe. It gave rise to a vogue of literature in the Oriental style and thus contributed to the rising phenomenon of Orientalism. Some of Galland's scholarly colleagues even tried to imitate his success, such as Pétis de la Croix, who published a collection named *Les mille et un jours* (*The Thousand and One Days*, 1710–12), allegedly translating a collection copied from a manuscript in the possession of a Persian dervish, but in reality adapting a Turkish collection of tales from the Royal Library in Paris. In addition, Galland's translation furthered Orientalist studies in that scholars began to occupy themselves with the origin of the collection, its various tales, and the culture presented therein. Moreover, it initiated a search for complete manuscripts of the work that in turn resulted in complete manuscripts being produced, whether in the East, above all in Egypt, or in the West, where Arab scholars in Paris forged allegedly old manuscripts right before the eyes of their Orientalist superiors.

Scholarship has classified the Arabic manuscripts of the *Arabian Nights* into several groups, the most important of which was defined by French scholar Herman Zotenberg and has become known as "Zotenberg's Egyptian recension" (ZER). Other manuscripts with differing contents include the Wortley-Montague manuscript preserved in Oxford and the Reinhardt manuscript in Strassburg.

Printed Editions and English Translations. With the exception of the Breslau edition, ZER manuscripts formed the basis of most of the printed editions of the *Arabian Nights* prepared in the nineteenth century.

Calcutta I: Edited by Ahmad al-Shirwani. 2 vols. Calcutta, 1814–18.
Bulaq I: 2 vols. Bulaq (Cairo), 1835.
Calcutta II: Edited by W. H. Macnaghten. 4 vols. Calcutta, 1839–42.
Breslau: Edited by M. Habicht and H. L. Fleischer. 12 vols. Breslau, 1825–43.
Bulaq II: 4 vols. Bulaq (Cairo), 1862.

While Galland's French version had previously served almost exclusively as the source of reference for translations into other European languages, the publication of the printed editions greatly facilitated the translation of the *Arabian Nights* from the original texts. The best-known English language translations published in the nineteenth century are those prepared by Edward W. **Lane** and Richard Francis **Burton**. Lane's translation, published in three volumes in London (1839–41), largely follows the Bulaq I edition. While prepared by an excellent scholar of Arabic, the translation submits itself to Puritan Victorian morality by eliminating various objectionable scenes and even complete tales. Lane's translation is, moreover, supplied with profuse and often distracting ethnographic annotation, since he intended the book to be read as a mirror of Arabic customs. Burton's translation was published in ten volumes in "Benares" (London, 1885–86). While profiting to a considerable extent from the previous limited English edition by John Payne (1882–84), Burton took pleasure in employing archaic language and in stressing, rather than suppressing, any sexual undertones or explicit scenes to be found; in particular, his "Terminal Essay" is notorious for his predilection with sexual matters. While the bulk of his translation is based on the Calcutta II edition, he later published a six-volume installment of "Supplemental Nights" (1886–88) containing additional tales from other versions of the *Arabian Nights*. A third English-language translation was published by Powys Mathers (1937) based on the French version prepared by Joseph Charles **Mardrus** in sixteen volumes in Paris (1899–1904). Even though it has been reprinted numerous times until today, this translation is the least faithful to the Arabic original, as it contains numerous additions from a large variety of different sources, particularly in its later volumes. Meanwhile, the Mardrus version was widely acclaimed in France by famous writers André Gide and Marcel Proust and also contributed to the fame of the *Arabian Nights* in its English version. Since, according to modern critical standards, none of the available English versions of the *Arabian Nights* are satisfactory, Malcolm C. Lyons and Robert Irwin are currently preparing a new translation.

Characteristics

While the various versions of the *Arabian Nights* differ in content, particularly in their later parts, all of them contain both a specific frame tale and a largely identical initial set of stories. In the frame tale, Sheherazade tells her stories to the cruel king over consecutive nights. Sheherazade's stratagem of breaking off her tales at a critical point not only saved her life but also turned the frame tale into a powerful engine driving a potentially endless number of stories. Some of the earlier tales are closely linked to Sheherazade's own intention of saving her life by telling stories, such as the tale of "The Trader and the Jinnî," the tales told by the Qalandars in "The Porter and the Three Ladies of Baghdad," the tale of "The Three Apples," and "The Hunchback's Tale," including the tales of the Broker, the Reeve, the Jewish Doctor, the **Tailor**, and the Barber. In his programmatic essay on "Narrative-Men," Tzvetan Todorov has identified this device as one of the major individual characteristics of the *Arabian Nights*: to reveal who they are, the characters relate their experiences by telling stories. In this manner, telling a story signifies life, and, in consequence, the absence of narrative signifies death. As the characters are "merely narrative" who must narrate to be able to live, their **storytelling** generates the overwhelming abundance of embedding and embedded tales in the *Nights*. The device of having characters within a tale tell their own tales on subsequent levels creates a labyrinthine structure that greatly contributed to the fascination of the *Arabian Nights*, particularly among Western audiences.

As a consequence of the frame tale's narrative potential, and probably resulting from the fact that "complete" manuscripts of the *Arabian Nights* were not always available, the compilers of later versions incorporated tales of the most divergent categories, including **folktale**s, **fairy tale**s, romances, **religious tale**s, **didactic tale**s, **fable**s, jokes and **anecdote**s, many of which are culled from either classical Arabic literature or from numerous anonymous collections of tales. Research has classified those tales and their hypothetical origin or integration into several strata, including an Indian stratum, probably encompassing the "wiles of women" stories about extramarital sexual relations and some of the fables; an Iranian stratum, encompassing those tales closest to the European understanding of the fairy tale, in which wonder and magic occur on an unquestioned and natural level; a Baghdad stratum, encompassing tales of the Harun-cycle (see **Harun al-Rashid**) as well as jokes and anecdotes from the times of the Abbasid dynasty; and a Cairo stratum, encompassing Mamluk tales of deceit and roguery. These strata cannot be clearly separated; the collection rather resembles a palace, one from whose ruins new buildings were erected at consecutive periods. Moreover, several originally independent tales or collections were at some point integrated into the *Arabian Nights*, such as the Persian *Sindbad-Name* (also known in the West by way of its Latin version *Dolopathos*), the tales of Sindbad's travels (already integrated into a seventeenth-century Turkish manuscript), or the lengthy romance of 'Umar ibn al-Nu'mân. Even some European translators could not resist the temptation to enlarge the repertoire of the *Arabian Nights* by adding tales from extraneous sources. Burton added, from an unidentified source, the jocular tale about a man whose breaking wind led to a new reckoning of time, and Mardrus exploited various works of historical literature as well as recent contemporary collections of folktales and fairy tales from the Arab world.

A major characteristic of the narrative universe presented in the *Arabian Nights* is the predominance of the ethical values of the merchant class, who probably constituted the major audience for oral **performance**s of tales from the *Arabian Nights* in their indigenous context. This led Aboubakr Chraïbi to classify the *Arabian Nights,* in allusion to the widespread literary genre of "mirror for princes," as a "mirror for merchants." Though the *Arabian Nights* is by no means a unified collection, its tales convey to some extent an image of social life in the Muslim world, particularly in Egypt in the Mamluk period. One should, however, beware of taking the *Arabian Nights* as an ethnographic manual, as was popular in Victorian England following Lane's translation. In particular, the playful atmosphere of the *Arabian Nights* relating to licentious behavior in terms of sexuality or the consuming of intoxicating beverages and drugs rather than advocating a tolerant or permissive atmosphere expresses compensation and wishful thinking. Its enthusiastic reception in Europe in all likelihood is due to the rigorous social standards reigning there at the time.

The Impact of the Arabian Nights

The impact of the *Arabian Nights* on Western creative imagination can hardly be overestimated. Elements from the frame tale of the *Arabian Nights* were already mirrored in Italian Renaissance literature long before Galland, in Giovanni Sercambi's *Novella d'Astolfo* (c. 1400), and in canto 28 of Ludovico Ariosto's *Orlando furioso* (1516), suggesting the possibility of a transfer by way of **oral tradition**. With the tremendous success of Galland's translation, hardly a major European writer of the eighteenth and nineteenth centuries could avoid being in some way or other influenced by *Arabian Nights*. By way of recreations in oral performance or public reading from printed tales, many of which were published as separate **chapbook**s, the tales from *Arabian Nights* also reached the more illiterate strata of society, and some of its stories have since become stock tales of European folk literature.

In the twentieth century, many images and tales from the *Arabian Nights* form an integral constituent of European and world culture. The collection as a whole is regarded as the quintessential expression of well-being, a matrix similar to the European notion of Cock-aigne (an imaginary land of great luxury and ease), with an added spice of (imagined) unin-hibited sexuality. Popular imagery includes the number 1001, denoting an endless amount, the image of the jinnî who is released from the bottle and cannot be controlled anymore (from the "Tale of the Fisherman and the Jinnî"), or the wording "Open, Sesame" (from the tale of "Ali Baba and the Forty Robbers"). The three best-known tales from the *Arabian Nights*, namely "Aladdin," "Ali Baba," and "Sindbad," have moreover gained fame as mod-ern trade names for purposes that popular imagination would spontaneously link with their content: "Aladdin" serves as a trade name for bail bonds and **Internet** search engines, Ali Baba is probably the most famous label for "Oriental" restaurants in the West, and Sindbad is a common name for travel companies, particularly for single males. *See also Arabian Nights* Films; Film and Video; Pasolini, Pier Paolo; *Popeye the Sailor*; Reiniger, Lotte.

Further Readings: Ali, Muhsin Jassim. *Scheherazade in England: A Study of Nineteenth-Century English Criticism of the Arabian Nights.* Boulder, CO: Three Continents, 1981; Caracciolo, Peter L., ed. *The Arabian Nights in English Literature: Studies in the Reception of the Thousand and One Nights into British Culture.* New York: St. Martin's, 1988; Gerhardt, Mia I. *The Art of Story-Telling: A Literary Study of the Thousand and One Nights.* Leiden: Brill, 1963; Irwin, Robert. *The Arabian Nights: A Com-panion.* London: I. B. Tauris, 2004; Mahdi, Muhsin. *The Thousand and One Nights* (Alf Layla wa-Layla) *from the Earliest Known Sources.* 3 volumes. Leiden: Brill, 1984–94; Marzolph, Ulrich, ed. *The Arabian Nights in Transnational Perspective.* Detroit: Wayne State University Press, 2007; ———, ed. *The Arabian Nights Reader.* Detroit: Wayne State University Press, 2005; ———, and Richard van Leeuwen, eds. *The Arabian Nights Encyclopedia.* 2 volumes. Santa Barbara, CA: ABC-CLIO, 2004; Pinault, David. *Story-Telling Techniques in the Arabian Nights.* Leiden: Brill, 1992.

Ulrich Marzolph

Arabian Nights Films

No film faithfully recreates all the tales in the ***Arabian Nights***, or the *Thousand and One Nights*, mainly because they are so numerous, but also because some would be objectionable to a modern sensibility. Still, they have inspired a large number of short films, full-length features, and **television** series that explicitly or implicitly use their characters, settings, and storytelling devices—especially the **frame narrative** and tales within tales. The range of cinematic approaches to the *Nights* adopted over ten decades is well shown by an account of four films whose titles claim kinship with the overall collection.

By the first half of the nineteenth century, the written *Nights*, in **translation**, was popular across Europe. British stage **pantomime**s capitalized on this by making frequent use of such tales as "**Aladdin**" and "**Ali Baba**," treating them just as it treated Charles **Perrault**'s "**Cinderella**" (1697), Jonathan Swift's *Gulliver's Travels* (1726), or Daniel Defoe's *Robinson Crusoe* (1719). That is, they were turned into vehicles for a medley of songs, acrobatics, star turns, topical jokes, **cross-dressing**, slapstick, dancing girls, and, above all, grandiose stage designs and marvelous illusions. Visiting London in the 1880s, future French filmmaker Georges **Méliès** enjoyed and noted these elements in shows he saw at the Egyptian Hall.

A decade later, back in Paris, Méliès was a pioneer in the development of cinema, often turning for source material to tried and trusted stage stories and techniques, enhancing them with camera tricks such as image substitution. One of numerous productions in this vein was *Le palais des mille et une nuits* (*The Palace of the Thousand and One Nights/Arabian Nights,* France, 1905).

Méliès was not interested in any particular tale from the *Nights*. He simply wanted a setting for which he could devise amazing cinematographic effects, sumptuous costumes, and spectacular tableaux. Only after those elements were under construction did he think about creating a storyline and characters to go into the spaces being created. What he came up with was a generic *Nights*-style quest, depicted in thirty black-and-white tableaux, lasting twenty-eight minutes.

It begins with a **prince** asking an Indian rajah for his daughter's hand. The rajah rejects him angrily because he is penniless; in any case, the **princess** is already promised to a wealthy usurer. Help comes from a **sorcerer** accidentally liberated by the prince from imprisonment inside an incense burner; the socerer shows his gratitude by giving the prince an invincible magic sword and telling him of a treasure that will satisfy even the Rajah. When the prince seeks support from the goddess Shiva, she transforms herself from stone into flesh, and then causes an ornate pavilion to emerge from the ground. Out of it, led by a blue **dwarf**, come the boatmen of the Sacred River, who row the prince to an impenetrable forest, protected by nymphs and a high priest. There, a **Fairy** of Gold leads him to a crystal grotto, but he meets strong resistance: genies create flames, smoke, and explosions to drive him away, and when this fails, an army of dancing skeletons joins the assault. Subsequent tableaux show the prince using his sword to vanquish a **dragon** and a host of giant toads before reaching a temple full of dancing girls. Climactically, surrounded by the splendors of the palace, he is told his courage has earned a fabulous reward. With it he returns home, arriving just in time to save the princess from a forced **marriage** to the usurer.

As the synopsis indicates, *The Palace of the Thousand and One Nights* glances only lightly at the literary source texts, the main direct reference being the liberated genie, taken from the tale of Aladdin. Being silent, the film's primary aim was to exploit the appeal of *Nights'* exotic visual iconography. It thus left plenty of other aspects of *Nights*—characters, themes, morality—for later filmmakers to bring to the screen.

Méliès's basic narrative scheme of the hero undergoing fantastic trials and winning a princess prefigured Douglas Fairbanks's *The Thief of Bagdad* (USA, 1924), Lotte Reiniger's silhouette animation feature *Die Abenteuer des Prinzen Achmed (The Adventures of Prince Achmed*, Germany, 1926) and Alexander Korda's Oscar-winning revision of *The Thief of Bagdad* (UK/USA, 1940). In this last version, because it had Technicolor, sound, and the child-star Sabu/Abu, lay the seed of a new cinema genre: the eastern. Easterns appropriated some elements of *Nights* but not the use of magic. Instead, they foregrounded physical adventure and prowess, like swashbucklers. The difference with easterns was that they were played out on sand rather than greensward, with scimitars rather than rapiers, supporting or deposing caliphs and sultans rather than **king**s and emperors.

This blend of Oriental setting with athletic action sequences was first seen in *Arabian Nights* (USA, 1942, directed by John Rawlins), which imported Sabu/Abu from the Korda film to reprise the role of the hero's resourceful young friend. This time the dispossessed ruler needing help is **Harun al-Rashid**, the rightful Caliph of Bagdad, who has been dethroned by his jealous half-brother. Harun takes refuge in a circus, where he befriends Ali, an acrobat (Sabu), and falls in love with dancer **Sheherazade**. They stage a mock funeral for Harun, hoping to throw his pursuers off the scent, but the ruse misfires when they are all captured and sold as slaves far away. Escaping, they pass through dangers and conflicts and finally return to Bagdad, where Harun is restored to the caliphate and marries Sheherazade.

In addition to stars, romance, acrobatics, swordplay, and dancing, the *Arabian Nights* offered comedy in the shape of a retired, rambling old sailor **Sindbad** and an Aladdin who is always yearning for the good old days when he used to have such a wonderful lamp.

This combination of elements proved a hit with wartime cinema audiences and spawned several more easterns. *Ali Baba and the Forty Thieves* (USA, 1944, directed by Arthur Lubin) featured the same tropes in a story about an underground resistance movement (the Thieves) fighting against tyrannical Nazi-style Mongols. After the war, *The Prince Who Was a Thief* (USA, 1951, directed by Rudolph Mate), set in thirteenth-century Tangiers, featured a **thief** who has royal lineage but does not know it. He thinks himself in love with the beautiful but shallow Princess Yasmin until a fellow thief, Yussef, shows him his true affection is for Tina, a street entertainer.

Not till the 1970s did the cinema take a deeper look into the heart of the *Nights* and try to get beyond the exoticism of flashing scimitars, flying carpets, gigantic djinns, and noble **thieves**. None of these elements is to be found in Pier Paolo **Pasolini**'s *Il fiore delle Mille e una notte* (*Arabian Nights*, Italy/Spain, 1974). The clue to Pasolini's intentions is missing from the English title; as his original suggests, he sought to re-create *The Flower of the Thousand and One Nights*.

For Pasolini, the *Arabian Nights* was the final part of the film series Trilogy of Life, the other two being based on Giovanni **Boccaccio**'s *Decameron* (1349–50) and Geoffrey **Chaucer**'s *Canterbury Tales* (c. 1387). With these films he sought to create cinema that would celebrate the energy and lack of inhibition, as he perceived it, of the precapitalist world. Visiting Yemen to plan his *Nights* film, he wrote about the "miserable consumerism" he saw everywhere and predicted imminent "cultural genocide" for Yemenis.

In accordance with his purpose in making this film, it was shot simply and quickly; Pasolini did much of the camera work himself, recording no sound—that was added later. He moved the camera as little as possible, not wishing to impose his own meaning on the objects and action in front of it. He built no sets, preferring existing locations found in Yemen, Persia, Nepal, or Eritrea—after they had been cleared of all plastic objects, tin cans, television sets, or anything else produced in a factory. He used almost no special effects; those he did use were unsophisticated (for example, a simple superimposition of one piece of film over another to show a djinni and his captive flying, upright, over a desert). A few professional actors and a small crew traveled with him from country to country, but mostly he found his cast among the villagers who lived where he was filming.

This preindustrial approach to filmmaking included a respect for the integrity of his sources. Even with a running time of 128 minutes, he could use only a few of the 468 tales available; those he chose are transposed to the screen with close adherence to the dialogue and incidents of the written text. Only in matters of **sex** and **violence** is there any serious directorial editing. For example, in the frame story of the slave girl Zumurrud and her master/lover Nur ed Din, she is suddenly abducted, leaving Nur ed Din with no idea how to find her. At this point he is helped, in the written text, by an old woman who demands nothing by way of payment, whereas in the film help comes from a young woman who wants sex in return for her efforts, and provokes a matching desire in Nur ed Din. Such exuberant, laughing celebration of youthful sexuality is a recurrent **motif** in the film.

In relation to violence, Pasolini goes the other way, playing it down compared to what is in the written text. At the end of Zumurrud's ordeal she has been made ruler of a city and in that capacity has to pronounce **punishment** on the men responsible for her earlier abduction and threatened gang rape. In the source material she ordains 100 blows on the soles of each foot, 1,000 lashes, flaying, then the flesh and bones to be burned and covered with offal and ordure. Such detailed relish shown by a beautiful young woman in the infliction of suffering and **death** did not fit Pasolini's vision: he simply shows a brief shot of the culprits tied to a cross and left to die.

With these aims and in this style, Pasolini weaves a web of interlocking tales, tales within tales, tales within tales within tales, tales invoked but not shown (Zumurrud's would-be rapists are specified as numbering forty), and parts of tales (a short **jest** about metaphorical names for male and female genitals is extracted from the fourteen pages of "The Porter and the Three Girls of Bagdad").

The longest unbroken tale is that of Aziz and his cousin Aziza, told by Aziz himself to a man he meets in the desert. Aziz was once meant to marry Aziza, with whom he had grown up, but on the morning of the ceremony he saw the mysterious Badur from a distance and, longing to have her, missed his wedding. Under Aziza's selfless tutelage, he goes through a long series of secret communications and assignations with Badur, and when he attains his desire, Aziza commits suicide. He is then forced into marriage and fatherhood with a third woman, Ertay; and when after a year he gets back to Badur, she castrates him. Finally he realizes how much he loved Aziza. In the original tale, its moral as expressed by Aziza is (in Richard Francis **Burton**'s translation): "Faith is fair; unfaith is foul." Pasolini, however, omits this and reinforces his refusal to impose meanings in his film by attaching the epigraph: "Fidelity is splendid, but no more than infidelity."

In total contrast to Pasolini's film was *Arabian Nights* (USA/Germany, 2000, directed by Steve Barron), a three-hour television miniseries shown in several countries. It has a galaxy of stars; it used forty-eight specially constructed studio sets; and it employed state-of-the-art visual effects. Above all, it differs from Pasolini in being very concerned with applying editorial guidelines to the writing, shooting, dialogue, and soundtrack so that the chosen texts yield a precise meaning. This is essential because the traditional framing story, of Sheherazade telling her husband tales every night, is expanded so that she is no longer simply trying to save herself from being beheaded: she wants to help him overcome the feelings of guilt and betrayal that have made him depressed, black-hearted, and seemingly mad. (A back story gradually reveals that five years earlier, Shahryar's first wife had betrayed him with his brother, and that he had killed her unintentionally.) The stories Sheherazade tells are chosen for their capacity to illustrate a **moral** that she wants Shahryar to reflect on, as part of the rehabilitation she seeks for him.

She begins with the tale of Ali Baba, implicitly suggesting that Shahryar could identify with Black Coda, the heartless, ruthless leader of the Forty Thieves. Several times during the dramatization of the tale, the film cuts back to the storyteller, pointing up its meaning: "Well, Ali had something that his brother Kasim never had—a good heart."

From this concentration on good and bad hearts, Sheherazade moves on to "The Tale of the Hunchback," about a king's favorite jester, who suddenly appears to die while at dinner with a **tailor** and his wife. Not wishing to be blamed, they carry him to a Jewish doctor nearby, who assumes the death is his fault and gets rid of the body as soon as possible. A Chinese visitor to the city and a hymn-singing Christian also get involved but try not to get blamed. However, the Christian is accused, tried, found guilty, and about to be hanged, at which point the Chinese visitor, the doctor, and the tailor all rush forward to claim they are guilty. They are saved by the sudden arrival of the King, who pardons them all, saying it must have been an accident. "The moral of this tale," comments Sheherazade to Shahryar, "is that they all learned to take responsibility for their actions." (In the original written text it turns out that the hunchback is not really dead at all, but the film omits that twist.)

Three more tales are shown in this style. Shahryar is invited to perceive Mustappa, Aladdin's phony uncle, as a man who lost everything because he could not control his temper. Then, while Shahryar's brother is massing forces for an assault on the city, Sheherazade rolls out the story of "The Sultan and the Beggar," with Shahryar playing the beggar who proves within just one day to be a better ruler than the real sultan, because he is in touch with the common people. Finally, "The Story of Three Brothers" shows that "men united do better than men divided." At this, with newfound self-confidence and love in his heart for Sheherazade, Shahryar uses the lessons of the tales—plus some of their protagonists' cunning tricks—to rout his brother and secure his throne.

In the epilogue, Sheherazade tells their children "The Tale of Sultan Shahryar," which must surely end with this moral: Ignore the old tales at your peril—there is much truth to be learned from them. ***See also*** Animation; Film and Video; *Popeye the Sailor*; Silent Films and Fairy Tales; Thief of Bagdad Films.

Further Readings: Breteque, François de la. "Les contes de Georges Méliès." *Contes et légendes à l'écran*. Special issue of *CinémAction* 116 (2005): 62–71; Ezra, Elizabeth. *Georges Méliès: The Birth of the Auteur*. Manchester: Manchester University Press, 2000; Haase, Donald. "The *Arabian Nights*, Visual Culture, and Early German Cinema." *The* Arabian Nights *in Transnational Perspective*. Edited by Ulrich Marzolph. Detroit: Wayne State University Press, 2007. 245–60; Irwin, Robert. "*A Thousand and One Nights* at the Movies." *New Perspectives on Arabian Nights: Ideological Variations and Narrative Horizons*. Edited by Wen-chin Ouyang and Geert Jan van Gelder. New York: Routledge, 2005. 91–102; Richards, Jeffrey. *Swordsmen of the Screen: From Douglas Fairbanks to Michael York*. London: Routledge, 1977; Robinson, David. *Georges Méliès: Father of Film Fantasy*. London: British Film Institute/ Museum of the Moving Image, 1993; Rohdie, Sam. *The Passion of Pier Paolo Pasolini*. Bloomington: Indiana University Press, 1995.

Terry Staples

Archetype

The concept of the "archetype" refers in a general sense to motifs, themes, characters, plots, or generic forms that are considered to be exemplary types or prototypes. However, the term "archetype" is most frequently and specifically associated with Carl Gustav **Jung**'s evolutionary model of the psyche. Jungian archetypes are forms that originate in the collective unconscious and appear across cultures as images and patterns in dreams and other creative outlets. The most important archetypal figures for fairy-tale and **folklore** studies are the shadow, wise old man, great mother, **witch**, anima, animus, and **trickster**.

Jung's evolutionary model of the psyche has four major components: the self, the ego, the personal unconscious, and the collective unconscious. Jung believed that just as all human beings share a common physiological heritage through evolution, they also inherit a common psychic structure from the evolution of the brain—the instinctual patterns that Jung called archetypes. These archetypes are the contents of the collective unconscious, the largest component of the psyche in the Jungian model. Jung also described a personal unconscious, which contains the psychic contents that are dissociated or repressed throughout an individual's lifetime. The key differences between the two layers of the unconscious are that the contents of the personal unconscious are unique to the individual and were once accessible to ego consciousness, whereas the archetypal contents of the collective unconscious are universal and were never originally accessible to ego consciousness. The ego is the smallest component of the psyche and comprises the conscious awareness of the individual. The totality of the psyche, conscious and unconscious, is termed the self.

It is possible to think of the collective unconscious as containing a genetic blueprint for psychic stability and wholeness, as well as a set of potentialities for responding to the outer world. Once the individual or collective psyche strays too far from the blueprint (an excessive amount of externalization, repression, or both), archetypal imagery and figures burst into consciousness through dreams and other creative activities. The purpose of the archetypes' appearance is to expose the ego to previously inaccessible content. One possible consequence of this exposure is the restoration of balance and gradual reintegration of dissociated content into the self—a process Jung called individuation. Whereas dreams manifest archetypal complexes of relevance to the individual, creative traditions such as fairy tales expose dissociated psychic content to an entire society, offering a type of group therapy.

In fairy tales an unlikely protagonist must usually journey beyond the familiar world into the realm of the unfamiliar. Often the unfamiliar is depicted as a forest, subterranean, or marine environment. Such imagery indicates an encounter with the collective unconscious, as these regions are hidden from the light of consciousness and civilization; instead, these darker areas team with fauna, whose behavior is tied to instinct. Beings that emerge from the trees and the depths, the instinctual realm of the collective unconscious, are culturally specific manifestations of the archetypes. It is important to note that the manifest forms in fairy tales are not actual archetypes—it is better to think of them as blankets cast over the archetypes, giving temporary shape to the mutable structures beneath.

A common archetype encountered in the unfamiliar realm of the fairy tale is the shadow. The shadow is the receptacle of universal psychic contents that have been dissociated from ego consciousness because of their social unacceptability. The contents that are cast into the shadow do not vanish from the psyche; rather, they resurface as projections upon others. The traits of the shadow that surface in fairy tales are typically extreme and associated with a society's sense of evil, especially murderous and incestuous drives. The ultimate role of the fairy-tale protagonist is to confront and defeat this figure; the parallel psychological function is the exposure and reintegration of dissociated content that has been repressed in the shadow and projected onto a villainous other. Frequently, the protagonist will defeat a proxy shadow in the form of a doppelgänger. The most familiar doubling of the shadow in fairy tales is the evil stepmother-wicked witch dyad. The duplication of female figures may also, depending on the individual tale, point to a **mother** complex (the great mother is a Janus-faced archetype that displays both nourishing and destructive tendencies) or an anima complex. The anima is the unconscious feminine component of the male psyche, and the animus is the corresponding masculine component in **women**. When these components are heavily repressed, they are typically projected onto members of the opposite sex.

The protagonist almost always requires help to successfully confront the shadow. Assistance frequently comes from a manifestation of the archetype of the wise old man. The old man appears at the protagonist's most desperate hour to deliver the sage advice that enables the protagonist to move forward. Psychologically, the old man provides information not accessible to the protagonist's ego consciousness. Jung describes this function as an endopsychic automatism—akin to a flash of inspiration. Assistance may also come in the form of animal helpers. From a Jungian point of view, this indicates the activation of human instincts, since the animals come from the forest, the unfamiliar realm of the collective unconscious.

More significant to folklore and mythology than the fairy tale is the archetype of the trickster. The trickster is a duplicitous figure, typically a creature that is half animal and half divine; a player and victim of cruel pranks; and a curios mix of **devil** and savior. A fool that defies authority, the trickster appears when the old social order is in crisis and traditional authority most vulnerable. The trickster's foolery and deceits may unintentionally cause the collapse of the old order, thus allowing the rise of the new. In this way, the trickster becomes an unlikely cultural hero by exposing repressed contents to the light of consciousness and allowing for their reintegration, much like the protagonist of the fairy tale. *See also* Franz, Marie-Louise von; Myth; Psychological Approaches; Trauma and Therapy.

Further Readings: Franz, Marie-Louise von. *Archetypal Patterns in Fairy Tales.* Toronto: Inner City Books, 1997; ———. *The Interpretation of Fairy Tales.* Revised edition. Boston: Shambhala, 1996; ———. *Shadow and Evil in Fairytales.* Dallas: Spring, 1974; Jung, Carl Gustav. *The Archetypes and the Collective Unconscious.* Translated by R. F. C. Hull. Edited by Sir Herbert Read et al. 2nd edition. Vol. 9.1. New York: Princeton University Press, 1990.

R. Seth C. Knox

Archives

An archives can be defined as a place in which public records or historical documents are kept, or simply as a compilation of records. In either case, an archives contains materials that are deemed important to ensure the continuity of societal **memory** for future research needs. In an archives with specific relevance for folktale and fairy-tale studies, the resources can consist of written records (for example, transcriptions of orally performed tales, field-workers' notes, correspondence, and manuscripts), images (such as **illustration**s), artifacts (for example, games, toys, or other items of material culture), or sound or visual recordings of storytellers performing in their typical settings. Although not strictly archival materials, many folkloristic archives contain first editions or other publications of works by fairy-tale authors and scholars.

Archives can be themed, such as the one devoted to the Brothers **Grimm** at the Brüder Grimm-Museum (http://www.grimms.de). Located in the Murhardsche Library of the University of Kassel, the Brüder Grimm-Archiv houses a collection of the Grimms' documents, original manuscripts, and other artifacts. The museum's library, housed with the archives, has a rich collection of books and other materials related to the study of the Grimms' lives and wide-ranging work. Together, the library and archives include valuable resources for the study of the Grimms' tales and the fairy tale generally.

Similar archives facilitate research on the tales of Hans Christian **Andersen**. The Royal Library of Denmark houses all of the original Andersen manuscripts; whereas, the Hans Christian Andersen Center, a part of the University of Southern Denmark, contains micro-film copies of the originals and serves as a portal for international research (http://www.andersen.sdu.dk/index_e.html). Additional manuscripts of his fairy tales and other works, along with his paper cuttings, drawings, and other materials, are housed in the Odense City Museums, which also makes many items available for viewing online (http://www.museum.odense.dk/H_C_Andersen.aspx).

Libraries and universities maintain many important archives. Princeton University's Cotsen Children's Library contains 23,000 items, including a 1697 first edition of Charles **Perrault**'s *Histoires ou contes du temps passé* (*Tales and Stories of the Past,* 1697). Princeton, in a more traditional archival setting, also holds a large assortment of George **Cruikshank**'s artwork that includes manuscripts and prints. The Bodleian Library, University of Oxford, in the United Kingdom, has a 30,000-piece collection of **Broadside Ballad**s available for searching online (http://www.bodley.ox.ac.uk/ballads/ballads.htm); and the British Library has an extensive collection of folktale and fairy-tale material. Among the most interesting is the online gallery "Turning the Pages," where the viewer can leaf through the pages of the original manuscript of *Alice in Wonderland*, annotated, written, and illustrated by Lewis **Carroll** (http://www.bl.uk/onlinegallery/ttp/ttpbooks.html). The Beinecke Rare Book and Manuscript Library of Yale University has an extensive J. M. **Barrie** Collection, as well as the L. Frank **Baum** Collection, the Oscar **Wilde** Collection, and correspondence, manuscripts, and other papers pertaining to Alfred Lord **Tennyson**, among others.

An especially noteworthy archives for oral narrative research is the collection of Turkish tales housed at the Special Collections Library at Texas Tech University. Beginning in 1961, the founders of the archives—Ahmet E. Uysal, Warren S. Walker, and Barbara K. Walker—started collecting narratives from the field and eventually donated their work to Texas Tech, where the collection became known as the Uysal-Walker Archive of Turkish Oral Narrative. Available online, the collection contains Turkish oral narratives and their translations (http://aton.ttu.edu/).

An important German resource for folk-narrative research is the Wossidlo Archive housed at the University of Rostock (http://www.phf.uni-rostock.de/ivk/). From 1883 to 1939, Richard **Wossidlo**, one of the most significant field researchers of European ethnography, traveled throughout his native Mecklenburg collecting the cultural knowledge of his fellow Mecklenburgians. His notes in the local dialect became the basis of the archives, which systematically documents folktales, folk songs, proverbs and sayings, regional customs, folk beliefs, folk medicine, regional cuisine, clothing, housing, and the lives of children, peasants, wage workers, fishermen, and craftsmen. This archives also contains Wossidlo's correspondence relating to his academic career, communications between Wossidlo and his assistants, and his personal journals. The University of Rostock is also home to Wossidlo's ethnological library. With 11,500 books and 2,800 journals, the library is one of the largest dedicated to folkloric researches in the area.

The U.S. Library of Congress accommodates The American Folklife Center, which has extensive holdings of worldwide folk culture housed in the Archive of Folk Culture (http://www.loc.gov/folklife/). The Folklife Center has a remarkable collection of audio tales of the supernatural, as well as a selection of papers, recordings, and ephemera of folk collector Zora Neale **Hurston**. Its notable international holdings include "Telapna: We—Zuni Verbal Art," a documentation of fifteen Zuni storytellers; the "Literatura de Cordel Brazilian **Chapbook** Collection"; and the "Four Masters of Chinese **Storytelling** Video Collection." Some of the center's collections are available online (http://www.loc.gov/folklife/onlinecollections.html).

International folk-narrative research has benefited in a very significant way from the archives maintained in Göttingen by the editors of the voluminous *Enzyklopädie des Märchens* (*Encyclopedia of the Folktale,* 1975–). In support of the *Enzyklopädie*'s broad historical and comparative scope, the editorial team has compiled extensive text archives relying on source material and collections from all over the world (http://wwwuser.gwdg.de/~enzmaer/).

Increasingly, archives reside solely on the World Wide Web. Many of these **Internet** archives are maintained by educational institutions. At the University of Pittsburgh, a several sites created and maintained by D. L. Ashliman archive numerous folkloric texts in electronic format (http://www.pitt.edu/~dash/folktexts.html; http://www.pitt.edu/~dash/folk-texts2.html). Archives dedicated to single **tale type**s are found at the University of Southern Mississippi Web site. *The Cinderella Project* archives texts and images pertaining to English versions of the Cinderella tale type (http://www.usm.edu/english/fairytales/cinderella/cinderella.html), and *The Little Red Riding Hood Project* does the same for ATU 333 (http://www.usm.edu/english/fairytales/lrrh/lrrhhome.htm). Although not affiliated with a university, the *SurLaLune Fairy Tales* Web site is a nonprofit educational site that archives the history of fairy tales. Relying on texts, translations, and images in the public domain, the site includes annotated tales, illustrations, texts of fairy-tale collections, and other kinds of information about authors, collectors, illustrators, and scholars (http://www.surlalunefairy-tales.com/). *See also* Fieldwork; Loorits, Oskar.

Further Readings: Bartis, Peter. *Folklife Sourcebook: A Directory of Folklife Resources in the United States.* 3rd edition, revised and expanded. Washington, D.C.: American Folklife Center, Library of Congress, 1997. Available online: http://www.loc.gov/folklife/source/index.html; Becker, Karin. "Picturing Our Past: An Archive Constructs a National Culture." *Journal of American Folklore* 105 (1992): 3–18; Lloyd, Timothy. *The Archive of Folk Culture: The National Collection of American and World Folklore.* Washington, D.C.: American Folklife Center, Library of Congress, 1992.

Helen J. Callow

Arnim, Bettina von (1785–1859)

Bettina von Arnim (née Brentano) contributed as author, supporter, and activist to the development of the German **fairy tale**. She assisted her brother Clemens **Brentano**, her fiancé Achim von Arnim, and Jacob and Wilhelm **Grimm** with their collections of folk songs and folktales. She later incorporated elements of the **folktale** and the **literary fairy tale** into her own writing and coauthored fairy tales with her daughter, Gisela von **Arnim**.

Bettina von Arnim penned her first tales in 1808 while helping Brentano and Achim von Arnim collect folksongs. The "Einsiedlermärchen" ("Hermit's Tale") was a fragment her fiancé completed and published under his name. While "Die blinde Königstochter" ("The Blind Princess") and "Hans ohne Bart" ("Beardless Hans") were versions of oral tales, Arnim wrote a fourth tale herself. Although extant manuscript versions are untitled, it was first published in 1913 as "Der Königssohn" ("The King's Son"). The modern English translation of this tale redirects attention to the central character with its title, "The Queen's Son." This story of a woman's quest in nature includes traditional folktale elements, the romantic wish for harmony between nature and humankind, and a model for an enlightened ruler.

After raising seven children, Arnim wrote and published actively, incorporating fairy-tale elements into her texts. The **motif** of **Cupid and Psyche** is central to *Goethes Briefwechsel mit einem Kinde* (*Goethe's Correspondence with a Child,* 1835). Arnim fantasized her own land of milk and honey in *Die Günderode* (1840) and included a fairy-tale autobiography in *Clemens Brentano's Frühlingskranz (Clemens Brentano's Spring Wreath,* 1844). As reflections of Arnim's political activism, the revolutionary magpie in *Dies Buch gehört dem König* (*This Book Belongs to the King,* 1843) and the socialist fairy tale "Der Häckebeutel" ("The Tale of the Lucky Purse," 1962) offer ironic twists on the themes of the indiscrete bird and the inexhaustible purse.

Arnim was a close friend of Jacob and Wilhelm Grimm, and the Grimms expressed their gratitude for her support in their ***Kinder- und Hausmärchen*** (*Children's and Household*

*Tale*s, 1812–15). They dedicated the first edition of their work to "Frau Elizabeth von Arnim" in honor of the birth of her first son. The third edition of 1837 paid homage to her "unconquerable youth." In the subsequent editions of 1840 and 1843, the Grimms acknowledged her efforts on their behalf in the wake of the brothers' political difficulties in Göttingen.

In years preceding the 1848 revolution, Bettina participated in Gisela von Arnim's literary **salon** and coauthored with her *Das Leben der Hochgräfin Gritta von Rattenzuhausbeiuns* (*The Life of High Countess Gritta von Ratsinourhouse.*) Today, scholars consider Bettina von Arnim's life and work significant not only for the development of the German fairy tale but also for the history of **feminist tales**. *See also* German Tales.

Further Readings: Arnim, Bettina von. "The Queen's Son." 1990. *The Queen's Mirror: Fairy Tales by German Women, 1780-1900.* Edited and translated by Shawn Jarvis and Jeannine Blackwell. Lincoln: Nebraska Press University Press, 2001. 111–16; Arnim, Bettina and Gisela von. *The Life of High Countess Gritta von Ratsinourhouse.* Translated by Lisa Ohm. Lincoln: Nebraska University Press, 1999; Blackwell, Jeannine. "German Fairy Tales: A User's Manual; Translations of Six Frames and Fragments by Romantic Women." *Fairy Tales and Feminism: New Approaches.* Edited by Donald Haase. Detroit: Wayne State University Press, 2004. 73–111; Morris-Keitel, Helen G. "The Audience Should Be King: Bettina Brentano-von Arnim's 'Tale of the Lucky Purse.'" *Marvels & Tales* 11 (1997): 48–60.

Lisabeth Hock

Arnim, Gisela von (1827–1889)

Gisela von Arnim had a deep understanding of the European fairy-tale tradition, and as an author and playwright, she often fashioned protofeminist revisions of its narratives. Von Arnim's fairy-tale production spans several decades and often bridges public and private spheres, as well as adult and juvenile audiences.

In the 1840s Biedermeier salon, the *Kaffeterkreis* (The Coffee Circle), von Arnim wrote tales for a semiprivate audience. In the same period, she coauthored with her mother, Bettina von **Arnim**, the female-Robinsonade/fairy-tale novel *Das Leben der Hochgräfin Gritta von Rattenzuhausbeiuns (The Life of the High Countess Gritta von Ratsinourhouse)* for publication, although it was never released. A decade later, she penned private epistolary fairy tales to her nephew with a **frame narrative** reminiscent of the *Arabian Nights*, and she began writing stage dramas based on **saga** material published by Jacob and Wilhelm **Grimm** or transmitted by the Romantics. "Das Licht" ("The Light," 1870) is her one published children's fairy-tale play. Her works take a critical look at fairy-tale paradigms and offer different models for socialization and **gender** relations. *See also* Salon.

Further Readings: Arnim, Bettina and Gisela von. *The Life of High Countess Gritta von Ratsinourhouse.* Translated by Lisa Ohm. Lincoln: University of Nebraska Press, 1999; Arnim, Gisela von. "The Rose Cloud." Trans. Shawn C. Jarvis. *Marvels and Tales* 11 (1997): 134–59; Jarvis, Shawn C. "Trivial Pursuit? Women Deconstructing the Grimmian Model in the *Kaffeterkreis*." *The Reception of Grimms' Fairy Tales: Essays on Responses, Reactions, and Revisions.* Edited by Donald Haase. Detroit: Wayne State University Press, 1993. 102–26.

Shawn C. Jarvis

Art

Over the centuries, fairy tales have inspired artists around the world. When fairy tales are incorporated into art forms other than literary art forms, the results are diverse and often spectacular. The art created through the lens of fairy tales ranges from explicit visual retellings of tales to more abstract, formal suggestions of them. That is, sometimes a particular fairy tale will be referred to explicitly in an artwork—its plot or characters are clearly depicted and the artwork is titled after the story. Yet often an artwork simply has what might be called a fairy-tale feel: a sense of lucid enchantment and what might be called riotous order. Much fairy-tale art comprises an imaginative response to fairy tales in general, rather than a literal representation of a particular story's main events. In this latter sense, visual art relates strongly to Max **Lüthi**'s assertion that the art of fairy tales resides in their form.

While this entry provides a chronological grand tour of examples from around the world, the possible content for a survey of fairy-tale art is as limitless as the literary field of fairy tales itself. It is important to note that in many cultures, from the third century on, art has had a fascination with the fantastic. However, this article concerns itself primarily with the eighteenth century and beyond, when most explicit fairy-tale art may be identified. An inclusive, comprehensive history of fairy-tale art has yet to be written and is called for.

Early Examples

While fairy-tale **motif**s may be identified prior to the coining of the term fairy tale—for example, a sixteenth-century woodcut of a donkey producing dung of gold, which might suggest "Donkeyskin" or "The Goose That Laid a Golden Egg"—the explicit influences on this art would more appropriately be identified as mythology and religion than fairy tales. Until the late eighteenth century, at least, fairy tales were not considered proper subject matter for serious and publicly ambitious high art. However, at least two specific movements from before the eighteenth century deserve mention.

Dutch artist Quinten Massys's painting "A Grotesque Old Woman" (1525–30) is a good example of a growing European fascination with the grotesque. In the painting the female face is distorted and seemingly unreal. The painting is predictive of future images of female fairy-tale villains such as **witch**es, stepmothers, and **queen**s in fairy-tale **illustration** and **animation** (although Massys's renderings avoid the clichés that often haunt such depictions today). Famous Italian artist Leonardo da Vinci also produced a series of fascinating studies of grotesque human heads in the late fifteenth and early sixteenth centuries. These drawings merge the clinical with the supernatural—a suffusion that one also

Lewis Carroll's photograph of Agnes Weld dressed as Little Red Riding Hood. [Princeton University Library]

finds in fairy tales. Grotesquerie shares fairy-tales' matter-of-fact relationship to the alarming.

Widely known sixteenth-century artist Hieronymous Bosch filled his horrifying, sublime canvases with imaginary worlds. These obsessive allegorical visions lend themselves well to readings through prominent aesthetic components of many fairy tales: exaggerated detail, **violence**, dreamlike narrative, repetitive motifs, and recurring characters. One of his most famous works, "The Garden of Earthly Delights" (1504), contains a typically dazzling yet precise landscape—full of binaries, it is explosive and serene at once. Drenched with otherworldly details such as magical architecture and glow, this painting reads like a fairy tale. It is a triptych, reminiscent of the serial nature of fairy tales and their interest in threes (see **Numbers**).

New awareness of nature's detail—made possible by the microscope, invented in the sixteenth century—spawned excitement about minute details. An enthusiasm for fairy tales and their collapsing of scale—where a mouse or small bird may be equal to that of a giant or human—appears naturally to evolve from this fervor for minutiae. A new kind of painting with exquisite attention to realism began to emerge, and this superrealism had the interesting effect of making that realistic world appear supernatural. Eighteenth-century artist Henry Fuseli drew from William **Shakespeare** to produce lush works such as "Titania and Bottom" (c. 1790) and "Titania's Awakening" (c. 1785–90), works that foreground enchantment as their main theme. In their relationship to each other, and to previous stories, these particular paintings connect to the nature of fairy tales as retold tales—endlessly reproducible tales—a motif that shows up from this time forward in fairy-tale art.

The Romantic Period

Romanticism, a turn-of-the-century European and American movement inspired in part by a rejection of aristocratic social and political norms, gave rise to visual techniques emphasizing wonder in nature. Artists from this time often had friendships and collaborative working relationships with writers explicitly exploring elements of wonder, including E. T. A. **Hoffmann** and Mary Shelley. In Germany, translations of Shakespeare's plays, which contain elements of **folklore** and fairy stories, influenced artists greatly. Romantic art also celebrates sublimity and heroic individuals. While realist in impulse, the exaggerated wonder in nature as depicted in Romantic art has the effect of fairy tales.

As an example one might look at Spanish artist Francisco de Goya's paintings, which often portrayed melancholy creatures; these images, while not necessarily evoking particular fairy tales, have a distinctly fairy-tale feel noted by many art historians. They have been called "monstrously

Kiki Smith, *Born*, 2002. Lithograph on moldmade T. H. Saunders paper. [Copyright © Kiki Smith, courtesy of PaceWildenstein, New York]

lifelike." Marina Warner has also drawn the parallel between fairy tales and Goya's art when she suggested that the ogre father depicted in "Saturn Devouring His Son" (1819) is reminiscent of "the **Bluebeard** of fairy tales" (Warner, 51).

One of the most important English Romantic writers and artists, William Blake, produced seven hauntingly beautiful illuminated books referred to as a group as the "Urizen books," the first of which is dated 1794. This series remains in very high esteem with contemporary print-makers and other artists as a work of printmaking genius. In the Urizen books, Blake presented an elaborate, original enchanted world, with biblical, mythic, and folkloric elements. Urizen's major motifs—oppression and liberation, and sexual dynamics—are those of fairy tales. Urizen (which stood for "your reason") was, like many literary fairy tales of the period (especially in Germany), a political work, a visual story/poem railing against the rational, materialistic age in which he found himself. The fantastic worlds in which Blake's "illuminated books" are set were populated—like the fairy tale—variously by humans (including children), animals, angels, giants, and **fairies**—including Oberon and Titania in *The Song of Los* (1795).

In the early nineteenth century, specific fairy tales had not yet become a major focus of painters, as they would later in the century in the remarkable work of artists such as Moritz von **Schwind**, who, in the 1850s and 1860s, "told" entire tales in cycles of paintings. However, at least three paintings invoking the story of "**Little Red Riding Hood**" testify in England to an emerging interest. In 1783, Maria Cosway presented a painting based on the tale, which was followed by portraits painted by John Hoppner and John Opie. Then, around 1821, Thomas Lawrence produced a portrait of "Emily Andersen: Little Red Riding Hood." Lawrence depicts his young subject in a bright "red riding hood," clearly invoking the soon-to-be classic tale. Lawrence's painting—along with those by Cosway, Hoppner, and Opie—not only confirms that the story of "Little Red Riding Hood" was well known in England by the late eighteenth and early nineteenth centuries; it also prefigures, perhaps, the interest that visual artists would soon show in the fairy tale as the genre grew in popularity throughout the nineteenth century.

The Victorian Period

One of the first movements that can be identified as overtly engaged with fairy-tale themes is the Pre-Raphaelite movement, founded in England in 1848. Many of the painters associated with the Pre-Raphaelites (who, in fairy-tale form, called themselves "The Pre-Raphaelite Brotherhood," or PRB), depicted folkloric characters in their works—**mermaid**s, sirens, and witches. Yet more significantly, the Pre-Raphaelite obsession with nature, literary symbolism, and **color** make their works exceptionally fairy-tale-like, even if these works lack the sparseness and abstraction so strongly associated with many traditional folktales and fairy tales. The exaggerated realism of pre-Raphaelite painting lends itself well to fairy tales: in such an artwork, a small bird might appear to be a giant, rendered in painstaking detail. The Pre-Raphaelites lived a consciously bohemian lifestyle, and as a result, art history books about the Pre-Raphaelites read as if they are fairy tales themselves—mentioning dreams, marmots, and muses.

Some of the more prominent pre-Raphaelites include Edward Burne-Jones, John William Waterhouse, and Dante Gabriel Rossetti, whose sister, Christina Georgina **Rossetti**, wrote the fairy-tale poem "Goblin Market" (1862). Richard Dadd's painting "Titania and Oberon," while featuring fairies—not an element of traditional fairy tales—is still a good example of the obsessive minutae of tale-like work from this time. Ford Madox Ford, Lewis **Carroll**, and E. **Nesbit**, all authors of fairy-tale literature, were friends with the Pre-Raphaelites.

Throughout the nineteenth century, fairy tales began to show up with more overt frequency in visual art, spreading, with the publication of Jacob and Wilhelm **Grimm**'s *Kinder- und Hausmärchen* (*Children's and Household Tales*, 1812–15) into the realm of illustration. Book illustration, in fact, constitutes the most obvious, prolific, and popular form of fairy-tale art (and for that reason has its own entry in this encyclopedia). Thomas Sully, Gustave **Doré**, Walter **Crane**, Arthur **Rackham**, George **Cruikshank**, Edmund **Dulac**, Kay **Neilsen**, Walton Ford, and James Ensor are examples of Victorian and post-Victorian artists working intricately with fairy tales. Cruikshank's exquisite mid-century illustrations of Grimms' tales were at the time considered the most important etchings to have been produced since Rembrandt.

Bosch's great influence on fairy-tale art shows up in the notable work of John Fitzgerald, an English painter whose paintings of odd miniature monsters—birdlike and beautifully creepy—were even framed unusually, with twigs (for example, "Fairies in a Bird's Nest," c. 1860). Again, while not referring to specific fairy tales—unlike Rackham's exquisite illustrations, for example—Fitzgerald's paintings are significant in their obvious and unique appreciation of enchantment stories. In fact, Fitzgerald's nickname at the time was "Fairy Fitzgerald." Richard Doyle's "The Fairy Tree" (1868) is also an exemplar of the range of aesthetics fairy-tale motifs inspired at this time, and it is a much more whimsical work, with a dreamlike element that became more common in the next century.

The Victorian era also saw a proliferation of fairy art, which points to a growing interest in enchantment. This includes a popular wave of fairy paintings—enchanting works depicting girls with wings, circle dances, and miniature people riding rabbits. Two British teens (not formal artists) captured the imagination of their nation, producing photographs of fairies—the so-called Cottingley fairies—for a hoax that persuaded many as to their authenticity. Today, the photographs' fake quality gives them a prescient Pop Art feel. Lewis Carroll's photographic portrait of Agnes Grace Weld as "Little Red" (1857) is riveting for its plain and homely style. Its subtlety predicts that of the late twentieth century's fairy-tale art.

The Twentieth Century and Beyond

Perhaps the most vivid example of fairy tale art in the early twentieth century is Surrealism. Dedicated to the relationship between dreams and the imagination, Surrealism—an art movement founded in France by André Breton in 1924—produced what can unquestionably be considered fairy-tale works. The unconventional imagery in a Surrealist painting such as "Eine kleine Nachtmusik" (1943) by Dorothea Tanning evokes a fairy-tale with its subject: young girls on the verge of sexual maturation drape themselves together near a giant flower, along a hallway of many doors. The world is askew; the world is bright and dark. This is a narrative of threat and promise, as in "Bluebeard" or "Donkeyskin." "Allegorie de Soie," a painting by Salvador Dalí, is another example of a fairy-tale-like Surrealist work: butterflies bigger than humans are in the foreground of the canvas, but they are not only large because they are near; the natural and the human world are on the same scale, as in a fairy tale. In the background, a magical figure appears, as if casting a spell. Surrealist artworks lend themselves to **psychological approaches**, and the Surrealist artists were interested in Freudianism. Yet Surrealism is interested in the collapsed nature of the conscious and unconscious worlds (rather than a separation between them), just as in fairy tales the magical and the real are collapsed.

Early in the twentieth century, American photographer Imogen Cunningham began producing photographs that have been included in many fairy-tale exhibitions. Of particular note are her portraits, from pictorialist work such as "My Mother Peeling Apples" (1910) to more experimental projects such as double-exposure portraits, including one of her mother made around 1923. In this untitled portrait, the mother's profile is veiled by a still life of a pewter pitcher filled with spoons (acting as a shining crown), and the relationship between positive and negative—one of fairy-tale's binary themes—is revealed. Even her flower photographs of magnolias and lilies have a fairy-tale feel, the flowers gigantic and glowing.

From the early twentieth century to the present, fairy tales have had an explosive effect on a vast range of contemporary art. The mid- to late twentieth century found many artists influenced by fairy tales, especially European and American artists, but also Japanese, German, Brazilian, Dutch, Czechoslovakian, and others. One may now begin to identify an explosive use of fairy-tale tropes. Common themes include **transformation**, abandonment, liberation, and suffering; and these themes are often rendered with exquisite abstraction. Much fairy-tale art from the mid-twentieth century to the present shares an ability to evoke wonder and danger with childlike strokes of painstaking awareness. The following narrative gives only a limited glimpse of some seminal works.

Overlapping with the Surrealists, but at odds with them, Joseph Cornell—who made box assemblages—produced delicate works such as "Pink Palace" (c. 1946–48) and "Setting for a Fairy Tale" (1942), which reference fairy-tale architecture, of course; but even his more abstract works evoke childlike wonder. He even called his muses—women who inspired his boxes—his *fées* (his fairies). In 1969, British artist David Hockney, inspired by the work of Rackham and Dulac, produced a series of prints based on six fairy tales. These are stand-alone images, rather than illustrations of the tales. One example is the image made from "Old Rinkrank," which it is said Hockney decided to make to solve the artistic challenge of drawing glass (which is transparent). Many art critics consider Hockney's fairy-tale prints to be among his most important work.

Kiki **Smith**, a German-born American artist, is one of the most significant fairy-tale artists of this time. She has made many works based on fairy tales, including sculptures, films, drawings, textiles, dolls, and prints. While Smith's work does often explicitly depict familiar tropes from fairy tales, she relies on abstraction to create intense scenes; effecting sparse color, her images evoke an intimate fairy-tale relationship between the human and animal worlds.

Other artists from this time period also explore fairy tales with great originality and **feminist** themes. Joan Jonas and Cindy Sherman both have worked from the violent tale "The Juniper Tree"—Jonas in an installation (1976) and Sherman in a series of photographs (of wax models). Perhaps Jonas's most-praised, beautiful installation is "Volcano Saga" (1985), based on an Icelandic folktale. African American artist Carrie Mae Weems has produced intense works drawn from fairy tales to explore questions of **gender** and **race**, as in the black-and-white photograph "Mirror, Mirror" (1987–88), which has the caption: "Looking into the mirror, the black woman asked, 'Mirror, Mirror on the wall, who's the finest of them all?' The Mirror answered, 'Snow White, you black bitch, and don't you forget it!'"

German artist Pipilotti Rist's postmodern video "Ever Is Over All" is an original fairy tale, featuring a woman skipping down a city street dressed as a princess (who resembles

Dorothy from the **film** version of *The Wizard of Oz*); she gleefully smashes car windshields. In "corpus," a temporary installation, Ann Hamilton designed a pink-glowing tale of loss, and viewers of the installation became the characters in it. Hamilton once sent artist Petah Coyne some human **hair**; Coyne then used it in one of her many voluptuous, yet disturbing, fairy-tale pieces—a thick braid hung on a wall.

Portuguese painter Paula **Rego**'s entire body of work can be read as a collection of fairy tales. Her work recalls grotesquerie with its extreme, angular, bawdy, strong-bodied subjects in tale-like tableaux. They cohabitate with aardvarks, pull at their hair, give **birth** to dogs, and live in chaotic harmony. German painter Anselm Kiefer's large-scale portraits such as "Brunhilde Sleeps," German painter Neo Rauch's Soviet-styled narratives, and American Kara Walker's giant cutouts all deserve notice in the context of recent fairy-tale art.

Today, Amy Cutler's visually accessible paintings are also intellectually challenging—filled with creepiness and light. Children come out of mouths, and people have horses strapped to their backs. Ruby Osorio has produced "Story of a Girl (Who Awakes Far, Far Away)," a fragmentary series that uses drawing, illustration, and sewing. Julie Heffernan produces neo-decadent self-portraits of the artist as a fairy-tale girl, as in "Self Portrait as Hotspot" (2004).

Visual artists continue to draw on fairy tales in a variety of ways, always keeping pace with new media and technologies. In one of the latest developments, American artist Joellyn Rock's "The Vasalisa Project" makes use of digital technology and the **Internet**. Having appeared both online and in print, Rock's "Bare Bones," a digital-art adaptation of "Vasilisa the Beautiful"—a Cinderella-type tale—attempts to "build a bridge for the fairy-tale audience between traditional media and digital media." *See also* Cartoons and Comics; Postmodernism; Schwind, Mortiz von.

Further Readings: Conger, Bill, Jan Susian, and Maria Tatar. *Pixerina Witcherina.* Normal: University Galleries of Illinois State University, 2002; Fahrenberg, W. P., and Armin Klein, eds. *Der Grimm auf Märchen: Motive Grimmscher Volksmärchen und Märchenhaftes in den aktuellen Künsten.* Marburg: Kulturamt der Stadt Marburg, 1985; Heiner, Heidi Anne. *SurLaLune Fairy Tale Illustration Gallery.* http://www.surlalunefairytales.com/illustrations/; Lawrence, Thomas. "Emily Anderson: Little Red Riding Hood." *Huntington Library, Art Collections, and Botanical Gardens.* Powered by eMuseum. http://emuseum.huntington.org/code/emuseum.asp; Osorio, Ruby. *Story of a Girl (Who Awakes Far, Far Away).* St. Louis: Contemporary Art Museum of St. Louis, 2005; Rock, Joellyn. "Bare Bones." *Marvels & Tales* 16 (2002): 233–63; ———. "The Vasalisa Project." 2001. http://www.rockingchair.org/; Warner, Marina. *No Go the Bogeyman: Scaring, Lulling, and Making Mock.* 1998. New York: Farrar, Straus and Giroux, 1999.

Kate Bernheimer

Asbjørnsen, Peter Christen (1812–1885)

Together with Jørgen **Moe**, Peter Christen Asbjørnsen is best known for the collection and publication of the classic *Norske folkeeventyr (Norwegian Folktales,* 1841–44). Asbjørnsen was born and grew up in Kristiania and met Moe at a university preparatory school in Ringerike when they were teenagers. Asbjørnsen began studying medicine but because of economic circumstances took a position as a live-in tutor for several years. Inspired by the example of the brothers **Grimm** in Germany, Asbjørnsen and Moe began **collecting** folktales and fairy tales. They published their first small collection in 1841, followed by additional collections in 1842, 1843, and 1844. The language and syntax of the folktales elicited some controversy since Asbjørnsen and Moe tried to recount the tales in the voices of the

Portrait of Peter Christen Asbjørnsen from *The Fairy World: Folk and Fairy Tales*, trans. H. L. Braekstad (Boston: D. Wolfe, Fiske and Co., 1900), p. xii. [Courtesy of the Eloise Ramsey Collection of Literature for Young People, University Libraries, Wayne State University]

people and utilized uniquely Norwegian words and style. Through his **editing** of subsequent editions over many years, Asbjørnsen made an important contribution to the development of a modern Norwegian written language. *Norwegian Folktales* holds a central place in the Norwegian literary canon and in Norwegian cultural life. Part of the enduring appeal of the stories lies in the numerous **illustration**s to the tales drawn by some of Norway's best artists, such as Theodor **Kittelsen** and Erik Werenskiold.

In addition to his collaboration with Moe, Asbjørnsen independently published two volumes of Norwegian **legend**s, *Norske huldreeventyr og folkesagn* (*Norwegian Hulder Fairy Tales and Folk Legends*, 1845–48). Most of the legends that Asbjørnsen collected are enclosed in literary **frame narratives**, in which an enlightened urban narrator undermines in various ways the legends told by fictional **folk** narrators. Asbjørnsen thought that it was important to preserve the legends, but he also wanted to eradicate the superstitions that were prevalent in nineteenth-century rural society. The stories in the *Norwegian Hulder Fairy Tales and Folk Legends* are actually literary short stories containing legendary material rather than faithful reconstructions from **informant**s. However, many Asbjørnsen and Moe anthologies include tales from *Norwegian Folktales* interspersed with stories from *Norwegian Hulder Fairy Tales and Folk Legends* without regard to authorship. Within Norway, *Norwegian Hulder Fairy Tales and Folk Legends* was an enormously influential text for many later Norwegian writers. Henrik Ibsen's *Peer Gynt*, for example, was based on a character of the same name in Asbjørnsen's story "Rensdyrjakt ved Rondene" ("A Reindeer Hunt in the Rondane Mountains").

In 1865, Moe turned his collection of folk material over to Asbjørnsen, who continued to revise and edit the folktale collections for the remainder of his life. In addition to collecting and publishing editions of the folktales and fairy tales, Asbjørnsen was a scientist who wrote and translated on topics of science and natural history. He studied forestry in Germany, served as a forester and manager of the Norwegian peat industry, and under a pseudonym published a cookbook, *Fornuftig Madstel* (*Sensible Cookery*, 1864). This led to the famous "porridge feud" with the sociologist Eilert Sundt, in which Sundt defended the peasants' method of making porridge (later shown to be correct), while Asbjørnsen criticized it as wasteful. *See also* Scandinavian Tales.

Further Readings: Christiansen, Reidar, ed. *Folktales of Norway.* Chicago: University of Chicago Press, 1964; Hult, Marte Hvam. *Framing a National Narrative: The Legend Collections of Peter Christen Asbjørnsen.* Detroit: Wayne State University Press, 2003.

Marte Hult

Asturias, Miguel Angel (1899–1974)

Due to his use of experimental narrative techniques and his artful combination of **myth** and realism, Miguel Angel Asturias is considered an important precursor of Latin American **magical realism**. His works combine severe criticisms of social inequalities and political oppression in his native Guatemala with the magical cosmovision of Mayan traditions. After writing in 1927 a Spanish version of the sacred text of the Mayas, the *Popol Vuh*, in 1930 Asturias published *Leyendas de Guatemala* (*Legends of Guatemala*), a collection of Mayan myths and **legend**s rendered in an intensely lyrical language.

His best-known novel, *El señor presidente* (*The President*, 1946), is the portrayal of a brutal dictatorship described in a hallucinatory, surreal style. Many critics consider *Hombres de maíz* (*Men of Maize,* 1949) as his best novel; it tells the story of an indigenous rebellion and the violent retaliation of the army. The novel integrates, both thematically and stylistically, Mayan myths and values and, above all, an indigenous perspective on the events. It is thus a summation of Asturias's political and aesthetic concerns. Asturias was awarded the Nobel Prize for Literature in 1967. *See also* Maya Tales.

Further Readings: Callan, Richard. *Miguel Angel Asturias.* New York: Twayne, 1970; Prieto, René. *Miguel Angel Asturias's Archaeology of Return.* Cambridge: Cambridge University Press, 1993.

Víctor Figueroa

Atwood, Margaret (1939–)

Canadian author Margaret Atwood has published more than thirty-five works, including **novel**s and collections of short fiction, poetry, and essays. She has also written several children's books and numerous journal articles. Her novels *The Handmaid's Tale* (1985), *Cat's Eye* (1988), *Alias Grace* (1996), and *Oryx and Crake* (2003) were shortlisted for the Booker Prize, which she won for *The Blind Assassin* in 2000. Among her many other awards are the Norwegian Order of Literary Merit, the French Chevalier dans L'Ordre des Arts et des Lettres, the Governor General's Award for *The Handmaid's Tale*, and the Giller Prize in Canada and the Premio Mondello in Italy for *Alias Grace*.

Whenever questioned in interviews or requested to write about the sources of her considerable literary output, Atwood designates her childhood reading and especially the unexpurgated *Grimms' Fairy Tales* (in the 1944 Pantheon edition introduced by Padraic Colum) as the most influential book she ever read. As Atwood readily acknowledges, the tales of Jacob and Wilhelm **Grimm** appear, with varying degrees of explicitness, throughout her work. These tales not only function as a fecund resource for allusions but also recur at the levels of theme, imagery, narrative structure, and characterization. Because her formative reading experiences included the complete Grimms' tales, in which there are many clever, active, and resourceful heroines, Atwood has a more favorable view of these tales than many contemporary critics. In her fiction and expository writings she expresses her concern with, and distaste for, the bowdlerization to which fairy tales are subjected—"pinkly illustrated versions of '**Cinderella**' or '**Sleeping Beauty**'" ("Of Souls," 23). For example, the narrator-protagonist of her **novel** *Surfacing* (1972) is a commercial artist who finds herself constrained to illustrate tales from which all "disturbing" elements have been removed and to provide the **princess**es with infantilized faces and emaciated torsos.

In addition to borrowing from the Brothers Grimm, Atwood's texts frequently echo other texts and contexts. Hans Christian **Andersen**'s **literary fairy tale**s, French-Canadian **folktale**s, indigenous North American **legends**, classical **myth**s, biblical narratives, and **children's literature** are all incorporated into her writings. Specific intertexts function differently in different works. Joan Foster's self-affirming, Ugly Duckling-like transformation in *Lady Oracle* (1976) requires a painful, Persephone-like separation from her **mother**. Whereas Atwood's immersion in a heterogeneous range of fairy tales as a child was empowering, she recognizes that the popular sanitized versions, with the passive feminine stereotypes and impossible expectations they promote, have been debilitating for many contemporary **women**. The psychical suffering and, in some cases, disintegration or breakdown experienced by her female protagonists (such as Marian MacAlpin in *Edible Woman* [1969], the unnamed narrator in *Surfacing*, Rennie Wilford in *Bodily Harm* [1981], and the Chase sisters, Iris and Laura, in *The Blind Assassin*) derive, at least in part, from the disparity between the fairy-tale and romance plots they have internalized and the harsh realities they encounter. Yet, although Atwood's Joan cultivates dreams of romantic surrender to dark, dashing men in cloaks, she operates like the third sister in the Grimms' "Fitcher's Bird," who outwits the wizard and rescues herself and her two sisters. In Atwood's fictional worlds, folktales, fairy tales, and myths are thus neither simply "good" nor "bad" but, rather, complex and central factors in her characters' lives. Her aesthetics of appropriation fully concedes the power of the past, while striving to challenge or loosen its grip on the present. She repeatedly transforms and reinvents what she adopts, as in her reinterpretation of the Homeric myth of Penelope and Odysseus, *The Penelopiad* (2005).

Whereas somber social and political implications are rarely absent from Atwood's treatment of her fairy-tale and mythic intertexts, humor and, above all, irony are also integral to her narrative revisions. In "Princess Prunella and the Purple Peanut," an ironically didactic and exuberant children's tale published in 1995, a pretty but pampered princess with a penchant for peppermint candies has her nose turned into a purple peanut as a punishment for her peevish behavior until, happily, she performs three positive deeds and meets her perfect princely partner. The story of Prunella is representative of the complexity of Atwood's treatment of the fairy-tale culture on which she draws. It simultaneously pays tribute to and parodies the genre of the **didactic tale**. It concedes the need for the socialization of young children—after all, it is a Wise Woman who transforms Princess Prunella's nose into a peanut and back again—while also underscoring that this shape-changing, developmental process (in a word, growing-up) may lead to an affirmative outcome. Yet because a pinheaded **prince**, "sporting a plaid pyjama top and a pair of preposterous plum-colored polka-dotted pants," is perhaps not such a prize, Atwood's tale also debunks the tradition of happy-ever-after endings with Prince Charming.

Another defining characteristic of Atwood's recourse to **folklore** and fairy tales is the interweaving of multiple **motif**s into a single text. In this respect her textual appropriations differ from such well-known works as Anne **Sexton**'s *Transformations* (1971), which take on one tale at a time. Although Atwood occasionally focuses on specific tales, as in the poem "The Robber Bridegroom" (from her 1984 collection *Interlunar*), which adopts the perspective of a serial killer operating under "red compulsion," for the most part her writing incorporates diverse and sometimes competing stories within a particular narrative frame. In *Lady Oracle*, for example, Joan's retrospectively narrated life story becomes thoroughly enmeshed not only in Andersen's "The Ugly Duckling" but also in "**The Red Shoes**" (both the tale and film version) and "The Little Mermaid," as well as in the Grimms' "Rapunzel" and the gothic apparatus of "Fitcher's Bird" and "The Robber Bridegroom." This listing of fairy-tale intertexts for *Lady Oracle* is far from exhaustive, and even a cursory analysis of Atwood's other works yields similarly resonant results. As Atwood affirms, her exposure to "a large chunk of these tales at an early age, before the manicured versions had hit the stands" ("Of Souls" 23), has left an indelible impression on her art. *See also* Feminism; Feminist Tales; Intertextuality.

Further Readings: Atwood, Margaret. "Of Souls as Birds." *Mirror, Mirror on the Wall: Women Writers Explore Their Favorite Fairy Tales.* Edited by Kate Bernheimer. New York: Anchor, 1998. 22–38; Bacchilega, Cristina. *Postmodern Fairy Tales: Gender and Narrative Strategies.* Philadelphia: University of Pennsylvania Press, 1997; Tatar, Maria. *Secrets beyond the Door: The Story of Bluebeard and His Wives.* Princeton, NJ: Princeton University Press, 2004; Wilson, Sharon Rose. *Margaret Atwood's Fairy-Tale Sexual Politics.* Jackson: University Press of Mississippi, 1993.

Shuli Barzilai

Aucassin et Nicolette

Composed by an unknown author, *Aucassin et Nicolette* is an early thirteenth-century French **cante fable**—or *chantefable* (song-story)—alternating prose narrative passages and couplets in verse. It tells the love story of Aucassin, the son of a count, and Nicolette, a young Saracen captive. Disapproving of their union, Aucassin's father has Nicolette imprisoned. When Nicolette escapes, Aucassin joins her in the forest. While eloping, however, they are captured by Saracen pirates. Separated from Aucassin, Nicolette is taken to Carthage, where she learns that she is a princess. To avoid being married off, she escapes to Provence. Disguised as a minstrel telling her adventures with a song, she is recognized by Aucassin, and they are finally reunited and married.

Unusual for the time, this cante fable constitutes a **parody** of medieval chivalric romance. Described as a timid prince who lacks courage, falls from his horses, and weeps frequently, Aucassin is the antithesis of a knight. Nicolette, on the other hand, is the one who takes charge. She escapes on her own and demonstrates great courage in overcoming several dangers. Endowed with magical healing powers, she heals Aucassin's injuries. Thanks to her perseverance, the couple is eventually reunited. Disregarding all literary and social conventions by presenting a Saracen female protagonist who is superior in intelligence and talent to her Christian suitor, the author sings the praises of women's love and physical beauty.

With only one extant manuscript, this song-story exemplifies the genre of the cante fable and serves as a unique example of oral literature created by medieval minstrels. In folklore and fairy-tale studies, scholars have often noted that the **motif**s, form, and narrative style of *Aucassin et Nicolette* suggest its relationship to **oral tradition** and the **folktale**. *See also* Middle Ages.

Further Reading: Sargent-Baur, Barbara Nelson, and Robert Francis Cook. *Aucassin et Nicolette: A Critical Bibliography.* London: Grant and Cutler, 1981.

Harold Neemann

Aulnoy, Marie-Catherine d' (1650/51–1705)

Marie-Catherine d'Aulnoy was the most prolific and one of the most prominent fairy-tale writers of late seventeenth-century France. Coming from a family of old Norman nobility, d'Aulnoy was forced to marry in 1666 the recently ennobled François de la Motte, Baron d'Aulnoy. A libertine, gambler, and thirty years her senior, the baron was hardly an ideal husband for the young Marie-Catherine. Perhaps instigated by her mother, Madame de Gudane, d'Aulnoy, her mother, and their two lovers, Charles de La Moizière and Jacques-Antoine de Courboyer, plotted to get the baron convicted of lese majesté, an offense against the dignity of a reigning sovereign which carried the death penalty. The plot failed miserably. La Moizière and Courboyer were executed, Madame de Gudane fled the country, and d'Aulnoy (recently having given birth) was briefly jailed but eventually left the country by 1672. Though little information is available on this period of d'Aulnoy's life, she likely spent time in Flanders, England, and Spain, a speculation to which her *Mémoires de la cour d'Espagne* (*Memoirs of the Court of Spain*, 1690), *Relation du voyage d'Espagne* (*Travels into Spain*, 1691), and *Mémoires de la cour d'Angleterre* (*Memoirs of the Court of England*, 1695) all lend credence.

D'Aulnoy definitively resettled in Paris by at least 1690, and in 1692 was frequenting the **salon** of the marquise de Lambert along with other future fairy-tale writers such as Catherine **Bernard**, Charlotte-Rose de Caumont de **La Force**, and Henriette-Julie de Castelnau, Comtesse de **Murat**. She also held salons at her own home during this period, as noted by

Portrait of Marie-Catherine d'Aulnoy from *D'Aulnoy's Fairy Tales*, trans. J. R. Planché (Philadelphia: David McKay, n.d.), vii. [Courtesy of the Eloise Ramsey Collection of Literature for Young People, University Libraries, Wayne State University]

her friend the journalist Anne-Marguerite Petit Dunoyer. At this time, d'Aulnoy launched her publishing career with travel memoirs and historical novels. In 1690, the same year her *Memoirs of the Court of Spain* appeared, d'Aulnoy published her first of three historical novels, *L'histoire d'Hypolite, comte de Duglas* (1690), in which she inserted the first French **literary fairy tale** to appear in France, "L'île de la félicité" ("The Island of Happiness"). Generally given this privilege, Charles **Perrault** did not in fact publish his first tale until 1693. It was only after having established her reputation as a popular author in both France and England that d'Aulnoy issued her first volume of *Les contes des fées* (*Tales of the Fairies*, 1697), a title that in fact introduced the very expression **conte de fées** into the French language.

Dedicated to the Princess Palatine, sister-in-law of Louis XIV, *Tales of the Fairies* was published in four volumes. The first two are straightforward tale collections, containing popular stories like "L'oiseau bleu" ("The Blue Bird"), "L'oranger et l'abeille" ("The Bee and the Orange Tree"), and "Le rameau d'or" ("The Golden Branch"). In the tradition of her Italian influences Giambattista **Basile** and Giovan Francesco **Straparola**, d'Aulnoy used

frame narratives to recount the tales of volumes three and four. Her Spanish **novella**s that frame the tales, "Don Gabriel Ponce de Léon" and "Don Fernand de Tolède," playfully weave together themes from the novellas with those of the tales themselves, which often concern how to overcome obstacles to finding happiness with one's true love. In 1698, d'Aulnoy produced another four-volume collection, *Contes nouveaux ou les fées à la mode* (*New Tales, or Fairies in Fashion*), again using a framing device, this time a novella entitled "Le nouveau gentilhomme bourgeois" ("The New Bourgeois Gentleman"), which blends elements of Molière and Miguel de Cervantes Saavedra.

Given her skill as a writer of historical romance and the fact that she framed her tales with novellas, it should come as no surprise that stylistically d'Aulnoy drew heavily from the tradition of the **novel** and novella to write her tales, whose length and baroque detail contrast with Perrault's much shorter and succinct stories. Novelistic melodrama, however, is often tempered by d'Aulnoy's sense of humor and irony. Thematically d'Aulnoy celebrated the nobility, who often need the support of fairies to maintain their position and identity. In "Gracieuse et Percinet," for instance, the Princess Gracieuse is persecuted by Grognon, of ambiguous social background. Borrowing from Straparola's "Ancilotto, King of Provino" to write "La Princesse Belle-Étoile et le Prince Chéri," d'Aulnoy replaced Straparola's lowborn heroines with **princess**es living like **peasant**s who eventually recover their noble identity. Even in d'Aulnoy's version of "**Cinderella**," "Finette Cendron" (which also blends elements from Perrault's "Little **Thumbling**"), the heroine is a princess from a fallen family whose position is reestablished by the end of the tale. In d'Aulnoy's corpus there are no rags-to-riches stories, so common in Straparola and Perrault.

Along with the nobility, d'Aulnoy works also celebrate the power and camaraderie of aristocratic **women**. "La Belle aux cheveux d'or" ("Beauty with the Golden **Hair**"), for instance, rules independently and crowns her **king** at the end of the tale. White **Cat** of "La chatte blanche" offers her true love **magic object**s and entire kingdoms. In "La bonne petite souris" ("The Good Little Mouse"), a princess, her **mother** the **queen**, and a good **fairy** overcome a cruel usurper to retake the throne. Figures of strong women abound: Amazonians appear in "Le Prince Lutin" and "The Bee and the Orange Tree"; and in "Belle-Belle, ou le chevalier Fortuné" ("Belle-Belle, or the Fortunate Knight"), the heroine disguises herself as a knight to fight in her **father**'s name. Often the tales' feminocentric kingdoms resemble salons in that only those who adhere to norms of civility are welcomed: the violent winds, for instance, are excluded from Félicité's island. D'Aulnoy's tales enjoyed popularity until the late nineteenth century, when the aristocratic society she so often celebrated saw its own decline. Her tales, however, made an invaluable contribution to the development of the literary fairy tale in western Europe. *See also* Cross-Dressing; French Tales; Pig; Woman Warrior.

Further Readings: Duggan, Anne E. "Nature and Culture in the Fairy Tale of Marie-Catherine d'Aulnoy." *Marvels & Tales* 15 (2001): 149–67; ———. *Salonnières, Furies, and Fairies: The Politics of Gender and Cultural Change in Absolutist France*. Newark: University of Delaware Press, 2005; Hannon, Patricia. *Fabulous Identities: Women's Fairy Tales in Seventeenth-Century France*. Atlanta: Rodopi, 1998; Mainil, Jean. *Madame d'Aulnoy et le rire des fées: Essai sur la subversion féerique et le merveilleux comique sous l'Ancien Régime*. Paris: Kimé, 2001; Mcleod, Glenda K. "Writer of Fantasy: Madame d'Aulnoy." *Women Writers of the Seventeenth Century*. Athens: University of Georgia Press, 1989. 91–99; Seifert, Lewis C. *Fairy Tales, Sexuality, and Gender in France, 1690–1715: Nostaligic Utopias*. Cambridge: Cambridge University Press, 1996.

Anne E. Duggan

Auneuil, Louise de Bossigny, Comtesse d' (d. c. 1700)

Louise de Bossigny, Comtesse d'Auneuil was a French author of fairy tales whose life remains mostly unknown. The only information about d'Auneil, provided in *Le cabinet des fées* (*The Fairies' Cabinet,* 1785–89), refers to her considerable social status and her Parisian **salon**, where she hosted women writers in particular.

Her collection *La tiranie des fées détruite* (*The Tyranny of the Fairies Destroyed,* 1702) opens with a tale of the same title. By referring to the misdeeds that certain fairies committed in previous stories, d'Auneuil constructs a narrative framework indicative of the fairy-tale genre. Announcing the destruction of the fairies' reign only to reinstate their power in the subsequent tales, the author plays on the narrative functions assumed by fairy characters so prominent in **French tales**.

D'Auneuil's stories attest to women's importance in the production of fairy tales between 1690 and 1715 and the popularity of the genre in French society during that period. Several of her tales appeared in periodical booklets entitled *Nouvelles du temps* (*Stories of the Time,* 1702–3), which were intended primarily for women readers. Resembling **etiologic tale**s dealing with social customs, some of the stories without happy endings seem to refute traditional views of female happiness in marriage.

Her last work, *Les chevaliers errans* (*The Errant Knights,* 1709), presents some tales modeled largely after medieval chivalric and marvelous narratives, such as those by Ariosto and Boiardo, while others elaborate on popular Oriental themes.

Further Reading: Robert, Raymonde. *Le conte de fées littéraire en France de la fin du XVIIe à la fin du XVIIIe siècle.* Paris: Champion, 2002.

Harold Neemann

Australian and Aotearoan/New Zealand Tales

Situated as neighbors in the Southeast Asia Pacific region, both Australia and Aotearoa/New Zealand were settled by predominantly Anglo-Celtic cultures in the eighteenth and nineteenth centuries, respectively. While there are similarities between the two societies, there are also differences fundamental to any account of folktale. Most obviously, the peoples inhabiting these lands prior to European settlement were entirely distinct. Australian Aborigines migrated into Australia via South Asia probably around 60,000 years ago and can lay claim to having the longest continuous cultural history of any living group of people. Their origin **myth**s, nevertheless, are deeply connected to the place and land of habitation, such that the shape of the land as seen in mountains, rivers, and so on, remains a map of the metaphysical events that brought the landscape into being. In contrast, it is currently thought that New Zealand (commonly referred to by modern Maori people as *Aotearoa*) was first settled by a calculated migration from East Polynesia (the Southern Cook and Society Islands region) in the mid-fourteenth century. Maori religious beliefs thus share many elements with other Polynesian peoples while their specific traditions include both discovery or origin traditions and migration and settlement traditions. Linked to the Pacific geographically, historically, and politically, contemporary New Zealand defines itself as a Pacific nation, and is a major migrant destination for non-Maori Polynesian people (currently 5 percent of the population). In contrast, Australia is much more closely linked to Asia.

The more recent European-derived populations of the two countries have many parallels but diverged from the point of settlement. Australia was initially set up as a penal colony, with free settlers coming later, whereas New Zealand was settled by free settlers. Local **folklore** in both places evolved in response to historical events shaped by different social conditions, such as the presence in Australia of an underclass (largely Irish) not particularly loyal to the British crown, added to by a disruptive influx of diverse peoples during the mid-nineteenth-century gold rush. The significant place held in Australian folklore, art, and literature by the nineteenth-century Irish outlaw Ned Kelly, who depicted himself as a champion of those oppressed by unjust, oppressive authorities, is symptomatic of a perceived disregard for authority amongst many Australians.

As settler societies, the two countries differ most radically in how indigenous peoples were treated in the colonial era. Declared an empty land (*terra nullius*), Australia was appropriated by discovery and conquest, whereas New Zealand joined the British Empire through the Treaty of Waitangi (1840) signed between the British Crown and a majority of Maori chiefs. The Maori people were thus granted rights not to be extended to Aboriginal Australians for almost two centuries after the arrival of Europeans. An immediate consequence for our knowledge of their beliefs and traditions is that Maori scholars such as Te Rangikaheke were already writing down materials from **oral tradition** by the late 1840s. In contrast, when Katie Langloh Parker published her first collection of Aboriginal (specifically Yularoi) stories, *Australian Legendary Tales* (1896), she worked from European perspectives and did not respect the confidentiality expected by her **informant**s. Maori tradition has of course suffered much Western appropriation, but Australian Aborigines exercised little control over their own stories until late in the twentieth century.

With respect to both indigenous cultures, the term "**folktale**" is apt to be inappropriate when applied to mythic or legendary material, which cannot be regarded merely as folktale or entertainment. One of the central Maori narratives, for example, the myth cycle pertaining to the **trickster** god Maui, deals with key beliefs about the land and **death**. In one form of Maori theology, humans partake of the whole movement of the universe by identifying themselves with spiritual powers and thereby derive the meaning of their existence. Thus ritual chants concerning firemaking or death, for example, derive power from direct reference to Maui.

All Australian Aboriginal stories are linked with the "Dreamtime" or "Dreaming," a complex network of knowledge, faith, and practices that derive from stories of creation and determine the spiritual and physical aspects of Aboriginal life. As a repository of all narratives, the Dreaming tells of the origin of the universe and of human beings and other creatures, and of the roles of all things within the cosmos. The land, plants, and animals were given their form by "Ancestor Spirits" who had taken on human or other forms. These spirits established the structures of human society and, as they traversed the country in human or animal form, created distinctive features such as rivers or hills. In a secondary meaning, "Dreaming" can be used to refer to the beliefs or spirituality of a particular group, as determined by the actions of Ancestor Spirits. For instance, an indigenous Australian might say that they have Emu Dreaming, or Lizard Dreaming, or Honey Ant Dreaming, or another Dreaming pertinent to their "country." While it may suggest a variety of meanings among different Aboriginal people, the Dreaming everywhere defines the structures of society, the rules for social behavior, the ceremonies and rituals to be performed, the stories to be told, and the pictures to be drawn and conserved to sustain the well-being of the country. The Dreaming is thus inextricably bound to the land. Because Aboriginal people do not own the land but are part of it, it is their duty to respect and look after it.

Having done their work, the Ancestor Spirits metamorphosed into animals or natural phenomena and remain present in these forms. The stories about them are handed down as part of a particular Dreaming. Thus, what to an outsider might appear to be merely a type of "just so" story may instead perform many functions at once: it defines the bond between people and place; it may inculcate practices of land management (for example, to regulate how much **food** can be taken from an area and at what season); or it may teach proper behavior to younger members of the group. Stories are deemed to be owned by members of the Dreaming in which they occur. Many involve spiritual secrets and may be classified as "**Men**'s Business" or "**Women**'s Business," and it is not permitted to tell these tales to members of the other sex.

In contemporary Australia it is now usual practice that a story is not retold without the explicit permission of its owners. This practice also extends to artwork and images, which are often the repositories of spiritual knowledge.

Rainbow Snake stories are a good example. Grounded in knowledge of a snake's habitat and behavior, such stories mesh with culturally prescribed belief and action, engage with symbolism and myth (relating to the creative and destructive power of nature, for example), and extend to secret sacred domains (separated in turn into male and female concerns). Hence some aspects of the stories and their symbolism are restricted to initiated persons while others are effectively in the public domain. Rainbow Snake stories have been commonly retold as children's picture books, mediating indigenous culture to white Australian culture (a leading example, from 1975, is *The Rainbow Serpent* by Goobalathaldin, published under the name Dick Roughsey).

Some stories involve spirit beings that resemble humans in many ways and have interactions with them. Examples are the *mimi, mamu,* or *mogwoi*—beings that live within rocks and caves in northern Australia. They are credited with teaching Aboriginal people how to hunt and cook and how to make rock paintings. Such beings are often hostile or predatory and always unpredictable. A careless hunter may find himself in danger of being eaten, and in several stories young wives who run away (perhaps only hoping to return to their parents) encounter a *mamu* or *mogwoi*, and undergo captivity and usually rape. Whatever arcane symbolic significance such stories may have, they also serve to reinforce notions of proper social behavior.

As with indigenous Australians, the mythic-religious system of Maori culture shaped and sanctioned the social behavior of its people. Inherited from a Polynesian homeland and modified during centuries of isolation in the cooler New Zealand environment, the mythic-religious system embodies beliefs about the origin of the universe and hence of gods, human beings, and all natural phenomena and living things. Knowledge of this system was sustained by story and genealogical narrative, as were also the local traditions about the migration and settlement that established the Maori in New Zealand. Each tribe (*iwi*) or subtribe (*hapu*) had its own narratives of origin, which variously emphasized a great ancestor and/or the specific name of the canoe (*waka*) on which the group's ancestors arrived in New Zealand from the mythical homeland, Hawaiiki. The word *waka* is thence commonly used to denote confederations of *iwi* descended from the people of one canoe. These oral history traditions determined and validated social hierarchy, possession of territory, and relationships with other groups, although not all *iwi* emphasized their descent from a particular canoe to the same extent.

Genesis stories have been retold as folktales. There are tales of struggles between heroes and various giant creatures, journeys to the underworld, and conflicts between human and spirit beings. The richest sources of folktale material in Maori story, however, are the cycles about the demigods Maui (the trickster god) and Tawhaki (god of thunder and lighting). The stories varied widely amongst different *iwi*, and hence have a great potential for retelling. Tawhaki is best known for his feat of climbing a vine to the heaven where, in some versions, he gains great wisdom and is reunited with his estranged wife, Hapai. There is also a version in which Tawhaki is killed in an attempt to fly to heaven.

Maui is a more complex being. As a descendent of the gods but less than a god, Maui is the subject of stories that are important but not sacred and are open to **adaptation**. They nevertheless take place at that time mostly in mythic Hawaiiki. Among numerous stories in the Maui cycle, five are particularly notable: stories of his **birth** and **childhood**, his capture of the sun, his bringing of fire to the people, his creation of the islands of New Zealand, and his bizarre death. Because he is a trickster hero, representations of him may be quite ambivalent, and his combination of human virtues and vices and capacity to represent conflicting ideologies offer great latitude for retelling his stories in different ways and with varying emphases. As often with trickster figures, events surrounding his birth are unusual. He is usually depicted as having been either aborted or born prematurely, the fifth and last son of Taranga, who wraps his body in a twist of her **hair** and casts it into the sea. The sky god Rangi reaches down and takes him up into the sky where he is nursed back to life, and where he spends his childhood. Rangi teaches him many magical skills.

When Maui eventually goes to find his **mother** and **family**, his mother does not at first recognize him but later treats him with special favoritism, thus angering his **brothers**. Margaret Orbell notes that immediately after joining his family, Maui displays his true character: "He achieves his ends through trickery, very often, and by breaking the rules … he performs no feats of arms, concerns himself often with practical, domestic matters, and tends to do things the 'wrong,' non-prestigious way" (*Concise Encyclopedia,* 114). The combination of trickster and culture hero is clearly evident in the story of fire. Having mischievously quenched all the fires of his people, Maui is sent to the underworld to bring new fire. There he provokes Mahuika, the guardian of fire, and in anger she flings fire into the treetops. After that, fire could always be made by rubbing sticks together.

Maui performs some of his major feats with the help of a magic jawbone that he has obtained from an ancestress in the underworld, either by theft or cajolement. In some accounts this is the jawbone of his grandmother. Thus, when he is angered by the speed at which the sun crosses the sky, he takes his brothers and many strong ropes to snare and hold the sun, and then Maui beats the sun into submission with the jawbone, even breaking some of his legs. The sun consequently travels more slowly. Maui also uses the jawbone as a fishhook and succeeds in pulling up a mass from the ocean bottom, which becomes the North Island of New Zealand. His canoe then is transformed into the South Island.

Motivated by arrogance, mischief, or anger, rather than by a desire to bestow any benefit, this trickster-cum-culture hero impacts the world in quite diverse ways. His career comes to an end when he makes the overconfident boast that he will destroy Hine-nui-te-po, the giant goddess of death. Having learned where she lies sleeping, he sets out on his quest with a group of birds as companions. His objective is to creep into the vagina of Hine-nui-te-po as she sleeps, pass through her body, remove her life force, and exit through her mouth. To avoid being killed by the sharp obsidian teeth that surround her vagina, he instructs his bird companions that they must not laugh until they see him emerge, lest they wake her. The sight is so comical, however, that the fantail is unable to contain his laughter,

Hine-nui-te-po wakes and closes her legs, and Maui perishes. Thus instead of bestowing the gift of immortality on the world, Maui ensures the certainty of death.

The stories about heroes such as Maui or Tawhaki still resonate in contemporary New Zealand, as seen in their use as intertexts and analogues in the highly successful recent film *Whale Rider* (2002), winner of BAFTA and Sundance awards, amongst others. The film, based on the 1987 novel by Maori writer Witi **Ihimaera**, deftly combines a coming of age narrative with allusions to these tales.

As remarked above, the white settler populations of Australia and New Zealand have developed local folk narratives in relation to diverse experiences of migration and settlement. Such tales are better known from folk songs, **ballad**s, **storytelling**, **tall tale**s, superstitions, or everyday idioms that have entered the language, and have not produced what might be considered a distinctive body of folktales. Thus New Zealand folk songs deal with experiences of the gold rush or the Great Depression, and railway and mining disasters. Australia has songs from the penal era and songs and stories dealing with rural life, especially the romanticized figure of the drover, traveling the roads with his mob of sheep or cattle. Poet and short-story writer Henry Lawson documented (and often originated) much of this folklore in his poems and stories. More recently, folklorists such as Bill Scott have begun assembling collections of **urban legend**s. *See also* Colonialism; Pacific Island Tales; *Pear ta ma 'on maf.*

Further Readings: Berndt, Ronald M., and Catherine H. Berndt. *The Speaking Land: Myth and Story in Aboriginal Australia.* Ringwood, Victoria: Penguin Books, 1989; Orbell, Margaret. *A Concise Encyclopedia of Maori Myth and Legend.* Christchurch: Canterbury University Press, 1998; ———, trans. *Traditional Maori Stories.* 1992. Auckland: Reed New Zealand, 1997; Scott, Bill, ed. *Lies, Flies and Strange Big Fish: Tall Tales from the Bush.* St. Leonards, New South Wales: Allen & Unwin, 2000; ———. *Pelicans and Chihuahuas and Other Urban Legends.* St. Lucia, Queensland: University of Queensland Press, 1996.

John Stephens

Authenticity

The term "authenticity" derives from the Greek *authentes,* which means both "one who acts with authority" and "made by one's own hand." Although an important concept in Western philosophy, the term proper only entered fields of cultural research as of the 1960s, when critical reflection on scholarly canon formation set in. A subsequent historiographic turn in folkloristics, cultural anthropology, and related fields demonstrated, however, that a vocabulary connoting authenticity had been fundamentally important in constituting not just "**folklore**" and with it "folk narrative" as a category. Rather, a search for the genuine, real, or unspoiled was shown to have been also a driving force in the huge social, economic, and political transformations starting in the eighteenth century. These transformations initiated the "tradition/modernity" dynamic that has provided a foil through which to look at the world in social life as much as in scholarship. The notion of "authenticity," generally associated with "tradition," has played a considerable role in this dynamic. Economically, industrialization introduced mass production, surrounding the uniqueness of the handmade object as much as the orally told tale with an aura of authenticity. Socially and politically, the French Revolution aimed for a democratization of politics, sought to overthrow the estate system, and in the process sowed the seeds of the notion of citizens as authentic individuals capable of self-determination. Romantic nationalists in turn hoped to find an alternate foundation for states to replace the elite language and culture of monarchies. They found it in oral literature. **Epic**s and other narrative forms seemed to express in unspoiled, vernacular, indigenous languages both the art and history of a people. They were (and in some instances continue to be) seen as the authentic cultural foundation for nation building. This group-based variant of authenticity dominated also in cultural scholarship until the late twentieth century.

The first and thus paradigmatic example for the "discovery" of folk poetry and the power of its presumed authenticity were the Gaelic epic poems "Finegal" (1762) and "Temora" (1763). They were attributed to Ossian, a Gaelic bard, and had been "found," restored, and prepared for publication by James Macpherson. Although Macpherson was soon suspected of having published a fraud, and while the "Ossian controversy" reappeared regularly in intellectual disputes, the impact of Ossian's poems on a transforming Europe was phenomenal. Even in **translation**, Ossian presented precisely the kind of example of raw, vernacular poetry of deep history that could represent the national aspiration of a hitherto subjected people. Johann Gottfried Herder devoted an enthusiastic essay to a translated Ossian in 1773. He developed a vocabulary of authenticity, ranging from the genuine and wild to the raw and timeless, to encapsulate the nature of the voice of the highland **folk** as transported by this Gaelic Homer. Without a doubt, the encounter with the work fueled Herder's influential call to collect "the voices of people in song," as his collection of folk songs, published in 1774, was named. This appeal to collect and restore folk poetry as the authentic representation of the spirit of a people was taken up throughout Europe and beyond, and its results contributed to and in some cases figured prominently in the construction of new national identities, as did the the national epic the *Kalevala* in Finland.

In folklore, and particularly folk-narrative scholarship, authenticity became an important measuring rod, in part because the political relevance of the material was continually demonstrated, and also because throughout the nineteenth and early twentieth centuries, disciplines throughout all fields of research aimed to establish scientific standards. As concepts, "authenticity" or "genuineness" evoke their opposite—the fake or spurious. Thus, in the collection of **folktale**s, epics, and other genres, increasing weight was placed on demonstrating that the source material was authentic—gathered from the lips of the people and wrested from sources that were clearly unspoiled. Philological as well as editorial practices were developed to ascertain such authenticity. In more ethnographically oriented branches of research, scholars attributed authenticity predominantly to narratives collected among people living "traditionally," without access to technology and thus more likely to be truthful guardians of ancient heritages. In the 1960s, the problems inherent to such dichotomous thinking began to appear. Richard M. **Dorson**'s attacks against popular and commercially successful narrative collections initiated a debate about "**fakelore**" and, in European contexts, "folklorismus" lasting for decades. It sharpened a dichotomous divide throughout folklore scholarship. Some scholars felt it to be their task to act as arbiters of authenticity (for example, folktales told orally only by individuals with ethnic credentials), while others sought to show how preserving the authentic was the surest path to render it inauthentic.

This crisis of authenticity was overcome, at least in academic discourse, through the following changes in perspective and approach: (1) Scholars came to include the role played by different media of communication in the transmission and traditionalization of folk narratives. In the process, they had to also acknowledge the profound impact of tale **collectors**, **editors**, and translators on narrative continuity and change. (2) Scholars developed an increasing interest in synchronic rather than diachronic questions. Context and **performance** came to be seen as key elements for understanding folk narrative and from this vantage point, as each instance of narration is unique. Change came to be recognized as an intrinsic element of traditional processes. (3) Cultural scholarship began to include the market and with it the commoditization of cultural goods and practices as an important facet of local and global life. Rather than condemning folktales, **legend**s, and other genres popularized in books, comics, **film**s, and so forth, scholars began to include the study of **adaptation**s and transformations and their underlying economic and sociopolitical intentions. In giving up the elusive tasks of delineating what is authenticity, scholars began to ask who needs authenticity, when, and for what purpose. *See also* Nationalism.

Further Readings: Bendix, Regina. *In Search of Authenticity: The Formation of Folklore Studies.* Madison: University of Wisconsin Press, 1997; Berman, Marshall. *The Politics of Authenticity: Radical Individualism and the Emergence of Modern Society.* New York: Atheneum, 1972; Trilling, Lionel. *Sincerity and Authenticity.* London: Oxford University Press, 1972.

Regina Bendix

Avery, Frederick 'Tex' (1908–1980)

An American cartoon director, Tex Avery is known for his animated adaptations of fairy-tale material. Avery began his directing career at Warner Bros. **animation** studios, and it was there that he began directing cartoons based on fairy-tale material. Avery directed four fairy-tale cartoons for Warner Bros. The first two, *Little Red Walking Hood* (1937) and *Cinderella Meets Fella* (1938), were satirical versions of these classic tales. In both cartoons, Avery accentuates the implicit sexual tensions of the fairy tale and makes his characters aware of the story frame, trends which would continue in his work.

Avery's next fairy-tale cartoons for Warner Bros., *The Bear's Tale* (1940) and *A Gander at Mother Goose* (1940), are both works of reflexive fairy-tale pastiche, in which separate fairy tales are combined. In the former, Goldilocks and **Little Red Riding Hood** take on a bear and a wolf with all characters aware of the story frame. In the latter, Avery sends up a number of short fairy tales, including a mouthwash advertisement with the Three Little Pigs.

After leaving Warner Bros. for MGM, Avery made four more fairy-tale cartoons. His first, *Blitz Wolf* (1942), adapted the story of the Three Little Pigs to the backdrop of World War II, with a Hitleresque wolf. Avery's three remaining fairy-tale cartoons were quite similar. In *Red Hot Riding Hood* (1943), *Swing Shift Cinderella* (1945), and *Little Rural Riding Hood* (1949), Avery's wolf is interested in the mature heroines not as meals but as mates. *See also* Frame Narrative; Sex, Sexuality; Werewolf, Wolf, Wolves.

Further Reading: Morris, Gary. "Goosing Mother Goose." *Bright Lights Film Journal* 22 (Sept. 1998). http://www.brightlightsfilm.com/22/texaverytales.html.

B. Grantham Aldred

Aztec Tales

The word "Aztec" refers to the speakers of Nahua languages who live in central and eastern Mexico. There are two principal dialects of Nahua: Nahuatl, spoken in the modern state of Guerrero and in the valleys of Mexico and Tlaxcala-Puebla, and Nahuat, spoken on the edges of the highlands near the Gulf Coast. Some historians restrict the definition of Aztec to those speakers of Nahuatl who claim they came from the mythical land of Atzlan and founded the city of Tenochtitlan in 1324 or 1345 in the Valley of Mexico.

The sources for Aztec or Nahua tales include a small number of picture books that survived the Spanish Conquest of Mexico and a larger number of stories Nahuatl scribes wrote under the direction of friars. Some of the friars, such as Bernardino de Sahagún, a Franciscan, learned Nahuatl and trained Nahuatl men to write their stories in their native language using the Roman alphabet. The anonymous authors left a number of texts that provide an invaluable glimpse into the way the Nahuas imagined their universe shortly after the Spanish had completed the Conquest of Tenochtitlan in 1521.

Michel Graulich and Alfredo López Austin begin their interpretations of Aztec mythology with the story in the reconstructed *Codex Telleriano-Remensis*. The story begins with a goddess who picked a flower and broke the branch from the tree in Tamoanchan. At that time, all of the gods lived in the celestial realm of Tamoanchan, where male and female forces lived in harmony personified by the God of Two, Ometeotl. The God of Two sometimes appeared as a separate male god, Tonacateuctli, and female goddess, Tonacacihuatl. The God of Two had the power of procreation, which the goddess Xochiquetzal, in one version, usurped when she picked the flower and broke the branch of the tree in Tamoanchan. Her act infuriated the God of Two, who banished her to earth where she gave birth to the corn god, Cinteotl, from whose body sprang many edible plants.

The themes found in this story include a state of harmony, an act of pride, a rupture, and a new state of being. These themes appear in many of the Aztec of Nahua tales that were written under the friars' direction. In the opinion of many scholars, the ancient Nahuas organized the events in their tales according to a cyclical notion of **time** patterned after the life cycles of corn and human beings, and the rotation of cosmic bodies such as the sun, the moon, and the Pleiades.

When applied to human history, the tales describe cycles of vigorous nomads with little culture taking over agricultural civilizations that had become decadent and lost their vigor. The story of the priest king Topiltzin Quetzalcoatl is a very good example of the Aztecs' cyclical conception of human history. According to the version of this story that John Bierhorst translated into English from Nahuatl, Topiltzin Quetzalcoatl was a highly disciplined young man who fasted and regularly carried out penis-piercing rituals. However, he too committed an act of pride when he drank too much pulque (a fermented drink made from the juice of the maguey plant) and called for his sister, with whom he wants to have sex. The sinister Smoking Mirror god, Tezcatlipoca, had tricked him into drinking the pulque, but no matter. Topiltzin Quetzalcoatl was now going into his decline. He later left the golden age city of Tollan he had ruled and became the morning star, and the city itself eventually collapsed. Some scholars identify it as the ancient and beautiful ceremonial center of Teotihuacan (125 to 675 CE). Henry B. Nicholson found more **variant**s of the Topiltzin Quetzalcoatl story in the ancient record than of any other tale, which is one indication of its importance to the Nahuas of that time.

The Aztecs extended their cyclical conception of history far back into the past, and their stories include accounts of the prior eras of creation or suns. The number and the sequence of suns vary with the source, but Graulich believes that Nahuas originally had four suns, and the Aztecs of Tenochtitlan added a fifth as they rewrote history when they became the dominant ethnic group in the Valley of Mexico. The number four represents the four cardinal directions in the

Aztecs' quadrilateral view of their universe. One important origin **myth** from sixteenth-century sources tells of the origin of the fourth sun, which took place in Teotihuacan, the ancient urban ceremonial city that came to a violent end around 675 AD. The gods gathered in Teotihuacan after the end of the third era and decided that the lordly Tecciztecatl should jump into a pyre, take the fire into the sky, and become the fourth sun. However, Tecciztecatl was cowardly and, fearing the heat from the pyre, he failed after four attempts. The gods then turned to the more humble Nanahuatl, who jumped into the pyre on the first try and carried most of the fire into the sky. He became the fourth sun, and Tecciztecatl took the rest of the fire and became the moon. The lordly Tecciztecatl, who dressed in fine clothes and also performed penis-piercing rituals (with a jade needle), is a symbol of the agriculturalists who had lost their vigor.

The Aztecs told several other stories of how gods created the final race of humankind. One of the better-known tales related how Quetzalcoatl descended into the land of the dead, Mictlan, and gathered the bones of those who had perished at the end of the third era of creation. One his way out of Mictlan, he was intercepted and fell, breaking the bones. This accident accounts for why humans have joints. He took the bones to his wife, Cihuacoatl-Quilatzli, who ground them on her grinding stone. Quetzalcoatl used blood from his penis to create the final race of humankind.

Humans had nothing to eat because corn that had come from the body of Cinteotl was locked inside Sustenance Mountain. Quetzalcoatl spotted an ant carrying a kernel of corn out of the mountain, so he turned himself into an ant, fetched a kernel, and took it to the gods in Tamoanchan. The gods tasted it, decided it was good, and consulted the calendar to see who would break open the mountain. They discovered it would be Nanahuatl, who opened the mountain and released different kinds of corn, plus beans and the herb amaranth.

The Aztecs of Tenochtitlan added stories about their patron god, Huitzilopochtli, who spoke to his **mother** from inside her womb. He was born wearing full warrior garb and soon killed his 400 siblings. They were jealous when their mother became pregnant after a ball of down entered her breast. Huitzilopochtli killed his sister, Coyolxauhqui, an act that scholars have interpreted in a number of ways. Some believe it was the justification for human sacrifice that had become very widespread, particularly in Tenochtitlan. June Nash noted that this story marks the rise of militarism and the beginning of a period of male dominance as the Aztecs expanded their empire through warfare. Nash cites evidence that the Nahuas, prior to the rise of Tenochtitlan, had worshipped a goddess who resembled the Hopi spider woman.

The sixteenth-century sources on Aztec mythology came primarily from the descendents of the elite who attended schools the friars had established in the Valley of Mexico. Other stories probably circulated among the rural farmers or macehualli who grew the food and provided much of the tribute for the Aztec empire. The sixteenth-century sources allude to other tales that may have circulated among the macehualli. One is an Orpheus myth involving Piltzinteuctli, the consort of the goddess Xochiquetzal who picked the flower and broke the branch from the tree in Tamoanchan.

Contemporary versions of Orpheus tales describe a man who loves, with a great passion, a woman who dies and goes to the land of the dead. The stories are **cautionary tale**s warning about the effects of emotional excess, particularly love as desire. Usually they describe what can go wrong in a relationship between a man and a woman: the woman may not love the man the way he loves her, or the woman may die and leave the man despondent in the land of the living. Emotional excess, particularly love as desire, is the basis of many transgressions, including Topiltzin Quetzalcoatl's call for his sister under the influence of too much pulque.

Contemporary speakers of Aztec languages also tell tales about the acquisition of corn-planting knowledge, an event that seems logically to follow from the tale of Sustenance Mountain. Usually the tale begins as the first rain god plants a cornfield with the kernels that came out of Sustenance Mountain. The other rain gods ask him how he planted his corn, but he does not tell the truth. Instead, he instructs them to roast the corn first, and then he tells them to boil it in lime and bury it in one large hole. When the rain gods see that nothing sprouts after two attempts, they blow down the first rain god's cornfield. The first rain god demands that they glue the broken stalks back together with their mucous, and then he tells them to soak the kernels in water for a day and then plant each kernel in a separate hole.

Many stories of rain gods or quiyahteomeh still circulate in contemporary Aztec **oral tradition**, and some of them are probably very old. No one has found the sixteenth-century versions primarily because there is a poor record of stories from the macehualli who lived outside the major ceremonial centers such as Tenochtitlan. Some of the stories that circulate among Nahuas living near the Gulf Coast resemble those found on ancient Mayan pottery. Among them are variants of the story of Xochiquetzal and her consort Piltzinteuctli, the mother and father of the corn god Cinteotl.

Contemporary Nahuas tell other stories that have no apparent parallels in the ancient sources and do not appear in Spanish oral tradition. Nevertheless, they describe a cyclical conception of history patterned after the life cycle of the corn plant. While that cycle is patterned after natural rhythms, some of the stories reveal how humans can speed it up by acts of emotional excess that can bring about the end of a state of harmony. One example that comes from a Nahuat-speaking storyteller in the northern sierra of Puebla tells of a young married couple that loved each other too much. While they playfully toss banana leaves, the boy picks up a small snake and throws it to his bride. After pitching the snake back and forth more than four times, the snake bites the wife on her breast and she dies. More than four represents overabundance and is a sure sign of trouble. The husband's parents, acting on their own emotional excess, beat their son to death in a blind fury. The story ends with the near-complete destruction of an extended **family**.

Many other tales that circulate in contemporary Aztec oral tradition are reworked versions of popular European **folktale**s. They include "The **Bear's Son**," "**Cinderella**," and "**Hansel and Gretel**." Aztec narrators have made radical changes to make them fit the cyclical conception of history they had expressed in the myths found in the sixteenth-century sources. In some cases, the Aztecs have created entirely new tales by changing **Spanish tales** into myths.

The Aztec versions of "The Bear's Son" begin much like the Spanish stories. A bear (or a monkey) kidnaps a woman and takes her to his cave in the wilderness. They have a child who becomes a very unruly boy. When told in Spain, the story describes the boy's socialization into a gallant man after he redeems himself by vanquishing the **devil**. When recounted by contemporary Aztecs, the story is about the **birth** and life of the captain of the rain gods, Nanahuatl, the hero mentioned earlier. Nanahuatl remains an unruly force of nature, wrecking havoc by causing a flood like the one that ended an earlier era of creation.

Contemporary Aztecs have changed other popular European folktales to fit a family structure based on the relationship between a **father** and son and sexual avoidance between a brother and sister. The importance of the father-son relationship is apparent in the way that Aztec storytellers have changed the Spanish story of "Cinderella." In Spain, the story describes a **prince** who falls in love with a woman for her beauty and pursues her until they marry. Among the Nahuat, their relationship ends when Cinderella goes off with another man, and her son sets out to find his father. The man's search for his father resembles Topiltzin Quetzalcoatl's search for his father.

Aztec versions of "Hansel and Gretel" are tragic love stories of a brother and sister. The Aztecs frequently represent the sister with ambivalence as a prohibited object of a man's desire. Nahuat storytellers have reworked the "Hansel and Gretel" stories to express their ambivalence. Usually the brother and sister begin by helping each other survive after their father abandons them in the wilderness. In one representative example, a Spanish-speaking man seduces Gretel, awakening her **sexuality**, so she must separate from Hansel. Gretel disappears from the plot, and the story continues with the adventures of Hansel, who ends up becoming a rich man. However, this tale does not end happily because the father appears, asking for a handout. He resents the meager amount that Hansel gives him, and he uses the money to pay a priest to kill his son for being stingy. The story expresses several themes appearing in the ancient mythology: brother and sister ambivalence and sexual avoidance; the danger of excess emotion; and the cycle of history. *See also* Brothers; Etiologic Tale; Sisters.

Further Readings: Bierhorst, John, trans. *History and Mythology of the Aztecs: The Codex Chimalpopoca*. Tucson: University of Arizona Press, 1992; Graulich, Michel. *Myths of Ancient Mexico*. Norman: University of Oklahoma Press, 1997; López Austin, Alfredo. *Tamoanchan, Tlalocan: Places of Mist*. Niwot: University Press of Colorado, 1997; Nash, June. "Gendered Deities and the Survival of Culture." *History of Religions* 36 (1997): 333–56; Nicholson, Henry B. *Topiltzin Quetzalcoatl: The Once and Future Lord of the Toltecs*. Niwot: University Press of Colorado, 2001; Quiñones Keber, Eloise. *Codex Telleriano-Remensis: Ritual, Divination, and History in a Pictorial Aztec Manuscript*. Austin: University of Texas Press, 1995; Taggart, James M. *The Bear and His Sons: Masculinity in Spanish and Mexican Folktales*. Austin: University of Texas Press, 1997; ———. *Nahuat Myth and Social Structure*. 1983. Austin: University of Texas Press, 1997.

James M. Taggart

B

Baba Yaga

Baba Yaga is the notoriously ambiguous preeminent **witch** of Slavic **folklore**. Her name is synonymous with the Russian term *ved'ma* (witch) and its regional variants. She is a kind of a *genius loci* (protective spirit) for the values and associations that attach themselves to the **archetype** of "the witch in the forest" in Slavic tradition. However, she is more than a natural substitute or enhancement of any one witch. She is referred to as the aunt or mistress of all witches, demonstrating the degree to which she holds sway in the Russian imagination. In this regard, Marie-Louise von **Franz** has compared her to Hecate (Franz, 173). In many ways, Baba Yaga represents a kind of a synecdoche of the archetypes of Russian folklore, being one of the oldest and most persistent characters in Russian lore. She is linked to the **dragon**s, to which she is sometimes referred as a **mother**, to the spirits of the forest in which she resides, and to the border between life and **death**, over which she reigns. Baba Yaga is marked by her

Baba Yaga. Illustration by Dimitri Mitrokhin in *Old Peter's Russian Tales* by Arthur Ransome (New York: Frederick A. Stokes Company, 1917). [Courtesy of the Eloise Ramsey Collection of Literature for Young People, University Libraries, Wayne State University]

long nose, steel teeth, and bony physique. She is also known by her voracious cannibalistic appetite and by her unusual domicile. She can have a temperamental nature: in tales, she can be a helper or an adversary.

Baba Yaga's name can be translated as an honorific diminutive, meaning roughly "Granny Yaga." However, the best translation of Baba Yaga's status in English is neither "granny" nor any of the equivalent forms of address that convey a respect for **age** and status alone. The best translation of Baba Yaga's name and position is a word with more blended origins: "crone." Although "baba" is a diminution of the respectful "babushka" or "grandmother," it is also a referent that can be used as either a respectful term of address or a fierce curse. Although Baba Yaga is sometimes linked to children (not only in her guise as a cannibal, but also as the mother of daughters, but never sons), her main role is that of a feared and respected elder, and not of a beloved nurturer. She is also called "Baba Yaga Kostinaya Noga" (Baba Yaga Bony Leg), which scholars alternately associate either with her affiliation with the underworld or simply with its rhythmic Russian rhyming pattern.

Like the witches of other cultures, Baba Yaga's preferred method of transportation is a commonly used household implement. However, unlike western witches, rather than traveling upon a broom, she chooses to ride in a mortar, rowing with a pestle and using a broom to sweep away the tracks it leaves. Her home is a mobile hut perched upon chicken legs. Vladimir **Propp** posited the belief that the hut might serve as a cultural **memory** of rituals of **initiation**, reflecting Baba Yaga's history as a chthonic goddess. Baba Yaga's hut is located not only in the forest but, more specifically, in the land of the "thrice-nine kingdom," the home of the living dead, the realm that lies between the world of the living and the "thrice-ten kingdom," the land of the truly dead. Baba Yaga's first extant appearances in **art** and literature date to the eighteenth century. *See also* Cannibalism; Russian Tales; Slavic Tales.

Further Readings: Franz, Marie-Louise von. *The Feminine in Fairy Tales*. Boston: Shambhala, 1993; Johns, Andreas. *Baba Yaga: The Ambiguous Mother and Witch of the Russian Folktale*. New York: Peter Lang, 2004.

Helen Pilinovsky

Bachelier, Anne (1949–)

A French painter and illustrator, Anne Bachelier draws from mythological and **fairy** themes to craft her dreamy-nightmarish tableaux. These works recall the fantastic horror and elegance of *fin-de-siècle* painters. Influenced by the surrealist painter Léonor Fini, who herself produced a series of color silk screens entitled *Sultanes et magiciennes des Milles et une nuits* (*Sultans and Magicians from the Thousand and One Nights*, c. 1976), Bachelier fashions otherworldly creatures with mannerist features who inhabit eerie yet magical worlds. Her paintings and illustrations bring to mind the stylized work of Kay **Nielsen** and Edmund **Dulac**.

Bachelier's paintings are peopled with unicorns, **witch**es, gorgons, and chimera. It is no wonder that she was led to illustrate several fairy tales, including Robin **McKinley**'s *Rose Daughter: A Re-Telling of **Beauty and the Beast*** (1998) and Scot D. Ryersson and Michael Orlando Yaccarino's *The **Princess** of Wax: A Cruel Tale, Inspired by the Life of the Marchesa Casati* (*La Princesse de Cire: un conte cruel, inspiré d'après la vie de La Marchesa*

Casati, 2003), published in an English-French edition. In 2005 she illustrated a new edition of Lewis **Carroll**'s *Alice's Adventures in Wonderland: Through the Looking-Glass and What Alice Found There*. In all of these illustrations, Bachelier creates a sense of movement and transformation as she takes us into fantastic realms where human and animallike figures undergo a **transformation**.

Strong female characters figure prominently in Bachelier's *oeuvre*. This is most evident in the kitschy work, *The Princess of Wax*, written expressly for Bachelier to illustrate and inspired by the life of the eccentric Italian heiress Luisa Casati. Like her namesake, the marchesa of the tale strolls about with cheetahs while wearing nothing but furs. Her ennui leads her to contact a **sorceress**, who concocts a wax princess for the marchesa's entertainment. Like Nathaniel of E. T. A. **Hoffmann**'s "Der Sandman" ("The Sandman," 1817), the marchesa's ebony manservant Garbi falls in love with the wax doll. Bachelier's images make up for the weaknesses of the text. The book opens with a character holding back curtains as if welcoming the reader onto a stage or into a secret world. Even before coming upon the illustration depicting the masked ball, one gets the sense that all of the characters are wearing masks. They seem to share the lifeless gaze of the wax princess; and, like her, their forms betray a fundamental instability expressed by their sinuosity.

Alice's Adventures in Wonderland is a perfect venue for Bachelier's phantasmagoric illustrations. Whiskers waving to and fro, her Cheshire **Cat** swims in a purplish haze, while the table on which the tea party takes place hovers just above the earth. Materializing into a monstrous form, a Jabberwocky takes to the sky, a serpentine tail swinging behind it. Bachelier's paintings and illustrations, in which the fantastic finds no better expression, truly take us through the looking glass. *See also* Art; Illustration.

Further Reading: Anne Bachelier at CFM Gallery. http://www.cfmgallery.com/artists/Bachelier/index.html.

Anne E. Duggan

Balázs, Béla (1884–1949)

Béla Balázs, the pseudonym of Hungarian poet and cinema theorist Herbert Bauer, composed libretti for two of Béla **Bartók**'s works for the stage, the **opera** *A kékszakákállú herceg vára* (*Duke Bluebeard's Castle*, 1918) and the ballet *Fából faragott királyfii* (*The Wooden Prince*, 1917). The **Bluebeard** opera rewrites Charles **Perrault**'s well-known story into a psychological confrontation of woman and man, in which the heroine Judith guesses the duke's evil secret but suffers the same fate as the other **women**. *The Wooden Prince* is a contrived yet charming fairy tale in which a **prince** falls instantaneously in love with a **princess**. A **fairy** enchants the prince's staff into a wooden copy of himself, which attracts the princess and depresses the prince. Then the fairy transforms the flowers of the wood into new **clothing** for the prince, who now snubs the princess until she kneels to him in homage. At last he takes her in his arms, and they live happily ever after. Bartók's lavish **music** already shows the influence of the folk music that was to become more audible in his later compositions.

In addition to collaborating as a librettist with Bartók, Belázs helped to write the script for Leni Reifenstahl's film *Das blaue Licht* (*The Blue Light*, 1932). He also wrote and adapted fairy tales with political and social themes, many of them in German, including collections such as *Sieben Märchen* (*Seven Fairy Tales*, 1917), *Der Mantel der Träume* (*The Mantle of Dreams*, 1922), and *Das richtige Himmelblau* (*The Real Sky-Blue*, 1925), as well as the play, coauthored with German storyteller and children's book author Lisa Tetzner, *Hans Urian geht nach Brod* (*Hans Urian Goes in Search of Bread*, 1927).

Further Readings: Balázs, Béla. *The Mantle of Dreams*. Translated by George Leitmann. Tokyo: Kodansha International; New York: Harper & Row, 1974; Balázs, Béla. *The Real Sky-Blue*. London: J. Lane, 1936; Loewy. Hanno. *Béla Balász: Märchen, Ritual und Film*. Berlin: Verlag Vorwerk 8, 2003.

Lee Haring

Ballad

A ballad is a short poetic narrative that is traditionally performed musically. While stylistically similar to genres such as Mexican *corridos* or Finnish runes, the term "ballad" is generally limited to traditional songs of the British Isles. Ballads have been the subject of **folklore** study since the beginnings of the discipline. An integral part of the founding of the American Folklore Society, the study of these poetic narratives has had a great deal of influence on **folktale** studies.

Before the nineteenth century, ballad scholarship mainly consisted of collection, with Robert Harley's *The Bagford Ballads* (1878) and Bishop Thomas Percy's *Reliques of Ancient English Poetry* (1765) standing as the most prominent works. These contained edited versions of many different ballads and provided a base for later analysis. The study of the ballad shifted with the work of Francis James Child. An American scholar at Harvard University, Child's colleagues convinced him to apply scientific methods to ballads. For his work, Child chose to study English and Scottish ballad traditions, as they shared similar text and language as opposed to Irish ballad traditions. Child's work, *The English and Scottish Popular Ballads*, a five-volume set published between 1882 and 1898, grouped ballads into a single publication that focused heavily on variation, including many different versions of each individual ballad. Child concentrated on the poetic aspects of the ballad, ignoring in many cases the accompanying music. Child's work encouraged others to study ballads, including Cecil Sharp in his collection *English Folk Songs from the Southern Appalachians* (1932). Sharp examined the migration of ballad texts from the British Isles to the American mountains. Sharp's work differed from Child's in its focus on the musical aspects of the ballad, rather than the poetic.

While ballad scholarship has become less prominent in the late twentieth century, many authors have drawn on ballads as source material. One fairly straightforward **adaptation** is the *Book of Ballads* by Charles **Vess**. Vess' **graphic novel** adaptation, begun in 1995, includes versions of "Barbara Allen," "The Daemon Lover," and "The Galtee Farmer." A number of **fantasy** authors have produced versions of ballads. Prominent among these are Ellen **Kushner**'s *Thomas the Rhymer* (1990), Pamela **Dean**'s *Tam Lin* (1991), Jane **Yolen**'s *Tam Lin* (1990), and Diana Wynne **Jones**'s *Fire and Hemlock* (1985). The first three adapt ballads of the same title while the last draws on both "Thomas the Rhymer" and "Tam Lin."

Another area where ballads have achieved prominence is in the **music** industry. The ballad is one of the cornerstones of the folk music movement of the twentieth century. American musicians such as Woody Guthrie and Pete Seeger performed traditional ballads alongside original compositions. Joan Baez' version of "Henry Martin" on her 1960 self-titled album is a good example of a popular release of a traditional ballad. Publications such as *Sing Out*, which began in 1950, have spread traditional ballads to new audiences. While the traditional context of the ballad may have changed, ballads have stayed alive in popular music.

Further Reading: Hixon, Martha P. "Tam Lin, Fair Janet, and the Sexual Revolution: Traditional Ballads, Fairy Tales, and Twentieth-Century Children's Literature." *Marvels & Tales* 18 (2004): 67–92.

B. Grantham Aldred

Bârlea, Ovidiu (1917–1990)

Ovidiu Bârlea was a Romanian folklorist. After graduating from the University of Bucharest in the field of modern philology, he became a researcher and fieldworker at the Institute for Ethnography and Folklore. His *Antologie de proză populară epică* (*Anthology of Folk Epic Prose*, 3 vols., 1966) includes all forms of prose folk narratives in circulation at the time (for example, fairy tales, **legend**s, **anecdote**s, and stories). The introduction to the anthology is the most modern, comprehensive account of prose folk narratives in Romanian since the work of Bogdan Petriceicu Hașdeu on fairy tales in the third volume of the *Etymologicum Magnum Romaniae* (1893) and Lazăr Șăineanu's monograph *Basmele române* (*Romanian Fairy Tales*, 1895). Bârlea addresses the main problems of the genre, including its origins, narrative occasions, narrative types, and the relation of the tale to the creative individual, as well as to its regional and temporal contexts.

The anthology contains oral narratives that were collected from forty-nine storytellers belonging to all regions of the country. The narratives were recorded and rendered phonetically, noting peculiarities of dialect, gestures, mimicry, and vocal inflections. This method resulted in an extremely accurate written reproduction of oral narrative and is considered a model of scientific **collecting** and **editing** of folk prose. The volume contains detailed information about the informants and a summary in German of each text. Bârlea's other contributions to the field are *Mică enciclopedie a poveștilor românești* (*Little Encyclopaedia of Romanian Fairy Tales*, 1976) and his discussion of "Fairy Tale" in *Foclorul românesc* (*Romanian Folklore*, 1981).

Further Readings: Bârlea, Ovidiu. *Istoria folcloristicii românești*. București: Editura Enciclopedică, 1974; Datcu, Iordan. *Dicționarul etnologilor români*. Volume 2. București: Editura Saeculum I. O., 1998. 79–81.

Nicolae Constantinescu

Barrie, Sir James Matthew (1860–1937)

A Scottish playwright, novelist, and author of the children's classic *Peter Pan*, Sir James Matthew Barrie was born in Kirriemuir, Forfarshire, and educated at Edinburgh University. He worked as a journalist in Nottingham before moving to London in 1885, where he became a leading novelist and successful dramatist with plays such as *Quality Street* (1901) and *The Admirable Crichton* (1902). His most successful and enduring work is his 1904 play *Peter Pan, or The Boy Who Would Not Grow Up*. A modern fairy tale about a boy who insists on remaining a child and who lives in Neverland with other lost boys, *Peter*

Pan tells of Peter's visit to the Darling children's nursery and the adventures Wendy and her two **brothers** have with him when he flies them to his island. Perennially popular on the stage, a British staple for Christmas **pantomime**s, and widely adapted, notably by Walt **Disney** in 1953, Barrie's story has become a classic of **children's literature**.

The story of Peter Pan was in part inspired by Barrie's close friendship with the sons of Sylvia and Arthur Llewelyn Davies, to whom he became guardian in 1910, after their parents' deaths. The games he played with the boys and stories he told them of fairies, pirates, and adventures were integral to his fictional creation.

Now a figure of modern **myth**, Peter Pan initially appeared in Barrie's *The Little White Bird* (1902), an episodic **novel** for adults, from which he later extracted the Peter Pan chapters to form the children's book *Peter Pan in Kensington Gardens* (1906). These two incarnations portray Peter as a week-old baby who was spirited away from his **family** and returned to London's Kensington Gardens to live among the fairies and birds. In 1911, Barrie produced *Peter and Wendy*, a novel version of the 1904 play that includes satirical comment on Edwardian society and a narrative that addresses adults and children severally. In the book, more strongly than in the play, the **fairy** Tinker Bell is depicted as a voluptuous, sexy creature with a private boudoir who displays acute jealousy over Peter's relationship with Wendy.

Peter, the boy who would not grow up, is often explained biographically as reflecting Barrie's brother David who died at age thirteen in a skating accident, or as expressing Barrie's longing for children and discomfort with aspects of the adult world. Often seen as a tragic figure, Peter might therefore represent a child lost, a child longed for, or Barrie himself. Barrie also drew on fairy tales for his play *A Kiss for* **Cinderella** (1916), in which a servant dreams about going to a ball with a duke. *See also* Childhood and Children; Theater.

Further Readings: Birkin, Andrew. *J. M. Barrie and the Lost Boys.* 1979. New edition. London: Yale University Press, 2003; Jack, R. D. S. "Barrie, Sir James Matthew, Baronet (1860–1937)." *Oxford Dictionary of National Biography.* Edited by H. C. G. Matthew and Brian Harrison. Oxford: Oxford University Press, 2004; Rose, Jacqueline. *The Case of Peter Pan, or The Impossibility of Children's Fiction.* London: Macmillan, 1984.

Adrienne E. Gavin

Barthelme, Donald (1931–1989)

An American writer of experimental fiction, Donald Barthelme is best known for his ironic and witty short stories that were published extensively in the *New Yorker* magazine from the 1960s to the 1980s. Often characterized as one of the pioneers of literary **postmodernism**, Barthelme primarily rejected the conventions of traditional formats, his work being more engaged with the nature and processes of writing itself than with narrative logic. The predictable structure and form of the fairy tale lent itself well to subversion in Barthelme's parodic interpretations. His **novel** *Snow White* (1967) reinvents the tale in a contemporary urban setting with **Snow White** depicted as a tall, dark, seductive woman living in a collective with seven men. As with much of Barthelme's work, the novel's style is an example of **metafiction**—the text draws attention to itself through various writing practices such as addressing the reader directly, varying the typographical format, and employing extensive non sequiturs.

In contrast, in his short story "**Bluebeard**," included in his collection *Forty Stories* (1987), Barthelme writes in a conventional narrative form but subverts the fairy tale's motifs in an ironic critique of contemporary culture and social mores. The story features a wife who is not innately curious and does not conform to the traditional conventions of womanhood, much to the bewilderment of her husband. It concludes with Bluebeard insisting that she unlock the famous door; she smarts with disappointment that it does not after all contain the carcasses of her predecessors but rather an array of well-dressed zebras. *See also* Parody.

Further Readings: Patteson, Richard F. *Critical Essays on Donald Barthelme.* New York: Maxwell Macmillan International, 1992; Trachtenberg, Stanley. *Understanding Donald Barthelme.* Columbia: University of South Carolina Press, 1990.

Louise Speed

Bartók, Béla (1881–1945)

One of the twentieth century's major composers, the Hungarian Béla Bartók wrote three works for the stage that bear the influence of folktales and fairy tales: the **opera** *A kékszakákállú herceg vára* (*Duke **Bluebeard**'s Castle*, 1918) and the ballets *Fából faragott királyfi* (*The Wooden Prince*, 1917), and *Csodálatos mandarin* (*The Miraculous Mandarin*, 1926). The scenario of *The Miraculous Mandarin* was written by the poet Menyhért Lengyel and depicts a beautiful young woman held by three **thieves** who oblige her to entrap a wealthy Chinese man. After they rob and stab him, he survives until, as the composer wrote, "the girl fulfills the Mandarin's desire and he falls lifeless to the ground." The libretti for *Duke Bluebeard's Castle* and the scenario for *The Wooden Prince* were both written by Hungarian writer Béla **Balázs**. *Duke Bluebeard's Castle*, which owes a debt to Maruice **Maeterlinck**'s play *Ariane et Barbe-bleue* and, according to recent research, the German dramatist Friedrich Hebbel, has had a significant impact on subsequent literary **adaptation**s of the Bluebeard tale. *See also* Dance; Music.

Further Readings: Fábry, Andrea. "A Comparative Analysis of Text and Music and Gender and Audience in *Duke Bluebeard's Castle*" *CLCWeb: Comparative Literature and Culture: A WWWeb Journal* 1.4 (1999): n.p.; Grace, Sherrill E. "Courting Bluebeard with Bartók, Atwood, and Fowles: Modern Treatment of the Bluebeard Theme." *Journal of Modern Literature* 11 (1984): 245–62; Leafstedt, Carl S. *Inside Bluebeard's Castle: Music and Drama in Béla Bartók's Opera.* Oxford: Oxford University Press, 1999.

Lee Haring

Basile, Giambattista (1575–1632)

The Italian writer, poet, and courtier Giambattista Basile is today remembered for his groundbreaking book of fairy tales, *Lo cunto de li cunti overo lo trattenemiemto pe peccerille* (*The Tale of Tales, or Entertainment for Little Ones*), also known as the *Pentamerone*. Written in the early years of the seventeenth century and published posthumously in 1634–36, it is the first integral compilation of authored, **literary fairy tale**s in western Europe. It holds unique status in many other aspects, too. *The Tale of Tales* is a masterpiece of Italian literature written not in standard Italian but in the dialect of Naples. The fabulous dimensions depicted in its tales stand in marked contrast to the realistic representation that was the

Portrait of Giambattista Basile (1641). [Courtesy of the Eloise Ramsey Collection of Literature for Young People, University Libraries, Wayne State University]

heritage of Giovanni **Boccaccio** and the **novella** tradition, still dominant at Basile's time. It is a work that simultaneously evokes the world of seventeenth-century Naples—its landmarks, customs and daily rituals, and family and professional life—as well as conjuring forth a fantastic world whose absolute originality still holds strong today.

Basile was a man of multiple literary personas. He was born to a middle-class family of courtiers and artists outside of Naples, at the time a major European metropolis and center of the baroque. For the most part, Basile's life was that of a typical man of letters: as he migrated from patron to patron, he composed verse on command, organized court festivities and spectacles, was a member of several academies, and even briefly served as a soldier of fortune. He later held administrative positions in the Neapolitan provinces and ended his life with the title of count. His predominantly poetic output in Italian spanned diverse genres—from odes and madrigals to pastoral and religious works to musical dramas—and his scholarly work included philological and editorial projects. But in these busy years Basile also worked on two projects that took him far in spirit and letter from his Italian production. These were *Le muse napoletane* (*The Neapolitan Muses*, 1635), a series of nine satiric eclogues celebrating landmarks and institutions of Neapolitan popular culture, and his masterpiece, *The Tale of Tales*. Both were probably read aloud at the "courtly conversations" that were a pastime of the elite during this period.

The Tale of Tales is an expression of the interest in popular culture and folk traditions that culminated in the Renaissance, when single fairy tales began to be included in novella collections, such as Giovan Francesco **Straparola**'s *Le piacevoli notti* (*The Pleasant Nights*, 1550–53). It also marked a generic crossroads, constituting one of the last great expressions of the waning Italian novella tradition just as it signaled the start of the new narrative paradigm of the literary fairy tale. Basile did not merely transcribe the oral materials he most likely heard in and around Naples and on his travels. He re-elaborated them into singular versions, in many cases the first in literary form, of celebrated **tale type**s such as **Cinderella**, **Sleeping Beauty**, Rapunzel, All Fur, and **Hansel and Gretel**, all of which would be included in later collections like Charles **Perrault**'s *Histoires ou contes du temps passé* (*Stories or Tales of Past Times*, 1697) or Wilhelm and Jacob **Grimm**'s *Kinder- und Hausmärchen* (*Children's and Household Tales*, 1812–15).

The Tale of Tales shares many structural features with Boccaccio's *Decameron* (1349–50) and other novella and fairy-tale collections (the *Arabian Nights*, for instance), such as its framed structure, in which the urgent circumstances of one tale—in this case, also a fairy tale—generate the rest of the tales and lead to a resolution of the initial dilemma. Basile's **frame narrative** tells of a slave girl who deceitfully cheats Princess Zoza out of her predestined husband, Prince Tadeo, to which Zoza reacts by using a magic doll to cast a spell on the slave that makes her crave tales. Tadeo summons the ten best storytellers of his kingdom, all crones who grotesquely mirror the more noble storytellers of other collections, and they each tell one tale apiece for five days. At the end of the last day Zoza recounts her own story and takes her rightful place as wife to Tadeo, after which the slave is killed. The first four days open with banquets, songs, dances, and games, and conclude with eclogues, satiric dialogues that give full rein to Basile the moralist and commentator on social ills.

The fifty stories in *The Tale of Tales* are like no other fairy tales: just as informed by elite literary culture as by folkloric traditions and the formulas of orality; bawdy and irreverently comic but also tender and whimsical; acute in psychological characterization and at the same time encyclopedic in description. Basile engages critically with dominant discourses by deformatively citing the most diverse authors and traditions through his hyperbolic descriptions and pyrotechnical metaphoric play; this parodic **intertextuality** has as its preferred targets courtly culture and the canonical literary tradition. Thematically, too, the tales display a permeability of moral boundaries surprising in a genre so often given to explicitly drawn lessons. The humanity of the characters in *The Tale of Tales* is portrayed with a complexity that does not always meet our fairy-tale expectations. We find, for example, **simpleton** heroes with no redeeming qualities, active heroines whose intelligence turns events to their advantage, **king**s unable to live up to the demands of reign, and conventional antagonists—such as **ogre**s—often far from evil. With all of their irregularities and loose ends that manage, magically, to merge into a splendid portrait of creatures engaged in the grave and laborious, gratifying and joyful business of life, Basile's journeys of **initiation** ultimately bear a certain familiarity to our own conflicted dialogues with the world around us. *See also* Bawdy Tale; Italian Tales.

Further Readings: Basile, Giambattista. *Giambattista Basile's The Tale of Tales, or Entertainment for Little Ones.* Translated by Nancy Canepa. Detroit: Wayne State University Press, 2007; Canepa, Nancy. *From Court to Forest: Giambattista Basile's* Lo cunto de li cunti *and the Birth of the Literary Fairy Tale.* Detroit: Wayne State University Press, 1999; Picone, Michelangelo, and Alfred Messerli, eds. *Giovan Battista Basile e l'invenzione della fiaba.* Ravenna: Longo Editore, 2004; Rak, Michele. *Logica della fiaba: Fate, orchi, gioco, corte, fortuna, viaggio, capriccio, metamorfosi, corpo.* Milan: Mondadori, 2005.

Nancy Canepa

Bauer, Herbert. *See* Balázs, Béla

Baum, L. Frank (1856–1919)

Well known and beloved as the creator of the world of Oz, Lyman Frank Baum is an important figure of children's literary **fantasy**. His writing career, which stretched from the 1880s until his death, covered not only the first fourteen Oz books but other fantasies, collections of tales, plays, and a few adult novels, as well as children's books under various pseudonyms. His legacy extends beyond his books into the classic **film** *The Wizard of Oz* (1939) and its less well-known sequel, *Return to Oz* (1985), and into further explorations of Oz by other writers after his death, most notably by Ruth Plumly Thompson.

Baum's writing for children betrays a strong bias towards the forms and **motif**s of the fairy tale, although this is perhaps stronger in his non-Oz writings than in his best-known works. As the title of one of his early collections, *American Fairy Tales* (1901), suggests, he works deliberately to Americanize and update the familiar fantasy elements, infusing them with a playful sense of the contemporary, particularly in terms of technology. His *American Fairy Tales* have a cautionary and didactic flavor, and often hinge on the intrusion of **magic object**s into the mundane world. *The Master Key: An Electric Fairy Tale* (1901) is perhaps his most explicit rewriting of the magical in terms of science. While the Oz books are similarly concerned with talking creatures, magic objects, and various forms of quest, the pattern, repetition, and symbol of the fairy tale is more strongly marked in Baum's non-Oz fantasies, such as *The Magical Monarch of Mo* (1903) and *Queen Zixi of Ix* (1905). These deal, respectively, with the adventures of an extensive royal family and with the **fairy** gift of a wishing cloak. Thompson's Oz narratives after Baum's death tend to continue this increased fairy-tale flavor.

Dorothy's adventures in Oz in the first book, *The Wonderful Wizard of Oz* (1900), form the template for subsequent narratives: her quest is a journey through the magical realm, supported by **magic helper**s and companions, and with a strongly didactic message conveyed through symbolic and at times allegorical elements. Baum's other important linkage with fairy tales is in his deliberate construction of Oz as a fairy realm, ruled by the beautiful Princess Ozma. In the power, inscrutability, and benevolence of the exclusively female fairies, Baum parallels motifs from the French *conte de fées,* a resemblance strengthened by specific elements such as the use of wands, Glinda the Good's stork chariot, and Ozma's protective relationship with Dorothy.

Baum's fantasies at their best have a playful charm that mimics the wonder and simplicity of the fairy tale despite the elements of the modern. In later works, however, his whimsy becomes forced, and the stress of responding to the unceasing demands of his considerable child audience is evident. *See also* Children's Literature; North American Tales.

Further Readings: Rahn, Suzanne. *The Wizard of Oz: Shaping an Imaginary World.* New York: Twayne, 1998; Riley, Michael O. *Oz and Beyond: The Fantasy World of L. Frank Baum.* Lawrence: University Press of Kansas, 1997.

Jessica Tiffin

Bawdy Tale

Whereas the **erotic tale** tends to be considered a wholly literary construction, the bawdy tale is the sexual, scatological, or otherwise risqué strain of the oral narrative tradition. Often humorous or irreverent, those without famous literary **adaptation**s have been largely ignored in **tale-type** and **motif** indexes, and until the late twentieth century, they were often considered inappropriate for scholarly study. During the last decades of the nineteenth century and first of the twentieth, many bawdy tales and other forms of "obscene" **folklore** were published in the French yearbook *Kryptádia* (1883–1911) and the Swiss-German journal *Anthropophytéia* (1904–1913). Neither publication circulated widely in its own time, and many volumes are exceedingly rare today.

Bawdy tales, however, may be found in a variety of sources from the Middle Ages to the present. Geoffrey **Chaucer** and Giovanni **Boccaccio** adapt an eclectic sampling in their work, while many other bawdy stories appear as Old French **fabliaux**. More recently, volumes have appeared that include the bawdy tales collected by folklorists Aleksandr **Afanas'ev** and

Vance Randolph. In *Deep Down in the Jungle* (1970), Roger Abrahams makes the African American variety one of his central concerns. Although publication and scholarly analysis of bawdy tales have remained on the fringe of folkloristics in Europe and America, the popularity of the form itself, unsurprisingly, has never wavered. *See also* Sex, Sexuality.

Further Readings: Afanas'ev, Aleksandr. *Russian Secret Tales: Bawdy Tales of Old Russia.* New York: Brussel and Brussel, 1966; Randolph, Vance. *Pissing in the Snow and Other Ozark Folktales.* Chicago: University of Illinois Press, 1986.

Adam Zolkover

Bear's Son

As an overall title, The Bear's Son (Motif B635.1) has been applied to two groups of folktales in which a bear and his human wife have a male child. One group belongs to Europe and Asia, the other to British Columbia and the adjacent Yukon and southern Alaska.

In the Eurasian type, the child is a strong man who becomes a dragon slayer. With his companions, or brothers, he descends to a lower world where he overcomes monsters, **devils**, or a **dragon**, rescuing three **princess**es. After further adventures, he marries the youngest princess and becomes king. The type is known to folklorists as ATU 301, The Three Stolen Princesses (often combined with ATU 650A, Strong John, also called John the Bear, in which the hero survives punishing tests).

If the Eurasian tale is predominantly of male interest, the American versions may be considered a woman's story. Here a haughty young woman follows a bear to his wilderness den and becomes his wife. They produce twin sons, in some retellings several sons. The wife betrays her husband, he is killed, and she returns to civilization. In some variants she terrorizes the human community, bearlike, venting a murderous rage. The type is variously known as The Girl Who Married the Bear or The Bear Mother.

Both types have echoes in literature. The Eurasian tale can be detected in the eighth-century English epic *Beowulf,* particularly in the hero's descent to a lower region where he beheads the monster Grendel. The American tale resonates in Alice **Munro**'s short story "Cortes Island" (in *The Love of a Good Woman,* 1998), set in British Columbia: a haughty woman who has returned to civilization with her strange son following a wilderness episode in which she has betrayed her now-dead husband turns a venomous rage against her neighbors.

Such echoes call attention to the hero's name,

Four scenes from The Bear Mother. [Detail from Argillite Sculptures, Haida, Cunningham Collection, now deposited at the Prince Rupert Museum, BC, carvings by Charles Edenshaw © Canadian Museum of Civilization, photo Marius Barbeau, 1939, image number 87389]

Beowulf, literally "bee wolf," a kenning for "bear," and the avowal of the woman returned from the wilds of Cortes Island (up the coast from Vancouver) that her experience had been interesting, "if," as she puts it, "you call bears interesting."

In the field of cultural analysis the anthropologist James M. Taggart has used Hispanic versions of the Eurasian Bear's Son tale, as told by men, to cast light on the workings of masculinity in Old and New World settings. In the realm of politics, as reported in the *New York Times* (February 9, 1998), the Gitksan nation of British Columbia, whose version of the tale incorporates information on land use, has put forth The Bear Mother in court proceedings to press its claim to ownership of 22,000 square miles in the mountains north of Vancouver.

Further Readings: McClellan, Catharine. *The Girl Who Married the Bear: A Masterpiece of Indian Oral Tradition.* Ottawa: National Museums of Canada, 1970; Stitt, Michael J. *Beowulf and the Bear's Son: Epic, Saga, and Fairytale in Northern Germanic Tradition.* New York: Garland, 1992; Taggart, James M. *The Bear and His Sons: Masculinity in Spanish and Mexican Folktales.* Austin: University of Texas Press, 1997.

John Bierhorst

Beauty and the Beast

"Beauty and the Beast" is one of the most beloved and enduring fairy tales of our time. Although it was first published in 1740 in a French **novel** for young adults by Gabrielle-Suzanne Barbot de **Villeneuve**, similar **animal groom** stories existed in the **oral tradition** of cultures around the world long before. It is possible they took their inspiration from the primitive ritual of sacrificing a virgin to appease a menacing supernatural being or serpent. Beauties and beasts make their appearance in European, rural American, and Native American folklore, as well as in folktales from India, Turkey, Israel, Zimbabwe, China, Indonesia, Jamaica, Colombia, among others. Some of these tales are quite ancient. However, in a reversal of the more frequent pattern, the existing oral tradition did not influence the **literary fairy tale**. Instead, Villeneuve's original story—especially the widely disseminated version of it by Jeanne-Marie **Leprince de Beaumont** (1756)—has made a lasting mark on folk narrative.

Fairy Tale

Scholars have suggested that Villeneuve may have taken the general outlines of her novel from two late seventeenth-century antecedents, Marie-Catherine d'**Aulnoy**'s story "Le Mouton" ("The Ram," 1698) and Charles **Perrault**'s "Riquet à la houppe" ("Riquet with the Tuft," 1697), in which a beautiful maiden falls in love with an animal or a singularly unattractive man. These tales arose from the **salon** culture of the second half of the seventeenth century, where it was the custom to invent publishable stories based on **motif**s from the oral tradition, and they may have mediated between that tradition and Villeneuve's original work. It is impossible to know the story's true ancestry.

Nonetheless, it is clear that the plot and details of the tale sprang largely from Villeneuve's creative imagination and reflected the milieu in which she was writing. Villeneuve's novel not only tells the story of the meeting, separation, and **marriage** of Beauty and the Beast but also includes the history of the Beast's enchantment and the story of Beauty's genealogy, as well as multiple dream sequences and the involvement of several **fairies**. Other distinctive features are the elaborate descriptions of the Beast's palace, the monkeys and parrots who act as Beauty's servants, the Beast's forthright request that Beauty sleep with him, and Beauty's willingness to give up her handsome **prince** when his **mother** asserts that this merchant's daughter is beneath him.

Writing for young French ladies of the rising middle class or the aristocracy, Villeneuve utilized many characteristics of the salon tales of the previous century. Her story features a whole nation of independent and powerful fairies, known as "intelligences," whose demeanor and values are those of the aristocratic salon **women** whose culture is under attack in France in the late 1730s. This older generation of women exists in tension with a younger generation represented by Beauty's fairy mother, who prefers to marry a humble mortal (albeit a **king**) and raise her **family** on Happy Island, living out the new bourgeois ideal best exemplified by the social theories of Jean-Jacques Rousseau. Thus, even as it demonstrates what it means to be beautiful and heroic, Villeneuve's tale reflects a contemporary shift in social mores and presents a new set of ideals for women that conflict with the norms of the recent past.

Villeneuve's literary tale was quickly taken up by others. Beaumont eliminated most of the novel's subplots when she turned it into a concise **didactic tale** for children. The family histories, most of the dream sequences, and all but one of the fairies are gone, and a less-sexualized Beast now asks Beauty to be his wife. Beauty's humility, patience, generosity, kindness, and hard work are repeatedly underscored, while moral commentary rounds out the tale, as in the final statement that perfect happiness is "founded on virtue." Translated almost immediately into English and many other languages and distributed throughout Europe (from Germany, Denmark, Sweden, Iceland, Poland, and Russia to Greece, Italy, Czechoslovakia, and Spain), Beaumont's version was largely responsible for the **diffusion** of the tale and became the standard referent for most subsequent retellings, in both folk and literary traditions.

The nineteenth century saw the proliferation of versions of all sorts, some of them beautifully illustrated (and existing largely for the sake of the **illustration**s), others in inexpensive **chapbook** form. Some—most notably *Beauty and the Beast, or a Rough Outside with a Gentle Heart, A Poetical Version of an Ancient Tale* (1811), attributed to Charles Lamb— were in verse. Not all the retellings were intended for children: Albert Smith's satirical rhymed version, illustrated by Alfred Crowquill, features cartoon images of Beauty's **father** and **sisters** and claims to imitate "the Annual, Album, or Fashion-Book line." James Robinson **Planché**'s theatrical take on the tale, *Beauty and the Beast: A Grand, Comic, Romantic, Operatic, Melodramatic, Fairy Extravaganza in Two Acts* (1841), is an ironic and punning spoof in rhyming couplets for an adult audience. The slight Oriental flavor in Planché's play—in the name of the Beast/Prince, Azor—is inspired by late eighteenth-century French versions and lingers in several twentieth-century tales.

Most nineteenth-century retellings take off from Beaumont, but one of the best known and most influential—Andrew **Lang**'s "Beauty and the Beast," which appeared in the *Blue Fairy Book* (1889)—is a radical abridgement of Villeneuve. The *Blue Fairy Book* was so popular that it was reprinted well into the mid-twentieth century by Longman, Green, a publisher known for its Supplemental Reading series for schools. As this development suggests, by the end of the nineteenth century the separation between the literary tale for adults and the moralizing fairy tale for children—begun when Beaumont rewrote Villeneuve's tale— was complete.

Folktale Variants

The proliferation of literary and children's versions of "Beauty and the Beast" in the eighteenth and nineteenth centuries paralleled the dissemination of the folktale **variant**s. "Beauty and the Beast" is the eponymous example of **tale type** 425C in the Aarne-Thompson-Uther index of international folktales. This is one of several variants of the tale-type cycle known as The Search for the Lost Husband (ATU 425), another variant of which is the myth of **Cupid and Psyche** (linked to both ATU 425A, The Animal as Bridegroom, and to ATU 425B, Son of the Witch). It is easy to see the kinship between these two tales. Both involve the meeting of the supernatural or enchanted groom and the beautiful girl, their separation as a result of the girl's **transgression**, and their ultimate reunion. Unlike the Cupid and Psyche tale, however, where the emphasis is on the breaking of the taboo that forbids the young woman to look at her husband (the god of love), "Beauty and the Beast" emphasizes the animal qualities of the groom and his ultimate **transformation** from a monster into a human being.

The similarity and differences between "Beauty and the Beast" and "Cupid and Psyche" are representative of the relationship among variants of a single tale type. Thus, the many folktale versions of "Beauty and the Beast" exhibit different characters and motifs while adhering to a basic structural pattern. For example, they may describe the beast as a bear, dog, serpent, **pig**, or other creature; explain the meeting of the groom and the maiden as unwitting or intended; and cite different taboos and different means for disenchanting the beast.

In the Russian tale "The Enchanted Tsarevitch," the groom is a three-headed snake. The father meets the reptile when he retrieves a flower for his daughter and promises to give the snake whatever he first encounters when he arrives home; unwittingly, he has promised the girl. After several nights in the company of the snake, who comes to sleep in her bed, the girl returns home, where her older sisters convince her to stay too long. When she returns to the snake, he is lying dead in a pond, but her kisses revive him and transform him into a handsome prince, whom she marries.

In the Appalachian tale "A Bunch of Laurel Blooms for a Present," the girl voluntarily goes to the house of a **witch** in place of her father, who is being punished for picking flowers to give to his daughter. The witch installs the girl in a little house, where a huge toad-frog is her companion. He is kind to the girl, he cooks and keeps house, and, when she is asleep, he sheds his warty skin and becomes a handsome young man. One night the girl burns the skin, lifting the witch's spell, and the pair lives happily together among the laurel blooms. In this tale there is no transgression.

As these examples indicate, except for a few core elements involving family relationships and symbolic objects, the folktale, like the literary tale, is susceptible to an infinite number of variations.

Artistic Legacy

In addition to its oral transmission, "Beauty and the Beast" has been carried forward in a remarkable number of works of art. It has been made into many plays, often for performance by young people, and it has given rise to at least two **opera**s, *Zémire et Azor* by Jean-François Marmontel and André-Ernest-Modeste Grétry (created in 1771 at Fontainebleau and recreated as recently as 2003 in Liège) and Robert Moran's *Desert of Roses*, which premiered in Houston, Texas, in 1992. Two famous films—Jean Cocteau's ***La Belle et la Bête***

(1946) and the **Walt Disney Company**'s *Beauty and the Beast* (1991)—are based on the tale. It was featured in a **television** series (1987–90) in the United States and also in a Disney-produced musical on Broadway. Finally, this vital narrative has been retold in feminist and science-fiction versions that reflect the changing mores of the late twentieth and early twenty-first centuries.

Angela **Carter**'s short story, "The Tiger's Bride" (1979), imagines that a man loses his daughter and all his other possessions to a beast in a game of cards. The beautiful young woman (who displays her feistiness and feminist turn of mind as she narrates her adventure) is transferred to the beast's abode, a run-down palazzo in wintery northern Italy, where the horses are housed in the ruined dining room and the beast sleeps in a rudimentary den. The plot reverses the original storyline when the young virgin, rather than the beast, undergoes a **transformation**, shedding her **clothes** and eventually her skin to become a tiger like her mate.

In Tanith **Lee**'s "Beauty" (1983), a science-fiction tale that challenges racism and homophobia, Estár, the third daughter of Mercator Levin, undergoes a process of growing self-awareness and sexual awakening when she is transported to the dwelling of an alien who has a muscular catlike form. Always the outsider in her own family, she quickly adapts to her new surroundings and feels love for this beast, who seems to read her mind. As the story unfolds, Estár learns the secrets of this alien race and discovers that, although her outward appearance is different, she is one of them. She has been summoned home—to her real home among the black, leonine "aliens"—by the delivery of an unusual rose.

Although critics such as Jack **Zipes** have decried the way "Beauty and the Beast" and other classic fairy tales have been taken over by the culture industry and turned into uninspiring romances or cute animated films for blatantly commercial purposes, the retellings by Carter and Lee suggest that there are still people of various ages who want to create and read provocative new imaginings of the story.

Symbolism and Significance

There is no single, straightforward way to explain what makes "Beauty and the Beast" so durable. Scholars disagree about its significance and the reasons for its widespread and long-standing appeal.

As it has evolved, the story's significance has changed. In its original outlines, "Beauty and the Beast" may have delighted audiences with its image of a potentially open society in which middle-class daughters could marry aristocratic husbands who respected them and women could choose to enter into marriage more or less freely. In Villeneuve's novel, Beauty's actions (unlike Psyche's) are never commanded or forced. In a way that is difficult for present-day readers to comprehend, the original "Beauty and the Beast" reflects the eighteenth-century emphasis on individual rights and freedoms—and tentatively suggests that they might even be extended to women.

However, the Beast's passivity and Beauty's agency are not always central in the modern tales, even in the feminist retellings. Instead, some recent literary versions of the story emphasize issues of self-awareness and psychological development that are more in keeping with the theories of adolescence engendered in the wake of Sigmund **Freud**. Some promote acceptance of racial or sexual others and teach that fear stems from resisting knowledge and difference. "Beauty and the Beast" has always been a vehicle for its authors' social or political messages or the popular ideas of their time.

Setting aside this inevitable updating of the story, however, certain elements remain and ensure the tale's underlying stability. These are the persistent **archetype**s and symbolic objects that allow audiences to recognize the story despite its shifting external and time-bound trappings. Instead of being situated in a particular **time and place**, the action is removed from any locatable reality and becomes dreamlike. In most versions, the Beast's residence is surrounded by a garden that could be a kind of Eden; or it may be in a remote part of northern Italy, or in an alien compound somewhere on earth.

Furthermore, the fact that the principal characters are named for abstract qualities (Beauty) or generic beings (Beast) makes them available as types, rather than particular individuals, and signals the universal, allegorical import of the tale. Even in a modern retelling such as Lee's, where the names are changed, their abstraction is maintained: the Beauty figure, Estár, translates as "Psyche," and the Alien is said to have a name that can only be intuited, not uttered or written.

Perhaps most important, basic family relationships form the core of the tale, which wrestles with the problem of exogamy, or marrying out. The daughter must make a successful transition from living with her father to entering into an adult relationship with another man. The flower the girl requests, which leads to her meeting with the Beast, symbolizes this transition. It can be understood either as a figure for male power, which is in play between the father and his daughter's suitor, or as a sign of the young woman's sexual innocence, which will soon be lost. In the end, the tale's durability may be due to the very fact that its meanings are not spelled out; they are not fixed once and for all. ***See also*** Childhood and Children; Feminism; Feminist Tales; Sex and Sexuality.

Further Readings: Griswold, Jerry. *The Meanings of "Beauty and the Beast": A Handbook*. Peterborough, Ontario: Broadview Press, 2004; Hearne, Betsy, ed. *Beauties and Beasts*. Phoenix: Oryx Press, 1993; _____. *Beauty and the Beast: Visions and Revisions of an Old Tale*. Chicago: University of Chicago Press, 1989; Swahn, Jan-Öjvind. *The Tale of Cupid and Psyche*. Lund: CWK Gleerup, 1955; Warner, Marina. *From the Beast to the Blonde: On Fairy Tales and Their Tellers*. New York: Farrar, Straus and Giroux, 1994; Zipes, Jack. "The Origins of the Fairy Tale." *Fairy Tale as Myth/Myth as Fairy Tale*. Lexington: University Press of Kentucky, 1994. 17–48.

Virginia E. Swain

Beauty and the Beast (Television Series)

An American **television** series that ran for fifty-six episodes from September 1987 to August 1990, *Beauty and the Beast* was an adaptation of the popular tale of the same name (ATU 425C). While significant differences exist between the original folktale and the television series, similarities exist that are of interest to folktale scholars.

Strongly influenced visually by Jean Cocteau's 1946 film ***La Belle et la Bête***, especially in terms of costuming and makeup, the television show took place in a fictionalized New York City, where a community of outcasts lived beneath the streets in an area called "the Tunnels." In the first episode of the series, Catherine, a successful assistant district attorney played by Linda Hamilton, was mistaken for a defense witness, attacked by a pair of criminals, and left in Central Park to bleed to death. She was found there by Vincent, a leonine human played by Ron Perlman, who brought her to his home in the Tunnels, where he nursed her back to health. As a result, the two developed a supernatural empathic bond and began a romantic relationship, which formed the basis of the plot of the series.

Through the first two seasons, the series revolved around Vincent and Catherine's developing relationship and the dangers of Catherine's work, with Vincent utilizing his empathic bond and his preternatural senses to help Catherine in her battles against organized crime. In the third season, due to Linda Hamilton's desire to leave the show, Catherine was written out of the show and replaced with Diana Bennet, a police investigator with extrasensory perception played by Jo Anderson. She supplanted Catherine both as potential love interest and investigatory partner. Supporting characters in the show included other residents of the Tunnels and Catherine's co-workers.

The show attracted praise for its combination of television genres, with elements of crime drama and romantic drama mixed throughout. This focus on romantic storylines is credited by many with attracting a greater proportion of female audience members than for contemporary crime shows.

One of the interesting aspects of the series is the relation between the basic plot structure of the show and the fairy tale for which it is named. While the show retains a relationship between a bestial man and a beautiful woman, their relationship does not result in his **transformation**. Instead, the show focuses on the transformation of Catherine from selfish to altruistic due to Vincent's influence, thus establishing a magical transformation based on a shift of personality rather than a shift in appearance.

The show did not survive long after Hamilton's departure and was cancelled at the end of its third season, though a fan community has grown up around it with avid video exchanges occurring. A DVD collection of the first season was released on February 13, 2007. *See also* Beauty and the Beast.

Further Readings: Erb, Cynthia. "Another World or the World of an Other? The Space of Romance in Recent Versions of 'Beauty and the Beast.'" *Cinema Journal* 34.4 (1995): 50–70; Jenkins, Henry. "'It's Not a Fairy Tale Any More!' Gender, Genre, *Beauty and the Beast*." *Textual Poachers: Television Fans and Participatory Culture*. New York: Routledge, 1992. 120–51.

B. Grantham Aldred

Bechstein, Ludwig (1801–1860)

Ludwig Bechstein (originally christened Louis Clairant Hubert Bechstein) was a successful German poet and editor of **folktale**s and **legend**s. He was born in Weimar on November 24, 1801, as the illegitimate child of Johanna Carolina Dorothea Bechstein from Altenburg and the French emigrant Louis Hubert Dupontreau. Bechstein died in Meiningen on May 14, 1860.

After he dropped out of school, he completed an apprenticeship with a pharmacist. Thanks to the support of Duke Bernhard of Sachsen-Meiningen, he was able to study from 1829 to 1831 in Leipzig and Munich and became librarian in Meiningen in 1831. In 1840, Bechstein was appointed Court Counselor. In 1844, he began systematizing the general **archives** relating to Henneberg. In 1848 he was appointed archivist and continued this work.

Bechstein was especially interested in older literature such as that of his role model Johann Karl August **Musäus**. He was the author of circuitous romantic religious **novella**s (*Sagennovellen* in German) such as the *Thüringische Volksmährchen* (*Thuringian Folktales*, 1823) and *Märchenbilder und Erzählungen* (*Fairy-Tale Scenes and Stories*, 1829). His *Deutsches Märchenbuch* (*German Fairy-Tale Book*, 1845) containing eighty folktales was a great success. Eleven editions (more than 70,000 copies) were published within eight years. The title was changed to *Ludwig Bechstein's Märchenbuch* (*Ludwig Bechstein's Fairy-Tale Book*) in 1853, and the book contained 174 illustrations by Ludwig **Richter**. By 1896, forty-five editions of *Ludwig Bechstein's Märchenbuch* had been published. Bechstein regarded himself as a poet and defended criticism of his **adaptation**s and revisions of older texts. He mainly directed his attention towards legends, and as a result a considerable number of them appear in his two books of folktales, particularly the sequel *Neues deutsches Märchenbuch* (*New German Fairy-Tale Book*, 1856) with fifty texts. Bechstein included in his work many folktales from the fourth edition (1840) of Jacob and Wilhelm **Grimm**s' *Kinder- und Hausmärchen* (*Children's and Household Tales*) after he had embellished them and changed some of the diction. In 1853, Bechstein incorporated still more tales from the *Kinder- und Hausmärchen*, such as "Das Rotkäppchen" ("**Little Red Riding Hood**") and "Der Wettlauf zwischen dem Hasen und dem Igel" ("The Race between the Hare and the Hedghog"), and removed those that reflected too much of a romantic style. In addition, Richter's drawings in Biedermeier style and the books' low price contributed significantly to the success of the two volumes.

Bechstein's other literary enterprises include editions of several volumes with Thuringian, Franconian, and Austrian legends (about 2,300 texts), that are pioneering works in the field of regional story **collecting** as well as an extensive *Deutsches Sagenbuch* (*German Legend Book*, 1853) with 1,000 regionally classified texts.

Bechstein's protagonists distinguish themselves by having timeless virtues such as modesty, industry, and diligence. However, compared to the folktales of the Brothers Grimm, a change in themes and **motif**s is conspicuous that is apparently related to the impact of the many legends that have been incorporated into this collection. Bechstein's heroes and heroines have to accomplish fewer impossible tasks, and they have to face fewer tests than heroes in other folktales. Likewise, they are neither at the disposal of the next world, nor do they have to obey it unconditionally. The protagonists are characterized only to a minimal extent by such negative qualities as hardheartedness or pride.

Courting is a frequent subject. The bride, however, is rarely abducted in Bechstein's folktales, and, accordingly, there is no task to find the right suitor. Rescues rarely occur. There are fewer **witch**es, giants, or **dwarves** as opponents from the next world. Malevolent antagonists are not severely punished but instead are spared. When Bechstein depicts scenes of everyday life and talks about **clothing**, he reveals a love for detail through his explanations of fashion trinkets. Songs and rhymes to liven up the plot are less important for Bechstein than for the Brothers Grimm. Bechstein strives to maintain the form of his literary models. Humor, satire, and irony are common stylistic devices in his tales. Social criticism and a personal evaluation of current affairs are also interspersed throughout his works.

Folktales by the Brothers Grimm have their own special character. Their everlasting fascination hinges on their high degree of abstraction and sublimation. Similarly, although their diction might be less appealing than that of the Grimms' tales, Bechstein's folktales are also individual literary achievements in their own right. When folktale scholarship was established at the end of the nineteenth century, Bechstein had few supporters. Considerable criticism arose, particularly from educators, with regard to the language used in Bechstein's works and literary adaptations. Franz Heyden's critique in 1908 had perhaps the strongest influence, and this negative assessment contributed to the relative obscurity of Bechstein's folktales today.

Nevertheless, Bechstein's ingenious alterations of even well-known tales and his skill for discovering new folktales and legends should not be underestimated. Bechstein's folktales are precious evidence of the spirit of his times and have maintained their individuality up to the present day. *See also* German Tales.

Further Readings: Bottigheimer, Ruth B. "Ludwig Bechstein's Fairy Tales: Nineteenth Century Bestsellers and Bürgerlichkeit." *Internationales Archiv für Sozialgeschichte der deutschen Literatur* 15.2 (1990): 55–88; Heyden, Franz. "Grimm oder Bechstein? Zur Kritik der Bechsteinschen Märchen." *Jugendschriften-Warte* 6 (1908): 13–15; 8 (1908): 22–24; *Ludwig Bechstein: Dichter, Sammler, Forscher; Festschrift zum 200. Geburtstag.* Ed. Hennebergisches Museum Kloster Veßra. 2 volumes. Meiningen-Münnerstadt: Kloster Veßra, 2001; Mederer, Hanns-Peter. *Stoffe aus Mythen: Ludwig Bechstein als Kulturhistoriker, Novellist und Romanautor.* Wiesbaden: Deutscher Universitäts-Verlag, 2002; Schmidt-Knaebel, Susanne. "Ludwig Bechstein als Märchenautor: Die vier Anthologien im Überblick." *LiLi: Zeitschrift für Literaturwissenschaft und Linguistik* 37.130 (2003): 137–60; Uther, Hans-Jörg. "Ludwig Bechstein und seine Märchen." *Palmblätter* 9 (2001): 29–53; _____, ed. *Märchenbuch: Nach der Ausgabe von 1857, textkritisch revidiert und durch Register erschlossen.* By Ludwig Bechstein. München: Diederichs, 1997; _____, ed. *Neues deutsches Märchenbuch: Nach der Ausgabe von 1856, textkritisch revidiert und durch Register erschlossen.* By Ludwig Bechstein. München: Diederichs, 1997.

Hans-Jörg Uther

Bécquer, Gustavo Adolfo (1836–1870)

The most intimate of Spanish Romantic poets, Gustavo Adolfo Bécquer also wrote some of the most lyrically pictorial tales of his era. His seventeen *Leyendas* (*Legends*, 1858–64; 1871) recall the fantasy of E. T. A. **Hoffmann** and Edgar Allan Poe. Based partly on Spanish **oral tradition**, partly on themes and **motif**s from other Western literatures, Bécquer's **legend**s are variously set in bygone ages, haunted ruins, majestic cathedrals, and idyllic landscapes. The supernatural plays a central role in "La cruz del diablo" ("The Devil's Cross," 1860) when a suit of armor donned by the **devil** is melted down and forged into a cross. "Los ojos verdes" ("The Green Eyes," 1861) tells of the young hunter who, bewitched by a beautiful green-eyed nymph, falls to his death in a lake. "Maese Pérez el organista" ("Master Pérez the Organist," 1861) and "La ajorca de oro" ("The Gold Bracelet," 1861) exemplify divine intervention. "El Miserere" ("The Miserere," 1962) and "La corza blanca" ("The White Doe," 1863) portray humans in altered forms, changed into ghosts in the former and into an animal in the latter. With the genies of wind and water, precious stones, and two **sisters**, "El gnomo" ("The Gnome," 1863) is a fairy tale evoking "The Fairies" of Charles **Perrault**. *See also* Spanish Tales.

Further Readings: Bécquer, Gustavo Adolfo. *Legends and Letters.* Translated by Robert M. Fedorchek. Lewisburg: Bucknell University Press, 1995; Bynum, Brant. *Romantic Imagination in the Works of Gustavo Adolfo Bécquer.* Chapel Hill: University of North Carolina Press, 1994.

Robert M. Fedorchek

Beech Mountain Jack Tale

"Beech Mountain Jack tale" has developed as a term to characterize the continuation and flowering of Jack tale telling in two mountain counties, Watauga and Avery, in northwestern North Carolina. Members of the Hicks, Harmon, and Ward families, often descendants of a notable late nineteenth-century teller, Council Harmon, continued telling these **märchen** in home settings. The tales' scholarly discovery and popularity, particularly after the publication of Richard Chase's *The Jack Tales* in 1943, led to the recognition of exceptional public storytellers in **performance** contexts ranging from schools to regional and national festivals into the twenty-first century.

Family members associated the tales with Council Harmon (1806–96), a fun-loving character who had learned them from his grandfather, Samuel "Big Sammy" Hicks (1753–1835). For a time in his later years, Council Harmon lived with his granddaughter, Jane Hicks Gentry, who had moved to the Hot Springs area, near Asheville.

Gentry (1863–1925), whose **ballad** repertory was collected by Cecil Sharp, told the Jack tales as entertainment for her children doing farmwork and did folk song and story programs at the Dorland Institute, a local settlement school. University of Tennessee sociology graduate student Isabel Gordon Carter collected what Gentry called "Old Jack, Will, and Tom tales" from her and in 1925 published their texts in "Mountain White Folk-Lore: Tales from the Southern Blue Ridge" in the *Journal of American Folklore*. Gentry handed down her tales to daughter Maud Gentry Long (1893–1984), who continued telling them. She recorded her repertory for the Library of Congress in 1947.

In 1935, Marshall Ward, a student at Appalachian State Teachers College in Boone, North Carolina, met Richard Chase, who was looking for old folk songs. Ward informed Chase of the existence of "old stories handed down from generation to generation ... mostly about a boy named Jack and his two brothers, Will and Tom" (Chase, vii). Chase began to visit Watauga County, collecting tales and then rewriting them and other variants collected in southwest Virginia as eighteen narratives in *The Jack Tales*. The book included black-and-white drawings by Berkley Williams, Jr., of Jack in various settings. It became extremely popular and has continuously been in print since its publication in 1943, going through at least thirty-eight printings and becoming a favorite school and library reading, including reading aloud for children's programs. Chase himself became a revivalist performer of the tales, often touring for school and university programs. He tried to establish a center for **storytelling** in Watauga County, but the venture was defeated by local opposition to his presence.

Storytelling as an important form of traditional family entertainment and work diversion among farm families in Watauga and Avery counties continued into the late twentieth century. Chase's book and his subsequent *Grandfather Tales: American-English Folk Tales* (1948) provided a validation for the worth of the local tales. These probably led to the local genre terms "**Jack tales**" and "Grandfather tales," but also may have affected their form. School performances by local tellers became popular. Ray Hicks and Stanley Hicks became frequent school visitors, while Marshall Ward used the tales for teaching fifth grade at the Banner Elk Elementary School in Avery County. The storytelling revival and promotion of folk arts led to more festival appearances by these three local tellers. Other recent tradition bearers include Frank Proffitt, Jr., and Orville Hicks.

Ray Hicks (1922–2003) probably was the best known of the contemporary tellers of the Beech Mountain Jack tale. Celebrated in the media, adulated at the Jonesborough, Tennessee, National Storytelling Festival, and documented in film and video, Ray and his home on the lower slope of Beech Mountain became iconic representatives of old mountain ways, and his Jack tales became famous.

Although the styles of contemporary tellers of the Beech Mountain tale have striking differences, ranging from Marshall Ward's educational elaborations and Ray Hicks's idiosyncratic digressions to Orville Hicks's more compact performances, all characterize the **trickster** Jack as a good-natured, laid-back hero, which certainly reflects local cultural norms. Often tellers preface their stories with comments on the importance of the tales to their family tradition and describe home contexts where they learned them. The Appalachian dialect of performances is especially distinct, using older verb forms such as *cloom* as the past tense of *climb* and "a-prefixing" to express intensive action (for example, "Jack was a-runnin"). While some recent analysis has stressed similarities to Chase as indicative of the influence of a written text, tellers such as Ray and Orville Hicks strongly deny influences from Chase's book.

The popularity of the Beech Mountain Jack tale has led to spin-offs in other media. Tom **Davenport** adapted "Jack and the Rich Man's Girl" into the film "Jack and the Dentist's Daughter" using an African American cast. Caldecott Medal-winning children's author Gale Haley wrote her own version of the tales. Ferrum College in Virginia and the arts center Appalshop in Kentucky have produced dramatic versions.

More recent scholarly attention has recognized the distribution of the traditional Jack tales outside of the area, downplaying the special nature of the local Beech Mountain tradition. However, the enduring appeal of the tales among a set of especially notable local tellers has led to important appreciation; Ray and Stanley Hicks won National Endowment for the Arts National Heritage Fellowships in 1983.

Further Readings: *Appalachian Storyteller: Ray Hicks Series.* 5 DVDs. Produced by Luke Barrow. Chip Taylor Communications, nd; Chase, Richard. *The Jack Tales.* Boston: Houghton-Mifflin, 1943; *Jack Tales Issue.* Special issue of *North Carolina Folklore Journal* 26.2 (September 1978): 51–143; Lindahl, Carl, ed. *Perspectives on the Jack Tales and Other North American Märchen.* Bloomington: Folklore Institute, Indiana University, 2001; McCarthy, William Bernard, ed. *Jack in Two Worlds: Contemporary North American Tales and Their Tellers.* Chapel Hill: University of North Carolina Press, 1994; *Ray and Rosa Hicks: The Last of the Old-Time Storytellers.* DVD. Produced by Charles and Jane Hadley, 2000.

Thomas McGowan

La Belle et la Bête (1946)

In his classic black-and-white film, *La Belle et la Bête* (*Beauty and the Beast*, 1946), the French artist, playwright, novelist, poet, and director Jean Cocteau claims to base his story on the eighteenth-century children's tale of the same name by Jeanne-Marie **Leprince de Beaumont**. However, several obvious differences between the alleged source and the film make it clear that this work emanates in large part from Cocteau's own imagination and embodies his visual aesthetic. The film is regarded as one of Cocteau's most important works, and it has influenced not only other filmmakers in France but also the **Walt Disney Company**'s rendition of *Beauty and the Beast* (1991).

Cocteau utilizes the basic plotlines of the **family** drama handed down from Leprince de Beaumont—the initial encounter between the Beast and Beauty's **father** when the merchant plucks a rose for his daughter, the girl's decision to save her father's life by entering the Beast's palace as a substitute for him, her uncertainty regarding the Beast's intentions, the Beast's near-demise when she fails to return from a visit to her family, and the ultimate **transformation** of the Beast into the handsome **Prince** who makes Beauty his bride. But the director transforms the story's impact with the addition of new characters and subplots, and shifts the focus away from the young woman's development onto the male characters, particularly their similarities and differences.

Jean Marais as La Bête and Josette Day as Belle in the 1946 French film *La Belle et la Bête*. [Lopert Pictures Corporation/Photofest]

Undoubtedly, the most important new character in the film is Beauty's handsome suitor, Avenant (whose name means "attractive" in French). This young man, played by Cocteau's longtime associate and lover, Jean Marais, is not an ideal match for Beauty despite his looks, inasmuch as he is a ruffian who attempts to force himself on his beloved in a near rape. Avenant's actions prefigure those of the Beast (also played by Jean Marais), who twice appears on the threshold of Beauty's bedroom covered with blood from the animals he has killed and eaten. The Beast's carnal instincts, first signaled in the film by a close-up of a mutilated doe, are an unmistakable sign of his potential to harm his beautiful prisoner. The Beast seems poised to carry out this threat each time he appears at Beauty's doorstep or carries her into her bedroom.

Furthermore, the film's conclusion, in which the Beast becomes the handsome Prince (again played by Jean Marais), contains a double lesson for **men**. First, Avenant is brought low. Acting on the assumption that if the Beast is no longer rich, he will lose his hold over Beauty, Avenant tries to break into the glass pavilion that houses the Beast's wealth. But this transgressive act, symbolic of Avenant's earlier attempted rape, brings about his own violent **death**: he is shot by an arrow from the bow of Diana, the goddess of chastity, who guards this spot. Dying, Avenant is transformed into an animal just at the moment when the Beast comes to life as a prince through Beauty's ministrations. In an unexpected twist, the gentlemanly Prince has the features of the handsome Avenant, while the treacherous Avenant now looks exactly like the Beast.

In these departures from Leprince de Beaumont's chaste version of the tale, Cocteau lays the emphasis on the dangerous and demeaning aspect of sexual desire, which can make a man a beast. At the same time, but in a less convincing manner, he asserts the more positive implication of the tale—that a man can become better through love. Instead of a lesson for **women**, emphasizing the benefits of self-sacrifice or the need to put aside a girlish attachment to the father in favor of a mature love relation, Cocteau's film may be read as a **cautionary tale** for men, urging against rough machismo and in favor of a civilized masculinity. However, as the conclusion of the film is both rapid and histrionic, and because the conventional, even dandyish Prince is so much less impressive than the Beast, many commentators have interpreted the film as a critique of heterosexuality.

Unlike Leprince de Beaumont's story, Cocteau's film is hardly a **fable** for children. Yet he begins *La Belle et la Bête* with a written preface asking his adult viewers to adopt the attitude of a child and suspend intellectual judgment as they watch the story unfold. He hoped that the public would react to the film as if it were a compelling dream, accepting its surreal atmosphere and symbolic objects as elements of a different, but vital and valid world. Cocteau often spoke of creation as capturing a dream and argued that a work of art could make an impact without being completely understood.

Cocteau did not choose **Beauty and the Beast** as his subject because of its unreality, however. Cocteau capitalized on the fact that films can make the invisible visible, and he wanted to replace narrative with lived experience, making the filmgoer's experience of the film its own reality. In *La Belle et la Bête*, these aesthetic principles are especially evident in the mysterious, eerie interior of the Beast's castle, where disembodied arms holding chandeliers and decorative herms on the mantelpiece turn their eyes to follow Beauty's movements. If the artist is merely a servant of the mysterious forces within him, as Cocteau claimed, then this film about a forceful Beast harboring his secrets in a dark, inscrutable place may be understood as a mythical, yet ultimately "real" representation of Cocteau's own artistic process. *See also* Film and Video; Sex, Sexuality.

Further Readings: Cocteau, Jean. *Beauty and the Beast: Diary of a Film.* Translated by Ronald Duncan. New York: Dover, 1972; _____. *Diary of an Unknown.* Translated by Jesse Browner. New York: Paragon House, 1988.

Virginia E. Swain

Benavente, Jacinto (1866–1954)

Jacinto Benavente, the prolific, Nobel-Prize–winning Spanish playwright, composed a number of plays with fairy-tale themes. In 1909, he established a **theater** for children in Madrid, offering *El príncipe que todo lo aprendió en los libros* (*The Prince Who Learned Everything from Books*) as the opening production. This comedy features a young Don Quixote of a **prince** who travels through the world expecting things to be just as in fairy tales—with almost disastrous results. The play became a children's classic. This was followed by the one-act children's plays "Ganarse la vida" ("To Earn a Living," 1909) and "El nietecito" ("The Grandson," 1910), the latter based on Jacob and Wilhelm **Grimm**s' "Der alte Großvater und der Enkel" ("The Old Man and His Grandson," 1812). In 1919, he returned to children's themes with *La cenicienta* (**Cinderella**) and *Y va de cuento ...* (*And Now a Story ...*), the first based on Charles **Perrault** and the latter incorporating elements of various fairy tales. In 1934, he wrote his masterful *La novia de nieve* (*The Snow Bride*), which combines the Russian **motif** of the Snow Maiden (*Snegurochka*) with the plot of "**Sleeping Beauty**." Benavente injected into these plays a sometimes-whimsical element of social satire and political consciousness for the alert adults in the audience. Benavente also composed a number of plays for adults in which **king**s, **princess**es, magic, and mythical kingdoms serve his agenda of social and political commentary. Examples are *El dragón de fuego* (*Fire **Dragon***, 1904), *La escuela de las princesas* (*The School for Princesses*, 1909), and *La noche illuminada* (*A Night of Lights*, 1927).

Further Readings: Días, José A. *Jacinto Benavente and His Theatre.* Long Island City, NY: Las Americas Publishing, 1972; Peñuelas, Marcelino C. *Jacinto Benavente.* Translated by Kay Engler. New York: Twayne, 1968.

William Bernard McCarthy

Benfey, Theodor (1809–1881)

Theodor Benfey was a German scholar of Sanskrit who helped establish the discipline of comparative philology, and whose edition of the **Panchatantra** (1859) inspired a generation of folklorists interested in the migrations of tales. He was born in Göttingen in 1809 to a Jewish merchant family, and at the age of sixteen began his university studies, which he undertook at Göttingen and Munich. He earned a doctorate in 1828. In 1830, he moved to Frankfurt, in 1832 to Heidelberg, and in 1834 returned to Göttingen. During this time, his interests shifted from classical and Semitic languages to Sanskrit. His academic career moved slowly until 1848, when he converted to Christianity; he was then appointed associate and later full professor. His main publications include a grammar of Sanskrit (1852); his edition of the *Panchatantra* (1859) in two volumes, of which the first traced the diffusion of the book from India westward to Europe and offered studies of individual tales; and a history of linguistics and philology, *Geschichte der Sprachwissenschaft und orientalischen Philologie in Deutschland* (*History of Linguistics and Oriental Philology in Germany*, 1869). His papers are collected in the posthumous *Kleinere Schriften* (*Short Writings*, 1892). He also edited, for the three years of its life, a journal devoted to comparative philology, *Orient und Occident* (1862–65).

Benfey's importance for folktale studies lies in his work with the *Panchatantra* and his subsequent writings. He was so impressed by the wealth of narrative material in the Sanskrit tradition and especially the Buddhist resources (**Jātaka**s and other writings) that he came to see in them something close to the original of much European narrative folklore; this is the theory of Indian origins, of which he was the originator. He envisioned some material traveling through Tibet, via Buddhist channels, to the Mongols, and then carried by the Mongols to Europe at a later date (in the thirteenth and fourteenth centuries), but did make an exception for animal fable, which thanks to **Aesop** was clearly documented in the Greek tradition before the Sanskrit florescence. This theory held sway for a time, but was eventually abandoned in the face of growing evidence; Emmanuel Cosquin and Andrew **Lang** were two of the most effective critics. It may be noted, however, that in much of the medieval Arabic and Persian material that Benfey examined in the context of his comparative work, the trope of an Indian origin for fabulous tales is a given. *See also* South Asian Tales.

Further Reading: Benfey, Theodor. *Der Pantschatantra: Fünf Bücher indischer Fabeln, Märchen und Erzählungen*. 2 volumes. Leipzig: F. A. Brockhaus, 1859.

Stephen Belcher

Bernard, Catherine (c. 1663–1712)

Born in Rouen to a wealthy Protestant family, French author Catherine Bernard produced works that reflect her familiarity with fashionable seventeenth-century intellectual society. Her first novel, *Frédéric de Sicile* (1680), though written in the literary style popular at the time, was unsuccessful. Bernard experienced more success after moving to Paris, where she wrote numerous prizewinning poems. She also published a short story, two plays, and three more historical novels, which were praised for their delicacy of emotions.

Bernard's fourth **novel**, *Inès de Cordoue* (1696), is noteworthy not only for its place in the tradition of works such as Madame de Lafayette's *La Princesse de Clèves* (1678), but also for featuring two original fairy tales. Set in the court of King Phillip II of Spain, the novel centers around the admirers of the French-born queen who frequent her salons. One such **salon** features a competition in the composition of fairy tales between the work's heroine, Inès, and her rival, Léonore. Inès's composition "Le Prince Rosier" ("Prince Rosebush") tells the story of a cursed **princess** who falls in love with an enchanted rosebush. The rosebush is transformed into a prince, who later ruins his hopes for a happy marriage to the princess by confessing a "slight weakness" for the queen of the Island of Youth. The prince asks fairies to return him to his flowery form to escape the princess's jealousy. The tale explains why roses give off the heady fragrance that would torment the unfortunate princess all of her life.

Léonore's composition "Riquet à la houppe" ("Riquet with the Tuft") is a variation on the **Beauty and the Beast** theme, exploring an encounter between a beautiful but dull-witted princess and a clever but hideous gnome. The story is similar to Charles **Perrault**'s tale of the same name, published in 1697: in both versions, Riquet helps the princess to find intelligence, under the condition that she eventually marry him. As in "Prince Rosebush," however, Bernard defies the conventional "happily ever after" ending. While in Perrault's tale, Riquet ultimately becomes handsome and beloved by his wife, in Bernard's tale, Riquet remains disgusting to the princess, who endures life in his underground kingdom only through frequent visits from her lover. When Riquet learns the truth, he transforms his wife's lover into a gnome identical to himself, and the bewildered princess spends the rest of her life unable to distinguish between the two. Léonore suggests slyly that the end is fitting, since lovers "nearly always become husbands" anyway.

Inès de Cordoue places Bernard in the tradition of the French *conteuses* like Marie-Catherine d'**Aulnoy** and Marie-Jeanne **Lhéritier de Villandon**, prolific authors of fairy tales during the 1690s. Scholars have also used this novel as evidence that the salon was one crucial source of fairy tales, pointing to educated women, rather than illiterate peasant women, as creators of these stories. *See also* French Tales.

Further Reading: Piva, Franco. "A la récherche de Catherine Bernard." *Oeuvres de Catherine Bernard, I.* Fasano: Schena, 1993. 15–47.

Elizabeth Wanning Harries

Beskow, Elsa (1874–1953)

Elsa Beskow was one of the most prominent authors and illustrators of Swedish **children's literature** of her time. In her stories, she combines reality with fairy-tale characters, such as trolls, **elves**, **fairies**, **witch**es, and talking animals. Her picture-book **illustration**s of nature, especially the Swedish countryside and the forest, are classic. Beskow was a trained artist. Her detailed art nouveau illustrations, most likely inspired by Walter **Crane**'s drawings, offer detailed and decorative images of nature and bourgeois small-town life.

Beskow's first book, *Sagan om den lilla, lilla gumman* (*The Story of the Little, Little Old Lady*), appeared in 1897. Although her stories are regarded as representative of an idyllic period in Swedish children's literature, they caused controversy when they were first published. *Tomtebobarnen* (*The Little Elves of Elf Nook*, 1910) was criticized for being too intimidating for children. A prominent theme in Beskow's works concerns the relationships among children, animals, and enchanted nature. This theme is evident in Beskow's breakthrough work, *Puttes äfventyr i blåbärslandet* (*Peter in Blueberry Land*, 1901), which advises young readers to show consideration for nature. The forest is described as a magical place, an image influenced by Nordic national Romanticism. Relationships between children young people and adults as well as independent children are depicted in *Pelles nya kläder* (*Pelle's New Suit*, 1912), a story that also emphasizes the importance of honest work. ***See also*** Childhood and Children; Nationalism.

Further Reading: Hammar, Stina. *Solägget: Fantasi och verklighet i Elsa Beskows konst.* Stockholm: Albert Bonniers Förlag, 2002.

Elina Druker

Bettelheim, Bruno (1903–1990)

Bruno Bettelheim was an Austrian-born American psychiatrist and author of *The Uses of Enchantment* (1976). This neo-Freudian study and international bestseller has immensely influenced popular fairy-tale studies and the general public's appreciation of the fairy tale. In an introductory chapter and several more elaborate case studies, Bettelheim argues for the tales' therapeutic function and importance in childhood education. Like dreams, fairy tales address the subconscious of children and help the young deal with their unspoken fears and desires, such as sibling rivalry and oedipal conflicts ("**Beauty and the Beast**"), ambivalent feelings towards their parents ("**Snow White**"), or oral regression ("**Hansel and Gretel**"). According to Bettelheim, the fairy tale—because of its long **oral tradition**—possesses a unique healing and liberating power, which he thought contemporary **children's literature** lacked. Essential are the fairy tale's optimism and happy endings: the good are rewarded, and the bad cruelly punished. Children, who identify with the protagonist of the tale, will feel relieved and reassured that their problems can be similarly vanquished. Bettelheim warns against fairy-tale **illustration**s and the efforts of parents to explain the stories' deeper meaning since both may interfere with the child's fantasy and subconscious understanding of the fairy tale's message. The addition of an explicit **moral**, the presence of irony, and the deletion of vulgar elements gave Bettelheim cause to disapprove of most of Charles **Perrault**'s tales. He preferred instead the tales of Jacob and Wilhelm **Grimm**.

Bettelheim promoted fairy tales at a time when they were criticized by pedagogues and feminists. Although his study was influential, it came under fire immediately after its appearance. Bettelheim's methodology was criticized for being unscientific, biased, and even harmful to children. His generalizations about children's responses to fairy tales (disregarding varieties linked to sex, age, social and historical background) have been refuted by empirical studies by researchers such as Arthur Applebee, Basil Bernstein, and Patricia Guérin Thomas. Moreover, Bettelheim was reproached for his ignorance of other fairy-tale scholarship, particularly on the genesis of the Grimms' collection and the sociohistorical context in which the tales originated. His scientific ethos was questioned by critics such as Alan **Dundes**, who pointed out the striking congruencies between *The Uses of Enchantment* and previous psychoanalytic studies, most notably Julius Heuscher's *Psychiatric Study of Fairy Tales* (1963). Others, such as Jack **Zipes** and Maria Tatar, objected to Bettelheim's moralistic approach to fairy tales and to his use of the Freudian idea of reversal, which often leads to blaming the victim, usually women and children. ***See also*** Freud, Sigmund; Psychological Approaches; Trauma and Therapy.

Further Readings: Dundes, Alan. "Bruno Bettelheim's Uses of Enchantment and Abuses of Scholarship." *Journal of American Folklore* 104 (1991): 74–83; Tucker, Nicholas. "Dr. Bettelheim and Enchantment." *Signal* 43 (1984): 33–41; Zipes, Jack. "On the Use and Abuse of Folk and Fairy Tales with Children: Bruno Bettelheim's Moralistic Magic Wand." In *Breaking the Magic Spell: Radical Theories of Folk and Fairy Tales*. Revised edition. Lexington: University Press of Kentucky, 2002. 179–205.

Vanessa Joosen

Bible, Bible Tale

Bible tales derive largely from two sources: mythological traditions and oral/folk traditions. The former is largely confined to tales or talelike stories appearing within the canonical scriptures, and the latter develops in extracanonical tales. Mythological tales preserved in the Bible are often variations of other ancient **myth**s common in much of the Near East, whereas Bible tales originating in folk traditions tend to arise within individual communities and continue to develop as a dynamic form of **storytelling** in modern times.

Most of the mythological material in the Bible that can be categorized as tales is found within the first eleven chapters of Genesis. They involve a level of interaction between humans, divine beings, half-divine creatures, and talking animals that one normally encounters in fairy tales. The tale of the Garden of Eden (Gen. 2.4–3.24) is a clear example of this, as Adam and Eve have direct conversations with God; a talking serpent plays the role of a **trickster**; God fashions **clothing** for his human creations; and God assigns a cherubim with a flaming sword to guard the tree of life in Eden. In the tale of the tower of Babel (Gen. 11.1–10), God descends from heaven to explore a city, only to feel threatened by the people's seemingly limitless abilities. God's response is to magically multiply the only language of the people into a myriad of tongues and scatter them over the earth. There is a bit of irony in Yahweh's performance as a trickster god, for the inhabitants of the city had built their tower as part of a plan to avoid being scattered over the earth.

The tale of Noah and the world flood (Gen. 6–9) has close parallels with other ancient deluge stories, such as those found in the Akkadian **epic**s of Atrahasis and **Gilgamesh**. The most striking fantastical elements of this tale include the Nephilim (a half-divine race of giants parented by women and angels), a box-shaped boat containing examples of every nonmarine species, a worldwide flood, and animal **magic helper**s (a raven and dove). The pseudepigraphic Ethiopic Book of Enoch expands the origins and gruesome crimes of the antediluvian Nephilim into a tale of its own. Extracanonical and apocryphal texts provide a rich source of Bible tales that are often of a legendary nature.

Modern Bible tales also have the quality of **legend**. Often preserved through **oral tradition** (but also recorded in forms such as children's Bibles), these tales typically add supplementary material to biblical stories. In modern variations of the tale of Noah, people mock him for building his ark. This event is absent from the Genesis account, but it would ring true to modern people who feel their faith is mocked in a secular world. The dynamic oral tradition of Bible tales adapts biblical stories to make them relevant and familiar to new audiences. *See also* Etiologic Tale; Religious Tale; Saint's Legend.

Further Reading: Bowman, Marion. "Vernacular Religion and Nature: The 'Bible of the Folk' Tradition in Newfoundland." *Folklore* 114.3 (2003): 285–95.

R. Seth C. Knox

La bibliothèque bleue

During the seventeenth and the eighteenth centuries, a wealth of cheaply printed **chapbook**s circulated first in a number of cities and then throughout the rural areas of France. These sold for the equivalent of a few cents by peddlers traveling from village to village. In the beginning of the seventeenth century, Nicolas Oudot, from Troyes in the Champagne area, invented them. They quickly became immensely popular in Normandy (Rouen and Caen), Paris, and Lyons. A century later, more than 150 printers in seventy different locations in France were printing those simple, cheaply produced, and poorly bound blue books, which, over time, shaped the mentalities of the economically disadvantaged and uneducated or less-educated people. This form of literature sold by peddlers is called in French *la bibliothèque bleue* ("blue," it is assumed, because of the cheap blue-gray paper that served as a cover).

If chapbooks were a source of contempt and mockery for an educated elite, they nonetheless touched a whole social group who had no access to erudite culture: farmers, small village notabilities, parishioners, artisans, and peasants. Books were rare and costly for underprivileged and mostly illiterate or semiliterate populations. The easily available, crudely illustrated volumes that made up *la bibliothèque bleue* were read many times during long winter evenings. Those who could not read listened to and memorized them, and the contents were even copied down by those who could write.

Borrowing from the great classics of literature as well as from folk culture, the rich corpus of *la bibliothèque bleue* provides insight into the popular culture of France's *Ancien Régime* and the imaginations of countless workers, craftsmen, peasants, merchants, and shopkeepers. Tales of chivalry and fairy tales were adapted from the rich repertoire of the fairy mythology and the pagan tales of marvels, as well as from the classic authors of **literary fairy tale**s. Charles **Perrault**'s fairy tales, originally published in 1697, appeared in chapbook editions as early as 1723, often featuring each tale in separate opuscules (smaller, minor works). Alongside "**Cinderella**," "**Blue Beard**," and "**Puss in Boots**," Gargantua and **Till Eulenspiegel** were also popular heroes in those **adaptation**s written for the most part by anonymous authors. An even larger number of blue books were of a pseudoscientific nature: conduct books, almanacs, calendars, recipe books, and manuals; handbooks for cooking, gardening, and healing; and advice on how to find a wife, raise children, or grow medicinal herbs. Many contained a wealth of practical knowledge about nature and the human body. The largest portion of *la bibliothèque bleue* consisted of religious books faithful to the teachings of the Counter-Reformation. Books of hymns, lives of saints, or commentaries on the Gospels all were intended to exemplify the Christian moral values of faith, honesty, loyalty, and friendship.

In the nineteenth century, the printed press with daily and weekly newspapers and magazines offered other forms of instruction, entertainment, and evasion, and thus contributed to the progressive disappearance of *la bibliothèque bleue*.

Further Readings: Andriès, Lise, and Geneviève Bollème. *La bibliothèque bleue: Littérature de colportage*. Paris: Robert Laffont, 2003; Mandrou, Robert. *De la culture populaire aux XVIIe et XVIIIe siècles*. Paris: Stock, 1964.

Claire L. Malarte-Feldman

Bilibin, Ivan (1876–1942)

Ivan Bilibin, who is generally regarded as the leading star of the Russian folk art movement at the beginning of the twentieth century, was born in Tarkhovka, not far from St.

Petersburg. **Art** studies under the great artist Il'ya Repin and the works of painter Viktor Vasnetsov, which were exhibited in 1898, had a crucial influence on Bilibin's choice of career. In 1898, he spent the summer in a remote village outside the city of Tver painting and reading Aleksandr **Afanas'ev**'s collection of Russian folktales. The watercolors he brought back with him attracted the attention of the government Department for the Production of State Documents, who wanted him to illustrate a series of Russian folktales. Among the tales, published between 1899 and 1902, were *Ivan-tsarevich, Zhar-ptitsa i sery volk* (*Ivan The Tsar's Son, the Firebird, and the Grey Wolf*); *Vasilisa prekasnaya* (*Vasilisa the Beautiful*); *Peryshko Finista yasna-sokola* (*The Feather of Finist the Falcon*); *Mariya Morevna*; *Tsarevna-Lyagushka* (*The Frog Princess*); and the lyrical *Belaya utochka* (*The White Duck*). He was invited to join *Mir iskusstva* (*World of Art*), a magazine and an artistic movement, founded in 1898, which mainly promoted the principles of art nouveau. From 1902 to 1904, Bilibin traveled in the Russian north, where he was fascinated with old wooden architecture and **folklore**. The influences are clearly to be seen in his **illustration**s for Aleksandr **Pushkin**'s *Skazka o care tsaltane* (*The Tale of Tsar Saltan*), which appeared in 1905. By now, Bilibin was also involved with set and costume design for the **theater**. His contribution in 1908 to the staging of Nikolai **Rimsky-Korsakov**'s opera *Zolotoi petushok* (*The Golden Cockerel*), based on Pushkin's fairy tale, became proof of his true mastery. The fact that he had illustrated the story a year earlier was probably significant.

Disappointed in the October Revolution of 1917 and wishing to experience something different, Bilibin went to Egypt in 1920, where he painted for the Greek colony. In 1925, he moved to Paris, where he devoted himself to decoration of private mansions and Orthodox churches. He also illustrated collections of Russian and French folktales. Eleven years later, his longing for Russia became too strong. Bilibin returned to his homeland in 1936 despite Stalin's increasing repression and was immediately appointed professor of graphic art at the Leningrad Institute. Along with the professorship, he continued to work for theatrical productions and illustrated a collection of heroic tales.

Bilibin's style is considered as native to his land, a style that incorporates traditional Russians designs and motifs from the world in which he grew up. He also unites ornament with unexpected perspectives, and his fascination for Japanese print can be discerned. His unerring sense of place, the forests and mountains of old Russia, and his ability to bring a sense of reality into the imaginary make Bilibin simultaneously traditional and innovative.

Further Reading: Golynets, Sergei. *Ivan Bilibin*. Translated by Glenys Ann Kozlov. New York: H. N. Abrams, 1982.

Janina Orlov

Birth

Birth is one of the many reproductive themes commonly found in folktales and fairy tales. The rich variety of plot devices demonstrates the persistence of a global preoccupation with understanding and controlling human fertility. Modern medical science may have unraveled many secrets of the procreative process, but superstition, magic, divine intervention, folk remedy, prayer, and trickery have a long and diverse cultural history as aids to procuring healthy sons and daughters. In many tales, birth validates marital unions and elevates both men and women within social and religious orders. Conversely, problems with conception,

Illustration by Dora Polster for "The Juniper Tree" from
Deutsche Märchen gesammelt durch die Brüder Grimm, ed. M.
Thilo-Luyken (Ebenhausen bei München: Langewiesche-Brandt,
1916; n.p.: Brentano's, n.d.), 184.

superfecundity, unusual pregnancies, maternal **death**, and the delivery of extraordinary offspring signal domestic conflict, lowering status, and necessitating intervention.

Birth in Folktales

Many **folktale**s with birth **motif**s have their roots in ancient creation **myth**s and **legend**s that venerate females for their ability to perform the supreme act of childbearing. These powerful **women** include Semmersuaq of Eskimo lore, Princess Pari in Korean legend, and the **sisters** in the Acoma tribe's "Emerging into the Upper World." **Etiologic tale**s frequently use unusual births to explain the origin of natural phenomena. Examples include the emergence of the Japanese islands in "Izamani and Iganaki," appetite in the West African "Anansi Gives Nyame a Child," and the oddest species on the planet in "How Platypuses Came to Australia." Birth narratives from antiquity employ unusual pregnancies and magical conceptions to herald the arrival of warriors and heroes. A childless **queen** conceives after eating only a portion of the **infertility** remedy intended for her in the Indian tale, "Prince Half-a-Son." Though deformed, her child makes the most of his physical condition, besting his **brothers** and winning the **king**'s crown and the maiden in the end. In Hadland Davis's telling of "Issun-Boshi," a tiny warrior is born to poor and elderly parents; neither his unusual birth nor diminutive stature prevent him from defeating demons, winning a wife, and bringing wealth to his family.

Birth motifs may function as a metaphor for a spiritual or emotional awakening as characters fall, burrow, and push their way through openings to assume new identities and responsibilities. In the Inuit tale "Kakuarshuk," the lonely heroine digs her way to the other side of the world where she endures both physical and emotional torment before becoming a **mother**. However, the vast majority of folktales assume that birth naturally follows **marriage** with the goal of cementing unions and producing heirs. Completion of the reproductive cycle in folk narratives assures the protection of parents in old age as well as a secure future for the **family**, tribe, or kingdom. It is also common to find that folktales identify parents by lineage or vocation since these factors determine social status and marriageability. In the Indian tale "Parwati and the Beggar-Man," a high-ranking Brahman's primary parenting duty is to find suitable husbands for his daughters; when one rejects his aid and selects a beggar outside her class, she is disowned. Often marriage beyond the confines of a proscribed community or class has negative consequences for resulting children; these difficulties are commonly overcome through divine intervention or personal struggle. In the Czech folktale "The Three Golden Hairs," a king commits many crimes as he tries in vain to prevent the marriage of his only daughter to a charcoal-burner's son; the intervention of the boy's godmother and his own brave deeds secure his survival. From the Himalayas comes Kim Narayan's retelling of "The Floating Flower," a tale in which an adopted son's station at birth makes him unsuitable to take his **father**'s crown; his true identity proves that he can assume his birthright. Many marriages succeed despite differences over rank, and both maids and gardeners are able to transcend their stations at birth and marry well, subverting social and economic expectations.

The harsh realities of preindustrial societies also meant that mothers died in childbirth. In the folktale context, this scenario sets the stage for cruel stepmothers, jealous siblings, passive fathers, and valiant survivors. The Russian tales of **Baba Yaga** recount the trials of a young girl whose mother's death and father's remarriage require that she outwit her cruel stepmother through kind and clever attentions to a repulsive witch. "The Frog Maiden" is a Burmese tale of an animal-daughter beloved by her mother but cruelly taunted by her stepmother and sisters. The Sudanese tale "Achol and Her Adoptive Lioness Mother" recounts the life of a girl who is abandoned in the wilderness by her half-brothers, only to find a loving surrogate mother in a devoted lioness.

Twins, multiple births, and too many mouths to feed are reproductive problems that receive a variety of treatments based on cultural and religious attitudes. The introduction to the Norwegian tale "East o' the Sun and West o' the Moon" describes the increased burden placed a family's resources by a surfeit of children. In the Greek tale "Mundig," an infertile wife asks a dervish for a child only to be given so many chickpea babies that she is driven to destroy them; all but one die before she salvages a son to put to work around the farm. The multiple births that open Ludwig Bechstein's "Nine Children at One Time" compel a woman toward evil; she is in such fear of her husband's reaction to her brood that she arranges their murder and is punished for it. But twin sons can also be regarded as an abundance of riches. In the Hebrew tale "The Blessings of a Hidden Saint" and Italo Calvino's Italian "Monkey Palace," competition threatens to divide twins brothers, though in the end they are handsomely rewarded for their mutual love and respect.

Finally there is no greater shame for a folktale couple than to fail at childbearing. In the classic context, the inability to give birth is yet another narrative obstacle to tackle and overcome.

Birth in Literary Fairy Tales

Since the genre's earliest beginnings, pregnancy and childbirth have figured regularly in the **literary fairy tale**. Representations of birth tend to center on four general themes. First, classical fairy tales often begin with reference to a royal couple's infertility, which is cured by a marvelous intervention (the goodwill of a kind **fairy**; some form of bartering on the part of wishful parents or family members; an oracle-like consultation or revelation in a dream; etc.). By way of example, one-quarter of Marie-Catherine d'**Aulnoy**'s tales and one-third of those by Henriette-Julie de Castelnau, Comtesse de **Murat** open with an infertile couple. Second, from the earliest medieval tales to more recent postmodernist variants, pregnancy and childbirth are frequently inflected with a narrative stress on desire and obstacles to desire whether physical or material. In Marie-Jeanne **Lhéritier de Villandon**'s "Discrete Princess or the Adventures of Finette," for instance, three sisters are locked in a tower to protect their virtue. Finette's two sisters each succumb to the seductions of the cunning prince called Rich-Craft and quickly find themselves pregnant. In other tales, the fate of the soon-to-be born child is negatively influenced by the mother's uncontrollable cravings during pregnancy (for example, Giambattista **Basile**'s "Petrosinella" and d'Aulnoy's "White Cat"). From Giovan Francesco **Straparola**'s "Tebaldo" to Jacob and Wilhelm **Grimm**'s "All Fur," and Anne **Sexton**'s "Briar Rose," **incest** similarly presents itself as one of the most insidious desires and often carries with it concerns about birth and bloodlines. Third, pregnancy and birth are frequently marked by **gender** preferences. Little girls seem to be born most frequently to fairy-tale queens. Scholarship, particularly on the late seventeenth-century French fairy tale, has consistently demonstrated the ways in which female-centered narratives—the strategic function of the birth of girls in fairy tales—is part of larger concerns surrounding gender politics in the private and public spheres of the periods in which the tales were written. Finally, monstrosity at birth or shortly following birth is frequently a theme associated with fairy tales in which childbirth and fertility are featured. D'Aulnoy's "Prince Marcassion" and "Babiole" suggest, for example, the power of ill-intentioned fairies to transform and torment the newborn, who will then spend the remainder of the narrative overcoming the obstacles of their monstrous form to find love.

Violence and suffering are often associated with pregnancy and childbirth, particularly in early stories. In d'Aulnoy's tales pregnant women are locked in towers or tormented by vicious fairies ("The Beneficient Frog" and "The Spring Princess"). Others die miserably in childbirth ("Fortunée"). Later tales, such as the Grimm's "Juniper Tree," create direct intersections between **blood** and birth when an infertile woman cuts her finger and makes a **wish** upon the blood that falls on the new snow: "If only I had a child as red as blood and as white as snow."

As this bloody precursor to childbirth in the Grimm's often-brutal tales suggest, fairy-tale births are frequently connected to the specific aesthetics of the fairy tale at specific moments in time. For example, recent scholarship has explored the ways in which tales written before the seventeenth century tend to focus on passive representations of women and their reproductive bodies. In a medieval variant of "Sleeping Beauty," *Perceforest* (c. 1337–44), Zelladine is raped in her sleep and is awakened only with her newborn child sucks on her finger and removes the splinter that had put her to sleep. In seventeenth-century Italy, Basile's "Sun, Moon, and Talia" in *Lo cunto de le cunti* (*The Tale of Tales*, 1634–36) describes a similar somnolent pregnancy, which results instead in twins. Moreover, the frame story of *The Tale of Tales* centers on the cravings of a pregnant woman who, in the last tale of the collection, is buried alive still with child. In these early tales (authored most often by men), pregnancy is generally represented in tandem with a narrative of disempowerment; mothers-to-be have little say over their own bodies. By the late seventeenth century, however, discourses of birth appear to shift to include a new valorization of the female reproductive body and its abilities to trouble existing power structures. As the eighteenth century approached, representations of pregnancy and birth were often bifurcated in ways that either reflect the parodic turn in the tale (mocking, in the case of Jean-Jacques Rousseau's "The Queen Fantasque," the breakneck speed at which children are conceived and born in earlier tales) or in ways that de-emphasize reproduction and **sexuality** more generally in favor of the instructive socialization of young girls in the years leading up to their eventual marriage (for example, the absence of pregnancy and childbirth in tales such as Jeanne-Marie **Leprince de Beaumont**'s "Beauty and the Beast"). It is in the postmodern, feminist rewritings of more traditional tales by writers such as Margaret

Atwood and Angela **Carter** that female protagonists take full control of their own fertility and sensual desire. *See also* Animal Bride, Animal Groom; Changeling; Childhood and Children; Feminist Tales; Postmodernism.

Further Readings: Bottigheimer, Ruth B. "Fertility Control and the Birth of the Modern European Fairy-Tale Heroine." *Fairy Tales and Feminism: New Approaches.* Edited by Donald Haase. Detroit: Wayne State University Press, 2004. 37–51; McGilvray, D. B. "Sexual Power and Fertility in Sri Lanka." *Ethnography of Fertility and Birth.* Edited by Carol P. MacCormack. 2nd edition. Prospect Heights, IL: Waveland Press, 1994. 62–72; Rank, Otto, ed. *Myth of the Birth of the Hero and Other Writings.* Edited by Philip Freund. New York: Vintage Books, 1964. 12–96; Röhrich, Lutz. *Folktales and Reality.* Translated by Peter Tokofsky. Bloomington: Indiana University Press, 1991. 72–73, 104–107; Tatar, Maria. "Daughters of Eve: Fairy-Tale Heroines and Their Seven Sins." *Off with Their Heads: Fairy Tales and the Culture of Childhood.* Princeton, NJ: Princeton University Press, 1993. 94–119; Tucker, Holly. *Pregnant Fictions: Childbirth and the Fairy Tale in Early-Modern France.* Detroit: Wayne State University Press, 2003.

Joanna Beall and Holly Tucker

Bland, Edith. *See* Nesbit, E.

Das blaue Licht (1932)

Directed by Leni Riefenstahl, *Das blaue Licht* (*The Blue Light*, 1932) is a film evocation of the German folklore tradition (though not related to the **Grimm** tale of that name) using visual language more than verbal to tell a tale of treasure lost and found.

In the 1920s, former dancer Leni Riefenstahl became an established international star through roles in mountain films such as *Die weiße Hölle von Piz Palü* (*The White Hell of Piz Palu*, directed by Arnold Fanck, 1929). Having thus learned something of filmmaking, she desired to move away from Fanck's realist narratives in modern settings and instead create a romantic **legend** in harmony with the beauty and purity of the Dolomite mountains. This aspiration led to *The Blue Light*.

Coscripted with Marxist writer Béla **Balázs**, the film shows how, long ago, in a poor mountain village called Santa Maria, the inhabitants see blue rays emanating from a perilous peak at every full moon. Young men, drawn to reach it, fall and die; only Junta, a persecuted outcast (Riefenstahl), knows a way up. One day she is followed, and her secret route discovered. Scaling the peak, villagers find a cavern filled with crystals—the source of the reflected blue light—that bring wealth to Santa Maria. Horrified by the desecration, Junta loses her footing and plunges to her **death**, to be commemorated over the years as the savior of the village.

Thematically, the film is more complex and contradictory than legends from the **oral tradition**. Junta's self-imposed mission to guard the crystals foreshadows later environmental concerns, while raising a political question about the private hoarding of assets that could benefit society. Similarly, when Junta is alive, the villagers cast stones and bar her from the church; but when she is dead they venerate her **memory**.

Equally important to Riefenstahl were the visuals, her initial impetus. She constantly downplayed dialogue and sought to build the mood and tell the tale by finding, or creating, beautiful black-and-white images: sunlight on waterfall spray; Junta in silhouette climbing a sheer rock face, backlit by the moon; reflections in shimmering water; lanterns carried through the dark; mist rising; the sun's rays piercing trees; the long shadows of men on the move; the grizzled granite faces of the villagers; crystals scintillating in the cavern; and the moon slowly disappearing behind clouds.

The Blue Light brought Riefenstahl critical and commercial success. One of many who admired its technique was Adolf Hitler, who asked her to direct documentaries about two Nazi party rallies. The results, notably *Triumph des Willens* (*Triumph of the Will*, 1934), associated her name forever with Nazi propaganda. In the aftermath of World War II, Riefenstahl spent four years in military detention and was judged guilty of having had Nazi sympathies, after which she was unable to raise money for film production. She did however produce a reedited version of *The Blue Light*, under the new title *Die Hexe von Santa Maria* (*The Witch of Santa Maria*, 1952). *See also* Film and Video.

Further Readings: Bach, Steven. *Leni: The Life and Work of Leni Riefenstahl*. New York: Knopf, 2007; Berg-Pan, Renata. *Leni Riefenstahl*. Boston: Twayne, 1980; Hinton, David B. *The Films of Leni Riefenstahl*. Lanham, MD: Scarecrow Press, 2000; Riefenstahl, Leni. *Leni Riefenstahl–A Memoir*. New York: St. Martin's Press, 1992.

Terry Staples

Block, Francesca Lia (1962–)

Francesca Lia Block is an American author of magic-realist novels and **adaptation**s of **myth**s and fairy tales. Block made her debut with *Weetzie Bat* (1989), a bestselling young adult novel, followed by several sequels in which Block relocates fairy-tale elements, such as three **wish**es or a gingerbread house, to twentieth-century Los Angeles. The same setting is used for some stories in *The Rose and the Beast* (2000), Block's collection of nine fairy-tale adaptations. She establishes a contrast between the fairy-tale realm and harsh reality: in "Charm," **Sleeping Beauty** becomes a drug addict, stabbed with a needle by Old-Woman-Heroin; in "Wolf," **Little Red Riding Hood** murders her sexually abusive stepfather.

Although Block's language appears simple, her stories are not, often mixing several layers of reality, dream, and magic. Most tales are rewritten from the point of view of a female character, to which Block adds psychological depth: **Cinderella** toils hard and tells stories to silence the voices in her head, and Thumbelina's mother is overprotective because she has lost several babies. Female bonding is a central theme in all of Block's tales, as is the healing power of love and friendship. By contrast, traditional patterns and norms for **family**, **gender**, and identity are shown to be arbitrary and restrictive. *See also* Feminism; Feminist Tales; Gay and Lesbian Fairy Tales; Magical Realism; Young Adult Fiction.

Further Readings: Russel, David L. "Young Adult Fairy Tales for the New Age: Francesca Lia Block's *The Rose and the Beast*." *Children's Literature in Education* 33.2 (2002): 107–15; Susina, Jan. "The Rebirth of the Postmodern Flâneur: Notes on the Postmodern Landscape of Francesca Lia Block's *Weetzie Bat*." *Marvels & Tales* 16 (2002): 188–200.

Vanessa Joosen

Blood

"The life of all flesh is its blood" (Lev. 17.14)—this hoary notion permeates **folklore**, from Homer to modern **wonder tale**s and **fairy tale**s. Because the life juice conspicuously flows, wonder tales use it to depict life's streams and transitions—a central preoccupation in this genre absorbed with **initiation**.

Wonder tales depict blood flows in two basic guises. First, there is the theme of human incorporation through **cannibalism**, which mostly depicts the blood of **women** circulating down the generations. Indeed, wonder-tale heroines regularly incorporate, or otherwise inherit, the life juice of their elders. This pattern suggests that women bear the essence of life, manifest in blood, which (being of limited supply) must quit old women to invest younger ones.

Second, blood spills out in life crises, in sex-specific ways. Women present lifeblood on menarche, defloration, and giving **birth**; **men** relate to spilled blood in wars and hunts. In both cases, liminal periods show as enchantment, which is usually a blood condition. This is an important point. A pubertal maiden will fall into red-tinted enchantment (possibly asleep or otherwise alienated) in her **father**'s abode or else will appear shut in a tower/well/glass mountain, or yet she will be delivered to some lunar beast, such as a **dragon**. Moreover, virtually all brides undergo blood-related enchantment after giving birth. Bridegrooms, on the other hand, fall into maternal regression while spilling blood. An animal bridegroom will slay every bride his mother brings him, or else will leave his bride and retreat to his **mother**'s realm in the otherworld, there to spend his days hunting (often wearing a blood-stained shirt). Newlywed **king**s—while the wife gives birth—retreat to war and exclusive communication with mother.

This means enchanted heroes and heroines are under the empire of their own blood, in the twofold sense that they are entangled in kin knots and actually shed blood (in sex-specific ways, as observed). Note one consequence: If enchantment is a lapse into both bleeding and kin confinement, then active married life and disenchantment are as one. Indeed, not only does the disenchanting kiss of Prince Charming involve "reaping the fruits of love" (to use Giambattista **Basile**'s florid expression from "Sun, Moon, and Talia"), but maidens, to disenchant a snake **prince**, eventually share his bed, too.

Because blood is at the core of initiation in wonder tales, and myriad themes build on it, blood enchantment is variously expressed. In other words, there is blood symbolism in wonder tales, and awareness of this is requisite. One foremost blood image is flowers. The connection is evident in the constant semantic convergence between *flow* and *flower* (English), *fluer* and *fleur* (French), *fluir* and *flor* (Portuguese), and *Blut* and *Blüte* (German). Along this semantic drift, any wonder-tale maiden associated with flowers is marked to see her blood flow. Beauty's request of a rose seals her fate to marry the Beast; **Little Red Riding Hood** is often laden with flowers as she enters the forest house, there to join a **werewolf** or **wolf** in bed; and another flowery maiden, Brier Rose (that is, **Sleeping Beauty**), pricks a finger at age fifteen, then falls asleep until the elected husband passes through her blooming flowers to, literally, deflower her (to which both Basile and independent oral versions testify).

These examples actually show two other symbols. One is finger slashing. Just as Brier Rose's pricked finger foreshadows defloration, so does the pricked finger of **Snow White**'s mother presage conception. The other is blushing sleep. Enchanted Sleeping Beauty displays carnation cheeks and coral lips, just as Snow White presents red cheeks.

Although redness as a rule connotes blood, it need not appear. In another trend, both enclosure in round structures (such as towers and wells) and display of disheveled **hair** (or shaggy furs) are constant images of bloody enchantment. Both sets of images converge in maiden abductions by dragons (or serpents, or werewolves, or cognate figures). Dragons, indeed, belong in a host of lunar figures standing for cyclic time. Such figures unify the dynamics of sloughing snakes, alternating werewolves, moon phases, and women's menstrual cycles under the common idea of renewal through **death**. In this view, periodic bleeding amounts to skin shifting and to enchantment, understood as death-in-life, followed by renascence. This is why pubertal heroines appear wearing beastly cloaks, are absconded by dragons or werewolves, or else turned into snakes and the like, whereas disenchantment happens in the guise of hair grooming and combing, shedding of ragged cloaks or furs, exiting a dragon's lair/body/ shape—and, of course, defloration. Muteness and blindness are also forms of enchantment, and heroines so afflicted intimate blood one way or the other.

The centrality of blood abides in Angela **Carter**'s postmodern rewriting of fairy tales. In this universe, Snow White, on fading out of existence into white snow, leaves behind a defloration bloodstain and a rose. Similarly, Red Riding Hood is white as snow insofar as she does not bleed; but the shawl granny hands down to her is as red as the blood she must spill and is also "the colour of poppies, the colour of sacrifices, the colour of her menses" (Carter, "The Company of Wolves"). In the same trend, it is after the dead mother transfuses her own blood to **Cinderella** that the latter can find a man ("Ashputtle or the Mother's Ghost"). And Carter's rendering of the **Bluebeard** tale ("The Bloody Chamber" from her anthology of the same name) posits blood at the innermost core of the mysteries of **marriage**.

Overall, Carter's use of a stained key for transposing immemorial themes into tales for modern times is true to the initiation pattern of wonder tales, and it establishes creative **transformation** between heretofore wonder tales and postmodern fairy tales. Because blood conspicuously flows, tales—old and new—use it to say "transitions" with flowers. *See also* Animal Bride, Animal Groom; Gender; Postmodernism; Sex, Sexuality.

Further Readings: Cardigos, Isabel. *In and Out of Enchantment: Blood Symbolism and Gender in Portuguese Fairytales.* Helsinki: Academia Scientiarum Fennica, 1996; Carter, Angela. *Burning your Boats: The Collected Short Stories.* Harmondsworth: Penguin Books, 1995; Knight, Chris. *Decoding Fairy Tales.* London: Lionel Sims/Radical Anthropology Group, 2004. http://www.radicalanthropologygroup.org/ pub_decoding_fairytales.pdf.

Francisco Vaz da Silva

Bluebeard

First appearing as "La barbe bleue" in Charles **Perrault**'s *Histoires ou contes du temps passé* (*Stories or Tales of Times Past,* 1697), the story of "Bluebeard" is in the cycle known as Maiden-Killer (ATU 312). In Perrault's tale, a wealthy serial murderer of wives puts his latest spouse to a test of obedience by giving her the key to a **forbidden room** but admonishing her not to enter. Driven by curiosity, she unlocks the door to discover a bloody chamber filled with the remains of her predecessors. When she drops the key in horror, the indelible bloodstain ultimately betrays her trespass. Her brothers rescue her and kill Bluebeard. Theses theme of prohibition and **transgression**, the fatal effects of curiosity, and the questioning of the happily-ever-after view of **marriage** form the staple of critical reception that continues to spin off rewritings and **adaptation**s.

Perrault's tale was widely translated and retold. Available as early as 1760 in German, "Bluebeard" appeared across the European continent in collections from England to Russia. Although Jacob and Wilhelm **Grimm** included it in the 1812 volume of their *Kinder- und Hausmärhcne* (*Children's and Household Tales*), they subsequently abandoned it as too

French. Later editions of Grimms' tales reflected two narrative strands: the clever girl's triumph in "Der Räuberbräutigam" ("The Robber Bridegroom") and "Fitchers Vogel" ("Fitcher's Bird") and the dire consequences of female curiosity in "Marienkind" ("The Virgin Mary's Child").

Folklorists account for variants of "Bluebeard" from Catalonia to Iceland, Greece to Puerto Rico and even the West Indies. The contents of the forbidden chamber may be dead previous wives, bodies of unspecified **gender**, body parts, a **prince**, and in one **variant**, the portal to hell. The indelible **blood**stain may mark a key ("Bluebeard"), an egg ("Fitcher's Bird"), or occasionally a ball or rose. Sundry helpers or her own resourcefulness effects the rescue of the endangered maiden. The various versions remain relatively stable in the presence of the bloody chamber, the breaking of a taboo, and the deliverance of the woman.

There has been wide speculation on Perrault's sources. Many scholars suggest the **ballad**s of maiden kidnappers circulating in Europe in the sixteenth century or the "Mr. Fox" tale in England. Others believe Perrault, who wrote hagiographies, may have been inspired by the St. Gilda **legend** recounting how the sixth-century saint revived the beheaded Tryphine, slain by her husband Comorre/Cunmar when he discovered she was with child. (Interestingly, the vignette for "Bluebeard" in the first edition of Perrault's *Stories* resembles the popular iconography of female martyrdoms, and a 1704 fresco in a chapel dedicated to St. Tryphine in St. Nicolas de Bieuzy shows six scenes from Perrault's story). The most commonly cited source is the historic figure of Gilles de Rais (1404–40), a one-time comrade-in-arms to Joan of Arc (he was also a notorious pederast and murdered more than 140 children). This interpretation gained currency with the late Romantic revival of de Rais as a literary figure. Still others focus on the title of the tale and cite explanations of the name. In the sixteenth century, "Barbe-bleue" signified a man with a raven black beard, a seducer of **women**; the Grimms speculated that Bluebeard, in search of a cure for his blue beard, bathed in vats of blood for medicinal purposes.

Stories about sinister spouses, forbidden knowledge gained at great cost, and the effects of female curiosity have many mythical, biblical, and literary precursors in Western civilization. Bluebeard's wife has sisters in Eve, Lot's wife, Psyche, and Pandora. Forbidden-chamber stories are also common: in Giambattista Basile's *Lo cunto de li cunti* (*The Tale of Tales*, 1634–36), Princess Marchetta may enter any room but the one for which she holds the key, and Prince Agib, in the *Arabian Nights*, has 100 keys to 100 doors and may open all, save the golden one. One critic suggests a link between the murderous Bluebeard and **King** Shahriyar from that Arabian collection, although it was not available in French until seven years after Perrault's work.

"Bluebeard" has experienced a rich tradition in the performance and visual arts. Premiered in 1789 as an **opera** by Michel-Jean Sedaine and André Ernest Modeste Grétry, the "Bluebeard" libretto continued to inspire adaptations and other works throughout the nineteenth and twentieth centuries. Maurice **Maeterlinck**'s 1899 play *Ariane et Barbe-bleue* inspired operas by Paul Dukas (1907) and Béla **Bartók** (1918), which in turn inspired Pina Bausch's ballet of 1977. Numerous plays appeared, starting with Ludwig **Tieck**'s *Ritter Blaubart* (*Knight Bluebeard*) in 1797. The tale even came to the United States in the form of musicals and melodramas from England. Between 1785 and 1815, "Bluebeard" took sixth in the number of stagings in the five principal American theatrical centers, with 163 performances. (These required extensive costuming and set designs, reflecting the **illustration** history of the tale with a scimitar-wielding, pantalooned "foreigner.") Sometimes the material was parodied, as is evidenced by a number of highly popular German comedies; sometimes its proscriptive allure castigating female curiosity was exploited, as in the nineteenth-century American *tableaux vivants* emphasizing scenes of the duly punished curious women and their passive submission to death. Bluebeard has even made it to the silver screen, as early as 1901 with Georges **Méliès**'s nine-minute, silent comic version, in 1947 with Charlie Chaplin's *Monsieur Verdoux,* and in numerous other **Bluebeard films**.

One major aspect of the tale—the focus on the female's breaking of the taboo rather than the serial crimes of the husband—has been the fulcrum of feminist rewritings. Perhaps the most characteristic and influential postmodern and feminist fairy-tale retellings are the title stories of Angela **Carter**'s *The Bloody Chamber* (1979) and Margaret **Atwood**'s *Bluebeard's Egg* (1983). *See also* Dance; Feminism; Feminist Tales; Punishment and Reward.

Further Readings: Davies, Mererid Puw. *The Tale of Bluebeard in German Literature from the Eighteenth Century to the Present.* Oxford: Oxford University Press, 2001; Hartland, E. Sidney. "The Forbidden Chamber." *Folk-Lore Journal* 3 (1885): 193–242; Tatar, Maria. *Secrets beyond the Door: The Story of Bluebeard and his Wives.* Princeton, NJ: Princeton University Press, 2004.

Shawn C. Jarvis

Bluebeard Films

The traffic between fairy tales and films has always been heavy, but the **Bluebeard** story has made its way with unprecedented speed and reliability into cinematic culture. Unlike "**Snow White**" or "The Little Mermaid," "Bluebeard" appears in adult features ranging from romantic comedies to *film noir* and seems just as much at ease in the mode of burlesque slapstick as high horror. Seductive and barbaric, charismatic and deceptive, charming and secretive, the character creates melodrama and mystery wherever he goes. His wife, by turns curious and shrewd, anxious and nervous, or crafty and sly, is driven by a desire for forbidden knowledge about her husband and his past. "Bluebeard" deviates from the fairy-tale norm by beginning with marriage rather than ending with it. It explores the dark side of the social institution, showing how it can be haunted by the threat of murder.

That the Bluebeard story lends itself to the medium of cinema becomes evident not only from the frequency of its **adaptation** but also from its early appearance on screen. Georges **Méliès**, perhaps under the influence of Jacques Offenbach's 1866 operetta *Barbe-Bleue*, capitalized on opportunities for comic inflections of the horror story in his 1901 film. Méliès himself played the film's Bluebeard, who perishes in the end under the swords of the wife's **brothers**. The film ends with high-spirited verve in multiple marriages, after the dead wives are resurrected by a goblin who provides suitable marriage partners for all seven of the now-merry widows.

A precursor of cinematic horror plots, the Bluebeard story gives us a killer who is propelled by psychotic rage, the abject victims of his frenzied compulsion to repeat, a "final girl" who either saves herself or arranges her own rescue, and the classic "terrible place" that harbors grisly evidence of the killer's derangement. Yet Bluebeard remained the stuff of comedy until the 1940s, with two versions of the witty and theatrical *Bluebeard's Eighth Wife* made in 1923 and 1938—the latter by Ernst Lubitsch. It was only during the war era that Hollywood began to take Bluebeard seriously, recycling the story in ways that are not always easy to detect.

In the 1940s, Holly-wood began staging end-less variations on the anxiety and excitement attending marriage to a stranger. This was, after all, a time of social crisis, when women were marry-ing men who were real strangers (soldiers anxious to take vows before going off to war) and when it was dawning on women that the men to whom they were married had become strangers (soldiers who had experienced the dark horrors of combat). Blue-beard provided the perfect plot apparatus for working through marital crises experienced by men and

David Niven and Claudette Colbert in the 1938 film *Bluebeard's Eighth Wife.* [Paramount Pictures/Photofest]

women whose lives had been unsettled by the war.

The proliferation of Bluebeard films in the 1940s, beginning with Alfred Hitchcock's *Rebecca* (1940) through George Cukor's *Gaslight* (1944) to Fritz Lang's *Secret beyond the Door* (1948), is mirrored in the multiple titles used to designate them: "paranoid woman's film," "wife-in-distress cycle," "woman-plus-habitation," "gaslight genre," and "Freudian feminist melodrama." What is new about these films is their emphasis on the woman as in-vestigator and her commitment to finding the key to the mystery of her husband's behavior, even as she is menaced by the threat of murder. Active and adventurous, Bluebeard's wife becomes a sleuth with Freudian flair, "a love-smitten analyst playing a dream detective," as Dr. Peterson is called in Hitchcock's *Spellbound* (1945).

Cukor's *Gaslight*, with Ingrid Bergman in the role of the beleaguered Paula, explicitly refers to the Bluebeard story in its opening scenes and builds its plot on the tension between terror and desire that characterizes Bluebeard films. Lang's *Secret beyond the Door* shows the wife as Freudian analyst, asking herself "What goes on in his mind?" and worrying about why her husband keeps that mind "locked." To solve the mystery of Mark's strange behavior, Celia must probe and reveal her husband's secrets, undoing the harm done by childhood trauma. If Lang's *Secret beyond the Door* emphasized the role of the wife as ana-lyst, other films like Hitchcock's *Notorious* (1946) position the wife as professional investi-gator, a sleuth who uses her investigative skills to get to the bottom of a mystery even as she succumbs to the charms of her coconspirator.

If Bluebeard's wife dominates films of the 1940s, her husband emerges as something of a cultural hero in movies of the postwar era, with Charlie Chaplin's *Monsieur Verdoux* (1947) setting the tone. He portrays a man who, even when he murders, does so for the sake of a higher cause. Hitchcock's *Shadow of a Doubt* (1943) takes up the same themes, with a murderer who may be less sympathetic, but who manages to bring glamour and excitement to small-town America.

Bluebeard's reputation as a lady-killer in both senses of the term was emphasized in a remarkable series of films that engage with the relationship between artistic creativity and sexual performance. An artist who needs **violence** to reinvigorate his art, the Bluebeard figures in Edgar G. Ulmer's *Bluebeard* (1944), Peter Godfrey's *The Two Mrs. Carrolls* (1947), and Edward Dmytryk's *Bluebeard* (1972) are all charismatic characters for whom the sacrifice of beautiful women becomes the necessary condition for creative success.

Jane Campion's *The Piano* (1993), like many Bluebeard films, was not explicitly planned as a reworking of the Bluebeard story, although Campion quickly became aware of how powerfully the film had guided her scriptwriting. Campion offers a feminist critique of the Bluebeard story by reversing the roles of the characters, with a wife who harbors a secret and a husband who is driven by curiosity and the desire for mastery. *The Piano* unsettles the **gender** roles delegated to husband and wife in the Bluebeard story and reconfigures the nexus of desire, passion, trust, and betrayal embedded in the story. It is joined by many other films ranging from Helma Sanders-Brahms's *Deutschland, bleiche Mutter* (*Germany, Pale Mother,* 1980) to Zhang Yimou's *Dà hóng dēnglóng gāogāo guà* (*Raise the Red Lantern,* 1991) that alter, adapt, transform, and borrow from a folktale that helps us with the cultural work of understanding what can go wrong in marriages. *See also* Feminism; Feminist Tales; Film and Video; Freud, Sigmund; Opera.

Further Readings: Benson, Stephen. *Cycles of Influence: Fiction, Folktale, Theory.* Detroit: Wayne State University Press, 2003; Davies, Mererid Puw. *The Tale of Bluebeard in German Literature from the Eighteenth Century to the Present.* New York: Oxford University Press, 2001; Doane, Mary Ann. *The Desire to Desire: The Woman's Film of the 1940s.* Bloomington: Indiana University Press, 1987; Hermansson, Casie. *Reading Feminist Intertextuality through Bluebeard Stories.* Lewiston, NY: Edwin Mellen, 2001; Tatar, Maria. *Secrets beyond the Door: The Story of Bluebeard and His Wives.* Princeton, NJ: Princeton University Press, 2004.

Maria Tatar

The Blue Light. See Das blaue Licht

Bly, Robert (1926–)

Major American poet and translator Robert Bly is also the author of the bestselling *Iron John: A Book about Men* (1990), which explicates the fairy tale "Iron John" and inspired the late twentieth-century men's movement in the United States. In this and subsequent books, Bly spells out mythopoetic interpretations of fairy tales, finding in them a key to understanding psychosocial struggles, especially as played out in American society. "Iron John" is thus a tale about the male's need to reclaim the inner "wild man" to secure his psychic health in the face (or wake) of the women's movement. In an important critique, Jack **Zipes** argues that Bly appropriates the tale to create a new **myth** rather than interpreting the tale in accordance with the historical circumstances of the tale's production.

Bly's *The Sibling Society* (1996) identifies an increasing repudiation of authority figures as a problem in both Western and non-Western culture. Here Bly turns to "Jack and the Beanstalk" to examine the problematic situation of living in a fatherless society and to critique a consumer culture whose rampant appetites are akin to those of the Giant. Bly also invokes the Hindu myth of Ganesha's creation as a worthwhile study of father-son relations. *The Maiden King*, which Bly published in 1998 with coauthor and longtime collaborator Marion Woodman, draws from the Russian tale "The Maiden Czar" to promote the psychosocial value of uniting archetypically masculine and feminine principles. *See also* Archetype; Father; Feminism; Men; Women.

Further Reading: Zipes, Jack. "Spreading Myths about Iron John." *Fairy Tale as Myth/Myth as Fairy Tale.* Lexington: University of Kentucky Press, 1994. 96–118.

Lori Schroeder Haslem

Boccaccio, Giovanni (1313–1375)

The Italian writer and humanist Giovanni Boccaccio authored significant works in virtually all genres. His masterwork, the *Decameron* (1349–50), a framed **novella** collection, greatly influenced European storytelling. The **frame narrative**, modeled on Eastern collections such as the ***Arabian Nights***, recounts the ravages of the plague (the Black Death of 1348), from which a group of ten noble youths take refuge in the countryside outside Florence and console themselves in **storytelling**. The influences on Boccaccio's work were multiple, including, as for many medieval authors, popular folktales and fairy tales. It was in the stories of fortune, love, and human enterprise of the *Decameron* that these traditions entered full force into Italian narrative.

In particular, the tales of Day 2, dedicated to the workings of fortune, and Day 5, love stories with happy endings, often incorporate structural elements of the fairy tale. Tale 2.3, for example, is a rags-to-riches story of three **brothers**, sons of messer Tebaldo of Florence; and "Andreuccio of Perugia" (2.5) includes a tripartite series of trials. Others include "Giletta of Nerbona" (3.9), which features a savvy young woman who works a difficult situation to her advantage. The last tale, "Griselda and the Marquis of Saluzzo" (10.10), combines **motif**s common to the **Cinderella** and **Beauty and the Beast tale type**s and found later rewritings in the work of Geoffrey **Chaucer**, Giambattista **Basile**, and Charles **Perrault**. *See also* Italian Tales; Middle Ages; Pasolini, Pier Paolo.

Further Readings: Papio, Michael, and Massimo Riva, eds. *Decameron Web.* http://www.brown.edu/ Departments/Italian_Studies/dweb/dweb.shtml; Petrini, Mario. *La fiaba di magia nella letteratura italiana.* Udine: Del Bianco Editore, 1983.

Nancy Canepa

Böhl de Faber, Cecilia (1796–1877)

Born in Switzerland of a Spanish-Irish mother and a German father, Cecilia Böhl de Faber—who used the pen name Fernán Caballero—is one of the great **women** writers of nineteenth-century Spain. Having spent most of her life in Andalusia (southern Spain), she became steeped in that province's **oral tradition**s and her interest in national **folklore** led her to give written form and legitimacy to many of the Spanish **folktales** and **fairy tales** of her time.

Although many of her stories originally appeared in literary magazines and newspapers, she collected them and released them in two important books: *Cuentos y poesías populares andaluzas* (*Popular Andalusian Tales and Poems*, 1859) and *Cuentos de encantamiento*

(*Stories of Enchantment*, 1877). Both have ties to tales that exist in other Western cultures and countries. *Popular Andalusian Tales and Poems* contains an important preface in which Böhl de Faber makes reference to the "inexhaustible popular muse," that is, the oral traditions from which she gathered the nuclei of her stories, fashioned and reworked to her literary tastes. In the same preface, she states: "The mine [Andalusia] from which we have dug these precious materials is not the only one in existence; each province, each town, each village has its own, and they are beginning to be worked." On a lesser scale she was a collector like the brothers **Grimm**, and credit is due her for making the first methodical attempt in modern times to begin preserving the rich vein of **Spanish tales** as envisioned by Juan **Valera**.

Popular Andalusian Tales and Poems contains stories reflecting Spanish **variant**s of the European folktale tradition. "Las ánimas" ("The Souls in Purgatory") is a variant of **tale type** ATU 501, The Three Old Spinning Women, and stands as an example of her adaptation of traditional folktales found in other cultures. "The Souls in Purgatory" is especially reminiscent of a **spinning** tale by the Brothers Grimm, "Die drei Spinnerinnen" ("The Three Spinners," 1819). In Böhl de Faber's version, a hapless girl must please a wealthy gentleman, and in the Grimms' tale she must please a queen, but in both versions three supernatural helpers come to the girl's aid. In Grimms' tale, the helpers take the form of three deformed women representing fortuitous intervention or possibly female solidarity, whereas in Böhl de Faber's variant they appear as three souls from purgatory, suggesting faith in salvation.

In another tale, "Juan Soldado" (literally, "John Soldier"), the title character leaves the military with very little recompense after many years of faithful service to his king. However, because of the soldier's generosity to Saint Peter and Jesus, Christ rewards him in such a manner that he is able to fill his knapsack with anything, at will, thereby thwarting **devil**s big and small and, in the end, browbeating Saint Peter to enter heaven. "Juan Holgado y la Muerte" ("Juan Holgado and Death") draws on the tale type of godfather-death (ATU 332) that is found in Grimm, Antonio de **Trueba**'s work, and other European tale collections. The tale relates the adventures of a bumpkin-turned-doctor as a result of his pact with **death**. "La suegra del diablo" ("The Devil's Mother-in-Law") is the story of a lazy girl whose mother exclaims in frustration when her daughter mentions marriage, "I hope to God you marry the devil!" Lo and behold, shortly thereafter, the evil one appears in disguise, woos the girl, and they do indeed marry. However, it is to his eternal regret, as his mother-in-law bests him by capturing him in a bottle.

In *Stories of Enchantment*, Böhl de Faber continued to make her own contributions to the genres and tale types populating the European folktale tradition. "La niña de los tres maridos" ("The Girl with Three Husbands") and "Bella-Flor" ("Lovely-Flower") are tales with a strong moral thrust. The first tells of a headstrong daughter who outwits her **father**, and the second features a talking horse and holds that virtue and goodness will be rewarded. "El pájaro de la verdad" ("The Bird of Truth") is a much more substantial tale that shares elements with Eustache Le Noble's "L'oiseau de vérité" ("The Bird of Truth," 1700) and to a lesser extent "De drei Vügelkens" ("The Three Little Birds," 1815) from the Grimms' collection. Central to Böhl de Faber's version is that nobody can kill the Bird of Truth because it cannot die, and if it cannot die, the truth cannot die. "Los deseos" ("The Wishes") is a variation on Charles **Perrault**'s "Les souhaits ridicules" ("The Foolish Wishes," 1693), and includes the incident of the sausage attaching itself to the angry wife's nose.

Further Readings: Böhl de Faber, Cecilia. "The Bird of Truth." Translated by Robert M. Fedorchek. *Marvels & Tales* 16 (2002): 73–83; _____. "The Devil's Mother-in-Law." Translated by Robert M.

Fedorchek. *Marvels & Tales* 15 (2001): 192–201; Fedorchek, Robert M., trans. *Stories of Enchantment from Nineteenth-Century Spain*. Lewisburg, NY: Bucknell University Press, 2002; Klibbe, Lawrence. *Fernán Caballero*. New York: Twayne, 1973.

Robert M. Fedorchek

Bolte, Johannes (1858–1937)

Johannes Bolte was a German scholar who represented in his time a new generation of narrative scholarship. Bolte's studies in Berlin and Leipzig embraced not only classical philology and archeology but also German literature, especially that of the sixteenth and seventeenth centuries. His expertise in diverse disciplines and genres and his knowledge of both folk traditions and literature—coupled with his comparative methodology—enabled him to make significant contributions to the comparative study of folktales and their **motif**s.

A prolific scholar, Bolte published many important works, including editions of sixteenth-century jestbooks and humorous tales that paved the way for new research on these genres. His most momentous work, however, is found in the annotations to Jacob and Wilhelm **Grimm**'s fairy tales that he published in collaboration with the Slavic scholar Jiří **Polívka**. Published in five volumes between 1913 and 1932, the *Anmerkungen zu den Kinder- und Hausmärchen der Brüder Grimm* (*Annotations to Grimms' Children's and Household Tales*) significantly expands the Grimms' own annotations by further documenting sources and international **variant**s of the brothers' tales. This was especially critical at the time, when scholars practicing the **historic-geographic method** were interested in documenting **tale type**s and tracking their **diffusion**. In a broader context, however, the work's importance lies in its serving as a foundational resource for the comparative study of European folktales.

During his career of nearly sixty years, Bolte also served as president of the Berliner Vereins für Volkskunde (Berlin Society for Folklore) and edited the *Zeitschrift des Vereins für Volkskunde* (*Journal of the Society for Folklore*). His distinguished scholarship earned him membership in the Preußische Akademie der Wissenschaften (Prussian Academy of Sciences). *See also* Köhler, Reinhold.

Further Reading: Bolte, Johannes, and Georg Polívka. *Anmerkungen zu den Kinder- und Hausmärchen der Brüder Grimm*. 5 volumes. 1913–32. Hildesheim: Olms, 1963.

Donald Haase

Bonardi, Luigi. *See* Malerba, Luigi

Boratav, Pertev Naili (1907–1998)

A renowned theorist and dedicated teacher of Turkish **folklore**, Pertev Naili Boratav founded folkloristics as an academic discipline in Turkey. Boratav's attempts to institutionalize folklore were misunderstood by extremist nationalists, who accused him of disseminating socialist ideas and forced his move to Paris in 1952. Boratav's folktale research was shaped by his professors Georges Dumézil and Fuad Köprülü and by the writings of Arnold van Gennep. In his study of the epic *Köroğlu* (1931), Boratav considered the sociohistorical factors that shaped the work as well as its **performance**.

In *Halk hikayeleri halk hikayeciliği* (*Folk Narratives and Folk Narration*, 1946), Boratav deals with the composition and performance of *hikaye*, a narrative form of prose and poetry. Not widely known among English-speaking folklorists, Boratav's book on the *hikaye* anticipates the study of folklore as performance. Modifying the methodology of Antti **Aarne**, Boratav and coauthor Wolfram Eberhard published *Typen türkischer Volksmärchen* (*Types of the Turkish Folktale*, 1953), a major contribution to the classification of Turkish folktales. Whereas Aarne aimed at an overarching classification of international folklore texts, Eberhard and Boratav argued that folklorists could pursue cross-cultural research only after understanding the materials of a particular culture. Boratav published numerous editions of folklore texts, studies of **oral tradition,** and works on method and theory in folklore. His important books on Turkish tales have been translated into European languages.

Further Readings: Birkalan, Hande. "Pertev Naili Boratav and His Contributions to Turkish Folklore." Master's thesis. Indiana University, 1995; _____. "Nachrichten: Pertev Naili Boratav (1907–1998)." *Fabula* 45 (2004): 113–17; _____. "Pertev Naili Boratav, Turkish Politics, and the University Events." *Turkish Studies Association Bulletin* 25.1 (2001): 39–60.

Hande Birkalan-Gedik

Borges, Jorge Luis (1899–1986)

Jorge Luis Borges was an Argentinean writer of **poetry**, essays, and short stories who drew inspiration from **myth** and the tales of many different cultures and traditions. One of the most important books resonating within his work is the *Arabian Nights*. Most famous for his story collections *Ficciones* (*Fictions,* 1944) and *El Aleph* (*The Aleph,* 1949), both of which can be described as literature of the fantastic, Borges is also well known for short stories such as "Las ruinas circulares" ("The Circular Ruins," 1941), "Pierre Menard, autor del Quijote" ("Pierre Menard, Author of the *Quixote*," 1941), and "El jardín de senderos que se bifurcan" ("The Garden of the Forking Paths," 1941). His poetry, which he wrote over a sixty-year period, is less well-known, but considered by many to be some of his best work.

One of the most innovative writers of Latin American fiction and poetry, and an early practitioner of **magical realism**, Borges exerted a powerful force in reforming the Spanish language. His prose is precise, compact, and direct, at times deceptively simple, yet abounds in psychological and philosophical subtlety as well as the frequent use of **archetype**, **intertextuality**, and **frame narrative**. Throughout his career as a writer, Borges maintained a consistent interest in a number of topics. These concerns can be characterized as falling into two general categories. The first is a love of things Argentine, such as the country's great plains, the Pampa, and their cowboys (called gauchos), whose proximity to **death** Borges often portrays, and which seems to have fascinated him. Despite Borges's fascination with the Pampan landscape and its violent and elemental gauchos, his broader attraction to Argentine life and literature found its focus in Buenos Aires, a city he both loved and knew intimately and where he spent much of his life.

Borges's second enduring interest can be classified as philosophical and a likely precursor of **postmodernism**, though his thought ranges widely over metaphysics, history, religion, **art**, and literature. Borges was an erudite individual, and early on he gained a reputation as a difficult writer who wrote not for the masses but for a select few scholars or literary critics. Borges's short stories are nevertheless accessible to those willing to approach them patiently, and they offer insight into the one of the most creative literary minds of the twentieth century. The persistent themes in his short stories (destiny, time, and infinity) occur throughout the entire corpus of his work. However, Borges avoids merely clothing ideas in literary format; instead, he carefully constructs tales whose plots flow relentlessly to their conclusion. His elegant integration of complex philosophical concerns and the striking artistic unity of his stories are testaments to his skill as a writer. *See also* Fantasy.

Further Readings: Bloom, Harold. *Jorge Luis Borges.* Broomhall, PA: Chelsea House, 2002; Borges, Jorge Luis. *Borges: Collected Fictions.* Translated by Andrew Hurley. New York: Penguin, 1999; Di Giovanni, Norman Thomas. *The Lesson of the Master: On Borges and His Work.* New York: Continuum, 2003; Rodríguez Monegal, Emir. *Jorge Luis Borges: A Literary Biography.* New York: Paragon, 1988.

Howard Giskin

Bošković-Stulli, Maja (1922–)

Maja Bošković-Stulli is a Croatian Slavic scholar, folklorist, and literary historian who collected and analyzed Croatian **folktale**s and folk songs, examined the stylistic differences between the **epic** and the lyric dominant forms, and studied **legend**s, fairy tales, **proverbs** and **riddle**s, all in historical, cultural, and geographical context. Bošković-Stulli published twenty-one books, many of them collections. She analyzed the characteristics of Croatian **oral tradition** in Dinaric, Adriatic-Mediterranean, Pannonian, central European areas, and in the border regions, especially those between Croatia and Slovenia with bilingual informants. She collected and analyzed texts from all Croatian dialects, including narratives of Croatians living in Bosnia, Hungary, Slovakia, and Moravia. Her work contributed to the development of contemporary folklore theory in Croatia. In addition, she interpreted works of Croatian writers and their intertwining with oral tradition.

Bošković-Stulli graduated in Belgrade in 1950 and received her doctorate in Zagreb in 1961. She worked at the Croatian Academy of and Arts from 1951 to 1952 and at the Institute of Ethnology and Folklore Research (formerly the Institute of Folk Art) in Zagreb from 1952 to 1979. For many years, she edited the Croatian ethnological journal *Narodna umjetnost* (*Folk Art*) and served on the editorial board of the international journal *Fabula*. She was among the founders of the International Society for Folk Narrative Research and took an active part in the *Enzyklopädie des Märchens* (*Encyclopedia of the Folktale*). One of her important books was a collection entitled *Kroatische Volksmärchen* (*Croatian Folktales,* 1975), written in German, which was later translated into Japanese. *See also* Slavic Tales.

Further Reading: Matičetov, Milko. "Bošković-Stulli, Maja." *Enzyklopädie des Märchens.* Edited by Kurt Ranke et al. Volume 2. Berlin: Walter de Gruyter, 1979. 634–36.

Mojca Ramšak

Brentano, Clemens (1778–1842)

Clemens Brentano, a German Romantic writer, is known both for his collection of folk songs and for his own fairy tales. Though he studied mining (in Halle), medicine (in Jena), and philosophy (in Göttingen, where he met his friend, later collaborator, and brother-in-law Achim von Arnim), Brentano's primary interest was literature. His novel *Godwi* (1801), published under the pseudonym "Maria," combines a narrative in letters with interspersed poems, including his well-known ballad "Zu Bacharach am Rheine" ("Bacharch on the Rhein").

From 1804 to 1809, Brentano worked with Arnim in Heidelberg, editing the *Zeitung für Einsiedler* (*Journal for Hermits*) and the important collection of German folk songs, *Des Knaben Wunderhorn* (*The Boy's Magic Horn*, 1805–08), which was dedicated to Johann Wolfgang von **Goethe.** Arnim and Brentano hoped to "salvage" the songs as evidence of vanishing German traditions and as an antidote to contemporary German culture and to the Napoleonic invasions. They found written versions of these songs in old **broadside**s, medieval chronicles, Renaissance collections, and more recent compilations. Many of the songs that the **editors** claimed to have heard orally (marked as "mündlich") actually came from written sources as well, often with substantial changes and additions. They even included several poems written by Brentano, like "Großmutter Schlangenköchin" ("Grandmother the Snake Cook") and "Des Schneiders Feyerabend" ("The Tailor's Holiday"), because they believed his work captured the simple vocabulary, meter, and verse forms of traditional songs. Their aim was to reinvent an endangered tradition, though they did not attempt to include the music of the songs.

Their collection, as well as Arnim's long essay on folk songs in the first volume and Johann Gottfried Herder's theories, helped inspire the Brothers **Grimm** to begin **collecting** folktales. (The preface of the first edition of their *Kinder- und Hausmärchen* [*Children's and Household Tales*, 1812–15], echoes Arnim's essay in both content and imagery.) Brentano also corresponded with the Grimms about folktales, sending them examples he had gathered for his own projected collection. They sent him the first drafts of some of their tales in 1810, a manuscript eventually found in Brentano's papers in a monastery in Ölenberg in the early 1920s. This Ölenberg manuscript has been invaluable to scholars in tracing the editorial changes the Grimms made before publication.

Later in his career, Brentano turned to Christian themes and conservative, nationalistic, sometimes anti-Semitic politics. He resisted publication of his own **märchen**, fine examples of the Romantic-era fairy tale, and most of these appeared only after his death. *Italienische Märchen* (*Italian Fairy Tales*), begun in 1805, is an **adaptation** for children of tales from Giambattista **Basile.** *Rheinmärchen* (*Rhein Fairy Tales*), begun in 1809, combines an overarching tale of the heroic miller Radlauf with traditional **legend**s of the Lorelei and the river Rhine itself. A friend published two tales in the journal *Iris* in 1827, to Brentano's distress. In 1838, he himself published one tale adapted from Basile, "Gockel, Hinkel, und Gackeleia," in an expanded form, with lithographs from his own sketches. *See also* German Tales.

Further Reading: Lampart, Fabian. "The Turn to History and the *Volk*: Brentano, Arnim, and the Grimm Brothers." *The Literature of German Romanticism.* Edited by Dennis Mahoney. Rochester, NY: Camden House, 2004. 168–89.

Elizabeth Wanning Harries

Brentano-von Arnim, Bettina. *See* Arnim, Bettina von

Brier Rose. *See* Sleeping Beauty

Briggs, Katharine M. (1898–1980)

Collector, belletrist, novelist, anthologist, and raconteur, Katharine M. Briggs was best known for her many volumes about fairy lore and British folktales in general. The daughter of the watercolorist Ernest Briggs, Katharine grew up in London and Perthshire, and was among the first to receive the bachelor's degree from St. Margaret's Hall Oxford (in 1921). After her service in World War II, she returned to Oxford and finished her doctor of philosophy degree in 1952.

With her two sisters, she created a theatrical troupe that traveled in rural England and Scotland. They performed in mime, dramatized short plays based on ballads and fairy legends, and adapted the *commedia delle' arte* (comedy of humors) for countryside presentations.

Most of her voluminous literary production had to do with fairy lore: plays, poems, and finally the well-received *Anatomy of Puck: An Examination of Fairy Beliefs Among Shakespeare's Contemporaries and Successors* (1959). She was awarded a doctor of letters from Oxford in 1965, having published a number of scholarly studies as well as children's books. She is best known for the four-volume *Dictionary of British Folk-Tales in the English Language* (1970–71).

Briggs lived for many years with her sisters at the Barn House, Burford, Oxfordshire, along with many cats. Her house was a mecca for visiting folklorists. She worked long and hard to organize and to stabilize the British Folklore Society, serving in many capacities, culminating in the presidency for three years. *See also* Faerie and Fairy Lore.

Further Reading: Davidson, H. R. Ellis. *Katharine Briggs: Story-Teller.* Cambridge: Lutterworth Press, 1986.

Roger D. Abrahams

Broadside

Printed sheets of paper pasted publicly and sold in the streets, the broadside was one of the most common forms of distribution of news, tales, and **ballad**s in Europe from the sixteenth to the nineteenth centuries. While a printed medium, the informal editing and printing processes allowed more variation than in most written works.

Broadsides were one of the earliest forms of popular print media. Traditionally limited to works printed on a single, one-sided page, broadsides arose in Europe in the late fifteenth century with the development of the printing press, which made duplication easy, quick, and cheap. Sheets printed on both sides or folded into booklike form are distinguished as "broadsheets." Typically broadsides included not only text but also illustrations and were distributed with two main purposes: to inform and to entertain. As a means of disseminating information, broadsides were used for the official publication of information such as royal edicts or legal announcements, for the spread of religious teachings and accounts of miracles, for the dissemination of news about wars or distant events, and for political rhetoric such as campaign speeches. In this way, the broadside was the ancestor to both newspaper and pamphlet.

In terms of entertainment, broadsides played an important role in the development of mass culture. Broadsides, especially in England, frequently would be distributed with lyrics to ballads or popular songs drawing on folktale material. These lyrics could be learned by the public and thus enter the common repertoire. Many ballads achieved wide distribution through this format. While the broadside was not a medium in which folktales per se were generally disseminated, it does frequently reference popular **legend**s, **religious tale**s, **saint's legend**s, **jest**s, and other forms. *See also* Chapbook.

Further Reading: Preston, Cathy Lynn, and Michael J. Preston. *The Other Print Tradition: Essays on Chapbooks, Broadsides, and Related Ephemera.* Garland: New York, 1995.

B. Grantham Aldred

Brontë, Charlotte (1816–1855)

English author Charlotte Brontë, best known for her novel *Jane Eyre* (1847), was the oldest of three sisters, all of whom became novelists. Practically every Brontë biographer has told the story of how twelve toy soldiers stimulated the creativity of four motherless children. Charlotte and her brother Branwell competed as chief animators of figures they entrusted to the *Arabian Nights* genii called called Tallii (Charlotte), Branni (Branwell), Emmii (Emily), and Annii (Anne), whose magical might fuelled the collaborative narratives that ensued.

The romances that the Brontë sisters published in 1847 retain traces of these youthful collaborations. But Charlotte's *Jane Eyre* appealed to Victorian readers more than Anne's realistic *Agnes Grey* or Emily's eerie *Wuthering Heights* because—despite its lightning bolts, ominous dreams, and disembodied voices—the **novel** steadily domesticates its supernaturalism. Its reliance on traditional fairy tales such as "**Cinderella**," "**Bluebeard**," and "**Beauty and the Beast**" aids this domestication. Jane is immediately cast as an orphaned stepchild. She is denied the approval of a **mother** who prefers her dull children to the imaginative cinder-waif she degrades. It is Rochester who shares Jane's grasp of fairy lore by identifying her with England's vanished "little people" and by disguising himself as a godmotherly gypsy *vielle*. Although he plays Bluebeard by barring the room that holds the shards of his married past, he also impersonates Jeanne-Marie **Leprince de Beaumont**'s Beast when he welcomes Jane's frank answer to his question, "Do you think me handsome?" and when, at the novel's end, he gratefully allows her to "rehumanize" a torpid, shaggy creature. *See also* Faerie and Fairy Lore; Forbidden Room.

Further Reading: Rowe, Karen. "'Fairy-born and human-bred': Jane Eyre's Education in Romance." *The Voyage In.* Edited by Elizabeth Abel, Marianne Hirsch, and Elizabeth Langland. Hanover, NH: University Press of New England, 1983. 69–89.

U. C. Knoepflmacher

Brothers

The German proverb "Brothers love one another like knife points" finds countless illustrations in folktales from around the world. Folkloric evidence suggests that rivalry between siblings of the same **gender** is a nearly universal condition. Competition between brothers constitutes an archetypal building block in **myth** and **folklore**. The account of the mortal feud between Cain and Abel is among the best known of all scriptural stories; furthermore, the narrative widely considered to be the world's oldest surviving fairy tale, "Anpu and Bata" from Egypt (thirteenth century BCE), is constructed around the conflict between two brothers.

Diverse problems contribute to the discord among brothers in folklore. Principal among these are disputes over an inheritance and competition for a bride. Many folktales reflect an inheritance tradition based on primogeniture, where the oldest son is the expected sole heir. However, in fairy tales he nearly always fails to fulfill the conditions set by the father, as does the second oldest (typically there are three contestants); the youngest brother, against all expectations, gains the prize.

Folktales of type ATU 402, The Animal Bride, recorded in **variant**s from around the world, provide relevant examples. Typically, to determine his heir, a **father** assigns a series of tasks to his three sons. The youngest, aided by a **magic helper** in animal form, wins each contest, much to the dismay of his father and brothers, all of whom consider him to be a **simpleton**. In the end, the youngest brother's helper (in truth an enchanted **princess**) turns into a beautiful human bride. Similarly, folktales of type ATU 551, Water of Life, also with international distribution, tell of an ailing father who sends his three sons on a quest for a remedy, promising his kingdom to the one who succeeds. The older brothers fail, usually because of pride, whereas the youngest one brings home the required item, thus securing his father's blessing and legacy.

Another **tale type** featuring a reversal of traditional expectations is the widely distributed family of **Puss in Boots** tales (ATU 545B). Best known in Charles **Perrault**'s version "Le maitre chat ou le chat botté" ("The Master Cat, or Puss in Boots"), this tale typically begins with the death of a father and the unequal distribution of his estate. As Perrault relates, the oldest brother receives the father's mill, the second a donkey, and the third a **cat**. Dismayed, the youngest bemoans the fact that his older brothers can join forces and earn a living from their inheritance, whereas his share is seemingly worthless. However, in good fairy-tale fashion, the cat becomes an extraordinary helper, who through trickery and magic leads his once-disadvantaged master to wealth, power, and **marriage** to a princess.

Competition for the same bride is the foremost conflict in many fairy tales about brothers. Here too it is virtually always the youngest brother who emerges victorious. Typical are tales of type ATU 610, The Healing Fruits, of which the opening episode in "Der Vogel Greif" ("The Griffin") by Jacob and Wilhelm **Grimm** is exemplary. A **king** promises his daughter to any man who can cure her of a severe illness. Three brothers make the attempt with an offering of their finest apples. The oldest, underway to the castle, is asked by a mysterious stranger what his basket contains, to which he replies, "Frog's legs." Upon arrival, he discovers that his sarcastic remark has come true. Similarly, the second brother tells the stranger that his basket is filled with hog bristles, and his lie also comes true. The youngest brother tries his luck as well, telling the old man that he is carrying apples to cure the princess. His naïve response comes true, and following additional adventures he marries the princess and becomes king.

In many fairy tales, fraternal rivalry extends into adulthood. One of the world's most widely distributed tales, ATU 613, The Two Travelers (Truth and Falsehood), often features two brothers, one of whom represents good, the other evil. Giambattista **Basile**'s introduction of the two characters, in his tale "Li dui fratielle" ("The Two Brothers"), is typical: "Marcuccio and Parmiero are two brothers, the one rich and wicked, the other poor and virtuous." In these tales, the evil brother temporarily gains the upper hand, but through magic intervention and good luck, the virtuous brother always prevails.

Similarly, in one of the best-known of all **trickster** tales, ATU 1535, The Rich and the Poor Farmer, the antagonists are often adult brothers, sometimes curiously having the same name, as in Hans Christian **Andersen**'s "Lille Claus og store Claus" ("Little Claus and Big Claus") or its Norwegian counterpart from the collection of Peter Christen **Asbjørnsen** and Jørgen **Moe**, "Store-Per og Vesle-Per" ("Big Peter and Little Peter"). This tale opens with a wealthy farmer abusing his impoverished brother. However, the victim quickly turns the wealthy man's greed against him, not only impoverishing him, but ultimately causing his **death**.

Similarly, tale type ATU 954, The Forty Thieves (Ali Baba), known from the **Arabian Nights**, begins with a description of two married brothers, one rich and selfish, the other poor and virtuous. The poor brother, Ali Baba, by chance discovers a **thieves'** treasure cave that can be opened with the magic command "Open, Sesame!" and takes enough wealth from it to meet his family's needs. With time, his envious brother also learns the secret and sneaks into the cave. But, overcome with greed, he forgets the magic word; the thieves catch him inside and kill him.

Denoting the rigid gender roles of most traditional cultures, there are relatively few conflicts between opposite-sexed siblings in folktales. Sisters often cooperate with and support their brothers, as exemplified in the well-known tales of type ATU 327A, **Hansel and Gretel**; ATU 450, Little Brother and Little Sister; and ATU 451, The Maiden Who Seeks Her Brothers. Conversely, the famous tale "**Blue Beard**" (ATU 312, Maiden-Killer), best known in Perrault's version "La barbe bleue," depicts a young woman captured by a serial killer. Her brothers rescue her at the last minute. **See also** Egyptian Tales; Family; Sisters; Twins.
Further Reading: El-Shamy, Hasan. "Siblings in Alf layla wa-laylah." Marvels & Tales 18 (2004): 170–86.

D. L. Ashliman

Brothers Grimm. *See* Grimm, Jacob; Grimm, Wilhelm; *Kinder- und Hausmärchen*

Brothers Grimm in Biopics

In the screen appearances of Wilhelm and Jacob **Grimm** as characters, they are always shown as brothers, but beyond that there is no attempt to be totally faithful to their documented biographies.

Despite its title, *The Wonderful World of the Brothers Grimm* (directed by Henry Levin and George Pal, 1962) is not primarily about the Grimms. It is about Cinerama, a then-new cinematographic process that was trying to attract people away from **television** by showing films on a screen that was not simply wide (ninety feet from edge to edge) but also curved. In a Cinerama film, the director's job was to exploit the system's ability to make the audience feel like they are at the very heart of the action.

Matt Damon starring as Will Grimm with Monica Bellucci as Queen Mirror in the 2005 movie *The Brothers Grimm*. [Dimension Films/Miramax Films/Photofest]

The narrative of this particular Cinerama drama revolves round two German brothers who have financial problems because one of them, Wilhelm, has a growing family to maintain. Against their will, they earn money by researching a local duke's family history: Wilhelm would rather be out collecting tales from people and writing them down for the next generation; solemn long-term bachelor Jacob, feeling the first stirrings of romance, would prefer to focus on the object of his affections.

Within this context, there arise dramatizations of three tales that Wilhelm is shown as either hearing and recording, or telling to children. Their content does not relate particularly to the Grimms' lives. The tales are chosen because they offer Cineramic fun and excitement. In "The Dancing **Princess**" (Grimms' "Die zertanzten Schuhe," or "The Worn-Out Dancing Shoes," with twelve princesses), a **king** wants to know what his daughter does every night, and he promises her hand in **marriage** to the first man to find out. In another story, Wilhelm himself plays one of his characters—a cobbler with a deadline problem, in "The Cobbler and the Elves" (from Grimms' "Die Wichtelmänner," or "The Elves")—with Puppetoons (wooden models animated frame by frame) as the **elves**. Finally, an old woman tells him the story of "The Singing Bone" (Grimms' "Der singende Knochen") with its vainglorious knight, ill-treated servant, and fire-breathing **dragon**.

While listening to this, Wilhelm becomes ill, and in his delirium has a vision of Rumpelstiltskin and other as-yet-uncollected characters, all begging him to capture their stories before it is too late. At this, he recovers quickly and produces several books of tales, while Jacob writes about subjects more likely to pay the bills. At the end, Wilhelm is publicly honored, and Jacob rekindles his old flame.

In the following decade, Jacob and Wilhelm transferred from the largest screen to the smallest, singing and dancing their way through the 1977 family-oriented U.S. television musical *Once Upon a Brothers Grimm* (directed by Norman Campbell). Passing through a forest, the brothers disagree about the relationship between the tales they have collected and the world about them: Jacob proclaims, in song, that, "Life is not a fairy tale." This debate is then fleshed out by the gradual appearance, in the forest, of a host of familiar Grimm characters, including eight dancing princesses (played by the Los Angeles Ballet Company), Rumpelstiltskin, the Bremen Town musicians, **Hansel and Gretel**, **Little Red Riding Hood,** and many others. After these encounters (and being turned into a swan), Jacob changes his tune: now, "Life can be a fairy tale."

The major film inspired by this duo, *The Brothers Grimm* (directed by Terry Gilliam, 2005), likewise presents them as contrasts, but this time Jake is the one who first begins to take the **oral tradition** seriously. They are no longer scholars; they have become hucksters, making a living by charging credulous villagers high rates for capturing ghosts—ghosts that they themselves have created.

The film posits a time when local oral traditions and beliefs are being displaced by nineteenth-century print-based national culture—but the old world is not quite dead yet. When the brothers are employed to unmask what is believed to be another group of scammers, who keep sending a wolfman to abduct girls from a village, Will is simply impressed by how well funded their rivals seem. However, Jake realizes that what they are dealing with, in the forest of moving trees and the castle of the sleeping Thuringian **queen**, is not a fake product of mechanical wizardry, but authentic enchantment. What ultimately saves them from defeat at the hands of the evil queen is their subliminal knowledge of the rules of the game, imbibed with their mother's milk. Even Will comes to realize that he knows where he is. "You can stop this! You know the story!" he shouts at Jake in a moment of danger. At the climax, their pursuer Cavaldi has the same perception: "Wait! I know this story. The spell can be broken with a kiss of true love—but it must be true love, otherwise it will be the kiss of death!"

Along the way, the dialogue invokes a myriad of tales (not every one necessarily from Grimm): "Jack and the Beanstalk," "Little Red Riding Hood," "**Cinderella**," "Hansel and Gretel," "**Snow White**," "**The Frog King**," "The Gingerbread Man"—even "The Princess on the Pea" (one of Hans Christian **Andersen**'s). Through its conclusion, the film validates the notion that these and other folktales contain truths of many kinds and sets up a future in which, it is implied, Will and Jake will return to being scholars and seek to preserve the nascent nation's oral heritage—though not till they have settled the question of whether either of them can pass the test and be worthy to claim the fair Angelica, who taught them how to get through the enchanted forest.

The Grimms' other film appearance is literally a walk-on part. It occurs in *Ever After* (directed by Andy Tennant, 1998), which approaches the same issue—fairy-tale truth—from a different angle. Arriving at an imposing palace, the Grimms are ushered in to see an elderly queen who tells them she admires their collection of folktales—except "Cinderella." In response, one brother acknowledges that Charles **Perrault**'s version, with its fairy godmother and pumpkins (not found in Grimm) is preferred by some; and the other raises the old question of whether Cinderella's **shoe**s were made of glass or fur. This prompts the queen to say she can settle that question immediately, and she produces a slipper made of glass. Through this slipper, and a portrait of a young woman, the audience is taken into the sixteenth century and the story of Danielle, her father, his new wife, the new wife's two daughters, the royal **prince**, and Leonardo da Vinci. At the end of the film, it transpires that the queen offering this revision is Danielle's own great-great-granddaughter. The Grimms leave the castle with her last words echoing in their ears: "The point is that Cinderella and her prince were not mere rumors . . . they did indeed live." What the Grimms intend to do with this kind of truth is not clear; as the credits roll, they enter their carriage and drive off without a word. *See also* Andersen, Hans Christian, in Biopics; Cinderella Films; Film and Video.

Further Readings: Gerstner, Hermann. *Die Brüder Grimm: Ihr Leben und Werk in Selbstzeugnissen, Briefen und Aufzeichnungen.* Ebenhausen bei München: W. Langewiesche-Brandt, 1952; Tatar, Maria. "Fairy Tales in the Age of Terror: What Terry Gilliam Helps to Remind Us about an Ancient Genre." *Slate,* September 22, 2005. http://www.slate.com/id/2126727/; Zipes, Jack. "Once There Were Two Brothers Named Grimm: A Reintroduction." *The Brothers Grimm: From Enchanted Forests to the Modern World.* 2nd edition. New York: Palgrave McMillan, 2002. 1–24.

Terry Staples

Broumas, Olga (1949–)

Born and raised in the Greek island of Syros, the poet and translator Olga Broumas came to the United States in 1967 with the Fulbright program to study architecture at the University of Pennsylvania. Immediately following, she received a master of fine arts degree in creative writing with a minor in dance from the University of Oregon. In 1982, she earned a massage therapist license, a skill that she combines with the teaching of **poetry** and creative writing.

Broumas published her first book in Greek at the age of eighteen (*Anisychies* [*Anxieties*, 1967]), after which she began to write and publish her poetry in English. With her first poetry collection, *Beginning with O* (1977), Broumas won the Yale Series of Younger Poets Award, the first nonnative speaker of English to receive this honor. She has published several major collections of poetry, which were collectively published in *Rave: Poems 1975–1999* (1999). She has also translated into English poems from the Greek poet and Nobel laureate Odysseas Elytis (her most recent effort being *Eros, Eros, Eros: Selected and Last Poems*, 1998).

Well-known fairy tales with female protagonists have been one of the inspirational sources for Broumas's poetry. The poems "**Beauty and the Beast**," "**Cinderella**," "**Rapunzel**," "**Sleeping Beauty**," "Rumpelstiltskin," "**Little Red Riding Hood**," and "**Snow White**" in *Beginning with O* offer a contemporary lyrical transformation of classical fairy tales and sometimes explicitly invoke the fairy-tale poetry published by Anne **Sexton** in *Transformations* (1971). For Broumas, the tales become a vehicle to express her feminist and lesbian views and demonstrate her own idea of women's role in society. "Cinderella," for instance, is a metaphor of "a woman alone/in a house of men." The unlucky victim heroine, who calls herself "a woman coopted by promises," prefers to return to her prior situation, back to the ashes, to escape from her unfulfilled life in the royal chambers. The poem "Sleeping Beauty" can be read in the context of Broumas's openly lesbian views. Amidst the "City-center, mid-traffic" a woman awakens another woman—the poem's speaker—from her sleep with a "public kiss" that "shocked the pedestrians." In "Little Red Riding Hood" and "Snow White," Broumas thematizes the mother-daughter relationship. In "Little Red Riding Hood," the heroine would return to her "Mother, landscape / of [her] heart"; and in "Snow White," the daughter asks to be received again by her mother. Generally, a hedonistic style and erotic scenes characterize Broumas's poetry, as clearly demonstrated in the poems "Beauty and the Beast," "Rapunzel," and "Rumpelstiltskin." *See also* Erotic Tales; Gay and Lesbian Fairy Tales; Sex, Sexuality.

Further Reading: Rose, Ellen Cronan. "Through the Looking Glass: When Women Tell Fairy Tales." *The Voyage In: Fictions of Female Development.* Edited by Elizabeth Abel, Marianne Hirsch, and Elizabeth Langland. Hanover, NH: University Press of New England, 1983. 209–27.

Maria Kaliambou

Browne, Anthony (1946–)

Anthony Browne is a British artist, illustrator, and author of picture books. He is the winner of several Kate Greenaway Medals and the Hans Christian Andersen Award for illustration in 2000. While his picture books range from humorous, everyday stories to surrealistic dreamlike narratives expressing the innermost feelings and fears of young children, many of them contain fairy-tale images and connotations. The forest is his favorite setting, and a variety of fairy-tale figures appear mysteriously in the backgrounds. He uses familiar fairy-tale motifs such as magic mirrors in *Through the Magic Mirror* (1976) and **transformation**s in *Piggybook* (1986), employing mostly visual means to convey the sense of the supernatural.

One of Browne's earliest works was *Hansel and Gretel* (1981) in which images add a significant new dimension to the story. Not only do the interiors, including an electric bulb and a television set, create a stunning contrast to the fairy-tale atmosphere of the forest and the witch's house, but the obvious similarity of the stepmother and the witch, enhanced by several pictorial devices, suggests a different, rather symbolic interpretation of the story. The stepmother, hardly characterized in the verbal narrative of the Brothers **Grimm** other than as being wicked, is in Browne's version presented as vain and selfish. Her rich garments and luxury objects contradict the verbal statements of the family's poverty. The book is a superb example of an artist's creative approach to illustrating a traditional fairy tale.

In *The Tunnel* (1989), perhaps Browne's best book, he offers a more refined variation on the **Hansel and Gretel** theme. While employing an original plot in a contemporary setting, the book evokes the fairy tale with the motif of a sacrificial girl rescuing her brother. It also contains a multitude of visual details alluding to **Little Red Riding Hood** in the girl's attire, and to a generic tale of a child entering an enchanted forest. Interestingly, the source of the evil enchantment is never featured, which prompts a sense of an internal rather than external landscape.

One of Browne's most recent books, *Into the Forest* (2004), already by its title suggests a further exploration of the fairy-tale theme and setting. In it, Browne plays with **gender**, placing a boy in the traditional Little Red Riding Hood role; but more importantly, he lets his protagonist meet characters from a number of well-known fairy tales, without naming them, thus inviting the reader into a game of recognition. In the imagery, he uses abundant self-quotations providing pleasurable recollections for an experienced Browne reader. A clever combination of color and black-and-white drawings hints at possible psychological interpretations and leave much to the reader's imagination. ***See also*** Illustration; Psychological Approaches.

Further Readings: Doonan, Jane. "Drawing Out Ideas: A Second Decade of the Work of Anthony Browne." *The Lion and the Unicorn* 23 (1998) 1: 30–56; _____. "The Object Lesson: Picture Books of Anthony Browne." *Word and Image* 2 (1986): 159–72; Perrot, Jean. "An English Promenade." *Bookbird* 38 (2000) 3: 11–16

Maria Nikolajeva

Burnett, Frances Eliza Hodgson (1849–1924)

As an Englishwoman who became a best-selling writer after moving to the United States, Frances Eliza Hodgson Burnett not only capitalized on her knowledge of British social mores but also on texts she had memorized as a child. Prominent among these were fairy tales she shrewdly enlisted when, as "Mrs. Burnett" and mother of two sons, she followed her adult novels with even more successful juvenile texts. The two Burnett novels most widely read (and most frequently filmed) today, *The Secret Garden* (1911) and *A Little Princess* (1905), deftly naturalize and revitalize fairy tale **motifs**. "Sleeping Beauty" is evoked when Mary Lennox awakens both a dormant garden and a bedridden young "**prince.**" "**Cinderella**" is recast when "**Princess** Sara" continues to act as a benevolent godmother to needy girls even after she is herself degraded as a cinder girl who must be redeemed by the "magic" of a genielike Ram Dass.

Burnett's initial ventures into the genre of the **literary fairy tale** were more derivative and less effective. Her three-part "The Story of Prince Fairyfoot" (1890) merely bloated a tale already told in *Granny's Wonderful Chair* (1856) by Frances Browne. Claiming to have forgotten the name of the book she had received when "six or seven," Burnett aborted a planned collection of "Stories from the Lost Fairy-Book, Re-told by the Child Who Read

Them." Thereafter, she would rely on imaginative characters like Sara Crewe to recast stories such as Hans Christian **Andersen**'s "The Little Mermaid."

Further Readings: Carpenter, Angelica Shirley, and Jean Shirley. *Frances Hodgson Burnett: Beyond the Secret Garden.* Minneapolis: Lerner Publications Company, 1990; Gruner, Elizabeth Rose. "Cinderella, Marie Antoinette, and Sara: Roles and Role Models in *A Little Princess.*" *Lion and the Unicorn* 22 (1998): 163–87; Laski, Marghanita. *Mrs. Ewing, Mrs. Molesworth and Mrs. Hodgson Burnett.* Edited by Hebert van Thal. London: Arthur Barker Ltd., 1950; Reimer, Mavis. "Making Princesses, Re-Making *A Little Princess.*" *Voices of the Other: Children's Literature and the Post-Colonial Context.* Edited by Roderick McGillis. New York: Garland, 1999. 111–34.

U.C. Knoepflmacher

Burton, Richard Francis (1821–1890)

A British explorer, translator, author, and Orientalist who knew many languages and traveled extensively, Richard Francis Burton was an enigmatic and fascinating figure who produced two especially important works for folktale and fairy-tale studies. His translation of the **Arabian Nights** (*The Book of the Thousand Nights and a Night,* first published in 1885–88) is still considered by some to be the standard English version. Burton's text shocked readers in Victorian England and in Europe because of its explicit sensuality and the way it heightened a combination of sex, violence, and glamour. If it true, as some scholars believe, that nothing has influenced the modern Western imagination more than the *Arabian Nights,* then Burton's role in that process is substantial. His second important work is the translation of a cycle of Indian folktales popularly known as *Baital pachisi* (literally, *Twenty-Five Tales of a Vampire*). Burton's version, titled *Vikram and the Vampire, or Tales of Hindu Devilry,* was first published in 1870. In his preface, Burton argued that this cycle of tales influenced the making of the *Arabian Nights* and the stories of Giovanni **Boccaccio**.

Burton belongs to that generation of adventurers who traveled before **colonialism** became an established system. He went to India in 1842 as a soldier for the East India Company and found himself in Sindh in the northwestern part of the subcontinent. Burton was not a regular soldier—he was connected to a powerful family, had been thrown out of Oxford University for misconduct, and had come to India with other intentions—specifically of experiencing the Orient. He roamed around the bazaars of Sindh dressed as a local, learned the regional language, and gained knowledge of the people's lives. The contemporary author Christopher Ondaatje has visited the same sites and revealed the ongoing existence of practices described by Burton.

Burton precedes the emergence of British colonial administrator as scholars and folklore collectors in Asia and Africa by a decade. His translations reflect a combination of attraction to the exotic narratives, irreverence toward the worldviews embedded in them, and a satirical angle that is subdued but ever present. This is especially pronounced in the translation of *Vikram and the Vampire,* but in the *Arabian Nights* his style is more perfected. He reveals almost nothing about his method—neither the original text nor help by native scholars. Burton is also renowned for his travels in Africa and his expedition to locate the source of the Nile.

Further Readings: Burton, Sir Richard F., trans. *Vikram and the Vampire, or Tales of Hindu Devilry.* 1870. New York: Dover, 1969; Lovell, Mary S. *A Rage to Live: A Biography of Richard and Isabel Burton.* New York: Norton, 1998; McLynn, Frank. *Burton: Snow Upon the Desert.* London: John

Murray Publishing, 1993; Ondaatje, Christopher. *Sindh Revisited: A Journey in the Footsteps of Sir Richard Francis Burton: The India Years.* Toronto: HarperCollins, 1996.

Sadhana Naithani

Burton, Tim (1958–)

American filmmaker Tim Burton is well known for his dark, magical, and slightly twisted cinematic fantasies. Both his stop-motion animation and live-action works have a characteristic visual feel that invokes the gothic and grotesque. While Burton's strongest influences are in horror, his work tends to be both symbolic and psychological, textured as **fable** or **myth** rather than realist narrative, and a recurring and self-conscious interest in folktale and **storytelling** can be found throughout his films.

Burton's somewhat unlikely start was in animating for the **Walt Disney Company**, which funded his training at the California Institute of the Arts. However, while he produced several animated shorts for the studio, his vision was always significantly different than Disney's cleaner and more saccharine feel, and some of his projects were never released. Notable from Burton's Disney phase were his animated short *Vincent* (1982), an homage to Vincent Price and Edgar Allen Poe that was filmed in an ironically German expressionist style, and *Frankenweenie* (1984), a live-action, tongue-in-cheek retelling of the Frankenstein story, in which a boy reanimates his dead dog. Both these works exemplify Burton's affection for gothic horror films and his ability to visually reference classics of the genre.

In this early phase, Burton created his most overtly fairy-tale works. He directed an episode of Shelley **Duvall**'s *Faerie Tale Theatre*, *Aladdin and his Wonderful Lamp* (1982), which followed the series' tendency towards a lively, humorous treatment with an all-star cast. He also created an animated short of *Hansel and Gretel* (1982), which used elements of Japanese culture and myth, and which aired only once on the Disney channel. Working within the clean-cut confines and expectations of the fairy-tale genre seems to have been somewhat cramping to Burton's highly personal vision, however, and subsequent projects made more use of his own concepts and darker visual sense. A similar sense of conceptual disjunction can be seen in Burton's version of *Planet of the Apes* (2001), an artistic and box-office failure, which suggests that the themes and symbols of the story were alien to its director. Other affectionate parodies of science fiction themes are more successful, notably the manic energy of *Mars Attacks!* (1996) and the loving exploration of the science fiction B-movie in *Ed Wood* (1994).

The most common word applied to Burton's oeuvre by critics is probably "fable," a categorization that points toward the reductionist, essentialist, and nonrealist mode in which he works. A strong thread of the magical in his films allows their operation largely in terms of myth and symbol, so that characters and plots are often universal rather than specific. His recurring use of both the musical format and stop-motion animation, in works such as *The Nightmare before Christmas* (1993) and *Corpse Bride* (2005), reaffirms this tendency towards emblematic, antirealist narrative. His excursion into the superhero genre with *Batman* (1989) and *Batman Returns* (1992) acknowledges the power of a modern myth and allows space for a typically exaggerated play with the capacity for symbol in the superhero motifs; Burton's villains must be among the most playfully excessive of the genre. The *Batman* films also continue Burton's tendency to figure the symbolic hero as a grotesque outsider, as seen in

Nightmare, Ed Wood, Beetlejuice (1988), *Edward Scissorhands* (1990), and *Sleepy Hollow* (1999). At the extreme edge of otherness, Burton's films explore themes of **death** and life after death. The dead and their world are, however, often comically dark, with a carnivalesque grotesquerie that renders their offbeat morbidity energetically amusing as well as disturbing. Even the fearsome Hessian of *Sleepy Hollow* manages a kind of manic glee.

The edgy darkness of Burton's vision means that many of his films are adult rather than children's fables, although his involvement with projects such as *James and the Giant Peach* (1996) and *Charlie and the Chocolate Factory* (2005) suggests that he has something in common with Roald **Dahl**'s macabre sense of **childhood**. Like Dahl, and to a certain extent like fairy tale itself, Burton's films create images of **violence** and horror that are cushioned by the fablelike unreality of their context and by a symmetrical sense of ultimate justice, as well as being lightened by his essentially comic vision. The classic Burton forest, twisted, shadowed and magical, is not so conceptually different from that of the Brothers **Grimm**. It is worth noting, however, that some of Burton's most-simplified work is also his most adult. In particular, the illustrated poems in the collection *The Melancholy Death of Oysterboy* (1997) deal in highly twisted and macabre terms with themes of family, **sexuality**, and death.

The fablelike construction of Burton's films is also often linked to the folkloric. *Sleepy Hollow*, for example, is an explicit attempt to rediscover and celebrate the essentially American folk **legend** of the Headless Horseman. *The Nightmare Before Christmas* uses the folk narratives of various holidays, particularly Christmas and Halloween; *Corpse Bride* transforms the legend of the accidental, supernatural bride into a winsome carnival. As with his use of classic science fiction themes, Burton relies on audience recognition of and response to such narratives, grounding his works in the familiar and universal. He thus tends to draw attention to, and hence celebrate, storytellers and artists, frequently, for some reason, named Edward: Edward Scissorhands and his ice and plant sculptures, the turgid pulp narratives of Ed Wood, and, most explicitly, the tales of Edward Bloom in *Big Fish* (2003). *Big Fish* is Burton's most sustained investigation of the nature of storytelling, and hence, the nature of reality. His tale-spinning Bloom is a **trickster** magician, capable of transforming the mundane into the magical through the power of narrative. The film reproduces Burton's familiar themes—dark woods, grotesque characters, a fablelike simplicity of narrative—but with a more self-conscious spin that lends postmodern insistence to Burton's ongoing message: the validity of the imaginative over the real. *See also* Animation; Film and Video.

Further Readings: McMahan, Alison. *The Films of Tim Burton: Animating Live Action in Contemporary Hollywood.* New York: Continuum, 2005; Petrie, Duncan. "But What If Beauty Is a Beast? Doubles, Transformations and Fairy Tale Motifs in *Batman Returns.*" *Cinema and the Realms of Enchantment: Lectures, Seminars and Essays by Marina Warner and Others.* Edited by Duncan Petrie. London: British Film Institute, 1993. 98–110.

Jessica Tiffin

Busk, Rachel Harriette (1831–1907)

An English traveler and amateur **folklore** collector, Rachel Harriette Busk is one of the few nineteenth-century folklorists to make Italian folk narratives accessible to an English-speaking audience. Born in London, she lived primarily in Rome after 1862 and published one of the first collections of that city's folklore under the title *The Folk-Lore of Rome,*

Collected by Word of Mouth from the People (1874). Her inability to identify an Italian **Grimm** inspired this collection, which is organized into four parts: *favole* (**fairy tale**s); *esempj* (**saints' legend**s and moral tales); family, local, and supernatural **legend**s; and *ciarpe* (gossip and humorous **anecdote**s). Busk also collected **folktale**s from Spain's interior villages, anonymously publishing two collections of tales as *Patrañas, or Spanish Stories, Legendary and Traditional* (1870) and *Household Tales from the Land of Hofer, or Popular Myths of Tirol* (1871); and she translated Asian folklore from German materials under the title *Sagas from the Far East, or Kalmouk and Mongolian Traditionary Tales* (1873).

Like many nineteenth-century folklorists, Busk's collecting efforts were motivated by a romanticized love of land, scenery, and the primitive character of the people. This perspective is apparent in her traveler's guide to the Tirol region, *The Valleys of Tirol: Their Traditions and Customs, and How to Visit Them* (1874). Busk was strongly influenced by Sicilian folklorist Giuseppe **Pitrè**, who selected and translated the Sicilian texts included in her work *The Folk-Songs of Italy* (1887). *See also* Italian Tales.

Further Reading: Dorson, Richard M. "The Overseas Folklorists." *The British Folklorists: A History*. Chicago: University of Chicago Press, 1968. 332–91.

Linda J. Lee

Byatt, A. S. (1936–)

British novelist and critic Antonia Susan Byatt is probably best known for her Booker Prize-winning **novel** *Possession* (1990), which exemplifies her ongoing interest in self-conscious narrative and generic traditions, including fairy tales and **folklore**. Her background as an academic underpins her rigorous and intellectual operation as a writer; her highly self-aware use of narrative, together with her interest in **intertextuality** and **metafiction**, align her firmly with **postmodernism**. Stylistically, she has a deceptively flat, apparently unadorned voice that tends towards simple statements but is nonetheless astonishingly vivid, concrete, and richly visual. Her narrative style is above all peculiarly suited to the telling of fairy tale, and she has published a translation of Marie-Catherine d'**Aulnoy**'s French fairy tale "Le serpentin vert" (1698) under the title "The Great Green Worm" (1994). However, she has written numerous novels and collections of short stories with a realist focus in addition to her critical and journalistic works.

Intertexuality is a recurring feature of Byatt's writing; her academic foci include Iris Murdoch, Samuel Taylor Coleridge, and Robert Browning, but a general sense of artistic reference pervades her work, forming both the theme and matter of her stories. Central intertexts in her writing are romance, Victorian literature and poetry (*Possession*), biography (*The Biographer's Tale*, 2000), painting (*Still Life*, 1978; *The Matisse Stories*, 1993; *Elementals*, 1998), science ("Morpho Eugenia," *Angels and Insects*, 1992), and even pornography (*Babel Tower*, 1996). The fairy tale, while clearly an important interest, is thus simply one aspect of her interest in literature and, more generally, in the notion of art as both a reflection and a refraction of human experience, an act of creation that exposes and invents the world. The tendency towards images of ice, glass, and snow in Byatt's work functions as an ongoing dramatization of this process. Her critical writings explore this in more detail, particularly in the collection *On Histories and Stories* (2000), which reflects not only her love of literature but her ability to theorize about it in complex, often symbolic terms.

Integral to Byatt's consciousness of narrative is her tendency towards **frame narrative** and the embedding of story within story. *Possession* contains **poetry**, fairy tale, and even literary criticism, while the Frederica series of novels (*The Virgin in the Garden*, 1978; *Still Life*, 1985; *Babel Tower*, 1996; and *A Whistling Woman*, 2002) embeds fragmentary and entire novels in its otherwise realistic world. Even shorter tales, such as "Morpho Eugenia," "The Story of the Eldest Princess," and "The Djinn in the Nightingale's Eye," form frames for folkloric and fairy-tale stories. This speaks directly to Byatt's metafictional awareness of narrative as artifact, her tendency to problematize her own fiction by drawing attention to the issue of fictionality. *Possession* itself embeds particularly interesting fairy tales, among them an introspective retelling of "The Glass Coffin" from the Brothers **Grimm,** which stresses the notion of craft and artistry, and "The Threshold," an Arthurian fragment that presents the adventuring knight at a moment of symbolic choice with echoes of William **Shakespeare** as well as fairy tale. "Gode's Story" is a **ghost story** told by an old Breton woman, an exercise in the oral voice that resonates eerily with the frame tale.

The subsequent reprinting of "The Glass Coffin" and "Gode's Story" in *The Djinn in the Nightingale's Eye* (1994), a collection of five fairy tales, points to the importance of framing in Byatt's lexicon, as the tales become considerably less complex and resonant without their interaction with a framing narrative. The collection is rounded out by "Dragon's Breath," written to commemorate Sarajevo and, in its implied equation of dragons and war, more allegory than fairy tale; and by two of Byatt's most postmodern and self-conscious tales, "The Story of the Eldest Princess" and "The Djinn in the Nightingale's Eye." Both use fairy tales with a semiautobiographical resonance; the "reading Princess" of the first story is, like Byatt, an eldest child all too aware of narrative bias toward the third child, and the heroine of "Djinn" is herself a narratologist and writer. "Eldest Princess" is a considerably freeing response to narrative predestination, powerfully validating **women**'s storytelling as personal self-determination. "Djinn" is a playful, often ironic exploration of metafiction as criticism, its *Arabian Nights* **wish**-granting scenario concerned with the implications of narrative as entrapment in the real as well as the fictional sense, life itself as a death-bounded scenario shaped by cultural imperatives.

While Byatt's other short-story collections have a more realist focus than *Djinn*, images of the marvelous drift in and out of their colorful, meticulously observed worlds. *Elementals* includes "A Lamia in the Cevennes," in which a potential fairy bride is ultimately rejected by an artist obsessed with the otherness and mystery that will vanish with her **transformation**; it is a story of the perceptive, fulfilled artist aware of the importance of not revealing or explaining the numinous. "Crocodile Tears" makes satisfying use of the **magic helper** tale, in this case the helper who turns out to be the dead man whose corpse was compassionately buried by the hero; the **death** imagery of the fairy tale is fruitfully applied to the emotional isolation suffered by the bereaved protagonist. The most obviously fairy-tale narrative in this collection, however, is "Cold," whose symbolically polarized desert **prince** and icewoman **princess** enact a **fable** not only of **sexuality** and **gender** balance but of artistry and the importance of artistic creation as a medium for continuing life itself. In *Little Black Book of Stories* (2003), Byatt provides other fairy-tale themes, particularly the monster/**dragon** and lost innocence of "The Thing in the Forest," and the **parable** of aging in "A Stone Woman," which explores with measured and beautiful deliberation the fairy-tale motif of a person transformed to stone. ***See also*** Feminist Tales.

Further Readings: Byatt, A. S., trans. "The Great Green Worm." By Marie-Catherine d'Aulnoy. *Wonder Tales.* Edited by Marina Warner. New York: Frarrar, Straus and Giroux, 1996. 189–229; Franken,

Christien. *A. S. Byatt: Art, Authorship, Creativity.* Houndmills: Palgrave, 2001; Sanchez, Victoria. "A. S. Byatt's *Possession*: A Fairytale Romance." *Southern Folklore* 52.1 (1995): 33–52; Todd, Richard. *Writers and Their Work: A. S. Byatt.* Plymouth: Northcote House, 1997.

Jessica Tiffin

Bye Bye Chaperon Rouge (1989)

An international Canadian-Hungarian coproduction directed by the acclaimed Hungarian director Márta Mészáros in 1989, the film *Bye Bye Chaperon Rouge* (also known as *Bye Bye Red Riding Hood*) offers a contemporary retelling of the story of **Little Red Riding Hood**. Filmed in Hungarian, under the title *Piroska és a farkas*, with French-, English-, Polish-, and Hungarian-speaking actors, it was dubbed in English and French. Shot in Quebec, it starred a six-year-old novice actress, Fanny Lauzier. *Bye Bye Chaperon Rouge* is the ninth film in an ambitious series of family films, Contes pour tous/Tales for All, by the Quebec producer Rock Demers, who seeks to provide youth with alternatives to the violent films of American cinema.

Although the movie is intended for a general audience, it appeals particularly to adolescent viewers. It is a coming-of-age film that explores the social and psychological problems of today's adolescents: peer acceptance, love, independence, and fears about growing up. For years, Mészáros had wanted to do a Red Riding Hood film, as she was fond of the **Grimm** brothers' version as a child. She felt a personal connection to this tale of a fatherless girl trying to cope in an alien world, since her own father died in a Soviet prison during her childhood. In the film, Fanny is a ten-year-old who has lived in the forest with her meteorologist mother ever since her father left them six years earlier. She has still not come to terms with her father's abandonment. Intergenerational female relationships are explored in this retelling that adds a fourth generation. One day on the way to visit her grandmother and great-grandmother, Fanny has three encounters with males that change her life forever. In turn, she meets a charming talking **wolf**, a city boy who awakens new feelings in her, and an ornithologist who is a stand-in for the Grimms' hunter. Fanny mistakes the ornithologist for her father, but he is, in fact, her mother's secret boyfriend. In the film, the two characters are played by Jan Nowicki, the Polish actor who is Mészáros's third husband. In addition, Nowicki's eyes were transposed to the face of the wolf, played by a malamute painted silver. *Bye Bye Chaperon Rouge* does not recount a single visit to the grandmother's but superposes several trips over a period of a number of months, resulting in an intricate pattern of repetitions and variations. Fantasy blends with reality in this retelling that actualizes the classic tale without losing its mythical meaning. The open ending of this complex film leaves viewers wondering if Little Red Riding Hood and her grandmother were, in fact, eaten by the wolf. A novel based on the film, also titled *Bye Bye Chaperon Rouge*, was published by Viviane Julien in the juvenile series Contes pour tous/Tales for All by Les Éditions Québec/Amérique in 1989, and the following year the English-language edition of the novel, *Bye Bye Red Riding Hood*, appeared. *See also* Film and Video.

Further Reading: Peary, Gerald. "Little Red Ridinghood." *Sight and Sound* 57 (Summer 1988): 150.

Sandra L. Beckett

C

Caballero, Fernán. *See* Böhl de Faber, Cecilia

Le cabinet des fées

Le cabinet des fées, ou Collection choisie des contes des fées, et autres contes merveilleux (*The Fairies' Cabinet, or Collection Chosen from Fairy Tales and Other Tales of Wonder,* 41 vols., 1785–89) is the most influential compilation of French **literary fairy tale**s of the late seventeenth through the mid-eighteenth centuries. Selected, edited, and critiqued by Charles-Joseph, Chevalier de **Mayer** between 1785 and 1789, the *Cabinet* marked approximately 100 years of literary fairy tales written in a tradition that began with late seventeenth-century writers such as Charles **Perrault** and Marie-Catherine d'**Aulnoy**. It extended through the "Orientalism" begun with the first translations of the ***Arabian Nights*** in 1704 by Antoine **Galland**, and culminated with the moralists and romance writers of the middle and late eighteenth century. By the time Mayer gathered his stories, interest in fairy tales had largely died with the **salon**s that had given them life. A century earlier, these salons had been a primarily female movement dedicated to the cultivation of politeness and propriety among the aristocracy. The French ***conte de fée***s (fairy tale) of this period expressed some of this emphasis upon courteous and decent behavior. However, as upper-class society learned the lessons of the salons, the salons themselves slowly declined, and the literary forms they had spawned began to seem increasingly old-fashioned and unappealing.

Many of the stories reflected their upper-class provenance. The vast majority of the protagonists are aristocrats (although they sometimes do not realize their identity until the end of the tale). Even more strikingly, the universe of the tales is largely matriarchal, ruled by female **fairies** and human enchantresses. The dominance of empowered feminine characters implies a greater esteem for **women** than did much of contemporary literature and was a crucial part of the morality Mayer saw in the tales. He rejected *contes licencieux* (**bawdy tale**s) as violating the respect for women promoted by salon culture.

The society that engendered fairy stories had already changed considerably and was moving toward a crisis in the 1780s. Mayer hoped to save the best of the tales for future generations. He modeled his collection on several other encyclopedic works being produced in the eighteenth century, including several similarly titled collections of fairy tales in both French and German: *Le cabinet des fées* (1711), *Les cabinets des fées* (1731–35), and *Das Cabinet der Feen* (1761–65), although Mayer gathered more fairy tales than anyone before him.

That Mayer intended his compilation primarily to save the genre for future readers is borne out by his explanation of why the works of major writers like François-Marie Arouet de Voltaire do not appear. He explained that such tales would continue to be read for ages to come based on the fame of their authors, while the works of those he included were, for the most part, more inclined to disappear through neglect. He noted that some were already becoming hard to find. The collection grew beyond its original proposed length of thirty volumes, suggesting that Mayer was interested in assembling as much material as he possibly could. While publishing his collection, he gathered enough to extend the number first to thirty-seven volumes (thirty-six of the tales) and then to forty-one. As a result of this final extension, volume thirty-seven, intended to conclude the collection with scholarly notes, is actually followed by four more volumes of tales added at the end.

However, the *Cabinet* was not only an attempt to save individual tales in danger of being lost, for Mayer included many that seemed unlikely to be forgotten. Generally, the better-known tales he incorporated were important enough to serve as landmarks among the genres of *conte de fées* and *conte oriental* (Orientalist fairy tale). Most notably, Perrault's tales appear in the first volume and receive their own preface (a distinction not accorded to any other works in the collection), while d'Aulnoy's tales appear in the second and third volumes. Mayer included Galland's translations and Jean-Marie **Leprince de Beaumont**'s tales, including *La Belle et la Bête* (*Beauty and the Beast*), which had already been translated into other languages. Such works proved important in the development of the fairy tale and therefore worth including in a collection intended to preserve and promote the genre overall.

Mayer collected the works of forty authors into forty volumes of tales, with the thirty-seventh devoted to biographical and critical notes on 100 fairy and Orientalist authors, including sixty whose fairy tales and romances were not represented. This list appears to be a reference to allow readers to search for more fairy-tale authors and their works, for Mayer included in the notes appreciative discussions and even summaries of many of their literary works. The biographical information was as well researched as he could manage although the level of detail proves uneven, especially for the more obscure writers.

Mayer packaged his collection in as complete and aesthetically satisfying a form as he could. He commissioned Clément-Pierre Marillier to draw three **illustration**s per volume, which were in turn engraved by thirty-one different artists. The books were published in Amsterdam and were readily available to international readers.

The *Cabinet* ensured that many individual fairy tales and the artistic genre would survive the turmoil of revolutionary France, and helped both the Romantics and later audiences rediscover both the tales and their authors. That the tales are still accessible today suggests Mayer's considerable success in achieving his goal. The *Cabinet* helped reinvigorate fairy tales as a literary form both inside and outside of France. ***See also*** French Tales.

Further Reading: Barchilon, Jacques. *Le conte merveilleux français de 1690 à 1790: Cent ans de féerie et de poésie ignorées de l'histoire littéraire*. Paris: Champion, 1975.

Paul James Buczkowski

Cabrera, Lydia (1899–1991)

Lydia Cabrera dedicated her life to the study of Afro-Cuban **folklore** and to the compilation and retelling of stories and traditions of the black populations on the island. Although

Cabrera did not have formal ethnographic training, during a stay in Paris as the daughter of a well-off Cuban family, she became involved in cubist and surrealist circles, and their interest in so-called primitive art awakened her desire to study the African traditions on her native island. Back in Cuba, and with the help of some of the former black servants of her family, she started writing down stories and traditions that African slaves had brought with them to the island. Cabrera, however, did not simply transcribe the stories; she embellished them and infused them with her own preoccupations (such as the incorporation of a feminine perspective). Thus, these short stories are literary works in their own right. Her best-known collection of short stories is *Cuentos negros de Cuba* (*Black Tales from Cuba*, 1940). In addition to her fiction, Cabrera wrote studies of Afro-Cuban religious syncretic beliefs, of which the most important one is *El Monte* (*The Mount*, 1954). *See also* Latin American Tales; Race and Ethnicity.

Further Readings: Rodríguez-Mangual, Edna M. *Lydia Cabrera and the Construction of an Afro-Cuban Cultural Identity*. Chapel Hill: University of North Carolina Press, 2004; Soto, Sara. *Magia e historia en los "Cuentos negros," "Por qué" y "Ayapá" de Lydia Cabrera*. Miami: Ediciones Universal, 1988.

Víctor Figueroa

Calvino, Italo (1923–1985)

The Italian writer, critic, and editor Italo Calvino, author of the monumental *Fiabe italiane* (*Italian Folktales*, 1956), was born in Cuba to Italian parents and spent his youth in San Remo, on the Ligurian Riviera. During World War II, he fought in the Resistance, and he embarked on his various careers immediately afterward: in 1947, he went to work for the Turin press Einaudi and the Communist Party, and began publishing his first works. As a writer, Calvino was initially influenced by the neorealist movement; later, during the years he lived in Paris (1964–80), he was part of the experimental Oulipo literary group.

Calvino is one of the most influential and widely read literary figures of the twentieth century. The fame of this "writer's writer," as he has been called, derives principally from his short stories and novels, in which he exhibits a consummate ability to unite brilliant storytelling with reflection on the nature of the combinatorial mechanics of narration itself. From his earliest works, Calvino sensed an affinity between the interplay of variety and repetition present in folktales and fairy tales and the narrative dynamic that he aspired to in his own writing, in which the marvelous and the everyday merge in stories structurally informed by familiar folkloric paradigms. Calvino's use of the "once upon a time" marvelous is, however, directed toward finding meaning in the here-and-now. His first novel, *Il sentiero dei nidi di ragno* (*The Path to the Nest of Spiders*, 1947), is a tale of the Resistance as seen through the eyes of a young boy; the trilogy *I nostri antennati* (*Our Ancestors*), which includes *Il visconte dimezzato* (*The Cloven Viscount*, 1952), *Il barone rampante* (*The Baron in the Trees*, 1957), *and Il cavaliere inesistente* (*The Nonexistent Knight*, 1959), are allegories on modern life populated by fabulous heroes; and the stories of *Marcovaldo* (1963), which feature the encounters of the bewildered Marcovaldo and family with contemporary urban life, have the flavor of dystopic fairy tales. Even if later works such as *Le città invisibili* (*Invisible Cities*, 1972), *Se una notte d'inverno un viaggiatore* (*If on a Winter's Night a Traveler*, 1979), and *Palomar* (*Mr. Palomar*, 1983) move away from the fairy tale in content, formally they continue to draw on its narrative potentialities.

The 1950s witnessed, in Europe, a revival of interest in folk traditions. In Italy, which had been a nation for less than a century and a republic only since the end of World War II, the need for a creative reelaboration of these traditions was especially felt. In 1954, Calvino was asked by the publisher Einaudi to compile a collection of Italian folktales. Recognizing the lack of a master collection like that of the Brothers **Grimm**, even though Italy was home to the earliest recorded **literary fairy tale**s in Europe, he set to work on *Fiabe italiane* (*Italian Folktales*, 1956). The collection contains 200 tales, just like the Grimms'; the guiding criteria in choosing the tales were variety of major **tale type**s—*Folktales* includes about fifty—and geographical representation; there are tales from all twenty Italian regions, plus Corsica. Fairy tales that incorporate magic predominate; also included are religious and local **legend**s, **novella**s, animal **fable**s, and **anecdote**s. Calvino did not use **informant**s but selected his materials primarily from nineteenth-century anthologies such as Giuseppe **Pitrè**'s *Fiabe, novelle e racconti popolari siciliani* (*Fairy Tales, Novellas, and Popular Tales of Sicily*, 1875) and Gherardo Nerucci's *Sessanta novelle popolari montalesi* (*Sixty Popular Tales from Montale*, 1880). The recasting of this material by imposing "stylistic unity," integrating **variant**s so as to produce the "most unusual, beautiful, and original texts," and in some cases translating tales in dialect into Italian has been compared to the Grimms', although Calvino openly discussed his "halfway scientific" method and indicated the specific changes he made in the abundant notes of *Folktales* (Calvino, xix). In the words of a Tuscan proverb that Calvino quotes, "The tale is not beautiful if nothing is added to it" (xxi). Calvino asserted that he had the right to produce variants, too.

In the introduction to *Folktales*, Calvino maintains that **Italian tales** are as varied and rich as those of Northern Europe; they are endowed with an "unparalleled grace, wit, and unity of design" (xvii) and possess certain unique features, such as enterprising and active female protagonists, an acute sense of beauty, "a continuous quiver of love" and sensuality, the preference for harmony and the "healing solution" (xxix) over cruelty, a "tendency to dwell on the wondrous" (xxx), and an ever-present dialectic between the fantastic and the real. Fairy tales are, at the end, not only the thematic and structural model for all stories, but a key to interpreting the world. The magic they showcase is a complement to human strengths we all possess; even further, they reflect, symbolically, authentic social and political desires and tensions. This is what Calvino means when he says that "folktales are real": they treat all of human experience in their "catalog of the potential destinies of men and women" (xviii); here we find "the arbitrary division of humans, albeit in essence equal, into **king**s and poor people; the persecution of the innocent and their subsequent vindication" (xviii–ix); "love unrecognized when first encountered and then no sooner experienced than lost"; and "having one's existence predetermined by complex and unknown forces" (xix). The vital lessons that folktales offer are that self-liberation comes through the liberation of others, that perseverance and a pure heart are the keys to salvation and victory; that beauty "can be masked by the humble, ugly guise of a frog"; and that the "infinite possibilities of mutation" (xix) are what unify the human and natural worlds.

Calvino's last work, published posthumously, was *Six Memos for the Next Millennium* (1988), a series of lectures to be delivered at Harvard University. It should come as no surprise that the six qualities that are for Calvino the essence of literature—lightness, quickness, exactitude, visibility, multiplicity, and consistency—all find themselves at home in the folktale as well. ***See also*** Collecting, Collectors; Editing, Editors.

Further Readings: Bacchilega, Cristina. "Calvino's Journey: Modern Transformations of Folktale, Story, and Myth." *Journal of Folklore Research* 26 (1989): 81–98; Benson, Stephen. *Cycles of Influence: Fiction, Folktale, Theory.* Detroit: Wayne State University Press, 2003; Calvino, Italo. Introduction. *Italian Folktales.* Translated by George Martin. New York: Harcourt Brace Jovanovich, 1980. xv–xxxii.

Nancy Canepa

Cannibalism

Cannibalism is a staple of fairy tales. Stith **Thompson**'s remark that **ogre**s are anthropomorphic and Vladimir **Propp**'s point that such creatures represent parental figures imply that cannibalism looms large in realm of fairy tales. Even if we focus exclusively on the actual (or attempted) eating of people, the theme appears in at least ten tale types (ATU 311, 315A, 327, 333, 334, 410, 425B, 510, 720, and 894). Moreover, cannibalistic imagery has survived literary sanitization and can be found, for example, in Giambattista **Basile**'s "Sun, Moon, and Talia" and "The Golden Root"; in Charles **Perrault**'s "**Sleeping Beauty**" and "Little **Thumbling**"; and in Jacob and Wilhelm **Grimm**'s "**Hansel and Gretel**," "The Juniper Tree," "Foundling," and "**Snow White**."

Thompson's remark that ogres are anthropomorphic draws attention to the fact that fairy-tale ogres are usually supernatural creatures. Eaters of visiting "living souls" include **witch**es, giants, and other dwellers of the liminal house in the forest as much as the sun, the moon, and other denizens of the faraway otherworld. This trait suggests the voraciousness of the realm of **death**/enchantment; it also hints the regurgitation/rebirth symbolism of disenchantment. Indeed, to be engulfed in enchantment or swallowed by a monster amounts to entering the world of the dead; and, conversely, to shed a skin amounts to exiting a beast, that is, to be regurgitated—disenchanted, reborn—to the world of the living.

Furthermore, Propp's point that ogres are parental figures implies cannibalism is rife among kin. This is true in three basic senses. First, **women** in different generations often ingest one another. Maturing girls eat their elders and, conversely, older women try to cannibalize young rivals. Recall the little girl's ingestion of granny's meat and blood in "The Story of Grandmother" (a variant of ATU 333, Little Red Riding Hood), a (step)**mother**'s attempt to eat Snow White's liver, and a mother-in-law's craving to taste Sleeping Beauty (and her children) in a stew (in Perrault's version of that tale). Underlying all such cases is the notion that fertility, being a limited good, must quit older women to invest younger ones. The incorporation of older women by maidens symbolizes such intergenerational flux. Conversely, attempted ingestion of young rivals by aging women denotes clinging to fading feminine powers. Second, on the male side this pattern shrinks down to unwitting absorption of a son by a man, which hinges on the idea of seed pathetically regressing to its source due to **punishment**—usually meted out by a woman. Third, many cases of cannibalism involve heterosexual kin consumption. In accordance with widespread homology between eating and **sex**, this connotes **incest**. Hence, Bengt Holbek showed that maiden-eating **dragon**s are symbols of **father**/daughter entanglements. Stories of sibling cannibalism draw on the same metaphor.

In sum, cannibalism connotes passage and transubstantiation, death and renovation, and encodes reflections on feminine power and kin entanglements—that is, on such own-**blood** conditions as fairy tales often translate as enchantment. In a fundamental sense, cannibalism is indeed a staple of fairy tales. ***See also*** Birth; Food; Infertility; Transformation.

Further Readings: Holbek, Bengt. "The Language of Fairy Tales." *Nordic Folklore: Recent Studies.* Edited by Reimund Kvideland and Henning Sehmsdorf. Bloomington: Indiana University Press, 1989. 40–62; Verdier, Yvonne. "Little Red Riding Hood in Oral Tradition." *Marvels & Tales* 11 (1997): 101–23.

Francisco Vaz da Silva

Cante Fable

The cante fable (also "cantefable" or "chantefable") is a narrative sequence that contains alternating prose and verse. Examples occur in the traditional literature and **folklore** of many languages—including Japanese and Chinese in the East, Irish and Icelandic in the West, and Hindu, Arabic, and others.

Often the cante fable is a deliberate composition in this form, with the import of the story being told in prose and the interspersed stanzas of verse representing the speech of characters at the high points of drama or of special insight. In the realm of literature, stage drama may be composed totally in rhetorical prose or even in rhymed verse, and the practice of varying prose and verse in that literary genre is a deliberate technique to keep the audience's attention. It is rare for a whole novel to be composed in verse form, but there are examples of the cante fable structure for such, especially in ancient and medieval literatures.

The dual methods of performing narrative—as instanced by ordinary oral storytellers on the one hand and through versified or **ballad** form on the other—have long existed side by side, so it is natural that there should be some crossover in structure. A ballad may be poorly remembered, or it may be thought necessary to give extra background detail to its narrative, so passages in prose may be inserted between quatrains or other groups of versified lines. Contrariwise, a storyteller may find it useful to memorize some parts of a tale in verse or may insert verse into a narrative to show how accomplished a word artist he or she is. There are of course many examples of literary or oral poets composing a narrative in skillfully combined prose and verse as a deliberate tour de force. The picaresque narrative sequence concerning the Rajah Rasàlu in Indian Punjabi tradition is a case in point.

Much more prevalent in folklore is a shorter type of cante fable which is usually referred to as a "stave **anecdote**." This is a brief story in which a poet or other wise person or being composes some extempore verse as the culmination of the event described. Such lines—usually in the form of a quatrain—settle the point at issue through compelling wisdom, or may win the argument or belittle the opponent in a manner approved of by the teller and the audience. There are also folk **legend**s that pit the wits of celebrated poets against each other, having them compete at describing some event, satirize each other, or pose and answer versified **riddle**s. The prevalence of such verbal duels varies from culture to culture, but it can be generally noted that the closer the literary stream is to the oral one, the richer in dexterity the verses tend to be. In some contexts, such as frequently in the Gaelic lore of Ireland and Scotland, and in Icelandic, the verse uttered by the poet in such anecdotes was represented as having magical power. ***See also*** *Aucassin et Nicolette*; Middle Ages.

Further Readings: Ó hÓgáin, Dáithí. *The Hero in Irish Folk History.* Dublin: Gill & Macmillan, 1985. 216–70; Reinhard, John R. "The Literary Background of the Chantefable." *Speculum* 1 (1926): 157–69;

Swynnerton, Charles. *Romantic Tales from the Panjâb with Indian Nights' Entertainment.* 1908. New Delhi: Asian Educational Services, 2004. 51–151.

Dáithí Ó hÓgáin

Čapek, Karel (1890–1938)

Karel Čapek was a Czechoslovak journalist, playwright, producer, and novelist internationally known and recognized for his futuristic play *R.U.R* (1920). First staged in the Theatre Guild in New York City in 1922, *R.U.R.* uses the term "robot" for the first time, a word invented by Čapek's brother Josef. His first two poems, titled "Prosté motivy" ("Simple Motives"), were published in 1904 while he was a student in Brno. Until his death, Čapek wrote on many topics and in a variety of genres, including literature, politics, insects, detectives, science fiction, travel, gardening, and fairy tales. Whatever the genre, all his works are typically entertaining, mind opening, and educational. As a liberal and close friend of President T. G. Masaryk, he always denied the utopia of communism and rejected fascism, which placed him high on the Nazi's blacklist when they entered Czechoslovakia in 1939. Refusing to flee the country when the threat was imminent, he died of pneumonia three months before the Nazi invasion. His brother Josef, also a journalist, gifted painter, and cartoonist, collaborated with Čapek on numerous works as a writer or illustrator. Josef was sent to the Bergen-Belsen concentration camp, where he died in 1945.

Devatero Pohádek (*Nine Fairy Tales,* 1932) consists of fairy tales written by Karel and Josef Čapek and illustrated by Josef. They display an everyday world, generally contemporary or recently past, filled with literary or real people, such as Sherlock Holmes and Hollywood stars, and creatures such as fairies or fairy dogs, magicians, sprites, birds that encounter angels, and animals who speak. Most of the tales take place in Czechoslovakia, in Prague, and in other various villages, with creatures or animals wandering in foreign countries. The geographical details are accurate and often linked to the living conditions of their inhabitants. A sprite from Prague, for example, is well off and sometimes even owns a motorboat, while his counterpart in Havlovice lives in a mud puddle. However, there is no animosity among different social classes, a theme conspicuously absent from Čapek's work and politics. Most of the fairy tales address children directly, but their political and social messages and moral lessons are presented in a manner typical of Čapek's satire, making them educational and appealing to a wide range of readers. The tales sometimes reference God, and many deal with the old world's confrontation with the new technological advances being experienced at the beginning of the twentieth century. The plots follow folk tradition, where ordinary people become heroes and innocence ultimately triumphs. Several fairy tales are imaginative **etiologic tale**s, explaining for example why birds can fly and chickens cannot, why dogs dig holes in the ground, or how God created humans as a god that dogs could smell. The language of the tales binds every element together. Written in colloquial Czech with the sparkle of the spoken word, the tales are rich in wordplay, verbal games, and lists. In this respect Čapek's fairy tales could be compared with those of Giambattista **Basile**, with which they share—besides the coarse, witty language—many characteristics and techniques.

Further Readings: Bradbrook, Bohuslava R. *Karel Čapek: In Pursuit of Truth, Tolerance, and Trust.* Brighton: Sussex Academic Press, 1998; Čapek, Karel. *Nine Fairy Tales: And One More Thrown In for Good Measure.* Translated by Dagmar Herrmann. Evanston, IL: Northwestern University Press, 1990;

Makin, Michael, and Jindřich Toman, eds. *On Karel Čapek: A Michigan Slavic Colloquium*. Ann Arbor: Michigan Slavic Publications, 1992.

Charlotte Trinquet

Capuana, Luigi (1839–1915)

Luigi Capuana was born in Catania, Sicily. After abandoning law studies, he embarked upon a career as writer, journalist, and playwright. Together with his fellow Sicilian Giovanni Verga, he was one of the protagonists of the *verismo*, or regional realism, movement, and as such embraced the expressive value of folkloric material, recognizing the similarities between the "impersonal" voice that was an essential element of *verismo* style and the narrative techniques of **folktale**s. As a novelist, he also published nearly twenty volumes of short prose, including *Profumo* (*Perfume*, 1890) and *Il Marchese di Roccaverdina* (*The Marquis of Roccaverdina*, 1901).

Capuana was also a prolific author and editor of **children's literature**, especially fairy tales. But the author's familiarity with Sicilian **folklore** and the work of folklorists such as Giuseppe **Pitrè** did not prevent him from creating his own unique tales through the "restoration" of traditional folk **motif**s and **tale type**s, the integration of literary materials, and the use of humor, whimsical fantasy, and realistic detail. The most important of Capuana's collections of fairy tales are *C'era una volta* (*Once upon a Time*, 1882, enlarged in 1889), *Il regno delle fate* (*The Kingdom of Fairies*, 1883), *La reginotta* (*The Princess*, 1883), *Il Racconta-fiabe* (*The Fairy Tale-Teller*, 1894), *Chi vuole fiabe, chi vuole?* (*Who Wants Fairy Tales, Who Wants Them?*, 1908), and *Le ultime fiabe* (*The Last Fairy Tales*, 1919). He also wrote fairy-tale plays such as *Spera di sole: Commedia per burattini* (*Sunbeam: A Comedy for Marionettes*, 1898).

In *Once upon a Time*, Capuana's most significant rewriting of the fairy tale, we find, together with the standard characters and motifs of the fairy tale, down-and-out protagonists whose battles consist of their all too real search for food and shelter, as well as **magic helper**s and royalty who resemble familiar relatives engaged in the mundane details of everyday life.

The tales of *Once Upon a Time* include "Le arance d'oro" ("The Golden Oranges"), "Ranocchino" ("Little Froggy"), "Cecina" ("Little Chick Pea"), "I tre anelli" ("The Three Rings"), "La Fontana della bellezza" ("The Fountain of Beauty"), "L'uovo nero" ("The Black Egg"), "Serpentina" ("Little Snake Girl"), "Testa di Rospo" ("Toad-Head"), "Il racconta-fiabe" ("The Fairy Tale-Teller"), and ten others. The last tale in particular suggestively illustrates Capuana's personal approach to his primary materials. It features a storyteller who, tired of telling the same old Cinderellas and Sleeping Beauties, meets up with some fairies in a wood as he is searching for new material. They send him to the wizard Tre-pi (a transposition of the folklorist Pitrè's name), but Tre-pi refuses to impart any of his narrative riches, instead directing him to Fairy Fantasy, who in turn offers him magical gifts that cause him to spew tales whenever he opens his mouth. His young audience tires of these tales, however, and he offers them to Tre-pi for his collection; but as they are changing hands, the tales turn into "a handful of flies," and the teller concludes that his search for new stories is futile. The entire tale thus sums up the dialectic, common at the end of the nineteenth century, between folklorists concerned with collecting and recording traditional tales before they disappeared, and innovative authors like Capuana, who affirm, through their original works, the potential for the creative regeneration of tradition. *See also* Italian Tales.

Further Readings: Cocchiara, Giuseppe. *Popolo e letteratura in Italia*. Turin: Einaudi, 1959; Marchese, Giuseppe. *Capuana poeta della vita*. Palermo: Ando, 1964.

Nancy Canepa

Carroll, Lewis (1832–1898)

Lewis Carroll is the famous pen name of Charles Lutwidge Dodgson, the Victorian writer, photographer, and Oxford mathematician responsible for *Alice's Adventures in Wonderland* (1865) and *Through the Looking-Glass and What Alice Found There* (1872). These classic children's narratives are not fairy tales, but looser and more wandering narratives, which use the framework of dreaming to rationalize their nonsense logic and dissolution of familiar structures.

While the first *Alice* book was written to amuse the seven-year-old Alice Liddell, daughter of the dean of Christ Church, in fact Carroll's writing includes levels of **parody**, satire, and mathematical puzzles which are not readily accessible to children. Carroll's somewhat obsessive friendships with female children are well documented by both his numerous surviving letters and his photographs, and are generally taken to be the retreat of a shy and socially inept man from the demands of adult interaction. Certainly he shows a genuine and playful sympathy for the child's imagination, and is notable among Victorian children's writers in that the dream narratives of the *Alice* books are subversive of Victorian society and mores, rather than offering the more usual moralizing tone.

Carroll was a close friend of Victorian fantasist George **MacDonald**, but Carroll's work is somewhat different from MacDonald's and from the bulk of Victorian fantasy for children. **Motif**s in the *Alice* books are recognizable from fairy tales—a child wandering with a vague sense of quest in a magical landscape of **king**s and **queen**s, **magic object**s, and talking animals—but their potentially fairy-tale nature is disrupted by Carroll's disintegrated logic. Where a strong sense of pattern does underpin the narratives, it tends to come from structures such as games (cards and chess), mathematics, or Victorian poetry, which are rather different from fairy tale. On the other hand, Carroll's ongoing invocation of familiar nursery rhymes, with their mythic and magical characters and essential situations (the Lion and the Unicorn, or Tweedledum and Tweedledee facing the Monstrous Crow), does provide some sense of folkloric narrative. In particular, the often savage and summary worlds of Wonderland and the Looking Glass, rife with curiously distanced threats of violence and extinction, bear some comparison with the ritualized brutality of older folkloric forms.

Lewis Carroll. [Library of Congress]

With the exception of the extended poetical nonsense quest *The Hunting of the Snark* (1876), Carroll's other writings have never achieved the popularity of the *Alice* books. His two novels with more explicitly fairy-tale content are *Sylvie and Bruno* (1889) and *Sylvie and Bruno Concluded* (1893). Intended for adults, these are considerably more moralistic and sentimental than the *Alice* books, and their focus on the children of a ruler in Fairyland is no more than a loose rationalization for a similar kind of disconnected dream-narrative based around an adult love story. **See also** Children's Literature; Mirror; Pig.

Further Readings: Demurova, Nina. "Toward a Definition of *Alice*'s Genre: The Folktale and Fairy-Tale Connections." *Lewis Carroll: A Celebration; Essays on the Occasion of the 150th Anniversary of the Birth of Charles Lutwidge Dodgson.* Edited by Edward Guiliano. New York: Potter, 1982. 75–88; Reichertz, Ronald. *The Making of the Alice Books: Lewis Carroll's Uses of Earlier Children's Literature.* Montreal: McGill-Queen's University Press, 1997.

Jessica Tiffin

Carter, Angela (1940–1992)

A vivid and original presence in British literature, Angela Carter—during her sadly foreshortened career—produced a motley array of novels, short stories, essays, radio and film scripts, and journalistic pieces. Stylistic and generic influences in her writing include **magical realism**, the marvelous, the Gothic, surrealism, science fiction, and cinema. There is also a strong thread of **folklore** and fairy tale in her work. Her writing is characterized by rich, sumptuous textures, linguistic and symbolic excess, and a maverick political sensibility that generates narratives in a continual state of flux. Her shifting indeterminacy shares techniques and sensibilities with **postmodernism**. She is at all times a self-aware feminist with particular interests in female subjectivity and power, but her unabashed interest in heterosexuality and the sensuous, expressed as it is with her earthy vitality, humor, and irreverence, led her to run afoul of some feminist critics. Her interest in genre narratives, particularly, is a fruitful ground for investigation of the inextricability of female desire from patriarchal processes. She is always provocative, never definitive, in her political explorations.

Folklore and fairy tale are both explicit and implicit in much of Carter's writing. Early works include two children's fairy tales, "Miss Z The Dark Young Lady" and "The Donkey Prince" (both 1970). These are playful pieces that self-consciously render traditional animal **motif**s with humor and vividness, and which feature tough, self-reliant heroines. *Sea Cat and Dragon King* (2000) is a similarly fantastic undersea **fable**. Another children's picture book, *Comic and Curious Cats* (1979), brings together her recurring themes of elaborate, mischievous language and magical beasts. Later, she published her own **translation** of Charles **Perrault**'s fairy tales (*The Fairy Tales of Charles Perrault*, 1977), giving them a warm, down-to-earth voice that stresses Perrault's qualities of social awareness and practicality. She also edited several collections of folklore and modern short stories, including the two volumes of the *Virago Book of Fairy Tales* (1990 and 1992) and *Wayward Girls and Wicked Women* (1986). The Virago collections are more folkloric in tone, whereas *Wayward Girls* features literary tales that have a marvelous, fablelike edge despite their realism; all three, however, are deliberate and gleeful assemblages that celebrate female power and wit across a variety of cultural scenarios.

Carter's 1979 collection, *The Bloody Chamber and Other Stories*, establishes the fairy-tale form as her richest arena for subversion, exploration, and play. Its ten tales are mostly retellings of Perrault, although with some excursions into other sources. They include versions of highly recognizable classics such as "**Bluebeard**," "**Beauty and the Beast**," "**Sleeping Beauty**," and "**Little Red Riding Hood**." Carter's tales use the symbols and scenarios of the classic fairy tales to explore different approaches to **women**'s subjectivity and desire, with a weighting toward marvelous beasts as a symbolic exploration of **sexuality**. This political project is particularly interesting when considered in conjunction with Carter's polemical work, *The Sadeian Woman: An Exercise in Cultural History* (1979). In this response to the Marquis de Sade, she demonstrates a powerfully demythologizing vision of sexuality divorced from its social and reproductive functions. *The Bloody Chamber*'s tales grope for a similar vision, attempting to transgress and restate the culturally defined parameters of sexuality. In particular, two "Beauty and the Beast" narratives exist as inverted images, "The Courtship of Mr. Lyon" presenting the complete eradication of desire versus its complete validation, although outside the confines of culture, in "The Tiger's Bride." The collection's strong use of **intertextuality** is consequently important: elements of erotic romance, the Gothic, Romanticism, and other textual traditions provide powerful stereotypes of female identity that illuminate and intersect with those of the fairy tale itself. Thus "The Bloody Chamber" presents a sadomasochistic relationship that explores, through a deliberately nineteenth-century erotic narrative, women's submission to male sexual experience. A comic version of legitimized desire is found in "**Puss-in-Boots**," whose **trickster cat** enables a baroque, operatic version of sexual gratification divorced from emotional or social consequence. The red, white, and black **motif**s of "**Snow White**" are updated to a chill Freudian parable in "The Snow Child," while "The Lady of the House of Love" explores the static and doomed entrapment of the Sleeping Beauty as brooding gothic vampire, the ultimately devouring feminine, equally lost whether her **prince** is rescuer or victim. The collection's final three stories are variations on the Red Riding Hood theme, the wolf becoming both threatening male sexuality and an image of female power in a series of complex, shifting visions that return to a more earthy folkloric expression, in sharp contrast to the deliberate artifice of the literary in earlier stories. The **werewolf** motif becomes the centerpiece in Carter's film script for Neil Jordan's *The Company of Wolves* (1984), a sumptuous visual realization both of Carter's fantastic vision and of her **gender** interests.

While *The Bloody Chamber* is Carter's most sustained engagement with fairy-tale forms, the familiar motifs and structures resonate throughout her writing, both as symbolic underpinnings to novels and in the fablelike, essentialist structure of her short stories. Explicit fairy-tale rewrites occur in other collections, notably the horribly enlivened puppet in "The Loves of Lady Purple" (*Fireworks: Nine Profane Pieces*, 1974) and the female rivalries and mutilated girls of "Ashputtle, or The **Mother**'s Ghost" in *American Ghosts and Old World Wonders* (1993). Carter's novels, with their tendency toward magical realism, feature more generalized images of the marvelous, often the symbolic literally embodied: the winged woman of *Nights at the Circus* (1984), the nightmarish, mythical, and science-fictional dreamscapes of *The Infernal Desire Machines of Doctor Hoffman* (1972). An awareness of structured narrative, genre, and tradition can be found in disparate elements such as the dystopian melodrama of *Heroes and Villains* (1969) or the fantastic cinematic of *The Passion of New Eve* (1977). Carter's writing returns again and again to dreams, **transformation**s, quests, monsters—the toolbox of symbolic fable. *See also* Feminism; Feminist Tales; Film and Video.

Further Readings: Bacchilega, Cristina. *Postmodern Fairy Tales: Gender and Narrative Strategies*. Philadelphia: University of Pennsylvania, 1997; Roemer, Danielle M., and Cristina Bacchilega, eds. *Angela*

Carter and the Fairy Tale. Detroit: Wayne State University Press, 2001; Sheets, Robin Ann. "Pornography, Fairy Tales, and Feminism: Angela Carter's 'The Bloody Chamber.'" *Journal of the History of Sexuality* 1 (1991): 633–57.

Jessica Tiffin

Cartoons and Comics

Folktales and fairy tales have long inspired visual representations—from **chapbook**s and **broadside**s, which illustrated the text of popular folk narratives with images, to children's picture books, illustrated editions, and the fairy-tale **art** of so-called high culture. The history of **illustration** shows how artists have been repeatedly inspired to illustrate the major **motif**s and episodes of folktales and fairy tales. The *Kinder- und Hausmärchen* (*Children's and Household Tales*, 1812–15) of Jacob and Wilhelm **Grimm** in particular have found many illustrators, from their brother Ludwig Emil **Grimm** and Ludwig **Richter** in the nineteenth century to important contemporary artists such as Tomi **Ungerer** and Maurice **Sendak**. But while the colorful depictions of these illustrators recreate the world of the fairy tales, cartoonists deal with the tales quite differently in their humorous or satirical drawings. With fairy tales being the most popular traditional narratives since the second half of the nineteenth century, cartoonists have created revealing images that place the perfect world of classical fairy tales in striking contrast with imperfect reality. They usually ignore the positive ending of traditional tales and instead concentrate on special scenes interpreted as signs of a troubled society. These innovative reinterpretations in the mass media of newspapers and magazines concentrate on such problems as hate, greed, cruelty, insensitivity, dishonesty, deception, vanity, selfishness, distrust, irresponsibility, jealousy, and so on. But this is not to say that there are not also those cartoons that react with much humor to some of the well-known fairy-tale **motif**s.

While almost all magazines and newspapers include cartoons and comic strips based on folktales or fairy tales, the *New Yorker* magazine has excelled in the publication of not only humorous but also satirical fairy-tale cartoons, with magazines like *Good Housekeeping*, *Saturday Review*, *Better Homes and Gardens*, *Cosmopolitan*, *Mad*, *Woman's Day*, *Fortune*, and others from the United States following suit. This is also true for such satirical publications as *Simplicissimus*, *Kladderadatsch*, *Fliegende Blätter*, and *Eulenspiegel* from Germany, *Punch* from Great Britain, *Krokodil* from Russia, and *Nebelspalter* from Switzerland. In addition, most newspapers around the world have comic sections that carry cartoons and comic strips into many homes, and since readers will be acquainted with the allusions to folk narratives, meaningful humorous or satirical communication is taking place.

Some of the cartoons and comic strips merely allude to fairy tales in general, as demonstrated by the following captions and lines: "Steve's stepmother isn't wicked. She gave us cookies"; "I fulfill my own wishes!"; "I love fairy tales! Read me 'Thin Thighs in 30 Seconds a Day!'"; "Don't you shush me! I've never heard such fairy tales!"; "It [the fairy tale] sounds a little too perfect. What's the downside?" and "No, my life was not always a fairy tale—yours?" There are also many cartoons that play off the standard introductory formula: "You read me that before, so now it's 'Twice upon a time,' right?"; "If it starts with 'once upon a time' I'm leaving"; "Once upon a time, once upon a time! When was it, anyway?"; "'Once upon a time ...' That's the way all the good stories begin"; "Are you sure this is a children's story? It didn't begin with 'Once upon a time'"; and "How many years ago was 'Once upon a time'?" And there are also those captions that refer to the formulaic ending of fairy tales: "You're not even trying to live happily ever after!"; "Doesn't anybody ever live happily ever after without gettin' married?"; "And they lived happily ever after—she in New York, he in L.A."; "And they lived happily for quite some time"; "And so the prince and the princess used condoms and had safe sex and lived happily ever after"; and "They lived happily ever after—except for the age thing." Of course, there is also a caption of a cartoon depicting someone trying to write the shortest possible short story: "One upon a time, they lived happily ever after."

It should be noted that most cartoons and comic strips react to a dozen fairy tales at best, mainly "The **Frog King**," "**Cinderella**," "**Hansel and Gretel**," "**Little Red Riding Hood**," "Rapunzel," "Rumpelstiltskin," "**Sleeping Beauty**," and "**Snow White**." Occasionally one also finds references to Hans Christian **Andersen**'s "The Emperor's New Clothes" and "The Princess on the Pea." Folktales are depicted much less frequently, with the exception of the ever-popular "Pied Piper of Hamelin." The ambiguous figure of the piper who first clears the city of rats and then lures children away has found many modern reinterpretations, with such figures as Napoleon, Adolf Hitler, Joseph Stalin, Henry Kissinger, the Ayatolla Khomeini, Margaret Thatcher, Ronald Reagan, and others being depicted as evil or good leaders. In fact, political movements such as communism and national socialism have been represented as negative Pied Pipers, while such modern commodities as the radio and **television** have also been depicted as Pied Pipers leading people astray from an active life. But the ambiguous Pied Piper as a positive or negative symbol can also be a rock musician, a famous athlete, a good teacher, or an evil terrorist, giving the cartoonists ample opportunity to make sociopolitical statements both in the drawing and the caption.

There are numerous articles and books that have included cartoons and comic strips, especially regarding "The Frog King" and "Little Red Riding Hood." The well-known cartoonist Gary Larsen could easily put together an entire book of his many "Far Side" illustrations based on fairy-tale motifs, and the same is true for the creators of such well-known cartoons and comic strips as "The Family Circus," "Dennis, the Menace," "Hi and Lois," "Peanuts," "Blondie," and "Garfield." There is even a comic strip entitled "Mother Goose & Grimm," which bases its individual frames on fairy tales, nursery rhymes, **proverbs**, and other verbal folklore genres. But here are at least a few telling captions from such fairy-tale cartoons that show the multifaceted possibilities of modern reinterpretations of standard fairy-tale motifs: "How 'bout once more with feeling?" ("The Frog King"); "All right, dear . . . have fun, but remember, your Visa card expires at midnight" ("Cinderella"); "Here's your pizza, ma'am. My . . . what big eyes you have" ("Little Red Riding Hood"); "Tell me the truth, mirror . . . do I look like I'm forty?"—"No, not anymore" ("Snow White"); "We should've left a trail of bread crumbs. All these condos look just like granddad's" ("Hansel and Gretel"); "Well, I've spun the entire natural ecosystem into gold. Now what?" ("Rumpelstiltskin"); "With every snip of the scissors she felt a renewed sense of freedom. And she lived happily ever after" ("Rapunzel"); and "Could you leave out the kissing part?" ("Sleeping Beauty").

As expected, there is a definite predominance of sexually oriented cartoons in the modern mass media. While they might be rather innocuous in mainstream magazines, they can also be quite explicit or crude in such erotic magazines as *Playboy*, *Penthouse*, and *Hustler*. Drawings in which the indirect and metaphorical **sexuality** of fairy tales is intentionally translated into commercial exploitation of crude sex can be regarded only as pornographic. But there are also those tasteful and merely suggestive reinterpretations that make some of these cartoons humorous commentaries on sexual politics, **gender** issues, and erotic pleasures (see **Erotic Tales**). A few captions tell this modern story: "Not bad, child, not bad, but you'll never catch a prince like that—stick these apples down the front of your gown and I'll give the wand another wave" ("Cinderella"); "Come back later, honey. Grandma's entertaining a gentleman caller right now" ("Little Red Riding Hood"); "Perhaps you could break the spell if you'd kiss me someplace other than the mouth" ("The Frog King"); "When you come to 'kiss'— that's a euphemism" ("Sleeping Beauty"); "I don't feel like it now that you're up here—I've got a headache" ("Rapunzel"); "Do you still feel a pea under the mattress, my lady?" ("The Princess on the Pea"); and "Snow White withheld her favors this morning, so we all got up Grumpy" ("Snow White"). Obviously, the drawings add much to make these captions come alive, but it is worth mentioning that in these particular cases none are grossly obscene.

Despite this obvious preoccupation with sexual matters that most certainly add fuel to the fire of **psychological approaches** to fairy tales, the mass media also include many social and political caricatures characterized by satire, sarcasm, and cynicism. Such illustrators as Olaf Gulbransson, Horst Haitzinger, Tony Auth, and Patrick Oliphant often depict known politicians or celebrities in their caricatures, thus going from indirect to direct confrontation and ridicule. Recent U.S. presidents, but also internationally recognized politicians and celebrities like Indira Ghandi, Prince Charles, Mikhail Gorbachev, Madonna, and many others have all been attacked or ridiculed in fairy-tale caricatures. One of the most common motifs is to place the person in front of a **mirror** and to have him or her ask that famous question: "Mirror, mirror on the wall, who is the fairest of them all?"—whereupon they receive an appropriately negative response. But if one is not exactly beautiful, one can, of course, alter the questions accordingly in the hope of getting at least some recognition, as for example in "Mirror, mirror, on the wall, who is the most unselfconsciously hipper-than-thou-almost-over-thirty-type-person of them all?"; "Who's the greatest Mom of them all?"; "Well, then, who is the most intelligent?"; "Mirror, mirror on the wall, who's the most successful regional manager of computer-systems analysis in East Orange, New Jersey?"; "Mirror, mirror on the wall, am I still a 10?"; "Mirror, mirror on the wall, who will rise and who will fall?"; "Mirror, mirror on the wall, who's the fairest at the mall?"; and "Mirror, mirror on the wall, who's the most optimistic of them all?"

But there are also those cartoons that depict certain persons, especially politicians, with revealing captions, as for example: "And so Mr. Reagan and Mr. Andropov threw away all their silly nuclear weapons and they all lived happily ever after"; "My, Grandma Gorbachev, what a witty sense of humor you have and, ooooh Grandma Gorbachev, what a charming personality you have and, gosh, Grandma Gorbachev, what great big teeth you have" ("Little Red Riding Hood"); and "Hi, my name is Mario [Cuomo, former governor of New York]. Don't kiss me or I'll turn into a candidate and if there's one thing I don't want to be it's a candidate. Hi, my name is Mario. Don't kiss me ..." ("The Frog King").

Finally, cartoonists have also had their fun in referring to several fairy tales at once to make social commentaries. Relating to the annual award ceremonies of the American Academy of Motion Pictures, the caption of one of these cartoons read befittingly: "Nominees for the hand of Prince Charming are Cinderella in 'Cinderella,' Rosamond in 'Sleeping Beauty,' Goldilocks in 'The Three Bears,' Beauty in 'Beauty and the Beast,' and Rapunzel in 'Rapunzel.' The envelope, please." There are also the captions of two cartoons comparing the **violence** of fairy tales with that of modern society: "Snow White kidnapped. Prince released from spell. Tailor kills seven. Those are the headlines. I'll be back in a moment with the details" and "Witches poisoning princesses, giants falling off beanstalks, wolves terrorizing pigs ... and you complain about violence on TV!?" Little wonder then that yet another cartoon example contains this caption addressing the Brothers Grimm: "You and your brother portray a great many wicked giants in these tales of yours, Herr Grimm. Do you think you could balance them by depicting a couple of good ones?"

The result is clearly that in many of the cartoons and comic strips, the perfect world of the fairy tales is placed into question, usually by also indirectly commenting on social issues and concerns. Again, the following captions with their drawings tell general but also more specific stories about modern life and communication: "They don't cast spells like they used to" ("The Frog King"); "Gingerbread? Really? How did you get a mortgage?" ("Hansel and Gretel"); "Actually I'm not a Prince exactly. I'm a Pretender. Will that do?" ("Snow White"); "Why do I have to kiss her awake? Why can't I just punch her one?" ("Sleeping Beauty"); "It is beautiful, Rapunzel, but we don't need it anymore, and it's a fire hazard" ("Rapunzel"); "Forget the gown. This is my best disco outfit" ("Cinderella"); and "My, Grandma, what a big-shot attorney you have" ("Little Red Riding Hood"). Such disenchanted cartoons and caricatures show the dissatisfaction with the sociopolitical situation, but by basing their criticism on traditional fairy-tale motifs, they also refer, if only indirectly, to the way it could and should be.

Because fairy tales continue to resonate in popular consciousness, the relationship between fairy tales and comics remains a vital one, especially in an era when being culturally literate also means being visually literate. Innovative creative work has created a productive new dynamic between traditional tales and visual art in the late twentieth and early twenty-first centuries. Comic art such as Art **Spiegelman**'s *Maus* books (1986–91) has revitalized the relation between the fairy tale and comic book; and the **graphic novel**, which frequently adapts the material of folktales and fairy tales for its combination of printed narrative and sequential images, has become immensely popular around the world, leading to new forms of fairy-tale production and reception that deserve further examination by scholars. *See also* Japanese Popular Culture; Mizuno Junko; Vess, Charles.

Further Readings: Flanagan, John T. "Grim Stories: Folklore in Cartoons." *Midwestern Journal of Language and Folklore* 1 (1975): 20–26; Horn, Katalin. "Märchenmotive und gezeichneter Witz: Einige Möglichkeiten der Adaption." *Österreichische Zeitschrift für Volkskunde* 37 (1983): 209–37; Mieder, Wolfgang, ed. *Grimms Märchen—modern: Prosa, Gedichte, Karikaturen.* Stuttgart: Philipp Reclam, 1979; _____. "Survival Forms of 'Little Red Riding Hood' in Modern Society." *International Folklore Review* 2 (1982): 23–40; _____. *Tradition and Innovation in Folk Literature.* Hanover, NH: University Press of New England, 1987; _____. *Der Rattenfänger von Hameln: Die Sage in Literatur, Medien und Karikaturen.* Wien: Edition Praesens, 2002; Röhrich, Lutz. "Wandlungen des Märchens in den modernen Bildmedien: Comics und Cartoons." *Märchen in unserer Zeit.* Edited by Hans-Jörg Uther. München: Eugen Diederichs, 1990. 11–26; Smith, Grace Partridge. "The Plight of the Folktale in the Comics." *Southern Folklore Quarterly* 16 (1952): 124–27; Zipes, Jack, ed. *The Trials and Tribulations of Little Red Riding Hood.* 2nd edition. New York: Routledge, 1993.

Wolfgang Mieder

Castroviejo, Concha (1910–1995)

A Spanish journalist, critic, novelist, and short-story writer, Castroviejo published two books of children's stories: *El jardín de las siete puertas* (*The Garden with Seven Gates,*

1961) and *Los días de Lina* (*Lina's Days*, 1971). *The Garden with Seven Gates* is a collection of fourteen stories and one minidrama that firmly established the author as a teller of contemporary fairy-tale-like narratives.

Featuring talking birds, child protagonists, and extraordinary occurrences, these tales speak to fantasies and fears that are common throughout life, which means that although they are peopled with child characters, they are not for youth alone. A fairy tale reminiscent of the Brothers **Grimm** is "La tejedora de sueños" ("The Weaver of Dreams"), a story about a much-criticized little girl who finds happiness in an unusual calling, in a house in the woods that has seven chimneys issuing seven different colors of smoke. "Una sirena y un corregidor, 500 vecinos y un mirlo cantor" ("A Mermaid and a Magistrate, 500 Neighbors, and a Singing Blackbird") describes a beautiful siren and shows that haughtiness comes at a price. "Barú y el gigante" ("Barú and the Giant"), about a giant who gathers pearls, censures royal greed and slavery. The story "El zopilote presumido" ("The Conceited Buzzard") cautions against arrogance and presumptuousness. *See also* Children's Literature; Spanish Tales.

Further Reading: Castroviejo, Concha. *The Garden with Seven Gates.* Translated by Robert M. Fedorchek. Lewisburg: Bucknell University Press, 2004.

Robert M. Fedorchek

Cat

Domestic cats appear in the earliest known **myth**s and folktales as representations of the highest deities, such as the Egyptian goddess Bast, the first image of which dates back to 2000 BCE. The cult of Bast was connected with joy and merrymaking, and this role is reflected in later lore of most cultures. For instance, the cat's proximity to gods is emphasized in Norse mythology, where Freya, the goddess of love, is carried in a chariot drawn by cats.

Parallel to Bast, the cat was featured in Egyptian mythology as one of the many incarnations of the solar god Ra, who struggles against and kills an evil serpent. The amalgamation of the cat and the dragonslayer has left traces in Oriental as well as European **folklore**, where the **motif** often got inverted. While sometimes the hero metamorphosed into a cat, often it was the antagonist who underwent this **transformation**, especially into a black cat. This ambiguity explains the twofold status of cats in folklore, where they appear as both benevolent and evil.

Before cats spread to Europe, they often appeared in stories as mythical creatures, alongside **dragon**s, unicorns, and basilisks. Until the late eighteenth century, the generic origin of cats was unclear; they were thought to be related to reptiles and birds. Rudyard Kipling's **etiologic tale** "The Cat Who Walked by Himself" from *Just So Stories* (1902) depicts cats as unreliable and independent as opposed to dogs, which are man's true friends.

The practical uses of domestic cats as mousers contributed to their positive reputation, and in this capacity they were carried throughout the world on conquerors' and merchants' vessels. This is reflected in the British tale of Dick Whittington, who makes his fortune by sending a cat on his master's ship. The ship ends up in Africa, where a local king buys the wonderful animal who can deliver his country from rodents.

During the **Middle Ages** in Europe, cats became associated with evil powers. This was based partly on popular beliefs about cats' lewdness and partly on their Christian association with Satan. In the European tradition of Last Supper paintings, a cat represents Judas. Such attitudes led to cats being linked to **witch**es. Indeed, black cats, together with ravens, frequently appear in folktales as witches' familiars (such as Grimalkin, a cat from Celtic lore, also featured in *Macbeth*), and witches themselves even turn into cats. An evil cat monster appears in King Arthur stories. In Slavic folklore, Bayun-Cat is a giant hostile black cat that imposes irresistible sleepiness on people, often by telling tales or singing songs. This image is, however, ambiguous since it portrays the cat as creative and wise, as also reflected in later literary works such as E. T. A. **Hoffmann**'s *Lebensansichten des Katers Murr* (*The Life and Opinions of Cat Murr*, 1820–22). The cat's mystifying nature is perhaps best expressed in the figure of the Cheshire cat in Lewis **Carroll**'s *Alice in Wonderland* (1865). A widely recognized trait ascribed to cats is that they have nine lives, apparently referring to their remarkable resilience. The view of cats as evil led to incredible cruelties toward them, including the Great Cat Massacre in France in the 1730s. During witch hunts, cats were burned together with their mistresses.

By the beginning of the nineteenth century, the cat's repute was exculpated, and cats became popular pets in upper- and middle-class families, as reflected in numerous nursery rhymes, **fable**s (for example, "The Mouse Who Put the Bell on the Cat"), **cartoons**, children's stories, and picture books. Cats became benign and often sweet characters in folklore adapted to children's and family reading.

The most famous fairy-tale cat is undoubtedly **Puss in Boots**, a **trickster** figure featured in Charles **Perrault**'s collection (1697) but also known in other cultures, where the same role is played by other animals—for instance, by a fox in Slavic folktales. Puss in Boots is endowed with human intelligence and speech. That he walks upright and wears a pair of boots puts him closer to human beings, even though he retains his feline cunning, agility, and hunting skills, which again underscores the cat's mysterious, double nature.

Cats appear in a number of well-known **animal tale**s, such as "The Bremen Town Musicians" and "The Cat and the Mouse in Partnership," in stories involving helpful animals, and in tales based on the magical bride/bridegroom motif, including the Irish story of Cuculin/Cuchulainn and Marie-Catherine d'**Aulnoy**'s "La chatte blanche" ("The White Cat," 1698), a female contemporary of Puss in Boots. Not unexpectedly, tomcats are frequently portrayed in fairy tales as adventurous and mischievous, while she-cats are connected to feminine witchcraft, shape shifting, mystery, and sexuality. A cat of indiscernible gender is featured in "The Story of Grandmother," a version of "**Little Red Riding Hood**." Here the cat is the voice of conscience, accusing the girl of eating her granny's flesh and drinking her blood. Taking into account the conventional connection between old women and their cats, this peripheral character may be the murdered grandmother's soul (or totem), similar to the bird in some versions of the **Cinderella** story. An enigmatic British tale is "The King of the Cats," which suggests that cats have a secret realm of their own; in a Scandinavian version of the tale, the cat is a disguised troll. A reminiscence of this tale can be found in **children's literature**, for instance, in *Carbonel* (1955) by Barbara Sleigh.

In modern fairy tales and **fantasy**, the cat is widely featured as a **magic helper** and bearer of magic powers, especially assisting the hero in transportation between the everyday and the magical realm. Some children's authors such as Lloyd **Alexander** and Diana Wynne **Jones** are especially fond of feline characters, and generally cats are among the most popular characters in children's literature. *The Cat in the Hat* (1957) by Dr. Seuss employs the trickster and magic helper aspect of the folkloric cat. In contrast, in C. S. Lewis's Narnia stories, a cat becomes a traitor and is denied salvation. Images of cats originating in folklore are also found in works by Edgar Allan Poe, Charles Baudelaire, T. S. Eliot, and Mikhail Bulgakov. *See also* Animal Bride, Animal Groom.

Further Readings: Briggs, Katharine M. *Nine Lives: Cats in Folklore.* London: Routledge & Kegan Paul, 1980; Holmgren, Virginia C. *Cats in Fact and Folklore.* New York: Howell, 1996.

Maria Nikolajeva

Cautionary Tale

A cautionary tale is a narrative that demonstrates the consequences of wrongdoing and thus reinforces moral and behavioral norms. Cautionary tales tend to have unhappy endings. For example, earlier versions of the **Little Red Riding Hood** story (ATU 333) concluded with the tragic death of the girl, who was eaten up by the wolf. In folklore, the tale warned children against the dangers of the forest—about encountering predators and werewolves and getting lost in the wilderness. Charles **Perrault** adjusted the tale to an urban setting by adding a moral for young ladies that cautioned them against talking with dangerous strangers—that is, men who would pursue and seduce them sexually.

The **fable** and **exemplum** also serve as pedagogical tools by teaching moral lessons. Many **legend**s admonish listeners to follow approved rules of behavior. Supernatural agents, such as the **devil** who appears to card players, dancers, drunkards, and people who work on Sundays and other holidays, typically administer the punishment meted out in legends. Often legends about ghosts caution that the sins people have committed during their lifetime turn them into restless dead who cannot find peace in the grave. Many **urban legend**s also bear warnings (about drugs, AIDS, etc.) that confirm the moral standards of society. Cautionary tales thus do not constitute a uniform genre but refer to various narratives with didactic plots. *See also* Didactic Tale.

Further Readings: Dundes, Alan, ed. *Little Red Riding Hood: A Casebook.* Madison: University of Wisconsin Press, 1989; Rumpf, Marianne. *Ursprung und Entstehung von Warn- und Schreckmärchen.* Helsinki: Suomalainen Tiedeakatemia, 1955.

Ülo Valk

Cazotte, Jacques (1719–1792)

French writer Jacques Cazotte is the author of about twenty tales, ballads, memoirs, and novels. Born in Dijon, Cazotte started his literary career in 1740 when he arrived in Paris to assume his functions as naval prosecutor. After traveling to different French towns and colonies where he suffered scurvy and almost became blind, he returned to France, retired to his house in Pierry, near Epernay, and married a Creole in 1761. Being a fervent royalist, in 1791 he wrote a series of letters to a friend denouncing the revolution and forming plans against it, which sent him to the guillotine a year later.

After arriving in Paris in 1740, he published two parodies of Oriental tales, *La patte du chat, conte Zinzinois* (*The Cat's Paw, Zinzinois Tale,* 1740) and *Les mille et une fadaises* (*The Thousand and One Trifles,* 1742). Back in Paris between 1751 and 1754, Cazotte wrote a series of poems and two defenses of French music. However, it is really only when he finally settled in France in 1759 that his literary carrier developed. With the publication of *Le Diable amoureux* (*The Devil in Love,* 1772), his masterpiece, Cazotte reinterpreted the marvelous in black magic with polemic, satire, and burlesque, drawing from contemporary occultist beliefs. Furthermore, he posed the question of the relationship between humans and supernatural beings, reality and the unknown world, and, already anticipating Charles **Nodier**, the real world and the realm of dreams. Given his influence on nineteenth-century writers like E. T. A. **Hoffmann**, Théophile **Gautier**, and Gérard de Nerval, Cazotte could be considered the true initiator of modern fantastic literature.

Le Diable amoureux tells the story of a young Spanish officer, Alvare, seeking to meet supernatural spirits. Initiated by one of his mates into the practice of the occult, he is left alone in the Herculaneum ruins. Conquered by his courage, the devil presents himself to Alvare in the form of a sylph called Biondetta, who gives him absolute submission. After being finally seduced, Alvare consents to marry her, and the devil reveals his real identity, returning to his primitive form of a camel. At this moment, Alvare wakes up, unable to decide if this was a dream or reality. Following the publication of the novel, Cazotte was approached by members of the Martinès of Pasqually society, which initiated him into the science of the occult. He later also belonged to the Saint Martin society and stayed true to his beliefs until his death.

In 1788, inspired by *Le cabinet des fees* (*The Fairies' Cabinet,* 1785–89), Cazotte published in Geneva the *Continuation des Mille et une nuits: Le diable en Arabie* (*Continuation of the Thousand and One Nights: The Devil in Arabia*), a compilation of Oriental tales, some of which profess Martinist theosophy. *See also Arabian Nights.*

Further Readings: Milner, Max. *Le diable dans la littérature française de Cazotte à Baudelaire, 1772–1861.* Paris: J. Corti, 1960; Décote, Georges. *L'itinéraire de Jacques Cazotte, 1719–1792: De la fiction littéraire au mysticisme politique.* Genève: Droz, 1984; Sadan, Joseph. "Jacques Cazotte, His Her Xaïloun, and Hamîda the Kaslân: A Unique Feature of Cazotte's 'Continuation' of the *Arabian Nights* and a Newly Discovered Arabic Source That Inspired His Novel on Xaïloun." *Marvels & Tales* 18 (2004): 286–99.

Charlotte Trinquet

Celtic Tales

Celtic tales encompass stories popular among people who speak Celtic languages. The term "Celtic" is basically a linguistic one, referring to a family of languages spoken at the time of the rise of the Roman Empire in much of central and western Europe, and in parts of eastern Europe and Asia Minor. The surviving Celtic languages are all in the extreme west of Europe—the Gaelic group native to Ireland, Scotland, and the Isle of Man; and the Britonic group native to Wales, Cornwall, and Brittany.

The traditional **folklore**s of the three Gaelic languages are directly connected with each other, and to a lesser extent the traditional folklores of the three Britonic languages are connected. The two language groups share few distinctive traditions between them, however. The Irish and Welsh folklore traditions, for instance, can properly be compared only within the general heritage of folklore in western Europe. Speaking strictly and properly of Celtic tales, one must confine oneself to whatever survivals there are of ancient common Celtic lore—mostly mythical materials. In terms of evidence from within the Celtic languages

Illustration by John Batten for "The Vision of MacConglinney" in *More Celtic Fairy Tales* by Joseph Jacobs (London: David Nutt, 1894), p. 73. [Courtesy of the Eloise Ramsey Collection of Literature for Young People, University Libraries, Wayne State University]

themselves, Irish literature is the earliest, beginning in the sixth century CE. Welsh literature began a few generations later, and the other Celtic languages were not written down until the **Middle Ages**.

The usual division of the year in the Irish language is *ó Shamhain go Bealtaine, is ó Bhealtaine go Samhain*—that is, "from November to May, and from May to November." This indicates that there are two halves to the year—the dark half and then the bright half following it. This is of ancient origin, for the druids of the continental Celts taught that they were all descended from "the same **father**" and they computed "the night before the day." The druids also taught that one should hold the dead in great respect, and that **death** was merely the "middle point" between this life and the afterlife. Such a belief system was quite theoretical—that their chief deity was an ancestral father, that this deity was on the far side of death, and that the living community was closely bound up with the departed. Yet another principle can be read from all of this—namely, that the context of the dead was darkness and that precedence was given by the living community to that dark side over their own appropriate side of light. Night and day are divided in a similar manner—the night as the dark half coming first and the day as the bright half coming second.

The ancestral god of the Celts was called **dago-Devos*, meaning "good sky," which name gives the Irish Daghdha, a personage who had the title "father of all." The term Devos itself was cognate with the name of the father deity in other Indo-European languages, names such as Dyâus, Deus, Jovis, Zeus, and Tiw. Similarly, the Daghdha was connected to the sun, which was imagined as his "eye." In this solar form, he could easily tend to the needs of both dead and living. He went underground at night to lighten the darkness of the otherworld, and by day he lit up the world of the living. From his function, he could be called by either of two nicknames—as patron of light and wisdom he was *Vindos ("the bright one"), and as lord of the dead and obscurity he was *Dhuosnos ("the dark one").

In European antiquity, aspects of the pre-Celtic religions were assimilated to the Celtic belief system. For example, in Ireland the great tumulus at Newgrange predated Celtic culture in Ireland by 3,000 years. Leading persons of pre-Celtic communities were buried there, and the renewal of the sun at midwinter was symbol to them of social renewal. When the Celtic language and its associated ideas came to predominate, it was natural that this tumulus would be claimed as the residence of the Daghdha. According to a story written down in the Middle Ages, the Daghdha had a very handsome son called Aenghus, and this son asked him for a loan of the Brugh for a night and a day. This was granted, but then Aenghus kept the Brugh, stating that "it is in nights and days that life is spent." Another name for Aenghus was Macán, the Irish cognate of the Welsh Mabon, which comes from the Celtic Maponos ("revered son"), a deity from both Gaul and Britain in ancient times. In Welsh tradition, Mabon was a wondrous youth and hunter, and his **mother** was Modron, from the ancient Celtic Matrona ("revered mother"), patroness of the Marne River. Clearly, in the Irish and Welsh traditions of Macán/Mabon, we are dealing with fallout from ancient lore concerning the father and mother deities and their patronage of society in the form of the ideal son.

The Celtic storytellers were more than willing to develop the contrast between darkness and light to create new narratives. In Welsh literature, for instance, there are accounts of seasonal contests between characters who represent Annwyfn (the underworld) and Gwynn (a name derived from Vindos and cognate with the Irish "Fionn"). In Irish literature, there are two bulls, the dark one Donn Cuailnge and the white one Finnbheannach, fighting each other in the Ulster Cycle **epic**. Furthermore, in Irish folklore, battles are fought each May and November between the Munster and Connacht **fairies** under their leaders Donn Fírinne and Fionnbharra.

The most celebrated of the characters called Fionn was Fionn mac Cumhaill, a mythical seer-warrior who is to the fore in tradition all over the Gaelic world. As a derivative of the god of wisdom, he is born a wonder child who gains magical knowledge from the habit of sucking his thumb, an ability that remains with him through his life. He was early associated with bands of young hunter-warriors called Fianna, and Gaelic literature and folklore in both Ireland and Scotland is replete with stories about the adventures of Fionn and his Fianna band—characters such as Diarmaid, Goll, Caoilte, Oisín, and Oscar. Through the prose poems written in English in the eighteenth century by the Scottish writer James Macpherson, this lore has influenced modern Romantic literature in many languages.

Where the sun sinks in the west is where the border between this world and the otherworld was imagined to be. Already in continental Celtic lore, the emphasis was on otherworld places far out to sea, where the souls of the dead depart with the setting sun. In Ireland, "The House of Donn" was the name of a great sea rock off the southwest coast, a stone shaped like a dolmen through which the sun shines as it sinks. It was considered the place where the dead go to join Donn (from the Celtic *Dhuosnos) the father deity as lord of the dead. Again, in the folklore of Celtic-speaking peoples from Brittany to Ireland, there are strong traditions of an otherworld island, or of a sunken city, off the western coast.

It is apparent that the oldest of all such beliefs concerned a glass rock in the western sea, where darkness and light encounter each other. Early on, this idea was dramatized in story, and the plot used was that of a primordial battle—a contest between two sets of deities at the beginning of the world. This was a far-flung plot, and Indo-European **variant**s of it are found in Greek, Norse, Hindu, and other mythologies. In Ireland, the deities set against each other were called the Tuatha Dé Danann and the Fomhóire. The former meant "people of the goddess Danu," and the latter "under-spirits." The two sets of deities dramatized the people of light and the people of darkness, but the earlier understanding that they were complementary to each other had faded.

This great primordial battle was imagined to have happened on Tory Island, off the Donegal coast. That island's name was Tor-Inis, with "tor" meaning a tower or a pillar, but that location was changed to a plain full of rocks in County Sligo known as Magh Tuireadh ("the plain of the pillars"). In that battle, the Tuatha Dé Danann vanquished the Fomhóire. Balar was **king** of the Fomhóire, Nuadhu was king of the Tuatha Dé, but their leader in battle was the young hero Lugh. Lugh in Ireland is a survival of the ancient Celtic deity Lugus. He was patron of many places that were in ancient times called *Lugudunon* ("fortress of

Lugus"); this was variously corrupted in later times into the toponymics Laon, Lauzun, Laudun, Loudon, and Leiden. The most significant of all these places is the French city of Lyon, where there was once a great autumn festival. This harvest festival is still called Lughnasa in Irish. The hero himself is often called *Lugh Lámhfhada* (the epithet meaning "long armed"), and in medieval Welsh literature his cognate is called *Lleu Llawgyffes* ("dexterously armed"). The name of the ancient deity is found also in place names in Britain and Ireland—such as Carlyle (Caer Liwelydd) and Louth (Lughbhaidh).

According to a Roman account, the Gauls had a god like Mercurius: "They assert that it was he who invented all the arts, that he is a guide on every road and journey, and they consider him the strongest influence in all matters of finance and commerce." This must have been Lugus, for the most likely meaning of his name was "swearer" or "guarantor." In Old Irish literature, Lugh was given the pseudonym *Samhildánach*, meaning that he had all of the arts in his power. It was said that he invented ball games, board games, and horse racing, and that he had consummate skill in many trades, including smithcraft, music, poetry, magic, and healing. In battle, Lugh slew Balar, who had a deadly eye that destroyed all upon which it looked. In folklore versions of the story, we are told that Balar had just one daughter, and that it was prophesied to him that if she gave **birth**, the child would kill him. Despite his best efforts, she became pregnant by a young man of the Tuatha Dé, and when Balar realized this, he ordered the child killed as soon as it was born. His servants took pity on the baby boy, set it adrift on the sea in a basket, and it was rescued. That baby was Lugh. The etymology of Balar's name (earlier *Belerios) has been identified as "blazing" or the like, and the emphasis on his eye indicates that Balar was in origin symbolic of the scorching sun or of a thunderbolt that could damage the harvest.

The story's plot must have come to prehistoric Ireland in as part of the cult of Lugus. This plot does not seem to properly belong to the lore of western Europe, but it was prevalent in the ancient Middle East, where ancient versions of it were told of characters such as Sargon, Moses, Cyros, and the mythical Perseus. It is reasonable to assume that the Celts of Gaul heard a version of the plot from the Greeks—whose colony at Marseilles dated from the sixth century BCE—and applied it to their divine hero of Lyon. Lugus (also called Esus in ancient times) appears to have been an aspect of the father deity that periodically contended with another aspect that had the guise of the thunder god Taranis. The likelihood, then, is that Belerios was another name for Taranis, and that the **myth** of the combat between Lugus and Taranis spread throughout western Celtdom and became the contest of Lugh with Balar in Irish tradition.

"Gobannonos" seems to have been the name of an ancient continental god of smithcraft, and such a god occurs in Wales in the form Govannon and in Ireland as Goibhniu. Many places in Ireland are said to have been the sites of the latter's smithy. He also had a wonderful cow called the Glas Ghoibhneann ("the grey of Goibhniu"), which gave a stupendous amount of milk. She would fill any vessel placed under her, but it is said that a malicious person once used a sieve instead, and the cow died trying to fill it. This tragic story of the Glas Ghoibhneann was told in folklore all over Ireland, and **variant**s also were known in Britain. It seems to reflect an old myth of a goddess in bovine shape, such as the river Boyne or Bóinn, which comes from a Celtic Bouvinda, meaning "cowlike and wisdom giving." Goibhniu himself is better known in folklore under another variation of his name—Gobán, or in full the Gobán Saor. The literature claimed that the Gobán was "the best smith who ever lived," and stories of his adventures are told in folklore throughout Ireland and Gaelic

Scotland. His ubiquity in lore probably sprang from the idea that wherever great skill was evident, the spirit of the deity was present.

The **motif** of a mystical island was strongly instanced in early Celtic Britain by lore of a mythical personage called Manawydan, a deity believed to reside on the Isle of Man. In Ireland, this personage was called Manannán, and the Irish Sea between Ireland and Wales was his flowery garden. The fish were his calves and lambs, and the surging waves were his white-maned horses. Lore of him survived in both Wales and Ireland to recent times. Many stories portray him as a marvelous mariner or as a wizard who came from the sea to help heroes in their adventures or to play tricks on humans.

There was a tendency throughout the whole ancient Celtic world to associate the mother goddess with rivers, and many epithets for her became river names in their own right. The conscious identification of rivers and landscapes with goddesses or otherworldly **women** survived strongly in Ireland, where ancient rituals for the inauguration of kings and chieftains were based on such ideas. It would appear that, according to rhetoric used on such occasions, the paternal solar deity was relinquishing the possession of the land goddess to the ruler who was being installed. This led to folklore about particular fairy queens protecting various families and districts, and indeed to the belief that the banshee (that is, *bean sí* or "woman of the otherworld") laments before the death of every person of Gaelic descent.

The land goddess in less colorful form was referred to as a "hag," or old woman, and throughout the Gaelic world, "the Hag of Beare" (Cailleach Bhéarra) was celebrated in story. This mysterious old woman, whose name associates her with the Béarra peninsula in southwest Ireland, is said to have lived longer than anyone else, and she was full of wisdom and had very keen eyesight, capable of seeing things over huge distances. It is said that she placed in their present position many rocks in the countryside and many islands off the shore; she often appears as a skilled thresher or mower. This is more in the nature of entertaining stories, however, and the patronage of agriculture is more seriously attributed to Saint Brighid, a sixth-century holy woman who has in tradition taken on much of the cult associated with her goddess namesake. The ancient Brigenta, which became Brighid in Irish, was a goddess name meaning "the highest one" and was known throughout the Celtic world from Spain to Britain. The Irish St. Brighid is the patroness of spring, and the protectress of all young things—both human and animal.

Much debris from ancient tradition survived in medieval epical lore. In the stories of the Ulster heroes, for example, the champion Cú Chulainn exhibits the battle frenzy attested from the warrior cults of continental Celtdom, while the battle crow (Cath-Bhadhbh) who haunts his battlefield in search of carrion has her ancient continental parallel called Catu-Boduva. The great Connacht **queen** Meadhbh ("she who intoxicates") is the symbol of sovereignty, and parallels the continental Meduva; and other leading characters, such as Fearghus mac Róich and Conchobhar, have names that echo the rituals and rhetoric of early kingship. The famous Arthur, of Welsh lore and later international medieval romance, may have been a historical figure, but his legendary image owes something to a continental bear god Artaios; while the horse lore associated in Wales with the lady Rhiannon and in Ireland with the Mór-Ríoghain or "Macha" derives from an ancient continental cult of the equine goddess Epona, often referred to as Rigana ("the queen"). The strongest tendency was for ancient Celtic cultic material to be reformulated in medieval times as adventurous tales of conflicts and of love and romance. The most celebrated of these utilize the three-cornered plot of an old man competing with a young man for the favors of a young lady—in the Gaelic world the story of Fionn, Diarmaid, and Gráinne in the Fianna Cycle and of Conchobhar, Naoise, and Deirdre in the Ulster Cycle; while in the Britonic world the characters are Marc'h, Tristan, and Iseult.

Much has been written of the ways in which lore has developed and altered in Celtic-speaking areas through the centuries, being influenced by international wonder tales and by colorful migratory **legend**s. Some examples of persistence were given above, but more generally the original Celtic cultic lore has been obscured and superseded. What does remain is the Celtic taste for color and ornateness, a factor which has guaranteed that adopted international lore has been preserved with unusual vivacity in these western European areas. *See also* Gregory, Lady Isabella Augusta Persse; Yeats, William Butler.

Further Readings: Bromwich, Rachel. *Trioedd Ynys Prydein: The Triads of the Island of Britain*. Cardiff: University of Wales Press, 2006; Dillon, Myles. *Early Irish Literature*. Chicago: University of Chicago Press, 1948; Jackson, Kenneth Hurlstone. *The International Tale and Early Welsh Tradition*. Cardiff: University of Wales Press, 1961; Koch, John T., and John Carey. *The Celtic Heroic Age*. Andover: Celtic Studies Publications, 1995; Ó hÓgáin, Dáithí. *The Lore of Ireland*. Cord: The Collins Press, 2006; Rees, Alwyn, and Brinley Rees. *Celtic Heritage*. London: Thames & Hudson, 1961.

Dáithí Ó hÓgáin

Chain Tale

A large body of folktales reflects the everyday observation that things don't just happen: they are caused. Furthermore, a seemingly inconsequential act can release a series of larger causes and effects. Storytellers everywhere have delighted in describing such chains, many of which have unintended and tragic results.

Unhappy chains are often initiated by small and well-intentioned acts. One such tale is "The Death of Mosquito" as recorded by Brenda E. F. Beck and others in *Folktales of India* (1987), and documented in variants around the world (ATU 2022, The Death of the Little Hen). A rat and a mosquito live happily together as husband and wife. One day, the rat embraces his wife, and she accidentally slips into his nose, causing him to sneeze, which kills her. Other beings respond to the mosquito's **death**, causing injury to themselves, ultimately all because of an innocent and loving embrace between husband and wife.

Not all chain tales end tragically. The **tale type** known as The Old Woman and Her Pig (ATU 2030), told in numerous international variants, characteristically ends with the woman getting her stubborn **pig** to jump over a stile, but only after a succession of events involving a dog, a stick, fire, water, a cow, a butcher, and others. Whether they end tragically or happily, most chain tales have only the sparsest of plots. More important than the story itself is its **performance**, which typically develops into a tongue-twisting progression that only a skilled storyteller can successfully deliver. *See also* Cumulative Tale.

Further Reading: Thompson, Stith. "Formula Tales." *The Folktale*. 1946. Berkeley: University of California Press, 1977. 229–344.

D. L. Ashliman

Chamisso, Adalbert von (1781–1838)

The German author and natural scientist Adalbert von Chamisso, along with E. T. A. **Hoffmann** and Ludwig **Tieck**, was a major purveyor of the Romantic **literary fairy tale**.

Chamisso's most famous contribution to the genre was *Peter Schlemihls wundersame Geschichte* (*The Wonderful History of Peter Schlemihl*, 1814), a fantastic-realist fairy-tale **novella**, whose protagonist sells his shadow for a magic purse filled with money. The symbolism of the story conveys the author's feelings of homelessness and search for a social and national identity.

A post-revolutionary expatriate whose family fled France in 1792, Chamisso was torn between his French heritage and his growing German engagement, first as an officer in the Prussian army and later as an author writing in German. In spite of his wealth, the shadowless Schlemihl, the object of fear and contempt, is a lonely and miserable figure. A number of satirical-ironic scenes depict Schlemihl's fruitless efforts to be integrated into human and social life. Finally, Schlemihl becomes a natural scientist travelling the globe in his seven-league boots. Hans Christian **Andersen** seized the motif of alienation and in "The Shadow" (1847) developed the idea into a philosophical tale in which nihilism and materialism demonically grow out of idealism, conquering spirituality.

Chamisso also wrote Biedermeier poetry, which was frequently set to music by Romantic-era composers, who produced socially engaged lyrical comments on the conditions of living, and translated Andersen's poetry into German. *See also* German Tales.

Further Readings: Haase, Donald. "Adalbert von Chamisso." *Supernatural Fiction Writers.* Edited by Everett F. Bleiler. Volume 1. New York: Scribners, 1984. 91–95; Hildebrandt, Alexandra. *Die Poesie des Fremden: Neue Einblicke in Adalbert von Chamissos "Peter Schlemihls wundersame Geschichte."* Eschborn: Klotz, 1998.

Helene Høyrup

Chamoiseau, Patrick (1953–)

A leading figure among Francophone Caribbean writers, Patrick Chamoiseau has shown considerable interest in the **folklore** and **storytelling** of the region. Born and raised in Martinique, he studied law and became a social worker for troubled youths. He has continued this work alongside his prolific and celebrated career as a writer of novels, plays, essays, and fairy tales. Perhaps best known for his novel *Texaco* (1992), for which he received the Prix Goncourt, Chamoiseau has produced among other works vaguely historical novels that accentuate the existential plight of inhabitants of the Antilles. Although woven into the fabric of his entire œuvre, Antillean storytelling and folklore gain particular prominence in his play, *Manman Dlo contre la fée Carabosse* (*Manman Dlo against the Fairy Carabosse*, 1982) and his collections of fairy tales, *Au temps de l'antan: Contes du pays Martinique* (*Creole Folktales*, 1988) and *Emerveilles* (*Marvels*, 1998). Chamoiseau is a major spokesperson for

Patrick Chamoiseau. [Giraud Philipe/Corbis Sygma]

créolité (Creoleness), an aesthetic and political movement promoting the diverse and syncretic social, cultural, and linguistic forms of Creole peoples as a means of resisting postcolonial power. As examples of these forms and this resistance, Caribbean folklore and storytelling play a central role in Chamoiseau's understanding of Creoleness.

Chamoiseau repeatedly uses the figure of the slave storyteller (*conteur*) from the colonial era as a model for both the theory and practice of Creole writing. For Chamoiseau, the slave storyteller serves as inspiration because he melded African stories and material specific to the Caribbean experience, but also because he offered an ambiguous resistance to the slave master. But it is especially the storyteller's reliance on orality that Chamoiseau finds to be most productive. In both his theoretical writings and his fiction, orality holds multiple meanings: Creole **authenticity**, polysemicity, and indeterminacy (as opposed to the monolithic and static nature of Western writing and postcolonial power, according to Chamoiseau). Furthermore, the oral storytelling of the slave *conteur* evokes a supernatural power that for Chamoiseau becomes a metaphor for social and cultural transformation inherent in the concept of Creoleness. Ultimately, though, the slave storyteller is not a model to which Chamoiseau limits himself, but rather one he seeks to appropriate into his writing, thus transcending, at least in part, the opposition between orality and writing.

Even as folktale and fairy-tale **motif**s permeate many of his other texts, both explicitly and implicitly, three of Chamoiseau's works can be classified as fairy tales per se. In his play *Manman Dlo against the Fairy Carabosse*, one of his first published works, Chamoiseau stages the conflict between Creole and Western cultures through a struggle between Manman Dlo, a supernatural character from Caribbean folklore, and the fairy Carabosse, a character in French fairy tales by Marie-Catherine d'**Aulnoy** and Charles **Perrault**, among others. Alongside a confrontation of two cultures, the Manman Dlo/Carabosse opposition allegorizes the political struggle of Caribbean peoples against Western colonial and postcolonial hegemony. In his collections *Creole Folktales* and *Marvels*, Chamoiseau rewrites folktales from the French Caribbean oral tradition. Although ostensibly for children (the two collections appeared in French series of **children's literature**), the tales are often written in a dense prose that wavers between standard and regional Caribbean French and often includes Creole words and phrases. Notable as well is the prominent, self-conscious narration that foregrounds the figure of the storyteller and his ambiguous relation to the stories. Like storytellers in the Caribbean **oral tradition**, Chamoiseau's narrator frequently distances himself from his tales, producing a comic effect but also inciting readers to reflect critically on their own interpretations. But the narrator's ambivalence does not put into question the status of the magical setting, as is the case in many other fairy tales; on the contrary, it accentuates the importance of traditional beliefs and the failure of many of the characters to take them seriously. Hence, Chamoiseau's narrator serves to reiterate and revalorize a traditional Caribbean culture under siege from numerous Western influences.

If only implicitly, Chamoiseau also makes comparisons with well-known Western folktale and fairy-tale plots and characters. Most of the stories in the two prose collections bear obvious resemblance to stories of the Western fairy-tale canon, such as "**Bluebeard**," "**Cinderella**," "**Little Red Riding Hood**," and "**Thumbling**," among others. Yet Chamoiseau's tales remain solidly anchored in the historical and social contexts of the French Antilles, not only with his cast of characters but also with the themes he employs. Two of these are given particular prominence: hunger and language. Congruent with the physical conditions under which slaves lived in colonial times, Caribbean oral traditions foreground hunger, and Chamoiseau retains this emphasis in his own versions. It could be argued, however, that his tales use this theme to emphasize literal and historical but also metaphorical meanings of hunger, which then signifies a desire for food, but also for Creole autonomy and authenticity. Although not as prominent as hunger in Creole oral narratives, language and especially its transformative powers are an important leitmotif in Chamoiseau's fairy tales. Frequently, these powers are illustrated through their characters' use of Creole verses or incantations, which effect magical turns of events, either for good or harm. Chamoiseau thus reiterates in his fairy-tale settings the importance he places throughout his work on the recovery of Creole and the role language can play in valorizing Creoleness. *See also* Colonialism; Négritude, Créolité, and Folktale.

Further Reading: Lewis C. Seifert. "Orality, History and 'Creoleness' in Patrick Chamoiseau's Creole Folktales." *Marvels & Tales* 16 (2002): 214–30.

Lewis C. Seifert

Changeling

Involving a complex mix of beliefs dealing with interactions between humans and the supernatural, a **changeling** is a wizened, deformed, insatiable, and frequently old **fairy** that has been exchanged for an often-unbaptised human child. Changeling narratives have been most heavily recorded in the North Atlantic regions—Scandinavia, the British Isles, Germany, and Newfoundland—but have more far-reaching parallels generally dealing with unexplained abductions of children. Because they are short, involve supernatural encounters, and are expressions of belief, changeling narratives are most often classified as **legend**s and are listed as Migratory Legend 5085 by Reidar Thoralf Christiansen. The typical changeling tale is reflected in **Grimm**s' "Die Wichtelmänner" ("The Elves," 1812). Stith Thompson's *Motif-Index of Folk-Literature* provides the most comprehensive description of changeling narratives in its list of **motif**s from F320 (Fairies carry people away to fairyland), through F321.5 (Fairies appear in a house and offer to dance with child). However, the motifs immediately following these in the *Motif-Index* point to the structural similarities between changeling narratives and stories dealing with the abduction of women by otherworldly beings (for example, Motif F322, Fairies steal man's wife and carry her to fairyland).

The typical changeling narrative involves: (1) the abduction of a child, usually due to the inattention of the **mother** or caretaker but motivated by the fairies' desire for human infants; (2) the substitution of a deformed, old fairy for the child; (3) the ensuing chaos that the changeling brings to the household—eating and screaming and generally failing to thrive; (4) the suspicion that the human baby has been exchanged and the seeking of advice; (5) the various remedies either to trick the changeling into revealing its true nature or to force the fairy parents to rescue their own from harm; and (6) the eventual return of the child to its parents. The concept of exchange lies at the heart of changeling tales. First comes the exchange of the desirable for the undesirable—young for old, a productive potential for a drain on the family economy. Then comes the reversal, the undoing of the exchange, which restores the desirable.

Scholars have put forth diverse analyses of the changeling complex, beginning with the idea that it offers an explanation of **birth** defects, deformities, and the failure-to-thrive syndrome. Whereas some view changeling narratives as adult justifications of child abuse, neglect, and infanticide, others suggest just the opposite: that the stories constitute **cautionary**

tales admonishing inattentive or negligent mothers not to leave their children unattended. Some interpretations stress the liminal and vulnerable position of the unbaptised and therefore unincorporated child, while still others consider the changeling complex in the general context of supernatural encounters. This places changeling narratives into a much larger corpus of stories involving human-fairy interactions, which serve as commentaries on otherwise inexplicable events in ordinary life.

Most modern adaptations, with the exception of Selma **Lagerlöf**'s more traditional "Bortbytingen" ("The Changeling," 1915), focus on a child's abduction by fairies or trolls and the subsequent journey to the otherworld and retrieval of the child by its older sister— for example, Maurice **Sendak**'s *Outside Over There* (1981), Ursula K. **Le Guin**'s *A Ride on the Red Mare's Back* (1992), and Jim **Henson**'s film *Labyrinth* (1986). *See also* Childhood and Children; Disability; Faerie and Fairy Lore.

Further Readings: Christiansen, Reidar Thoralf. *The Migratory Legends: A Proposed List of Types with a Systematic Catalogue of the Norwegian Variants*. 1958. Helsinki: Academia Scientiarum Fennica, 1992; Narváez, Peter, ed. *The Good People: New Fairylore Essays*. New York: Garland, 1991.

JoAnn Conrad

Chapbook

Printed little volumes for popular reading, chapbooks were common in several western European languages. These books contained a wide variety of reading material, ranging from stories about the heroes of ancient Greek and Roman literature to accounts of philosophers, saints, and noted historical personages, and to picaresque tales of rogues and entertaining rascals. The term "chapbook" first came into vogue for such publications in the early nineteenth century. It was derived from "chapman," the usual word for the type of trader or peddler who sold them at fairs or markets and in other public places.

The publishing of small inexpensive tracts began in France near the end of the fifteenth century and soon after became common in Germany, the Netherlands, and England. The German chapbooks—*Volksbücher*—contained prose versions of medieval romances and other miscellaneous tales; and in Germany, the Netherlands, and France, the adventures of the entertaining **trickster Till Eulenspiegel** were especially popular. From the seventeenth century onward, a wide variety of chapbooks were available in England, and they spread to Ireland, America, and other places where material in English was read. Some of the favorites among these chapbooks were "The Seven Champions of Christendom," "The Seven Wise Masters of Rome," "The History of Guy of Warwick," "Doctor Faustus," the ubiquitous Eulenspiegel in the guise of "Owlglass," and "George Buchanan, the King's Fool," as well as the plays of William **Shakespeare** and the prose works of Jonathan Swift, Henry Fielding, and other well-known writers.

Also in chapbook form were accounts of Robin Hood and a variety of other outlaws, including contemporaneous highwaymen and pirates. Written versions of **folktale**s such as "Jack the Giant-Killer" and "**Sleeping Beauty**" were featured, and, in the early eighteenth century, the *Arabian Nights* became available in short and simplified form. This included a variety of joke books and collections of comical stories from many sources—including **anecdote**s from earlier literature, short humorous folktales, **jest**s with temporary or limited currency, and quaint fictional or semi-fictional accounts. It is interesting to note that the stories that had a lasting effect were usually those that already existed in **folklore** or were similar to folklore in type.

It was inevitable that popular reading material of this kind would exert a strong influence on oral **storytelling**. Because of this, folklore researchers must take into account the possible origin of a narrative in a chapbook or alternately the influence of a chapbook variant on a story preexisting in the lore of a particular area. In some cases—for instance, a mid-eighteenth-century Irish chapbook by James Cosgrave entitled "Irish Rogues and Raparees"—the writer collected **legend**s from living folklore and included them in his book, which in turn tended to eclipse the earlier oral versions of these same legends. In general, the chapbooks provide a unique opportunity for folklore scholars, in that they can be used as definite sources of lore, against which oral derivatives and independent variants can be assessed. This allows for the investigation of plot variations and development in **oral tradition**, as well as for analysis of folk sentiment, humor, and fancy. *See also* Broadside.

Further Readings: Ashton, John. *Chap-books of the Eighteenth Century.* 1882. New York: B. Blom, 1966; Neuburg, Victor E. *Popular Literature: A History and Guide from the Beginning of Printing to the Year 1897.* Harmondsworth: Penguin Books, 1977; Preston, Cathy Lynn, and Michael J. Preston. *The Other Print Tradition: Essays on Chapbooks, Broadsides, and Related Ephemera.* Garland: New York, 1995.

Dáithí Ó hÓgáin

Charm. *See* Incantation

Chaucer, Geoffrey (c. 1343–1400)

Throughout his work, Geoffrey Chaucer utilized a mix of European **folktale**s, reworking them from oral or literary sources to generate many of his most memorable poems. Certainly this is true of his best-known work, *The Canterbury Tales*, which he began around 1387. The characters in this **frame narrative**, pilgrims traveling to the shrine of the late Thomas Beckett, engage in a **storytelling** contest to pass the time. The stories recounted are not uniformly traditional, but many do have prior medieval analogues and have a recorded oral life, even up to the present.

Perhaps the most widely known of Chaucer's folktale retellings is "The Pardoner's Tale" (ATU 763, The Treasure Finders Who Murder One Another), which has seen many adaptations, including the 1948 film by John Huston, *The Treasure of the Sierra Madre*. Other retellings include "The Miller's Tale" (ATU 1361, The Flood), "The Reeve's Tale" (ATU 1363, Tale of the Cradle), and "The Clerk's Tale" (ATU 887, Griselda), which appears in Giovanni **Boccaccio**'s *Decameron* (1349–50) and in Charles **Perrrault**'s "Griselidis" (1691). The concordance with Boccaccio is hardly happenstance. Literary evidence suggests that many of Chaucer's tales, as well as the frame narrative form itself, can be traced to Italy, where Chaucer was part of a military expedition in 1373. *See also* Fabliau, Fabliaux; Middle Ages.

Further Readings: Benson, Larry D., and Theodore M. Anderson. *The Literary Context of Chaucer's Fabliaux: Texts and Translations.* New York: Bobbs-Merrill, 1971; Bryan, William Frank, ed. *Sources and Analogues of Chaucer's Canterbury Tales.* Chicago: University of Chicago Press, 1941.

Adam Zolkover

Childhood and Children

In 1962, Philippe Ariès, in his *Centuries of Childhood,* asserted that the category of the "child" was a cultural construction that emerged in Europe in the seventeenth century and came to full fruition in the eighteenth century. Prior to that time, Ariès argued, what might now be clearly seen as a child was merely a small person, with limited economic potential, and the separate and protected sphere of childhood did not exist. Subsequent biological and developmental justifications of the category of childhood were, thus, motivated by this underlying social and historical shift, which was primarily economic in its derivation, and are the processes by which the category of the child has become naturalized. Although the constructionist argument is highly controversial and contested, it does question the presumption of a biological category of "the child" and further suggests that even though there may be some biological aspects of childhood that differentiate children from adults, the meanings that are ascribed to these categories are historically and culturally contingent.

The coincidence of the rise of this new conceptualization of childhood, one that ultimately relegated real children to their own separate sphere, with many other radical social changes sweeping seventeenth- and eighteenth-century Europe, points to its ideological underpinnings. These changes, it has been argued, are a result of those same forces—the move to capitalism, reorganization of social structure, consumerism, modernization, **nationalism**, and literacy—from which both the field and the concept of **folklore** emerged, as well as the category of "the **folk**" and "the child," the development of a separate **children's literature**, and the subsequent relegation of the folktale/fairy tale to this new genre. The intersections and relays between these phenomena, often held distinct, and their interrelationship within an ideological milieu, are significant and essential.

The complicated relationship between the study of folklore and folklore itself is caught up in the transition to modernity, not only in the by-now well-ingrained discussions of literacy, the rise of the middle class, and changes in social structure, but by a changing attitude toward wonder and wonders in the natural world. By the eighteenth century, wonder, the stock in trade of the fairy tale, had shifted from being a favored object of contemplation of the elite in Europe to being seen as that which defined the "folk," prompting its banishment to the margins of elite discourse—wonder became relegated to the "vulgar." The logic of this conceptualization of the vulgar still underscores much of folklore scholarship today, and is certainly critical to it historically: into the vulgar were dumped a host of characters— **women**, the elderly, **peasant**s, illiterates, and children—the stock characters in the folklore about folklore. These constituted, in the case of women and peasants, the ideal **informant**s, and in the case of children, the intended audience. Thus children, folk, and peasants were all embraced into an evolutionary, developmental premise. As such, they were all not only empty signifiers to be filled with meaning, they also were awaiting the paternalistic guidance and stewardship of the institutional and academic elite.

Folklore and childhood were also linked in their ambiguous relationship to the dual impulses of rationalism and Romanticism, the intertwined discourses of modernity. Folklore was seen to be in need of **collecting**, recording, **editing**, archiving, managing, and indexing, with the underlying presumption that if collected and ordered it could be maintained, analyzed, and even reproduced—a rationalist enterprise. Similarly, children were seen as malleable, open to socialization and acculturation according to a rational plan—that of the educational institutions. On the other hand, both the constructed notions of the folk and the child were seen as Romantic palliatives to an increasingly modern, industrial, and impersonal world. Children and the folk were the sites of innocence, purity, and **authenticity**, which could be tapped into as a corrective to the contamination of cosmopolitan, urban life. Nevertheless, real children and real folk were disciplined into the rationalist enterprise.

The rise of the nuclear **family** and the bourgeoisie in early modernity also led to a dramatic restructuring of social relations. The nuclear family, typified by the "male breadwinner/female bread maker" dyad, became the most economically productive unit in terms of industrial capitalism, providing a support system for the now wage-earning and away-from-home husband, while structuring all family members' lives around a workday logic, into which fit the institutionalized child, socialized to eventually become a productive member of society. In this system, not only are children institutionalized and socialized, they are separated from the world of adults, and become economically dependent. The ideological enforcement of this nuclear family model was carried out through the mobilization of folklore, in particular the folktale and fairy tale, in two distinct and yet complementary strands. First, the **literary fairy tale** gradually came to embody the power of romantic/thematic love, essential in the trope of love at first sight—a love that is mysterious and based primarily on superficial qualities. The imperative of thematic love, reiterated in the fairy tale and subsequently in the **novel** and **film**, tended to obscure the economic motivation of the modern nuclear family. Secondly, the fairy tale was co-opted into the newly emerging, much broader category of children's literature, with the intention of socializing the developmentally immature child. Thus the fairy tale gradually came to manifest those stylistic and content characteristics of the larger genre, and as such was purged of elements inappropriate to the construction of childhood as a site of innocence. This particularly included sexual references, since the concept of "innocence" is dependent not only on the denial of childhood **sexuality**, but also furthers the emptying of this emblematic child of its own agency, leaving it open to be filled with adult projections and expectations.

This merging of written folktales and fairy tales with children's literature further exemplifies the tension in the construction of childhood as both the site of innocence and the object of socialization. Editorial changes in tales to conform to generic convention likewise follow a larger ideological premise. The removal of sexual material in tales for children speaks to the notion of "appropriateness" derived from a developmental model. Further, the elimination of aspects of the grotesque, particularly when used subversively, disallows agency and resistance, and encourages conformity. Increasingly violent aspects of the tales, when converted to literary tales targeted toward children, however, tended to invest punishment with a higher moral purpose, thus underscoring the authority of patriarchal institutions, as well as serving as exemplary and/or **cautionary tale**s.

The Historical Relationship between the Literary Fairy Tale and Childhood

The development of the canonical literary fairy tale and the development of the modern notion of childhood are inextricably intertwined and emerge simultaneously in the context of the rise of modernity in Europe. Although the origins of the literary fairy tale are often placed in the French salons of the late seventeenth and early eighteenth centuries, and although the majority of these tales, written by aristocratic female authors, were associated neither with the subsequent emergence of the notion of the folk nor the construction of the child, it is the work of one author of this period, Charles **Perrault,** that has been integrated into the canon of the literary fairy tale and associated with the transformation of the fairy tale into a child-oriented genre. In his *Histoires ou contes du temps passé* (*Stories or Tales of Times Past,* 1697)—which includes a frontispiece identifying the tales as "contes de ma mère l'oye" ("tales of my **Mother Goose**")—Perrault established the persistent connection between these tales, an audience of children, and the female, peasant tellers, thus, in one move, linking again the primitive, illiterate folk developmentally with the unformed, illiterate, innocent (and malleable) child. Perrault's simple prose, in an imitation of an imagined folk speech, was praised subsequently in the 1812 preface to the **Grimm**s' *Kinder- und Hausmärchen* (*Children's and Household Tales*) as being authentically derived from oral sources, and, in a circular fashion, became the standard for the signs of authenticity and orality. This purity and authenticity located this text clearly in the Grimms' Romantic-rhetorical sphere, and yet, Perrault was also insistently didactic, summing up each tale with a short moral. His simple language, in circular logic, also came to be seen as suitable for the developmental level of children, as opposed to the longer, more complex, and elaborate prose of his contemporary female authors.

Although Perrault's work ultimately was associated with children's literature, with didactic intent in a simple language that mimicked not only the "folk" but also a childlike simplicity, it was Jeanne-Marie **Leprince de Beaumont** who was the first to write explicitly for children, as in her 1757 *Magasin des enfants* (translated in 1759 as *The Young Misses' Magazine*). Leprince de Beaumont's work is situated in what Jack **Zipes** refers to as the third vogue in the French literary fairy tale—that period in which the fairy tale is fully institutionalized and adapted to do the work of childhood socialization. These stories, in particular Leprince de Beaumont's rendition of "**Beauty and the Beast**," emphasized the proper upbringing for young girls, stressing that happiness depends on industriousness, self-sacrifice, modesty, and diligence. The books celebrate self-denial, domesticity, passivity, and a particular inflection of "femininity" as read through newly emerging middle-class sensibilities. Ultimately, the goal was **marriage**, and selflessness was underscored as the desired feminine attribute, with the promise of thematic love serving as the incentive. Ideologically, these tales are linked to the rise of the middle class, and convey a middle-class morality, stressing imbalanced male-female relationships, domesticity, and dependence for women. They also embody the notion of the "perfect girl" in normative models of beauty that include silence, passivity, and duty.

During this period, children's' literature was beginning to carve out childhood as a unique consumer group, a target audience with its own market potential well beyond that for specialized publications, and yet one still motivated toward the instruction of middle-class subjects. In 1744, John Newberry published *A Little Pretty Pocket Book*, which "endorsed a productive discipline ... as it hails acculturation and accommodation" (quoted in Tatar, xvi). The conceptual category of childhood is fully entrenched in this market; the goal of publications is to produce normal, well-adjusted, and productive (and consuming) adults along a predetermined developmental design. This was even more emphatically underscored with ideals of universal subjecthood and universal literacy, embodied in the first Elementary Education Act in England in 1870, which shifted the responsibility of education and literacy to the state, further institutionalizing childhood.

The overlapping of the ideas of childhood socialization, Romantic-era notions of authenticity, and the standardization and canonization of the fairy-tale corpus directed at children was further enhanced by the work of the Grimms. Their *Kinder- und Hausmärchen* served as the model for fairy tales directed specifically at children for generations. The Grimms' use of a markedly simple and implicitly pure and authentic language not only served as a marker of the oral lore of the folk but also was indicative of the presumed state of purity and emptiness of childhood, which was thus available for the explicitly ideological messages embedded in the texts.

It is the model of the Grimms that has maintained up to the current **adaptation**s of classic fairy tales by Walt **Disney** and the **Walt Disney Company** but is also the basis of most folklore scholarship on the fairy tale until recent years. It is necessary to mention in this context the still-circulating theories of Bruno **Bettelheim**. In *The Uses of Enchantment: The Meaning and Importance of Fairy Tales* (1976), Bettelheim uses a short selection of the tales from the Grimms to discuss the psychoanalytic meaning from what he assumes is a child's point of view, and, in ironic and circular logic, rearticulates the evolutionary, developmental premise (following Jean Piaget and Sigmund **Freud**). Arguing the child's perspective from the imagined child/folk speech adapted by the Grimms, Bettelheim finds latent meanings in the tales that reinscribe the modern cultural logic affirming patriarchal prerogative, exonerating the acts of the father while blaming those of the child, fitting into the greater cultural Oedipal logic, and further enshrining the male academic/expert as the location of redemption. *See also* Didactic Tale; Exemplum, Exempla; Pedagogy; Psychological Approaches.

Further Readings: Ariès, Philippe. *Centuries of Childhood.* Translated by Robert Baldick. New York: Random House, 1962; Freudenburg, Rachel. "Illustrating Childhood—'Hansel and Gretel.'" *Marvels & Tales* 12 (1998): 263–318; Shavit, Zohar. "The Concept of Childhood and Children's Folktales: Test Case—'Little Red Riding Hood.'" *Little Red Riding Hood: A Casebook.* Edited by Alan Dundes. Madison: University of Wisconsin Press, 1989. 129–58; Tatar, Maria. *Off with Their Heads! Fairy Tales and the Culture of Childhood.* Princeton, NJ: Princeton University Press, 1992; Zipes, Jack. *Happily Ever After: Fairy Tales, Children, and the Culture Industry.* New York: Routledge, 1997.

JoAnn Conrad

Children's and Household Tales. See Kinder- und Hausmärchen

Children's Literature

One of the greatest misconceptions about folktales has been that they are a natural part of children's literature. Indeed, most of the overview works, historical surveys, and handbooks on children's literature start with folktales, also called "traditional stories." In their original form, however, most folktales, magic stories as well as everyday tales, are considered by some to be highly inappropriate for young readers. They contain such elements as lewdness, extreme **violence**, **cannibalism**, rape, **incest**, and so on. Many folktales, especially Oriental (for example, *Panchatantra* and the *Arabian Nights*), are explicitly erotic (see **Erotic Tales**). **Trickster** tales contain dubious **moral**s, and **anecdote**s mocking the **clergy** subvert the power of the church. The early Western **literary fairy tale**s, for instance, those by Marie-Catherine d'**Aulnoy** in late seventeenth-century France, were not addressed to children, and fairy tales as a genre were not considered particularly suitable for a young audience.

The reason folktales and fairy tales became part of children's reading (rather than children's literature as such) lies in the fact that by the eighteenth century, **childhood** was successively acknowledged as a separate part of human life with its own interests and needs. Prior to that, children would be present while stories were told or read at familial and social occasions; they might also listen to their nurses' and governesses' yarns. When children's literature began emerging as a specific category, with obvious didactic and instructive purposes, educators were obliged to look for texts that suited the current requirements for desirable reading matter for the young. Selected folktales and fairy tales matched these requirements on several bases. First, they were relatively simple in their narrative structure of home-adventure-return home, which subsequently became the most common plot in children's fiction. Second, they were clear and explicit in their moral values, expressing unequivocal views on good and evil. Third, most fairy tales feature a happy ending, which was connected with the concept of children's literature as optimistic—a notion that is still alive today. Finally, folktales and fairy tales focus on the ultimate triumph of the underdog, the youngest son or daughter (alternatively the oldest, depending on the cultural premises), the poor orphan, and the hero of unknown origin, who prove more virtuous, courageous, and imaginative than their initially more-fortunate rivals. This oppressed position of the folktale hero corresponds to the powerless state of the child in most cultures and societies. According to many scholars, folktales reflect the **initiation** rite. Incorporating folktales into children's reading thus became part of the child's socialization.

Changing Attitudes Toward Fairy Tales As Children's Reading

Educators happily included folktales and fairy tales in the reading matter for children at its very first appearance as detached from general literature, mainly due to the absence of other sources. Presumably, among the very first Western collections of fairy tales overtly addressed to children was Charles **Perrault**'s *Contes ou histories du temps passé* (*Stories or Tales of Times Past*, 1697), in which he adapted a number of popular French folktales to the current ethics of the upper class. The stories included in this volume have become the most famous children's fairy tales ever, among them "Sleeping Beauty," "**Little Red Riding Hood**," "**Cinderella**," and "**Puss in Boots**." The tales were heavily modified to fit the prevailing view on child education and purified from the most offensive elements, present in the oral versions. They were permeated by didacticism, and equipped with proper moral conclusions, and these traits paved the way for their subsequent reception as children's literature. At the same time, these tales contained irony and a certain playful eroticism that certainly spoke to adults rather than children. So there is good reason to conclude that Perrault's primary audience was in fact adults, and that the ostensible appeal to children served also as a cover for introducing folktales into literary culture. Thus, this early collection already demonstrates one of the most essential characteristics of children's literature: its inevitable double address.

The Age of Enlightenment brought forward ardent adversaries of fairy tales as children's reading. Jean-Jacques Rousseau especially considered fairy tales directly dangerous and harmful for children because of their dubious morals and, in the first place, their unrealistic representation of the world.

Romanticism combined interest for **folklore** with adoration of the child as pure and innocent, which resulted in many scholarly collections of folktales being adapted for children. Among these, Jacob and Wilhelm **Grimm**'s *Kinder- und Hausmärchen* (*Children's and Household Tales*, 1812–15) is the most famous, but it is far from unique. The Grimms retold a great number of German folktales, adapting them to the governing pedagogical ideas. The nature of **adaptation**, which also characterizes most other collections addressed to children, follows several directions. Stepmothers substitute for biological **mother**s in folktales such as "**Snow White**" and "**Hansel and Gretel**," which ostensibly were less offensive. In "Little Red Riding Hood," the girl and the grandmother are saved by a hunter, which enhances the patriarchal social order and supposedly makes young girls differentiate between wild and civilized males. On the other hand, the Grimms did not hesitate to add some gruesome details, absent from, for instance, Perrault's volume. In their version of "Cinderella," graphic depictions of the evil **sisters** appear, as they cut off their toes and heels to squeeze their feet into the slipper, and the birds pick out their eyes as punishment in the end. Generally, the castigation of the villain is ruthless; **punishment**s include dancing in red-hot **shoe**s, being rolled in a barrel with spikes nailed inward, or being torn apart bound to galloping horses. "The Juniper Tree" has instances of violence and cannibalism.

The treasury of more or less anonymous "world fairy tales for children" normally contains less-offensive versions of the common tales, such as Perrault's rather than Grimms' "Cinderella" and Grimms' rather than Perrault's "Little Red Riding Hood." In twentieth-century publications of the Grimm tales overtly aimed at children, a limited number of tales is habitually selected, the most popular being "The **Frog King**," "Rapunzel" (often heavily abridged and purged of violence), "Hansel and Gretel," "The Bremen Town Musicians," "Brier Rose" (a version of "Sleeping Beauty"), and "Snow White." This fact contributed to the later picture of the Grimm Brothers as child-friendly, pleasurable storytellers. Further, their tales are perceived as genuine folktales, collected from poor people, which, as Grimm scholars have repeatedly shown, is far from the truth. Even their original versions were already stripped of the most inappropriate details.

Since the Grimm tales were quickly translated into many languages, they were also immediately integrated into children's reading all over the world and remain among "children's classics" today, parallel with, or instead of, national collections. The latter originated likewise from the combination of the Romantic fascination with folk traditions and the need for reading matter for children. Scholarly collections of folktales provided ample material for retellings and adaptations. In England, Andrew **Lang**'s and Joseph **Jacobs**'s collections became models for further compilers, contributing to children's reading with "Jack and the Beanstalk" and "Jack the Giant Killer," as well as a number of tales from continental Europe, such as "Tom Tit Tot" ("Rumpelstiltskin") and "The Pied Piper." From Scandinavia, Peter Christian **Asbjørnsen a**nd Jørgen **Moe**'s *Norske folkeeventyr* (*Norwegian Folktales,* 1841–44) achieved international recognition, with its specific local flavor, while the stories themselves were again well known in other countries, for instance, "Valemon the White Bear" (the story of the magical bridegroom) and "The Giant Who Had No Heart in His Body." The impact on children's literature can primarily be seen in its function as reading matter for Norwegian children in their own language at a time when Danish influence was still tangible and when Norway was in union with Sweden. The original collection was not intended for young audiences, but many of the tales were soon afterward published in children's magazines, anthologies, and school primers. The first collection published specifically for children, *Eventyrbog for børn* (*A Book of Children's Fairy Tales*), appeared in 1883 and was edited by Asbjørnsen himself. This edition and two subsequent volumes (1884–87) were constantly reprinted; often the language in them was revised. The original folktales from the Asbjørnsen and Moe collection lacked any moral or didactic closure. Therefore, they were not always considered suitable as children's reading.

In *Russkie detskie skazki* (*Russian Children's Tales*, 1870), Aleksandr **Afanas'ev** included **animal tale**s, **magic tale**s, and humorous tales from his scholarly collection, carefully adjusting the language and excluding everything unsuitable for children. The most original Russian tale features the wicked witch **Baba Yaga**, who lives in a hut on chicken legs and flies around in a mortar. From the *Arabian Nights*, several tales became incorporated into the Western children's canon, such as "**Aladdin**" and "**Ali Baba** and the Forty **Thieves**," presumably as being the least odious. The **frame narrative** about the skillful storyteller **Sheherazade**, if published at all in children's editions, is heavily purged of its bawdy elements. In *Fairy Tales and the Art of Subversion* (1983), Jack **Zipes** outlines how the versions of various fairy-tales correspond to and reflect the sociocultural values and the status of childhood in the society that produces them.

The common denominator of all the tales that finally became integrated into children's literature is that they are stories of maturation, focused on quests and difficult tasks. The ending is frequently enthronement and **marriage**, which is perhaps alien to childhood but symbolizes the empowerment of the oppressed.

Basically, each country and culture started its own children's literature by adapting local folktales and translating the most famous stories by Perrault and the Grimms. In some cases, as in North American and Australia, immigrant populations have partly imported the European treasury and partly—and only quite recently—turned to the rich cultures and traditions of the indigenous population. In some countries, such as China, fairy tales are still considered the only suitable reading matter for younger children before they are mature enough for realistic prose. In many African countries, **myth**s and fairy tales are more or less the only native children's literature.

In the Western countries, the appropriateness of fairy tales for children created violent debates at various periods. In Russia, for instance, in the 1920s, militant educators attempted to banish fairy tales as part of the old, bourgeois heritage. Kornei **Chukovsky**, a leading Soviet children's writer, as well as critic and translator, initiated what he called the "struggle for the fairy tale," insisting on the importance of folktales and fairy tales in childhood education. Fairy tales played a special role in totalitarian countries in the twentieth century. Under the Soviet occupation of the Baltic countries and during the existence of communist satellites in Eastern Europe (1945–91), when all culture was subject to close censorship and children's literature was considered primarily an ideological implement, fairy tales, often with allegorical undertones, became a powerful vehicle of subversive national literature.

During the radical 1960s and 1970s, most western European countries experienced a strong interrogation of fairy tales in favor of contemporary socially engaged children's and youth literature. Today, fairy tales enjoy a relatively high status. They are included in teachers' training, and publishers all over the world release new collections in various adaptations. Moreover, Western publishers as well as educators have discovered the golden mine of Oriental, African, and other folktale traditions, resulting in children's books such as Robert D. San Souci's *Sootface: An Ojibwa Cinderella Story* (1994), Shirley Climo's *The Egyptian Cinderella* (1989), Adeline Yen Mah's *Chinese Cinderella* (1999), and so on. These publications reflect the desire for multicultural experience in contemporary children's education.

Literary Fairy Tales

Although **literary fairy tale**s were written in France as early as the seventeenth century, few of them were included in children's reading, possibly with the exception of "**Beauty and the Beast**," which was abridged and adapted. In the Western world, Hans Christian **Andersen** has been accorded the honorable label of "the father of the literary fairy tale." Between 1835 and 1872, he published four collections that were an immediate, unprecedented success and that were translated into many languages during his lifetime. Yet, only a handful of his fairy tales and stories are widely read by young audiences today, including "The Tinder Box,"

"Thumbelina," "The Ugly Duckling," "The Little Mermaid," "The Steadfast Tin Soldier," and "The Snow Queen."

The sources of Andersen's stories were mostly Danish folktales, collected and retold by his immediate predecessors, whose aim was to preserve, classify and study them. Andersen was primarily a writer, and his objective was to create new literary works based on folklore, although some of his fairy tales also have their origins in ancient poetry or medieval European literature. He also found inspiration in the literary fairy tales by the German Romantics, such as E. T. A. **Hoffmann** and Adalbert von **Chamisso**.

There are several ways in which Andersen may have created the genre of the literary fairy tale for children. First, he gave the fairy tale a personal touch. Many of his stories open in a matter-of-fact way instead of with the traditional "Once upon a time," and their characters, including **king**s and **prince**s, speak a colloquial, everyday language. This feature became the trademark of Andersen's style. Quite a number of his early fairy tales are retellings of traditional folktales; in Andersen's rendering, however, they reveal a definite uniqueness and brilliant irony. Kings wear battered slippers and personally open gates of their kingdoms; **princess**es read newspapers and roast chicken; and many supernatural creatures in later tales behave and talk like ordinary people. An explicit narrative voice, commenting on the events and addressing the listener, is another characteristic trait of Andersen's tales. On the other hand, there are no conventional morals in the tales, possibly with the exception of "The Red Shoes" or "The Girl Who Trod on a Loaf," which are rarely included in children's editions. Many tales persistently explore the theme of true and false art, as in "The Swineherd" and more subtly in "The Nightingale." This aspect, too, is addressed to adults rather than children. Physical and spiritual suffering are accentuated in several tales, but they are either excluded in children's editions or adapted. Thus, in some versions, the Little Match Girl is adopted by a nice **family**.

In addition, Andersen brought the fairy tale into the everyday. His first original tale, "Little Ida's Flowers," reminds one of Hoffmann's tales in its elaborate combination of the ordinary and the fantastic, its nocturnal magical **transformation**s, and its use of the child as a narrative lens. Still closer to Hoffmann is "The Steadfast Tin Soldier" with its animation of toys. However, in both tales, Andersen's melancholy view of life is revealed. Both end tragically, thus questioning the essence of children's literature as depending on happy endings. These may be counterbalanced by more conventional stories of trials and reward such as "Thumbelina" or "The Snow Queen," the latter based on a popular Norse **legend** of the Ice Maiden and featuring the invincible power of love. The origins of the title figure in "Ole Lukkøje" (translated into English as "Willie Winkie," "The Sandman," "The Dustman," or "Old Luke"; the name means literally "Ole, close your eyes," Ole being a boy's name) harks back to a character from German folklore, the Sandmännchen, a little man or **dwarf** who makes children fall sleep. He may be viewed as one of Andersen's many self-portraits as a skillful storyteller.

In one group of fairy tales, Andersen went still further in animating the material world around him and introducing everyday objects as protagonists, which in twentieth-century children's literature led to a vast genre of animated toy and doll stories. Andersen's animal tales are also radically different from traditional **fable**s. "The Ugly Duckling" is one of his many camouflaged autobiographies. The animals, including the protagonist, possess human traits, views and, emotions, making the story a poignant account of the road from humiliation through suffering to well-deserved bliss.

Another programmatic fairy tale is "The Little Mermaid," based on a medieval **ballad**, eagerly exploited by Romantic poets. Andersen, however, reversed the roles and, downplaying the ballad's juxtaposition of the Christian versus the pagan, created a beautiful and tragic story of impossible love. The essence of the tale lies well beyond a young reader's grasp, even though it can also be appreciated more superficially. The **mermaid**'s desire for the prince is connected with her desire for an immortal soul, which she can obtain only by marrying a human. She has to make a great sacrifice to achieve her goal; her loss of voice is irreversible, and her acquisition of legs instead of a tail causes enormous physical suffering. In the end, although she has endured so much to win the love of the prince, she does not live happily ever after with her beloved. Yet—and this is the peculiar kind of hope inherent in Andersen's works—she is given a second chance as she joins the Daughters of the Air and can receive her immortal soul as a reward for good deeds. The philosophical implication of the story is completely gone from the movie of the **Walt Disney Company**, as well as from many retellings.

While most of Andersen's fairy tales are firmly set in his home country and often mention concrete topographical details, such as the Round Tower, the landmark of Copenhagen, some tales have exotic settings: China in "The Nightingale" or unspecified southern countries in "The Shadow," probably echoing Andersen's frequent visits to Italy. The latter tale, based loosely on a story by German Romantic author Adalbert von Chamisso, is probably the most enigmatic and disturbing in Andersen's oeuvre, not only because it depicts evil triumphing over good, but also because it explores the darkest sides of the human psyche. Quite a few tales show similar dual address, especially in their satirical undertones, as in "The Emperor's New Clothes." Most of these aspects disappear in children's editions.

Despite such careless treatment, Andersen's impact on children's literature cannot be overestimated. His fairy tales have been translated into dozens of languages, often in a horrendously corrupted and oversimplified manner, and his most famous characters, such as the Little Mermaid, the Little Match Girl, and the Ugly Duckling, are known all over the world. His fairy tales have been made into picture books, plays, **film**s, **opera**s, and merchandise, and many children's writers have acknowledged their debt to Andersen as model and inspiration.

Another, lesser-known Nordic storyteller was the Finno-Swedish professor Zacharias **Topelius**, whose eight-volume collection *Läsning för barn* (*Reading for Children*, 1865–96) is the first truly national children's work published in the Swedish language. It contains a variety of magic tales, local legends, moral stories, and animal tales. Everyday settings and events are intertwined in his stories with romantic and fantastic motifs to suit the educational purposes of the time. Some of his fairy tales, showing clear influence from Andersen, are still read today.

Among English-language authors, George **MacDonald** can be pointed out as an early creator of literary fairy tales. Some are based on known plots, for instance, "The Giant's Heart" (1867), and some develop them and add unexpected elements, such as unusual curses in "The Light Princess" (1864) and "Little Daylight" (1871), while "The Golden Key" (1867) is highly original, with its enigmatic philosophical ending. The status of MacDonald's fairy tales as children's literature is debatable, yet they paved the way for later writers, not least E. **Nesbit**, who is rightfully called the creator of modern literary fairy tales and fantasy. Nesbit was also inspired by Kenneth Grahame's "The Reluctant Dragon" from his childhood memoir *Dream Days* (1898), an upside-down tale about a romantically minded **dragon** that refuses to fight St. George. Due to financial difficulties, Nesbit produced a whole series of fractured fairy tales, first published in magazines, and later collected in *The Book of Dragons* (1900) and *Nine Unlikely Tales for Children* (1901). The essentially new feature in Nesbit's tales, compared to earlier authors, was that she introduced tokens of her own time, such as elevators, telephones, diving bells, or cars, into traditional fairy-tale settings, thus violating the genre's norms.

Fantasy

Fantasy, a genre often treated in handbooks on children's literature together with literary fairy tales, or under the misleading label "modern fairy tales," is another example of folktales' overall impact on children's literature. Indeed, a sharp border between fairy tales and fantasy is impossible and normally unnecessary to draw. Roger Sale's study, for instance, bears the title *Fairy Tales and After: From Snow White to E. B. White* (1978), although it is primarily focused on fantasy **novel**s; Jack Zipes makes no differentiation in *When Dreams Came True: Classical Fairy Tales and Their Tradition* (1999) and his other critical works.

Historically, fantasy grew out of fairy tales and myths, but its specific feature is some form of anchoring in the everyday world. Hoffmann's *Nußknacker und Mausekönig* (*The Nutcracker and the Mouse King*, 1816) is acknowledged as the first fantasy explicitly addressed to children, mainly because the protagonist is a little girl. Carlo **Collodi**'s *Le avventure di Pinocchio* (*The Adventures of Pinocchio*, 1881–83), with its puppet as the central character, adhered to this tradition and well as Andersen's toy stories. In the English-speaking world, however, priority is given to Lewis **Carroll**'s *Alice's Adventures in Wonderland* (1865), accompanied by Charles Kingsley's *Water Babies* (1863) and George MacDonald's *At the Back of the North Wind* (1871). Nesbit followed the path of her predecessors; however, she brought magic into the everyday world rather than sent her characters into magical realms. Thus, her famous fantasy novels *Five Children and It* (1902), *The Phoenix and the Carpet* (1904), and *The Enchanted Castle* (1907) reveal visible links to the folktale about three wishes, in which the last **wish** has to be used to eliminate the fatal consequences of the first two. *The Story of the Amulet* (1906) features a **magic object**, and *The House of Arden* (1908) has a **magic helper**. This tendency to bring magical agents into the ordinary lives of children has been developed by many twentieth-century fantasy writers, notably Pamela Travers in *Mary Poppins* (1934).

By contrast, the most famous American children's fantasy novel, *The Wonderful Wizard of Oz* (1900) by L. Frank **Baum**, closely follows the traditional fairy-tale pattern, in which the heroine is transported into a faraway magical country, exposed to hardship, assisted by helpers, pursued by enemies, and finally gets her heart's desire. Unlike the traditional fairy tale, in which the hero is enthroned in the new realm, Dorothy returns to her own world and is completely disempowered. This ending has become the most common in twentieth-century fantasy for children, present in such classics as Sir James Matthew **Barrie**'s play *Peter Pan* (1904), Eric Linklater's *The Wind in the Moon* (1944), C. S. **Lewis**'s *The Lion, the Witch and the War*drobe (1950), and Michael **Ende**'s *Die unendliche Geschichte* (***The Neverending Story***, 1979).

Roald **Dahl**'s *Charlie and the Chocolate Factory* (1964) replays the theme of the virtuous hero wining over less-worthy rivals. In one of the most recent successes in the fantasy genre, J. K. **Rowling**'s Harry Potter series (1997–2007), more or less every possible trait inherent in fairy tales can be found. Philip **Pullman**'s *His Dark Materials* trilogy (1995–2000) is more sophisticated in setting, characterization, and message, yet it also carries some the basic fairy-tale elements, including magical agents, objects, good and evil, and quests.

Animal fantasy, such as *The Wind in the Willows* (1908) by Kenneth Grahame, *Bambi* (1923) by Felix Salten, and *Winnie-the-Pooh* (1926) by A. A. Milne (it can be argued whether the characters are animals or toys), has obviously developed from animal folktales and fables. However, many contemporary children's animal stories have more in common with magic folktales than animal tales, such as the story of the little orphan Babar, who becomes king (*The Story of Babar, the Little Elephant,* by Jean de Brunhoff, 1931), while Arnold Lobel's "Frog and Toad" tales are merely everyday stories in which children are disguised as animals. *The Mouse and His Child* (1967) by Russell **Hoban** alludes to Andersen but also features a traditional fairy-tale quest for a better life.

The remarkable feature of fantasy for children is that it enjoys a higher status within children's literature than in general literature, where it is treated as formula fiction. Apparently, fantasy is considered suitable for children on the same premises as folktales and fairy tales, mostly as a vehicle for socialization.

Realistic Fiction

It is perhaps difficult and challenging to discern fairy-tale traits in so-called realistic fiction for children, yet in some genres they are evident. Scholars have pointed out the similarity in structure between fairy tales and adventure stories, in which the hero—often a poor orphan—leaves home, experiences trials, takes on quests, meets enemies and helpers, and returns home in triumph, with wealth and a "princess" as his reward. Many of these stories, originally not intended exclusively for children, have entered the canon of children's literature, sometimes abridged. Robert Louis **Stevenson**'s *Treasure Island* (1883) is the best example. Historical novels by Sir Walter Scott also show a similar pattern, as well do stories by Captain Maryatt, Mayne Reid, and G. A. Henty. Among books addressed primarily to children, Mark **Twain**'s *The Adventures of Tom Sawyer* (1876) can be mentioned. In addition, more-recent novels, such as Mordechai Richler's *Jacob Two-Two Meets the Hooded Fang* (1975), are modeled after the Jack the Giant Killer story, and so on.

Mystery novels, whether addressed to boys, such as the Hardy Boys series, or to girls, such as the Nancy Drew books, and the many adventures of the fearless Biggles series adhere to the same narrative structure. Adventure stories borrow from fairy tales not only plot and stereotypical stock characters but also motifs such as the struggle between good and evil, clear-cut borders between heroes and villains, exotic settings corresponding to fairy-tale dark forests and faraway realms, and the inevitable success and reward of the hero. The convenient removal of parents, necessary for the hero's freedom of action, is another common feature of fairy tales and adventure stories.

On the other hand, books for girls, widely popular in the beginning of the twentieth century and still written and enjoyed today, show clear similarities with another type of folktale, portraying girls who wait for the right man, reject false pretenders, and display moral superiority over less-virtuous rivals. Basically, they follow the "Beauty and the Beast" plot (the **animal bridegroom**). Girl fiction does not have to exhibit explicit fairy-tale elements for us to recognize them anyway, for instance, in such classics as *Little Women* (1868) and *Anne of Green Gables* (1908). Children's career stories, such as Noel Streatfeild's "Shoe books" (*Ballet Shoes*, 1936, and others), display a clear fairy-tale plot of "Cinderella" type. Such novels have been successfully analyzed in terms of Vladimir **Propp**'s **function** sequence and character gallery. The archetypal fairy-tale orphan turns up regularly in children's fiction, for instance, in *The Foundling* (1878; also known as *The Adventures of Remi*) by Hector Malot, or *Heidi* (1881) by Johanna Spyri.

Contemporary realistic stories for children have naturally gone still farther from folktales, yet they, too, frequently reveal traits obviously inherited from fairy-tale plots. Formula fiction in particular is close to folktales with its stereotypical plots and character. Some of the fundamental human relationships explored by folktales, such as **mother**/daughter ("Snow White," "Cinderella," and "Rapunzel"), **father**/daughter ("All-Fur"), and father/son ("Puss in Boots" and "Jack the Giant Killer"), constitute central conflicts in contemporary psychological novels for children. Children's book characters still struggle against evil, not least the dark sides of their own psyche; they still go on quests, even though these may be inner quests; they are still abandoned by parents and discover parent substitutes; and they still have helpers and friends among their peers and among adults. Their goals continue to be maturation and entering adulthood. The stories, with some exceptions, still have fairy-tale happy endings. Finally, recurrent allusions to fairy tales create an additional symbolic level in everyday situations. Katherine Paterson's *The Great Gilly Hopkins* (1978) is an excellent illustration of all these features. Thus, while realistic stories for children may seem radically different from folktales, upon closer examination, they demonstrate the same basic plots and the same core characters, merely with deeper psychological dimensions.

Parody and Fractured Tales

Although fractured fairy tales are often connected with the postmodern stage of literature, in fact they go back to *mundus inversus* folktales that exist in all cultures. However, it is true that **parody**, irony, and intentional intertextual bands in children's books increased during the last decades of the twentieth century. **Feminist fairy tales** have explored the inverted **gender** roles (Robert Munsch and Michael Martchenko's *The Paper Bag Princess*, 1980), and socialist fairy tales have exposed class structures; yet most fractured tales seem merely to play with fairy-tale patterns for pleasure and amusement, consciously addressing both children and adults. These trends are apparently the result of extensive academic study of folktales and fairy tales from various perspectives.

Last but not least, picture books based on fairy tales have brought alien elements into well-known stories, both in words and images. Among these, Jon Scieszka's and Lane Smith's *The Stinky Man Cheese* (1992) is perhaps the most famous. However, Scieszka and Smith's *The True Story of the Three Little Pigs* (1989), Eugene Trivizas and Helen Oxenbury's *The Three Little Wolves and the Big Bad Pig* (1993), Babette Cole's *Prince Cinders* (1987), and Ellen Jackson and Kevin O'Malley's *Cinder Edna* (1994) are equally worth attention in this respect. Anthony **Browne**'s *The Tunnel* (1989) and *Into the Forest* (2004) are not exactly fractured tales but contain many folktale elements that enhance the psychological depth of the plot. **Metafiction** has become a conspicuous trait of modern illustrated fairy tales, such as David Wiesner's *The Three Pigs* (2001). The wordless picture book by **Anno** Mitsumasa, *Anno's Journey* (1977), has numerous visual allusions to famous European folktales. Another recent trend in fracturing tales is children's novels loosely based on famous fairy tales, such as *Ella Enchanted* (1997) by Gail Carson Levine.

Disney As the New Channel for Children's Fairy Tales

In the modern era, fairy tales have invaded children's culture through the productions of Walt **Disney** and the Walt Disney Company. These include *Snow White* (1937), *Pinocchio* (1940), *Cinderella* (1950), *Alice in Wonderland* (1951), *Peter Pan* (1953), *The Little*

Mermaid (1989), *Beauty and the Beast* (1991), and *Aladdin* (1992). Frequently, the Disney film versions, adapted to the morals of the American middle class, are substantially better known than the originals. Unhappy or ambivalent endings are eliminated, as are graphic details and anything that may appear offensive. Plots are simpler and more action-oriented, while personal conflicts and inner quests are made explicit, resulting in the introduction of new, external enemies. The movies are subsequently made into mass-market picture books that push the original stories out of bookshops, libraries, and the young generation's encyclopedic knowledge. ***See also*** Didactic Tale; Illustration; Pedagogy.

Further Readings: Lurie, Alison. *Boys and Girls Forever: Children's Classics from Cinderella to Harry Potter*. New York: Penguin, 2003; Nodelman, Perry, ed. *Fairy Tales, Fables, Myths, Legends and Poetry*. Volume 2 of *Touchstones: Reflections on the Best in Children's Literature*. West Lafayette, IN: Children's Literature Association, 1987; Nodelman, Perry, and Mavis Reimer. *The Pleasures of Children's Literature*. 3rd edition. Boston: Allyn and Bacon, 2003; Sale, Roger. *Fairy Tales and After: From Snow White to E. B. White*. Cambridge: Cambridge University Press, 1978; Shavit, Zohar. "The Concept of Childhood and Children's Folktales: Test Case—'Little Red Riding Hood.'" *Little Red Riding Hood: A Casebook*. Edited by Alan Dundes. Madison: University of Wisconsin Press, 1989. 129–58; Stephens, John, and Robyn McCallum. *Retelling Stories, Framing Culture: Traditional Story and Metanarratives in Children's Literature*. New York: Garland, 1998; Tatar, Maria. *Off With Their Heads! Fairy Tales and the Culture of Childhood*. Princeton, NJ: Princeton University Press, 1992; Zipes, Jack. *Fairy Tales and the Art of Subversion: The Classical Genre for Children and the Process of Civilization*. New York: Wildman Press, 1983; _____. *When Dreams Came True: Classical Fairy Tales and Their Tradition*. New York: Routledge, 1999.

Maria Nikolajeva

Chinese Tales

History of Chinese Folktales and Storytelling

As in other lands and cultures around the world, China has an enduring history of folktales and **storytelling**. In China, **oral tradition** has always intertwined with the literary tradition. This distinctive feature of mutual nurturing and the long history of Chinese literacy have made the works of literati a rich resource in tracing the history, genealogy, and the written records of Chinese tales.

Scholars regard the early decades of the post-Hàn era (around the third to fourth centuries) as one of the most influential times in the history of Chinese tales. First, the spread of Buddhism and its growing influence among the literati promoted the emergence of the collections of Buddhist miracle tales, an important source of Chinese religious tales. The included translation from various Indian or central Asian languages in early Buddhist literature also facilitated the study of the **diffusion** of tales in history. Second, another important tradition related to folktales emerged in this era, the so-called *zhìguài* (literally "documenting strangeness"). Literati recorded and reported marvels and anomalies as **anecdote**s or historical events. The collections of the supernatural and unusual that they compiled, often containing brief outlines of contemporary tales, helped to establish and maintain one of the earliest written repertoires of Chinese folktales.

In the following centuries, from the Jìn (265–420) to Qīng (1644–1911) dynasty, the influence of this tradition continued among literati. Documenting oral tales and anecdotes in personal notes, casual storytelling, and creating literary tales and fictions in both classical and vernacular languages remained an important aspect of the literary tradition. While the historical trace of oral tradition could easily vanish, some historical records and literary works, such as *Tàipíng Guǎng Jì* (*Taiping Comprehensive Collections*, 978), *Xī Yóu Jì* (*Journey to the West*, 1592), *Fēngshén Yǎnyì* (*The Investiture of Gods*, around 1567–1619), and *Liáo Zhāi Zhì Yì* (*Strange Stories from a Scholar's Studio*, 1679), consisted of abundant **myth**s, oral tales, and religious beliefs popular in their times. The works were so embraced by the **folk** in the marketplace that they often passed into the repertoire of Chinese folktales and professional storytelling.

Compared to the written historical sources of folktales, there is relatively less premodern documentation of Chinese storytelling. Although archaeological material shows that an entertaining form in the Hàn court (206 BCE–220 CE) had a strong affinity with storytelling, scholars commonly agree that *Sújiǎng* (popular sermons in Buddhist temples) in the Táng dynasty (618–907) directly related to the later maturity of professional storytelling in the Sòng dynasty (960–1279). Historical documents show that, in the capital of Sòng, storytelling was regularly performed in the vernacular language in well-defined urban entertainment centers. It included various genres, such as history, Buddhist scripture, warfare, and marvels. Storytellers also had training techniques and written scripts, but they often improvised in performance. In the Qīng dynasty (1644–1911), storytelling experienced its second developmental peak. Professional storytelling became more sophisticated with more variety. Regional, linguistic, and musical differences formed a rich repertoire of schools, genres, and performance formats. Tales of both oral and literary origin, especially the famed traditional stories from the previous dynasties, were more fully developed in this era in terms of plots and characters. Many of them uphold their vitality in contemporary China. Nowadays, professional storytelling is quite visible in many regions and vigorously incorporates mass media into performance to spread its influence.

Collection and Classification

Despite rich historical resources, the systematic collection and documentation of Chinese tales did not begin until the early twentieth century, when **folklore** emerged as a discipline in modern China (from 1911 onwards). Modern Chinese folklorists have conducted three major phases of folktale **collecting**—from 1919 to 1937, from 1952 to 1965, and from 1985 to the present, corresponding to three major transitional eras in the history of modern China.

The early twentieth century saw a declining and powerless China facing internal warfare and the military and economic invasion of Western powers. The rise of folklore at that time was largely related to the nationalistic feelings of intellectual elites, who searched for a new, vital source among the people to build a new national language, literature, and nation-state. It is not surprising that the social and aesthetic values of folktales, such as **women**'s social status reflected in folklore, were emphasized for nationalistic tasks and social reforms. Folktale collections that were published in short-lived journals were often collected through **fieldwork** and were respectable in terms of their numbers and **authenticity**.

The second high point in the collecting of folktales came right after the founding of the People's Republic of China. During the 1950s and 1960s, a time when the peasants and working class were leaders, there was great enthusiasm for collecting ethnic and folk literature from the people. While the published collections were often selective or polished for ideological purposes, radical changes to essential story elements were infrequent.

After the devastating Cultural Revolution (1966–76), China experienced a wave of cultural revival. In the 1980s, Chinese folklorists launched an unprecedented movement to collect folklore with the support of the state. Their intention was to document folktales from all of the nationalities and regions in contemporary China and to compile the most comprehensive collection in history. The result was *Zhōngguó Mínjiān Gùshì Jíchéng* (*The Comprehensive Collections of Chinese Folktales*; hereafter, *Jíchéng*), under the editorship of Zhōng Jìngwén. With one volume per province, *Jíchéng* when completed will encompass thirty volumes, twenty-four of which have been published in China since 1991. The tales are categorized as myths, **legend**s, **animal tale**s, tales of magic (**wonder tale**s), and **joke**s. They are collected and documented by trained folklorists and the staffs of local cultural bureaus. Ethnographic information about tales and storytellers is provided.

Predating the work of Chinese folklorists, the collecting of Chinese folktales by Westerners can be dated at least to the mid- and late nineteenth century. Many of the earliest collections were compiled by missionaries who had direct knowledge of oral lore. For example, Adele M. Fielde, the author of *Chinese Nights Entertainment* (1893), provided rich details about collecting and recording tales from the people in local dialect in her article "The Character of Chinese Folktales" (1895). She also briefly analyzed the local folk beliefs and social life reflected in the tales. Albert L. Shelton, the author of *Tibetan Folk Tales* (1925), gathered his data around the tents and campfires of the Tibetan people.

Later influential collections, such as Wolfram Eberhard's *Chinese Fairy Tales and Folk Tales* (1937) and *Folktales of China* (1965), display an approach that relies on both fieldwork and folktale publications in Chinese. There are also some recent collections coming from the direct translation of selected tales in Chinese anthologies. This approach significantly broadens the Western view of Chinese folktales by directly introducing Chinese texts. However, for academic research, compilers and **editor**s need to provide careful annotations and ethnographic information. In this respect, Eberhard's *Folktales of China* stands as a good example by including information about the origin of the tales, drawing attention to related customs or beliefs, and identifying **tale type**s in the international tradition.

One consistent interest that underlies Western collection of Chinese tales is to understand the Chinese modes of thoughts and the relation between Chinese tales and their international counterparts. Thus, the work of scholars has been characterized by a comparative perspective and active efforts to classify Chinese tales. In 1937, Eberhard published *Typen Chinesischer Volksmärchen* (*Types of Chinese Folktales*), one of the earliest tale-type indexes devoted to Chinese folktales. In 1978, based on the vast number of Chinese publications from before the 1970s (about 7,000 tales), Nai-tung Ting produced the most comprehensive and thorough classification of Chinese folktales, published as *A Type Index of Chinese Folktales*. Ting's systematic index, based on the European Aarne-Thompson (since 2004 the Aarne-Thompson-Uther) tale-type system, brings Chinese folktales and the international tradition under one frame and provides detailed descriptions and impressive bibliographic material. Recently, Chinese and Taiwanese scholars have tried to create a new tale-type index, which aims to include the newly compiled *Jíchéng* collections and stress the intrinsic cultural-narrative characteristics of Chinese folktales.

Comparability and Distinctiveness of Chinese Folktales

The classification of Chinese folktales in the international tradition reveals that Chinese folktales consistently interact with tales from other lands and, at the same time, develop their own distinctive features. Depending on their relation with international tradition, Chinese folktales can be roughly divided into three categories.

The first category consists of folktales that can be identified with the Indo-European tale types and contain the same essential events and plots. Nonetheless, the texts of these tales often bear distinct cultural details and messages. For example, the **prince** or **princess**, a popular character in the European tale tradition, often appears in Chinese folktales as a son or daughter of the rich or noble. In the commonly shared tales of sibling rivalry, the older brother (or his wife) or sister is usually identified as the villain and the suffering hero or heroine as the younger one. This feature emphasizes the responsibility of the older siblings to the younger ones in Chinese morality. The tales about a journey to search for treasure, advice, or answers to questions (ATU 461, Three Hairs from the Devil's Beard) often include, in Chinese versions, a distinctive plot called The Condition in Ting's index (Ting 461A). The protagonist can ask only a certain number of questions and eventually does not get a chance to ask his own. The popularity of this plot highlights the cultural message that the protagonist is rewarded because he believes that the others' interests are more important than his own.

The second category includes folktales that have developed regional and cultural deviations and are often entangled with tale types that are widely distributed in China. Two representative and famous examples are the tale types **Little Red Riding Hood** (ATU 333) and **Cinderella** (ATU 510A). The common Chinese title of the tale known in the West as "Little Red Riding Hood" is "Tiger or Wolf Grandma." The earliest written record of this tale occurs no later than the mid-eighteenth century, and the story circulates popularly among various nationalities and regions in contemporary China. Although the Chinese version has the essential theme involving the violation of a warning and the encounter with danger, it nonetheless exists as a contrastive subtype (Ting 333C) to the tale as it appears in the European tradition. The main characters in Chinese versions are almost exclusively siblings rather than a helpless little girl, and the **wolf** or tiger (or bear) is punished or killed by the children at the end. "Tiger or Wolf Grandma" not only runs counter to the tragedy of "Little Red Riding Hood" but also shatters the central conflict based on **gender** in the European versions. It gives prominence to the self-salvation of children, the power of wit, and the decisive role of the oldest sibling in protecting the younger.

"Cinderella," one of the most beloved tales worldwide, does not enjoy wide popularity in China despite the fact that China maintains the earliest written record of this tale anywhere in the world. Cinderella, under the name of Yè Xiàn, first appeared in the collection of Duàn Chéngshì (803–863) and experienced the same series of plots as her Western cousin. However, in the Chinese versions that are currently available, the tales appear more often than not in combined form (ATU 510A + Ting 433D, Snake Husband), such as the version published in Eberhard's *Folktales of China*. The focus of the tale shifts to the murder of the heroine at the hand of her jealous stepsister after her **marriage** and how the heroine's soul engages in a series of magical **transformation**s to be recognized by her husband. The Chinese tale highlights the moral contrast between the two **sisters** and presents a strong and intelligent Cinderella who overcomes many difficulties to regain her own identity and status.

The third category of Chinese folktales encompasses those that are particularly popular among the Chinese people or peculiar to China. Folktales as a form of human creative expression, whether indigenous or mixed, convey the worldview and ideologies of their storytellers and audience. Scholars have noticed that, besides "Tiger or Wolf Grandma" and "Snake Husband" mentioned above, certain tale types and Chinese subtypes have a special position in the repertoire of Chinese folktales.

One such group is the immortal or supernatural wife (Ting 400A, 400B, 400C, and 400D, Chinese subtypes of ATU 400, The Man on a Quest for His Lost Wife), for which the written record dates back to at least the fourth century. The tales contain the popular **motif** of the **Swan Maiden** (Motif D361.1) but emphasize the man's miserable premarital life and his married life. The heroine—a bird, **fairy**, snail, goose, or fox—often appears in human form to do household work for an orphaned or outcast young man of high morals. The marriage brings the man a warm and materially abundant **family** and children. The wife often disappears at the end. In a departure from other tales of magic, in this tale type the wife's magic is presented in the context of helping the man change his economic status and to fulfill his social role as a husband and **father**. In some cases, such as in the most representative tale "Cowherd and Weaving Maiden" (Ting 400A + ATU 313, The Magic Flight), wherein the couple is persecuted by an outside force, it is often the wife's supernatural power that helps her husband protect the family. The wife's devotion and heroic deeds often transform a tale of magic into a tale of romantic love.

Tales about wit are another very popular category of Chinese folktales. Many of these tales present the contrasting images of "stupid son-in-law" and "clever daughter-in-law or woman." For example, the tale type The Forgotten Word (ATU 1687) has a wide distribution throughout the world, and in Chinese versions, the fool is usually a son-in-law. In other tales, he fails to say the right words on the right occasions, mistakes his mother-in-law for his wife, or is controlled by his wife at home. The clever daughter-in-law or woman, on the contrary, is capable in both domestic and social spheres because of her strategy, skills, and intelligence. She is also often literate and knowledgeable and ridicules or challenges men of learning or of high social status. The popularity of these tales, together with those of the supernatural wife mentioned above, opens a window onto the complex representation of women in Chinese folklore.

Other popular tales peculiar to the Chinese cultural context often contain deeply held cultural values or references to specific customs, beliefs, or events in Chinese history. For example, the tale type The Dog Plows Farms (Ting 503E; Chinese subtype of ATU 503, The Gifts of the Little People) features the struggles over inheritance that often occur between **brothers** in Chinese society, the traditional farming life, and the moral lesson that the wicked and greedy will be punished. In "Cowherd and Weaving Maiden," romantic love and the capable, skillful fairy are linked to a female worship ritual for dexterity and adeptness on the seventh day of the seventh month in the Chinese lunar calendar. The tale of "Mèng Jiāngnǚ" or "The Faithful Lady Meng" in Eberhard's *Folktales of China* (Ting 888C, Faithful Wife Revenges Husband's Death) is based on the historical background of building the Great Wall in the Qín dynasty (221–206 BCE). Mèng's husband is seized and carried away to build the Great Wall and later dies of hard labor. Mèng travels thousands of miles to search for her husband only to discover the tragic news. Her weeping causes part of the Great Wall to collapse. After avenging her husband's death, she commits suicide.

Research on Chinese Tales

The long history and rich written records of Chinese folktales provide a basis for productive historical-geographical research in this field (see **Historic-Geographic Method**). The Chinese repertoire, as in the case of "Cinderella," helps scholars to look beyond the conventional Indo-European tale cycles and create a broader view of the origin, distribution, and diffusion of folktales. In China, this approach has been adopted to trace the transformation of individual tales in the Chinese cultural context. One representative example is the groundbreaking research carried out in the 1920s and 1930s by Gù Jiégāng on the tales of "The Faithful Lady Meng." Gù lists the circulation systems of the tales, historically and geographically, over the past 2,000 years. Furthermore, combining tales and related customs, beliefs, and historical contexts from different historical periods, he studies the changes in the plots and other details of the stories and examines how the imagination and values of the people influenced the development and themes of the tales. Gù's historical-geographical research provides a rich cultural background and illuminates not only the diffusion of the tales but also why and how the tales were transformed.

Folktale scholars have also drawn attention to the mutual nurturing between oral and written traditions in Chinese literary history. The role and relationship between literacy and orality in the growth and circulation of folktales has become an important topic. Scholars with a historical-textual perspective approach this topic by comparing the works of literati in premodern China with modern oral versions of individual tales. This approach helps detect the literary origins and influence of folktales and the historical process of cross-borrowing between literary and oral traditions. Other scholars have focused on the **performance** of storytelling and the life stories of storytellers in contemporary China. Research has shown that storytellers often consciously base their tales on literary works and insert classical literature (for example, poems) to create atmosphere or underline the main theme in their performances. At the same time, their performances follow the audience-centered techniques and formulas of telling stories. Literacy and orality are woven together as a continuum rather than as a split or dichotomy.

Chinese folktale research has also been concerned with issues raised by **feminism** and questions of gender. In contrast to the stereotypical image of Chinese women as submissive and passive, the heroines in folktales present a complicated picture. A Chinese heroine might be a **woman warrior** like Mùlán, a beautiful and capable fairy with supernatural power, a faithful and strong wife like Lady Meng, or a smart daughter-in-law. Recent research has been undertaken to understand the representation of women in both classical literature and folktales comparatively to explore alternative definitions of womanhood and gender roles in the Chinese oral tradition.

The progress made since the 1980s in compiling *Jíchéng* as a major resource for the study of folktales has prompted another new direction in Chinese folk narrative research in China. Folklorists are now actively conducting research on newly discovered storytellers and storytelling events. Folktales are not regarded solely as texts or isolated performances but as a living cultural ingredient in the historical and cultural cosmos of local regions. Folklorists study the role of folktales and folktale events in the development of temple fairs, village or community history, and in other cultural contexts. At the same time, Chinese folklorists are engaged in writing the history of popular tale types in China. Using the new texts provided by the collection *Jíchéng*, scholars are tracing the historical transformation of tale types and their motifs. These efforts are paving the way for an updated and comprehensive tale-type index of Chinese folktales in the future. *See also* Pú Sōnglíng; Wú Chéng'ēn.

Further Readings: Børdahl, Vibeke, ed. *The Eternal Storyteller: Oral Literature in Modern China.* Richmond, Surrey: Curzon Press, 1999; Chan, Leo Tak-hung. "Text and Talk: Classical Literary Tales in Traditional China and the Context of Casual Oral Storytelling." *Asian Folklore Studies* 56 (1997): 33–63; Eberhard, Wolfram, ed. *Folktales of China.* Chicago: University of Chicago Press, 1965; Gernant, Karen, trans. *Imagining Women: Fujian Folk Tales*. New York: Interlink Books, 1995; Gjertson, Donald E. "The Early Chinese Buddhist Miracle Tale: A Preliminary Survey." *Journal of the American Oriental Society* 101 (1981): 287–301; Gù, Jiégāng. *Mèngjiāngnǚ Gùshì Yánjiū Jí*. Shanghai: Guji Press, 1984; Liú, Shǒuhuá, ed. *Zhōngguó Mínjiān Gùshì Lèixíng Yánjiū*. Wuhan: Huazhong Normal University, 2002; Ting, Nai-tung. *The Cinderella Cycle in China and Indo-China*. Helsinki: Academia Scientiarum Fennica, 1974; Ting, Nai-tung. *A Type Index of Chinese Folktales: In the Oral Tradition and Major Works of Non-Religious Classical Literature*. Helsinki: Academia Scientiarum Fennica, 1978.

Jing Li

Chukovsky, Kornei (1882–1969)

Kornei Chukovsky, the pseudonym of Nikolai Korneichukov, is usually referred to as the greatest name in modern Russian **children's literature**. Although he is well regarded as a literary scholar, critic, translator, and essayist, his work as a poet for children is considered extraordinary.

Born as an illegitimate son in St. Petersburg, he was raised in Odessa by his mother, under very poor conditions. Still, he managed to graduate from secondary school and began work as a journalist for the *Odessa News* in 1901. From 1903 to 1905 he served as a correspondent in London, where he became familiar with the writings of Edward Lear and Lewis **Carroll**, as well as with the tradition of nursery rhymes. Back in St. Petersburg, he published the satirical journal *The Signal* and started to write literary criticism. In 1911, he published *Materyam o detskikh zhurnalakh* (*To Mothers about Journals for Children*), a collection of critical articles on contemporary children's literature. Encouraged by Maksim Gorky, Chukovsky, together with the publishing house Parus, produced the anthology *Yolka* (*The Christmas Tree*) in 1918. This was the first example of a collaboration between representatives of children's literature and the literary avant-garde. By then he had also developed a great interest in the speech of small children, which in 1928 resulted in the popular study *Malen'kie deti* (*Small Children*), later renamed *Ot dvukh do pyati* (*From Two to Five*) and republished in twenty editions.

His real breakthrough occurred in 1917. Like many classics for children, the poem "Krokodil" ("The Crocodile") of that year was created in a real-life situation. While traveling home with his sick son accompanied by the clicking of the train's wheels, Chukovsky made up a story about a cigar-smoking crocodile who strolls along Nevsky Prospekt swallowing policemen and dogs until the brave Vasya comes along, defeats the villain, and sends him back to Africa. In the second part of the poem, man has become an oppressor and war breaks out between humans and animals. As is always the case in Chukovsky's works, the story ends in peace and harmony. The animals captured in the zoo are set free on the condition that they will only eat porridge and drink yogurt kefir. Most of the characteristics of Chukovsky's **poetry** are present already in "Krokodil." Vivid and unusual images, play and improvisation, distinct rhymes, and a precise rhythm formulate the encounter of tradition and innovation and anthropomorphism and protagonists, whose predecessors can be found in folktales.

The verse tale "Tarakanishche" ("The Giant Roach," 1923) once again illustrates the struggle between a despot and his subjects. A similar case is shown in "Mukhina Svad'ba" ("The Wedding of the Fly," 1924), wherein a spider decides to eat the bride but is beheaded by a brave mosquito. In "Moidodyr" ("Wash 'Em Clean," 1923), a careless boy is haunted by the commander of bath sponges, while "Chudo-derevo" ("The Wondrous Tree," 1924) and "Telefon" ("The Telephone," 1926) stand out as Chukovsky's most advanced poems within the tradition of nonsense, showing the influence of Russian futurism and **folklore.** *See also* Russian Tales.

Further Reading: Bode, Andreas. "Humor in the Lyrical Stories for Children of Samuel Marshak and Korney Chukovsky." Translated by Martha Baker. *Lion and the Unicorn* 13.2 (1989): 34–55.

Janina Orlov

Cinderella

Best known in the canonical versions by Charles **Perrault** and the Brothers **Grimm,** Cinderella is the widely distributed **tale type** classified as ATU 510A in the Aarne-Thompson-Uther index of folktales. The oldest identified variant of the Cinderella story is Duàn Chéngshì's "Yè Xiàn," which was written in China around 850 CE. Here Cinderella's **magic helper** takes the form of a fish, which is the reincarnation of her deceased **mother.** Several other elements of Perrault's French version of 1697 are already present in "Yè Xiàn," including the evil stepmother, the royal ball, and the small slipper. Other variants of the Cinderella story can be found all over the world: from the Japanese "Benizara and Kakezara" and the Russian "Burenushka, the Little Red Cow" to the Brazilian "Dona Labismina" and the African "The Maiden, the Frog, and the Chief's Son." The rags-to-riches tale (or rather riches-to-rags-to-riches) appears to be one of the most popular story formats. It also lies at the heart of many classic literary works, such as Charlotte **Brontë**'s *Jane Eyre* (1847) and Frances Eliza Hodgson **Burnett**'s *A Little Princess* (1905), and is used in several more recent stories and **film**s, such as *Pretty Woman* (1990) and *Maid in Manhattan* (2002).

Best-Known Versions

Giambattista **Basile**'s *Lo cunto de li cunti* (*The Tale of Tales*, 1634–36) contains an early variant of "Cinderella" called "La gatta Cenerentola" ("The Cinderella Cat"). The protagonist, Zezolla, takes the advice of her governess and breaks her stepmother's neck with the lid of a chest. Her governess, Carmosina, then takes the place of her stepmother, and it turns out that she had been hiding six daughters of her own. Again, Zezolla is treated with cruelty, and her name is changed to "Cinderella Cat." She asks her **father** to commend her to the **fairies** and to send her a gift. She gets a date tree,

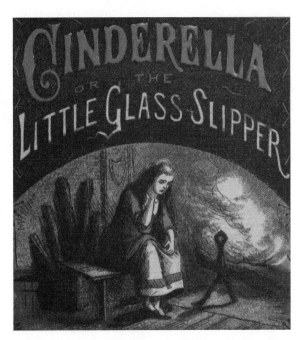

The cover of *Cinderella or The Little Glass Slipper* in the Little Dot Series (New York: McLoughlin Brothers, 1887). [Courtesy of the Eloise Ramsey Collection of Literature for Young People, University Libraries, Wayne State University]

which magically dresses her like a **queen**. The **king** falls in love with Zezolla but is unable to discover her identity until she loses one of her pattens, the decorated covers of her shoes. Since she is the only one whom it fits, he makes her his queen.

Charles Perrault's "Cendrillon," which also served as the basis for Andrew **Lang**'s *Blue Fairy Book* (1889) and for Walt **Disney**'s animated film (1950), was first published in his *Histoires ou conte de temps passé* (*Stories or Tales of Times Past*, 1697). Cinderella is the only daughter of a widower. When he remarries, she is treated poorly by her stepsisters and stepmother in particular. This comes to a climax when the **prince** organizes a ball. Although Perrault's extremely good-hearted and humble Cinderella claims that it would be fitting for her to join such an occasion, she starts crying when her stepsisters leave for the dance. Her fairy godmother brings solace: with her magic wand, she turns a pumpkin into a coach, six mice into horses, a rat into a coachman, and six lizards into footmen. After giving Cinderella a beautiful gown, she warns her to come home before midnight, when the magic spell will end. For three nights in a row, Cinderella dances with the prince, but runs away before midnight. On the last night, however, she loses one of her glass slippers, which the prince retrieves. (Scholars disagree on whether Perrault intended the slipper to be made from glass, or whether this was a misunderstanding based on the French word *vair*, a type of fur that sounds very similar to *verre*, or glass.) The prince claims that he will marry whomever the slipper fits. When his servant comes to Cinderella's house, she asks to try it on after her sisters, and the shoe fits. As Perrault's Cinderella is a forgiving character, she does not hold any grudge against her stepsisters but lets them marry two noblemen from her new husband's court. Perrault adds two *moralités*—**moral**s—to his tale: in the first, he stresses that "good grace" is worth more than mere beauty. In the second, he adds that one needs a good godmother or godfather to succeed in life.

The Grimms' version of Cinderella, titled "Aschenputtel" ("Ash Girl," 1812), opens with a scene by the mother's deathbed, in which she tells her daughter that if the girl stays pious and good, she will always be with her. This already indicates two major differences between the versions by Grimm and Perrault: Cinderella's biological mother is much more prominent in the Grimm tale, and greater emphasis is placed on religion. Cinderella visits her mother's grave every day, even when her father remarries. As in Perrault's tale, Cinderella is ill treated by her stepmother and stepsisters: the Grimms describe in great detail all of the dirty tasks that she is forced to do. In contrast to Perrault's tale, Cinderella's father makes several appearances during the rest of Grimms' story. When he has to travel to a fair, Cinderella asks him to bring her the first twig that hits his hat. He brings her a hazel twig, which she plants on her mother's grave and from which grows a beautiful tree, watered with her tears. The birds that live in this tree will be crucial to the further development of the plot. When the king organizes a ball, Cinderella's stepmother sets her several difficult tasks, such as sorting lentils from ashes. She accomplishes these with the help of the birds but is still forbidden to go.

Unlike Perrault's persecuted heroine, the Grimms' Cinderella receives no help from a fairy godmother, nor does she get a coach and coachmen. Instead she retrieves a beautiful outfit from the birds in the hazel tree. As in Perrault's tale, she visits the ball three times and wins the prince's heart. The warning to leave the ball before midnight is lacking in the Grimms' version, however; Cinderella decides for herself that it is time to go. The prince follows her, but each time she hides from him: first in the dovecote, then in a pear tree. Each time her father wonders whether it is his daughter hiding there, and so he chops down her hiding place. On the final night, the prince covers the staircase with pitch and is thus able to retrieve Cinderella's golden **shoe**. In the next episodes, the Grimms' version has several added moments of cruelty in comparison to Perrault's. In a vain attempt to trick the prince, Cinderella's stepmother urges her daughters to cut off their toes and heels so that the shoe will fit. They are revealed by the birds, however, that draw the prince's attention to the **blood** that oozes from the shoe. When the shoe is placed on Cinderella's foot and fits perfectly, the birds reassure the prince that this time he has chosen the right bride. At the end of the tale, the Brothers Grimm add another cruel **punishment**: two doves come to peck out the stepsisters' eyes as they walk Cinderella to and from the church.

Disney's animated picture based on Perrault's "Cinderella" appeared in 1950. In contrast to the versions of Grimm and Perrault, Disney makes the stepsisters extremely ugly and dumb. They are dominated by Cinderella's stepmother, who is given a demonic dimension compared to a happy, chubby fairy godmother. Cinderella's father is completely absent. He is said to have died before the story begins and is thus liberated from all blame for his daughter's hardship.

Criticism

The earliest research on "Cinderella" mainly involved **collecting variant**s of the folktale from different parts of the world and attempting to trace the origin and development of the story. Marian Roalfe Cox published her important collection in 1893 under the explanatory title *Cinderella: Three Hundred and Forty-Five Variants of Cinderella, Catskin, and Cap o' Rushes*. In 1951, Swedish folklorist Anna Birgitta Rooth published her *Cinderella Cycle* with more than 700 variants.

Feminists have critiqued the tale of "Cinderella" as promoting passivity and victim behavior in **women**. In *Women Hating* (1974), Andrea Dworkin defends Cinderella's cruel stepmother: she knows how patriarchal society works and has to cripple her daughters to arrange a good **marriage** for them. On the basis of a speech analysis of "Cinderella" in the variants by Basile, Perrault, and several editions of the Brothers Grimm's **Kinder- und Hausmärchen** (*Children's and Household Tales*), Ruth B. Bottigheimer found that direct speech shifted from women to **men** and from good to bad girls: thus Cinderella is gradually silenced. Moreover, although her father's role is increased in the Grimm editions, he is acquitted of any blame for his daughter's hardship. Other critics value the **gender** relationships in "Cinderella" more positively. August Nitschke believes that the story originated in the **oral tradition** of a prehistoric matrilineal society, a view shared by Heide Göttner-Abendroth in her book *Die Göttin und ihr Heros* (1980; translated as *The Goddess and Her Heroes*, 1995). Göttner-Abendroth explains how the tale was adapted by patriarchy: symbols of female rituals were subdued, patrilineal marriage was introduced, and female power was demonized. Jack **Zipes** finds traces of the matriarchic societies in Basile, Perrault, and the Brothers Grimm's variants, for instance, in the fairy godmother or the connection between the helping birds and the heroine's dead mother.

In her book *From the Beast to the Blonde* (1994), Marina Warner interprets "Cinderella" with reference to the sociohistorical context in which Perrault and Grimm were writing. She links the figures of the stepmother and the godmother to that of the mother-in-law, who often needed to live with her son's **family** and could be both an assistant and adversary to the young wife. Moreover, placing these tales in the tradition of old wives' tales, Warner argues that the fairy godmother may symbolically represent the voice of the elderly woman telling the story.

The Cinderella **motif** has been taken on by feminists and psychologists to explain victim behavior and find a cure for it. Colette Dowling's *The Cinderella Complex* (1981) deals with "women's hidden fear of independence," as the subtitle suggests. Psychoanalyst Bruno **Bettelheim**, in *The Uses of Enchantment: The Meaning and Importance of Fairy Tales*, 1976), sees sibling rivalry as central to the tale: the stepsisters are exaggerated symbolic representations of a child's real siblings. The real source of Cinderella's misery is not her sisters, however, but her parents. Bettelheim interprets Cinderella as a jealous child who projects her feelings of resentment onto other people in the family. He links her degradation as a maid to feelings of guilt and uncleanliness at the end of the oedipal period.

Modern Interpretations

As one of Western culture's most-popular fairy tales, "Cinderella" has frequently been adapted, rewritten, and parodied. Several authors and illustrators have relocated the story to different historical periods. Shirley Hughes' *Ella's Big Chance* (2003), Lynn and David Roberts *Cinderella: An Art Deco Love Story* (2001), and Roberto **Innocenti**'s **illustration**s to Perrault's *Cendrillon* all set the tale in the 1920s and make use of ample details in their illustrations of the fashion and architecture of that period. Gregory **Maguire**'s *Confessions of an Ugly Stepsister* (1999) sets the tale in seventeenth-century Holland. Apart from fundamentally changing the relationship between the stepsisters to one of friendship rather than jealousy, Maguire includes reflections on painting, **art**, and **storytelling** in his **novel**.

Other authors have chosen to relocate the tale to another culture, alluding to the multiple occurrences of "Cinderella" variants around the world. Examples of this are Shirley Climo's *Egyptian Cinderella* (1989); Tom **Davenport**'s live-action film *Ashpet: An American Cinderella* (1990); Alan Schroeder's *Smoky Mountain Rose: An Appalachian Cinderella* (1997); Robert D. San Souci and Brian Pinkney's Caribbean Cinderella, *Cendrillon* (1998); and Jude Daly's *Fair, Brown & Trembling: An Irish Cinderella Story* (2000).

Retellings that update the tale to a twentieth-century setting show that sibling rivalry and struggles with stepparents are timeless. In the Irish author Siobhán Parkinson's *Sisters ... No Way!* (1996), the tale is told twice, as the reader is presented with diary extracts from both Cinderella and her stepsister. Both girls have problems with their parents' new marriage, especially since it is hurried by the arrival of a new baby. Frances Minters' *Cinder-Elly* (1994) is a humorous rap version of "Cinderella," set in late-twentieth-century New York. Sibling rivalry is once again the central theme: Cinder-Elly feels bad because her older siblings have much more freedom than she. She is simply deemed too young to go to the ball, which here takes the form of a basketball game.

Several picture books and humorous retellings for children turn "Cinderella" into an **animal tale**. The titles of Gregory Maguire's "Cinder Elephant" (2004) and Janet Perlman's *Cinderella Penguin, or the Little Glass Flipper* (1992) speak for themselves. In Jennifer Rae's "Cindersmelly" (1998), all the characters are dogs. Tony Johnston and James Warhola's grotesque picture book *Bigfoot Cinderella* (1998) reverses the theme of the tiny slipper: here Cinderella is the person with the biggest rather than the smallest feet. Such reversals are common in retellings for the young, also with regard to gender. Babette Cole's *Prince Cinders* (1987), a picture book about a male Cinderella in which the glass slipper is replaced with a pair of tight jeans, has become a children's classic. Ellen Jackson's *Cinder Edna* (1994) contrasts two Cinderella figures: one is the traditional character from Perrault's tale, the other, Edna, is an active and happy girl who does not need magic to find her way in the world. With her retelling, Jackson makes a point that Bettelheim also makes in his interpretation: it is unknown whether the prince and Cinderella really love each other at the end of the story. Cinder Edna, by contrast, shares with her new husband a love for jokes and the environment.

Retellings of "Cinderella" for an adult audience are often written from a feminist perspective. Emma **Donoghue**'s "Tale of the Shoe" (1997) describes Cinderella's struggle to live up to the expectations of society, while at the same time she develops feelings for her godmother, here a friend of her mother's. Barbara **Walker** (*Feminist Fairy Tales*, 1996) draws on feminist beliefs that the tale contains traces of former matriarchal cultures: Cinderella's biological mother is a priestess of the Underground Goddess, her stepmother is the evil Christiana. The story thus becomes an allegory of the battle between paganism and Christianity, as well as a commentary on matriarchal and patriarchal societies. *See also* Cinderella Films; Feminism; Feminist Tales.

Further Readings: Bottigheimer, Ruth. "Cinderella." *Grimms' Bad Girls and Bold Boys: The Moral and Social Vision of the Tales.* New Haven, CT: Yale University Press, 1987. 57–70; Dundes, Alan, ed. *Cinderella: A Folklore Casebook.* Madison: University of Wisconsin Press, 1982; MacMath, Russ. "Recasting Cinderella: How Pictures Tell the Tale." *Bookbird* 32.4 (1994): 29–34; Nitschke, August. "Aschenputtel aus der Sicht der historischen Verhaltensforschung." *Und wenn sie nicht gestorben sind . . .: Perspektiven auf das Märchen.* Edited by Helmut Brackert. Frankfurt a.M.: Suhrkamp, 1980. 71–88; Parsons, Linda T. "Ella Evolving: Cinderella Stories and the Construction of Gender- Appropriate Behavior." *Children's Literature in Education* 35 (2004): 135–54; Philip, Neil, ed. *The Cinderella Story: The Origins and Variations of the Story Known as "Cinderella."* London: Penguin, 1989; Tatar, Maria. "Tyranny at Home: 'Catskin' and 'Cinderella.'" *Off With Their Heads! Fairy Tales and the Culture of Childhood.* Princeton, NJ: Princeton University Press, 1992. 120–39; Warner, Marina. "Absent Mothers: Cinderella." *From the Beast to the Blonde: On Fairy Tales and Their Tellers.* London: Chatto and Windus, 1994. 201–17; Zipes, Jack. "Semantic Shifts of Power in Folk and Fairy Tales: Cinderella and the Consequences." *The Brothers Grimm: From Enchanted Forests to the Modern World.* 2nd edition. New York: Palgrave MacMillan, 2002. 187–205.

Vanessa Joosen

Cinderella Films

The tale of **Cinderella** (ATU 510A) is said to be the story that has most often been made into **film**. If one is to take into account not only the literal versions of the tale for the screen, but also the number of films that are more or less overtly influenced by it, then the task of compiling the filmic avatars of that famous fairy-tale heroine becomes virtually impossible. The success of this story in cinema seems to be due to the same reasons that make it so attractive in its literary renditions by Jacob and Wilhelm **Grimm** or Charles **Perrault**, among others. However, on-screen Cinderellas do have a few other assets to help them succeed.

On the one hand, taking into account that film versions of Cinderella are specially targeted at a feminine audience usually trained to accept traditional **gender** roles as the most desirable ones, it is not surprising to find out that many female spectators enjoy the story of Cinderella as a substitutive ritual. In other words, the films offer them the chance to experience, if only vicariously, the magic of courtship, of being beautiful and desirable, and of transcending loneliness and poverty. On the other hand, the fact that the story of Cinderella shows the ascent of the main character from rags to riches, that it glorifies romantic love, and that it ends in **marriage** as the epitome of the happy ending may explain why this tale seems to be so much in keeping with Hollywood's narrative spirit. Because of this congeniality, Hollywood has produced hundreds of Cinderellas, and the industry's pervasive influence has disseminated its numerous **princess**es throughout the world, thus socializing the audience to accept the role models they are offered.

From the beginnings of film history it is possible to find silent **adaptation**s of the Cinderella story in black and white. The French experimental filmmaker Georges **Méliès** produced the first with his *Cendrillon (Cinderella)* in 1899. Other silent versions were to follow: *Cinderella*, directed by the American James Kirkwood, appeared in 1914; *Aschenputtel (Cinderella)*, a silhouette film directed by the German Lotte **Reiniger**, was first shown in 1922; *A Kiss for Cinderella*, by the American film director Herbert Brenon, came out in 1925; and in 1926, another American, Alfred E. Green, offered his own rendition of the Cinderella story in *Ella Cinders*.

From then onward, the talkies offered renewed adaptations of the story, both in the United States and in many other countries. The Japanese film director Kenji Mizoguchi, for example, used the Cinderella tale in films such as *Naniwa hika* (*Naniwa Elegy*, 1936), *Gion no shimai* (*Sisters of the Gion*, 1936), and *Saikaku ichidai onna* (*The Life of Oharu*, 1952). For his part, the Russian Grigory Aleksandrov is responsible for a musical originally entitled *Cinderella*, which was later retitled *Svetly put'* (*The Radiant Path*, 1940) at Stalin's request. Federico Fellini directed *Le notti di Cabiria* (*Nights of Cabiria*) in 1957. In 1964, George Sherman directed a Spanish film titled *La Nueva Cenicienta* (*The New Cinderella*), and in 1973, the Czech director Václav Vorlícek made his film *Tri orisky pro Popelku* (*Three Wishes for Cinderella*).

Nevertheless, it is the American film industry in general and Hollywood in particular that have most often contributed to the omnipresence of Cinderellas on the screen. Many outstanding film directors have made their particular renditions of the fairy tale. Certain directors have chosen to produce versions that are largely dependent on the literary sources, as their titles clearly show. Among these we find Walt **Disney**'s *Cinderella* (1950) and many other adaptations, such as *The Glass Slipper* (directed by Charles Walters, 1955), *Cinderella* (directed by Ralph Nelson, 1957), *Cinderefella* (directed by Frank Tashlin, 1960), and *The Slipper and the Rose* (directed by Bryan Forbes, 1976).

On the other side of the spectrum one can find films that are not as close to the literary source but are nevertheless greatly influenced by some of the tale's most outstanding features, such as the presence of a poor or victimized female character who rises on the social scale by means of love. They are sometimes free versions that depart from the magic and fantastic elements of the fairy tale and on certain occasions even from its romantic and festive mood. In this sense, Alfred Hitchcock's *Rebecca* (1940) can be said to be partially influenced by the Cinderella story, as are many films by Frank Capra (*Lady for a Day*, 1933; *Mr Deeds goes to Town*, 1936; and *A Pocketful of Miracles*, 1961, among others). The same applies to a number of movies by Mitchell Leisen (for example, *Hand Across the Table*, 1935; *Easy Living*, 1937; *Midnight*, 1939; and *Masquerade in Mexico*, 1945), as well as to many others, including Lloyd Bacon's *42nd Street* (1933), Stanley Donen and Gene Kelly's *Singin' in the Rain* (1952), Laurence Olivier's *The Prince and the Showgirl* (1957),

Vincente Minnelli's *The Reluctant Debutante* (1958), and Robert Wise's *The Sound of Music* (1965).

Just as a great number of important directors have turned to the Cinderella story, many well-known actresses and actors have likewise specialized in playing the role of Cinderella and Prince Charming, respectively. In recent decades, for example, Harrison Ford has become a princelike character in films such as *Working Girl* (directed by Mike Nichols, 1988) and the remake of *Sabrina* (directed by Sydney Pollack, 1995). Audrey Hepburn, for her part, became the princess par excellence in most of her films. In *Roman Holiday* (directed by William Wyler, 1953), she played the role of a princess in disguise, a Cinderella-in-reverse; however, in other plays such as *Sabrina* (directed by Billy Wilder, 1954), *Funny Face* (directed by Stanley Donen, 1957), or *My Fair Lady* (directed by George Cukor, 1964) she is a proper Cinderella in that her initial disadvantages are eventually overcome by virtue of her falling in love with and being loved by a "**prince**" who is superior to her in social status, age, experience, culture, and, of course, economic power. Hepburn's glamorous makeover in films such as these have made her the model for the cinematic Cinderella, a role to which she might partly owe her status as a cultural icon in the Western world.

For the past twenty or thirty years, attempts of many feminist critics have failed to reduce the desirability of the Cinderella story both in its literary and in its movie versions on the grounds that it offers a negative role model for women. As a result, this fairy-tale princess continues to appeal to each new generation, a circumstance from which the film industry of the last few decades has profited greatly. The list of recent movies that have revisited the tale of Cinderella in a more or less obvious way is, once again, a never-ending story. Among the most successful and better known titles are Nichols's *Working Girl* and Pollack's *Sabrina*, as well as ***Pretty Woman*** (directed by Garry Marshall, 1990), *Stroke of Midnight* (also called *If the Shoe Fits*, directed by Tom Clegg, 1990), ***Ever After**: A Cinderella Story* (directed by Andy Tennant, 1998), *Maid in Manhattan* (directed by Wayne Wang, 2002), *What a Girl Wants* (directed by Dennie Gordon, 2003), *The Princess Diaries* (directed by Garry Marshall, 2001), *The Princess Diaries 2: Royal Engagement* (directed by Garry Marshall, 2004), *The Prince and Me* (directed by Martha Coolidge, 2004), *A Cinderella Story* (directed by Mark Rosman, 2004), and *Ella Enchanted* (directed by Tommy O'Haver, 2004).

In some of these films, it is possible to perceive an attempt to adapt their message to the ideology and cinematic language of the last decades, but the extent to which efforts of this kind have succeeded is quite dubious in most cases. The clearest instance of this accommodation to audience expectations in the late twentieth century and early twenty-first century has to do with the treatment given to **sex** and **sexuality**. Generally speaking, modern revisions of Cinderella are far from being prudish in this respect. Thus, they usually have a number of scenes in which the main characters kiss each other passionately and make love. Whereas the Cinderellas impersonated by Audrey Hepburn had to wait until they were married to do so, more modern Cinderellas such as Jeniffer López in *Maid in Manhattan* are no longer worried about virginity. For that reason, they sometimes have premarital relationships with their respective princes, and, on other occasions, instead of marrying the prince they simply move in with him.

The professional profiles of modern Cinderellas is another aspect that might be affected by contemporary expectations of what women can offer to society as part of the workforce. However, in most cases, the improvement with respect to classical Cinderellas is rather subtle, if not nonexistent. Hepburn's roles in her Cinderella films make her a flower girl in Covent

Garden (*My Fair Lady*), a shop assistant who first sells books in New York and ends up working as a model in Paris (*Funny Face*), and a student of cookery in Paris (*Sabrina*). For her part, Julia Roberts in *Pretty Woman* plays the role of a prostitute, so this modern Cinderella's professional profile is no breakthrough. But in the 1995 remake of *Sabrina*, Julia Ormond becomes an assistant photographer, so here it seems obvious that the scriptwriter and the film director considered it appropriate not to relegate Sabrina to traditionally feminine activities, such as cooking, but to let her explore other fields as well. Nevertheless, her inexperience is made obvious, as is her need to learn from her male mentor, a professional photographer. In *Working Girl*, Melanie Griffith plays the role of a submissive secretary whose intelligence will help her get promotion at the firm where she works, even though she will be promoted only after her "prince," Harrison Ford, intercedes on her behalf. In *If the Shoe Fits*, Jennifer Grey is a shoe designer who aspires to be recognized as such by a famous fashion designer, Salvitore (Rob Lowe), who will nevertheless be unable to actually see her until she is magically transformed into a glamorous model by her fairy godmother. In *Maid in Manhattan*, Jennifer López plays the role of a maid who is afraid of applying for a better job.

With respect to the modern Cinderella's discursive practices, there is also little deviation from the classic tale, though some changes may be perceived, particularly in *Ever After*. In this film, Drew Barrymore plays the role of a Cinderella who likes to read, even though she does not seem to have read any book except Thomas More's *Utopia*. Because of her fondness for literature, she has developed a mind of her own and is able to give rational justifications for her actions. In some scenes, she even dares to refute her prince's words, but it should be noted that she only answers back when she is given permission to do so. Similarly, in *Maid in Manhattan*, Marisa Ventura (Jennifer López) has her own ideas about politics, social welfare, racial and class issues, among other topics, but she never speaks unless her prince, Congressman Christopher Marshall (Ralph Fiennes), begs her to tell him what she is thinking. Despite this subtle development in some modern Cinderellas' capacity to express their own points of view, it is nevertheless true that they are far more articulate than their predecessors. In *My Fair Lady*, for example, Eliza Doolittle (Audrey Hepburn) shows an inability to utter more than polite expressions or set phrases once Professor Higgins (Rex Harrison) has transformed her into a princess. Likewise, in *Funny Face*, Dick Avery (Fred Astaire), falls in love with the photographer Jo Stockton (Audrey Hepburn), and robs his model not only of her own ideas, but also of her feelings.

The degree of action undertaken by modern Cinderellas is also a reason for concern, since, once again, most contemporary movie revisions depart relatively little from their classical models. The only significant exception to this rule is the role played by Drew Barrymore in *Ever After*.

In most films, Cinderellas wait for their prince to rescue them from their situation of disadvantage. Even Marisa Ventura in *Maid in Manhattan* modestly disappears from her prince's life when he discovers that she has assumed someone else's personality. When the prince finally forgives her, he finds her sitting in the basement of the hotel where she now works. He then takes her up, and, offering no words for this sudden change, starts kissing her, much to her joy. These shots are actually quite similar to the final scene in *Funny Face*. Dick Avery searches for Jo Stockton and finally finds her in tears near a church, where he embraces and kisses her, thus helping her recover the happiness she had lost. In *Ever After*, however, the action undertaken by Danielle de Barbarac (Drew Barrymore) is such, that she is first responsible for rescuing the prince from a group of gypsies who had kidnapped him, and then, at the end of the film, for gaining her own freedom.

Another aspect that can be noted with respect to modern Cinderellas is that their classical discrimination on the basis of their inferior social class has become more complex, at least in the case of *Maid in Manhattan*. In this film, the fact that Marisa Ventura is an immigrant from Puerto Rico, a single mother, and a person of mixed **race**, apart from a working-class woman who has always lived in the Bronx, introduces other reasons that modern Cinderellas may be discriminated against. Thus, racial and ethnic issues, together with immigrant status and single motherhood, complicate Marisa's situation a great deal. However, her prince does not reject her on account of all these circumstances, but because she lied to him by pretending to be a rich guest at the hotel, although this is not exactly the case. First of all, the fact that in one scene Marshall is unable to perceive Marisa's attractiveness in her work uniform shows that economic status still plays an important role in enhancing women's desirability, and that therefore social classes do matter. Secondly, the film narrative shows that racial discrimination is also at play, because even though the movie seems progressive enough to permit an interracial relationship between the Anglo-Saxon Marshall and the Latin American Marisa, it nevertheless adheres to Hollywood's racial code. The white man has the prerogative to first approach and finally accept the ethnic woman, not the other way around. Besides, she must have a controlled sexuality, one that is not too dangerous for the white man. Thus, the character of Marisa, despite being played by the sex symbol Jennifer López, is only slightly sexualized, inasmuch as it seems to harmonize with her role as both a devoted mother and an important politician's consort. *See also* Feminism.

Further Readings: Balló, Jordi, and Xavier Pérez. "La ascensión por el amor: La Cenicienta." *La semilla inmortal: Los argumentos universales en el cine.* Barcelona: Anagrama, 1997. 193–207; Preston, Cathy Lynn. "Disrupting the Boundaries of Genre and Gender: Postmodernism and the Fairy Tale." *Fairy Tales and Feminism: New Approaches.* Edited by Donald Haase. Detroit: Wayne State University Press, 2004. 197–212.

Carolina Fernández-Rodríguez

Cinderfella (1960)

Directed by Frank Tashlin, the American movie *Cinderfella* (1960) is a twist on the traditional **Cinderella** fairy tale. The plot conveys the familiar story but with **gender** reversals that affect most characters. Jerry Lewis plays the role of poor Fella, who, after his father's death, has been left at the mercy of his stepmother and his two stepbrothers. While Fella works as a servant for his greedy steprelatives, they try to restore their dwindling fortune by searching for a treasure Fella's father hid before he died, as well as by planning a ball in honor of Princess Charmein in the hope that she will marry one of the stepbrothers. Eventually, the intervention of Fella's fairy godfather helps the protagonist win the princess's love for himself. According to his fairy godfather, the point of having Fella marry the princess is to rectify the wrongs brought about by the original Cinderella story, which leaves the stepsisters frustrated at not winning the prince's love and at having to marry other men, whom they abuse out of resentment. Fella is therefore called to act for husbands as an avenging agent, since he, a mere **simpleton**, is allowed to marry the princess.

The film received mixed reviews, though most of them agreed that its pace was uneven, that the editing process left some gaps in the plot, and that Lewis's songs did not contribute to the film's quality. Nevertheless, many reviews agreed that it had some amusing scenes, some handsome sets, and a few memorable performances. *See also* Cinderella Films.

Further Readings: *Cinderfella.* Directed by Frank Tashlin. 1960. DVD. Paramount, 2004; Clark, Randall. "Frank Tashlin." *American Screenwriters: Second Series.* Edited by Randall Clark. Volume 44 of *Dictionary of Literary Biography.* Detroit: Gale, 1986. 378–84; Garcia, Roge, and Bernard Eisenschitz, eds. *Frank Tashlin.* London: Éditions du Festival international du film de Locarno in collaboration with the British Film Institute, 1994.

Carolina Fernández-Rodríguez

Clarke, Susanna (1959–)

Susanna Clarke's reputation rests on her long **novel**, *Jonathan Strange & Mr Norrell* (2004). Set in early nineteenth-century England and Europe, it deals in a realistic manner (echoing Jane Austen) with a revival of magic and various encounters with the realm of **faerie**.

The daughter of a Methodist minister, Clarke spent a nomadic childhood in northern England and Scotland; she was educated at St Hilda's, Oxford. Between 1993 and 2003, while an editor at Simon and Schuster's Cambridge office and working on their cookery list, Clarke composed her magnum opus. In 2006, she published a collection of fairy tales, *The Ladies of Grace Adieu.*

The eponymous heroes of *Jonathan Strange & Mr Norrell* are magicians. The setting is the early nineteenth century, when, in the novel's alternative version of English history, the practice of magic has died out and become of merely antiquarian interest. Several hundred years earlier, however, the north of England had been ruled by John Uskglass, the Raven King, a powerful magician who had close dealings with the realm of faeries. Clarke combines this alternative history, dominated by magic, with a conventional treatment of history, including real people and events (for example, the Duke of Wellington, mad King George, Lord Byron, the Peninsular War, and Waterloo). The "reality effect" is heightened by extensive footnotes purporting to derive from scholarly works about magic and **folklore**.

The novel begins with the merely theoretical York Society of Magicians being astounded by Gilbert Norrell's ability, unheard of in modern times, to do practical magic. Norrell has acquired this ability through his large collection of books of magic kept locked away in his library. Inspired by the prophecy of Vinculus, later revealed actually to *be* the one great book of magic that Norrell cannot find (Vinculus has the magic script inscribed on his body), Jonathan Strange becomes the second practical magician of modern times. His magical powers are derived from instinct, rather than from the books, which Norrell continues to hide even after Strange has become his pupil.

Anxious to promote a revival of magic, Norrell gains influence by restoring to life the fiancée of Pole, a politician, through a bargain with a powerful **fairy**, referred to only as "the gentleman with the thistle-down hair." The price is that Mrs. Pole must make nightly visits to faerie. Strange's wife also becomes enchanted and disappears into faerie. Meanwhile, Strange's spells purportedly determine the outcome of the Peninsular War and the Battle of Waterloo. After a breach with Norrell, Strange visits Venice, where he conjures up a magical darkness. Back in England, Strange is aided by Norrell (their differences notwithstanding), Vinculus, and Pole's servant Stephen Black, on whom the fairy has designs. The Raven King is summoned, the fairy defeated, and the enchanted women released. Strange and Norrell are themselves enchanted, disappearing into the darkness.

Further Readings: "Susanna Clarke." *Contemporary Authors Online.* Gale Literary Databases. Thomson Gale, 2006; "The Three Susanna Clarkes." *Locus: The Magazine of the Science Fiction and Fantasy Field* 54.4 (April 2005): 6–7.

William Gray

Classical Antiquity

Ancient Greek and Roman literature teems with stories furnishing information about the presence of traditional narratives of different sorts in antiquity as well as their use and transmission. Folk-narrative scholars from the early nineteenth century to the present day have asked whether the Greeks and Romans had **folktale**s, including **fairy tale**s, and, if so, what they were like.

These questions have received different answers due in part to a lack of clarity regarding genre categories. Genre terms are frequently incommensurate from language to language, and scholars differ in their employment of them, For some investigators, key terms such as "folktale" and "**märchen**" are synonymous and interchangeable, whereas for others they are not. Moreover, the meanings of such terms are fluid, having changed and shifted over the past two centuries.

For the present purpose, folktales are traditional tales of any sort to which no serious question of historicity attaches. Competent members of the community in which the tales are told understand them to be fictions. Folktales differ in this respect from **myth**s and **legend**s, which are traditional belief-narratives whose historicity it is at least thinkable for competent persons to discuss.

Folktale is consequently an umbrella term that covers more than one kind of tale. Instead of asking whether the Greeks and Romans told folktales, it is more useful to ask what kinds of folktales (if any) are attested to in classical literature. Characteristic forms of the folktale in modern **oral tradition** include the following: **animal tale**s, humorous tales, formula tales, **religious tale**s, **novella**s (or realistic tales), tales of the stupid **ogre**, and fairy tales (or magic tales or **wonder tale**s). Some kinds of tale (for example, the humorous narratives known as **tall tale**s) may be thought of as being true subgenres of the folktale in that they are felt to constitute a distinct class of tale, whereas others (for example, religious tales) are merely convenient thematic groupings.

Animal Tales

Animal tales are abundant in classical literature. Consisting of one or two episodes, they are structurally simple. The characters are partially analogized to human beings in that they eat like animals but are gifted with human speech. An instance is the familiar tale of the town and country mice (ATU 112, Country Mouse Visits Town Mouse):

> A country mouse invited an old acquaintance of his, a town mouse, to dine with him in his humble country quarters. The country mouse offered the best fare he had, which was rustic and modest. His visitor could scarcely bear to touch this humble fare and urged his host to leave his hard country life and accompany him to the city. The country mouse was persuaded, and the two mice journeyed to town under cover of darkness. Making themselves comfortable in a mansion well stocked with food, they were dining luxuriously when they were terrified by the sudden slamming of a door and the barking of watchdogs. The country mouse departed for home, declaring that he preferred his humble abode and rustic food. (Horace, *Satires* 2.6)

Most ancient animal tales are recounted as **Aesopic fables**, called simply "Aesopic tales" by the Greeks and Romans. However, animal tales and fables are not identical, for although animals are the principal actors in most fables, other characters such as humans, deities, or plants also appear. Any brief and simple tale whose plot lent itself to illustrating a point of practical wisdom could be recounted as a fable.

Humorous Tales

Humorous narratives often focus upon the actions of a clever person or of a stupid one, or both. At one extreme is the numskull tale (or noodle tale), a distinct and simple class of tale that presents the amusing actions of persons who are foolish to the point of absurdity (see **Simpleton**). Many numskull tales are preserved in a Greek joke book from late antiquity known as *Philogelos*, or *Laughter-Lover*. Below is an example of such a tale:

> Two numskulls wished to hide from invading soldiers. One went down a well, and the other hid in the reeds. When the soldiers lowered a helmet down into the well to draw some water, the numskull in the well thought that a **soldier** was coming down, and begged the soldier to spare him; as a result the man was captured. When the soldiers remarked that if he had remained silent, they would have passed him by, the other numskull said: "Then pass me by, since I'm staying silent." (*Philogelos* 96)

According to Greek tradition, the entire citizenry of certain towns were particularly simple-minded, like the conventional communities of fools in various modern numskull traditions such as the silly inhabitants of the English village of Gotham. One such place was the Greek town of Cumae:

> A funeral for a prominent man was being held in Cumae. Arriving late, a stranger inquired: "Who is the deceased?" A Cumaean turned to him and said, pointing: "The fellow lying there on the bier." (*Philogelos* 154)

The opposite of the numskull is the **trickster** who achieves his or her ends by deceit, as in this tale (ATU 1525J, Thieves Cheated of Their Booty):

> A little boy sat crying beside a well. When a **thief** asked him what the matter was, the boy explained that the rope broke so that his golden pitcher fell into the well. The thief immediately stripped off his clothes and descended into the well, whereupon the boy made off with the man's clothes. (Avianus 25)

The tall tale is a simple narrative that features an outrageous exaggeration of one sort or another. For example (ATU 1889F, Frozen Words [Music] Thaw):

> There is a certain city that gets so cold in winter that words freeze as soon as people utter them; however, the words thaw in the summer, so that the citizens are able to hear what they conversed about during the winter. (Plutarch, *Moralia* 79A)

True Story, a whimsical work by Lucian of Samosata, is a repository of ancient Greek tall tales, recounted, as such tales often are, in the first person with tongue-in-cheek seriousness as if the narrator were recounting his own actual experiences.

Formula Tales

Several kinds of structurally unusual tales, principally **cumulative tale**s and catch tales, are known collectively as formula tales. Both kinds are found in classical authors. The following **anecdote** about the orator Demosthenes illustrates the telling of a catch tale (ATU 2200, Catch Tales) in **context**:

> Demosthenes once had difficulty getting the Athenians to be quiet and listen to him. When he finally got them quieted down, he recounted how one summer a young man hired a donkey to travel from Athens to Megara. At noon, both the young man and the donkey's owner sought relief from the sun's heat in the animal's shadow. Each kept pushing the other out, the owner declaring that the youth had rented only the donkey, not its shadow, and the young man saying that he had hired the donkey and so had all rights to it. Then Demosthenes began to walk away. The Athenians grabbed hold of him, asking him to finish the story. Demosthenes rebuked them, saying that although they were not willing to listen to him speak about serious matters, they were happy to hear him talk about a donkey's shadow. (Pseudo-Plutarch, *Lives of the Ten Orators* 848a)

The speaker's account of the dispute over the donkey's shadow seduces his listeners by its masquerading as a real tale, whereas it only is a device to trick them into appearing foolish.

Religious Tales

A number of tales are about the relationship between the human and the divine. For example (ATU 774K, St. Peter Stung by Bees):

> A ship and its passengers once sank down to the bottom of the sea. Observing this, a man reproached the gods for their injustice, saying that because merely one impious person had embarked upon the ship, many innocent persons had also met their **death**. As he was saying this, a colony of ants began to crawl on him, and after one of the ants bit him, he trampled most of the rest. The god Hermes then appeared, saying: "Can't you allow the gods to judge you humans the way you judge ants?" (Babrius 117)

Hermes plays the role of divine spokesman because, as the principal messenger of the gods, he regularly mediates between them and humans.

Novellas (Realistic Tales)

Several kinds of realistic tales are collectively known to folk-narrative scholars as "novellas" (or "novelle," from Italian, "short stories"). They focus upon romance, wisdom, trickery, and other themes. A humorous tale (ATU 1510, The Matron of Ephesus) that is also a novella combines most of these themes:

> A man died, leaving a beautiful widow who was inconsolable. Mourning at his tomb day and night, she soon became renowned for her remarkable faithfulness to her husband's memory. One day, several criminals were crucified not far from the man's tomb, and a soldier was posted to prevent the bodies of the crucified men from being removed. When he noticed the attractive widow, he felt an immediate and irresistible desire for her, and began to invent little excuses to visit her. She gradually accepted his company, and eventually they were spending their nights together in each other's arms inside the tomb. One morning, the soldier emerged from the tomb to discover that one of the bodies he was charged with guarding was missing. He anxiously explained his crisis to the widow. She told him not to fear. In order that her new lover not suffer punishment, she turned over to him the corpse of her late husband to fasten to the cross. (Phaedrus, *Appendix Perottina* 15)

The following novella has a domestic setting:

> Aesop, a slave of the philosopher Xanthos, was attending his master at a dinner party. Wishing to share some of his food with his wife, Xanthos gave a portion to Aesop, telling him: "Take this to her who is fond of me." Aesop went home, showed the food to his mistress, but then gave it to the family dog. When Xanthos came home, his wife wanted a divorce, angrily calling him a dog lover.

Asked to explain his actions, Aesop said that he had been instructed to give the food to her who is fond of Xanthos, and so gave it to Xanthos's dog. In support of his action, he pointed out that because of a trifling amount of food, Xanthos's wife was ready to leave him, whereas Xanthos could beat his dog and she would still come back to him, wagging her tail. (Anonymous, *Life of Aesop* 44–50)

The incident is based upon an international folktale (ATU 921B, Best Friend, Worst Enemy), which the unknown author must have adapted to his fictionalized biography of Aesop.

Fairy Tales (Magic Tales or Wonder Tales)

Typically, fairy tales are complex tales characterized by the presence of magic and an atmosphere of wonder. Many folk-narrative scholars prefer the analytic term "magic tale" or "wonder tale" to the more popular term "fairy tale" because fairies rarely appear in such tales.

The ancient narrative that most strikingly resembles a modern oral fairy tale is the story of **Cupid and Psyche**, recounted by the Roman author Lucius **Apuleius** in his novel, *Metamorphoses*, also known as *The Golden Ass*. At one point, an old woman consoles a young bride, who has been kidnapped by robbers, with a leisurely, charming tale of wonder and hope:

A **king** and **queen** had three daughters, of whom the youngest, Psyche, was extraordinarily beautiful. An oracle instructed the girl to attire herself for a **marriage** to a dreaded creature, and to proceed to a certain cliff. Once there, however, Psyche was conveyed gently by the West Wind to a wondrous palace, where she was attended by invisible servants. Her mysterious husband arrived that night and each night thereafter, slept with her, and departed before sunrise, warning her that if she should look at his face, she would lose him. Presently, Psyche came back into contact with her sisters, who in their jealousy told her that her husband was a serpent, whom they urged her to kill. So Psyche, oil lamp in hand, approached her sleeping husband that night but discovered that he was the god of love himself, Cupid. He awoke and angrily departed.

The tale goes on to tell of Psyche's long, arduous, and ultimately successful quest to find her husband again and to win over his hostile, witchlike **mother**, Venus. All ends happily with the marriage of the beautiful **princess** and her supernatural husband.

Most scholars see Apuleius's narrative as a literary **adaptation** of an ancient popular tale (ATU 425B, Son of the **Witch**), which the novelist has mythologized. But a staunch minority of scholars believes that Apuleius himself invented the tale, which for them is a **literary fairy tale** (*Kunstmärchen*), indeed the first of its kind.

One group of folktales not well attested in antiquity consists of tales of the stupid ogre. Stories of the stupid ogre are found in ancient sources as legends. This is the phenomenon of "genre variance," in which a narrative is told at one place or time in one genre and at another place or time in a different genre. There are in fact many stories that manifest genre variance, appearing in modern tradition as a folktale but in classical antiquity as a legend. For example, a modern folktale (ATU 1137, The Blinded Ogre) relates how a youth came to the dwelling of a one-eyed, cannibalistic giant, where he was held captive. The resourceful hero, pretending to know a cure for the giant's faulty eyesight, destroyed the giant's single eye by jabbing it with a spit or by pouring boiling liquid on it. After more trickery, the youth eventually escaped, taking with him the giant's treasure. In antiquity, this story is recounted as one of the adventures of the supposedly historical hero Odysseus. It appears first and most famously in Homer's *Odyssey*. The story illustrates a thorny problem in the history of traditional narratives. Does the modern international folktale of The Blinded Ogre derive from an ancient legend, or does the legend of Odysseus and the Cyclops represent a special development of a folktale? The historical relationship of ancient and modern stories that agree in plot but disagree in genre has been much discussed by scholars from Jacob and Wilhelm **Grimm** onwards, but no consensus has been reached. *See also* Greek Tales; Middle Ages; Ovid.

Further Readings: Anderson, Graham. *Fairytale in the Ancient World*. London: Routledge, 2000; Hansen, William. *Ariadne's Thread: A Guide to International Tales Found in Classical Literature*. Ithaca, NY: Cornell University Press, 2002; _____. "Homer and the Folktale." *A New Companion to Homer*. Edited by Ian Morris and Barry Powell. Leiden: Brill, 1997. 442–62; _____. "The Seer and the Computer: On *Philogelos* and Modern Jokes." *Classical Bulletin* 77 (2001): 87–102; Heldmann, Georg. *Märchen und Mythos in der Antike? Versuch einer Standortbestimmung*. Munich: K.G. Saur, 2000; Siegmund, Wolf-dietrich, ed. *Antiker Mythos in unseren Märchen*. Kassel: Erich Röth-Verlag, 1984.

William Hansen

Clemens, Samuel Langhorne. *See* Twain, Mark

Clergy

Religious leaders—priests, rabbis, mullahs, and such—as a rule do not fare well in folktales. Although the faith-promoting **religious tale** and **saint's legend** eulogizing holy men and women exist in all cultures, the orally transmitted lore of the people is replete with charges of hypocrisy and excess leveled against the clergy. An important function of **folklore** is to provide a socially acceptable platform from which taboos can be addressed. Speaking ill of "the Lord's anointed" is suppressed in all religions, but storytellers everywhere and throughout history have circumvented these restrictions.

International folktales abound in **jest**s and **anecdote**s about religious figures (ATU 1725–1849), and their portrayal is seldom positive. A notable exception is the Turkish Muslim cleric **Nasreddin** Hodja, whose self-effacing, pragmatic ways endear him to ordinary people everywhere, while at the same time casting unfavorable light on his dogmatic and self-righteous compatriots.

Taboos against criticizing religious leaders and those governing **sex** and **sexuality** come together in a large number of folktales, many of which were recorded in medieval and Renaissance tale collections. Reflecting secular values, they often recount in bawdy detail sexual exploits of the clergy. Giovanni **Boccaccio**'s *Decameron* (1349–50), Geoffrey **Chaucer**'s *Canterbury Tales* (c. 1387), Gian Francesco Poggio Bracciolini's *Liber facetiarum* (usually titled *Facetiae*, 1470), and Antoine de la Sale's *Cent nouvelles nouvelles* (translated as *One Hundred Merrie and Delightsome Stories*, c. 1462), to name a few prominent examples, present a shameless cast of priests, monks, and nuns artfully engaged in "good works" that defy any biblical definition.

A good example is the **tale type** Putting the Devil into Hell (ATU 1425), exemplified in Boccaccio's *Decameron* (3.10), and well represented among international folktales. In Boccaccio's version, a fourteen-year-old woman requests religious instruction from a "holy man." He complies with a lesson in theological anatomy, identifying his own "resurrection of the flesh" as the devil, and calling her corresponding part hell. Then with her permission he puts the devil into hell. A variation on this ribald classic is Aleksandr **Afanas'ev**'s "Putting the Pope in Rome."

Tales of type ATU 1424, Friar Adds Missing Nose, offer additional examples of naïve **women** exploited by the clergy. In this tale, a churchman warns a pregnant woman whose husband is away that her lack of sexual relations will result in a malformed child. He then volunteers to avert the tragedy by taking her husband's place, and the concerned woman gratefully accepts his offer. Literary versions of this tale appear in the collections of Poggio and others, and folkloric examples are found throughout Europe and beyond.

Gluttony is often paired with lust in tales of clerical misconduct. "Der alte Hildebrand" ("Old Hildebrand," ATU 1360C) as recorded by Jacob and Wilhelm **Grimm** in their *Kinder- und Hausmärchen* (*Children's and Household Tales*, 2nd ed, 1819), is an example. In this tale, a priest and a **peasant**'s wife conspire to trick her husband into leaving home on a pilgrimage to give the illicit couple time alone. Thinking themselves safe, the priest and the woman proceed to feast on the household's food. The excesses being practiced in the kitchen undoubtedly would soon lead to the bedroom, but the peasant unexpectedly returns home and drives the wayward priest away with blows.

Religious dogmatism is criticized in numerous folktales. Foremost among these are the tales of type ATU 756, The Three Green Twigs, popular since the **Middle Ages**. "Der Tannhäuser," as recorded in the Grimms' *Deutsche Sagen* (*German Legends*, 1816–18) is typical. Tannhäuser, following a sojourn with lovely women in the Mountain of Venus, confesses his sins to Pope Urban IV, asking for forgiveness. The pope responds by holding out a dried-up stick and stating that Tannhäuser would no sooner be forgiven than this stick would grow fresh leaves. Disheartened, Tannhäuser returns to the Mountain of Venus. Three days later, the pope's stick begins sprouting green leaves. Angelo S. Rappoport tells essentially the same story ("The Flourishing Staff," *The Folklore of the Jews*, 1937) about a rabbi refusing to accept the penance of a Jew who had left the faith.

In a related story popular in the Nordic countries, belonging to the tale type called Sin and Grace (ATU 755), a woman magically prevents the **birth** of children. Learning of her act, her husband (who is a pastor) casts her out, declaring that she shall no sooner be forgiven than flowers shall sprout from a slate roof. Years later, the woman returns as a beggar and dies during the night. The next morning, flowers miraculously are blossoming from the roof. The message in tales of type 755 and 756 is obvious: God is often more forgiving than are his self-proclaimed messengers.

An important responsibility of the clergy in many faiths is the preservation and practice of sacred rituals. This ostensibly requires substantial learning, but many folktales call into question the clerics' actual knowledge. Representative of this group are tales of type ATU 1848A, The Clergyman's Calendar. First recorded in Georg Wickram's *Das Rollwagenbüchlein* (*The Little Carriage Book*, 1555), this tale is known internationally. For example, J. E. Hanauer's *Folk-Lore of the Holy Land* (1907) includes a version titled "Fast Days and Festival Days." Here an orthodox priest keeps a tally of holy days by counting the number of peas in his pocket. His wife refills the pocket, inadvertently throwing off his count. Reaching his hand into his pocket, the priest exclaims aloud, "According to the peas there will be no feasts," thus revealing his ignorance to the congregation.

The common denominator of most tales critical of the clergy is condemnation of hypocrisy. Religious leaders of all faiths serve as moral arbiters, and those who fail to follow their own teachings find little sympathy. An example from Pakistan is "The Miserly Moslem Priest [Imam] and His Wife" from *Oral Tradition from the Indus* (1908) by J. F. A. McNair and Thomas Lambert Barlow. An imam preaches generosity in the mosque but forces his wife to lead a life of parsimony. Through trickery she exposes his hypocrisy and forces him to change his miserly ways. Thus, a woman rather than an official clergyman has the final moral word.

Further Readings: Röhrich, Lutz. "The Social Milieu." *Folktales and Reality*. Translated by Peter Tokofsky. Bloomington: Indiana University Press, 1991. 184–98; Thompson, Stith. "Parsons." *The Folktale.* 1946. Berkeley: University of California Press, 1977. 212–14.

D. L. Ashliman

Clothing

Clothing is significant in folktales and fairy tales in a variety of ways—as enchanted objects that confer magical power to the wearer; as disguise, to transform the wearer's appearance and fate; or as markers of identity for those characters closely identified with distinctive items of clothing or styles of dress.

Many magical items of apparel have figured in international tale traditions—including trousers, gloves, snowshoes, veils, and belts (Motifs D1050 through D1069). Such items are often coveted for their powers: for example, the magical cap or hood from German folk tradition—the *Tarnkappe* prized by the warriors in the **epic** *Nibelungenlied*—renders its wearer invisible. Both a "cloak of darkness" and "**shoe**s of swiftness" are featured in the Scottish travelers' tale "The King of England," collected by Hamish Henderson in 1954. In the **Grimm**s' "Der König vom goldenen Berge" ("The King of the Golden Mountain," 1815), magical boots and a cloak of invisibility form a part of the title character's inheritance. The cloak of invisibility makes another appearance in the Grimms' collection, in "Die zertanzten Schuhe" ("The Worn-Out Dancing Shoes," 1815). In this tale, the magical item is a gift to a far humbler character, a retired **soldier**, from a mysterious old woman later revealed to be a **witch**. The cloak is essential to the old soldier's revelation of the **princess**es' secret nightly escapades, and thus to his own social and economic rise when rewarded by the **king**.

Clothing, enchanted or wondrously luxurious, is sometimes a reward in itself. For example, in Italian versions of ATU 480, **The Kind and the Unkind Girls**, fine clothing or a body covered in gold is the prize given by an appreciative community of **cat**s to the generous sister who cares for them. But the enchantment attached to such magical attire is not always beneficial. Indeed, there are many cases in which clothing punishes, curses, or even kills its wearer. Examples include the six enchanted white silk shirts that transform stepsons into swans in the Grimms' "Die sechs Schwäne" ("The Six Swans," 1812). The stepmother in the Grimms' "Sneewittchen" ("**Snow White**," 1812) uses implements of female adornment, corset laces and hair combs, in her attempts to kill the princess—her own final **punishment** is to wear hot iron slippers until she drops dead. In Hans Christian **Andersen**'s literary tale "De røde sko" ("The Red Shoes," 1845), shoes likewise are more than simple adornments: the desired shoes prove to be fatal, serving as a commentary on female vanity and materialism.

Shoes and other items of clothing come to stand metonymically for their owners in many tales, perhaps most memorably in versions of ATU 510A, **Cinderella**, including Charles **Perrault**'s widely-known "Cendrillon ou la petite pantoufle de verre" ("Cinderella, or the Little Glass Slipper," 1697) and the Grimms' "Aschenputtel" (1812), but also "Fair, Brown, and Trembling" from Jeremiah Curtain's collection of Irish tales and more recently collected **variant**s like the Sudanese "Fatma the Beautiful" (Ahmed Al-Shahi, 1978), the Chilean "Maria Cinderella" (Yolando Pino-Saavedra, 1967), or the Japenese "Benizara and

Kakezara" (**Seki** Keigo, 1963). In a self-conscious parody of such metonymic substitution, Marie-Catherine d'**Aulnoy**'s **prince** in "Finette Cendron" (1697) falls passionately, fetishistically, in love with the shoe itself—never having seen its owner.

In both the narrated worlds of tales and in everyday social interactions, clothing is significant as an outward, visible signifier of identity. This is expressed in a fundamental way in the case of fairy-tale characters known by or named for a distinctive item of apparel or style of dress—such as Perrault's "Le petit chaperon rouge" ("**Little Red Riding Hood**," 1697) or the Norwegian "Lurvehette" ("Tatterhood," collected by Peter Christian **Asbjørnsen** and Jørgen **Moe**, 1841). Tales that feature sartorial description or that foreground specific items of apparel often use clothing as symbols of the wearer's **gender**, **age**, status, class, or sexual availability. As is the case in variants of Cinderella, items of clothing closely associated with particular characters can be key to rejecting imposters or to revealing true identities. For instance, in the Grimms' "Die zwölf Brüder" ("The Twelve **Brothers**," 1812), it is the princess's discovery of twelve white shirts that leads her to find and later to identify her exiled siblings.

Where clothing stands as metonymic identifier, changes in clothing may also play a significant role in the unfolding of plot—as characters disguise their bodies to conceal their own identities or adopt the dress/identities of others. Clothing can disguise a baker's youngest son as a nobleman, as in Giovan Francesco **Straparola**'s "Constantino Fortunato" (1553); offer a king access to the world of commoners, as in the Hungarian "King Mátyás and the Hussars" (collected by Bálint Bodnár, 1957); transform a princess into a nobleman, as in Henriette-Julie de Castelnau, Comtesse de **Murat**'s "Le sauvage" ("The Savage," 1699); turn beautiful daughters into beastly, liminal, socially marginalized figures—and render them safe from **incest**uous **father**s, as in worldwide variants of ATU 510B, Peau d'Asne.

Finally, the vagaries of fashion, vanity, social aspirations, and anxieties are central concerns of ATU 1620, The Emperor's New Clothes. In the well-known version by Hans Christian Andersen and in earlier accounts, such as those from fifteenth-century Turkish and Spanish **jest** books, a ruler's vanity and credulity are exposed, as is his dishonesty in claiming to see and admire garments that do not exist. Variants of this **tale type**—and, to a certain extent, all of the tales that employ clothing as important symbols—demonstrate a tacit understanding of clothing as a means by which social identities and social status are conveyed and negotiated, both for the viewer and the viewed. *See also* Cross-Dressing; Magic Object; Transformation.

Further Readings: Muhawi, Ibrahim. "Gender and Disguise in the Arabic *Cinderella*: A Study in the Cultural Dynamics of Representation." *Fabula* 42 (2001): 263–83; Scott, Carole. "Magical Dress: Clothing and Transformation in Folk Tales." *Children's Literature Association Quarterly* 21 (1996–97): 151–57; Walsh, Elizabeth. "The King in Disguise." *Folklore* 86 (1975): 3–24.

Jennifer Schacker

Cocchiara, Giuseppe (1904–1965)

Italian folklorist Giuseppe Cocchiara was born in Messina and spent most of his life in his native Sicily, where he served as director of the Pitrè Ethnographic Museum and was the professor of the history of popular traditions at the University of Palermo.

Cocchiara embraced a dynamic historicist vision in which the development of **folklore** in Europe was seen to have its origins far earlier than the period of nineteenth-century

nationalism, with its search for cultural identities and consequent interest in native popular traditions. Instead, Cocchiara posited its beginnings in the early modern period, when, as hegemonic Europe began to observe the populations of the New World, it also began to cultivate an interest in its own "others"—the "**folk**"—and thus to reconsider the history of its "innermost soul."

Unlike his mentor Giuseppe **Pitrè**, Cocchiara did little significant **collecting**. His prolific scholarly output included both wide-ranging studies on the origins and development of ethnography as well as investigations of specific folkloric topics. These include *Genesi di leggende* (*The Genesis of Legends*, 1941), *Storia degli dtudi delle tradizioni popolari in Italia* (*The History of the Study of Popular Traditions in Italy*, 1947), *Il mito del buon selvaggio* (*The Myth of the Noble Savage*, 1948), *Storia del folklore in Europa* (*The History of Folklore in Europe*, 1952), *Il paese di Cuccagna* (*The Land of Cockaigne*, 1956), *Il mondo alla rovescia* (*The World Upside Down*, 1963), and *Le origini della poesia popolare* (*The Origins of Popular Poetry*, 1966). ***See also*** Italian Tales.

Further Reading: Simeone, William. "Italian Folklore Scholars." *Journal of American Folklore* 74 (1961): 344–53.

Nancy Canepa

Collecting, Collectors

Collectors engage in the collecting of folkloric texts, such as oral narratives and poetic texts, to communicate them through other media. The process begins with the collecting of texts from **informant**s, typically in the context of **fieldwork**, and ultimately involves the transformation of the oral **performance**s into written or audio-visual texts when the collector, now acting as an editor, prepares the texts for publication or storage in an **archives**. The work of collecting forms the core of theoretical folkloristics: the history of collecting is the record of the methods used to compile folktales since the pioneering work of Jacob and Wilhelm **Grimm**; and the analytical study of collectors offers insights into the specific processes of collection. Over the last two centuries, the processes of collection and the ideas of collectors have been influenced by technological developments (such as the ability to make audio-visual recordings) and by ideological movements (such as **nationalism**). Moreover, the collection of folktales and the ideas of their collectors have influenced sociocultural histories of nations in major ways. In the history of the discipline of folkloristics, the methods of collectors have been analyzed and the collectors evaluated accordingly. For example, the pioneer collectors Jacob and Wilhelm **Grimm** have been criticized for the method they used and for the way their own contemporary consciousness and values influenced the versions of the tales that they published.

The colonial British collectors of Asian and African folklore have been critically analyzed for their representation of the **folk** and **folklore** of those continents. Some folklore collectors have been given the status of national heroes, such as Elias Lönnrot in Finland, especially for the work he did to preserve the *Kalevala*, the Finnish national **epic**. Important questions regarding the role of the collector arise from the social differences between the collectors and the people from whom they collect. In most cases, the relationship is of unequal social power, in which the collector's perception of the folk becomes dominant in the written or edited version. ***See also*** Authenticity; Colonialism; Editing, Editors.

Further Readings: Naithani, Sadhana. "Prefaced Space: Tales of the Colonial British Collectors of Indian Folklore." *Imagined States: Nationalism, Longing, and Utopia in Oral Cultures.* Edited by Luisa del Giudice and Gerald Porter. Logan: Utah State University Press, 2001. 64–79; Neumann, Siegfried. "The Brothers Grimm as Collectors and Editors of German Folktales." *The Reception of Grimms' Fairy Tales: Responses, Reactions, Revisions.* Edited by Donald Haase. Detroit: Wayne State University Press, 1993. 24–40.

Sadhana Naithani

Collodi, Carlo (1826–1890)

The Italian writer, journalist, and patriot Carlo Collodi authored the children's novel *Le avventure di Pinocchio* (*The Adventures of Pinocchio*, 1881–83), one of the most widely read and beloved books in the world.

Collodi was born Carlo Lorenzini in Florence to a family of modest means; his parents, who hailed from a small town in Tuscany that provided Lorenzini with his pseudonym, served a noble Florentine family. Collodi was educated in a seminary, but as a young man left religious life to work at an important bookstore in Florence, where he immersed himself in the cultural humus of the city. Soon after, he became active in the Risorgimento, the movement for Italian unification, fighting in the First War for Independence in 1848, and then later in the Second War of 1859. After 1848, Collodi took a job as a civil servant and embarked on his career as journalist and writer, founding newspapers such as *Il Lampione*, dedicated to political satire, and producing novels and comedies.

Collodi's first official encounter with fairy tales came in 1875, when the Florentine publisher Paggi commissioned him to translate a small collection of early French tales by Charles **Perrault** and others, issued as *I racconti delle fate* (*Fairy Tales*). In 1877, Collodi reworked a character from a children's book written several decades earlier, *Giannettino*, whose exuberant and mischievous hero in some way previews Pinocchio, and in 1878, continued his adventures in *Minuzzolo*. From 1880 to 1890, these characters appeared in nine more books for use in elementary schools. Collodi returned to experimentation with fairy-tale and fantastic material after *Pinocchio* as well, in 1887, with *Pipì o lo scimmiottino color di rosa* (*Pipì, or the Pink Monkey*).

In 1881, the children's weekly *Il Giornale per i bambini* asked Collodi for a story to be published in installments. Featuring a wily wooden puppet and originally called *La storia di un burattino* (*The Story of a Puppet*), it ran from July to October 1881, and ended after what is now chapter fifteen of the complete work. Collodi was persuaded to continue his tale, with the title *Le avventure di Pinocchio*, from February 1882 to January 1883; in 1883, *Pinocchio* was published in a single volume of thirty-six chapters, with pen-and-ink illustrations by Enrico Mazzanti. Four more editions followed before Collodi's death.

The late nineteenth century was a pivotal moment in the history of **children's literature** and of Italy. Drawing on the emergence of the study of folk traditions earlier in the century and the editions and collections of folktales and fairy tales that resulted, much children's writing of the time, such as *Pinocchio*, incorporated fairy-tale themes and **motif**s in highly innovative ways. Moreover, *Pinocchio* arrived shortly after Italian Unification (1860), and in light of Collodi's earlier experiences as a patriot and experiments with pedagogical literature, *Pinocchio* can be read as a somewhat ironic Bildungsroman (novel of development) for the new Italian subject—what he must undergo, the lessons he must learn, and, ultimately, the sacrifices he must make to become a proper member of society.

Collodi's original chapters begin with Pinocchio's "**birth**" from a piece of wood to the wood-carver Geppetto and are structured as a **cautionary tale**. The puppet immediately engages in every sort of mischief, causing his father to be sent to prison, killing the Talking Cricket, cutting school and selling his books to go to a puppet theater, and finally falling prey to two con men in the form of a fox and **cat**. Pinocchio pays for these wrongdoings by hanging at the end of chapter fifteen.

In chapter sixteen Pinocchio is revived, and his cycles of **transgression** and redemption resume. The Blue **Fairy**, a fairy-godmother figure who also takes on the role of sister and mother, assumes an ever-larger part in Pinocchio's reform, in which he is put to various tests as he traverses landscapes both fantastic and real. When Pinocchio finally realizes the advantages of changing his ways and in chapter thirty-six becomes a boy, his **transformation** has less of the flavor of a **utopia**n "happily-ever-after" tale than that of a coming-of-age story in a harsh and all-too-realistic world.

The interplay between the everyday and the marvelous, fairy-tale expectations and the contradiction of these is, in fact, laid out from the very first lines of *Pinocchio*: "Once upon a time there was ... ! 'A king!' my little readers will immediately say. No, children, you're wrong. Once upon a time there was a piece of wood." This dialectic persists as Pinocchio encounters impoverished Tuscan peasants, thinly veiled representatives of contemporary institutions, **Aesop**ian beasts, **magic helper**s, and *commedia dell'arte* characters, all in a story that shares a basic structure not only with fairy stories but also with the nineteenth-century **novel**. Physical hardships such as hunger, cold, and the threat of **death** punctuate Pinocchio's adventures in a world where indifference and injustice reign; even his adoptive family of Geppetto and the Blue Fairy cannot always guarantee him a safe haven.

Collodi's vision is ambivalent. Pinocchio's struggles between transgression and conformity, anarchic vitality and respect of the social compact, reflect the instinctive anxiety that all of us feel about maturing in an imperfect world and about, at the end, determining who the puppets really are. As the great critic Benedetto Croce commented, "The wood from which Pinocchio is carved is humanity itself."

Pinocchio has enjoyed phenomenal success. It has been translated into more than 100 languages, seen many theatrical and cinematic incarnations (such as Walt **Disney**'s animated film of 1940 and Roberto Benigni's live-action version of 2002), and been rewritten, extended, and otherwise reworked in countless ways. There is a veritable cottage industry of Pinocchio gadgets and toys, and even a sculpture theme park dedicated to him in the town of Collodi (see **Tourism**). Over the past several decades, studies and conferences on Pinocchio have proliferated, as have critical interpretations ranging from the theological to the psychoanalytic to the politico-historical, further proof of the irresistible appeal that Pinocchio continues to wield for young and old alike. *See also* Italian Tales.

Further Readings: Asor Rosa, Alberto. "Le avventure di Pinocchio: Storia di un burattino." *Letteratura italiana: Le opere III; Dall'Ottocento al Novecento*. Edited by Alberto Asor Rosa. Turin: Einaudi, 1995. 879–950; Perella, Nicolas J., trans. Introduction. *The Adventures of Pinocchio: Story of a Puppet*. By Carlo Collodi. Berkeley: University of California Press, 1986. 1–69; Wunderlich, Richard, and Thomas J. Morrissey. *Pinocchio Goes Postmodern: Perils of a Puppet in the United States*. New York: Routledge, 2002.

Nancy Canepa

Coloma, Luis (1851–1915)

A bon vivant who became a Jesuit after recovering from a near-fatal pistol wound, Luis Coloma wrote a series of *Lecturas recreativas* (*Recreational Readings*, 1884–87), one of which is subtitled *Cuentos para niños* (*Stories for Children*). Coloma was a friend of Cecilia **Böhl de Faber** and shared her interest in fairy tales and stories of wonder with a didactic twist, and this is reflected in the tales he wrote for children. "Pájaro verde" ("Green Bird") relates the **Cinderella**-like trials of Lelita, a comely maiden who suffers at the hands of her harsh stepmother and mean stepsisters until she meets a prince who transforms into a green bird. When the prince as a green bird is injured and disappears, Lelita roams the world in search of him. "Ratón Pérez" ("Pérez the Mouse") is a contemporary tale with social implications that was written for King Alfonso XIII of Spain when he was a child. The story abounds in humor and irony as it reveals the ravages of children's poverty to a future king. "Las tres perlas" ("The Three Pearls") is subtitled "Leyenda imitada del alemán" ("A Legend in Imitation of German Tales") and tells of the transcendence of a girl's faith. *See also* Didactic Tale; Spanish Tales.

Further Readings: Fedorchek, Robert M., trans. *Stories of Enchantment from Nineteenth-Century Spain.* Lewisburg: Bucknell University Press, 2002; Flynn, Gerard. *Luis Coloma.* Boston: Twayne, 1987.

Robert M. Fedorchek

Colonialism

While there have been many "colonial" systems in the history of humankind, the term refers here to the nineteenth-century phenomenon of European colonial control over other continents. Colonialism's relationship to the folktale involves three important components: the collection of folktales worldwide; the growth of the discipline of folkloristics; and the **performance** of folktales in the colonies. In a discourse parallel to that of Orientalism, colonial folktale **collectors** claimed that they were presenting to European readers the narratives of the common and "real" people of the empire—the rural "**folk**" of the colonies. Indeed, this claim was the tales' unique selling point and was especially relevant for India, which Orientalists depicted using ancient and classical images. The threefold relationship between colonialism and folktales is illustrated here by considering specifically the role of folktales in the British Empire.

Folktale Collection in the Colonies

The British Empire encompassed countries and cultures of the Asian, African, South American, and Australian continents. Folktale collections were compiled by British officers, missionaries, and women in almost all of the colonies of the empire, but most collections came from India and Africa. These collections of folktales published in the English language were translations of the tales that the British collectors were believed to have heard directly from the people who narrated them. Different collectors were **collecting** tales from different language zones and transforming them into English-language texts. Some collectors claimed to have remained close to the original narratives, while others took more liberties with the stories.

Contemporary research in colonial folkloristics has shown that these collections were guided by a variety of motives, adopted different methods, and were published for different kinds of readers. However, it is apparent from the large number of publications that there was interest in the subject among common readers as well as scholars in England and European countries.

Although the collectors were guided by different motives, the most common was the desire to understand the mentality of the people under their rule. Entertaining the readers back home was another popular reason. The method of collection was based on the use of the collectors' political and administrative power over the people. Narrators were very often summoned to the residence of the collector, and the precise job of recording was performed by another "native." The narrative was presumably written in the original language and translated at a later stage. Therefore, folktales of various colonized peoples started appearing in print in English even before they appeared in their native language. Another important aspect of the colonial method is the involvement of so-called native assistants. Although no generalizations can be drawn regarding the roles of these assistants, there is evidence that in certain cases, the tasks performed by these individuals far surpassed those of an assistant. This was the case with Pandit Ram Gharib Chaube in India, whose work with William Crooke was examined by Sadhana Naithani in her book *In Quest of Indian Folktales*. However, there were many British collectors, and some of them—such as William Crooke and Richard C. Temple in India and R. E. Dennet, Suthreland Rattray, Edwin Smith, and Andrew Dale in Africa—made significant contributions to the modern study of Indian and African folktales.

It is important to understand the role that the collecting of folktales played in the rise of the British Empire. The nineteenth-century British folklore collectors were guided by anthropological theories and believed that folktales revealed the social customs, attitudes, and mentality of people. As such, the text could be simply a source of pleasure or of making ostensibly definitive conclusions about the narrators. We thus find that colonial folktale collectors often gave vent to their racist and colonialist biases in the context of folktale gathering. Stories of cunning and deceit made them conclude that the people of India and Africa were inherently cunning. Stories of mystical powers made the collectors conclude that people were superstitious. The collecting of folktales also brought colonial rulers into contact with natives. Sometimes, this situation transcended the regular plane of colonial relations and enabled new levels of communication. The writings of colonial collectors exhibit appreciation for their narrators and their skills. Edwin Smith and Andrew Dale, collectors of folklore in Northern Rhodesia, were mesmerized by versatile African narrators. Interestingly, many collectors from different colonies said that the best narrators in their cultural zones were **women**, but they were not accessible by foreigner collectors. Some of the collectors produced more than one anthology and from more than one locale. Their collections became the basis of popular notions about "other" people among the British public. To them, Africa seemed to be a wild place, while India appeared to be lost in a past glory.

Colonialism and the Growth of Folkloristics

Until the middle of the nineteenth century, the documentation and study of folklore was primarily based on the European continent. It has become increasingly international since then. In other words, the concept of "folklore," the means of its collection, and the methods of its interpretation are internationally known, applicable, and comprehensible. Of course, the ideas of European Romanticism, which had spurred interest in oral culture and was the foundation of nineteenth-century folktale collections, also played an important role in motivating the colonizers to gather folklore. Whatever the case—whether they were guided by colonial reasons, such as the need to control people by better understanding their culture, or by the Romantic fascination with folktales—the colonizers' work led to the growth of folkloristics. Folktales are often very old, but the concept and study of folklore is a result of modernity. Colonialism led to the propagation of the term "folklore" across the world and to the movement of folktales across cultural and linguistic borders at an unprecedented speed.

Colonialism also paved the way for the growth of independent folklore collection movements. In the late nineteenth and early twentieth centuries, erstwhile British colonies such as Ireland and India were witnessing the rise of strong nationalist independence movements. The term that had entered the colonies with the British was now employed by these freedom fighters to assert their cultural identities. This marked the establishment of folklore studies in nations in Asia and Africa. In their postcolonial histories, folklore has been an issue in **politics**, education, and social welfare. While some of the former colonies, such as Ireland, have had strong developments in the study of folklore, others have yet to establish it as an academic field in a major way. India, for example, remains an important locale for folklore scholars; however, the institutions that study India's folklore are not commensurate with the wealth of folktales that the country possesses. This feature is not unconnected to colonial folkloristics. Colonial collectors, unlike their nineteenth-century counterparts in Europe, did not bother to develop the infrastructure for the study of folklore in the colony concerned. They collected materials in the colony and published them in England. Colonial folkloristics was colonial not because it was based in the context of colonialism, but because the collectors never cared for the field of their study. Africa and Asia were grounds for folktale collection but were not developed as centers of folklore research. Most former colonies still suffer from this deficit in the history of their folkloristics. The case of Ireland differs significantly, as Ireland had long been a partner in the expansion of the British Empire. Even today, colonial folklore collections continue to inform those interested about Indian or African folklore worldwide.

Colonialism spread a discipline that was based in Europe. Its terms, categories, methods, and theories of interpretation also became popular concepts in the study of other cultures. For example, "orality" might have been a relevant category to distinguish the expressions of "classical" and "folk" cultures, but in other locations, orality cut across these boundaries and was the dominant form of all cultural discourse.

Colonial folkloristics also helped the agenda of colonial rulers. On the one hand, folkloric scholarship gave the impression that colonial rulers cared about the culture of their subjects. On the other hand, it gave them the right to define the cultures of those colonized. Interestingly, the interpretations of colonial folklore collectors were close to the popular anthropological theories of the time. The major British folklore theorists were the anthropologists Andrew **Lang**, James Frazer, and E. Sidney Hartland. The folklore collectors themselves felt the urgency to gather folktales and theorize later. They felt that the concerned colony was changing quickly under colonial rule and, therefore, soon there would be no (native) folktales available to collect. Not surprisingly, then, some major perceptions about Indian folktales came from German scholars. The theoretical conclusions of Theodor **Benfy** regarding the age of Indian folktales generated much debate in England. Benfy suggested that India was the original homeland of European folk narratives, whereas many colonial collectors vehemently contested this idea.

Colonial folkloristics was a very interdisciplinary and intercultural phenomenon. It traversed the disciplines of history and anthropology as it tried to explain the history and society of the colonized subjects. The library collections of the Folklore Society of London are evidence of the amount of materials published in the form of books and articles. Although credit for the collections was often claimed by British collectors alone, these were in reality works produced by many people on both sides of the colonial divide.

Folktale Performance in the Colonies

Another dimension of the relationship between colonialism and folktales is at the level of performance. Performance requires performers, audiences, and sponsors. Smith and Dale tell of performers in northern Rhodesia who could mimic so many animals that a jungle once came alive in their narration of stories. Richard Carnac Temple relates the wandering narrators in the northern Indian state of Punjab who sang long versified **legend**s about true lovers. Throughout Africa and India, folktale performance was practiced in ritual and secular arenas of community life. Either way, in the colonies, the place of performers in society was definite, and the sponsorship was organized accordingly—whether in cash or in kind, whether paid by the local ruler or the audience. The channels of sponsorship were seriously disrupted by changes in these colonized societies. Native rulers were displaced, traditional religious authorities were undermined, and social structures were changed or transformed. This contributed negatively to local performance practices, and many vanished. Some colonial rulers banned performances connected with rituals they deemed unacceptable, and the practice came to an end.

Many performance practices survived, but colonialism often created stressful situations, which led to the transformation of all performance practices. The displacement that began in colonial times continues. For example, the *mirasis* (bards), from whom Richard C. Temple collected versified legends, were also bearers of local genealogies and land records. The British Empire used its information to write real-estate records, but this removed from the *mirasis* an important social role. Today they are paupers.

In summary, one can say that the colonial British folktale collectors added substantially to the global stock of printed folklore. Although folktales have traveled across cultures for centuries, colonial collectors worked at this consciously and put the folktales they gathered into a new **context**. A study of the **translation** methods used for these collections shows that frequently more than one language came into play. The text was often narrated in a dialect that the British collector could not understand. The native assistant could translate it into another link language between himself and the British collector, from which the English text then emerged. This text was printable and traveled around the world. It no longer mattered whether a given story was meant to be narrated on a particular occasion, by particular persons, and in a particular style. It was simply a text that symbolized an "other."

Some interesting aspects of the relation between colonialism and folktales are less-commonly known. For example, colonialism led to the creation of new folktales. It is easy to imagine that those colonized would have told stories about their new rulers. Surprisingly, these stories have not yet been systematically documented. In recently discovered tales from India, for example, the British are depicted as ghosts and harmful spirits (Naithani).

There is a positive aspect of colonial folktale collections: for many cultures and languages, they are often the first modern records of their traditional stories. More often than not, no other equally comprehensive records exist for the nineteenth century. The negative side is that these folktale collections are often colored by the biases of their collectors. When dealing with such collections, the researcher must closely analyze the interpretations of the collectors. As postcolonial theory and scholarship continue to develop, more serious analyses of colonial collectors and their collections should be published. *See also* African Tales; Anthropological Approaches; Editing, Editors; Frobenius, Leo; Nationalism; Négritude, Créolité, and Folktale; South Asian Tales.

Further Readings: Naithani, Sadhana. *In Quest of Indian Folktales: Pandit Ram Gharib Chaube and William Crooke.* Bloomington: Indiana University Press, 2006; Smith, Edwin, and Andrew Dale. *The Ila-Speaking Peoples of Northern Rhodesia.* 2 volumes. London: Macmillan, 1920; Temple, Richard Carnac. *The Legends of the Punjab.* 3 volumes. 1883–85. Patiala: Punjabi University Press, 1962.

Sadhana Naithani

Colors

The use of colors in **wonder tales** is both scant and stable, suggesting more hues than meets the eye. Max **Lüthi** once remarked that since most wonder-tale items are colorless, the colored few stand out sharply. Moreover, he noted that the standouts display clear and ultra-pure colors—such as white, black, and red—along with the hues of precious metals: gold, silver, and copper. Add the occasional shimmer of green or blue, and the chromatic list is about complete. Lüthi's point suggests, then, purposefulness in creating sharp contrasts. Why? The short answer is, because clear-cut colors are convenient pegs for genre-specific values.

Regarding the colors of precious metals, Vladimir **Propp** pointed out in *Istoricheskie korni volshebnoi skazki* (*Historical Roots of the Wondertale,* 1946) that golden hues connote the otherworld and, in particular, its solar essence. Propp also noted that the standard set of precious metals—copper, silver, and gold—refers to three kingdoms along the transition to the otherworld. Such transition is also marked by (among others) the realms of the stars, moon, and sun. Bright as the stars, silvery as the moon, and golden as the sun is a customary referent for dresses of silk, silver, and gold in the "**Cinderella**" cycle. The slaying of Russian **dragon**s often liberates the light of the stars, moon, and sun even as it frees **princess**es from underground castles of copper, silver, and gold. In sum, the three precious metals represent otherworldly sources of light and life befitting the cosmic framework of wonder tales.

All such guises of light find synthesis in white, which thus connotes otherworldly essence. Blue, the color of the sky and the sea, likewise intimates unearthly origin. Hence, meeting a white animal or a white lady in the forest signals otherworldly presence, and so does meeting donor figures garbed in blue. But white also stands for the mundane realm of the living as opposed to the chthonian sphere of darkness and **death**. Thus, heroes venturing underground leave the "white" world to find themselves in the "black" world. Indeed, black generally connotes infernal essence. Specifically, usurpers replacing enchanted characters are dark. Even the forest of enchantment is dark, not green.

This is important. Maidens delivered to **animal groom**s may choose between a black wedding dress foreshadowing their death or a green one heralding a joyful life. Green connotes prosperity even when the **devil**, acting as a donor, appears clad in this color. The green devil echoes the immemorial Green/Wild Man personifying vegetable vitality. Overall, whereas blackness bodes doom, green promises revival.

In the Wild Man of yore, green meets red. Of old, the *homo ferus* (wild) is also said to be *ferreus* (iron)—hence, of the color of rusty iron (as in **Grimm**s' "Der Eisenhans," or "Iron Hans"). **Oral tradition** also presents this colorful character as the hirsute, sometimes red-haired, son of a bear. The Wild Man appears in both green and red because, of course, his envelope is seasonal—green leaves predominate in summertime, and ragged hairs show in the winter. However, whereas green leaves indicate exuberant vitality, tangled **hair**/furs hint at the dormant state of enchantment wonder tales persistently associate with **blood**.

Indeed, wonder-tale **transformation**s include swinging between the world of the living and the realm of death, whence heroines and heroes acquire riches and vitality to take back to this world. In between the living and the dead, heroines and heroes undergo enchantment, which is a blood condition. Because red connotes an intermediary state between living whiteness and deadly blackness, it can be associated with both. (Also, red represents the realm of earthly blood as opposed to those of otherworldly whiteness and of infernal blackness, as when supernatural **ogre**s say they smell the hero's blood.) Structurally speaking, then, white, red, and black constitute the basic color triad of wonder tales.

Remarkably, this color triad also designates ideal maidens, deemed white as snow, red as blood, and black as a crow. On one hand, white stands for luminosity and untainted sheen, thus for heavenly essence and purity. But it appears tinged by red, for persistent red-on-white imagery underlies the **initiation** leitmotiv of maidens passing from the purity of infancy to the mature realm of procreation. On the other hand, black connotes death; but this, in wonder tales, is a prerequisite for rebirth. Indeed, enchantment is like reversible death, just as darkness foreshadows new light. Such primacy of death and darkness over life and light is a standard feature of cyclic models based on natural phenomena—recall the dark moon, out of which the "new" moon reappears periodically, or the black earth synthesizing tomb and womb. Moreover, persistent equivalence between such phenomena and **women**'s cycles shows in the Mother-Earth metaphor as well as in association between moon's returns and menstruation. All this suggests that depiction of ideal womanhood in terms of white, red, and black engages the theme of women's unique power to generate new life—out of death, as it appears—by means of cyclic blood.

In sum, the basic color triad concerns characters fallen into red enchantment, then to extract luminous riches from the black realm into the domain of light, as much as it connotes women's capacity to elicit white from black by means of red. Such parallelism between the cyclic pattern of wonder tales and ideal womanhood recalls Propp's assertion that all wonder tales are variations on the kidnapping of a princess by a dragon—a full-fledged image of cyclic time. In other words, one finds red at the heart of tale chromaticism, the full set of which describes cyclic transitions hinging on enchantment.

Further Readings: Berlin, Brent, and Paul Kay. *Basic Color Terms: Their Universality and Evolution.* Berkeley: University of California Press, 1991; Lüthi, Max. *The European Folktale: Form and Nature.* Translated by John D. Niles. Philadelphia: Institute for the Study of Human Issues, 1982. 24–36; Propp, Vladimir. *Morphology of the Folktale.* Translated by Laurence Scott. Revised and edited by Louis A. Wagner. 2nd edition. 1968. Austin: University of Texas Press, 1996. 92–117.

Francisco Vaz da Silva

Comics. *See* Cartoons and Comics

The Company of Wolves (1984)

Irish filmmaker Neil Jordan's sumptuous Red Riding Hood film, *The Company of Wolves*, is based on three tales from Angela **Carter**'s collection *The Bloody Chamber* (1979) and features a script by the author herself. While nominally a **werewolf** film in the tradition of gothic horror, it is an intelligent and densely textured cinematic work. Carter's original stories, "The Werewolf," "The Company of Wolves," and, to a lesser extent, "Wolf-Alice," are patched together in the script to explore issues of female **sexuality** and desire within a patriarchal universe, using images of the wolf and werewolf to represent the power, seduction, and threat of sexuality. Both tales and film thus infuse Charles **Perrault**'s "**Little Red Riding Hood**" with psychological depth, Freudian significance, and a heightened sense of erotic menace.

The film is particularly interesting in its framing of fantastic narrative both as oral **storytelling** and as dream. The Red Riding Hood character, Rosaleen, occupies a central space in the film, her encounter with the wolf forming a coherent narrative in which smaller werewolf narratives are embedded. At the same time, she has a dual identity, since the "Red Riding Hood" narrative is also itself framed as the dream of an adolescent child, sleeping fitfully in the fever of an awakening sexuality. While the dream narrative can work against

The wolf dinner party in the 1984 film *The Company of Wolves*. [Cannon Films/Photofest]

the flat acceptance that is characteristic of fairy tale, here it instead brings to prominence the symbolic significance of imagery that is simultaneously that of fairy tale and of Sigmund **Freud**. Jordan's rich visual canvas includes frequent, lingering shots of snakes, toads, giant trees, spiders, birds, and white roses slowly turning red. The film's mixture of visual styles is also validated by the dream framework. For instance, Rosaleen's medieval-village existence is seamlessly integrated not only with the trappings of eighteenth-century aristocracy, which deliberately invoke the classic French fairy tale, but also with the **devil**'s vintage motorcar. The overall effect is of a universalized dreamworld, a visual realization of an idealized fairy-tale setting that is both compelling and endlessly resonant.

Within the dream narrative, the story of Rosaleen forms an interior frame for embedded oral recitations, notable in that the storytellers are all **women**. Rosaleen's grandmother provides a cautionary note, representing the somewhat reactionary strictures of patriarchy that curtail women's sexual freedom in the service of social uniformity. Her tales thus include warnings about **men**, specifically men who embody sexual promise, and who thus exist on the fringes of society: a woman marries a werewolf and loses him to the forest on her wedding night, a boy encounters the devil in the forest at night and accepts the gift that brings out the wolf in him. The grandmother's tale telling is thus intrinsically the narrative of culture itself, told by a woman who has clearly adopted a patriarchal view of sexuality after a lifetime in that culture. Rosaleen's **mother** provides a contrast to this: her sense of the sexual is far more egalitarian, epitomized by her statement that "If there's a beast in men it meets its match in women, too." The process of gradual emancipation down the generations reaches its climax in Rosaleen, whose narratives of **transformation** are celebratory rather than cautionary: a **witch**-woman turning aristocratic men into wolves in revenge against the lover who discarded her, and a wolf-girl emerging from the deep well that links to the underground world of the subconscious, to meet with misunderstanding and fear, but also a tentative gesture toward reconciliation, in the above-ground world of culture. The film thus faithfully represents Carter's ongoing concern with the artificiality of social restraints, the constructs of culture in conflict with the self-determination of animal symbols. The figure of Rosaleen's werewolf, an urbane and charming gentleman in beautiful eighteenth-century costume, explicitly explores and attempts to reconcile this divide. He is clearly a far more desirable alternative to Rosaleen's freckled and naive village-boy suitor, whose social conditioning has come to replace the power of acknowledged sexuality represented by the animal.

While the film is a powerful and resonant piece of symbolic cinema, in its closing scenes, it becomes problematical for Carter's feminist exploration of sexuality via fairy tale. Rosaleen's story climaxes with an ending taken from Carter's story "The Tiger's Bride," that involves the transformation of the girl into beast rather than the humanizing of the beast into man. The wolfpack's joyous excursion into the winter woods suggests an abdication of the effort needed to be a free sexual entity within culture rather than outside it. More disturbingly, however, the resolution of the **frame narrative** is an unabashed horror trope, the wolves pouring through a picture in the sleeping girl's bedroom to waken her, screaming, in a classic image of phallic defloration. This is not the ending provided by Carter's film script, published in *The Curious Room* (1996), which has the awakened girl diving suddenly through the floor of her bedroom in a graceful appropriation of phallic penetration and authority, leaving her bedroom to be explored in her absence by the transformed wolf couple of her dream, rather than a threatening pack. Jordan's ending seems to deny the resolution provided by the dream narrative, overwriting its promise of sexual equality with the reasserted **gender** constraints of the horror genre, an essentially male vision of woman as victim, which affirms the masculine gaze of both director and camera. Despite this, however, the film stands as one of the most successful cinematic **adaptation**s of fairy tale—compelling, thought-provoking, and symbolically powerful. *See also* Cautionary Tale; Erotic Tales; Feminism; Feminist Tales; Film and Video.

Further Readings: Haase, Donald P. "Is Seeing Believing? Proverbs and the Film Adaptation of a Fairy Tale." *Proverbium* 7 (1990): 89–104; Zucker, Carole. "Sweetest Tongue Has Sharpest Tooth: The Dangers of Dreaming in Neil Jordan's *The Company of Wolves.*" *Literature Film Quarterly* 28 (2000): 66–71.

Jessica Tiffin

Comparative Method

It is always useful to know as much as possible concerning the origin, growth, and spread of an item of **folklore**—be it a belief, custom, narrative, or traditional saw. The fact that it is usually very difficult, and often quite impossible, to be precise on these issues does not negate the importance of the inquiry. Accordingly, folklore scholarship includes a long and continuing tradition of inquiry into the origin and dissemination of folklore, and the technique employed is known as the "comparative method."

The method is basically directed to two planes—the historical and the geographical. An attempt is made to identify as exhaustive a number of examples as possible of the particular item to be investigated—for example, as many **variant**s of a **tale type** as possible. On the historical plane, this entails all of the occurrences of the item in recorded written sources, and the dates of these sources are noted. On the geographical plane, the places where the item has been recorded, either in written or oral sources, are noted. The combined sources of information are considered to give insights into the growth and spread of the item, and these observations can be deepened by further details such as the context in which each example occurs and the sociocultural connections between the relevant communities possessing the lore. All of the collated information constitutes the "provenance" of the item.

Since the work of Jacob and Wilhelm **Grimm** in the nineteenth century, systematic exploration of folkloric data has been undertaken through comparison, and the culmination of this work in the area of folk narrative research has been the catalogue *Verzeichnis der Märchentypen* by Antti **Aarne** (1910), which was translated and enlarged by Stith **Thompson** in *The Types of the Folktale* (1928 and 1961) and then further developed by Hans-Jörg Uther in *The Types of International Folktales* (2004). An indispensable guide for students of the international folktale, this catalogue allots a number to each identifiable narrative plot, provides a synopsis of its main features, lists its basic **motif**s, and gives references to its occurrences in literary sources and in folklore anthologies from different countries. Those researchers who specialize in the comparative method are often referred to by scholars as "the historical-geographical school," and also sometimes (from the nationalities of Aarne and Thompson) as "the Finnish-American school."

One undeniable benefit of this comparative approach is that it specifies the available sources and groups them into manageable units, indicating the variations that appear to have come about in time and place. The method has not been without its critics, however. For one thing, it tends towards pictorial representation, where the concentration of instances as marked on a map can be misleading because it depends to a greater or lesser degree on the availability of samples. Since the provenance of literature itself varies from culture to culture, and since samples from actual folklore are dependent on the volume of collecting, which varies greatly from place to place, the actual evidence must necessarily be of a haphazard nature. The most that can be expected from the comparative method, therefore, is likelihood but not certainty, and this likelihood itself will vary according to context.

A more far-reaching, but less assured, criticism of the method questions the very premise that there are definite phenomena to be studied. Much does indeed depend on the role and purpose assigned to an item of lore within a particular culture, but to what extent such roles and purposes change the inherent nature of the item is itself a matter for investigation and can easily be accommodated within the comparative methodology. In the case of narrative, the idea—basic to the method—that a traditional story is a logical unit comprising a definite selection of motifs has been questioned by scholars of several schools, including formalists, structuralists, and functionalists. Oral storytellers do indeed have the ability, and sometimes an incentive, to vary plot-structures, to combine hitherto separate structures, or indeed to deliberately disassemble them and reassemble them as new constructs. A survey of the myriad of examples cited by Aarne and Thompson, however, bears witness to an extraordinary degree of consistency in the growth and spread of specific narratives. This is a strong argument in favor of the comparative method of study.

The method can also be used to good effect in investigating the various genres of oral **legend**, the distinctive plots of which tend not to be disseminated over such large areas as the folktales; and in the cases of mythical stories or hero-tales, in which dissemination can be an important factor but tends to be more concerned with partial borrowing. The shorter and simpler items of folklore may be bound to specific cultural contexts and therefore entail the possibility of **polygenesis**. It is obvious that the more complicated a plot's structure, the more assured is the argument for borrowing, and consequently the more reliable is the comparative method as a tool for analysis. *See also* Historic-Geographic Method; Monogenesis; Structuralism.

Further Readings: Aarne, Antti. *The Types of the Folktale: A Classification and Bibliography.* Translated and enlarged by Stith Thompson. 2nd revision. Helsinki: Academia Scientiarum Fennica, 1961; Dundes, Alan. "The Anthropologist and the Comparative Method." *Journal of Folklore Research* 23 (1986): 125–46; Sydow, Carl Wilhelm von. *Selected Papers on Folklore: Published on the Occasion of His 70th Birthday.* Copenhagen: Rosenkilde & Bagger, 1948; Thompson, Stith. *The Folktale.* 1946. Berkeley: University of California Press, 1977; _____. *Motif-Index of Folk-Literature.* Revised and enlarged edition. 6 volumes. Bloomington: Indiana University Press, 1955–58.

Dáithí Ó hÓgáin

Conduit Theory

The conduit/multiconduit theory was developed by Linda **Dégh** and Andrew Vázsonyi in an effort to explain why **folklore** genres persist throughout their transmission and dissemination. The theory holds that folkloric texts do not pass through a systematic track between senders and receivers; instead, they formulate their own specific chain linkages, called "conduits," which carry messages through society. The theory argues that these conduits consist of individuals united by analogous mindsets, such as those who react correspondingly to similar messages. Dégh and Vázsonyi suggest that these groups of individuals qualify as members of a similar proper conduit, which is essential for the continued transmission of the original texts. When a transmission is received by an appropriate conduit receiver, that recipient is likely to resend the message to other proper conduit members.

When a transmission is received by an inappropriate conduit receiver of the text, it will either cease to be resent, thereby reaching a dead end, or undergo modification to assume the characteristics of a new conduit by deviating from the original message. Conduit modification creates the opportunity for infinite personal variations of the original text by senders and receivers as they are shaped by **context**. Thus, the theory is contingent upon the transmission through interested parties who have the opportunity and willingness to interact. Conduit theory denotes that folklore transmission only occurs with interested participants and consequently enables uninterested parties to opt out.

Dégh and Vázsonyi assert that conduits unite persons with similar tastes and consequently aid in the formation of **folk** groups and regional identities. The individual's personal preferences (as evidenced through linking conduits) influence, shape, and reshape the regional, ethnic, and personal cache of ghost stories, **ballad**s, **tall tale**s, and **legend**s. The characteristics of a single genre can also amount to their own conduits, known as subconduits or microconduits. In a given community, folklore conduits typically function concurrently. Conduit theory holds that the transmission of folkloric texts leads to a complex multiconduit system that is essential to the folklore process.

Conduit theory debuted in *Folklore: Performance and Communication* (1975), in an article titled "The Hypothesis of Multi-Conduit Transmission in Folklore." While there have been critiques made on the lack of empirical evidence provided in this publication, conduit theory has gained credibility among scholars who utilize it to analyze various fields in the social sciences. ***See also*** Diffusion; Monogenesis; Polygenesis; Storytelling; Variant.

Further Readings: Dégh, Linda. *Legend and Belief: Dialectics of a Genre.* Bloomington: Indiana University Press, 2001; Dégh, Linda, and Andrew Vázsonyi. "The Hypothesis of Multi-Conduit Transmission in Folklore." *Folklore: Performance and Communication.* Edited by Dan Ben-Amos and Kenneth S. Goldstein. The Hague: Mouton, 1975. 207–54; Fine, Gary Alan. *Manufacturing Tales: Sex and Money in Contemporary Legends.* Knoxville: University of Tennessee Press, 1992.

Trevor J. Blank

Contamination

In folktale studies, "contamination" refers to the mixing of elements from one story into another. The notion of contamination stems from the arrangement of folktales into **tale type**s. Antti **Aarne,** in building the first version of what became the Aarne-Thompson-Uther index of folktale types, chose to take a complete narrative as a template for each type. Therefore, each tale type was defined on the basis of a particular set of **motif**s. But **folktales** actually shuffle motifs continuously, displaying ever-new **variant**s. Therefore, discrepancies became apparent between preset tale types and protean folktales.

Aarne attempted to resolve such discrepancies by postulating that "originally" every motif was part of one tale exclusively, so that motif mix-ups are due to latter borrowings between tales. He thought such borrowings result from corruption due to imperfect oral transmission. The rationale is as follows: Since **oral tradition** is based on **memory**, which is intrinsically faulty, new variants of tales become increasingly corrupted. As tellers forget motifs, materials from other stories tiptoe in. Therefore, contamination results from corruption, which is endemic in oral tradition.

In hindsight, the use of contamination in folkloristics is one byproduct of two rather simplistic ideas: that of tale types as real entities (as opposed to scholarly constructs) and that of oral tradition as corruption. Both ideas are outdated now; so is contamination, along with its melancholic assumption of once-upon-a-time purity or **authenticity**.

Further Readings: Dundes, Alan. "The Motif-Index and the Tale Type Index: A Critique." *Journal of Folklore Research* 34 (1997): 195–202; Thompson, Stith. "The Life History of a Folktale." *The Folktale.* 1946. Berkeley: University of California Press, 1977. 428–48; Zipes, Jack. "Cross Cultural Connections and the Contamination of the Classical Fairy Tale." *The Great Fairy Tale Tradition: From Straparola and Basile to the Brothers Grimm.* Edited by Jack Zipes. New York: Norton, 2001. 845–69.

Francisco Vaz da Silva

Conte de fées

"*Conte de fées*" is the expression used in French to signify "**fairy tale**." Its emergence in the French language came in 1697 with the publication of Marie-Catherine d'**Aulnoy**'s first volume of *Les contes des fées* (*Tales of the Fairies*). Notably it was the **salon** woman d'Aulnoy and not her better-known contemporary Charles **Perrault** who coined the expression. "**Fairy**" could refer to an aristocratic woman who presided over a Parisian salon, evidenced in Henriette-Julie de Castelnau, Comtesse de **Murat**'s preface to her *Histoires sublimes et allégoriques* (*Sublime and Allegorical Stories*, 1699). These early fairy tales implicitly celebrated the salon **women** who hosted **storytelling** games as well as the women who wrote them.

The term "*conte de fées*" surfaced during the great fairy-tale vogue of late seventeenth-century France, which introduced to the literary scene for the first time in history tales thoroughly imbibed with the marvelous and in which powerful fairies cast spells with their magic wands, magical forms of transportation carry heroes and heroines across the skies, and beautiful princesses inhabit magnificent castles. Although we think of such tropes as common currency when we hear the expression "fairy tale," in fact few such examples of the marvelous exist in tale tradition before the 1690s, and certainly not to the same extent. Indeed, it was in this period that our contemporary notion of "fairy tale" and all that the term evokes emerged.

See also Folktale; French Tales; Literary Fairy Tale; Märchen; Wonder Tale.

Further Readings: Harries, Elizabeth Wanning. "Introduction: Once, Not Long Ago." *Twice upon a Time: Women Writers and the History of the Fairy Tale.* Princeton, NJ: Princeton University Press, 2001. 1–18; Zipes, Jack. "Introduction: The Rise of the French Fairy Tale and the Decline of France." *Beauties, Beasts, and Enchantments: Classic French Fairy Tales.* Translated by Jack Zipes. New York: New American Library, 1989. 1–12.

Anne E. Duggan

Contemporary Legend. *See* Urban Legend

Context

"Context" derives from the Latin word *textere*, which means "to weave." In the broader sense, the term "context" means anything that comes with the text. A text, like a piece of textile, is woven together from the situation of a given **performance**: the audience, the individual performer, the knowledge and understanding of the social group, and the culture of the performer and audience. Since the 1960s in particular, when folklorists began emphasizing performance in response to developments in the field of sociolinguistics, context has been used as an analytical concept central to determining the conditions in which folkloric materials are composed, transmitted, and received. As utilized in **folklore** studies, contextual analysis strives for an interpretation, rather than description or mere explanation, of folkloric material.

The understanding of context as developed in the discipline of anthropology, especially by Bronislaw Malinowksi, found its way into folklore studies through the work of William Bascom. Malinowski's notions of "context of situation" and "context of culture," which he deemed essential to understanding a text, drew attention both to the specific situation in which a given text is produced or uttered and to the broader cultural system of which it is a part. These ideas of context and their importance to our understanding of texts demanded a new level of analysis and shifted the attention of folklorists from function to meaning, from explanation to interpretation. Alan **Dundes** sought to illuminate the nature of context for folklorists by considering it in relation to the terms "text" (a single version of an item of folklore) and "texture" (the text's linguistic features). According to Dundes, "The context of an item of folklore is the specific social situation in which that particular item is actually employed" (Dundes, 23). Dundes posited that the text and its textural features must be understood not only in relation to their context but also as being influenced by that context. Consequently, Dundes stressed that in **collecting** folklore, the documentation of not only the text but also its context is critical since context will give us information that helps us understand what significance a text has—why it is used—in a given social situation. Analyzing who is telling what to whom on which occasion and under which circumstances enables us to discern why the text takes the specific form that it does. Moreover, the fact that context shapes a text is for Dundes "evidence that a knowledge of context can explain variations in text and texture" (Dundes, 27). Knowledge of context better enables folklorists to interpret the variations among tales of the same **tale type**.

Context is obviously relevant to the act of **storytelling**. Applying a linguistic model of communication to storytelling events, Robert A. Georges underlined in 1969 that the message of each event is shaped by the interactions between the storyteller and listeners in reference to their social interrelationships, which are unique to each storytelling occasion. The role of context in storytelling had been recognized well before the 1960s, however. Representing an eastern European perspective on context, Mark Azadovskii had emphasized the role of the narrator in storytelling as early as 1926 in *Eine sibirische Märchenerzählerin*, an introduction to a revision of his fairy-tale collection from the upper Lena in Irkutsk in 1925. First translated into English in 1974 as *A Siberian Tale Teller*, Azadovskii's pioneering work found resonance among American folklorists only in the 1980s. Azadovskii presents the image of postrevolutionary storytellers, especially Natalia Vinokurova, an illiterate storyteller from whom Azadovskii collected more than fifty tales. Among Vinokurova's folktale characters were vagrants, some of whom were prisoners in the Upper Lena region. By analyzing the particular motifs of Vinokurova's art, Azadovskii detected that some motifs carried a particular historical context and that the storyteller's performance depended a great deal upon her psychological situation.

Linda Dégh is another folklorist representing an eastern European perspective on context. In *Folktales and Society*, which originally appeared in German in 1962 and was translated into English in 1969, Dégh focuses on the relationship among tale, narrator, and society. Her study demonstrates the effect of the narrator's personality and social position on the texts of the tales and illuminates the idea of "stability" or "continuity" within tradition. Continuity, it turns out, depends on both the narrator and the audience playing key roles in the social context. Narrators tell their favorite tales, but those stories to which the audience does not listen do not remain within the tradition. By seeking other tales that will appeal to their audience, the narrators preserve a corpus of tales in their repertoire.

Early scholars of folk narrative implicitly recognized that folktales could be shaped by what we now call "context" when they viewed folktales as the embodiment of social, cultural, and national characteristics. According to the eighteenth-century German writer Johann Gottfried Herder and the nineteenth-century Brothers **Grimm**, the style of folktales derived from the social and cultural contexts in which they were produced. Herder argued that that folk literature owed its style to peasants' close contacts with nature. Today—in the wake of **anthropological approaches**, **ethnographic approaches**, **sociohistorical approaches**, cultural studies, and sociocultural movements such as **feminism**—scholars take a wide range of social, cultural, and situational factors into account when considering context, including the age, gender, ethnicity, class, and socioeconomic status of the storyteller and audience. All of these play roles in determining the form, meaning, and function of the narrated materials. *See also* Fieldwork.

Further Readings: Azadovskii, Mark. *A Siberian Tale Teller.* Translated by James R. Dow. Austin: The University of Texas, 1974; Bausinger, Herman. "Zur Kontextforschung in der Folklorewissenschaft der Vereinigten Staaten von Amerika." *Jahrbuch für Volksliedforschung* 26 (1981): 11–14; Ben-Amos, Dan. "Context in Context." *Western Folklore* 52 (1993): 209–26; Dégh, Linda. *Folktales and Society: Story-Telling in a Hungarian Peasant Community.* Translated by Emily M. Schossberger. Expanded edition. Bloomington: Indiana University Press. 1989; Dundes, Alan. "Texture, Text, and Context." *Interpreting Folklore.* Bloomington: Indiana University Press, 1980. 20–32; Georges, Robert A. "Towards and Understanding of Storytelling Events." *Journal of American Folklore* 82 (1969): 313–28.

Hande Birkalan-Gedik

Coover, Robert (1932–)

One of the most inventive voices of late twentieth-century American literature, Robert Coover has produced a large body of fiction marked by a critical interest in the active role of popular cultural narratives in the lives and selves of those who consume them. Specific forms include baseball and sports, used in *The Universal Baseball Association* (1968), and the various modes of cinema, explored in *A Night at the Movies* (1987) and *Ghost Town* (1998). Coover's interest in narrative forms and their influence is nowhere more evident than in his engagement with the fairy tale, a genre to which he has returned intermittently throughout his writing. His credentials as a postmodernist experimenter were firmly established with the publication in 1969 of *Pricksongs and Descants*. This collection of short stories opens, fittingly, with "The Door: A Prologue of Sorts," a fractured, scatological take on "Jack and the Beanstalk" and **"Little Red Riding Hood."** Key Coover traits are already apparent in the use of the source narratives as an implicit backdrop against which are enacted a series of variations on central fairy-tale themes of innocence and experience, **transformation, death**, and, above all, desire. "The Gingerbread House," from the same volume, experiments further with narrative, consisting as it does of forty-two numbered sections, offering a cubist-like meditation on the first part of "**Hansel and Gretel**." These early fictions, together with the uncollected "The Dead Queen" (1973), a version of "**Snow White**," stand alongside Angela **Carter**'s *The Bloody Chamber* (1979) and Salman **Rushdie**'s *Shame* (1983) as key texts in the renaissance of English-language fairy-tale fiction in the 1970s and 1980s. Coover's writing is integral to this countertradition, of a piece with the questioning of ideologies of power and **gender** evident in Rushdie and Carter, but perhaps the more experimental in formal terms.

Coover's most ambitious engagement with the fairy tale is the **novel** *Pinocchio in Venice* (1991), a carnivalesque riposte to the moralizing of Carlo **Collodi**'s *Pinocchio* and, even more so, of Walt **Disney**'s cinematic adaptation of 1940. Specific source material is again used to spin a dense web of variations. Collodi's narrative tells of the taming, via transformation, of a wayward spirit, and it is this waywardness that comes back to haunt Coover's Pinocchio figure, aging art historian Professor Pinenut. Pinenut is a palimpsest of all the former lives of Pinocchio. Having devoted himself to the pursuit of absolute truth, he is now encircled by the forces and figures of mutability—that is, by the wayward powers of transformation on which the fairy tale, and so Pinocchio's own life, might be said to have been built. Coover is quite clearly of the same mind as Carter in feeling a need to argue furiously with Bruno **Bettelheim**'s conception of the fairy tale as a normative vehicle for successful socialization.

Coover taught experimental writing at Brown University for many years. He has been a firm advocate of the creative possibilities of hypertext, the early influence of which can be detected in the intertextual layering of *Pinocchio in Venice*. Yet it is in *Briar Rose* (1996), the first of two mid-length prose works, that the workings of hypertext are most clearly evident. Harking back to the numbered sections of "The Gingerbread House," *Briar Rose* comprises a series of single paragraph blocks that circle relentlessly around a familiar core scenario: the sleeping and dreaming beauty, her entangled but eager prince, and the witch-fairy who inhabits and fuels her dreams. As with the experiments of *Pricksongs and Descants*, narrative is frozen, with the characters caught in those moments of tension prior to the longed-for release of transformation and fulfillment. The space of the tale is constructed from its many forms, including those by Giambattista **Basile**, Charles **Perrault**, and Jacob and Wilhelm **Grimm**. Uniting these strands is the force of desire, including the need to make a name and settle down: the desire for desire to reach its end. Such easy outcomes are of course dismissed as just one more set of fictions. The storytelling crone is a classic Coover figure, a manipulative narrator who carries the burden of tradition with a mixture of sardonic humor and world-weary regret. Such an aged character allows Coover not only to incorporate a narrator within the narration, and so to acknowledge the folkloric heritage of the fairy tale, but also to play with a literal embodiment of the tradition. It is a technique used again in *Stepmother* (2004), another **novella**-length prose work, this time with a slightly more conventional acceptance of narrative. Again, the eponymous protagonist serves as a palimpsest of previous lives; and as with the crone of *Briar Rose*, Coover rescues the figure of demonized femininity. Alongside the scurrilous narrator are her current charge, an Old **Soldier**, the Reaper, and a shape-shifting **devil**. Reaper's Woods, in which much of tale is set, is a chaotic, magical space. The transformative aesthetic of the fairy tale is represented as an unruly force, well able to survive beyond the neat conclusions of didactic narrators. Whereas Coover's previous fairy-tale fictions have centered on particular source narratives, *Stepmother* takes the tradition itself as its object. The language is saturated with echoes and allusions, Coover once again holding the fairy tale to account for its erroneous symmetries and moralizing, while at the same time finding new fictional potential in its **motif**s, characters and, above all, in its desire-driven dramas. *See also* Intertextuality; Postmodernism.

Further Readings: Bacchilega, Cristina. "Folktales, Fictions and Meta-Fictions: Their Interaction in Robert Coover's *Pricksongs and Descants.*" *New York Folklore* 6.3–4 (1980): 171–84; _____. *Postmodern Fairy Tales: Gender and Narrative Strategies.* Philadelphia: University of Pennsylvania Press, 1997; Benson, Stephen. *Cycles of Influence: Fiction, Folktale, Theory.* Detroit: Wayne State University Press, 2003; Bond, Barbara. "Postmodern Mannerism: An Examination of Robert Coover's *Pinocchio in Venice.*" *Critique* 45 (2004): 273–92; Evenson, Brian. *Understanding Robert Coover.* Columbia: University of South Carolina Press, 2003; Redies, Sünje. "Return with New Complexities: Robert Coover's *Briar Rose.*" *Marvels & Tales* 18 (2004): 9–27.

Stephen Benson

Correia, Hélia (1949–)

Portuguese writer, novelist, dramatist, and poet, Hélia Correia manipulates the folktale and fairy-tale traditions in a variety of ways. In her **novel**, *O número dos vivos* (*The Number of the Living*, 1982) the author draws on **archetype**s from popular culture and dwells on themes such as life and **death**, love and immortality, and triumph over or defeat by patriarchy.

Although Correia's **novella**s are comparable in form and length to **fable**s and exemplary tales (or **exempla**), reminding us of the German **märchen**, her stories are unique. Set in a superstitious peasant community, *Montedemo* (*Devil's Mountain*, 1983) builds on Christian and pre-Christian elements in Portuguese popular beliefs to explore questions of social conditioning, **gender** relations, female identity, and sexuality. **Women** are central in Correia's work. **Oral tradition**s of **folklore** are often mediated through a feminine voice and emphasis is placed on female characters that embody the Great Mother archetype, as is the case with Teresinha Rosinha and Maruja in *Villa Celeste* (1985) and *A Fenda Erótica* (*The Erotic Fissure*, 1988).

Correia's more recent work reprises these **motif**s, focusing on traditional ways of life (*Insânia* [*Insanity*, 1996]), translating and adapting works that abound with fairy-tale characters (*Sonho de uma noite de verão* [*Midsummer Night's Dream*, 2003]), and writing original versions of popular folktales (*Fascinação* [*Fascination*, 2004]). *See also* Feminism; Feminist Tales.

Further Readings: Owen, Hilary. "Fairies and Witches in Hélia Correia." *Women, Literature, and Culture in the Portuguese-Speaking World.* Edited by Cláudia Pazos Alonso and Glória Fernandes. Lewiston: Edwin Mellen Press, 1996. 85–104; _____. "Hélia Correia's *Montedemo:* The Tale of an (Un)becoming Virgin." *Portuguese Women's Writing 1972 to 1986: Reincarnations of a Revolution.* Lewiston: Edwin Mellen Press, 2000. 57–72.

Ana Raquel Fernandes

Coyote

A **trickster** figure from **Native American tales** based on the species *Canis latrans*, Coyote is one of the most widespread folktale characters, with Coyote stories stretching from Canada to Central America and persisting in popular culture to the present day. Generally characterized as an anthropomorphic male, Coyote is the archetypal trickster in stories prevalent in many Native American cultures, including the Pima, Chippewa, Salish, Maya, Apache, Nez Perce, Blackfoot, Chumash, Pawnee, Ute, Thompson, Crow, Pueblo, and Navajo.

In the mode of many Native American tricksters, Coyote is the buffoonish hero who does good by accident. These tales tend to feature Coyote, motivated by his hunger and libido, falling victim to some sort of misfortune. Coyote is featured as the protagonist of some versions of "The Bungling Host" (Motif J2425), including the one in Stith **Thompson's** collection *Tales of the North American Indians* (1929). In this characteristic tale, Coyote hurts himself by attempting to imitate a trick by Bear. Coyote's misadventures, while comical, are generally intended to be educational, presenting foolish behavior as a contrast to proper behavior.

One of the complicated aspects of Coyote, as with many Native American trickster figures, is the lack of distinction between **folktale** and **myth** in Native American cultures. Coyote is featured in some tales as a creator figure, for instance creating humanity by rolling dung, and in some tales as a bungling character, being scared away by the voice of a mouse. Individual cultures may include both types of tale, thus making Coyote a hero of both myth and folktale.

Coyote has been adapted a number of times into modern **fantasy** literature. Christopher Moore's *Coyote Blue* (1994) adapts the tale to a modern context, with a Crow Indian insurance agent encountering the figure of Coyote. Coyote also appears in *Buffalo Gals and Other Animal Presences* (1987) by Ursula K. **Le Guin**, *Green Grass, Running Water* (1993) by Thomas King, and *New Coyote* (2005) by Michael Bergey. Bergey's **adaptation** uses science-fiction concepts to present a futuristic cyborg masquerading to Chumash Indians as their Coyote god. Many contemporary versions of Coyote have linked the traditional figure to the character Wile E. Coyote from Warner Bros. **animation**, implying a link between the folktale figure and the cartoon character. Interestingly, Coyote's generic ambiguity carries over to modern literature, with some tales presenting him as a god and some as a culture hero.

One of the interesting characteristics of Coyote is demonstrated by the controversy involving folklorist Barre Toelken and his Navajo **informant** Yellowman. Among the Navajo, who refer to Coyote as Ma'i, Coyote stories are traditionally told only during the winter months of the year; telling them outside this time period is against the belief system of the Navajo. Due to difficulties in limiting access to such materials to the Navajo winter, Toelken made the controversial decision to return his fieldwork tapes to Yellowman's family. *See also* Anansi.

Further Readings: Bright, William. *A Coyote Reader.* Berkeley: University of California Press, 1993; Cuadra Downing, Orlando, ed. *The Adventures of Don Coyote: American Indian Folk Tales.* New York: Exposition Press, 1955; Toelken, Barre. "The Yellowman Tapes, 1966–1997." *Journal of American Folklore* 111 (1998): 381–91.

B. Grantham Aldred

Craik, Dinah Maria Mulock (1826–1887)

An English writer who produced work in a wide variety of genres including fairy tales, Dinah Maria Mulock Craik was born in Hartshill near Stoke-on-Trent in Staffordshire. In 1839, she moved to London, where she studied, taught, and established a literary career, marrying George Lillie Craik in 1865. The author of the bestseller *John Halifax, Gentleman* (1856) and other novels, Craik also wrote fairy tales for children. *Alice Learmont: A Fairy Tale* (1852), inspired by Scottish **folklore**, tells of a girl stolen from her cradle by **fairies** and raised in their pleasurable but soulless world until she escapes into human womanhood via helping members of her **family** and being saved by her **mother**'s love.

Craik's popular anthology *The Fairy Book* (1863) includes traditional tales and some lesser-known stories. For her adopted daughter Dorothy she wrote *The Adventures of a Brownie as Told to My Child* (1872), which recounts children's adventures with a house **elf**, and *The Little Lame Prince and His Travelling Cloak* (1875), which tells of a lame **prince** regally usurped and imprisoned in a tower by his uncle. The prince is given a magic cloak by his fairy godmother that allows him to fly all over the world—looking but not touching anything. After his uncle's death, he becomes **king** and rules wisely. *See also* Changeling; Disability.

Further Readings: Mitchell, Sally. "Craik, Dinah Maria (1826-1887)." *Oxford Dictionary of National Biography.* Edited by H. C. G. Matthew and Brian Harrison. Oxford: Oxford University Press, 2004; _____. *Dinah Mulock Craik.* Boston: Twayne, 1983.

Adrienne E. Gavin

Crane, Walter (1845–1915)

An English illustrator, painter, and designer, Walter Crane was best known for his popular illustrations of fairy tales and children's stories. Born in Liverpool and raised in Torquay and London, Crane apprenticed as a wood engraver and in 1865 began illustrating a series of highly popular toy books for young children. Published by Routledge and printed by prominent woodblock color printer Edmund Evans, this inexpensive series made colored pictures more widely available and included fairy tales, nursery rhymes, and primers. Crane's illustrations for these books, including ***Beauty and the Beast, The Frog Prince***, ***Cinderella***, and *The **Sleeping Beauty*** in the Wood, established his fame as well as his distinctive style of **illustration**. Influenced by the aesthetic movement and Japanese prints, his images are characterized by attention to aesthetic fashions and furnishings. Crane used bright colors, bold lines, and lavish details that fill the picture. He also is known for his imaginative fantasy illustrations of anthropomorphized animals engaged in human activities. He often signed his work with his initials and an illustration of a crane.

Crane's later illustrations of fairy tales include those for his sister Lucy Crane's **translation** *Household Stories from the Collection of the Brothers **Grimm*** (1882). The illustrations therein are often regarded as his finest work. In elaborately detailed black and white, they interpret light and dark aspects of the tales and include headpieces and tailpieces, elegant initial letters, decorative frames, and incorporated text. He illustrated many other works of **children's literature** including fairy tales by several writers such as Mary Louisa **Molesworth**, Oscar **Wilde**'s *The Happy Prince and Other Tales* (1888), and Nathaniel **Hawthorne**'s *A Wonderbook for Boys and Girls* (1892). He also drew private illustrations for stories he told his children.

Crane wished his success to rest on his allegorical paintings, but it was for his children's book illustrations that he was best known. From the 1870s onward, he also became a leading decorative artist involved in the arts-and-crafts movement. He knew William Morris, became a socialist, and served as president of The Arts and Crafts Exhibition Society from 1888 to 1893 and again from 1896 to 1912. As a prominent, inventive, and prolific decorative artist, he designed textiles, stained glass, tiles, plasterwork, embroideries, and wallpaper, including wallpaper for nurseries. He wished to move beyond his connections with children and illustrated adult books in aesthetic style, such as an edition of Edmund Spenser's *Faerie Queene* (1894), and he wrote books on decorative **art** and illustration. He also became involved in art education at the Royal College of Art and Manchester Municipal School of Art.

Further Readings: Crawford, Alan. "Crane, Walter (1845–1915)." *Oxford Dictionary of National Biography*. Edited by H. C. G. Matthew and Brian Harrison. Oxford: Oxford University Press, 2004; Engen, Rodney K. *Walter Crane as a Book Illustrator*. London: Academy Editions, 1975; Smith, Greg, and Sarah Hyde, eds. *Walter Crane, 1845–1915: Artist, Designer, and Socialist*. London: University of Manchester, 1989.

Adrienne E. Gavin

Créolité. *See* Négritude, Créolité, and Folktale

Croker, Thomas Crofton (1798–1854)

An Irish antiquary and collector of Irish **folklore** and **legend**s, Thomas Crofton Croker was born in Cork and worked in a mercantile firm before moving to London, where he became a clerk in the Admiralty. From 1812 to 1815 and again in 1821, he traveled through southern Ireland (Munster) gathering **folktale**s, songs, legends, and **myth**s. In 1824, he published *Researches in the South of Ireland*. This was followed in 1825 by the anonymously published first volume of his *Fairy Legends and Traditions of the South of Ireland*, which was expanded and completed in two series in 1828 and published under Croker's name. A collected edition appeared in 1834. The **Grimm** brothers translated volume one into German shortly after it first appeared in 1825, and by the end of that year, it was in print, predated for 1826. In 1828, Croker included the Grimms' essay "On the Nature of the Elves" in volume three of his work, which focused on English and Welsh fairy lore. In 1828, a French translation of *Fairy Legends* was also produced.

Regarded as the earliest collection of Irish or British oral tales collected in the field, *Fairy Legends and Traditions of the South of Ireland* was reprinted widely throughout the nineteenth century and illustrated by artists such as George **Cruikshank** and Daniel Maclise. The stories influenced literary interpretations of Irish tales and helped expand interest in Irish myth. Croker had corresponded, for example, with the poet Thomas Moore at the time of his Irish travels, and Moore worked some of Croker's discoveries into editions of his *Irish Melodies*. In *Fairy Legends*, Croker emphasized a variety of fairy figures of Irish folklore, such as leprechauns, and the collection served as inspirational source material for poets and authors of the Irish literary revival. Croker's work brought traditional tales to a wider readership and was well regarded by early readers, including Sir Walter Scott. Later commentators, however, suggested that Croker had made the tales overly literary and inauthentically humorous.

Fairy Legends is Croker's most important work, but he also edited R. Adolphus Lynch's Killarney tales, *Legends of the Lakes,* in 1829, and helped inspire Thomas Keightley's *The Fairy Mythology* (1828). Additionally, he engaged in further historical and ethnographical investigations, published works such as *Popular Songs of Ireland* (1839), continued his career at the Admiralty, researched English drama, contributed to journals, helped found several historical societies, and was a member of the Royal Irish Academy and a fellow of the Society of Antiquaries of London. Croker had married in 1830 and his wife, Marianne Croker, a painter, illustrated and collaborated in his work, although her role has been given little recognition. *See also* Celtic Tales; Collecting, Collectors; Oral Tradition.

Further Readings: Croker, Thomas Crofton. *Fairy Legends and Traditions of the South of Ireland.* 1825. Edited by Neil C. Hultin and Warren U. Ober. Delmar, NY: Scholars' Facsimiles & Reprints, 1983; _____. *Fairy Legends and Traditions of the South of Ireland.* Edited by Thomas Wright. 1870. Ann Arbor: Scholars' Facsimiles & Reprints, 2001; Kosok, Heinz. "Thomas Crofton Croker's *Fairy Legends*: A Revaluation." *ABEI Journal: The Brazilian Journal of Irish Studies* 3 (June 2001): 63–76; Schacker, Jennifer. "Everything Is in the Telling: T. Crofton Croker's *Fairy Legends and Traditions of the South of Ireland.*" *National Dreams: The Remaking of Fairy Tales in Nineteenth-Century England.* Philadelphia: University of Pennsylvania Press, 2003. 46–77.

Adrienne E. Gavin

Cross-Dressing

Prohibited in many societies, cross-dressing, or wearing the **clothing** of the other sex, is nonetheless practiced or narrated around the world in ritual, **dance**, balladry, **theater**, **folktale**s, **fairy tale**s, short stories, and **novel**s. Transvestism, as it is also known, is an integral part of many folk ritual practices. In initiation rites for young boys, as well as comic theater and ceremonial dance in many clan cultures, **men** dress as **women**. Male transvestites are also the highlight of carnival celebrations in Europe and the Americas. From Greek theater to Kabuki and the Elizabethan English stage, prohibitions against women performers made male transvestites commonplace in dramatic performance. While cultural practice nearly always calls for men dressed as women, **legend** and literature prefer the cross-dressed woman. Legendary women such as Hua Mulan (fifth century balladry), Catalina de Erauso (1592–1650), and Mary Read (c. 1700–1720) passed as men to live a life of combat. Similarly, **epic** poetry and early romance feature women fighting in disguise, often against their own lovers, as in the case of Khvaju Kirmani's Humayun (fourteenth-century Persian manuscript) and Britomart of Spenser's *Faerie Queene* (1590–96).

Fairy tale and folktale, too, adore the story of the female transvestite (Motif K1837, Disguise of woman in man's clothes). While there are many types that feature cross-dressed girls, there is no tale type specific to male cross-dressing. Even as a **motif** male transvestism is quite rare. When it appears, male cross-dressing has neither the ennobling force of ritual transvestism nor the comic relief of carnivalesque disguise. Common among the few men who cross-dress in tales are the **devil**, adulterers, **thieves**, and the infamous **wolf** that tricks Little Red Riding Hood. All disguise themselves as women to escape justice, infiltrate enemy territory, or seduce their prey. Female cross-dressers appear as an entirely different cast of characters in tales, and they are generally heroic, clever, and virtuous. In the marvelous universe of tales, if men dress as women for reasons either dubious or humorous, when women dress as men, the transvestism serves a higher purpose.

Variations on the female transvestite theme occur in tales from China, India, Arabia, Iran, Romania, Armenia, Greece, Italy, France, Spain, England, and Chile. More intriguing than female transvestism in tales, however, is the remarkably similar form the theme takes across traditions. Transvestite heroines tend to be of noble birth and cross-dress out of necessity in response to disorder. In other words, female transvestites do not create disorder by shifting gender; rather they assume male power to restore legitimacy and stability, which male authorities in the story have failed to secure. Crises that call for female transvestism can take many forms, including everything from a domestic problem (a girl cross-dresses and runs away to avoid misalliance or to find her husband) to full-blown political catastrophe (with extraordinary helpers, the transvestite heroine vanquishes a threat to the crown).

The transvestite heroine resembles the classic underdog of the marvelous universe, who overcomes her limits through heroic or extraordinary means. In this case, her tactics involve passing as a man for a portion of the story. She is often the youngest of the family and must rely on her natural ingenuity and/or physical prowess to make her way, graced sometimes with a **fairy**'s magical intervention. Yet, cross-dressing stands apart from other tale theatricality such as metamorphosis or other forms of disguise and trickery. At least two features distinguish tale cross-dressing from these broader motifs common to **myth**, **legend**, and **folklore**. First, the cross-dressed girl/woman plays the role of heroine and hero in the story. Second, the girl masquerading as a man violates the most basic rules of social order: **gender** distinction and the dominance of the masculine over the feminine. Unlike the categories of rich/poor, noble/**peasant**, and human/animal, breached liberally in the realm of the marvelous, the hierarchy of the sexes remains a defining element of tale morphology (the active **prince** saves the passive maiden in distress) and is rarely reversed. Transvestite heroine tales alter the traditional romantic plot by sending the **princess** out on the prince's journey, but they tidy up the narrative in the end by returning her to female attire.

One set of motif variants has women pose as members of an elite social group, such as doctors, lawyers, wise men, or even monks. In one story of deception, a woman disguised as a man becomes pope (motif K1961.2.1, Woman in disguise becomes pope). Women who ascend to legal or religious functions do not necessarily cross-dress for this purpose, which is rather a means to an end. Instead, they become doctors or lawyers to find or free their husbands, or to prove themselves worthy of a prince. More common in the early modern period and after are tales that are classified in the ATU index as tales of magic and found in the category of Supernatural Helpers, where they are grouped together as tale type ATU 514 (The Shift of Sex) and those classified under as realistic tales (or **novella**s) and grouped together as a range of tale types collectively known as Proofs of Fidelity and Innocence (ATU 880–899). As the categories suggest, in these stories, the heroine embarks on a journey to prove or save herself, and ends in a romantic union. The most common female-to-male disguise in tales is that of the knight.

While there exist transvestite folktales that feature an actual metamorphosis (for example, Motif D11, Transformation woman to man), wherein the girl eventually turns into a man to legitimize her exploits, in most versions of the story, cross-dressing takes the form of temporary disguise. Unlike stories of sexual metamorphosis, tales of gender inversion turn on the ambiguity of the heroine/hero's identity. The woman or girl in disguise invariably betrays cultural habits or interests associated with femininity that pique the curiosity of other characters in the story. Attendant effects of this ambiguity, such as a suspicion and homoeroticism, are common. Often, she is suspected of being female and undergoes tests to prove her male sex identity (Motif H1578, Test of Sex: to discover person masking as of other sex). In some cases, when she arrives at court as a soldier, the queen falls in love with "him" and threatens to have him killed when he does not return her affections (ATU 514**, A Young Woman Disguised as a Man Is Wooed by the Queen). Transvestite tales inevitably end when the girl's identity is discovered, a dramatic event that resolves the ambiguity of the heroine's identity. Rather than leading to sanction, however, the revelation of her gender brings glory to the heroine and improves her social standing through a royal union that places her on the throne.

Famous among transvestite heroine tales for modern readers is the legend of Hua Mulan, popularized by Maxine Hong Kingston's novel *The* **Woman Warrior**: *Memoirs of a Girlhood Among Ghosts* (1975) and Disney's *Mulan* (1998) based on a modern version by Robert de Sans Souci. Renewed interest in French fairy tales has revived Marie-Catherine d'Aulnoy's "Belle-Belle, or the Chevalier Fortuné" (1696), which appears in Jack Zipes's *Beauties, Beasts, and Enchantment: Classic French Fairy Tales* (1989); and the novella, "The Counterfeit Marquise" (1695), attributed to the Abbé de Coisy and Charles Perrault, in Marina Warner's *Wonder Tales* (1994). At the turn of the twenty-first century, an ancient Japanese version of the transvestite tale produced as anime achieved cult status. In the popular *Cardcaptor Sakura* (1998), *Shojo Kakumoi Utena: Adolescence Mokushiroku* (1999), and *The Butterfly Lovers* (2003), heroines do not cross-dress in response to a social or political crisis, but with a personal goal in mind: to go to school and learn what the boys know.

Further Readings: Garber, Marjory. *Vested Interests: Cross-Dressing and Cultural Anxiety.* New York: Routledge, 1992; Husain, Shahrukh. *Handsome Heroines: Women as Men in Folklore.* New York: Anchor Books, 1996; Velay-Vallantin, Catherine. *La fille en garçon.* Carcassonne: GARAE/Hésiode, 1992.

Christine A. Jones

Crowley, John (1942–)

An American writer of science fiction, **fantasy**, and mainstream **novel**s, John Crowley produces challenging, intellectual work, characterized by beautiful prose and dense with ideas. He is very much a modern fabulist: characteristic concerns in his novels include history and memory, the notion of alternative worlds lying alongside our own, and a strong awareness of the mythological and folkloric.

Crowley most strongly investigates other worlds in the **faerie** realm of *Little, Big* (1981) and in the Aegypt series (*Aegypt: The Solitudes*, 1987; *Love and Sleep*, 1994; and *Daemonomania*, 2000), with its secret history of the world. *Little, Big* is Crowley's most overt exploration of the folkloric: **folklore**, fairy tales, and nursery rhymes weave in and out of the warm, sprawling narrative, which, in its depiction of the Drinkwaters, an eccentric country family whose many generations are subject to faerie intervention, has a Victorian feel. Significantly, the world of faerie is also the world of story, the human characters living with the pervading sense that that their lives are a fairy tale told by the fairies themselves. A similar sense of the importance of narrative is found in *Engine Summer* (1979), in which storytelling both enshrines history and designates status.

Many of Crowley's works have the flavor of **fable**, such as the symbolic use of red and black in *The Deep* (1975), or the humanized, postapocalyptic animals of *Beasts* (1976). The folkloric is more overt in his short stories, however, including a retelling of "The Green Child" (*Antiquities,* 1993) and the Scottish selkie story in *An Earthly Mother Sits and Sings* (2000). "Lost and Abandoned" (*Novelties and Souvenirs,* 2004) uses the recounting of "**Hansel and Gretel**" in a contemporary setting to work through issues of divorce and separation.

Further Reading: Shinn, Thelma J. "The Fable of Reality: Mythoptics in John Crowley's *Little, Big.*" *Extrapolation: A Journal of Science Fiction and Fantasy* 31 (1990): 5–14.

Jessica Tiffin

Cruikshank, George (1792–1878)

George Cruikshank was a Victorian caricaturist, cartoonist, and illustrator who became popular for his literary illustrations, including those for many fairy tales. Notably, Cruikshank illustrated Edgar **Taylor**'s *German Popular Stories* (1823–26), which offered English translations of selected tales from Jacob and Wilhelm **Grimm**'s 1819 edition of their ***Kinder- und Hausmärchen***. These illustrations added to the sense of narrative by depicting either the climactic moment of a tale or a moment crucial to the plot. For instance, in his picture for "The Elves and the Shoemaker," the **elves** dance wildly in their new clothes as the shoemaker and his wife watch. Typical of Cruikshank's illustrations, details such as the furnishings of the room place the fabulous elements in a familiar setting. The picture also typifies many of his early engravings in portraying the figures as caricatures. Cruikshank's work for Taylor helped launch a decades-long career illustrating fairy stories.

In 1853 and 1854, Cruikshank rewrote "Hop-O'-My-Thumb and the Seven-League Boots," "The History of Jack and the Bean-Stalk," and "**Cinderella** and the Glass Slipper," which he published as *George Cruikshank's Fairy Library*. In 1864, Cruikshank also published a version of "Puss in Boots," which he had evidently written earlier. He planned to add more tales but found relatively few readers. Cruikshank's retellings were bowdlerized. For instance, the **ogre**'s slaying his own

Jack brings the Giant prisoner to King Alfred.

George Cruikshank's illustration of "Jack and the Beanstalk" in *The Cruikshank Fairy-Book: Four Famous Stories with Forty Illustrations by George Cruikshank* (New York: G. P. Putnam's Sons, 1900). [Courtesy of the Eloise Ramsey Collection of Literature for Young People, University Libraries, Wayne State University]

children is absent from "Hop-O'-My-Thumb;" and he rewrote "Puss in Boots" to eliminate the dishonest behavior of characters. In particular, Cruikshank, whose family had suffered from alcoholism, depicted alcohol as a destructive force. In "Jack and the Bean-Stalk," drink accounts for the giant's cruelty; in "Cinderella and the Glass Slipper," the fairy godmother gives a temperance lecture to Cinderella's future father-in-law. These revisions have been condemned since their appearance. In his 1853 article, "Frauds on the Fairies," for instance, Charles **Dickens** mocked Cruikshank's didactic revisions and claimed that traditional tales promoted healthy mental development in children. Cruikshank countered his critics in an open letter by arguing that many writers had altered the tales and that the alterations did not lessen the appeal of the fantasy. A revised version of the letter was included in later editions of *Fairy Library*. Cruikshank's other revisions have attracted less criticism, such as his introduction of a character named Crooked Shanks at the end of "Puss in Boots."

Cruikshank's pictures for *Fairy Library* have usually been better received. Like much of his later work, they continue to display careful detail but also exhibit finer lines and shading. For instance, an illustration to "Jack and the Bean-Stalk" shows Cruikshank's altered conclusion for the story, in which Jack presents the captive Giant to Alfred the Great. Although some critics, including John **Ruskin**, have found Cruikshank's later illustrations to lack the vigor of his earlier work, others, including Dickens, have admired them for realizing the dramatic possibilities of fairy tales. *See also* Illustration.

Further Reading: Stone, Harry. "Dickens, Cruikshank, and Fairy Tales." *George Cruikshank: A Revaluation.* Edited by Robert L. Patten. Princeton: Princeton University Library, 1974. 213–47.

Paul James Buczkowski

Cumulative Tale

Repetition is an integral part of many art forms, including **storytelling**. Folktales of many types repeat (with variation) selected events, thus adding drama and a certain epic breadth to their basic plots. In a large family of tales (ATU 2000–2100, Cumulative Tales), repetition itself is the essential aesthetic element.

When given in verse, cumulative tales are akin to folksongs, as in tale type ATU 2010A, The Twelve Days (Gifts) of Christmas, with its incremental reiteration. Each of the twelve days brings a new gift with a restatement of all the previous days' gifts as well. The familiar American folksong "When I First Came to This Land" follows the same formula, with the immigrant's acquisitions accumulating one at a time, then added to an ever-growing list: "Called my duck 'out of luck'; called my cow 'no milk now'; called my shack 'break my back,'" and so on.

Some cumulative tales are limited in their extension only by the patience of storyteller and listener, giving them a kinship to the **nonsense tale**. For example, "Pulling Up the Turnip" (ATU 2044) from Aleksandr **Afanas'ev**'s collection of Russian fairy tales, tells of a turnip so large that grandfather cannot pull it up. One at a time, additional family members form an ever-growing chain to pull at the vegetable; animals too—including a puppy and a succession of beetles—join in, until finally they pull out the turnip. *See also* Chain Tales.

Further Reading: Thompson, Stith. "Cumulative Tales." *The Folktale.* 1946. Berkeley: University of California Press, 1977. 230–34.

D. L. Ashliman

Cupid and Psyche

Whether classified as **folktale**, **fairy tale**, **literary fairy tale**, or **myth**, the ancient story of Cupid and Psyche is one of the world's most enduring narratives, and its plot and characters find echoes in **art** and literature from the Renaissance to the present day. The literary tale of Cupid and Psyche originated as a framed story within the Latin **novel** *Metamorphoses* or the *Golden Ass* by Lucius **Apuleius** (c. 124–c. 170 CE). There is no single accepted source for Apuleius's creation, although he undoubtedly drew on existing folklore, myth, and iconographic representations, combining them in a new way. In *The Types of International Folktales* (2004) by Hans-Jörg Uther—the index used by folklorists to categorize **tale types**—the story is classified as ATU 425B, Son of the Witch, although it can also be associated with ATU 425A, The Animal as Bridegroom. Versions of the story are found worldwide, in regions as disparate as Scandinavia and Indonesia; but it was Apuleius's tale that perpetuated the story in the Western world.

Apuleius's work was known to pagan and Christian authors in centuries following his death, but it was only when an eleventh-century manuscript of the *Golden Ass* was discovered in Italy in the fourteenth century that its influence grew. The Italian storyteller Giovanni **Boccaccio** was one of the earliest European authors to spread Apuleius's fame. The Cupid and Psyche story became particularly popular after the *Golden Ass*'s first publication in Rome in 1469. The Italian painter Raphael's *Villa Farnesina* frescoes in Rome (begun in 1518 and unfinished) are perhaps the most famous visual representations of the story, which has also been taken up by countless authors, including the French fabulist Jean de **La Fontaine** in *Les amours de Psyché et de Cupidon* (*The Love of Psyche and Cupid,* 1669), the English Romantic poet John Keats in his "Ode to Psyche" (1820), and the American writer Joyce Carol Oates in her story "Cupid and Psyche" (1970), as well as by composers such as César Franck and Manuel de Falla.

A brief overview of the story's characters and **motif**s reveals its relationship to fairy tales such as "**Beauty and the Beast**." Psyche, youngest of three daughters of a royal couple, is the most beautiful young woman in the realm; but she is fated to become the bride of a horrid, snakelike creature with wings. (In fact, threatened by the girl's beauty, Venus has decreed that Psyche will fall in love with a monster and orders her son, Cupid, to make this happen. However, Cupid himself falls in love with Psyche.) Transported to an ornate palace from the mountaintop where her **family** abandons her, Psyche is welcomed by invisible attendants. At night Cupid enters her room, makes her his wife without disclosing his identity, and leaves before dawn. Reassured by her partner's gentleness, Psyche soon finds herself pregnant.

Meanwhile, her **sisters** search for her and, despite Cupid's warnings that they will bring about sorrow and destruction, she invites them to her new home. But the wicked sisters are envious of Psyche and plot to ruin her good fortune. They inquire about her husband's identity, and when she cannot enlighten them, they suggest that her husband is a wild beast who will soon eat her. They prevail upon Psyche to kill the creature that has repeatedly warned her not to gaze upon him. Lighting her lamp while her husband sleeps, the young woman discovers the winged god. A drop of oil on his shoulder awakens him, and he disappears. Distraught, Psyche determines to earn Cupid's love; but first she punishes her sisters by indirectly causing their **death**.

Venus is furious when she learns that Cupid has wed her rival. She locks up her disobedient son and turns her attention to Psyche, who must submit to her cruel **mother**-in-law if she is to win back her husband. Venus devises a series of trials, each more difficult and life-threatening than the next, culminating with the requirement that Psyche go to the Underworld and bring back a box containing Proserpine's beauty. Psyche fears for her life, but a tower tells her how to carry out her mission, warning only that she must never open the box.

Curious and incautious, Psyche disobeys the command, whereupon she falls into a deadly sleep. Rushing to her rescue, Cupid revives his beloved, who then completes this final task. Cupid obtains Jupiter's approval of his **marriage**, and Psyche becomes immortal. Venus is placated, Psyche delivers a daughter called Voluptas, and they all live happily ever after.

This family drama has universal appeal, and the fact that Apuleius's version allows for many different interpretations also has kept the tale alive. Modern classical scholars view Psyche's story as the key to understanding the *Golden Ass*, which they read as a pagan allegory of a soul lost and saved by the goddess Isis. Psyche's fatal curiosity parallels that of Lucius, the novel's protagonist, and both undergo a series of ordeals, including a kind of death, before they are redeemed through the gods' intervention. This reading draws on the Platonic idea of the union of the soul (Psyche) with love (Cupid/Eros), producing eternal joy (Voluptas). Christian commentators, including Fulgentius (468–533), have interpreted the tale in line with their belief that the soul is meant to be united with God, as the church is the bride of Christ. More recently, analysts in the Freudian and Jungian traditions, pursuing **psychological approaches** to the study of fairy tales, have read it as a story of (usually feminine) psychological or sexual development. Bruno **Bettelheim**, for example, claims that Psyche's experience symbolizes the necessary overcoming of a girl's sexual anxieties and the mature, hard-won union of **sexuality** and wisdom. *See also* Animal Bride, Animal Groom; Initiation.

Further Readings: Apuleius. *Cupid and Psyche*. Edited by E. J. Kenney. Cambridge: Cambridge University Press, 1990; Cavicchioli, Sonia. *The Tale of Cupid and Psyche: An Illustrated History*. New York: Braziller, 2002; Gollnick, James. *Love and the Soul: Psychological Interpretations of the Eros and Psyche Myth*. Waterloo, Ontario: Wilfrid Laurier University Press, 1992; Swahn, Jan-Öjvind. *The Tale of Cupid and Psyche*. Lund: CWK Gleerup, 1955.

Virginia E. Swain

D

Dadié, Bernard Binlin (1916–)

Bernard Binlin Dadié is a West African playwright, novelist, and **folktale** collector who published in French. Born in Assinie, Ivory Coast, of Agni ethnic origin, Dadié became a civil servant in the colonial administration in 1939 and served in Dakar, Senegal, until 1947. After returning to his home country, he became an activist in the independence movement, which brought him a jail sentence of sixteen months. From 1957 to 1985, Dadié held several senior ministerial offices, including the post of the country's minister of culture. His poetic, dramatic, and fictional writings take a stand against colonial oppression, negotiate between modern and traditional conditions, and issue African satirical perceptions of life in Paris, Rome, and New York.

Dadié published four editions of folktales: *Légendes africaines* (*African Legends,* 1954), *Le pagne noir: Contes africains* (1955; translated as *The Black Cloth: A Collection of African Folktales*, 1987), *Les belles histoires de Kacou Ananzè, l'araignée* (with André Terrisse; *The Wonderful Stories of Kacou Annanzè, the Spider*, 1963), and *Les contes de Koutou-as-Samala* (*The Tales of Koutou-as-Samala*, 1982). The *Legends,* which tell of interactions between animals and humans, are "a lie, but a lie that contains a teaching from which to profit, a lesson in prudence, generosity, patience, and indispensable wisdom for the guidance of mankind and necessary for the stability of the society," as Dadié stated in a lecture he gave during the First Congress of Black Writers and Artists in Paris 1956 ("Le rôle de la légende," 167). The principal character of the stories in *The Black Cloth* is Kacou Ananzè, a spider who is cunning, clever, skillful, and sly. In the first group of stories, he triumphs over his victims; in the second, he is punished for his egoism and thoughtlessness. The title of the collection derives from a story in which a cruel stepmother sends little Aiwa to wash the pitch-dark loincloth white. Aiwa sets out on a quest with many tests until her deceased mother relieves her by exchanging the black cloth for a white one. The other two collections constitute a schoolbook with didactic apparatus and an edition for young people. The latter contains the widespread story of a girl who chooses her husband on her own. He is just a skull that she must discover step by step and escape from in a dramatic flight, which is followed by insightful maturity.

Dadié's intention in these works is to edit the oral tales as an affirmation of African cultural identity and as an assertion of African literary values against colonial and postcolonial cultural estrangement. Accordingly, certain tales—for example "Les premiers aveugles" ("The First Blindmen") from *The Tales of Koutou-as-Samala*—can be interpreted in straight political terms. In his essays, Dadié has developed a comparative perspective on the humanism and universality of African tale themes, which are related to European tale traditions. In choosing the medium of writing, he did not opt for his mother tongue, Agni, but for French, a language of wider circulation in the Ivory Coast, West Africa, and the world. Dadié now stands alongside his contemporaries Birago **Diop** and Léopold Sédar Senghor. *See also* Anansi; Collecting, Collectors; Colonialism.

Further Readings: Dadié, Bernard Bilin. "Le conte, élément de solidarité et d'universalité." *Présence Africaine* 27–28 (1959): 69–80; _____. "Folklore and Literature." Translated by C. L. Patterson. *The Proceedings of the First International Congress of Africanists, Accra, 11th–18th December 1962*. Edited by Lalage Brown and Michael Crowder. Evanston: Northwestern University Press, 1964. 199–219; _____. "Le rôle de la légende dans la culture populaire des noirs d'Afrique." *Présence Africaine* 14–15 (1957): 165–74; Edebiri, Unionmwam, ed. *Bernard Dadié: Hommages et Études.* Ivry-sur-Seine: Nouvelles du Sud. 1992; Egonu, Iheanachor. "The Nature and Scope of Traditional Folk Literature." *Présence Africaine* 144 (1987): 109–17; Erickson, John D. *Nommo: African Fiction in French South of the Sahara.* York, SC: French Literature Publications, 1979. 35–90; Wynchank, Anny. "Transition from an Oral to a Written Literature in Francophone West Africa." *African Studies* 44.2 (1985): 189–95.

Thomas Geider

Dahl, Roald (1916–1990)

Roald Dahl was a best-selling British author of novels, short stories, and screen plays for adults and books and fairy-tale retellings for children. Intertextual references to fairy tales abound in Dahl's works: when James sows the magic seeds that produce his giant peach (*James and the Giant Peach*, 1961), or when Sophie travels to a land of man-eating giants (*The B.F.G,* 1982), the reader is reminded of "Jack and the Beanstalk." Other books draw on stock fairy-tale characters, such as *The Witches* (1983), or on typical folktale patterns, such as underdog protagonists who go on adventures, meet **magic helper**s, and end up living happily ever after.

In *Revolting Rhymes* (1982), illustrated by Quentin Blake, Dahl parodies six popular tales in humorous verse. His colloquial style, specked with curses and swear words, clashes with the solemn and sentimental tone of Jacob and Wilhelm **Grimm**, Hans Christian **Andersen**, and Charles **Perrault**. In "**Cinderella**," Dahl makes his antiauthoritarian view on education explicit, as well as his critique of the bourgeoisification of the fairy tale. The narrator explains that adults cooked up a "sappy" version of the story "Just to keep the children happy." He then continues to tell the "true" version of the tale, which now has a grotesquely bloody ending: the **prince** chops off several heads and calls Cinderella a "dirty slut." Although Dahl has often been accused of antifeminist attitudes, his Red Riding Hood is no easy

Roald Dahl. [Library of Congress]

victim: she shoots the **wolf** with a gun that she pulls from her knickers, and turns him into a wolfskin coat.

In *Rhyme Stew* (1989), the sequel to *Revolting Rhymes*, Dahl draws upon a varied collection of source material, from **fable**s ("The Tortoise and the Hare") to nursery legends ("Dick Whittington and His **Cat**"), as well as fairy tales and the **Arabian Nights**. Dahl's retelling of "**Hansel and Gretel**" explicitly attacks Wilhelm Grimm for adapting the tales and for his lack of humor. He goes along with Andersen's social satire in "The Emperor's New Clothes" but adds a different ending: the emperor freezes to death when he goes skiing without his **clothes**.

Traditionally, Dahl's books are beloved by children but disapproved of by parents and teachers. The folktale has been used in defense of Dahl's work: his use of scatological references, flat characterization, **violence**, and grotesque humor is said to be rooted in the **folk** tradition from which he drew inspiration. *See also* Anti-Fairy Tale; Children's Literature; Intertextuality; Parody.

Further Readings: Beckett, Sandra L. "Perverse, Pistol-Packing Riding Hoods." *Recycling Red Riding Hood.* New York: Routledge, 2002. 124–29; Culley, Jonathon. "Roald Dahl—'It's About Children and It's for Children'—But Is It Suitable?" *Children's Literature in Education* 22 (1991): 59–73; Tal, Eve. "Deconstructing the Peach: *James and the Giant Peach* as Post-Modern Fairy Tale." *Journal of the Fantastic in the Arts* 14 (2003): 265–76.

Vanessa Joosen

Dance

Although earlier productions of fairy-tale ballets were registered in dance history books and dictionaries—for example, **Cinderella** was choreographed by Charles Didelot for the Paris Opera Ballet in 1823—the genre blossomed with Marius Petipa's monumental pieces based on **literary fairy tale**s in late nineteenth-century Russia. Working for the St. Petersburg Imperial Theater and Maryinsky Company, he created **Sleeping Beauty** (1890); *The Nutcracker*, choreographed with his assistant Lev Ivanov (1892); *Cinderella* (1893), created with Ivanov and Italian choreographer Enrico Cechetti; **Bluebeard** (1896); and *The Magic Mirror* (1903).

The Romantic era of the beginning of nineteenth-century Europe, with its infatuation with the supernatural and the ethereal ideal of the ballerina, had set the ground for the fairy-tale ballet format. Nevertheless, it was only with Marius Petipa that fairy tales turned into prototypes for ballet librettos, as he managed to parallel the fairy tale's magical shifts with postures demanded by the ballet steps. The choreographer also depicted male and female dancers in a contrasting manner that reinforced **gender** notions perpetuated in the balletic world from then on. The ballerina became the center of all attention, gaining a status that was equivalent to that of the fairy-tale heroines in the literary stories, particularly since Charles **Perrault**'s tales of 1697. The notions of ballet as a graceful, pure, and feminized art became universal.

Examples of fairy tales turned into ballet productions abound. The first of George Balanchine's ballets to be shown in Paris in 1925 was *The Song of the Nightingale*, based on Hans Christian **Andersen**'s tale. *Le baiser de la fée (The Fairy's Kiss)* was choreographed by Balanchine in 1937 for the American Ballet Company and by Frederick Ashton for the

Sadler's Wells Ballet, while *Beauty and the Beast* was choreographed by John Crancko, also for the Sadler's Wells, in 1949. *Bluebeard,* after Petipa, was conceived by Michel Fokine in 1941 and produced by the Ballet Theater in New York.

Other specific fairy tales were used in an even larger number of productions. After Didelot and the St. Petersburg production of 1893 by Cecchetti, Ivanov, and Petipa, *Cinderella* was produced in 1938, choreographed by Michel Fokine for the Original Ballet Russe. There was also a 1945 production by Rostislav Zakharov for the Bolshoi Ballet in Moscow, the first to use Sergey Prokofiev's score; and also American productions, beginning with the one created for the National Ballet of Washington, D.C., by Ben Stevenson in 1970.

Peter and the Wolf, considered a contemporary fairy tale—it was created by Sergei Prokofiev himself in 1936 for orchestra—had a first ballet version conceived by Adolph Bolm for the Ballet Theater in 1940. Many other productions followed, such as Ivo Cramer's for the Norwegian National Ballet, Niels B. Larsen's for the Royal Danish Ballet in 1960, a 1969 version choreographed by Jacques D'Amboise for the New York City Ballet, and a 1992 **adaptation** by Michael Smuin for the American Ballet Theater.

Sleeping Beauty, after Petipa, was choreographed by Bronislava Nijinska (1960), as well as by Sergeyev for the Sadler's Wells in 1946, and a additional version was choreographed by Frederick Ashton and Ninette de Valois. Finally, T*he Nutcracker*, after Ivanov and under Petipa's auspices, was choreographed by Sergeyev for the Sadler's Wells in 1934. It was first presented in American stages in 1934 in a production of the Ballets Russes of Monte Carlo in 1940 and was restaged by Balanchine for the New York City Ballet in 1954.

While the fairy tale became almost a paradigm for the ballet, it was eventually rejected by the modern dance world. The modernist project in dance corresponded less to the experiments with abstraction developed in the visual arts and more to a search for essential emotions, social engagement, and expressive movement.

In the 1930s and 1940s, American choreographers such as Martha Graham and Doris Humphrey denied ballet's tendency to become a virtuosic showcase. Graham, for example, choreographed a cycle of dances based on Greek mythology dealing with **archetype**s of universal emotions, such as passion, guilt, and redemption, as well as symbolic marks of life's cycle.

In contrast, during the 1960s and 1970s, the urge for expression and drama launched by modern dancers was questioned and eventually abandoned by a new generation of choreographers known as the postmodern dance choreographers. During its initial developments, **postmodernism** in dance did not refer to the notions of historical references, pastiche, irony, and nostalgia, attributes associated with the postmodern condition in cultural history and art. In fact, the term "postmodern dance" has been coined by some dance critics, particularly Sally Banes and Noel Carroll, in reference to a generation's reaction to expression in modern dance as it was propagated by choreographers such as Martha Graham and Doris Humphrey.

Influenced by Merce Cunningham, choreographers such as Yvonne Rainer, Trisha Brown, Douglas Dunn, David Gordon, Laura Dean, and others proposed that the formalist quality of dance could be reason enough for choreography. Another idea was the use of pedestrian movements and clothing, a reaction against the elitist condition imposed by specifically trained bodies.

Since the mid-1980s, however, narrative has returned and become the center of preoccupations of the new dance generations. It has been again infatuated with content, meaning, and historical references. But the rebirth of narrative is not simply a return to older values or storytelling techniques. The way the new generation deals with narrative incorporates the developments of postmodern dance in its deliberate dismantling of literary devices, fragmentation, and ambiguity of interpretation. In contrast to the theatrical illusions fostered by Graham or Humphrey, the new choreographers create pieces that are partially expressive and partially abstract, playing with perception and interpretation.

The consistent use of narrative has become an anchor for representation, with the audiences being given recognizable material, which guarantees that they will remain dance patrons. For an appetite for meaning and conventions, fairy tales appear as exemplary narrative. In fact, the new dance choreographers' focus is not on the telling of the tale, but on experiments about how to narrate it. They profit from the fact that fairy tales are well-known narrative frames and play with them, using them to question artistic media, the relation of high art and mass cultures, gender roles,and political issues.

German *Tanztheater* (dance theater) choreographer Pina Bausch has been an inspiration for an entire generation of new dance choreographers worldwide. The presentation of harsh emotional content in Bausch's pieces allow other choreographers to make use of emotion too, as opposed to keeping dance as a structural, abstract art form. Unlike fairy-tale ballets, Bausch's *Bluebeard* (1977) does not follow a narrative line imposed by the **music**. Using only tape-recorded spurts of Béla **Bartók**'s one-act **opera**, *Bluebeard's Castle*, it develops an onslaught of movement metaphors of the impasse between the sexes.

In France, Maguy Marin has choreographed a new version of *Cinderella* (1985) for the Lyon Opera Ballet. Marin, who belongs to a contemporary generation of French choreographers named *danse nouvelle,* combines a background in classical ballet, modern dance, and **theater**. At first glance, Marin's *Cinderella* seems a cheerful, delicate modern ballet, with dancers as masked dolls retelling Perrault's fairy tale. Nevertheless, the work is loaded with an ironic comment about our cliché notions of prettiness, happiness, and **childhood**.

In the United States, many choreographers have been using fairy tales in jigsaw-puzzle ways, combining a generalized excitement toward **storytelling** with the pure formalist interplays developed by their postmodern predecessors of the 1960s and 1970s. The ballet company Kinematic's *The Handless Maiden* (1987) based on the **Grimm**s' "Das Mädchen ohne Hände" ("The Maiden without Hands") is a good example. The dance company formed by Tamar Kotoske, Maria Lakis, and Mary Richter combined different techniques to recreate this tale onstage. The work begins with the creation of scripts that are collages made with the libretto and other literary sources. The group then composes the movements under the voiced text, according to the sounds of the words. The result is astonishing.

The Nutcracker, based on E. T. A. **Hoffmann**'s literary fairy tale *Nußknacker und Mausekönig (The Nutcracker and the Mouse King,* 1816) is another fairy-tale classic that has been consistently staged by contemporary choreographers. One of its most intriguing versions is Mark Morris's *The Hard Nut* (1991), which uses Pyotr Il'ich **Tchaikovsky**'s music to build both a scary and a very ironic piece, with movements and costumes that remind us of the comic book's sensibility.

Further Reading: Canton, Katia. *The Fairytale Revisited: A Survey of the Evolution of the Tales, from Classical Literary Interpretations to Innovative Contemporary Dance-Theater Productions.* New York: Peter Lang, 1994.

Katia Canton

Daudet, Alphonse (1840–1897)

Born in Nîmes, Alphonse Daudet moved to Paris in 1857, and he started his career writing for newspapers before becoming known as a talented short-story writer and novelist. He is mostly remembered for his *Lettres de mon moulin* (*Letters from My Mill,* 1866), a collection of skillfully crafted tales that find their inspiration in the lore of Daudet's beloved Provence. Among them, "La chèvre de Monsieur Seguin" ("Mr. Seguin's Goat"), a children's favorite, is still published in illustrated editions in French and has been translated, like much of his work, into English. Daudet's genius lay in his ability to retell meridional **folktale**s in a pure French language and yet with a distinct southern style. The most famous regional tales that Daudet wrote can be found in the trilogy that he devoted to the adventures of a truculent Provençal character who likes to tell **tall tale**s and jokes: *Tartarin de Tarascon* (*Tartarin of Tarascon,* 1872), *Tartarin sur les Alpes* (*Tartarin on the Alps,* 1885), and *Port Tarascon* (1890).

In addition to his regionally inspired tales, Daudet published adaptations of well-known tales such as "**Little Red Riding Hood**" and "**Bluebeard**" to conform to the values of his time. This is evident in *Le roman du chaperon-rouge* (*The Novel of Red Riding Hood,* 1862), which—as the subtitle tells us—includes "scenes and fantasies," among them the title story and "Les sept pendues de barbe-bleue" ("The Seven Hanged Wives of Bluebeard"). Daudet's *Contes du lundi* (*Monday Tales,* 1875) offers stories that create a sharp image of France in the context of the Franco-Prussian war. Daudet wrote two children's stories that he dedicated to his son Lucien, *Les cigognes (The Storks)* in 1884 and *La Belle-Nivernaise* in 1886.

Further Reading: MacNamara, Matthew. "Some Oral Narrative Forms in *Lettres de mon moulin.*" *Modern Language Review* 67 (1972): 291–99.

Claire L. Malarte-Feldman

Davenport, Tom (1939–)

Tom Davenport, an independent filmmaker, produced some of the most innovative folktale **adaptation**s of the late twentieth century in his live-action film series, From the Brothers Grimm: American Versions of Folktale Classics. A native of Washington, D.C., and graduate of Yale University, Davenport spent several years studying Chinese and teaching English in Hong Kong and Taiwan. His work in New York with documentary filmmakers Richard Leacock and Don Pennebacker led to the production of his first independent film in 1969. In 1970, he settled in Delaplane, Virginia, where he works as a farmer, filmmaker, and film distributor. Since 1971, his wife, Mimi Davenport, has served as designer and artistic director for their independent company Davenport Films, which has produced documentaries about American folklife and eleven films in the folktale series.

While reading to his young sons, Davenport recognized how deeply traditional fairy tales appealed to the psychological needs of children. Realizing that historical scenes filmed in rural Virginia could seem like faraway magical settings to modern children, the Davenports produced ***Hansel and Gretel***: *An Appalachian Version* in 1975, a sixteen-minute film in which poor parents abandon their children during the Great Depression. Subsequent short films based on tales of the Brothers **Grimm** were *Rapunzel, Rapunzel* (1979), *The* ***Frog King*** (1980), *Bearskin, or The Man Who Didn't Wash for Seven Years* (1982), *The Goose Girl* (1983), and *Bristlelip* (1982).

Still photo from Tom Davenport's *Jack and the Dentist's Daughter*. [Copyright © Tom Davenport. Used by permission.]

The remaining five films are somewhat longer, more sophisticated productions (from forty to eighty-five minutes), with regional Appalachian sources as well as European antecedents. "Soldier Jack," "Ashpet," "Mutsmag," and "Jack and the Doctor's Girl" all appear in Richard Chase's Appalachian folktale collections from the 1940s. In 1983, Davenport adapted the last of these tales as *Jack and the Dentist's Daughter* with an African American cast because he thought Jack's humorous tricks to win the hand of a girl with a socially superior, disapproving father fit well into the **trickster** tradition in African American folklore.

The specific historical settings, with authentic costumes, props, songs, and other details, range from seventeenth-century colonial America in *The Goose Girl* to the Civil War in *Bearskin* and the World War II era in *Soldier Jack* (1988) and *Ashpet* (1990). Soldier Jack, a war veteran, saves the president's daughter and captures **death** in a sack until he realizes that dying naturally is better than aging eternally. In *Ashpet: An American **Cinderella***, a soldier instead of a **prince** woos the heroine, who develops self-reliance while a wise neighbor helps her recover the property, memories, and love of **storytelling** left by her dead **mother**.

Davenport's films contain humorous and satiric touches, such as the dinner scene in *The Frog King*, when a real frog splashing around on the table horrifies refined Victorian guests. But these films also retain the integrity and serious themes of old fairy tales. As the series developed, Davenport became most interested in appealing to the often-neglected audience of preteen and adolescent girls. Characters such as Ashpet, Mutzmag, and Willa, who rely less on magical help than their European counterparts, use inner strengths and ingenuity to overcome obstacles that are more realistic than fantastical. Gothic details in *Mutzmag: An Appalachian Folktale* (1992) create an atmosphere of terror as spunky Mutzmag outsmarts a **witch** and a giant (played by a large, violent man without elaborate special effects), while Mutzmag's role as narrator reassures the audience that she will triumph in the end. Mutzmag and most of the supporting roles were played by high school students from Madison County, North Carolina.

*Willa: An American **Snow White*** (1996) is a more polished, innovative feature-length adaptation of European and Appalachian folktales, blending real Virginia settings, historically accurate elements of American popular culture, and intertextual allusions to sources from William **Shakespeare** to Charles **Dickens** to classic movies about young heroines and jealous older **women**, such as *Sunset Boulevard* (1950) and *Rebecca* (1940). Its sources include "A Stepchild That Was Treated Mighty Bad," a Kentucky tale collected by Marie Campbell around 1935. The Snow White character, fleeing from a violent stepmother who is an aging actress, stays with three men in a traveling medicine show in 1915, before leaving with a young filmmaker headed for California. Her virtues and acting talents help raise the level of the entertainment and ethical standards in the rural medicine show.

In 1992, Davenport and writer Gary Carden, who coauthored the script of *Willa*, published storybook versions of all of the films except *Willa* in *From the Brothers Grimm: A Contemporary Retelling of American Folktales and Classic Stories*. Davenport encourages educators and others, especially teenagers, to explore **folklore** history and the processes of filmmaking. He provides a wealth of background material on the folkloric, literary, and cinematic origins of his films through articles, teaching guides, interviews, and Web sites. *The Making of the Frog King* (1981) and the three-part *Making Grimm Movies* (1993) are short films about creating fairy-tale illusions for low-budget films.

Early in its development, the series attracted support from arts foundations, the National Endowment for the Humanities, and the Corporation for Public Broadcasting. The films have appeared many times on educational **television** and won numerous awards, including, for *Willa,* the 1998 Andrew Carnegie Medal for Excellence in Children's Video. Critics such as Jack **Zipes** praise Davenport's experimental approach to providing thoughtful, original alternatives to Walt **Disney**'s fairy-tale films and empowering young people to understand modern media.

Many of Davenport's documentary films focus on Southern American folklife and oral history. They include films about storytellers, such as John E. Joines, Arthur "Peg Leg Sam" Jackson, and Louise Anderson (who played the wise helper in *Ashpet*). *The Ballad of Frankie Silver* (1996) explores a legendary North Carolina murder. *See also* African American Tales; Beech Mountain Jack Tale; Cinderella Films; Film and Video; Intertextuality; Jack Tales.

Further Readings: *Davenport Films & From the Brothers Grimm*. Davenport Films. http://www.davenportfilms.com; Manna, Anthony L. "The Americanization of the Brothers Grimm: Or, Tom Davenport's Film Adaptation of German Folktales." *Children's Literature Association Quarterly* 13 (1988): 142–45; Zipes, Jack. "Once upon a Time beyond Disney: Contemporary Fairy-Tale Films for Children." *Happily Ever After: Fairy Tales, Children, and the Culture Industry*. New York: Routledge, 1997. 89–110.

Tina L. Hanlon

Dazai Osamu (1909–1948)

Japanese author Dazai Osamu is best known for his highly autobiographical short stories and novels; he is also renowned for revising and retelling literary classics and canonical folktales and fairy tales. Born Tsushima Shūji in Kanagi, Aomori Prefecture, Dazai entered Tokyo Imperial University in 1930 to study French literature. Within six months of arriving in Tokyo, Dazai had abandoned his studies in favor of writing. He took his pen name in 1933, and his first collection, *Bannen* (*The Final Years*), appeared in 1936. Alongside the overtly autobiographical stories in *The Final Years*, there are others that draw less on personal experience and instead utilize fragments of folktales and **legend**s as well as narrative techniques derived from fairy tales. During World War II, Dazai continued to find inspiration by rewriting the work of earlier authors, including Friedrich Schiller, William **Shakespeare**, and Ihara Saikaku. Some of these stories have been collected in *Blue Bamboo* (1993), an anthology of Dazai's short fiction that also includes tales appropriated and retold from sources as diverse as Pú Sōnglíng and the **Grimm** brothers.

Dazai's enduring interest in the fairy-tale genre culminated in 1945 with the publication of the critically acclaimed *Otogizōshi* (*Fairy Tales*), a retelling of the popular **Japanese** tales "Kobutori" ("Taking the Wen Away"), "Urashima-san" ("The Tale of Urashima"), "Shitakiri suzume" ("The Tongue-Cut Sparrow"), and "Kachikachi yama" ("Crackling Mountain"). After the war, Dazai returned to his more familiar autobiographical mode to write his two best-selling novels, *Shayō* (*The Setting Sun*, 1947) and *Ningen shikkaku* (*No Longer Human*, 1948).

Further Readings: Dazai Osamu. *Crackling Mountain and Other Stories*. Translated by James O'Brien. Rutland, VT: Tuttle, 1989; Lyons, Phyllis I. *The Saga of Dazai Osamu: A Critical Study with Translations*. Stanford, CA: Stanford University Press, 1985.

Marc Sebastian-Jones

De Lint, Charles (1951–)

Canadian author Charles de Lint writes **novel**s and short stories that incorporate **motif**s from folk narrative—**myth**, **legend**, **ballad**, and **folktale**. De Lint's most notable creation is the mythical North American town of Newford, where characters from **Native American tales** and myths interact with creatures of European legends and folktales. Many of de Lint's characters are musicians, artists, social workers, and street people who are likely to violate interdictions and cross boundaries that lead to other worlds.

De Lint's works do not slavishly follow fairy-tale plots. His novel *Jack, the Giant-Killer* (1987) features urban heroine Jacky Rowan and her friend Kate Hazel. Jacky corresponds to the **trickster** Jack of European folktales, while Kate alludes to Kate Crackernuts. Other characters come from both fairy tales and legends: trolls, giants, and princes who change between human and swan shapes through nettle shirts.

His first Newford story collection, *Dreams Underfoot* (1993), is characteristic of his melding of folkloric genres and tropes from modern fiction. Most of the stories have bittersweet endings, differentiating them from the happy or didactic endings of their sources. "Our Lady of the Harbor" retells Hans Christian **Andersen**'s "The Little Mermaid," whereas "The Moon Is Drowning While I Sleep" plays with fairy-tale tropes in a modern heroine's dreams. Typically, de Lint uses folk narrative material to validate both tradition and creativity in the lives of his characters. ***See also*** Vess, Charles.

Further Readings: De Lint, Charles. *Dreams Underfoot*. New York: Orb, 1993; _____. *Jack, the Giant-Killer*. New York: Ace Books, 1987.

Jeana Jorgensen

De Morgan, Mary (1850–1907)

In a period noted for its evolving **literary fairy tale**, the British Victorian author Mary de Morgan played a central, comprehensive role. Coming of age in the era of Pre-Raphaelitism and its aesthetic descendants, having inherited the lore of the Brothers **Grimm** and John **Ruskin**, de Morgan honed her craft telling original tales to the William Morris, Edward Burne-Jones, and Kipling clans. De Morgan's first published collection, *On a Pincushion and Other Fairy Tales* (1877), featured woodcuts by her artist brother, William de Morgan. While respectful of their roots in **folktale**, these stories also translated contemporary issues such as the woman question ("A Toy Princess") and the wages of industrialism ("Siegfrid and Handa"). Other sturdy pieces include "The Seeds of Love" and "Through the

Fire." Walter **Crane** illustrated the even stronger second collection, *The Necklace of Princess Fiorimonde and Other Stories* (1880).

The trials of the human heart, the marketplace, and the body politic are explored in such memorable tales as the title story, "The Wanderings of Arasmon," "The Bread of Discontent," and "The Three Clever Kings." A third volume, *The Windfairies and Other Tales*, appeared in 1900. Though not as well known as its predecessors, it contains selections— "The Gipsy's Cup" and "The Ploughman and the Gnome"—worthy of joining de Morgan's anthologized tales. *See also* Children's Literature.

Further Reading: Fowler, James. "The Golden Harp: Mary de Morgan's Centrality in Victorian Fairy-Tale Literature." *Children's Literature* 33 (2005): 224–36.

James Fowler

Dean, Pamela (1953–)

Pamela Dean Dyer-Bennet, a founding member of the Scribblies, a Minneapolis-based writing group, is also affiliated with the Pre-Joycean Fellowship. Her writing, which is grounded in **folklore** and fairy tales and which stylistically hearkens back to the nineteenth century while set in a variety of times and places, certainly reflects both associations. Dean's first published works were stories in the Liavek shared-world anthologies published by Emma Bull and Will Shetterly. Appropriately, her Secret Country trilogy—including *The Secret Country* (1985), *The Hidden Land* (1986), and *The Whim of the Dragon* (1989)—concerned a similar conceit, as a friends' role-playing game became reality: Dean revisited the realm of *The Secret Country* in her 1994 stand-alone **fantasy** novel, *The Dubious Hills*.

Dean's next major work, the cult-classic novel *Tam Lin* (1991), ventured further into the realm of **faerie**, taking its basis from the sixteenth-century Scottish **ballad** of the same name. *Tam Lin* is set during the 1970s at Blackstock College (loosely based on Dean's own alma mater of Carleton College) and concerns the travails of one Janet Carter and her circle of friends. However, Janet's circle of friends includes more than just the typical assortment of eccentric, budding intellectuals; it also overlaps with the court of faerie, pursuing liberal arts degrees as a kind of entertainment while still, somehow, trying to meet the conditions of their necessary tithe to hell. Dean's other ballad-based novel, the young-adult-oriented *Juniper, Gentian and Rosemary* (1998), is more loosely based upon the Scottish ballad "Riddles Wisely Expounded." *See also* Young Adult Fiction.

Further Reading: Perry, Evelyn M. "The Ever-Vigilant Hero: Revaluing the Tale of Tam Lin." *Children's Folklore Review* 19.2 (1997): 31–49.

Helen Pilinovsky

Death

Death is, like all human conditions, such as **birth**, child/parent relationships, marriage, and procreation, an indispensable element in **folklore**, appearing in some way in most folktales and fairy tales. The origin of the **motif** is manifest in all world mythologies, explaining humankind's passage from immortality toward demise by some fatal incident, often offense and punishment (for example, the Bible's description of the Fall). Death is thus the most essential difference between gods and human beings. Folktale motifs involving death and rebirth are based on the archaic ideas of circular, cyclical time, as opposed to the linear, measurable time, in which death is definite and irreversible. The **myth**s of the dying and returning god are connected with the earliest solar and lunar worship, where the sun is devoured by a monster every day and reappears in the morning, while the moon is slowly dying and recovering during a month.

In the plot structure of folktales and fairy tales, death has several functions. Many tales begin with the death of one or both of the hero's parents, which radically changes the hero's status and initiates his maturation process. As the hero is usually the youngest son, the older brother takes over the deceased **father**'s position, while the hero has to depart in search of a better fortune. Alternatively, the remaining parent remarries, and the stepparent becomes the primary antagonist of the hero, trying to gain privileges for his or her own offspring. The dead parent can transform into an animal (such as a cow or a bird) and assist the oppressed orphan; a later version, more frequently employed in **literary fairy tale**s, is a substitute parent, such as a **fairy** godmother. At the end of the tale, the antagonist is sometimes punished by death, often of an extremely violent torture.

During his trials, the hero may encounter death in many shapes and situations. Peripheral characters are dispensable and killed off without much regret. A common motif is the hero being slain, devoured or even dismembered either by the antagonist or by envious rivals. This element goes back to the myth of the eternal return, in which death is not only reversible but necessary for the further welfare of humanity. Some **etiologic tale**s and myths trace the origin of a certain landscape in the scattered body parts of the hero; most often, the resurrected hero brings back fertility and prosperity to his people. In folktales, the **magic helper** provides some means to bring the hero back to life, such as the Water of Death (to glue the cut parts together; Motif E84) and the Water of Life (to revive him; Motif E80); or the hero is simply retrieved from the monster's belly unhurt (for example, "**Little Red Riding Hood**"). The hero recollects his experience as a deep long sleep, which reflects the archaic belief in the essential connection between the states of sleep and death. The tales of "**Snow White**" and "**Sleeping Beauty**" also reveal close association of temporary and permanent inactivity.

In tales involving the motif of the magical groom or bride, the hero is compelled to kill and dismember the animal spouse to disperse the spell. Death is thus perceived as the necessary transitional state between the enchantment and the true shape. Yet another universal motif is the hero descending into the realm of the dead, usually to bring back a deceased beloved (Orpheus); sometimes a **mother** tries to bring back her dead child. The endeavor fails as the hero breaks some form of prohibition: not to look back, not to talk, and so on. Accepting **food** in the realm of the dead has fatal consequences. In contrast, assisting someone dead brings generous reward. In the tale of The Grateful Dead (ATU 505), the hero rescues a corpse from defilement, and the dead becomes his magic helper.

Death also appears in folklore as a character, both male and female. In the Godfather Death **tale type** (ATU 332), a doctor makes a deal with death, who, by standing at the head or foot of a sickbed, indicates whether the patient will survive or die (Motif D1825.3.1). The doctor tries to cheat by turning the bed around and is punished by untimely death (Motif K557).

In literary fairy tales, the death motif can be modified, especially to accommodate the current views on death. In Romantic-era tales, with their typical notion of the innocent child, the death of the main character may be presented as a blessing, as in Hans Christian **Andersen**'s

"Den lille pige med svovlstikkerne" ("The Little Match Girl," 1846). Because of strong Christian values in Western **children's literature**, death was not perceived as a tragedy but as a welcome liberation from earthly worries, sometimes depicted symbolically, as in George **MacDonald**'s *At the Back of the North Wind* (1871). In "Den lille havfrue" ("The Little Mermaid," 1836), Andersen treats the fear of death through the **mermaid**'s longing for an immortal soul. At the same time, various Gothic tales widely exploited the motifs of living dead, corpse brides, vampires, and ghosts, all based on the vague border between life and death.

Modernization, urbanization, and higher standards of living in the Western world in the twentieth century made death into something alien and more terrifying. Many contemporary fairy tales and **fantasy** novels transform the folktale motif of death. Because death is still today perceived as the greatest imaginable evil and the utmost mystery, dark magical forces are always associated with death and are portrayed as destructive, as in J. R. R. **Tolkien**'s *Lord of the Rings* (1954–56). The pivotal point of C. S. **Lewis**'s *The Lion, the Witch, and the Wardrobe* (1950) is Aslan's sacrificial death and resurrection; Astrid **Lindgren**'s *Bröderna lejonhjärta* (*The Brothers Lionheart*, 1973) depicts death as a passage to a magical realm; and in Philip **Pullman**'s His Dark Materials (1995–2000), the protagonists meet their own personal death figures and descend into the realm of the dead. A comical figure of death appears in Terry **Pratchett**'s Discworld novels.

Further Readings: Ariès, Philippe. *Western Attitudes toward Death: From the Middle Ages to the Present.* Translated by Patricia M. Ranum. Baltimore: Johns Hopkins University Press, 1974; Eliade, Mircea. *The Myth of the Eternal Return.* London: Routledge & Kegan Paul, 1955; Frazer, James G. *Man, God, and Immortality.* London: Macmillan, 1927.

Maria Nikolajeva

DEFA Fairy-Tale Films

In the Soviet-controlled eastern part of defeated Germany, which was to become the German Democratic Republic (GDR) in 1949, the first full-length motion picture was produced in 1946, even before the state-operated Deutsche Film AG (German Film Company)—known as DEFA—was officially established in 1950. From the outset, films for younger audiences played a prominent role in the GDR's overall effort of forming a socialist society. Of the roughly 200 full-length children's films made in East Germany, 25 percent were **adaptation**s of fairy tales. The GDR, along with Japan, India, the Soviet Union, Czechoslovakia, and Great Britain, was one of only very few countries to produce children's films on a regular basis. Until the end of the GDR in 1990, children's films constituted approximately 20 percent of all full-length motion pictures produced. A studio for animated pictures with a focus on short films for children was created in Dresden in 1955. In 1971, the state-operated **television** network made the first full-length fairy-tale movie of its own, *Der kleine und der große Klaus* (*Little Claus and Big Claus*, directed by Celino Bleiweiss). In 1958, the GDR inaugurated its National Center for Children's Films and Television Productions (Nationales Zentrum für Kinderfilm und -fernsehen der DDR), which became a member of the UNESCO's Centre International du Film pour l'Enfance et la Jeunesse (CIFEJ) in 1960.

Film adaptations of fairy tales were not primarily geared toward grown-up audiences. Following the example of the Soviet Union, they were thought of as elements of a comprehensive educational strategy to guide young people on their way to socialism. The first two

DEFA fairy-tale films, however, were films intended for the entire family: *Das kalte Herz* (*The Cold Heart*, 1950, directed by Paul Verhoeven) and *Die Geschichte vom kleinen Muck* (*The Story of Little Mook*, 1953, directed by Wolfgang Staudte) were both adapted from nineteenth-century German tales by Wilhelm **Hauff**. These films won wide acclaim and were in fact exported worldwide. In the following decades, more than half of all fairy-tale films were adaptations of the well-known ***Kinder- und Hausmärchen*** (*Children's and Household Tales*), first published in 1812–15 by Jacob and Wilhelm Grimm. Another 20 percent were derived from the works of various, not necessarily German, fairy-tale authors such as Hans Christian **Andersen** (Danish), Hans Fallada (German), Theodor **Storm** (German), Samuil Marshak (Russian), and Václav Rezác (Czech). The fairy-tale plays by Soviet author Evgeny **Shvarts** strongly influenced the theoretical framework guiding DEFA's film production for young audiences. The remaining films were chiefly produced from original screenplays often based on children's books. Following the classification of Aarne-Thompson-Uther, the stories adapted for film mainly belong to the Tales of Magic (ATU 300–749), from which nineteen full-length motion pictures were drawn.

Between 1946 and 1990, fifteen different directors were involved in the making of full-length DEFA fairy-tale adaptations, including film productions for television. Siegfried Kolditz, for example, had directed **opera**s on stage before he began shooting motion pictures. When working with the DEFA, he mainly directed general entertainment pictures. His first fairy-tale film, *Die goldene Jurte* (*The Golden Tent*, 1961), a coproduction with the Mongolian Republic, was based on a Mongolian folktale. Its huge success with the general public was largely due to its opulent decor and exotic setting. Kolditz's further fairy-tale adaptations, *Schneewittchen* (**Snow White**, 1961) and *Frau Holle* (*Mrs. Holle*, 1963), were designed to reach the youngest audience. Filmed in somewhat simpler settings than his first production, they closely followed the texts by the Brothers Grimm.

Walter Beck began his career by filming documentaries, but he soon discovered that making children's films was his true calling. He shot more fairy-tale films than any other DEFA director and also wrote numerous articles delineating his theoretical ideas on fairy-tale adaptation, **pedagogy**, and socialist humanity. Between 1959 and 1990, he directed fifteen pictures for a younger audience, six of which were fairy-tale films. His adaptations of a number of Grimms' tales were particularly successful: *König Drosselbart* (*King Throstlebeard*, 1965), *Der Prinz hinter den sieben Meeren* (*The Prince beyond the Seven Seas*, 1982), and *Der Bärenhäuter* (*The Bear-Skinned Man*, 1986). His films triggered considerable controversy because their styles differed from mainstream fairy-tale adaptations. Since Beck wanted his young audience to remain aware of the artificial character of the fairy-tale world he presented to them, his movies were filmed entirely in the studio, without any location shooting involved.

Rainer Simon began his career with two very successful fairy-tale films: *Wie heiratet man einen König?* (*How to Marry a King*, 1969) and *Sechse kommen durch die Welt* (*Six Go round the World*, 1972). He is said to have turned his attention toward children's films to avoid disagreement with DEFA and Socialist Party authorities over issues of production and style in movies for the general public. The two fairy-tale films he made nevertheless caused heated discussions because they broke up the familiar dichotomy between good and evil, which structures the plot of most fairy tales. In Simon's films, the protagonists' actions are no longer predictable from a theoretical, that is, socialist point of view. He augmented the stories by including psychological motivation, wittiness, and a sense of humor. The celebrated fairy-tale films of Czech and Russian origin found their equal in these DEFA pictures.

In a socialist country such as the GDR, the guiding aesthetic principles of socialist realism even applied to fairy-tale films. While films were being shot or edited, they often had to be changed according to the cultural administration's ideas. Konrad Petzold's *Das Kleid* (*The Dress*, 1961), for example—an adaptation of "The Emperor's New Clothes"—was banned for political reasons and was released only in 1991. *See also* Film and Video; Mother Holle; Soviet Fairy-Tale Films.

Further Readings: Creeser, Rosemary. "Cocteau for Kids: Rediscovering *The Singing Ringing Tree.*" *Cinema and the Realms of Enchantment: Lectures, Seminars and Essays by Marina Warner and Others.* Edited by Duncan Petrie. London: British Film Institute, 1993. 111–24; *DEFA Film Library.* University of Massachusetts Amherst. http://www.umass.edu/defa/; König, Ingelore, Dieter Wiedemann, and Lothar Wolf, eds. *Zwischen Marx und Muck: DEFA-Filme für Kinder.* Berlin: Henschel, 1996.

Willi Höfig

Dégh, Linda (1920–)

Born in Hungary, Linda Dégh is one of the most prominent folktale scholars of the twentieth century. Her influential scholarship has focused primarily on the relationship among narratives, performers, and societies. One of Dégh's important early works is *Folktales and Society: Story-Telling in a Hungarian Peasant Community,* originally published in German as *Märchen, Erzähler und Erzählgemeinschaft dargestellt an der ungarischen Volksüberlieferung* (1962). In this volume, Dégh studies folktales based on their role in society, exploring connections to cultural identity, subject matter, and **performance** context. Drawing on Dégh's research among the Szekelers in Hungary, *Folktales and Society* established the roles that **märchen** played in European peasant life, where they served as more than simple entertainment.

After coming to America in the 1960s, Dégh began to focus more on **legend**s and personal narratives, but she returned to folktale work in her book *American Folklore and the Mass Media* (1994). Here, she examines how märchen are used in the American media. She considers in particular the influence that fairy tales and folktales have on gendered socialization and the ways in which models of wish fulfillment from märchen and legend are used in American **advertising**.

Dégh, who published frequently with her late husband Andrew Vazsonyi, has shown a great deal of versatility in her scholarship. Through the years, she has worked on two continents and in many different genres, and her influence on subsequent generations of scholars has been significant.

Further Readings: Dégh, Linda. *American Folklore and the Mass Media.* Bloomington: Indiana University Press. 1994; _____. *Folktales and Society: Story-Telling in a Hungarian Peasant Community.* Translated by Emily M. Schossberger. Expanded edition. Bloomington: Indiana University Press, 1989.

B. Grantham Aldred

Delarue, Paul (1889–1956)

Paul Delarue was a French folklorist whose efforts in compiling all of the **folktale** versions collected in France and Francophone countries during the late nineteenth and early twentieth centuries culminated in *Le conte populaire français: Catalogue raisonné des* *versions de France et des pays de langue française d'outre-mer* (*The French Folktale: Structured Catalog of Versions from France and French-Language Countries Overseas,* 4 vols., 1957–2000). This catalogue follows the Aarne-Thompson index of **tale type**s while adapting it to the French domain. Having edited and annotated the first volume, which included a history of the French folktale and a critical bibliography, Delarue died before its publication in 1957. The subsequent three volumes were published in 1964, 1976, and 1985–2000 by Marie-Louise **Tenèze** in keeping with Delarue's approach.

Delarue became first interested in the **folklore**, especially the folksongs, of his native Nivernais region while working as an elementary school teacher. In 1934, he began classifying the collection of the late folklorist Achille Millien. Delarue participated in the first international folklorist conference in Paris (1937) and soon became affiliated with the French Society of Ethnography. After World War II, his research focused increasingly on folktales. Delarue's extensive work on Charles **Perrault** centered on the relationship between **oral tradition** and **literary fairy tale**s. He also founded and directed two series on French and Francophone tales published by Editions Erasme. Delarue devoted much of his later life to compiling materials for the catalogue, which remains an invaluable reference work for students of French folk narratives and literary tales alike. *See also* Collecting, Collectors; French Tales.

Further Reading: Tenèze, Marie-Louise. "A la mémoire de Paul Delarue." *Arts et Traditions Populaires* 6 (1958): 289–307.

Harold Neemann

Deledda, Grazia (1871–1936)

The self-taught Italian writer and folklorist Grazia Deledda was born in Nuoro, Sardinia, and published more than forty volumes, primarily **novel**s and short stories. She won the Nobel Prize for Literature in 1926. Her noteworthy novels include *Elias Portolu* (1903), *Cenere* (*Ashes,* 1904), *Canne al vento* (*Reeds in the Wind,* 1913), and *La madre* (*The Mother,* 1920). Much of her early writing was in the style of Italian regional realism and as such integrated Sardinian customs, traditions, and **folklore** into its texture.

Deledda's interest in the traditional cultures of Sardinia, as well as her belief that, in this context, "Sardinia is the Cinderella of Italy and still awaits its fairy godmother," led her to gather and edit material that she compiled first in a collection of Sardinian **legend**s appearing in the journal *Vita Sarda* (1893) and then in the ethnographic study "Tradizioni popolari di Nuoro" ("Popular Traditions of Nuoro") published in the journal *Rivista delle Tradizioni Popolari Italiane* in 1894–95. In the latter, she covered topics such as **proverbs**, popular sayings, names, curses, oaths, popular poetry, nursery rhymes, lullabies, **riddle**s, games, superstitions, popular beliefs, rituals, and festivities.

Deledda's editing and original reworking of popular material demonstrated her interest in the intersections between legends and other narratives (**fairy tales**, for example), fantastic and realistic modes, and historical and supernatural or mythical characters, as well as her attraction to themes common to folk narrative, such as **transgression**, negotiation of violent passion, and socialization. *See also* Collecting, Collectors; Editing, Editors; Ethnographic Approaches.

Further Reading: Gunzberg, Lynn. "Ruralism, Folklore, and Grazia Deledda's Novels." *Modern Language Studies* 13.3 (1983): 112–22.

Nancy Canepa

Demófilo. *See* Machado y Alvarez, Antonio

Deulin, Charles (1827–1877)

Charles Deulin was the son of a poor tailor who lived in the Escaut, a region in the north of France whose **folklore** inspired his major works. Deulin's early career as the secretary of an enlightened notary and patron of the arts came to a sudden end after he eloped with the daughter of a notable local merchant. Deulin relocated to Paris, where he worked as a columnist for numerous French journals and reviews. However, Deulin found his real fame writing tales that drew on regional folklore and folktales. His first tale, "Le compère de la mort" ("Godfather Death"), was based on an oral tale that he had first adapted as a song.

His tales achieved both popular and critical success, so Deulin mined the rare resources and folk literature in the Library of the Arsenal in Paris for material that he could reshape into tales of his own. *Contes d'un buveur de bière* (*Tales of a Beer Drinker*, 1868) and its sequels *Contes du roi Cambrinus* (*Tales of King Cambrinus*, 1874) and *Histoires de petite ville* (*Village Stories*, 1875) constitute his most important collections of fairy tales. *Les contes de ma Mère l'Oye avant Perrault* (*The Tales of **Mother Goose** from before Perrault*), a scholarly work that explores Charles **Perrault**'s likely sources, was published in 1879, after his death. Deulin and his beer drinker remind us of his contemporary Alphonse **Daudet** and his windmill of Provence. Despite obvious differences between these writers, they both provide sharp yet personal evocations of the lore of their native regions, thanks to their skill at giving French language a distinctive regional twist.

Further Reading: Deulin, Charles. *Intégrale des contes.* Dondé-sur-l'Escant: Miroirs, 1992.

Claire L. Malarte-Feldman

Devil

According to Jewish, Christian, and Islamic beliefs, God and humans are opposed by a mighty enemy who is the personification of the powers of evil. He is known under several names, such as Satan (Hebrew for "adversary"), the devil (from the Greek *diabolos* for "slanderer"), and Lucifer (Latin for "light carrier"). The latter name refers to his former status as one of the archangels, who due to his pride revolted against God and was expelled from the heaven by the archangel Saint Michael. According to Christian **legend**s, minor angels who followed Lucifer were cast down from heaven together with their leader and turned into demons. This legend explains the origin of various spirits of nature in Christian folk religion.

The devil appears as an adversary to humans in literary and oral genres that range from scriptures, sermons, and **exempla** to fairy tales, legends, and jokes. Thus, in many **variant**s of the **tale type** The Three Stolen **Princess**es (ATU 301), the abductor is the devil, who is sometimes replaced with a monster or a **dragon**. Identification of the dragon with the devil has a parallel in the New Testament (Rev. 12). Thus, in European folktales about the slaying of the dragon by a young hero, his victory sometimes symbolizes defeating the devil, which was also the main mission of Christ. In religious legends, Christ descends into the inferno to chain Satan and to rescue the righteous, who were imprisoned in hell. The resurrection of Christ was interpreted as a victory over the devil, who had tempted Adam and Eve in the guise of a serpent. According to the **Bible** and to the interpretation of early church fathers, **death** entered the world due to the fall of the first humans, who were deceived by Satan, who gained power over them and subsequent generations. Early church fathers claimed that it was God's plan to save humankind from the power of Satan. Since he was not able to recognize Jesus as the Son of God, he was cheated by God and lost his legitimate power over humankind.

Some of the theological topics found in religious legends have parallels in folktales. The **motif** of cheating the stupid devil became particularly popular. In tales of the type called The Crop Division (ATU 1030), also known as "The Peasant and the Devil" in the version of the Brothers **Grimm**, the devil is cheated by a farmer, who promises him that part of the crop that grows above the ground. The farmer plants turnips, and the devil gets the leaves. The next year, the devil tries to be wiser and claims what grows beneath the ground. The farmer sows grain, and the devil is cheated again. In many versions of the story, the farmer's stupid partner is not the devil but a bear or a giant. This narrative belongs to the set of tale types about the stupid **ogre**, giant, or the devil (ATU 1000–1199). Replacing an ogre, a giant, or some other beast with the devil shows that he took over the role of opponent in many tales during Christianity's spread throughout Europe. Tales about outwitting the devil often have humorous overtones because the mighty adversary is depicted as a clumsy and even harmless creature. In the folktale, the devil sometimes seems more like a human than a diabolic character. This is in contrast to his appearance in church doctrines, which depict him as an aggressive demonic creature. In the tale type ATU 475, The Man as Heater of Hell's Kettle, a poor **soldier** works in hell for a good salary and discovers that his former cruel masters are in the kettles. Here the devil is a positive figure and even helps the hero to regain his money, of which he had been robbed. A good example is Grimms' "Des Teufels rußiger Bruder" ("The Devil's Sooty Brother," 1815).

The devil's character in **folklore** ranges from funny to evil, from a hero's helper to a demonic adversary. It seems that both humorous and **cautionary tale**s about the devil have spread parallel to each other. The dangerous and frightening devil is typical of legends, where encountering him can cause sickness and death. As a shape-shifter he can appear as a man, woman, or child, as a wild or domestic animal, a bird, a material object, or a fantastic creature that combines human and bestial traits (hooves, horns, tail, etc.). The most common **colors** associated with the devil are black and red. Many legends warn against his seemingly innocent guises and instruct listeners how to ward him off when he appears in everyday situations. Among the common means of defense are the Lord's Prayer and the sign of cross. There are many **didactic tale**s about the devil, who both seduces humans into sin and punishes them for immoral behavior. He appears at dance parties as a handsome youth who carries his merry partner to hell; in other legends, he punishes card players, drunkards, **witch**es, and other offenders. In many legends, the devil comes after the soul of a dying sinner, often with a black coach drawn by black horses. There is a strong link in folklore between riches and the devil, who can help to procure money. This is the topic of many legends about making a contract with the devil, who can guarantee wealth, success, and magical powers in return for one's soul. The didactic function prevails in legends about the repentance and frightening death of the person who enters into a contract with the devil. In other tales, the devil is cheated by the contractor, who can also be saved by the Virgin Mary, by prayer, or thanks to somebody's advice. *See also* Ghost Story; Jest and Joke; Religious Tale; Saint's Legend.

Further Readings: Röhrich, Lutz. "German Devil Tales and Devil Legends." *Journal of the Folklore Institute* 7.1 (1970): 21–35; Russell, Jeffrey Burton. *Lucifer: The Devil in the Middle Ages.* Ithaca, NY: Cornell University Press, 1984; Valk, Ülo. *The Black Gentleman: Manifestations of the Devil in Estonian Folk Religion.* Helsinki: Academia Scientiarum Fennica, 2001.

Ülo Valk

Dickens, Charles (1812–1870)

For the English novelist Charles Dickens, fairy tales and the *Arabian Nights* held a lifelong allure. His very first **novel**, *The Pickwick Papers* (1836–37), interpolated magical and surreal stories as a darker counterpoint to the sunny adventures of Mr. Pickwick and his comical friends. One of these, "The Story of the Goblins Who Stole a Sexton" (which appeared as the novel's tenth installment in December 1836), prefigures *A Christmas Carol* (1843): Gabriel Grub, a cynical sexton, becomes "an altered man" after his abduction by a goblin king and his cohorts. Dickens's later fictions, however, directly weave fairy-tale allusions into their plots. In *Little Dorrit* (1855–57), for example, the story of a shadow parted from its owner (derived from Hans Christian **Andersen**) plays an important symbolic role. In *Great Expectations* (1860–61), Magwitch is cast as Goblin, Bad Wolf, and Frog King before we discover that he has acted as a beneficent godparent.

In an 1853 essay called "Frauds on the Fairies," Dickens accused George **Cruikshank**, a former associate, of having violated the sanctity of fairy tales in his *Fairy Library* (1853–54). To mock Cruikshank's use of "**Cinderella**" as a temperance tract, Dickens himself deformed Charles **Perrault's** version of the tale into a satire of similarly "enlightened" but curiously American and protofeminist views. Dickens also adopted a female point of view when he pretended, more genially, that "The Magic Fishbone" (1868) had been written by a wishful little girl called Alice.

Further Reading: Stone, Harry. *Dickens and the Invisible World: Fairy Tales, Fantasy, and Novel-Making.* Bloomington: Indiana University Press, 1979.

U. C. Knoepflmacher

Didactic Tale

A didactic tale is a story that seeks to instruct an audience, especially in moral values. Didactic tales are found in all cultures and periods, and many genres of folk narrative can have a didactic thrust. In the Indo-European context, there have been narratives with didactic purposes since the earliest recorded tales such as the **Jātaka**s. A didactic orientation is evident in tales from the **Bible** and the Aesopic **fable** tradition, in the **exemplum** of the **Middle Ages**, and in the **literary fairy tale** during the early modern and modern periods. In the seventeenth century, French moralists created literary works that sought both to please and to instruct (*plaire et instruire*), thereby blurring the distinction between didactic and nondidactic tales. Jean de **La Fontaine**'s fables and the literary fairy tales of Charles **Perrault**, Marie-Catherine d'**Aulnoy**, Marie-Jeanne **Lhéritier de Villandon**, and Henriette-Julie de Castelnau, Comtesse de **Murat** are examples of narratives that are simultaneously instructive, entertaining, and aesthetically pleasing.

With the increased production of **children's literature** beginning in the eighteenth century, didactic tales once aimed at adult audiences now targeted children. For example, *Juttud ja Teggud* (*Tales and Deeds*, 1782), a didactic collection by the Estonian clergyman Friedrich Wilhelm von Willmann, drew on a wide range of sources, especially fables from **Aesop** and Martin Luther. The didacticizing of previously adult tales for children in also illustrated by Jeanne-Marie **Leprince de Beaumont**'s rewriting, in 1757, of Gabrielle-Suzanne de **Villeneuve**'s "Beauty and the Beast" (1740). In nineteenth-century Germany, the Brothers **Grimm** further developed this trend in their editing and rewriting of traditional tales. Grimms' version of "Little Red Riding Hood" transforms Perrault's **cautionary tale** for young ladies into a didactic tale for children. Whereas in Perrault's version the heroine dies for not being guarded and vigilant, in the Grimms' version the wolf is punished for committing the sin of gluttony. The heroine's good scare, however, is enough to teach her a moral lesson about acceptable behavior and obedience and to demonstrate the fluid relationship between cautionary and didactic tales.

Further Reading: Trinquet, Charlotte. "Le Petit Chaperon Rouge et les divers chemins qu'elle emprunte." *Studies in Modern and Classical Languages and Literatures* 6 (2004): 80–89.

Charlotte Trinquet

Diffusion

Diffusion is the transmission or spread of cultural traits from one location or group to another. Since the nineteenth century, diffusion has been one standard explanation for the recurrence of **folktale**s across cultures. Unlike the rival hypothesis of **polygenesis**, the hypothesis of diffusion makes no assumption regarding the human psyche. Rather, it attempts to map actual migrations of cultural traits. Therefore, its outlook is historical—and even genetic insofar as it assumes **monogenesis**, which posits a single time and place of origin.

Regarding folktales, diffusion's premises are evident in two main sets of proposals. Nineteenth-century authors such as Theodor **Benfey**, Emmanuel Cosquin, and Joseph **Jacobs** thought the uniformity of Eurasian folktales owes to diffusion from an original place of invention. In the early twentieth century, the so-called Finnish school proposed the **historic-geographic method** to reconstitute the "life history" of folktales. Ultimately, at stake in both cases was a genetic quest for "original" stories—either as invented in some named place, such as India, or as told for the first time at some yet unknown place to be ascertained via the historic-geographic method. While such quests for a largely hypothetical **urform** are no longer tenable, diffusion studies did draw valuable attention to actual folktale **variant**s and **motif**s as well as to their distribution patterns and cultural contexts.

Today, the benefit of hindsight suggests that the views of diffusion and polygenesis are not incompatible. Human imagination tends to be akin everywhere, and diffusion did take place, which suggests that modern scholars need adopt a layered view of human complexity to meaningfully engage cross-cultural similarities. *See also* Contamination; Oicotype.

Further Reading: Thompson, Stith. "The Life History of a Folktale." *The Folktale.* 1946. Berkeley: University of California Press, 1977. 428–48.

Francisco Vaz da Silva

Diop, Birago (1906–1989)

Author of the best-known collections of Western African folktales in French, Birago Diop belonged to the founding generation of Francophone African writers. Although he approached writing as a pastime (he was a practicing veterinarian his entire life, after being barred from medical studies by French colonial authorities), he was widely celebrated as a writer in both his native Senegal and in France. He is chiefly known for three volumes: *Les contes d'Amadou Koumba* (*The Tales of Amadou Koumba*, 1947); *Les nouveaux contes d'Amadou Koumba* (*The New Tales of Amadou Koumba*, 1958); and *Contes et lavanes* (*Tales and Enigmas*, 1963). Diop was intimately acquainted with members of the négritude movement, which sought to valorize African cultures and traditions in the face of Western assimilation and hegemony. The movement's leader, Léopold Sédar Senghor, wrote an enthusiastic preface for *The New Tales of Amadou Koumba* in which he praised Diop for preserving and recasting authentic African traditions by adapting them into a French literary medium. In spite of his connections to Senghor and others, Diop's tales are less overtly political than the works of most négritude writers.

In the introduction to his first volume, Diop explicitly credits his family's griot, Amadou Koumba N'Goum, for his tales (although he also evokes childhood memories of his grandmother's **storytelling** as inspiration). In point of fact, he also culls from widely divergent sources, including Bambara stories from Mali, Wolof stories from Senegal, and Mossi stories from the Upper Volta, all regions where he had lived while practicing veterinary medicine. The product of his wide knowledge of oral storytelling, his tales also incorporate, stylistically and formally, western European and particularly French literary traditions, with which he was also well acquainted. Written in elegant prose, Diop's tales do not seek to replicate an oral storytelling style, nor do they conform on the whole to the standard formulaic features of Western **literary fairy tale**s. Instead, they use a variety of narrative techniques (borrowed from the *nouvelle* or short story, especially) to highlight the sociofamilial organization of rural African societies as well as the animistic beliefs they once held, and to retell West African **etiologic tale**s, pseudohistorical stories, **legend**s, and animal **fable**s. This last genre constitutes fully one-half of his corpus and includes many characters that appear in French Caribbean and Louisiana **folklore**.

Prominent in Diop's tales is the use of irony, and especially tragic irony. In lieu of an explicit **moral**, it is more often the sudden reversal of fortune putting a character in a position he or she initially rejects that conveys the tale's latent message. Through irony, Diop underscores the cultural importance of traditional rites of passage (for example, in "Petit mari" ["Little Husband"]), but also of the respect due between husband and wife ("Le salaire" ["The Wages"]), parents and children ("Maman-Caïman" ["Mother Crocodile"]), and one friend and another ("L'os" ["The Bone"]), among other things. Diop's vivid and engaging portraits of traditional West African society have become classics in their own right and have been adapted both for the stage and the screen. ***See also*** African Tales; Négritude, Créolité, and Folktale.

Further Readings: Diop, Birago. *Tales of Amadou Koumba.* Translated by Dorothy S. Blair. London: Oxford University Press, 1966; Kane, Mohamadou. *Les contes d'Amadou Coumba: Du conte tradition-nel au conte moderne d'expression française.* Dakar: Université de Dakar, 1968.

Lewis C. Seifert

Disability

People who are categorized as "disabled" are, by definition, in some way severely impaired. Impairment can take different forms; restrictions in disabled people's movements may, for example, be due to missing or malformed limbs, or to spastic or mental disorders. How the disabled have been regarded and accordingly handled in society over time—ranging from complete rejection to the highest esteem—is related to the prevailing cultural and historical conditions at any one time or place.

On the one hand, contact with this group of people was regarded as inauspicious; those with physical defects conflicted with the supposed aesthetic harmony of the world, and an abnormal physical appearance was seen as an indication of a disharmony of the soul. Many folktales and **proverbs** reflect this way of thinking. On the other hand, the disabled were thought to bring luck or were considered to be particularly gifted lovers, as we learn from old songs. An increasingly positive attitude towards the disabled began to evolve at the dawn of the spread of the major religions. Thus, the Romans, ancient Greeks, and Jews for example integrated the phenomenon of disability into their religious worldview and inter-preted it as a sign from God. Moreover, contemporary accounts exist of the miraculous heal-ing of disabilities by Jesus Christ, Mohammed, and Buddha. In late sixteenth-century Europe, secular society also changed its attitude towards the disabled, who were finally rec-ognized as fully entitled citizens and granted rights, such as access to education.

When disability appears in early descriptions of the world, bestiaries, stories about nature, travel accounts, and literature about other countries and civilizations, it is linked with the con-cept of "otherness." In these writings, people and animals from foreign cultures are often char-acterized by physical deformities. This reflects the confrontation and conflict with the "foreign" and the "exotic" and shows that there is no limit to the imagination when projecting how people and animals from foreign countries may appear. Sometimes they are rendered as monsters or at least as strange creatures with various deformities. The folktale has a special position in this context. It is true that otherness in folktales also finds its expression in the depiction of charac-ters or animals with physical defects. However, the difference is that their deformities do not have a purely negative connotation. In fact, deformities can be the reason for the remarkable abilities of the disabled. Accordingly, disability is not detrimental to these figures but makes them superior to their normal counterparts. One example of this is the one-legged man who out-runs his two-legged competitors (ATU 513A, Six Go through the Whole World).

In spite of the possible advantage deriving from their impairment, the disabled in folktales are at the same time represented in a way that clearly evokes stereotypes of ugliness (which are also commonly found in **chapbook**s, **comics**, science-fiction literature, detective novels, horror legends, and children's books and are used to reinforce typologies of **age**, as, for example, with bugbears). Although the physical defect might grant them supernatural powers, this only underlines their otherness and their distance from the society of "normal beings." Moreover, as protagonists they are not necessarily likeable for their outstanding abilities, especially since these qualities often appear in conjunction with a ruthless determination to succeed. The ambiguous representation of the disabled in folktales is a clear indication that the otherness of disability always held a fascination for people but that a distanced and skeptical attitude prevailed.

In **legend**s, a physical handicap is regarded as a **punishment** imposed on the victim by other human beings or by the otherworld because social norms have in some way been violated. A permanent or temporary physical disability (including blindness) may be inflicted on humans in the form of miraculous punishments. This may occur, for example, when moral and ethical norms have been flouted (for example, leading to the amputation of a leg if someone has treated his mother badly) or when laws have been disregarded (for example, someone's hand might be crippled if he has stolen from the church, thereby committing sacrilege). Similarly, if a human being observes or comes into contact with a supernatural creature, he could also be subject to punishment (becoming a hunchback or paralyzed). In legends where disability is thus inflicted as a punishment, the prospect of disability is obviously intended as a deterrent to steer the readers into conforming to social conventions rather than as a demonstration of the principles of law. Hence, the **motif** of magic disability (in the sense that the disability is not congenital or due to an accident but intentionally inflicted) illustrates the repressive nature of legends. Human beings are completely at the mercy of powers from the otherworld (ATU 503, The Gifts of the Little People).

Moreover, the motif of disabling someone as a precautionary measure is also found in legends. Such drastic action might, for instance, be taken to secure someone's possessions and power before somebody else could lay hold of them, or to eliminate rivals. For similar reasons, jealousy among artists can lead to a master's mutilating his apprentice to hinder him from achieving greater success. When a victim exacts revenge on his tormentor, he or she prevents him from ever performing his abominable deeds again (as in the German **myth** of Wieland or the Akkadian myth *The Poor Man of Nippur* [ATU 1538, The Revenge of the Cheated Man]).

Being mutilated at the hands of another, however, is not the only means of becoming impaired and disabled. Self-mutilation also occurs, especially among groups whose religious beliefs promote self-harm as a means to avoid temptation. **Saints' legend**s depict many martyrs who maim themselves to preserve their celibacy and chastity (see also Matt. 18.8 and 19.12). There are three forms of self-mutilation: (1) crippling of the hand; (2) cutting off the nose, ears, tongue, or breasts; and (3) gouging out the eyes.

Disability and (magic) healing constitute one of the central topics of folktales and legends and often determine their plot structure. According to Max **Lüthi**, disability stands for "neediness," which manifests itself in the apparent helplessness of the hero or heroine. It is not always important, therefore, to know why the protagonists are handicapped, and the reason for their misfortune need not be mentioned. The information that they lack something and need help is sufficient to set the action in motion. Though Lüthi and Vladimir **Propp** follow different methodologies (phenomenology and **structuralism**, respectively), they both come to the same conclusion with regard to the basic **function**s of the folktale: a deficiency (Propp's functions VII and VIIa) must be made good (function XIX), both functions, of course, necessitating each other. This is consistent with the overall structure of folktales, which requires that a task be completed and a deficiency eliminated.

According to Hans-Jörg Uther, three basic functions can be identified: (1) an old, blind **king** regains his sight via a healing substance; (2) the defect is removed as a result of selfless behavior; and (3) the disability is caused by a criminal act. Concerning the first and the second functions, the heroes either procure the remedies themselves or receive advice as to how to heal their ailments. In this way, they receive help and are cured of their defects (often blindness). Though the selection of remedies (most often healing herbs, water of life, and lion's milk) is more limited than in folk medicine, it nevertheless suffices for a "happy" ending to the folktale. In the third basic function, the disabled blossom in spite of their defects, outgrow the malicious, and defeat stronger opponents. The message here is two-fold and not only reflects a tendency to protest in folktales but also demonstrates the desire to see wishes come true. Consistent with the irony typically found in folktales, the evil opponent harms himself. This form of compensatory justice insures that antagonists are punished. When the disability is only temporary, is subsequently healed, and is then used to the advantage of the affected person, the folktale creates role models for the disabled.

Disability can already be found as the target of mockery in classical Greek and Roman comedies as well as in derisive epigrams from antiquity. The defects of the disabled have a comic effect because they violate the conventions of harmonious proportions (the theory of contrast). Therefore, these defects are an ideal starting point for plots intended to create a humorous mood. Aristotle (*Poetics* 5.1449) was the first to draw attention to this phenomenon: the ridiculous is part of ugliness and, in turn, ugliness is the counterpart of the sublime. In short, physical defects provoke laughter (ATU 1536B, The Three Hunchback Brothers Drowned). Furthermore, **joke**s, legends and pictures may all at least superficially confirm the widespread belief that physical ailments are hereditary. **Broadside**s from the nineteenth century, for example, depict a husband's discovery of his wife committing adultery with a wooden-legged priest. Subsequently, she gives **birth** to a baby who also has a wooden leg.

If the function of jokes about the disabled (as with jokes about the insane) is reduced to breaking taboos—however absurd they may be—they then cease to be "comical" or "funny." Anton C. Zijderveld draws attention to the fact that jokes about the disabled often serve the purpose of breaking taboos relating to sociocultural structures. Even though grotesque jokes about the disabled are not often published in collections of jokes (due to the control mechanisms of the media), their real number is certainly considerably higher. In jokes, the disabled are placed in the most absurd situations: They appear as witnesses in court (ATU 1698, Deaf Persons and Their Foolish Answers), as one-eyed bridegrooms (ATU 1379***, One-Eyed Man Marries), as people cured through shock (ATU 1791, The Sexton Carries the Clergyman), or as courageous and valiant **soldier**s who carry their substitute leg around with them in a trunk. Tall tales relate the grotesque adventures of three disabled people as hunters: the blind man shoots a hare with a gun, the lame man catches the wounded animal, and finally, the naked man puts it into his pocket (ATU 1965, The Disabled Comrades). Such absurd stories have been popular since ancient times and appear frequently in folk literature dating from the late **Middle Ages**.

Nevertheless, disabled people are not always the object of ridicule in folktales; they are sometimes more than able to defend themselves with a quick-witted repartee. However, the protagonists are interchangeable (ATU 1620*, The Conversation of Two Handicapped Persons) in these stories categorized in Stith Thompson's *Motif-Index of Folk-Literature* as "clever verbal retorts" (Motif J1250–J1499). Being "different" in the broadest sense of the word is the basis for this kind of humor, which has enjoyed great popularity since time immemorial and is often related to the double meaning of words.

The portrayal of disability in folktales depends on the genre and is determined by certain rules. Thus, the attitude toward the disabled in legends, miracle plays, and **exempla** is dictated by basic notions of religion (duty to be merciful and charitable). The saintly healing of the disabled confirms that God and his representatives on earth are more powerful than either humans or matter (miracles of confirmation). Enduring excruciating torments and the resulting mutilation, whether it be self-inflicted or not, is regarded as serving a higher purpose. The primary aim of legends is to confirm given norms. This is demonstrated by the recurring motif of miraculous punishment, which can be interpreted as an effective means of divine and, implicitly, social control. In folktales, disabled characters who prove themselves to be worthy members of society can be healed of their disabilities by magic aides. In farcical stories, jokes about the disabled are mostly discriminatory. The disabled are put into grotesque situations where their defects appear distorted and are often reduced to absurdity. In popular tales, the negative portrayal of the disabled has largely disappeared, and they are generally regarded with sympathy and respect. Nevertheless, we should not ignore the fact that humor about the "defects" of the disabled, in particular aggressive jokes, are still virulent.

Further Readings: Azarnoff, Pat. *Health, Illness, and Disability: A Guide to Books for Children and Young Adults.* New York: Bowker, 1983; Conrad, JoAnn. "Polyphemus and Tepegöz Revisited: A Comparison of the Tales of the Blinding of the One-Eyed Ogre in Western and Turkish Traditions." *Fabula* 40 (1999): 278–97; *Enzyklopädie des Märchens.* Edited by Kurt Ranke et al. 11 volumes to date. Berlin: Walter de Gruyter, 1977– . (See the entries: "Blendung"; "Blind, Blindheit"; "Buckel, Buckligkeit"; "Einäugig, Einäugigkeit"; "Hinken, Hinkender"; "Krüppel"; "Lahmer und Blinder"; "Monstrum"; etc.); Goldberg. Christine. "The Blind Girl: A Misplaced Folktale." *Western Folklore* 55 (1996): 187–209; Hand, Wayland D. "The Curing of Blindness in Folktales." *Volksüberlieferung: Festschrift Kurt Ranke.* Edited by Fritz Harkort, Karel C. Peeters, and Robert Wildhaber. Göttingen: Schwartz, 1968. 81–87; Holden, Lynn. *Forms of Deformity.* Sheffield: Sheffield Academic Press, 1991; Lüthi, Max. "Gebrechliche und Behinderte im Volksmärchen." *Volksliteratur und Hochliteratur.* Bern: Francke, 1970. 48–62; Propp, Vladimir. *Morphology of the Folktale.* Translated by Laurence Scott. Revised and edited by Louis A. Wagner. 2nd edition. 1968. Austin: University of Texas Press, 1996; Uther, Hans-Jörg. *Behinderte in populären Erzählungen.* Berlin: Walter de Gruyter, 1981; Zijderveld, Anton C. *Humor und Gesellschaft: Eine Soziologie des Humors und des Lachens.* Graz: Styria, 1976.

Hans-Jörg Uther

Disney, Walt (1901–1966)

As the cofounder and creative head of the media and entertainment corporation that bears his name, Walter Elias Disney established his company's reputation for family-friendly fare by producing animated fairy-tale **film** adaptations. In the twentieth century, Walt, as he was referred to throughout his career, and by extension The **Walt Disney Company**, substantially shaped Hollywood animation studios and influenced **children's literature**, media, and culture. Disney's **adaptation**s of folktales and fairy tales, which celebrate technological innovations and reflect his middle-class American values, have become classic versions in their own right. His films also set expectations against which other versions of tales, earlier or later, print or visual, continue to be received.

Early Life and Career

What has become known as the Disney version of the fairy tale is rooted in the personal history of its founder, whose own life is often cast as an American fairy tale. Disney was born in Chicago to Elias and Flora Disney, and his youth was marked by the family's struggle to achieve economic stability and his father's entrepreneurial desires. During Disney's early childhood, the family worked a farm near the small Midwest town of Marceline, Missouri. As an adult, Disney would nostalgically revisit this period in early cartoon shorts, setting them in rural America and depicting anthropomorphized animals, and later in Marceline's reincarnation as Disneyland's Main Street, USA. When he was eight, the family moved to Kansas City, where Elias became a newspaper-route manager. Elias hired Disney and his older brother Roy, a move that established a lifelong partnership.

While in Kansas City, Disney became interested in **storytelling**, film, and cartooning. He enjoyed reading, notably works by Horatio Alger, Robert Louis Stevenson, and Mark Twain, and watching **silent films** with stars such as Charlie Chaplin, Mary Pickford, and Harold Lloyd. During this period, he began to consider a career as an artist. In 1917, when his family returned to Chicago, Disney briefly enrolled in classes at the Chicago Art Institute. Soon afterward, though, Disney lied about his age to become an ambulance driver for the Red Cross and serve in World War I. He informally worked as a cartoonist while serving in France and gained a reputation as a capable artist. In 1919, he returned to Kansas City and joined a commercial arts studio. There he met Ub Iwerks, a gifted technical artist and inventor. Disney and Iwerks formed Laugh-O-Grams and made several fairy-tale cartoon shorts, all of which rely on anthropomorphism and sight gags. Well-received Laugh-O-Grams include *Little Red Riding Hood* (1922), *The Four Musicians of Bremen* (1922), and *Puss in Boots* (1922). The company also started the live action-**animation** hybrid *Alice's Wonderland,* loosely based on Lewis **Carroll**'s fairy tale and featuring the adventures of Alice, a human girl in a cartoon world. Although these shorts were popular, distribution problems and Disney's general lack of business sense bankrupted the studio.

Undeterred, Disney relocated to Hollywood and convinced his brother Roy to invest in and manage the financial operations of the new Disney Brothers Studio. Iwerks joined this new endeavor, but as an animator rather than as a partner. Disney resurrected the Alice series as the *Alice Comedies* (1924–26), fifty-six cartoons based on the same scenario as *Alice's Wonderland*. *Alice's Comedies*, like its predecessor, was popular with audiences, and Disney earned recognition as an up-and-coming studio head who beat the odds. Even at this time, Disney's story as a Midwest son succeeding in Hollywood was being framed as a real-life fairy tale.

Early Studio Years and Short Cartoons

Although it enjoyed early success with the fairy tale, the studio did not emerge as dominant in Hollywood until Mickey Mouse first appeared in *Steamboat Willie* (1928). Mickey was created after the Disney Brothers Studio lost the rights to Oswald the Lucky Rabbit, the character who had replaced Alice. Accounts about Mickey Mouse's creation vary but generally credit the concept of Mickey Mouse to Disney and the character's execution to Iwerks. This distinction subtly acknowledges Disney was, at best, a mediocre animator and that his skills instead rested in his contributions as a film producer and entrepreneur—storytelling, generating ideas, recognizing others' talents, and encouraging innovation. These strengths helped Disney create an identifiable brand during the late 1920s and 1930s, when the studio focused on its Mickey Mouse and *Silly Symphonies* cartoons.

Although the Mickey Mouse shorts occasionally adapted fairy tales, such as *Thru the Mirror* (1936) and *Brave Little Tailor* (1938), they primarily offered gag-oriented narratives promoting the studio's central characters. The *Silly Symphonies* shorts, however, often used folktales and fairy tales to highlight technological innovations in the use of sound, music, and color. Both types of cartoons were popular, garnering industry recognition and technical awards. *The Three Little **Pig**s* (1933), with its catchy "Who's Afraid of the Big Bad **Wolf**?" song, received a particularly strong public following as it was considered a response to anxieties about the Depression and, later, to those surrounding World War II.

These animated shorts established the studio's implementation of its production model, aesthetic preferences, and technological developments. Disney developed a Taylorized production environment, including discrete units devoted to character animation, backgrounds, cleanup, color, photography, sound and music, and editing. This environment formalized the use of head animators, directors, and storyboards. The studio's emphasis on storytelling reflects Disney's own interest in realistic, personality-driven animation, sentimental narratives, and the musical genre. The studio also adapted, and continues to adapt, folktales and fairy tales and other texts associated with children's literature. Disney versions, as they are known, offer attractive if bland protagonists, truly villainous villains, comic sidekicks, anthropomorphized animals, and clear conflicts with happy resolutions. Equally important, the studio promotes its development of new technology to distinguish itself from other studios, a strategy utilized early in its history with the use of synchronized sound and movement in *Steamboat Willie,* Technicolor in *Flowers and Trees* (1932), and the multiplane camera (which provides animation with an illusion of depth) in *The Old Mill* (1937).

Feature Animation

In part due to their high production values and use of technological innovations, Disney's cartoons were commercially successful. Success let to expansion, with most of the profits folded back into the studio's development. By 1934, Disney had decided to make the first American full-length animated film. Shorts were increasingly expensive and a feature would explore animation's possibilities and challenge his animators. For this groundbreaking project, Disney chose another fairy-tale adaptation, *Snow White and the Seven Dwarfs* (1937).

The story surrounding ***Snow White***'s production has itself taken on fairy-tale qualities. Disney gathered his head animators, known as the Nine Old Men, to convince them of a feature's viability. The right story, a fairy tale, would provide the emotional complexity necessary to appeal to an audience. Disney told his version of *Snow White,* describing each scene and acting out each character. According to company legend, this nearly three-hour long performance inspired the animators' work and was even superior to the film. (Some sources suggest Disney's version was influenced by a 1916 silent-film version of *Snow White* that stars Marguerite Clark.)

Snow White introduced the studio's strategies for feature-length films. Disney was the producer turned auteur, his aesthetic preferences and ideologies the studio's Sweatbox sessions, in which Disney reviewed a film's progress with select animators, were common. Technological advancements, such as *Snow White's* use of the multiplane camera, were associated with aesthetic experimentation. Merchandising, a primary source of the studio's income by 1934, helped finance the project, and *Snow White* was the first film to have a fully operational campaign in place by its release. Despite the studio's belief in its undertaking, outsiders nicknamed *Snow White* "Disney's Folly," a label that reflected its risk to the studio. Most of the public's skepticism was related to the project's scope, as in its final form, *Snow White* would cost $1.5 million and consist of more than two million drawings.

The film's success, earning over $8 million in its initial release and a special Academy Award, provided the studio with its formula for features. Although the film suggests, in its opening shots of a book, a debt to the **Grimm**s' fairy tale, *Snow White* is not a close adaptation. The film is instead influenced by melodrama, early film, and vaudeville conventions, identifiable in its marked sentimentality, clearly demarcated characters, heightened emotions punctuated by **music**, and comic relief. It reflects Disney's middle-American ideology and is characterized by optimism, the reinforcement of traditional **gender** roles, and a democratic sensibility. Snow White's function as heroine is indicated by her beauty, innocence, and affinity with nature. In addition to attempting to kill Snow White, the **Queen**'s mature beauty suggests her evil nature and is confirmed in her transformation into the ugly Hag. Because she willingly nurtures them, Snow White's happiness and belief in true love become important to the secondary characters, the cute forest creatures and comically awkward **dwarves**. These supporting characters, in turn, willingly work for and protect Snow White in recognition of her innate goodness rather than because of her royal status. The handsome **prince**, although the focus of Snow White's romantic dreams, exists mainly to rescue Snow White with a kiss that seals the film's happy ending.

Snow White's success increased the pressure for other studios to emulate the Disney model, both in adapting fairy tales and in adopting its production modes. The Fleischer Brothers made the feature-length *Gulliver's Travels* (1939) and Bob Clampett released *Coal Black and de Sebben Dwarfs* (1943), a short **parody** with African American caricatures. But *Snow White* was the first feature, guaranteeing Disney's and the studio's reputations as the leading producers of animated family entertainment. The studio enhanced its reputation by continuing to adapt folktales and fairy tales and children's literature: *Pinocchio* (1940), *Dumbo* (1941), *Bambi* (1942), **Cinderella** (1950), *Alice in Wonderland* (1951), *Peter Pan* (1953), and **Sleeping Beauty** (1959), as well as the live action-animated hybrids *Song of the South* (1946) and *Mary Poppins* (1964).

While basic elements had been established by the shorts and *Snow White*, later films refined and varied the Disney version. Subsequent features increasingly employed a realist aesthetic, especially in realizing human characters, detailed backgrounds, and special effects. *Cinderella* and *Sleeping Beauty*, along with others produced after Disney's death, constitute what the corporation refers to as its "**princess** films." Like *Snow White*, they offer idealized heroines, their external beauty matched by an adherence to gender roles, and a focus on romantic, heterosexual relationships. *Pinocchio* and *Bambi* reinforce gender roles through their coming-of-age narratives of young boys and offer strong homosocial bonds between protagonists and their companions. The alternate worlds of *Alice in Wonderland, Peter Pan,* and *Mary Poppins* distinguish between the imaginative, even subversive, spaces of **childhood** and the domesticated space of adulthood and families in ways that emphasize the comfort and safety of the latter.

Disney's Expansion

The Disney Brothers Studio quickly expanded from primarily a film studio to a multimedia entertainment corporation. By the 1950s, The Walt Disney Company, as it has come to be known, entered the **television** market and planned its first theme park. These two expansions have been characterized as keystones in Disney's kingdom, a reference to the theme parks and to the company's debt to the fairy tale. Television helped promote and finance the company's diversification. The studio negotiated with ABC television to begin airing *Disneyland* in 1954, a series aimed at generating public interest in the California theme park, and the *Mickey Mouse Club* (1955–59), a series based on the children's fan club. Called "The

Happiest Place on Earth," Disneyland opened in 1955 and was organized into different lands; Fantasyland attractions are inspired by the animated films Disney adapted from fairy tales and children's literature. At Disneyland's center, serving as a gateway to Fantasyland and the park's architectural icon, is Sleeping Beauty's castle. As with studio operations, Disney was creatively involved in these projects and they reflect his ideological concerns. They reveal a tendency toward sentimentality and nostalgia, depict childhood as a time of innocence, anthropomorphize nature, and promote a belief in technology and industry. These concerns are presented through sanitized narratives that promote the company as clean, family fun.

Disney died on December 16, 1966, but the company is still influenced by his contributions as well as by a public perception of what it should produce using his name. Walt Disney World, the Florida theme-park resort under development at the time of his death, opened in 1971. Disney's original plan for a residential community, an Experimental Prototype Community of Tomorrow (Epcot), offered an entrepreneurial approach to solving urban problems; its controlled environment would have integrated technology, business, and innovation in ways similar to studio operations. Epcot, opened in 1982, is more closely modeled after Disneyland, a type of world's fair where technology and consumerism intersect and are presented as entertainment, a fairy tale of the future based on controlled narratives of the present.

Despite its expansion into other media and entertainment venues, the company returns periodically to the fairy-tale movie, invoking history as a means of reasserting its reputation. After several films supporting U.S. goodwill efforts in Latin America, the studio released *Cinderella*; this is also the period Disney's reputation as the compassionate father figure of his studio family was tarnished following the 1941 Screen Cartoonists Strike and his own 1946 testimony for the House Un-American Activities Committee (HUAC) investigations. Similarly, *Sleeping Beauty* was released after several years when company resources had been devoted to its television and theme-park enterprises to suggest the company's continued commitment to animation. A similar return to the corporation's fairy-tale roots can be found in post-Disney periods. *The Little **Mermaid*** (1989), followed by ***Beauty and the Beast*** (1991) and ***Aladdin*** (1992), ushered in the company's second golden age of animation. More recently, *Chicken Little* (2005) was marketed as evidence of the corporation's long-term commitment to computer-generated animation and as a response to increased competition from other Hollywood studios. The Walt Disney Company may now be as well known for its status as a global media and entertainment corporation as for its fairy-tale films, but, as its early history suggests, the company remains grounded in the success found, and the concerns expressed through, Disney's adaptation of the fairy tale. *See also* Tourism.

Further Readings: Bell, Elizabeth, Lynda Haas, and Laura Sells, eds. *From Mouse to Mermaid: The Politics of Film, Gender, and Culture.* Bloomington: Indiana University Press, 1995; Iwerks, Leslie, and John Kenworthy. *The Hand behind the Mouse: An Intimate Biography of the Man Walt Disney Called "The Greatest Animator in the World."* New York: Disney Editions, 2001; May, Jill P. "Walt Disney's Interpretation of Children's Literature." *Language Arts* 58.4 (April 1981): 463–72; Merritt, Russell, and J. B. Kaufman. *Walt in Wonderland: The Silent Films of Walt Disney.* 1991. Baltimore: Johns Hopkins University Press, 1993; Schickel, Richard. *The Disney Version: The Life, Times, Art, and Commerce of Walt Disney.* 1968. New York: Simon and Schuster, 1985; Wasko, Janet. *Understanding Disney: The Manufacture of Fantasy.* Cambridge: Polity, 2001; Watts, Steven. *The Magic Kingdom: Walt Disney and the American Way of Life.* Boston: Houghton Mifflin, 1997; Zipes, Jack. "Toward a Theory of the Fairy-Tale Film: The Case of *Pinocchio*." *Happily Ever After: Fairy Tales, Children, and the Culture Industry.* New York: Routledge, 1997. 61–87.

D. K. Peterson

Dodgson, Charles Lutwidge. *See* Carroll, Lewis

Donoghue, Emma (1969–)

An Irish-born author living in Canada, Emma Donoghue has published fairy-tale **adaptations**, **novel**s, radio plays, dramas, and literary histories and anthologies. Lesbian love is a recurrent theme in her nonfiction work *Passions between Women: British Lesbian Culture 1668–1801* (1993) and in her novels, such as *Stirfry* (1994), *Hood* (1995), and *Life Mask* (2004). This theme is also central to *Kissing the **Witch**: Old Tales in New Skins* (1997), which includes twelve adaptations of well-known fairy tales by Jacob and Wilhelm **Grimm**, Charles **Perrault**, Jeanne-Marie **Leprince de Beaumont**, and Hans Christian **Andersen**, as well as a newly invented fairy tale, "The Tale of the Kiss." The stories form a retrospective chain of first-person narratives: in each, a female fairy-tale character tells another woman her personal, "true" version of a well-known tale. *Kissing the Witch* displays the clear influence of feminist criticism.

The importance of female agency and finding one's own voice is a recurrent theme, most explicitly in the retelling of "The Little Mermaid," who is at first prepared to give up her voice for the love of a man. Traditionally, evil women such as **Snow White**'s stepmother or the witch in "**Hansel and Gretel**" find redemption, often at the cost of male characters. Several stories portray **women**'s struggles with their lesbian **sexuality**: **Cinderella**, for instance, tries her best to fall in love with the **prince** but eventually acknowledges her affection for her godmother. Donoghue has been praised for her concise style and imaginative power, which sheds new light on Western culture's most popular tales. *See also* Feminism; Feminist Tales; Gay and Lesbian Tales.

Further Readings: Donoghue, Emma. *Emma Donoghue Home Page.* http://www.emmadonoghue.com; Sellers, Susan. *Myth and Fairy Tale in Contemporary Women's Fiction.* New York: Palgrave, 2001.

Vanessa Joosen

Doré, Gustave (1832–1883)

Gustave Doré was a prolific French illustrator. Although he illustrated more than 200 books during his career, he is best known in the context of folktale and fairy-tale studies for his illustrations of Charles **Perrault**'s seventeenth-century fairy tales. A fertile artist, Doré worked primarily in the medium of the engraving, although he also produced a large number of sketches. Born in Strasbourg, Alsace-Lorraine, Doré developed, during his childhood, a fascination with supernatural tales that would influence his work in years to come. Attracted throughout his life to subjects that were both innocent and grotesque, he often created illustrations in which the two themes are contrasted.

Doré's first forays into **folklore** were in the genre of **legend**. In 1856 and 1857, he produced illustrations for *Les aventures du chevalier Jaufre et de la belle Brunissende* (*Jaufry the Knight and the Fair Brunissende*) by Jean Bernard Lafon (pseudonym: Mary Lafon), *La légende du Juif errant* (*The Legend of the Wandering Jew*) by Pierre DuPont, and *Fierabras: Legende nationale* by Lafon, all literary **adaptation**s of medieval legends. Subsequently, Doré illustrated literary works such as William **Shakespeare**'s *The Tempest* (1860) and Xavier Saintine's *La mythologie du Rhin et les contes de la mère-grand* (*Myths of the Rhine*, 1862) before undertaking the illustrations for *Contes de Perrault* (*Perrault's Fairy Tales*) in 1862.

These fairy-tale illustrations were richly detailed tableaus set in primeval European forests. Doré depicted the young protagonists of Perrault's tales as full of childlike innocence in a dark and scary world. His illustrations of **Little Red Riding Hood** and the **wolf**—their encounter in the forest and their lying together in the grandmother's bed in particular—have become icons for that tale.

Doré would go on to illustrate a number of literary classics, including Miguel de Cervantes Saavedra's *Don Quixote* (1863), Dante's *Divine Comedy* (1866), John Milton's *Paradise Lost* (1866), and Alfred Lord **Tennyson**'s *Idylls of the King* (1867–68). In 1865, Doré returned to the illustration of fairy tales, this time providing 300 illustrations based on the *Arabian Nights* for Mary Elizabeth Braddon's collection entitled *Aladdin; or, the Wonderful Lamp. Sindbad the Sailor; or, the Old Man of the Sea. Ali Baba; or, the Forty Thieves.* He followed this with illustrations for Jean de **La Fontaine**'s *Fables* in 1867, provid-

Engraving after Gustave Doré entitled *Help! The Marquis of Carabas Is Drowning.* [Courtesy of the Dover Pictorial Archives]

ing artistic accompaniment to both adaptations and new creations. Doré's illustrations—especially those he made for Perrault's fairy tales—have achieved considerable fame and appear repeatedly in numerous editions and studies of fairy tales. *See also* Illustration.

Further Reading: Malan, Dan. *Gustave Doré: Adrift on Dreams of Splendor.* St. Louis: Malan Classical Enterprises, 1995.

B. Grantham Aldred

Dorson, Richard M. (1916–1981)

Richard M. Dorson was the most active and influential university folklorist in the United States. He wrote many books and mentored many students through the Folklore Institute at Indiana University, which he headed. Both **folktale** and **legend** occupied his wide-ranging zeal. Trained as a historian, he advocated the study of American **folklore** in the context of American history. He also considered geography an important influence on narrative, as he showed in collections of folktales from Michigan and Arkansas. He set standards for **fieldwork** and taught the technique to others.

Dorson's exemplary annotation of the folktales he collected, and the volumes of the Folktales of the World series he edited, demonstrated his principles: verbatim transcription, background information about narrators, and a clear relation between newly recorded tales and previous publication by others, as well as reliance on the folklorist's **tale-type** and **motif** indexes. He opened several new areas for research: oral style of narrators, the identification of folklore in American literature, and the traditions of industrial workers and other occupational groups. Dorson was tireless as a university administrator, promoter of the academic study of folklore, and supervisor of dissertations. By organizing and attending international conferences, he established connections among folklorists in the United States, Europe, and Asia.

Further Readings: Dorson, Richard M. *America in Legend: Folklore from the Colonial Period to the Present.* New York: Pantheon Books, 1973; _____, ed. *Folktales Told around the World.* Chicago: University of Chicago Press, 1975; _____. *American Negro Folktales.* Greenwich, CT: Fawcett, 1967.

Lee Haring

Dragon

Dragons are quasi-universal creations of human imagination. They come under many designations and present various forms. You recognize one, whatever its name in a given culture, when you hear about a creature that systematically combines opposites. Dragons partake of the chthonian snake as well as of the uranian bird; they are terrestrial and aquatic, act by fire and water, and display male and female features. Moreover, while perennially deadly or dying, they portend renovation.

In the extremity of their contradictions, dragons display basic traits of cyclic time—time forever ranging through opposite phases and rewinding itself through periodic **death** and rebirth. Also, being attuned to the sovereign cycles of sun and moon, dragons also stand for divine kingship. Such features explain their centrality in the cycles of enchantment and disenchantment that **fairy tales** express by means of rags-to-royalty plots.

Indeed, slaying a fairy-tale dragon is a prime way to acquire a royal bride and become a **king.** Consider this in light of Vladimir **Propp**'s crucial observation in *Istoricheskie korni volshebnoi skazki* (*Historical Roots of the Wondertale,* 1946) that the dragon himself begets his killer, which implies that dragon slaying amounts to dragon rejuvenation (in agreement with

the folk notion that snakes rejuvenate through sloughing, and eagles self-renovate through molting). In this perspective, dragon killing amounts to kingship renovation. Moreover, Propp noted that swallowing is the essence of dragons. Such engulfing nature, in agreement with other feminine traits, recalls that heroes often kiss dragons to obtain a maiden—who appears, consequently, as the disenchanted dragon. Equivalence between kissing a dragon and spearing it highlights the

A dragon resting its head in the lap of a woman. Illustration from a 1912 edition of *Grimm's Fairy Tales.* [New York Public Library]

sexual undertone of the heroic act. In this perspective, dragon slaying amounts to marrying each king to the chthonian dragon-woman representing (under the guise of each new **queen**) the primordial owner of the land.

From another viewpoint, Bengt **Holbek** showed maiden-kidnapping dragons connote **father**/daughter entanglements. But the bisexual dragon is not only own-blood to the maiden—it is also the maiden herself, her very own **blood**, which is another way dragons express cyclic time. In a life-stage sense, while abduction by a dragon expresses primordial confinement in own (kin and menarcheal) blood, dragon slaying establishes marital rights and social ties. Moreover—such are the quirks of cyclic time—the dragon and its killer periodically reappear along with the lunar periodicity of **women**'s life, for it is when a fairy-tale maiden bleeds that a dragon abducts her and a savior arises.

In essence, dragons express death and rebirth, aboriginal beginnings and cyclic repetitions; they embody **transformation** and alternations. In the logic of fairy tales, as in the metaphysics of sacred kingship, self-defeat ultimately engenders victory: *Le roi est mort, vive le roi*—"the king is dead, long live the king." *See also* Cannibalism; Sex, Sexuality; Time and Place.

Further Readings: Coomaraswamy, Ananda. "On the Loathly Bride." *Speculum* 20 (1945): 391–404; Knight, Chris. "On the Dragon Wings of Time." *Maidens, Snakes and Dragon.* Edited by Chris Knight, Isabel Cardigos, and José Gabriel Pereira Bastos. London: Center for the Study of Imagination in Literature, 1991. 7–50.

Francisco Vaz da Silva

Drama. *See* Theater

Dudevant, Amandine-Aurore-Lucile, née Dupin. *See* Sand, George

Duffy, Carol Ann (1955–)

Born in Glasgow, Carol Ann Duffy is a critically acclaimed and popular poet, playwright, and editor who writes both for adults and children. Her poems characterized by demotic diction reveal a subversive and often satirical approach to subject matter and reflect on language itself. A revisionist take on traditional narratives, myth-making, and a drive towards storytelling is a salient feature of Duffy's later narrative poems. Her trademark dramatic monologue is successfully employed in *The World's Wife* (1999) in which, drawing on Greek mythology, the **Bible**, fairy tales, literature, history, and film, Duffy gives voices to such characters as Mrs. Midas, Queen Herod, Mrs. Beast, Mrs. Faust, Frau Freud, and Queen Kong, who present their versions of life behind the myth of famous men. Surreal **tall tale**s in *Feminine Gospels* (2002) continue the poet's exploration of the female condition.

A blend of realism, surrealism, and the grotesque creates an eerie world in Duffy's poems for children in *Meeting Midnight* (1999) and *The Oldest Girl in the World* (2000). The *Collected Grimm Tales* (2003), adapted without mollification by Duffy and dramatized by Tim Supple, revive both well-known and obscure originals in a contemporary idiom. Duffy's interest in the genre is also reflected in her own prose writings for children, *The Stolen Childhood and Other Dark Fairy Tales* (2003). *See also* Children's Literature; Feminist Tales; Poetry.

Further Readings: Duffy, Carol Ann. *New Selected Poems.* London: Picador, 2004; Rees-Jones, Deryn. *Carol Ann Duffy.* Plymouth: Northcote House, 1999; Rowland, Anthony, and Michelis Angelica, eds. *The Poetry of Carol Ann Duffy*: *"Choosing Tough Words."* Manchester: Manchester University Press, 2003.

Olga Holownia

Dulac, Edmund (1882–1953)

A French illustrator influenced by William Morris and Walter **Crane**, and a rival in the book market of Arthur **Rackham**, Edmund Dulac distinguished himself with his Oriental style. After studying art in Toulouse and Paris, by age twenty-two the anglophile Dulac made his way to London, where he received his first commission to illustrate the novels of the Brontë sisters. Like Rackham, Dulac contributed to the *Pall Mall Gazette* and exhibited his works at the Leicester Galleries, which later would commission him to illustrate a series of deluxe gift books published by Hodder and Stoughton.

The first of these was *The **Arabian Nights*** (1907), which contained fifty watercolors characterized by their earthy orange tones. In 1910, he produced illustrations for Sir Arthur Quiller-Couch's *The Sleeping Beauty and Other Tales from the Old French*, in which Dulac drew from Chinese and Japanese landscape painting as well as European Orientalist painting. The wife of **Bluebeard**, for instance, lounges on couches with her female guests, recalling scenes like Léon Belly's *Intérieur d'un harem* (c. 1865). For **"Cinderella"** and **"Sleeping Beauty,"** however, Dulac resorts to a more classical style, situating the characters in settings resembling an eighteenth-century French court. His illustrations for *The Snow Queen and Other Stories from Hans Andersen* (1911) also find inspiration in East Asian landscape painting, particularly evident in illustrations for "The Nightingale." Dulac would illustrate two more books of Oriental tales: *Princess Badoura* (1913), retold by Laurence **Housman**, and *Sindbad the Sailor and Other Stories from the Arabian Nights* (1914), whose illustrations draw from Persian art. During World War I, Dulac published *Edmund Dulac's Fairy Book: Fairy Tales of the Allied Nations* (1916), in which he adopts the style of each tale tradition represented. *See also* Art; Illustration.

An illustration of Bluebeard by Edmund Dulac. [Christie's Images/ Corbis]

Further Reading: White, Colin. *Edmund Dulac*. New York: Scribner, 1976.

Anne E. Duggan

Dumas, Philippe (1940–)

The French children's author and illustrator Philippe Dumas collaborates frequently with his friend, the author-illustrator Boris Moissard. In 1977, they published a collection of tales, *Contes à l'envers* (*Upside Down Tales*), in which a number of classic fairy tales are turned inside out. Their strategy is in the tradition of Gianni **Rodari**. Dumas and Moissard coauthored the book, but the small, black-and-white drawings embedded throughout the text were done entirely by Dumas. Their parodic inversions, full of playful irony, appeal to adults as well as children. Traditional **archetype**s and **motif**s are confronted with modern characters, settings, and situations.

Three of the five tales subvert well-known fairy tales by Charles **Perrault**. "La belle histoire de Blanche-Neige" ("The Beautiful Story of Snow White") pokes fun at feminist retellings. In a republic ruled by **women**, the president/evil stepmother is determined to eliminate her rival, but the intelligent and beautiful **Snow White** becomes the leader of male bandits in the forest, who eventually lead the **men** of the nation in a revolution. In "Le petit chaperon bleu marine" ("Little Navy Blue Riding Hood"), the wolf and the grandmother both become victims of an ambitious heroine, who takes her grandmother to the zoo at knifepoint and locks her in the wolf's cage. Wordplay is the catalyst of the reversion of "**Sleeping Beauty**," as "La belle au bois dormant" ("Sleeping Beauty of the Wood") becomes "La belle au doigt brulant" ("Beauty with the Burning Finger"). *See also* Feminist Tales; Illustration.

Further Reading: Malarte-Feldman, Claire-Lise. "The French Fairy-Tale Conspiracy." *Lion and the Unicorn* 12.2 (1988): 112–20.

Sandra L. Beckett

Dundes, Alan (1934–2005)

As one of the leading scholars in international folkloristics, Alan Dundes founded and directed the Folklore Program at the University of California at Berkeley, with the Berkeley Folklore **Archives** serving as a model for gathering various **folklore** materials from oral and written sources. Alan Dundes perhaps best expressed his own creative genius in presenting innovative interpretations of traditional materials by way of the book titled *Folklore Matters* (1989), with its ingenious double meaning depending on whether "matters" is read as a noun or verb. Dundes stated his personal credo in an epilogue to his book on *Bloody Mary in the Mirror: Essays in Psychoanalytic Folkloristics* (2002): "As a psychoanalytic folklorist, my professional goals are to make sense of nonsense, find a rationale for the irrational, and seek to make the unconscious conscious" (Dundes, 137).

His folkloristic publications are informed by a morphological, structural, and above all psychoanalytical approach to traditional texts and their **variant**s. They deal with literally all genres of verbal folklore, with an emphasis on **folktale**s, **fairy tale**s, **legend**s, **myth**s, **proverbs**, **joke**s, stereotypes, superstitions, and **riddle**s. Among his many books are numerous studies that apply Freudian psychology and folkloric theories to folktales and fairy tales and their multifaceted meanings. These books include *The Morphology of North American Indian Folktales* (1964), ***Cinderella***: *A Folklore Casebook* (1982), *Oedipus: A Folklore Casebook* (1983, with L. Edmunds), *Sacred Narrative: Readings in the Theory of Myth* (1984), *The Wandering Jew: Essays in the Interpretation of a Christian Legend* (1986, with Galit Hasan-Rokem), *The Flood Myth* (1988), ***Little Red Riding Hood***: *A Casebook* (1989), *The Blood Libel Legend: A Casebook in Anti-Semitic Folklore* (1991), and *Two Tales of Crow and Sparrow: A Freudian Folkloristic Essay on Caste and Untouchability* (1997). By applying the psychoanalytical idea of projective inversion to folklore texts from many languages and cultures, Dundes shows that they are part and parcel of human communication, cognition, and worldview.

Dundes influenced folklore studies throughout the world, arguing incessantly for the comparative, historical, and international scope of the discipline of folklore that is concerned with tradition and innovation as well as identification and interpretation. With books such as *The Study of Folklore* (1965), *International Folkloristics. Classic Contributions by the Founders of Folklore* (1999), and the four-volume set *Folklore: Critical Concepts in Literary and Cultural Studies* (2005), he helped to maintain the scholarly rigor of folklore scholarship in its multifaceted manifestations. *See also* Freud, Sigmund; Motifeme; Native American Tales; Propp, Vladimir; Psychological Approaches; Structuralism.

Further Readings: Bendix, Regina, and Rosemary Lévy Zumwalt, eds. *Folklore Interpreted: Essays in Honor of Alan Dundes.* New York: Garland Publishing, 1995; Boyer, L. Bryce, Ruth M. Boyer, and Stephen M. Sonnenberg, eds. *The Psychoanalytic Study of Society: Essays in Honor of Alan Dundes.* Hillsdale, NJ: The Analytic Press, 1993; Mieder, Wolfgang, ed. *Festschrift for Alan Dundes on the Occasion of His Sixtieth Birthday on September 8, 1994.* Burlington: The University of Vermont, 1994. Special issue of *Proverbium: Yearbook of International Proverb Scholarship* 11 (1994); _____. *"Best of All Possible Friends": Three Decades of Correspondence between the Folkorists Alan Dundes and Wolfgang Mieder.* Burlington: The University of Vermont, 2006.

Wolfgang Mieder

Dutch Tales

The term "Dutch tales" encompasses stories from three geographic areas: Flanders (the northern, Dutch-speaking part of Belgium), the Netherlands, and the West Frisian province, which is part of the Netherlands but has its own language and cultural tradition.

As in many other European countries, the **collecting** of Dutch **folktale**s started in the nineteenth century. Pioneering collectors were Nicolaus Westendorp and the German Johann Wilhelm Wolf. In 1843, Wolf published a collection called *Niederländische Sagen* (*Dutch Legends*), and in 1873–74 a two-volume study by G. D. J. Schotel appeared under the title *Vaderlandsche volksboeken en volkssprookjes van de vroegste tijden tot het einde der 18e eeuw* (*National Folklore Books and Folktales from the Earliest Time until the End of the Eighteenth Century*). In 1892, Gerrit Jan Boekenoogen launched an appeal for others to send him Dutch folktales, which he published in the journal *Volkskunde* (*Folklore*). Many of these tales came from a doctor named Cornelis Bakker, who had been told the tales by his patients (Meder, 43).

The collection of folktales from the Netherlands, however, remained fragmented. In contrast, the Frisian linguistic minority had a greater interest in preserving its cultural heritage. The collecting of Frisian tales also started in the nineteenth century with work by Tiede

Roelofs and Waling Dykstra, and was continued in the 1960s and 1970s by Dam Jaarsma and Ype Poortinga.

Like Frisian tales, Flemish fairy tales were often collected for romantic and nationalistic reasons. After the Belgian state was established in 1830, the Dutch language was threatened with suppression by a French elite. Under the impulse of the "Vlaamse Beweging" (Flemish Movement), folktales were collected to help shape cultural identity. The first Flemish collection was *Oude Kindervertelsels in den Brugschen Tongval* (*Old Children's Stories in the Dialect of Bruges*, 1868) by Adolf Lootens. Victor de Meyere gave a broader overview of Flemish folktales in his four-volume *De Vlaamsche Vertelselschat* (*The Flemish Story Treasury*, 1925–33).

All of these collections led to inventories and anthologies of fairy tales according to regional types. J. R. W. Sinninghe made a typology of Dutch fairy tales in 1943, Maurits de Meyer catalogued Flemish fairy tales in 1921, and Jurjen van der Kooi did the same for Frisian tales in 1984. Ton Dekker, Jurjen van der Kooi, and Theo Meder have noted that current knowledge about the folktale in the Netherlands (in contrast to Flanders) is still patchy. It can nevertheless be observed that most folktales told in Dutch probably did not originate in the Dutch-speaking areas but were borrowed from books and other cultures. The collector of Flemish fairy tales Maurits de Meyer argues that Flanders lies at the crossroads of the Germanic and Romance traditions and is thus related to both. What de Meyer finds exceptional, however, is the fact that humor dominates in the Flemish folk stories, as well as in **wonder tale**s and **animal tale**s. In the view of Jurjen van der Kooi, the Dutch, Flemish, and Frisian folktale tradition is clearly embedded in the West-European context: only few stories seem original creations of individual storytellers. In the Frisian provinces, the most common genre is the *Novellenmärchen*, or the "fairy-tale **novella**." According to van der Kooi, the high number of supernatural opponents in Dutch fairy tales is especially striking. The tale of magic is by far the most popular of all types in Flanders and is often combined with elements from "Schwankmärchen" (humorous folktales), **legend**s, and **didactic tale**s (Lox, 296). Harlinda Lox has also pointed out the popularity of pancakes in Flemish tales and the frequency with which the Walloons, the French-speaking Belgians, are mocked.

The 1970s saw a revival of the fairy tale: a great number of anthologies, both with Dutch and translated tales, were published. Although these collections helped to spread national and regional folktales among the general public, the most popular stories in the Dutch-speaking countries remain imported: the best known are translations or **adaptation**s from the Brothers **Grimm,** Charles **Perrault,** Hans Christian **Andersen,** and the *Arabian Nights*. The popularity of these tales further increased with movies from the **Walt Disney Company,** supermarket editions, cassettes, as well as with the Dutch fairy-tale theme park De Efteling (see **Tourism**). It features an attraction based on "De Indische Waterlelies" ("The Indian Water Lilies"), a tale by the Belgian former Queen Fabiola. As Fabiola was from Spanish descent, her collection was originally published as *Los doce cuentos maravillosos* (*The Twelve Marvelous Tales*, 1955) but became very popular in the Dutch translation from 1961.

A number of twentieth-century Dutch authors have been inspired by traditional folktales to write their own **literary fairy tale**s. Paul Biegel translated and adapted Czech fairy tales and stories by the Brothers Grimm. He also makes ample use of fairy-tale figures in his own fantastic stories for children, most notably in *De tuinen van Dorr* (*Dorr's Gardens*, 1969). Godfried Bomans was inspired by Hans Christian Andersen in creating his literary fairy tales, *Sprookjes* (*Fairy Tales*, 1946).

Since the late twentieth century, fairy-tale retellings have become a popular genre in Dutch fiction. The most influential works include Wim Hofman's *Zwart als inkt* (*Black as Ink*, 1998), a retelling of "**Snow White.**" Hofman reinterprets the story by putting Snow White's longing for her **mother**'s love at the heart of the narrative. The Flemish author Anne Provoost published her subversive retelling of Jeanne-Marie **Leprince de Beaumont**'s "**Beauty and the Beast**" in *De roos en het zwijn* (*The Rose and the Swine*, 2004), using elements from Giovan Francesco **Straparola**'s "The Pig King" and relocating the story to Antwerp in the Middle Ages. Since then, fairy-tale retellings have achieved a great vogue. "**Little Red Riding Hood**" turns out to be an especially popular character and has been recycled by many authors, including Pieter Gaudesaboos in *Roodlapje* (*Little Red Rag*, 2003) and Edward van de Vendel in *Rood Rood Roodkapje* (*Red Red Riding Hood*, 2003).

Further Readings: Buijnsters, P. J., and Leontine Buijnsters-Smets. *Lust en leerling: Geschiedenis van het Nederlandse kinderboek in de negentiende eeuw.* Zwolle: Waande, 2001; Dekker, Ton, Jurjen van der Kooi, and Theo Meder. *Van Aladdin tot Zwaan kleef aan: Lexicon van sprookjes.* Nijmegen: SUN, 1997; Fabiola. *The Twelve Marvellous Tales.* Translated by John P. Fitzgibbon. Illustrated by. Tayina. Madrid: Ediciones Sinople, 1961; Griffis, William Elliot. *Dutch Fairy Tales For Young Folks.* New York: Thomas Y. Crowell Co., 1919; Lox, Harlinda, trans. and ed. *Flämische Märchen.* München: Eugen Diederichs, 1999; Meder, Theodoor. "Nederlandse sprookjes in de negentiende en twintigste eeuw." *Tot volle wasdom.* Edited by Berry Dongelmans et al. Den Haag: Biblion, 2000. 31–46; Meyer, Maurits de. *Les contes populaires de la Flandre: Aperçu général de l'étude du conte populaire en Flandre et catalogue de toutes les variantes flamandes de contes populaires, d'après le catalogue des contes types par A. Aarne.* Helsinki: Suomalainen Tiedeakatemia, 1921; _____. *Vlaamse Sprookjes.* Illustrated by An Candaele. 1957. Antwerpen: Standaard Uitgeverij, 1995; van der Kooi, Jurjen. "Das Zaubermärchen im niederländischen (einschließlich flämischen) und westfriesischen Sprachberreich." *Märchen und Märchenforschung in Europa: Ein Handbuch.* Edited by Dieter Röth and Walter Kahn. Frankfurt a.M.: Haag und Herchen, 1993. 156–69.

Vanessa Joosen

Duvall, Shelley (1949–)

As the executive producer and host of *Shelley Duvall's Faerie Tale Theatre* (1982–87), Shelley Duvall brought twenty-seven acclaimed **adaptation**s of fairy tales to cable **television**. She has also produced several other notable children's television series, and has had a successful career as a film and television actress.

Born in Houston and named for Mary Shelley, the author of *Frankenstein* (1818), Duvall was selling cosmetics in a department store when she was unexpectedly cast by director Robert Altman in his film *Brewster McCloud* (1970), set in the Houston Astrodome. Duvall's waiflike appearance and assured screen presence brought her starring roles in subsequent Altman films, notably *Thieves Like Us* (1974), *3 Women* (1977), and *Popeye* (1980). She has also appeared in movies directed by such major directors as Woody Allen, Tim **Burton**, Stanley Kubrick, and Terry Gilliam.

As a longtime collector of illustrated fairy-tale books, Duvall thought there might be a market for high-quality programs based on those books. She was able to convince executives at Showtime, then a nascent cable network, to invest in this idea. The result was *Faerie Tale Theatre*, featuring hour-long adaptations of fairy tales and children's stories, starring top-name actors and actresses. From September 1982 to November 1987, there were many noteworthy performances: Jennifer Beals as **Cinderella**, Joan Collins as **Hansel and Gretel**'s stepmother, Carrie Fisher as Thumbelina, Mick Jagger as an emperor, James Earl Jones as a genie, Elizabeth McGovern as **Snow White**, Liza Minnelli as a **princess**, Tatum O'Neal as Goldilocks, Bernadette Peters as **Sleeping Beauty**, Christopher Reeve as a **prince**, Paul Reubens (aka Pee Wee Herman) as Pinocchio, Lee Remick as the Snow Queen, Susan Sarandon and Klaus Kinski as **Beauty and the Beast**, Harry Dean Stanton as Rip Van Winkle, Mary Steenburgen as **Little Red Riding Hood**, Robin Williams as the Frog Prince (see **Frog King**), and more. Duvall was also able to attract many top film-makers—such as Tim Burton, Francis Ford Coppola, Eric Idle, Ivan Passer, and Roger Vadim—to direct some of these programs.

Due to this success, Duvall was able to produce another series for Showtime, *Shelley Duvall's Tall Tales and Legends* (1985–86), based on folkloric characters. When *Faerie Tale Theatre* was sold into syndication for nearly $5 million in 1987, Duvall founded Think Entertainment, one of the first companies to develop and produce programs exclusively for cable networks, such as the Disney Channel, Home Box Office, Lifetime, Showtime, and Turner Network Television. One such series was *Shelly Duvall's Bedtime Stories* (1991–96), which presented animated versions of fairy-tale-like stories, such as *The Christmas Witch* and *The Little Rabbit Who Wanted Red Wings*. As both an actress and a producer, Duvall continues to find new ways to bring fairy tales to wider audiences. *See also* Animation; Film and Video.

Further Readings: Fanning, Deirdre. "The Shelley and Ted Show." *Forbes* 145 (February 5, 1990): 172–74; Haase, Donald. "Gold into Straw: Fairy Tale Movies for Children and the Culture Industry." *Lion and the Unicorn* 12.2 (1988): 193–207; Zipes, Jack. "Once upon a Time beyond Disney: Contemporary Fairy-Tale Films for Children." *Happily Ever After: Fairy Tales, Children, and the Culture Industry.* New York: Routledge, 1997. 89–110.

James I. Deutsch

Dvořák, Antonín (1841–1904)

A composer from what is now the Czech Republic, Antonín Dvořák composed a number of works influenced not only by Bohemian folk **music** but also by Slavic folktales. Dvořák was born near Prague in what was then the Austrian Empire and studied music from the age of six, eventually developing skills in the violin and the viola. His musical career took him to England and the United States, where he lived for several years, serving as director of the National Conservatory of Music in New York. Dvořák ultimately returned to his native Bohemia, serving as a conservatory director in Prague from 1901 to 1904.

Dvořák, a major figure of the Czech Romantic Movement, drew heavily on Bohemian **folklore** in his compositions. He earliest works based on folktale material were *Sirotek* and *Rozmarýna*, both from 1871 and based on poems by Karel Jaromír Erben that drew on folk-tale material from Czech history. Dvořák would return to Erben's folktale **adaptation**s in 1896 and 1897 with five symphonic poems, *Polednice (The Noon Witch)*, *Zlatý kolovrat (The Golden Spinning Wheel)*, *Houloubek (The Wild Dove)*, *Píseň bohatýrská (A Hero's Song)*, and *Vodník (The Water Goblin)*, all of which drew upon Erben's *Kytice z povřstí národních (A Bouquet of National Legends)* published in 1853. Dvořák also worked exten-sively with the work of author Božena Nřmcová, adapting her work into his **opera**s *Čert a Káča (The Devil and Kate*, 1899) and *Rusalka* (1901). Both of these works have librettos in

Czech, the first by Adolf Wenig and the second by Jaroslav Kvapil, and are based on Nřmcová's work with folktales, with *Rusalka* also drawing further on the work of Erben. These operas also show the influence of Richard Wagner on Dvořák, primarily in the selection of subject matter from the folkloric tradition in a Romantic-nationalist manner.

One interesting thing about Dvořák's works on folktale material is that he did not limit it to Czech subject matter but worked with the folklore of other cultures as well. *Čtyři písnř na slova srbské lidové poezie* (*Four Songs on Serbian Folk Poems*), which was initially performed in1872, showed some of Dvořák's affinity for Slavic material. This fondness was fully realized in the opera *Vanda* of 1875. Based on a Polish **legend** about a pagan **princess** who committed suicide because she had to marry a Christian German knight, *Vanda* is frequently interpreted as a metaphor for the Czech struggle against Austrian imperial domination. Dvořák's last major work drawing on folklore from elsewhere is his Ninth Symphony (1893), frequently referred to as the New World Symphony, due to its composition in the United States. While there is no clear consensus on Dvořák's influences in composition, many have cited Native American and African American music as heavily influencing Dvořák.

Further Reading: Clapham, John. "The Operas of Antonín Dvořák." *Proceedings of the Royal Musical Association* 84 (1957–58): 55–69.

B. Grantham Aldred

Dwarf, Dwarves

Dwarfs (or dwarves) commonly appear in folktales and fairy tales from northern Europe but are best known from Norse mythology, notably from the *Prose Edda* (c. 1220), a compilation of **myths**, **folklore**, and poetic forms by antiquarian Snorri Sturluson. Dwarfs are great craftsmen, and forged such major treasures as the mead of poetry, Odin's spear, the golden **hair** of Sif (wife of the god Thor), and especially Thor's hammer, which defended the realm of the gods from the chaos threatened by the frost giants. Dwarfs were also repositories of wisdom and masters of runes and magic songs. Short in stature, they lived in underground tunnels or within rocks and hence, like other dwellers underground, were thought to turn to stone if touched by sunlight. Subterranean habits are attributed to them in all Germanic cultures.

In folktale collections and retellings from the seventeenth to nineteenth centuries, dwarfs are mostly creatures of dubious purpose (as in "Rumpelstiltskin") or quite evil (Marie-Catherine d'**Aulnoy**'s "Le nain jaune" ["The Yellow Dwarf"]). The unfriendly dwarf in Jacob and Wilhelm **Grimm**'s "Schneeweißchen und Rosenrot" ("Snow White and Rose Red") fulfills a stereotype: he is long-bearded, bad-tempered, obsessed with wealth, lives under a rock, and a malevolent magic worker. However, in perhaps the best-known dwarf story, "**Snow White** and the Seven Dwarfs," the dwarfs are entirely benevolent.

Probably because of their chthonic associations, dwarfs are linked with the elements: in Norse mythology, four dwarfs, named North, East, South, and West, hold up the corners of the sky; in the Swiss tale, "The Dwarf in Search of Lodging," the dwarf apparently causes a flood and then prevents it from harming an old couple who had earlier given him **food** and shelter; and the dwarfs in Hallmark's made-for-**television** movie *Snow White: The Fairest of Them All* (directed by Caroline Thompson, 2001) are named for the days of the week and control the weather.

Modern **fantasy** literature (including role-playing games) follows J. R. R. **Tolkien**'s *The Hobbit* (1937) and *The Lord of the Rings* (1954–55) in depicting Norse-derived dwarfs (plural *dwarves* in Tolkien) as long-lived, bearded, often xenophobic, surly (especially in the proximity of traditional enemies such as **elves**, trolls, goblins, and orcs), and greedy for treasure. Their characteristic fighting weapon is a battle-axe (a common weapon in medieval Scandinavia). Tolkien was able to build on these limiting traits to depict character development of dwarf heroes into trustworthy and heroic members of a questing company.

Tolkien's propensity to define characters by race and class stereotypes has been parodied by Terry **Pratchett**'s depiction of dwarfs in his Discworld novels, most extensively in *The Fifth Elephant* (1999) and *Thud!* (2005). Pratchett follows Tolkien in identifying different dwarf clans, but his principal distinction is between those who remain in their underground homelands and those who migrate to the city, where they work as artificers but also spend a lot of time in dwarf bars singing nostalgic songs about gold and home. Further, picking up on an allusion in Tolkien to the indistinguishability of female dwarfs from male, Pratchett introduces the engaging character of Cheery Littlebottom, who outrages traditionalists by experimenting with **gender**-specific body appearance.

Further Readings: Gilmour, Simon J. "Die Figur des Zwerges in den *Kinder- und Hausmärchen* der Brüder Grimm." *Fabula* 34 (1993): 9–23; Natov, Roni. "The Dwarf Inside Us: A Reading of 'Rumpelstiltskin.'" *Lion and the Unicorn* 1.2 (1977): 71–76.

John Stephens

E

Eckert, Horst. *See* Janosch

Editing, Editors

The first task in preparing a collection of tales for publication is the selection of content, and in some instances this can be daunting. For example, Richard Francis **Burton**'s edition of the *Arabian Nights* (1885–88) fills sixteen large volumes, whereas any version of this work intended for popular consumption would contain only a small portion of this material. Further, in creating readable texts, editors may feel compelled to standardize dialects and to bring grammar, spelling, and punctuation to literary norms. However, scholars intending to provide authentic texts for linguistic or folkloric study will leave the texts in the form delivered by their **informant**s, possibly providing supplementary explanations of unfamiliar words and situations.

Restricted by censors, marketplace pressure, or both, publishers traditionally avoid words or descriptions deemed to be obscene, presenting editors with a dilemma when confronted by such expressions or episodes in the original texts. Many editors deem it their duty to replace objectionable words with euphemisms and to rewrite potentially offensive passages. "We have carefully removed every expression inappropriate for children," reassure Jacob and Wilhelm **Grimm**, in the foreword to the second edition of their *Kinder-und Hausmärchen* (*Children's and Household Tales*, 1812–15).

Finally, editors often assert the freedom to retell folktales to "improve" their aesthetic qualities, as successfully done—for example—in Italo **Calvino**'s *Fiabe italiane* (*Italian Folktales*, 1956), or to bring them into social conformity with a particular ethical or political view. *See also* Authenticity; Collecting, Collectors; Translation.

Further Readings: Ashliman, D. L. Censorship in Folklore. 2006. http://www.pitt.edu/dash/censor.html; Tatar, Maria. "Rewritten by Adults: The Inscription of Children's Literature." *Off with Their Heads! Fairy Tales and the Culture of Childhood*. Princeton, NJ: Princeton University Press, 1992. 3–21; Vandergrift, Kay E. Censorship of Mother Goose and Her Followers. 2006. http://eclipse.rutgers.edu/goose/censorship1.aspx; Zipes, Jack. "Once There Was a Time: An Introduction to the History and Ideology of Folk and Fairy Tales." *Breaking the Magic Spell: Radical Theories of Folk and Fairy Tales*. Austin: University of Texas Press, 1979. 1–19.

D. L. Ashliman

Egyptian Tales

Despite nearly two centuries of intensive research on ancient Egyptian religion, art, and literature, the orally communicated **folktale** remains shrouded in mystery. This uncertainty can be attributed to three factors: (1) Nearly all documents that have reached us from antiquity were produced by learned scribes and professional priests who, like their modern counterparts, seem to have disdained vernacular and informal oral **storytelling** and wrote in styles steeped in allegoric ambiguities. Moreover, most recorded narrative texts are fragmentary or incomplete. (2) As folktales, the relatively limited number of stories currently thought of as Egyptian received scant attention. Egyptologists did not use the perspectives or research methods known to **folklore** scholars, while students of the folktale dealt with only a few select ancient texts within the confines of preconceived European "theories." One such theory accorded the ability to create a **märchen** (fairy tale) for certain racial groups that excluded Egyptians. (3) There is an absence of folktale collections from modern times. Only a few collections, undertaken by European linguists, dealt with Egypt and neighboring lands that were within the cultural domain of ancient Egypt. Thus, the possible links between ancient texts and modern folktales has remained unexplored. (Note that this entry refers to **motif**s and **tale type**s developed by Hasan El-Shamy in *Folk Traditions of the Arab World* and *Types of the Folktale in the Arab World*. The sign § indicates a new motif or tale type. The sign ‡ indicates a newer motif or tale type developed after the publication of *Folk Traditions*.)

The existence of the folktale in ancient Egypt can only be inferred. Some tantalizing hints allude to social situations in which the oral folktale seems to have been present on the Egyptian scene, but no details were provided. One of these appears in "King Khufu and the Magicians" (Fourth Dynasty), wherein the story speaks of deities disguised as wandering musicians, who must have also sung hymns and praise songs (Motif K1817.3.2§, ‡Disguise as wandering musician [singer, bard, etc.]). This text also refers to "the telling of marvels known only to people of other times, but of which the truth cannot be guaranteed," thus indicating awareness of the narrative categories that are taken seriously and of those that are not. In addition, some drawings indicate the existence of ordinary **animal tale**s, but no accompanying texts were provided.

The ancient repertoire that survived reveals that virtually all of the texts belonged to the category of narratives that were taken seriously. These represented the realms (or genres) of belief (**myth**s/sacred accounts, religious **legend**s) and the factual (historical legends, personal experiences or **memorate**s, and business reports). Notably, the **epic** was not one of the forms in which Egyptians recorded their beliefs or history. Even the "Tale of Two **Brothers**" (ATU 318, The Faithless Wife), whose publication in 1852 established the link between ancient Egyptian narratives and folktales (*contes populaires*)—a genre not previously encountered in Egyptian records—may prove to have been a folk "myth." Some recent studies identify the main characters in the narrative, Anubis and Batu (also known as Anpu and Bata), as two local deities rather than ordinary humans.

The oldest tale, entitled "King Khufu and the Magicians," seems to have been recorded during the Twelfth Dynasty (2000–1785 BCE). It is based on Motif P470.0.1§, ‡Tale-teller needed (required)—so as to tell story (to sleepless ruler). The text links serially several independent stories and may be seen as a prototype of the **frame narrative** made famous by the *Arabian Nights*. The frame story corresponds to tale type 1920E1§, Contest: Strangest (Most Bizarre) Story Awarded Prize, a recurring theme in modern times. Constituent narratives correspond to tale types ATU 1359, Husband Outwits Adulteress and Lover; and 930E§, ‡Prophecy: Unborn Child (Infant) Predestined to Replace King. Another story includes the earliest occurrence of Motif D1551 (Waters magically divide and close) as a magical feat performed for a compassionate pharaoh.

One of the late—that is, recent—narratives of Egyptian antiquity harkens back to the Twenty-Sixth Dynasty (570–526 BCE). It tells of how a slave girl married Pharaoh Amasis as a result of a golden "slipper test" (Motif H36.1). The story, given as a historical fact, may be seen as the **urform** of ATU 510, Cinderella and Peau d'Âne. Another story of the late period, though depicting scenes from much older dynasties, is the tale of Rhampsinitus, the treasury master thief (ATU 950), reported by Herodotus the Greek historian (c. 484–425 BCE). Although this tale was acquired from Greek-Egyptian sources, it is probably the first ancient text collected from **oral tradition** wherein a travel guide acted as **informant**.

On the basis of evidence found in modern oral folk traditions in Egypt and surrounding nations, including sub-Saharan Africa, numerous tales may be viewed as deriving from ancient sacred/religious accounts (myths). In the myth of Isis and Osiris, we find components that may have provided the foundations for current folktales. These include types 758C§, Origin of Sibling Rivalry: conflict between siblings of the same sex began when one was favored over the other; and 932A§, The Sister Who Desires a Son Sired by Her Brother Achieves Her Goal: The Unsuspecting Brother (Motif K1843.5§, Sister masks as her brother's wife and sleeps with him). In the ancient context, the persona involved are the twin deities Osiris-Isis and Seth-Nephthys; in the Semitic religious context, the twins are Cain and his twin sister, and Able and his twin sister; while in Arab historical legends, the characters are the heroes Luqmân and Abu-Zaid, each deceived by his own sister. Likewise, the adventures of Isis in Byblos to secure her murdered husband's corpse have been shown to be related to the modern tales designated as type 591A§, The Thieving Starling; and AT 1442*, Stupid Queen's Unsuccessful Imitation of Magic. (She kills [burns] her own child).

Another ancient myth dating back to the New Kingdom (the Eighteenth, Nineteenth, and Twentieth dynasties, 1554–1085 BCE) describes aspects of the struggle between the deities Horus and Seth, under the title "The Blinding of Truth by Falsehood." This ancient account was shown to be the oldest form of the widespread modern tradition designated as ATU 613, The Two Travelers (Truth and Falsehood), and ATU 980*, The Painter and the Architect. In addition, current **trickster**s, such as Goha, and many of their deceitful deeds have been shown to duplicate episodes from these ancient struggles.

If the relationship between an ancient text and its modern counterpart appears evident in most of these cases, there are several instances where such ties may be assumed to exist or may be attributed to archetypal patterns of thought (as in **polygenesis**). For example, "The Prince and the Sphinx" describes how a dream led Thutmose IV, when still a young prince, to undertake the first act of restoring the neglected sacred relic, and how he consequently was rewarded with Egypt's throne. This very theme occurs daily in modern Egypt, where deceased "saints" come to their followers in visions and demand that a shrine be erected or properly maintained. Comparable to AT 506** (The Grateful Saint), this Egyptian pattern is also designated in *Types of the Folktale in the Arab World* as 760B§, ‡Restless Soul: Deceased cannot rest because of worldly concerns; his soul contacts the living to make wishes known.

These and other links between ancient Egyptian texts and modern folktales deserve further investigation by scholars. With new theoretical perspectives, modern folktale collections, and research tools such as motif and tale-type indexes representing the Arab world, scholars are poised to undertake the objective study of ancient Egypt's narrative traditions as folktales.

Further Readings: Brunner-Traut, Emma. *Altägyptische Märchen.* Düsseldorf: Diedrichs, 1965; Budge, Ernest A. Wallis, ed. and trans. *Egyptian Tales and Romances* London: T. Butterworth, 1931; El-Shamy, Hasan. *Folk Traditions of the Arab World: A Guide to Motif Classification.* 2 volumes. Bloomington: Indiana University Press, 1995; ———. *Folktales of Egypt: Collected, Translated, and Annotated with Middle Eastern and African Parallels.* Chicago: University of Chicago Press, 1980; ———. *Types of the Folktale in the Arab World: A Demographically Oriented Approach.* Bloomington: Indiana University Press, 2004; Hollis, Susan T. *The Ancient Egyptian "Tale of Two Brothers": The Oldest Fairy Tale in the World.* Norman: University of Oklahoma Press, 1990; Maspero, Gaston C., ed. *Popular Stories of Ancient Egypt.* Edited by Hasan El-Shamy. 2002. Oxford: Oxford University Press, 2004; Simpson, William Kelly, ed. *The Literature of Ancient Egypt.* New Haven, CT: Yale University Press, 1972.

Hasan El-Shamy

Eichendorff, Joseph Freiherr von (1788–1857)

A leading exponent of German Romanticism, Josepeh Freiherr von Eichendorff wrote **poetry** and **literary fairy tale**s that drew upon **motif**s and figures from German **folklore**. He was born into the impoverished Prussian aristocracy near Ratibor in Upper Silesia. He studied philosophy and law at the universities of Halle and Heidelberg, where he made the acquaintance of Achim von Arnim and Clemens **Brentano**. Literature provided a creative outlet and supplemented his income from the poorly paid civil-service jobs he held until his retirement in 1844.

Eichendorff is best known for lyrical poems resembling folk songs. Many of his poems were inspired by *Des Knaben Wunderhorn* (*The Boy's Magic Horn,* 1805–08), the collection of German folk songs edited by Arnim and Brentano. Reworking the Grimm **legend** and Brentano folk song of the "Loreley," whose beauty was said to cause sailors to drown in the Rhine, Eichendorff's poem "Waldgespräch" ("Forest Conversation") transported the legendary seductress to the quintessential Romantic location, the forest. His prose works often contained poetry, and Robert Schumann and Richard Strauss set several of his best-loved poems to **music**.

Eichendorff's most important **novella**s, *Das Marmorbild* (*The Marble Statue,* 1819) and *Aus dem Leben eines Taugenichts* (*Memoirs of a Good-For-Nothing,* 1826), both draw upon and subvert the conventions of the folktale and literary fairy tale. *The Marble Statue* relates the journey of Florio, the comic type of reluctant suitor who repeatedly fails to recognize his true love, Bianca. Whereas the obstacle to happiness in the folktale is external and often takes the form of a villain, prohibition, or curse, in *The Marble Statue*, the obstacle to the union of the lovers stems from the hero's unconscious fantasies and misguided ideals, which cause him to fall in love with a statue of the goddess Venus. The happy ending also distinguishes *The Marble Statue* from the literary fairy tales of Romantic authors such as E. T. A. **Hoffmann** and Ludwig **Tieck**, whose protagonists' stories end in despair or madness. In contrast to Hoffmann's tales in particular, Eichendorff's are more realistic and lighthearted.

Memoirs of a Good-For-Nothing most closely approximates a folktale, with the salient motif of the unpromising hero (Motif L100). Denounced by his **father** as a good-for-nothing and expelled from home, the lazy younger son of a miller goes out into the world to make his fortune. Although recreating the fairy-tale world and consistent in style with comic folk-tales such as **Grimm**s' "Hans im Glück" ("Lucky Hans," 1819), the first-person narration in *Memoirs of a Good-For-Nothing* clearly sets it apart from the narrative conventions of the folktale. Critics have seen the Romantic protest against bourgeois capitalism in the hero, a carefree artist and vagabond who refuses to adapt to social norms. ***See also*** German Tales.

Further Readings: Eichendorff, Joseph Freiherr von. "The Marble Statue." *German Literary Fairy Tales.* Edited by Frank G. Ryder. New York: Continuum, 1983. 133–71; McGlathery, James. "Magic and Desire in Eichendorff's *Das Marmorbild.*" *German Life and Letters* 42.3 (1989): 257–68.

Mary Beth Stein

Einfache Formen. *See* Simple Forms

Ekman, Fam (1946–)

A Norwegian author-illustrator born in Sweden, Fam Ekman has used fairy tales innovatively in sophisticated, postmodern picture books that challenge conventional views of the genre. Her intertextual play with fairy tales includes unusual, humorous allusions as well as highly original retellings. *Rödhatten og Ulven* (*Red Hat and the Wolf*, 1985) is a playful version of "Little Red Cap" that reverses the **gender** of the main characters, opposing a naïve little country boy and a seductive urban she-wolf in a red dress. It shows that girls are not the only ones at risk from **wolves**, which come in both sexes, thus counterbalancing certain feminist revisions that fall into new gender stereotypes. This retelling is enhanced by elegant, sequential frames which offer comedic scene-to-scene transitions. Ekman's unconventional fairy-tale characters are a blend of expressionism and **cartoons**.

A very homely **Little Red Riding Hood** appears unexpectedly in *Lommetørkleet* (*The Handkerchief*, 1999), adding a touch of color to almost monochromatic pages. In this whimsical story of a self-centered **cat** that abandons his owner, taking her handkerchief with him, Little Red Riding Hood wants to borrow the handkerchief to protect her picnic from the ants in the woods. Ekman's bold composition, distinctive collages, and quirky characters are well illustrated by *Skoen* (*Shoe*, 2001), a whimsical reworking of the **Cinderella** story, in which the fairy-tale character and her prince, a cleaning lady and an old bachelor respectively, are reunited in their golden years. ***See also*** Cross-Dressing; Postmodernism.

Further Reading: Beckett, Sandra L. *Recycling Red Riding Hood.* New York: Routledge, 2002. 174–82.

Sandra L. Beckett

El Dorado

The lore of El Dorado, "The Gilded One," enters history in the early 1500s, when rumors of a city of treasures began luring explorers into the vast interior of South America. Interest centered on the middle reach of the Amazon River, but there were expeditions to other areas as well, including Paraguay and the Guiana region. Gold objects from Peru, traded widely, seemed to confirm the reports of an as-yet-undiscovered realm, ripe for plunder.

The term "El Dorado" itself may be understood as referring to a native ruler covered in gold. The missionary-historian Pedro Simón's *Noticias historiales* (1617), notice 3, ch. 1, gives a full version of the **legend**. In former times, it is related, the Muisca, or Chibcha, of central Colombia observed a ritual of sacrifice in which gold and jewels were thrown into a sacred lake. Then a chieftain, his body coated with gold dust, rode out in a splendid canoe and was bathed in the waters until all of the gold had been washed away.

As an emblem of the fabulous—a beacon for either the foolhardy or the enterprising—El Dorado found a place in literature (for example, John Milton's *Paradise Lost,* book 11, l. 411; Voltaire's *Candide,* chs. 18–19; Edgar Allan Poe's "El Dorado"; and Willa Cather's *El Dorado: A Kansas Recessional*) and became the name of at least thirteen towns in Colombia, Brazil, Texas, Kansas, and elsewhere.

Further Readings: Silverberg, Robert. *The Golden Dream: Seekers of El Dorado.* 1967. Athens: Ohio University Press, 1996; Slater, Candace. *Entangled Edens.* Berkeley: University of California Press, 2002.

John Bierhorst

Elf, Elves

Elves are a variety of supernatural beings well known in both the British Isles and the Nordic countries from which they appear to have originated in the early **Middle Ages**. Commonly (if mistakenly) associated with **fairies** and often connected with various physical afflictions in later medieval and renaissance Britain, the original *álfar* (singular *álfr*; cf. *ælf* in Old English; and *alp* in Old High German) appear to have been regarded in Old Nordic belief

"The Barn Elves," illustrated by S. E. Wallter, in *Queer Folk: Seven Stories* by E. H. Knatchbull-Hugessen (London: Macmillan and Co., 1874), p. 267. [Courtesy of the Eloise Ramsey Collection of Literature for Young People, University Libraries, Wayne State University]

as near equals to the gods and giants, rather than nature spirits. Indeed, it has been argued that *álfar* was another name for certain fertility gods (Freyr, Freyja, and Njörðr) who were essentially worshipped in Sweden. (Indications in J. R. R. **Tolkien**'s *Silmarillion* [1977] suggest that he saw the same connections when creating the elves that form the core of his mythology.) One early Icelandic poet even talks of Swedish people holding elf sacrifices.

The root of the word *álfr* (elf) appears to come from Indo-European **albh* (cf. the Latin *albus*), meaning "white one," and various early references point to connections between the *álfar* and brightness. However, as time went on, the image of the original *álfar* began to change, not least through ecclesiastical influences that actively associated them with demons, if not fallen angels. The Icelandic historian Snorri Sturluson apparently had this angelic parallel in mind when he invented the idea of dark and light elves in his *Prose Edda* (c. 1220). (His original sources make no such division.) By the thirteenth century, and probably earlier in England, the *álfar* were beginning to blend with nature spirits that British and Nordic people had always believed inhabited the landscape. In Shakespeare's *A Midsummer Night's Dream* (3.1.134 and 3.3.151) the words "fairy" and "elf" are used interchangeably, and the same applied in Scotland where "elf" was more commonly used for those beings later known as "fairies."

While elves in the British Isles gradually diminished in size, those in the Nordic countries remained similar in appearance to humans, their only distinguishing marks being their good looks or (in Norway) their latterly acquired tails. The names for these beings have also changed. In Norway and Denmark, where they have blended with other supernatural beings such as farm guardians and trolls, they are often known as *troll*, *huldre* (hidden ones), or *underjordiske* (underground dwellers). In Iceland, where they are also called *huldufólk*, their homes tend to be in rocks above ground.

The chief characteristic of these beings in **legend**s and **memorate**s is that they live on the periphery of our world and regularly interact with humans, either by direct cooperation (the sharing of food or livestock, via requests for help with **birth**s) or by luring innocent men or women into illicit relationships. They are also known for stealing children and replacing them with **changeling**s. *See also* Faerie and Fairy Lore; Scandinavian Tales.

Further Readings: Hall, Alaric Timothy Peter. "The Meanings of *Elf* and Elves in Medieval England." Dissertation. University of Glasgow, 2005. http://www.alarichall.org.uk/phd.php; Lindow, John. *Handbook of Norse Mythology*. Santa Barbara, CA: ABC-CLIO, 2001. 109–10.

Terry Gunnell

Enchantress. *See* Sorcerer, Sorceress

Ende, Michael (1929–1995)

One of the most successful German authors in postwar Germany, Michael Ende wrote fantasy and **children's literature** that has been translated into more than forty languages and is read all over the world. The son of the surrealist painter Edgar Ende, he studied theater in Munich, pursued literary studies and the arts, and eventually started writing his own works of poetry and prose. Ende's formative years introduced him to Rudolf Steiner's esoteric understanding of the Brother **Grimm**s' fairy tales and also to Bertolt Brecht's drama theories. Working in many different genres—including drama, **poetry**, and short fiction—Ende is best known for his work as children's book author and writer of **fantasy** literature in which he attempts to infuse the everyday world with the remedial powers of poetry, **folklore**, and fairy tales.

Ende's earlier work includes two of his many prize-winning children's books, *Jim Knopf und Lukas der Lokomotivführer* (*Jim Button and Lukas the Engine Driver,* 1960), and *Jim Knopf und die Wilde 13* (*Jim Button and the Wild 13*, 1962), both of which relate the story of a black foundling's adventurous encounters with giants, **dragon**s, and pirates. These early novels were followed later by *Momo* (1973), about a little girl who saves her society from a group of gray gentlemen who attempt to steal people's time, and *Die unendliche Geschichte* (*The Neverending Story,* 1979), Ende's best known dual-world tale in which a boy enters a fantastic realm that first exists only in a book but then becomes powered by his own imagination.

Ende's attraction to the Romantic Movement and the Romantic fairy tale remained the foundation of his literary works. The fantastic realms in his tales are not so much an irreversible escape from the everyday world into a utopian counter reality; rather, they represent a state of mind where the infusion of meaningful poetry into a meaningless world becomes possible. Ende uses **motif**s of magic, talking animals, and the cryptic power of language to create new cultural myths for a technocratic society that has lost touch with nature. Reminiscent of his favorite Romantic poet **Novalis**, Ende's self-proclaimed lifelong quest was to find the one magic word that represented the socio-aesthetic founding principle of modern society and culture. To give new impulses to the everyday world, Ende often broke with established literary conventions. His prose and poetry texts usually defy established logics of story patterns, causalities, and rationalization.

One of the recurring characters in Ende's writings is the *Gaukler*, or juggler, an **archetype** that he used most prominently in *Das Gauklermärchen* (*The Circus Clowns' Fairy Tale*, 1982). Invoking the juggler, Ende suggests that his own fantastic literature is not a practical tool that can change the present order of society. Instead of formally reeducating the audience, Ende's works seek to enlighten the mind with a new self-reflexive vision and free play. *See also The NeverEnding Story.*

Further Reading: Haase, Donald. "Michael Ende." *Contemporary German Fiction Writers.* Second Series. Edited by Wolfgang D. Elfe and James Hardin. Detroit: Gale, 1988. 54–58.

Nicolay Ostrau

English Tales

Fewer **wonder tale**s have been found in England than in neighboring Ireland and Scotland, but the country is rich in other types of traditional narrative, especially local and historical **legend**s and humorous tales. Scholarly collections in recent decades have made many texts easily available. It is no longer possible to complain that England has no folktales.

Folktales in Preindustrial England

In the early and medieval periods, magical and fantastic **motif**s occur abundantly in works whose overall plots do not fit into the Aarne-Thompson folktale typology. Thus, the hero of the Anglo-Saxon **epic** *Beowulf* (c. 700–1000 CE) defends a house against an **ogre**, whom he defeats by tearing his arm off; then he plunges down through a pool to an underwater Otherworld, where he kills the ogre's mother. Many years later, he slays a **dragon**, but at the cost of his own life. There are similarities to an Irish and Scottish tale, "The Hand and the Child," to the **Bear's Son** subtype of ATU 301 (The Three Stolen Princesses), and to the widespread motifs of underwater worlds and dragon-slaying—but nobody could call *Beowulf* a **folktale**.

Again, there are plenty of marvels and enchantments in the Arthurian tales (often modeled on French sources), which Sir Thomas Malory wove together into *Le Morte d'Arthur* (printed in 1481). Others are found in the late medieval verse romances *Sir Guy of Warwick* and *Sir Bevis of Hampton,* about English legendary heroes, and *Huon of Bordeaux*, a translation from French; the latter is the earliest text to mention Oberon, king of the **fairies**. Walter Map's light-hearted miscellany *De Nugis Curialium* (*Courtiers' Trifles,* c. 1190) includes two **anecdote**s that have features well attested in international **fairy lore**. One tells how Herla, a (nonhistorical) early king of Britain, agreed to visit the underworld realm of a pigmy, where he was lavishly entertained. Upon returning to the human world, Herla found that almost 200 years had passed; those of his retinue who had dismounted had crumbled to dust (Motifs F377 and F378.1). Map's second story tells how Wild Edric, a historical English aristocrat contemporary with William the Conqueror, caught a fairy woman in a forest; she consented to be his wife provided he never taunted her about her origins, but years later he broke this taboo, and she vanished (Motif F302.6). William of Newburgh's *History of the Kings of England* (c. 1198) seriously asserts that, in Yorkshire, a man passing a certain hillock was offered a drink by the fairies feasting inside. He stole their precious cup, escaped pursuit, and gave the cup to King Henry I (1100–33), who in turn gave it to the King of Scotland. This is a perfect early example of the migratory legend ML 6045, Drinking Cup Stolen from the Fairies.

Two anonymous medieval poems entirely devoted to magical **fantasy** are "Sir Orfeo" and "Sir Gawain and the Green Knight," both from the fourteenth century. The former, which claims to be based on a Breton lay (a narrative poem), tells how Queen Heurodys is abducted into a sinister fairy world that is also a world of the dead, and how Orfeo sees her riding among a troupe of hunting fairies, follows them, and wins her back from the otherworld by his music (Motif F322.2). The latter tells how a gigantic Green Knight offers to let Gawain behead him if Gawain in turn allows himself to be beheaded a year later (a motif found also in medieval Irish tales); the bargain is accepted, but the Green Knight picks up his severed head and rides off. Gawain's courage, chastity, and truthfulness are further tested when he reaches the castle of the magically disguised knight and his enchantress wife.

Elizabethan plays provide evidence that some of the standard wonder tales were circulating in England during that period. The humor of George Peele's significantly titled *Old Wives' Tale* (1595) depends upon the audience's recognition of a medley of fragmented fairy-tale plots. These include a **king**'s daughter held captive by an enchanter and rescued by her two **brothers** (also used by John Milton in his masque *Comus,* 1634); a dead man (Motif E341) who helps the man who paid for his funeral to rescue a **princess** but tests him by asking that she be cut in half (ATU 505, The Grateful Dead); and a pair of half-sisters who go to a well in which floating heads ask, "Stroke me smooth and comb my head" (ATU 480, **The Kind and the Unkind Girls**).

In William **Shakespeare**'s *Much Ado About Nothing* (1599), Benedict jokingly quotes the tag, "It is not so, nor 'twas not so, but indeed God forbid it should be so," saying it is from an old tale. To explain this, a scholar in 1821 put on record the story "Mr. Fox," which he had learned from his great-aunt; it is an excellent **cante fable** version of ATU 955, The

Robber Bridegroom. Its popularity in England is confirmed by about a dozen shorter variants found as local legends. Folktale allusions probably also underlie the Fool's words in *King Lear* (1623), "Child Rowland to the dark tower came, / His word was still Fie foh and fum, / I smell the blood of a British man." The couplet is a common tag in tales about the killing of giants, but the first line is mysterious. In 1814, Robert Jamieson claimed that it refers to the story of the two brothers rescuing their sister, but the **ballad** he offered in evidence is no longer accepted as genuine.

Shakespeare had a decisive—some would say, damaging—influence on the way fairies were portrayed in English literature and **art**. When he put them on stage in *A Midsummer Night's Dream* (1595–96), and gave a playful description of Queen Mab in *Romeo and Juliet* (1597), wherein he spoke of them as very small, pretty, harmless creatures. His **Puck** (aka Robin Goodfellow) is still a mocking **trickster**, as in folk tradition, but never dangerous. Although Shakespeare must surely have known folktales, he never borrowed a plot from them.

Complete **märchen** begin to reach print in the seventeenth and eighteenth centuries. A **chapbook** entitled *Jack and the Giants* (c. 1750–60) is the earliest surviving version of the story of "Jack the Giant-Killer," a medley of "stupid ogre" and giant-killing episodes (including ATU 328, The Boy Steals the Ogre's Treasure; and ATU 1088, Eating/Drinking Contest), set in the reign of King Arthur. It was widely known in the eighteenth and nineteenth centuries, as literary allusions prove; some episodes were localized in Cornwall. A lively oral telling, dating from 1909, is given in Ella M. Leather's *The Folklore of Herefordshire* (1912). Equally popular was Jack and the Beanstalk (ATU 328A), but the surviving chapbooks (1807) are poor texts, so the best version is a recreation from childhood memories by the folklorist Joseph **Jacobs** in 1890. In Norfolk, a cycle of local tales about Tom Hickathrift was printed in a chapbook (c. 1660) and is still orally current; the tales describe his huge strength, which terrified every farmer he worked for, and how he fought and killed giants. *The History of Tom Thumb the Little* is a booklet of 1621 by "R. J." (probably Richard Johnson, 1573–1659?), but there are allusions to the story (ATU 700, **Thumbling**) several decades earlier. All of these publications catered to readers who liked down-to-earth stories, with humor and **violence**; none of the more romantic wonder tales were printed.

Native English versions of the latter certainly existed, but before anybody thought of **collecting** and printing them, a flood of foreign ones appeared—first those of Charles **Perrault**, Marie-Catherine d'**Aulnoy**, and Jeanne-Marie **Leprince de Beaumont**; then those of the Brothers **Grimm**; and finally those of Hans Christian **Andersen**. Selections from these were soon translated and printed in chapbooks and other cheap editions, as were a few stories from the *Arabian Nights*; they became thoroughly integrated into English popular culture, where their foreign origins were rapidly forgotten. The native wonder tales lived on, precariously, as oral stories told among working-class people, and sometimes by nursemaids to **children** of middle-class families, but publishers and scholars ignored them until late in the nineteenth century.

Folktale Collectors

Joseph Jacobs, in his *English Fairy Tales* of 1890, opens his introduction defiantly: "Who says that English folk have no fairy tales of their own?" In this book and its successor *More English Fairy Tales* (1894), Jacobs retold eighty-seven stories, from various sources and of varied types. There are märchen, including "Tom Tit Tot" and "Cap o' Rushes," which are good Suffolk versions of ATU 500, The Name of the Supernatural Helper, and ATU 510B, Peau d'Asne, both printed in an Ipswich newspaper in late 1870s. There is a group of village numskull stories, "The Wise Men of Gotham" (ATU 1213, 1287, and 1291); a few localized tales such as "The Pedlar of Swaffham" (ATU 1645, The Treasure at Home) and a Cornish version of ML 5070, Midwife to the Fairies; and some animal **fable**s, jocular anecdotes, and nursery tales. In his notes, Jacobs apologizes that these "scanty survivals ... for the present must serve as the best substitute that can be offered for an English Grimm." However, he hoped that others might still be found by regional **folklore** collectors.

There are in fact stories fitting into Aarne-Thompson-Uther's category Tales of Magic (ATU 300–749) that had been published before Jacobs wrote, and it is strange that he apparently did not know them, or did not think them relevant. One example is "Duffy and the Devil" (ATU 500, The Name of the Supernatural Helper), a Cornish tale from Robert Hunt's *Popular Romances of the West of England* (1865). Another, a version of "The Frog Prince" (ATU 440, The **Frog King** or Iron Henry) from Oxfordshire, was printed in the journal *Notes and Queries* on May 15, 1852.

A number of folktales are scattered through collections of regional and county folklore compiled in the late nineteenth and early twentieth centuries. Among them are several good stories from Derbyshire in Sidney O. Addy's *Household Tales with Other Traditional Remains* (1895), such as "The Little Red Hairy Man" (ATU 301, The Three Stolen Princesses) and "The Small-Tooth Dog" (ATU 425C, Beauty and the Beast). Other tales appeared in the journal *Folk-Lore*.

Gypsy travelers had, and still have, a strong tradition of **storytelling**, an art that they practice among themselves, not as a **performance** to entertain outsiders. Being constantly on the move throughout England and the Scottish Lowlands, they escaped the attention of regional folklore collectors. Some of their tales were printed in the specialist *Journal of the Gypsy Lore Society* and others in a collection by Dora Yates, *A Book of Gypsy Folk-Tales* (1948). Even more valuable are the unpublished manuscript notebooks of Thomas William Thompson, compiled in the first two decades of the twentieth century. Thompson recorded many long narratives from gypsy storytellers and gave detailed summaries of others. Some examples were printed by Katharine M. Briggs in her four-volume compilation, *A Dictionary of British Folk-Tales in the English Language* (1970–71), and by Neil Philip in his *English Folktales* (1992). These include "Lousy Jack and his Eleven Brothers" (a blend of ATU 551, Water of Life, and ATU 410, **Sleeping Beauty**); "Sorrow and Love" (ATU 425, The Search for the Lost Husband); "The Frog Sweetheart" (ATU 440); "Snow-White" (ATU 709, **Snow White**); "Doctor Foster" (ATU 955, The Robber Bridegroom); and "Mossycoat" (ATU 510B, Peau d'Asne). In Cumberland in 1914, a gypsy told Thompson "The Little Red Hairy Man" (ATU 301) in a version almost identical to the one Addy had found in Derbyshire twenty years earlier.

Contexts for Storytelling

One reason that the records are so scattered and scanty is that England did not have any tradition of formal gatherings for public storytelling and singing such as were common in Ireland and the Scottish Highlands. Only in Cornwall were there semiprofessional storytellers, namely the wandering droll-tellers of the early nineteenth century—men who tramped from one farm to the next and were welcomed for their music and tales. Some of their stories were related by Robert Hunt in his *Popular Romances of the West of England* (1865), though he chose to "improve" their style. Others were recounted rather more reliably by William Bottrell in *Traditions and Hearthside Stories of West Cornwall* (3 vols., 1870–80). Giant-killing was a common topic, though in Cornwall the hero's name was usually Tom, not Jack. Their narratives had many colorful details. For example, "The Droll of Lutey and the **Mermaid**" in Bottrell's collection, which was the favorite story of a blind storyteller called Uncle Anthony James, is a distant variant of ML 4080, The Seal Woman, told at considerable length. Similarly, Bottrell had often heard the story of "Tom the Giant-Killer" told by "an aged tinker of Lelant" who could spread the tale over three or four winter evenings; this storyteller would go into minute detail, and indulge in glowing descriptions of the treasures in the giant's castle, though he would carefully leave the traditional dialogue unchanged.

Passing references can be found to more casual storytelling situations. One writer in the 1830s describes how **men**, **women**, and children in the Yorkshire and Lancashire dales would gather in one house for a knitting session after the day's work was over, and as they knitted they would enjoy telling "all the old stories and traditions of the dale." He unfortunately does not say what these were. Henry Mayhew in *London Labour and the London Poor* (1861) gives a short, vigorous rendering of a version of ATU 1525, The Master **Thief**, here entitled "Clever Jack," which was told to him by an intelligent-looking sixteen-year-old boy in a London workhouse. The boy said the inmates would sometimes tell stories among themselves—romantic tales, **bawdy tale**s, and tales about "some big thief who was very clever at stealing." He added that they would always call the hero Jack.

By far the most commonly mentioned situation for storytelling was the domestic one, with older women as the narrators and children as the audience. Particularly significant in this connection is the role of the working-class nanny or nursemaid in a middle-class household; she would pass on the beliefs and stories of **oral tradition** to youngsters, some of whom in later life became writers themselves and put them on record. Charles **Dickens** is an outstanding example. In his essay "Nurse's Stories" in *The Uncommercial Traveller* (1860) and again in his Christmas story "The Holly Tree," he describes with comic gusto the sinister tales with which his nurse Mary Weller used to terrify him. They all involved crime and horror: an innkeeper who would cut a guest's throat as he slept, drop the body through a trapdoor, and bake it into pies; a murderous burglar who was identified by a clever servant girl who killed him with a red-hot poker; and so forth. They were said to be true, and some seem to have been brief, not unlike the genre we would now call contemporary legends or **urban legend**s. But the two longer ones that Dickens relates in full have much repetition of incident and of formulaic phrases, as in märchen narration. "Chips" is about a ship's carpenter who owes his skill to a pact with a demonic rat but fears that the rat will take him in the end; and so it does, since poor Chips, unlike other folktale heroes who have dealings with the **devil**, cannot escape the consequences. The stages of the tale are marked by a repeated rhyme. The superbly gruesome "Captain Murderer" is, as Dickens puts it, "an offshoot of the **Bluebeard** family," in which a bridegroom kills and eats a succession of young brides; it can also be seen as a rationalized version of ATU 311, Rescue by the Sister, but one in which the storyteller has rejected a happy ending. As Mary Weller tells it, both **sisters** die, but at least the second one ensures that the villain is spectacularly punished.

Doubtful Cases

No doubt there have always been some storytellers who changed traditional narratives to suit their personal tastes, and others whose tales do not fit into recognizable categories and patterns. Unless the folklorist who collects such nonstandard stories is known to be scrupulously accurate, doubts can arise over their **authenticity** as folklore. One group of tales presenting problems of this kind are the twelve "Legends of the Lincolnshire Cars" published by Marie Clothilde Balfour in *Folk-Lore* (1891)—"Cars" being a word for drained areas of fens. One story, "Tattercoats," is a poor variation on the **Cinderella** theme, but the rest are unlike any traditional tales in England or elsewhere. Some give hints of mythical themes and rural paganism; others have weird, ghoulish motifs. Although Balfour took them down in note form from **informant**s whom she names, the expanded versions she printed are in a thick dialect that later scholars have criticized as linguistically inaccurate. There is some suspicion that she tampered with the contents as well as the language, but Jacobs and Briggs accept them as authentic.

The work of Ruth Tongue is even more controversial, though it was accepted as authentic by Briggs, who included a lot of Tongue's material in her *Dictionary of British Folk-Tales in the English Language*. A retired teacher and theatrical producer, Tongue became known in Somerset in the 1960s as a lively performer of folktales and folksongs that she said she had learned there some fifty years earlier as a child. However, there is good reason to suspect that her sources were not always the pure oral traditions she claimed, and that her material was much embellished and recreated in her own personal style. Like Balfour, she relied heavily on quaint dialect. But unlike Balfour, her tone is sweet, not sinister, and her endings are invariably happy. Her stories are usually local legends and anecdotes, often featuring fairies and other supernatural beings and motifs, but not fully developed wonder tales.

Local and Migratory Legends

Local legends are far more abundant than märchen in English tradition; the 900 pages of Jennifer Westwood and Jacqueline Simpson's *The Lore of the Land* (2005) give a representative selection. In practice, the distinction between the two genres is not watertight. Sometimes a fairy-tale plot is attached, quite unchanged, to a particular locality. In "Duffy and the Devil," the Cornish version of ATU 500, the scene where a demon helper is overheard boasting of his unguessable name is set in the *fougou* (artificial cave) at Boleigh. More often, it is only the core motif of a märchen that is matched by a legend. For instance, many places have a local story about a man who kills a dragon, sometimes in straight combat but generally through some cunning device, but (unlike ATU 300, The Dragon-Slayer) none features a rescued princess, and only one example, in Jersey, has the impostor and the dragon-tongue proof.

Certain shorter narratives that have been given ATU numbers are commonly told in England as localized legends about specified persons and places and are often grouped in cycles. The fool **joke**s (ATU 1200–1349) told against the people of various villages are one example. Others are the cycles of anecdotes telling how some locally famous wizard, such as Jack o' Kent in Herefordshire or Tommy Lindrum in Lincolnshire, made a pact with the devil, used him as a servant, made a fool of him, and cheated him in the end (ATU 756b, 1030–59*). The tale of how the devil built a bridge for the price of a soul but got only a dog or **cat** as his pay (ATU 1191) is found at Kentchurch in Herefordshire, Tarr Steps in

Somerset, and Kirby Lonsdale in Westmorland. Cockerham in Lancashire has the story of a man who rashly summons the devil and gets rid of him by giving him an impossible task, weaving ropes of sand (ATU 1174). The very similar migratory legend ML 3020, Inexperienced Use of the Black Book (Sorcerer's Apprentice) is also found in Lancashire, told of schoolboys and their teacher at Bury; there, the impossible task is to count the letters in the church Bible.

The **tale type**s classified as "novelle" (see **Novella**) or "romantic tales," where the events are astonishing but not supernatural, are well represented among English local legends. Those recorded here, often in several different places, include ATU 736A, The Ring of Polycrates; ATU 939A, Killing the Returned Soldier; ATU 955, The Robber Bridegroom; ATU 956B, The Clever Maiden Alone at Home Kills the Robbers; ATU 960A, The Cranes of Ibycus; ATU 974, The Homecoming Husband (ML 8005, The Return of the Warrior); ATU 990, The Seemingly Dead Revives; and ATU 1645, The Treasure at Home.

Migratory legends—those that recur in many different places—are very common in England. Most of the types classified in *The Migratory Legends* (1958) by Reidar Thoralf Christensen on the basis of Norwegian material can be found here. Those relating to the devil include ML 3015, The Cardplayers and the Devil; and ML 3025, Carried by the Devil or by Evil Spirits. The latter is told in Northumberland of the medieval philosopher and alleged wizard Michael Scot, and in Wiltshire of St. Aldhelm, first Abbot of Malmesbury. ML 3070, The Devil and the Dancers, is used as an **etiologic tale** to account for certain groups of standing stones, in the form typified by the German medieval tale of the "Dancers of Kolbeck." The fullest English version is from Stanton Drew (Somerset), where it is said that Satan was a fiddler for a Sabbath-breaking wedding party, causing them to dance wildly and then turn to stone.

ML 3055, The Witch That Was Hurt, is extremely common. English versions tell how the **witch**, in the form of a hare, constantly eludes pursuit, until one day she is hurt on the hind leg just as she is taking refuge in her cottage; a corresponding wound on her human body gives away her secret. Legends found here that describe the interaction of fairies and humans include ML 5070, Midwife to the Fairies; ML 5080, **Food** from the Fairies; ML 5085, The **Changeling**; and ML 6045, Drinking Cup Stolen from the Fairies. There are several relating to house fairies—ML 6035, Fairies Assist a Farmer in His Work; 7010, The House-Fairy's Revenge for Being Teased; 7015, The New Suit; and 7020, Vain Attempt to Escape from the House-Fairy.

Other widespread stories explain landscape features as due to the actions of a giant or of the devil; for instance, that he set out to bury a town but was tricked into dropping his shovelful of earth elsewhere, or that he flung a large rock that missed its target, or dropped one through stupidity. All such stories are in the category ML 5020. Another type found again and again is ML 7060, Disputed Site for a Church. All such tales are intimately linked to topography and sometimes also to the supposed origin of place-names. Several places have versions of The Sleeping Warriors (also known as The King Under the Mountain), with King Arthur as the hero who will one day awaken; Christensen did not include this in his list, but Briggs provisionally numbered it ML 8009*. Tales of buried treasure (ML 8010) are abundant too, with well-known international motifs such as the supernatural animal treasure-guardian, the supernatural phenomena that scare away the treasure-seekers, and the ritual conditions (especially a rule of silence) that when broken cause the treasure to be lost at the last moment. Several of the same motifs occur in the equally common legends about church bells sunk in rivers, lakes, or the sea (ML 7070). The category for robber tales (ML 8025) is also well represented; one notable recurrent story (not listed by Christensen) is "The Hangman's Stone"—a thief who is carrying home a live sheep he has stolen stops to rest against a certain boulder, but while he sleeps the movements of the sheep cause the rope binding it to twist around the man's neck and choke him.

Among many ghost legends, two well-developed narrative types recur (see **Ghost Story**). One is attached to old houses where a skull is (or was) preserved and displayed; it explains why the person whose skull it is had insisted it be kept there and not buried, and how attempts to remove it caused psychic disturbances and were abandoned. The other type tells how a priest or group of priests confronted a fierce ghost that was terrorizing the locality, weakened it by fearless prayer, and then either shut it in a small box or bottle that was thrown in deep water, or set it some endless, impossible task. A few variants from the southwestern counties add that the ghost has escaped and is returning home, but only by the measure of one cock-stride per year. Clearly, the comparative rarity of märchen in England is balanced by an abundance of other forms of traditional narrative.

Literary Fairy Tales

Many English authors have written **literary fairy tales**, whether for children or for adults. In the Victorian period, they were often regarded as useful tools for teaching moral lessons to the young. John **Ruskin**'s *The King of the Golden River* (1851) and the stories of Mary Louisa **Molesworth** and Juliana Horatia **Ewing** are examples. Ewing's work is enlivened by a good sense of humor. Others used the genre in more personal and less-simplistic ways. These include William Makepeace **Thackeray**'s farcical *The Rose and the Ring* (1855); George **MacDonald**'s fantasies with strong allegorical and spiritual subtexts (*At the Back of the North Wind*, 1871; *The Princess and the Goblin*, 1872; and *The Princess and Curdie*, 1883); Charles Kingsley's chaotic but intermittently entertaining *The Water Babies* (1863); and Oscar **Wilde**'s elegant, melancholy tales in *The Happy Prince and Other Tales* (1888). From the early twentieth century, one can pick out as particularly successful E. **Nesbit**'s lively blend of fairy tale and adventure story in *Five Children and It* (1902), *The Phoenix and the Carpet* (1904), and *The Story of the Amulet* (1906); and from the 1950s, C. S. **Lewis**'s six books set in the imaginary world of Narnia, full of magical adventures and quests, with strong religious themes. Less well known, but far more powerful, is his adult version of the **Cupid and Psyche** story, *Till We Have Faces: A Myth Retold* (1956); it is narrated from the viewpoint of Psyche's ugly older sister, whose intensely possessive love for the girl is in fact an obstacle that both must painfully overcome before they can find salvation and joy in the divine love offered to them.

In recent decades, several writers of literary fairy tales have taken ultrafamiliar stories (for example, "Bluebeard," "Sleeping Beauty," and "**Little Red Riding Hood**") and rewritten them to convey feminist messages or to convey their possible sinister and/or erotic implications while preserving the atmosphere of magic and marvel. Important examples include Angela **Carter**'s *The Bloody Chamber and Other Stories* (1979); Tanith **Lee**'s *Red as Blood: Or Tales from the Sisters Grimmer* (1983); and Marina **Warner**'s *The Mermaids in the Basement* (1993). This approach is naturally linked to the numerous critiques produced by scholars since the 1970s on the **gender** stereotyping and patriarchal assumptions underlying traditional tales.

Fantasies based on fairy lore have flourished over the last fifty years. An early writer in this vein was Sylvia Townsend Warner, whose *Kingdoms of Elfin* (1977) described fairies as an elegant, sophisticated race, but coldhearted and cruel; her inspiration came from Irish and Scottish folk beliefs rather than märchen. Susanna **Clarke**'s *Jonathan Strange & Mr Norrell* (2004) presents a similar but even more sinister picture of the fairy world.

More popular are large-scale adventure fantasies set in complex imaginary worlds, appealing to older children and adults alike. Though the genre can trace some of its roots back to American "sword-and-sorcery" writing of the 1930s and 1940s (itself an offshoot of science fiction), the major influence has been that of J. R. R. **Tolkien**. His children's story *The Hobbit* (1937) is a fairly lighthearted quest story, but the three-volume *Lord of the Rings* (1954–55) is a darker study of good and evil and the proper use of power, written in a consciously archaic "high" style and full of motifs drawn from **epic**s and **myth**s. Despite its conventional happy ending, it has deeply melancholy undertones.

Other fine **novel**s in this genre include those of Alan **Garner**, who successfully blends the landscape and legends of his own home district with magical adventures (*The Weirdstone of Brisingamen*, 1960; *The Moon of Gomrath*, 1963; and *Elidor*, 1965); and the Earthsea quartet of Ursula **Le Guin** (*A Wizard of Earthsea*, 1968; *The Tombs of Atuan*, 1971; *The Farthest Shore*, 1972; and *Tehanu*, 1990). Also notable are the comic fantasies of Terry **Pratchett**'s ongoing Discworld series, which constantly borrow, adapt, parody, or allude to items of myth, fairy tale, and folklore. *Witches Abroad* (1991) pits three good witches against one ruthless one who controls people by locking them into the stereotypes of such fairy tales as "Cinderella," "The Frog King," and "Little Red Riding Hood"; *Lords and Ladies* (1992) reworks the plot of *A Midsummer Night's Dream*; *Hogfather* (1996) revolves around popular notions about Father Christmas and tooth fairies. Pratchett celebrates "narrativium," the power of a good story to get itself told again and again, to mold our imaginations, and to be acted out in real life. And the best stories begin and end as mythic, fairy-tale patterns.

Further Readings: Avery, Gillian. "Written for Children: Two Eighteenth-Century English Fairy Tales." *Marvels & Tales* 16 (2002): 143–55; Briggs, Katharine M. *A Dictionary of British Folk-Tales in the English Language: Incorporating the F. J. Norton Collection*. 4 volumes. London: Routledge and Kegan Paul, 1970–71; Jacobs, Joseph. *English Fairy Tales and More English Fairy Tales*. Edited by Donald Haase. Santa Barbara: ABC-CLIO, 2002; Knoepflmacher, U. C. *Ventures into Childland: Victorians, Fairy Tales, and Femininity*. Chicago: University of Chicago Press, 1998; Philip, Neil, ed. *The Penguin Book of English Folktales*. London: Penguin Books, 1992; Westwood, Jennifer, and Jacqueline Simpson. *The Lore of the Land: A Guide to England's Legends*. London: Penguin Books, 2005; Zipes, Jack. *Victorian Fairy Tales: The Revolt of the Elves*. New York: Methuen, 1987.

Jacqueline Simpson

Epic

Epic can be described as an oral or literary genre that powerfully memorializes a story of central significance and interest to a particular cultural group's identity, and that usually contains some amalgam of other genres (such as **fairy tale**, **folktale**, **saga**, charm, encomium, lament, prayer, **proverb**, catalogue, etc.). The term "epic" ultimately derives from Greek *epea* ("story"; sing. *epos* "utterance"), which in Homeric poetry designates a traditional heroic tale of the sort Demodocus is urged to sing to the Phaeacians (*Odyssey* 8.91). Epic may emphasize narrative as it characterizes action and central, often significant human, semidivine, or divine heroic figures (depending on the particular constituency). It is consequently often longer than other native genres. Epic may be poetic, though it need not resemble the *Iliad* or *Beowulf*, which follow rigid metrical schemes—"poetry" is not defined in the same way in every culture. An epic may be created orally, as with the South Slavic *Wedding of Mustajbey's Son Bećirbey*, and speak to its audience though the language of a long-standing, shared, **oral tradition** (metonymy). Alternatively, as with the *Aeneid*, the foremost national epic of the Romans, it may be a self-conscious literary work, which artificially and intentionally imitates or plays off its predecessors (the *Iliad*, *Odyssey*, and *Argonautica*). An epic may also lie at any point between an oral traditional and literary creation. Some epics, such as the Finnish ***Kalevala***, a creative literary synthesis of smaller genuine oral traditions, attempt to preserve and access oral tradition through written form.

The range of epic as genre has been greatly increased by the study of living oral epics, such as those from India (for example, the Tulu *Siri Epic),* North Asia (for example, Mongolian and Tibetan epics), and Africa (for example, *Mwindo Epic*). Further, cycles (circulating clusters of traditional stories) of epics, both ancient and modern, have been discovered on every continent, stretching far back in their inherent traditions. Moreover, diverse cultures have been borrowing **motif**s, themes, and story patterns from one another, suggesting that epics evolve to meet changing needs within the bounds of each culture's mores. As with folktales, epics can be seen to follow traditional patterns of presentation in their representation of significant cultural stories. Less helpfully, Western models have sometimes been used to exclude non-Western traditions. In such cases, the definition for "epic" has become prescriptive rather than descriptive. A more circumspect approach recognizes the work done by anthropologists and folklorists, who hear or read the "texts" of a cultural group (*ethnos*) from within as well as outside the given tradition. Only after such readings, in reality, is it possible to effectively compare epics from different cultures.

Further Readings: Foley, John Miles. *How to Read an Oral Poem*. Urbana: University of Illinois Press, 2002. With eCompanion at http://www.oraltradition.org/hrop; Foley, John Miles. "Epic as Genre." *The Cambridge Companion to Homer*. Edited by Robert Fowler. Cambridge: Cambridge University Press. 2004. 171–87; Martin, Richard. "Epic as Genre." *A Companion to Ancient Epic*. Edited by John Miles Foley. Oxford: Blackwell Publishing, 2005. 9–19.

Andrew E. Porter

Erdrich, Louise (1954–)

Louise Erdrich, a highly acclaimed Native American writer, has published eleven **novel**s, four children's books, three volumes of **poetry**, and three works of nonfiction. Erdrich often affirms that **storytelling**, and particularly traditional **folktale**s from her Ojibwe (Anishnaabe, Chippewa) and German heritage, inspire her work.

Erdrich considers herself primarily a storyteller. In her novels and poetry, she often evokes traditional characters, themes, patterns, and images from **myth** and folktale. Erdrich breathes new life into the tales and characters inspired by the Ojibwe corpus, such as the traditional **trickster** Nanabozho. In Erdrich's novels, the Nanapush family carries on his legacy through humor, ingenuity, and antics, as well as complexity of character and mastery of words and storytelling (see especially the original Nanapush in *Tracks* [1988] and *Four Souls* [2004]). Erdrich excels at incorporating multiple voices, creating complex characters and rich imagery, and writing lyrically. Her often-tragic themes are balanced by humor and beauty (see especially *Love Medicine* [1984]; *The Antelope Wife* [1998]; and *The Painted Drum* [2005]).

Most of Erdrich's novels center on a fictional community in North Dakota (nine of her eleven novels are set there), which features a reservation near the town of Argus. Her complex, successful, quirky, fictional North Dakota community leads many people to compare her to William Faulkner. However, the Native American themes in Erdrich's work and her writing style distinguish her as original. Prominent topics throughout her work include characters struggling to maintain traditions (or succeeding at doing so), while also negotiating the modern world and the powerful, mainstream, non-Native American society. Additionally, she often writes about the influence of the Roman Catholic Church upon her Native American community, and of characters searching for identity and meaning. In addition to incorporating characters and themes from traditional Ojibwe folktales, Erdrich has woven fabulous tales of German immigrants in *The Master Butcher's Singing Club* (2003) and *The Beet Queen* (1986).

Edrich grew up in North Dakota, spending time on the reservation with her maternal relatives but living primarily in Wahpeton with her parents, who taught at a Bureau of Indian Affairs School. Erdrich received a Bachelor of Arts degree from Dartmouth College and a Master of Arts in creative writing from Johns Hopkins University. For years, Erdrich lived in the Northeast with her husband writer Michael Dorris, who taught at Dartmouth. Since the couple's separation in the mid-1990s and Dorris's suicide in 1997, Erdrich has lived in Minneapolis. Along with writing full time, she runs a bookstore there. Erdrich often expresses a desire to more deeply understand both her Ojibwe and German heritage. She is a student of the Ojibwe language, which she often sprinkles into her fiction. *See also* Magical Realism; Native American Tales; Silko, Leslie Marmon.

Further Readings: Chavkin, Allan, ed. *The Chippewa Landscape of Louise Erdrich.* Tuscaloosa: University of Alabama Press, 1999; Jacobs, Connie A. *The Novels of Louise Erdrich: Stories of Her People.* New York: Peter Lang, 2001.

Mary Magoulick

Erotic Tales

Erotic tales—stories that are concerned explicitly with **sex** and **sexuality**—exist widely in both oral and literary traditions. A distinction may be drawn between erotic folktales that circulate orally and erotic tales that are literary creations or rewrites of previously adapted fairy tales. However, the study of erotic tales, whether in oral or literary tradition, is impeded by the lack of scholarly materials devoted to sexual **motif**s.

Collections of erotic folktales have appeared sporadically, regulated by censorship. Two examples of erotic folktale texts are Aleksander **Afanas'ev**'s *Russkie zavetnye skazki* (*Russian Forbidden Tales,* 1872; translated as *Russian Secret Tales: Bawdy Folktales of Old Russia*, 1966) and Vance Randolph's *Pissing in the Snow and Other Ozark Folktales* (1976). While these collections each have annotations, by Giuseppe **Pitrè** and Frank A. Hoffman respectively, their utility is hindered by the lack of a common referential system.

Other erotic folktales collected from **oral tradition** have appeared in journals devoted to "obscene" folklore: the French publication *Kryptadia* (1883–1911) and the German publication *Anthropophyteia* (1904–13).

Orally circulating erotic folktales tend to deal with earthy themes, including scatology and sex. Topics present in the collections of **bawdy tale**s by Afanas'ev and Randolph include feats of sexual prowess; premarital and extramarital sex; and **incest** both practiced and averted. Erotic folktales are underrepresented in each of the incarnations of the **tale-type** index, which can make comparative work difficult. Moreover, few collections contain contextual information surrounding folklore performances. Randolph's collection is notable for giving specific information about the teller of each folktale. Another important work is Roger Abrahams's *Deep Down in the Jungle: Negro Narrative Folklore from the Streets of Philadelphia* (1963), especially for its collection and analysis of **African American tales** that run the gamut from **joke**s to toasts and frequently incorporate some irreverent if not erotic elements.

Erotic fairy tales in the literary tradition are different from erotic folktales collected from oral tradition not only due to the degree of literary stylization and commodification present, but also because erotic fairy tales are largely based upon a closed body of texts: already well-known fairy tales. Moreover, erotic fairy tales are fluid in the forms they can take, ranging from romance novels to filmed pornography. An example of the former is Anne Rice's **Sleeping Beauty** trilogy (1983, 1984, and 1985), while an example of the latter is the pornographic video *The Punishment of Red Riding Hood* (1996).

Although there is a wealth of scholarship available on fairy tales, little of it pertains explicitly to sexual identities and relations, despite the fact that erotic tales have long played a significant role in the literary tradition. Examples of erotically charged literary tales are evident in the *Arabian Nights*—which is, after all, premised on an account of voyeurism and sexual betrayal—and in the Orientalist stories they inspired in Europe in the eighteenth century. Tales by Anthony **Hamilton**, Claude-Prosper de Crébillon, Jean de **La Fontaine**, and Denis Diderot offer good examples. Crébillon was imprisoned for writing the sexually charged tale "L'écumoire" ("The Skimmer," 1734). Diderot's "Les bijoux indiscrets" ("The Indiscreet Jewels," 1748), which involves a magic ring that can cause sexual organs to speak and reveal their activities, became widely known after it was published posthumously. Richard Francis **Burton**'s Victorian-era English translation of the *Arabian Nights*—published in 1885–88 by the Kama Shastra Society, a publisher of Indian erotica—took pains to exploit and intensify the work's sexual themes (in the narrative as well as in Burton's notes).

The **literary fairy tale** is a prime vehicle for the transformation of classic fairy tales into erotic fairy tales. Collections of erotic fairy tales are published and sold online and in bookstores; some are single-author collections of short stories, whereas others are anthologies featuring numerous authors and various styles of retellings. Four accessible collections are *Once upon a Time: Erotic Fairy Tales for Women*, edited by Michael Ford (1996); *Erotic Fairy Tales: A Romp through the Classics*, by Mitzi Szereto (2000); *The Empress's New Lingerie and Other Erotic Fairy Tales*, by Hillary Rollins (2001); and *Naughty Fairy Tales from A to Z*, edited by Alison Tyler (2003). These vary in how sexually explicit and normative they are; whether they feature heterosexual or homosexual interactions; and how closely they adhere to the structure and content of fairy tales.

Some of the erotic fairy tales that are published in short-story form revolve around a single sexual encounter, such as Szereto's version of "**Little Red Riding Hood**," which focuses more upon the heroine's sexual appeal than any actual sexual acts. Other tales feature multiple sexual encounters within the narrative, like Rollins's "**Snow White** and the Seven Dwarfs." The sexual encounters depicted range from what might be considered "normal" sex to the other end of the spectrum, as in a version of "**Cinderella**" in Michael Ford's collection that involves the use of restraints and other bondage gear.

The interactions between characters are sometimes heterosexual, as is the unspoken assumption in most fairy tales, and sometimes homosexual. In particular, **gay and lesbian fairy tales** are notable for their exploration of previously unquestioned relationships between characters of the same sex, as well as pairings that did not exist in the original versions of the fairy tales in question. For instance, a version of "Rapunzel" in the Ford collection explores a sexual relationship between the witch and Rapunzel—two characters who are not sexually connected in known variants of the fairy tale. The other possible homosexual alteration, substituting a character of a different **gender**, is more common in the four representative collections listed above. In Ford's anthology, **Puss in Boots** is a female servant who sexually serves her mistress; Jackie climbs a beanstalk to encounter a lesbian giant; and twelve butch lesbian **prince**s court the twelve dancing **princess**es.

The alterations in the degree of explicit sex and the sexual identities of characters are part of larger structural changes that occur in erotic fairy tales. Some tales conform strictly to the content and structure of the texts upon which they are based, while other erotic fairy tales are pastiche texts, in that they combine motifs from disparate fairy tales to achieve a fairy-tale feel. An example of a minor change to a fairy-tale plot would be substituting an act of kindness in a donor sequence with a sexual favor, as is the case in Szereto's "The Twelve Months." The degree to which an erotic fairy tale can be traced to a traditional text is related to the author's intent and the ideological implications of the tale. Collections of erotic fairy tales are often marketed toward **women**, listing female authors and depicting women on the covers.

Erotic folktales and fairy tales are especially provocative due to their subject matter, and studying them will illuminate shifting attitudes toward and performances of sex and gender in various societies. *See also* La Force, Charlotte-Rose de Caumont de; Pasolini, Pier Paolo.

Further Readings: Green, Rayna. Introduction. *Pissing in the Snow and Other Ozark Folktales.* By Vance Randolph. Urbana: University of Illinois Press, 1976. ix–xxix; Legman, Gershon. Introduction. *Russian Secret Tales: Bawdy Folktales of Old Russia.* By Aleksander Afanas'ev. 1966. Baltimore: Clearfield, 1998. v–xxxix.

Jeana Jorgensen

Ershov, Pyotr (1815–1869)

Pyotr Ershov's literary reputation rests mainly on his hilarious verse tale *Konyok gorbunok* (*The Little Humpbacked Horse*), which he wrote at the age of eighteen. While studying philosophy at the University of St. Petersburg, he presented his manuscript to the rector, Pyotr Pletnyov, a famous critic and poet. Pletnyov, in turn, showed the poem to his close friend, Aleksandr **Pushkin,** who invited Ershov to his home and gave him some friendly advice about the text. The first part was eventually published in the journal *Biblioteka dlya chteniya* in 1834, and the whole tale was printed as a separate book in the same year. There were ellipses in the place of many verses, however, since the censors had read it as a satire critical of the tsar. Success was immediate. The tale was, however, published in its complete form only in 1856. Brought up in Siberia, young Ershov traveled a great deal in his childhood. He listened to stories and tales, told by numerous coachmen, about marvels and the great past of Siberia. The tales, together with the mighty landscape, had an indelible impact and influenced all of his writings. In *The Little Humpbacked Horse*, Ershov brings forth familiar components from the Russian folk tradition in his own original way. The story is mainly based on the **motif** of the Golden-Maned Steed with Ivanushka the **Simpleton** as hero. It has become a classic of Russian **children's literature**. *See also* Russian Tales.

Further Reading: Jahn, Gary R. "Petr Pavlovich Ershov." *Russian Literature in the Age of Pushkin and Gogol: Poetry and Drama*. Edited by Christine A. Rydel. Detroit: Thomson Gale, 1999. 67–70.

Janina Orlov

Espinosa, Aurelio M. (1880–1958)

Aurelio M. Espinosa, scholar of Hispanic **folktale**s and comparative Hispanic **folklore**, was descended from the earliest Hispanic settlers of northern New Mexico and southern Colorado. In 1902, he graduated from the University of Colorado and began teaching Spanish at the University of New Mexico. In 1904, he received a Master of Arts degree from Colorado, and in 1909, a doctor of philosophy degree in Romance Languages from the University of Chicago. In 1910, he joined the faculty of Stanford University, where he chaired the Department of Romance Languages from 1932 until his retirement in 1947.

Eager to establish the relationship between the Hispanic folklore of New Mexico and Colorado and the folklore of Spain, Espinosa pioneered the field of comparative Hispanic folkloristics and linguistics. His first publication dedicated to New Mexican folklore as such was an eleven-part series in the *Journal of American Folklore* from 1910 to 1916, based on his own **fieldwork** and including two articles devoted to folktales. As Spanish editor for the American Folklore Society, he supervised the publication of a number of important folktale collections in the *Journal* and the Memoir series. Moreover, Juan B. Rael, collector-editor of one of the great Hispanic folktale collections, *Cuentos españoles de Colorado y de Nuevo Méjico* (*Spanish Tales from Colorado and New Mexico*, 1939–42), was his student at Stanford. Espinosa himself, over the years, published nearly 100 folktales from New Mexico, Colorado, and California.

Needing Spanish folktales for comparative study but finding no authoritative collections, Espinosa undertook a field trip to Spain in 1920, sponsored by the American Folklore Society. In less than five months, he collected more than 300 folktales from many parts of Spain, most of which he annotated and published in *Cuentos populares españoles, recogidos de la tradición oral de España* (*Spanish Popular Tales, Collected from the Oral Tradition of Spain*, 1923–26; rev. ed., 1946–47), which remains the standard collection of **Spanish tales**.

Among his numerous folktale studies, the most important group, perhaps, is a series devoted to the Tar Baby story (ATU 175, The Tarbaby and the Rabbit). In these articles and essays, he compares European, Latin American, and North American versions, establishes a typology, identifies characteristic traits of each type, and argues that the tale originated in India, coming to the New World via Europe and Africa. His folklore publications included other genres as well, and his *Romancero de Nuevo Méjico* (*Spanish Ballads from New Mexico*, 1953) remains a definitive collection.

Espinosa's folktale scholarship focused on dialectology and on understanding the interconnections among folk traditions. He produced extremely careful documentation, sometimes phonetic, of a huge body of folktales and other material from all levels of society, including members of his own extended family. Critics have noted, however, that he collected outside of the **context** of **performance**, suppressed names of sources, and focused on Spanish origin for folklore in southern Colorado and New Mexico, not on contemporary function or Mexican relationships. In these regards, he was a scholar of his own times.

Espinosa produced this folklore and dialect scholarship while pursuing a parallel career devoted to developing Spanish-language studies in the United States and at Stanford. He drew up standards to determine class level, compiled twenty-two textbooks, served as Spanish textbook editor for Oxford University Press, wrote articles, founded a professional association for instructors in Spanish, and edited its journal.

Espinosa served as president of the American Folklore Society (1924 and 1925) and held offices and associate editorships in several other societies. He received numerous honors from bodies in the United States and Latin American and from the Spanish government. His sons Aurelio, Jr., and Jose Manuel have also made notable contributions to folktale scholarship. *See also* Collecting, Collectors; Latin American Tales; North American Tales.

Further Readings: Briggs, Charles L. Review of *The Folklore of Spain in the American Southwest,* by Aurelio M. Espinosa. *Journal of American Folklore* 100 (1987): 236–37; Espinosa, Aurelio M. *The Folklore of Spain in the American Southwest: Traditional Spanish Folk Literature in Northern New Mexico and Southern Colorado.* Edited by J. Manuel Espinosa. Norman: University of Oklahoma Press, 1985.

William Bernard McCarthy

Estonian Tales

Estonian folktales—in the same way as **Finnish tales**—are situated at the crossroads of Western and Eastern folktale traditions, marking the end point of distribution for many Western tales in the East and Eastern tales in the West. Therefore, both the central European and the eastern Byzantine **variant**s of several **tale type**s are evident. For instance, both variants of tale type ATU 555, The **Fisherman and His Wife**, have been collected in Estonia—the classical European variant, as represented by the well-known **Grimm** version, and the one spread throughout eastern Europe and the Nordic countries, where the granter of the wishes is a sacred tree and the story ends like an etiological **legend,** with the husband and wife turning into bears (see **Etiologic Tale**).

The first period in which Estonian folktales were extensively collected covers primarily the end of the nineteenth century. In 1888, after Jakob Hurt had published his call for all people to gather **folklore**, he began receiving numerous texts collected by ordinary peasants, schoolmasters, tailors, and representatives of other professions. The collections of Hurt and Matthias Johann Eisen were later stored in the Estonian Folklore Archives, founded in 1927. This central **archives** holds more than 110,000 folktales and legends, including 3,000 **animal tale**s and more than 5,500 **wonder tale**s. The high points of **collecting** Estonian fairy tales occurred during the 1890s after Hurt's initiative and during the 1930s following the founding of the Estonian Folklore Archives.

The richest and most noticeable part of the Estonian tradition consists of folktales told by the Orthodox people in the Setu region in the southeastern corner of Estonia. With its great number of distinct tale types, even nowadays this region offers some possibilities for collecting traditional oral fairy tales. A unique Setu story is "Coal Porridge" (resembling type ATU 327, The Children and the **Ogre**) where a girl, turned as black as coal after eating coal porridge, goes to wash in the sea and is carried away by Old Nick, from whom her brother saves her. In addition to the Setu region, southern Estonia as a whole has been the richest place for collecting lesser-known stories. One example would be tale type ATU 843*, The Lazy Weaving Woman, which has a relatively small distribution and is also known only to Latvians and to the Votic people since they are Estonia's neighbors. In this tale, a weary weaver, who sees a tirelessly chipping woodpecker, is inspired by the bird to finish her own work.

An analysis of wonder tales collected in Estonia reveals that, in the nineteenth century, most tellers of these stories were **men**, whereas, beginning in the second decade of the twentieth century, wonder tales were mostly told by **women**. The main reason for this shift was probably the change in the popular understanding of the wonder tale. Previously aimed at adults, it was now intended for children. A striking number of stories still alive in oral folklore either are didactic or have a religious background. The same applies to the most widely collected tale type in Estonia—ATU 480, **The Kind and the Unkind Girls**—and its subtype ATU 480A, Girl and **Devil** in a Strange House, wherein an orphan goes to a sauna at midnight and Old Nick comes to propose her. The well-known stories about a very strong young man (ATU 650A, Strong John) are also known in Estonia, where the hero often bears the name Tugev Mats. There are numerous tales about a poor orphan girl who meets the **king**'s son in church (ATU 510), is turned into a cuckoo by her evil stepmother (ATU 720, The Juniper Tree), or is replaced with another girl by the stepmother (ATU 403, The Black and the White Bride). It is not rare for the orphan **motif** to blend with the **werewolf** motif (ATU 409, The Girl as Wolf). The top ten wonder tales in the archives also includes types ATU 300, The **Dragon**-Slayer; ATU 301, The Three Stolen Princesses; ATU 313, The Magic Flight; ATU 327, The Children and the Ogre; and ATU 530, The Princess on the Glass Mountain—all of which have been traditionally widespread in Europe.

The characters that the Estonian wonder tales often introduce are the sons and daughters of ordinary **peasant**s rather than children of royal blood. The same applies to relatively less-widely distributed **novella**s and legends. In the Estonian novella, the characters live in the countryside instead of towns, and the tales often include confrontations between a poor peasant and a lord of the manor, between an ordinary peasant girl and a king, or between a younger brother and a king's daughter.

The best-known animal tale is ATU 243*, The Crow Marries, which features a crow proposing to another crow and boasting about his nonexistent riches. Favorite characters in Estonian animal tales are the fox, the wolf (the two are often depicted as adversaries), and the bear. The best-known combination is the cycle of stories about the fox's ice-fishing activities (ATU 1+2+4).

Estonia's popular Stupid Ogre tales tell about the beloved character Kaval Ants (Crafty Hans). Among the category of **anecdote**s and **joke**s often told in Estonia is ATU 1525, The Master **Thief**, a story with wide international distribution. When Antti **Aarne**'s tale-type index was first published in 1910, The Foolish Bridegroom (ATU 1685) was the best-known joke in Estonia. Since then, however, a great amount of new material has been collected to fit this particular category, and typological research is currently underway to systematize the actual types.

Tales published at the end of the nineteenth century in books by Friedrich Reinhold **Kreutzwald**, Juhan Kunder, and other writers influenced the style and popularity of Estonian folktales. Some of these authors changed the stories considerably, often creating adaptations of a more literary nature. As a result, some tales in the archives echo a more literary mode of **storytelling** instead of an oral one.

Estonian folktales have been published in German by Oskar **Loorits** in *Estnische Volkserzählungen* (*Estonian Folk Narratives,* 1959) and by Richard Viidalepp in *Estnische Volksmärchen* (*Estonian Folktales,* 1980). Translations into English include *Estonian Folktales: The Heavenly Wedding* (2005), compiled by contemporary Estonian storytellers Piret Päär and Anne Türnpu.

Further Readings: Loorits, Oskar. "Some Notes on the Repertoire of the Estonian Folk-Tale." 1937. *Studies in Estonian Folkloristics and Ethnology: A Reader and Reflexive History.* Edited by Kristin Kuutma and Tiiu Jaago. Tartu: Tartu University Press, 2005. 217–39; Päär, Piret, and Anne Türnpu, comps. *Estonian Folktales: The Heavenly Wedding.* Tallinn: Varrak, 2005.

Risto Järv

Ethnicity. *See* Race and Ethnicity

Ethnographic Approaches

Collecting stories in **context**, either through interviews with storytellers or via observation and recording of storytelling performances, is the basis of most ethnographic approaches to folktales and fairy tales. These approaches, by the very nature of their field-research methods and underlying assumptions, often value oral narrative over the written or rewritten, but diverge in their specific concepts of story, **collecting** methodologies, and interpretations of **storytelling**.

Approaches focusing on comparative contexts, favored by nineteenth- and mid-twentieth-century literary scholars, trace the transmission of international folktales and fairy-tale texts through time and space, often to determine story origins, as summarized in folklorist and literary scholar Stith **Thompson**'s 1946 study *The Folktale.* Comparative researchers, drawing on **historic-geographic method**s not usually seen as ethnographic in their quest to map **tale type**s cross-culturally, have, nonetheless, gathered story texts from a variety of sources, including literary, historical, and archival documents, the latter often collected in the field, as well as from their own occasional **fieldwork**. For example, in her study of the worldwide distribution of the flood **motif** in myths and folktales, *The Raven and the Carcass* (1962), Swedish folklorist Anna Birgitta Rooth drew from literary sources as ancient as the Babylonian **epic** of **Gilgamesh** and the biblical Genesis and from her own field research with the Athabascan Indians of Alaska.

Approaches focusing on cultural contexts are rooted in twentieth-century **anthropological approaches** and were the first to draw on field research in earnest to assess how storytelling functions in communities. In his 1954 "Four Functions of Folklore," anthropologist William Bascom urged folklorists to consider the cultural matrices of the oral literatures they were examining so that they might understand the stories' meanings from native as well as analytic points of view. Full immersion into a community, ideally through participant observation and knowledge of the language, would allow ethnographers to assess the power of stories to entertain and educate and also to legitimate social values and institutions of specific cultures. This ethnographic model is exemplified in *Folktales and Society: Story-Telling in a Hungarian Peasant Community* (first published in German in 1962), Hungarian folklorist Linda **Dégh**'s long-term field study of storytelling among ethnic Hungarian communities.

Many folktale and fairy-tale collections for both children and adults presuppose a connection between folklore and culture, either explicitly or implicitly. For example, volumes in the University of Chicago's Folktales of the World Series—such as **Seki** Keigo's *Folktales of Japan* (1963) and Yolando Pino-Saavedra's *Folktales of Chile* (1967)—and in the Pantheon Fairy Tale and Folklore Library—such as Inea Bushnaq's *Arab Folktales* (1986) and Richard Erdoes and Alfonso Ortiz's *American Indian Myths and Legends* (1984)—often draw from ethnographic research, selected and edited by native scholars, and presented to readers as introductions to their respective cultures.

The sociocultural or sociohistorical perspectives of fairy-tale studies by the scholars Ruth B. Bottigheimer, Maria Tatar, and Jack **Zipes** also examine the cultural contexts in which stories have been embedded, albeit within a comparative, historical framework. Zipes's approach, in particular, although not ethnographic per se, includes analyzing the connections between field-collected oral tales and their literary counterparts, first articulated in his *Breaking the Magic Spell* (1979).

Approaches focusing on **performance** contexts, emerging in the latter half of the twentieth century, examine the immediate social situations in which storytellers and their listeners interact, rather than observing cultures as a whole. Researchers analyze individual storytelling acts to understand cultural differences and narrative variations *in situ*, one aspect of the "ethnography of speaking" movement as summarized in Richard Bauman's *Verbal Art as Performance* (1977). Attention to the details of storytellers' adaptations to different storytelling situations and to audiences' responses demands that ethnographers record each performance in its natural context, ideally using video as well as audio equipment if possible.

In his *Dynamics of Folklore* (1979), folklorist Barre Toelken discusses one performance of a story about the American Indian **trickster**, **Coyote**, told by Yellowman, a Navajo storyteller, to his children and visitors. Coyote, attempting to trick Skunk, loses his eyes in the branches of a pine tree. Toelken's account includes not only the literal transcription and translation of the Navajo text but also indications of the storyteller's gestures as well as his children's responses to that particular telling. Performance models of audience response to storytelling relate to reception theory in literary and fairy-tale criticism.

Approaches focusing on individual contexts have a long history, whether referring to psychoanalytic readings of folktales and fairy tales, to American anthropologists' studies of personality and culture, or to Russian and eastern European ethnologists' field studies of peasant narrators. Recent studies of storytellers, based on extensive long-term interviews over many years, include Toelken's study of Yellowman mentioned above, Henry Glassie's examination of northern Irish tellers and singers in his *Stars of Ballymenone* (2006), Kirin Narayan's analysis of a Hindu holy man's religious narratives in her *Storytellers, Saints, and Scoundrels* (1989), and Patricia Sawin's study of a North Carolina traditional singer and tale teller, *Listening for a Life* (2004).

Ideally, all of these ethnographic approaches examining comparative, cultural, performance, and individual contexts will inform studies and collections of folktales and fairy tales in a richly holistic way. ***See also*** Oral Theory.

Further Readings: Bascom, William. "The Four Functions of Folklore." *Journal of American Folklore* 67 (1954): 333–49; Bauman, Richard. *Verbal Art as Performance.* Prospect Heights: Waveland Press, 1977; Dégh, Linda. *Folktales and Society: Storytelling in a Hungarian Peasant Community.* Trans. Emily M. Schossberger. Expanded edition. Bloomington: Indiana University Press, 1989; Glassie, Henry. *The Stars of Ballymenone.* Bloomington: Indiana University Press, 2006; Haase, Donald. "Preface to the Special Issue on 'Jack Zipes and the Sociohistorical Study of Fairy Tales.'" *Marvels & Tales* 16 (2002): 127–31; Narayan, Kirin. *Storytellers, Saints, and Scoundrels: Folk Narrative in Hindu Religious Teaching.* Philadelphia: University of Pennsylvania Press, 1989; Oring, Elliott. "Folk Narrative." *Folk Groups and Folklore Genres: An Introduction.* Edited by Elliott Oring. Logan: Utah State University Press, 1986. 121–45; Rooth, Anna Birgetta. *The Raven and the Carcass: An Investigation of a Motif in the Deluge Myth in Europe, Asia and North America.* Helsinki: Academia Scientiarum Fennica, 1962; Sawin, Patricia. *Listening for a Life: A Dialogic Ethnography of Bessie Eldreth through Her Songs and Stories.* Logan: Utah State University Press, 2004; Thompson, Stith. *The Folktale.* 1946. Berkeley: University of California Press, 1977; Toelken, Barre. "The Folk Performance." *The Dynamics of Folklore.* Revised and expanded edition. Logan: Utah State University Press, 1996. 117–56; Zipes, Jack. *Breaking the Magic Spell: Radical Theories of Folk and Fairy Tales.* Revised and expanded edition. Lexington: University Press of Kentucky, 2002.

Janet L. Langlois

Etiologic Tale

Derived from Greek (*aitiologia*) and Latin (*aetiologia*), the term "etiology" (also "aetiology") means "knowledge about causes." Etiologic tales explain the origin of various phenomena, including animals, plants, natural objects, buildings, cultural institutions, and humans. They exist in all cultures and derive from mythical thinking. Some etiological tales have been canonized by world religions as sacred narratives. The first chapters of the **Bible** relate the creation of the cosmos and the world with its inhabitants, and about establishing the rules of human behavior, thus forming the foundation for civilization. Etiologic tales do not form a uniform genre that expresses belief but only a broad set of narratives, sometimes with humorous overtones.

In Christian **folklore**, biblical etiologic tales were supplemented by stories about God and the **devil** creating the world together, with the evil one imitating the work of God but making ugly, dangerous, or unpleasant phenomena (God creates humans, whereas the devil creates an ape; God makes a bee, the devil makes a fly, etc.). Some folktales include an etiologic **motif** at the end. Thus, in the **tale type** ATU 2, Tail-Fisher, Fox advises Bear to fish with his tail through a hole in the ice. His tail is frozen and remains in the ice, which explains why Bear has a short tail. It is common to etiologic tales that they are linked with objects in the outside world. *See also* Aztec Tales; Myth.

Further Reading: Johns, Andreas. "Slavic Creation Narratives: The Sacred and the Comic." *Fabula* 46 (2005): 257–90.

Ülo Valk

Ever After (1998)

Ever After (1998) is the title of a live-action fairy-tale film version of "**Cinderella**," produced by Twentieth Century Fox and directed by Andy Tennant. The presence of stars such as Drew Barrymore and Angelica Huston underlines the film's status as a big-budget studio release. *Ever After* combines an unabashed appeal of the Hollywood notion of fairy-tale romance with a self-conscious determination to update the Cinderella narrative to more modern ideas of realism and feminist principles. Ultimately, because of this combination, the film is flawed and confused.

By placing the Cinderella narrative within a deliberately historicized setting—that of sixteenth-century France—the film underlines its deliberate play with realism. All traces of the magical are eradicated from the story, which becomes instead an exercise in social and psychological conflict. Accordingly, the eventual happy ending is based on understanding rather than revelation, achieved by mundane rather than magical intervention. The replacement of the fairy godmother with Leonardo da Vinci is partially playful but nonetheless reinforces the claim of realism. However, the haziness of the film's historical setting and its tendency to diverge wildly from actual history flaw this process. After all, the real Prince Henry certainly did not marry a provincial nobody.

In some ways, the notion of realism is likewise highlighted by the film's framing, in which the Brothers **Grimm** are told the "real" story of Cinderella by the Queen of France. She thus authenticates it both as a historical document concerning her ancestors and as a genuine **women**'s story in opposition to the male narrative power represented by the Brothers Grimm. However, this self-conscious metafictional play acts against the film's repeated claims of reality, following the general tendency of embedded narrative to emphasize the fictionality of the story against the comparative realism of the **frame narrative**. The attempt to update the characters of both Danielle, who is the film's Cinderella figure, and her Prince Henry flounders against the strength of fairy-tale expectation. Danielle is a feisty feminist heroine to Henry's conflicted ineffectuality, but both are ultimately constrained and defined by their fairy-tale roles.

Ever After may attempt to deny its status as fairy-tale narrative, but is in fact a particularly strong example of the genre, reinforced not only by adherence to the familiar terms of Cinderella's story but also by the expectations of the Hollywood fairy-tale romance, which ultimately overcome the film's attempt at subversion. *See also* Brothers Grimm in Biopics; Cinderella Films; Feminism; Film and Video; Metafiction.

Further Readings: Gruner, Elisabeth Rose. "Saving 'Cinderella': History and Story in *Ashpet* and *Ever After*." *Children's Literature* 31 (2003): 142–54; Preston, Cathy Lynn. "Disrupting the Boundaries of Genre and Gender: Postmodernism and the Fairy Tale." *Fairy Tales and Feminism: New Approaches.* Edited by Donald Haase. Detroit: Wayne State University Press, 2004. 197–212; Stephens, John, and Robyn McCallum. "Utopia, Dystopia, and Cultural Controversy in *Ever After* and *The Grimm Brothers' Snow White*." *Marvels & Tales* 16 (2002): 201–13.

Jessica Tiffin

Ewald, Carl (1856–1908)

Danish author Carl Ewald produced more than twenty volumes of fairy tales for children. Originally published in Denmark between 1882 and 1909, they became popular around the world. As a young man, Ewald taught natural history in Copenhagen, and in the spirit of Charles Darwin and natural science, his fairy tales aim to teach children the mechanisms of evolution and natural laws. Cultivating a modern **fantasy** form, fairy tales such as *Fem nye eventyr* (*Five New Fairy Tales*, 1894; translated as *The Old Post and Other Nature Stories*, 1909) were conceived as modernized versions of Hans Christian **Andersen**'s Romantic tales.

Blending the use of imagination with a clearly didactic purpose, Ewald reappropriated the fairy-tale genre to fit a contemporary focus on education as amusement. The fairy tales reflect a naturalist, scientific outlook rooted in an urban middle-class perspective, and they distinguish themselves from earlier nineteenth-century fairy-tale traditions such as the **folktale**s collected by Svend **Grundtvig** in the service of preserving national **folklore**. Ewald's fantasy tales, for example, often replace Romantic or traditional **myth** by inventing a modernist mythology of nature, frequently describing human and social states or processes as exposed to natural laws.

In *Eventyrskrinet* (*The Fairy-Tale Shrine*, 1906), Ewald retold traditional Danish **legend**s and folktales, and in 1905, he published a new translation of **Grimm**'s fairy tales into Danish. *See also* Scandinavian Tales.

Further Reading: Rossel, Sven H., ed. *A History of Danish Literature*. Lincoln: University of Nebraska Press, 1992.

Helene Høyrup

Ewing, Juliana Horatia (1841–1885)

As chief contributor to her mother's *Aunt Judy's Magazine*, the short-lived Julie Gatty, who married Major Alexander Ewing, becoming Juliana Horatia Ewing, quickly established herself as one of Victorian England's foremost authors of children's stories. Although she retained the mixture of moralism and **fantasy** that Margaret Scott Gatty had successfully used in *Parables from Nature* (1855–71), the inventiveness of Ewing's fairy tales far surpassed that of her mother's *The Fairy Godmothers* (1851). Ewing's brilliant first fairy tale "The Brownies" (1865) was illustrated by an admiring George **Cruikshank**, as were "Amelia and the Dwarfs," "Benjy in Beastland," and "Timothy's Shoes" (all published in 1870 in *Aunt Judy's Magazine*). The amused narrator of these stories often seems more distanced from adult parents or guardians than from the derelict children who profit from their contact with supernatural and natural agents. Ewing channels the vitality of a bratty Amelia or of the defiant Timothy into more socially acceptable channels. She even is willing to redeem the unsavory Benjy, who looks "like something ending in jy or gy, or rather dgy, such as *podgy* [or] smudgy, having that cloudy, slovenly look (like a slate *smudged* instead of washed)."

Whereas an exquisitely crafted longer story like "Amelia and the Dwarfs" was based on an oral Irish folktale akin to one later reproduced by Ruth Sawyer as "Wee Meg Barnileg and the Fairies," Ewing began to fashion compact folktales of her very own from 1870 until 1876, finally collecting them in 1882's *Old Fashioned Fairy Tales* near the end of her brief career. These stories, she explained in the preface, relied on what we would now call universal **archetype**s and **myth**s "common" to different folk cultures. Setting herself in opposition to John **Ruskin**, whose 1868 essay on "Fairy Tales" had demanded the restoration of pristine and unrevised **fable**s, she enlists her "old-fashioned" tales to dramatize a conflict between inimical realms: wanting to annoy "the whole stupid [human] race," a water sprite in "The Nix in Mischief" causes a girl to be falsely accused of incompetence; even after the child's good name is reinstated, however, she must share the marginality of creatures whom humans have unfairly "banished" from all too "many waters." In "The Hillman and Housewife," Ewing even allows a rightly vindictive goblin to punish the mean-spirited **peasant** woman who tried to cheat him. But sometimes humans familiar with these alternate realities can act as intermediaries. In "The First Wife's Wedding Ring," a "small weazened old woman" teaches a young man how to outwit a greedy and treacherous giant. Like the female slave who helped Amelia thwart the **dwarf**s who had captured her, this mentoria possesses no magical powers. But her experience allows others to be schooled in the art of deception. By coming in contact with the fantastic, innocents can become wiser and warier adults.

Further Readings: Knoepflmacher, U. C. "Repairing Female Authority: Ewing's 'Amelia and the Dwarfs.'" *Ventures into Childland: Victorians, Fairy Tales, and Femininity.* Chicago: Chicago University Press, 1998. 378–423; Sawyer, Ruth. "Wee Meg Barnileg and the Fairies." *The Way of the Story Teller.* Revised edition. 1962. London: George G. Harrap, 1990. 205–16.

U. C. Knoepflmacher

Exemplum, Exempla

"Exemplum" is a medieval Latin term for an illustrative story or **anecdote**, the sort of material that can be inserted into a sermon or discourse to serve a larger argument. It is typically a very short story with a pithy point. Medieval collections of exempla were compiled to provide resources for speakers, and some of the anecdotes recorded in this way constitute evidence for narrative material, often from the **oral tradition** of the time, and thus also evidence for early forms of **folktale**s and **legend**s. The practice may also have some relationship to the Arabic *adab* literature, in which actions or sayings of the Prophet Muhammad were explicated for moral guidance; the connection may be most evident through Spanish works such as the *Disciplina clericalis* of Petrus Alfonsi (c. 1100 CE) or *El Conde Lucanor* (*Count Lucanor*, c. 1335) of Juan Manuel. In England and Germany, the best-known collection was the **Gesta Romanorum** (*Deeds of the Romans*), of which hundreds of manuscripts survive, with great variation among them. The book is best known from its earliest printed forms, which contain some 150 stories with accompanying moral interpretations.

Earlier collections of moral anecdotes were more explicitly devoted to theological material and explication; by contrast, the *Gesta* seems to be a collection intended for entertainment. Medieval **frame narrative**s such as the *Seven Sages* (eastern and western branches) or the Arabic *Kalila and Dimna*, which were in circulation before the Latin collections were compiled, also illustrate the use of stories as parts of a larger argument, although often their value is tangential to the argument, and some of the stories from these collections are to be found in Europe. *See also* Didactic Tale; Moral; Religious Tale.

Further Readings: Hermes, Eberhard, ed. and trans. *The "Disciplina clericalis" of Petrus Alfonsi.* Berkeley: University of California Press, 1977; Swan, Charles, trans., and Wynnard Hooper, ed. *Gesta Romanorum, or Entertaining Moral Stories.* 1876. New York: Dover Publications, 1959.

Stephen Belcher

F

Fable

The fable is a short allegorical tale featuring animals, men, gods, and even inanimate objects as characters in a plot that illuminates a moral truth about the human condition or human behaviors. A **moral** is usually, though not always, explicitly stated at the end of a fable and is meant to give the preceding tale its full force. Fables can be written in prose or verse, though they usually appear in prose. They are designed to ring with truth and to produce insight even while presenting characters and situations that are quite obviously fictional. Indeed, in some cases, such insight can outlast the tale's particulars, as with the term "sour grapes," which refers to **Aesop**'s fable about the fox that concludes that the grapes he cannot reach must (therefore) be sour and consequently undesirable.

Perhaps the best-known fables are those by Aesop, a freed Greek slave who lived in the sixth century BCE and who is credited with 200 fables. But the form can be traced back to even earlier times, being found in the Egyptian papyri of about 1500 BCE and later in the works of Hesiod in the eighth century BCE. The *Panchatantra*, a collection of Indian fables in Sanskrit, dates to about the third or fourth century CE, though it too is rooted (orally) in even earlier times. As the centuries progressed, the beast fable—drawing mainly on Aesop—emerged as a particularly popular type in Western literature. Closely related to the beast fable in the West is the beast legend, perhaps most clearly preserved in the stories of **Reynard the Fox**, celebrated hero of the medieval beast epics and increasingly popular after about 1150. The French, who contributed most to the original story, produced *Le roman de Renart* (c. 1175–1250). Thus, the fox that turns up in many beast fables is also given some cultural dimension by the simultaneous development of Reynard as the legendary and notoriously wily contestant in an epic hunt. Another legendary version of the fox as foe appears centuries later with the **Uncle Remus** stories, **African American tales** compiled by Joel Chandler **Harris** in the nineteenth century.

Other notable fables include those penned by the seventeenth-century Frenchman Jean de **La Fontaine**, who borrows heavily from Aesop and displays an unapologetic love of rural life and an embrace of hedonistic principles. His fables were widely translated and imitated throughout Europe during the seventeenth and eighteenth centuries. Important fables from the twentieth century include George Orwell's politically charged beast fable *Animal Farm* (1945), humorist James **Thurber**'s *Fables for Our Times* (1940), and Richard Adams's environmentally conscious novel *Watership Down* (1972). *See also* Exemplum, Exempla; Fabliau, Fabliaux; Parable.

Further Reading: Blackham, H. J. *The Fable as Literature*. London: Athlone, 1985.

Lori Schroeder Haslem

Fabliau, Fabliaux

The fabliau is a short narrative, typically in verse, about the extraordinary incidents that may befall ordinary people, who are frequently depicted as foolish or ridiculous. The original fabliaux were verse tales written in the vernacular from the early period of northern French literature (from the twelfth to fourteenth centuries), but similar tales—which sometimes blur the generic boundaries—are also found elsewhere in western Europe. *Dame Sirith* and Geoffrey **Chaucer**'s *Canterbury Tales* are the main Middle English examples; Middle High German analogues to the French fabliaux are referred to as *Mähren* or *Schwänke*; and the Middle Dutch fabliaux are known as *boerden*. From medieval Italian literature, the most striking example is the **novella**, as in Giovanni **Boccaccio**'s *Decameron* (1349–50). The fourteenth-century Spanish *Libro de buen amor* (*The Book of Good Love*) of Juan Ruiz also contains notable examples.

Fabliaux had considerable popular currency and were often used to convey valuable moral lessons. The fabliau is brief. Its plot follows a simple structure, and its characters embody clearly identifiable social and professional stereotypes: the cunning wife, the cuckolded husband, the lover, the prostitute, the priest, the knight, the squire, and the jongleur (traveling entertainer), all given to practicing deceit and misleading one another. Although the term "fabliau" derives from the Latin *fabula*, fabliaux differ significantly in their content and intention from the **Aesop**ic **fable** tradition. Notwithstanding any underlying didactic purpose, these stories are intended to provoke laughter. A number of interrelated themes recur in the fabliaux: unbridled sexual appetite, adultery, sexual naivety, fetishism, and jokes about corpses and lower bodily functions. Accordingly, the fabliaux and its related genres are often characterized by bawdy humor. *See also* Bawdy Tale; Clergy; Erotic Tales; Jest and Joke; Moral; Sex, Sexuality.

Further Reading: Hines, John. *The Fabliau in English*. London: Longman, 1993.

Ana Raquel Fernandes

Faerie and Fairy Lore

Faerie, or fairyland, is the realm thought to be populated by fairies. The *Oxford English Dictionary* defines "fairies" as "supernatural beings ... popularly supposed to have magical powers, and to meddle for good or evil in the affairs of men." Whatever their names, all share certain traits: generally invisible, they have the power of "glamour," the ability to make themselves visible or to enchant or hypnotize; they are ordinarily smaller than mortals—and they are always somehow "other" than human. They may be helpful and benign, destructive and malevolent, or simply capricious and mischievous.

The origin of fairies is much debated. Traditional Christian religious and popular views of fairies connected them to the fallen angels, deluded by Satan, who did not have the strength to choose God or the **devil**. Thus, they were ejected from heaven yet not condemned to hell. Some fell into the sea, becoming the mer-creatures of the waters; some dropped into the caverns of the earth and became goblins, kobolds, gnomes, or **dwarf**s; some fell into woods and forests becoming **elves**, pixies, and the like. Another similar idea was that they were the children of Adam and Eve, whose existence the couple denied when inquired about by God. Still others suggested that they were the pre-Adamite inhabitants of earth. In short, these commentators saw them as a morally indeterminate "second race" inhabiting the world alongside humans.

Another common belief in Europe was that fairies were a special category of the dead. In *British Fairy Origins* (1946), Lewis Spence argued for their connection to a cult of the dead on the basis of their sizes, similar dwelling places, and the frequently identical tales and rituals associated with both groups. Some thought them the spirits of the ancient druids or of the pagans who had died before the possibility of salvation through Christ. A more contemporary explanation, offered by modern occultists, is that they are the souls of the recent dead awaiting reincarnation or transportation to the astral plane.

Yet another theory holds that fairies are diluted versions of the ancient deities of a given country or of nature spirits from the early stages of civilization. Gods and heroes—reduced in stature and importance as new beliefs supersede old ones—become the elfin peoples. Euhemerists (believers in an historical basis for **myth** and **folklore**) suggest that fairies are derived from folk memories of earlier or aboriginal inhabitants of a country, long after its conquest by its present inhabitants.

Modern spiritualists, theosophists, and Rosicrucians (members of a secret order who seek esoteric knowledge) have added to origin theories by suggesting that fairies are the elementals (spirits of the four elements) of Paracelsus (c. 1500), and later alchemists and magicians and the agents present in psychical phenomena. Sir Arthur Conan Doyle, whose book *The Coming of the Fairies* (1921) placed photographs of elfin creatures in the glare of publicity, thought them lifeforms existing on another branch of the tree of evolution—little nature spirits whose special function was to tend plants and flowers.

No single explanation of their genesis covers all varieties, for fairies range from the beautiful, godlike Tuatha De Danann of the Irish to the tailed, grotesque little creatures known in southern Africa as tokoloshes. However, there is some consensus about their habitats, behaviors, and characteristics. Fairylands may be located within prehistoric burial places, as with the Irish Sidhe (a *sidhe* is a burial mound), within mountains as with the "Little People" of Mount Kilimanjaro, within caves, forests, or even under water. Wherever fairyland, or faerie, is located, it is a world without change, decay, illness, or aging, a realm without time; or rather, with a sense of time different from the human, as one fairy day may be 100 mortal years.

Elfin behavior is best described as capricious and amoral. Fairies love and reward cleanliness and order, yet have no qualms about stealing from mortals; they are known to take the "goodness" or essence out of human **food**. Yet they are generous and reward mortals who aid them. Passionate about protecting their privacy, they severely punish those who spy on them or visit them uninvited, yet they are capable of great hospitality. As befits creatures linked to fertility, they are often wanton and highly sexual in nature; they take mortal lovers at whim and can literally destroy them with amorous actions. They must always be treated with caution and, above all, with politeness and respect. At their worst, they are capable of considerable evil; they can paralyze with elf-shot or fairy-stroke, cause madness, and kill humans. Many of their actions, however, fall between these categories. They love mischief and are fond of pranks.

Fairy **infertility** may explain their kidnapping of human infants, substitution of their own imperfect offspring, and frequent abduction of women to serve as midwives, nurses, or breeders. Tales of changed children and of fairy **changeling**s abound. Other frequently told stories deal with the love between mortals and fairies. These often follow patterns similar to tales of **animal bride**s and **animal groom**s. There are numerous accounts of mortals visiting the fairy realm and a host of homier **legend**s of fairies asking for and gaining human aid.

However, **fairy tale**s (**märchen**) and tales about fairies (often legends or **memorate**s) are not the same thing. Nursery tales often lack fairies, and accounts of encounters with them are often devoid of the elements of märchen. Moreover, the fairies in Geoffrey **Chaucer**'s *Canterbury Tales* and William **Shakespeare**'s plays are amalgams of **folklore** and literary conventions. The **literary fairy tale** or *conte de fées* of French seventeenth-century society compounds the mixture both by giving the "fairy tale" its name and by adding to the ranks of supernatural creatures. The authored French stories of the seventeenth century are the sources of the benevolent fairy godmother, and of aristocratic, powerful female supernatural creatures whose magic can make or break the fortunes—especially the loves—of mortals. Utilized and rendered mystical in the literary fairy tales of the German Romantics, fairy creatures passed into the mainstream culture of Europe.

Even in the twenty-first century, fairy lore is not yet dead. The resemblance of the small grey creatures from UFOs to the fairies has given the transformed elfin races a new and only slightly different life. *See also* Fairy, Fairies.

Further Readings: Briggs, Katharine M. *The Fairies in English Tradition and Literature.* Chicago: University of Chicago Press, 1967; Silver, Carole G. *Strange and Secret Peoples: Fairies and Victorian Consciousness.* New York: Oxford University Press, 1999.

Carole G. Silver

Fagunwa, Daniel Orowole (1903–1963)

Daniel Orowole Fagunwa was a Nigerian educator and writer who authored folktale **novella**s in his mother tongue, Yoruba. Born into a Christian family in Òkè-Igbó in western Nigeria, he worked as a teacher and headmaster in Oyo, Lagos, and Benin City from 1929 to 1946. Following studies in England, he became education officer of western Nigeria. After retiring in 1959, he worked as an agent for Heinemann publishing until his death in 1963 in Baro, northern Nigeria. His five books expand Yoruba folktales into novellas that show great similarity. Significantly, Fagunwa combined the Yoruba narratives with plots, **motif**s, and **moral**s from classical Greek mythology, Aesopean **fable**s, Shakespearean plays, the *Arabian Nights*, and Christian literature such as John Bunyan's *The Pilgrim's Progress.* Thematically, the novellas tell of treachery and retribution, perseverance and love, thereby dwelling heavily upon the weird and supernatural.

His debut novella, *Ògbójù ode nínú Igbó Irúnmalè* (1938), was frequently reprinted and served as a schoolbook for generations of Yoruba pupils. A congenial translation by Wole Soyinka was published as *The Forest of a Thousand Daemons* (1968). Two further novellas also were translated into English: *Igbó Olódùmarè* (1949), translated by G. A. Ajadi as *The Forest of God* (1985); and *Ìrìnkèrindò nínú Igbó Elégbèje* (1954), translated by D. Adeniyi as *Expedition to the Mount of Thought* (1994). Two other novellas in Yoruba remain untranslated: *Ìrèké-oníbùdó* (*The Cane of the Guardian*, 1949) and *Àdììtú Olódùmarè*

(The Secret of the Almighty, 1961). Fagunwa's writings served as models for the novellas of his Yoruba compatriot Amos **Tutuola**.

Further Readings: Ajadi, Gabriel Ajiboye. "A Critical Introduction for and an Annotated Translation of D. O. Fagunwa's 'Igbó Olódùmarè (The Forest of God).'" Dissertation. Ball State University, 1985; Bamgbose, Ayo. *The Novels of D. O. Fagunwa.* Benin City: Ethiope, 1974.

Thomas Geider

Fairy, Fairies

The origin of the word "fairy" or more directly of the word "fay," from late Latin *fata* or *fatae*, earlier *fatum* (fate[s]), gives us some indication of the nature and powers ascribed to these supernatural creatures. The word connects the thirteen enchantresses who stood beside the cradle of **Sleeping Beauty** with their ancient foremothers, the Fates, who stood beside the cradle of Meleager in Greek mythology. All are female; all are as powerful as the gods themselves in presiding over human destiny. In the **Middle Ages**, however, the word "fairy" had several meanings: enchantment itself (magic or illusion), the realm where enchanted beings dwelt (often written as "**faerie**"), and the supernatural inhabitants of that land. Sir Walter Scott and others incorrectly believed the name was derived from the *peris* of Persian **myth** on the basis of a false etymology (that *peri* equals *feerie*). Thomas Keightley, whose Victorian work *The Fairy Mythology, Illustrative of the Romance and Superstition of Various Countries* (1850) is still much used, categorized fairies as "distinct from men and from the higher orders of divinities." But whether they are called "fairies," "fays," "fées" (French), "weise Frauen" (German, "wise women"), "little people," or "good folk," they share certain traits. Generally invisible, fairies have the power of "glamour," the ability to change shape and size and to make themselves visible to enchant or hypnotize. **Folklore** sources envision them as smaller than humans—ranging from a few inches to four feet. In both folklore and fairy tale, they may be seen as helpful and benign, destructive and malevolent, or merely capricious and mischievous. **Folktale**s and **literary fairy tale**s alike indicate their importance to humans as **magic helper**s or powerful opponents or both. Yet fairies have limitations; although they are thought to excel mortals in power, knowledge, and longevity, they too are subject to **death**.

The "good people" (as they are euphemistically called) are often believed to live in subterranean lands or within mounds, hills, or mountains, but they may also reside under water or in remote woods and wilds. Prominent in the lore of western Europe, especially in Celtic areas such as Ireland, Scotland, Cornwall, and Brittany, they are also important in Germany and Scandinavia as **elves**, nisses, neks, kobalds, and nixies. Some folklorists divide the elfin peoples into two categories regardless of nationality: solitary fairies, often malignant and unpleasant, and trooping fairies, varied in attributes but tending to be less antisocial and more benign in their relations with humans. Under various names, types of fairies are found in Asia and North America (among Native Americans), among the Maoris of New Zealand and the aboriginal peoples of Australia, and throughout Africa. Whatever their forms—and these range from the elegant willow-tree fairy of Japan to the mischievous *tokoloshes* of southern Africa—all share in the power and mystery associated with supernatural creatures. *See also Conte de fées*; Faerie and Fairy Lore.

Further Readings: Briggs, Katharine. *A Dictionary of Fairies: Hobgoblins, Brownies, Bogies, and Other Supernatural Creatures.* Harmondsworth: Penguin, 1977; Purkiss, Diane. *At the Bottom of the Garden: A Dark History of Fairies, Hobgoblins, and Other Troublesome Things.* New York: New York

University Press, 2000; Silver, Carole G. *Strange and Secret Peoples: Fairies and Victorian Consciousness.* New York: Oxford University Press, 1999.

Carole G. Silver

Fairy Tale

Despite its currency and apparent simplicity, the term "fairy tale" resists a universally accepted or universally satisfying definition. For some, the term denotes a specific narrative form with easily identified characteristics, but for others it suggests not a singular genre but an umbrella category under which a variety of other forms may be grouped. Definitions of "fairy tale" often tend to include a litany of characteristics to account for the fact the term has been applied to stories as diverse as "**Cinderella**," "**Little Red Riding Hood**," "**Hansel and Gretel**," "Jack and the Beanstalk," "Lucky Hans," "**Bluebeard**," and "Henny-Penny." As Elizabeth Wanning Harries has noted, "Nothing is more difficult than to try to define the fairy tale in twenty-five words or less" (Harries, 6).

One approach to understanding the sense and scope of "fairy tale" has been to define not the term per se but its equivalents in other languages. This maneuver is an implicit admission of the English term's deficiency and degree of difficulty. Of course, the substitute terms may not be precisely equivalent and may be problematic in their own right. It is commonplace, for example, to point out that "fairy tale" was originally a late-eighteenth-century English translation of "*conte de fées,*" a term that appeared in France in 1697 to describe the literary tales of Marie-Catherine d'**Aulnoy** and then those of her contemporaries. Meaning literally "tale of/about fairies," *conte de fées* may offer the potential of sharpening the denotation of "fairy tale," but only if we historicize the term and limit it to denoting only those kinds of seventeenth- and eighteenth-century **French tales** to which its French equivalent originally referred. As a practical matter, given the broad popularity of the term, that would be a losing proposition. At the same time, when taken to be more inclusive, both the terms *conte de fées* and "fairy tale" are problematic since, as so many have pointed out, not all fairy tales include fairies. So using *conte de fées* to help define the fairy tale is historically relevant and illuminating but does little to clarify what the fairy tale has come to mean and how it should be defined.

Scholars have also tried to get to the heart of "fairy tale" by avoiding it and substituting the German word "**Märchen**." Dissatisfied with "fairy tale," Stith Thompson—like many others—proposed märchen as a superior alternative (that is, märchen means what fairy tale *should* mean). In fact, the term "märchen" has entered into the English lexicon and now functions as part of a transnational terminology among folklorists and literary scholars. "Märchen" can imply a wide range of genres—namely, all of those diverse narrative forms included in the seventh edition of Jacob and Wilhelm **Grimm**s' foundational fairy-tale collection, *Kinder-und Hausmärchen* (*Children's and Household Tales,* 1857): the **animal tale**, **fable**, **etiologic tale**, **jest**, **wonder tale**, **exemplum**, **religious tale**, and so on. In compound forms, "märchen" also has the advantage of offering us the designations *Volksmärchen* (**folktale**) and *Kunstmärchen* (**literary fairy tale**), which does help to clarify terminology by making a useful distinction. English-language scholars frequently use "folktale" to refer to tales from **oral tradition** and "fairy tale" to designate written tales. This rough opposition of folktale and fairy tale, which places orality and literature at the opposite ends of an axis, can be useful, especially if it allows for the interaction of oral and written forms along that axis. For example, *Buchmärchen* (book tale), sitting midway between the oral and the literary, is a word that has been used to designate tales from oral tradition that have been transcribed and published. Using the terms "folktale" and "fairy tale" in this way, as two kinds of märchen, is initially helpful in roughing out the distinction between oral and literary narratives, but thinking of them as the endpoints on a linear axis or scale makes them the alpha and omega of folktale and fairy-tale studies; and it does not take into account the relation of other forms and nonverbal media to the folktale and fairy tale. In fact, the privileged distinction between *Volksmärchen*/folktale and *Kunstmärchen*/literary fairy tale defines these genres first and foremost in terms of the *medium* in which each appears—the oral versus the written. Using the medium of narration to distinguish one kind of tale from another does not get to the heart of determining the essential *generic* characteristics of fairy tale.

In proposing the German word "märchen" as an alternative to the English term "fairy tale," Thompson has in mind another *märchen*-compound—the *Zaubermärchen,* that is, the magic or wonder tale. Thompson's definition states that a märchen "is a tale of some length involving a succession of **motif**s or episodes. It moves in an unreal world, without definite locality or definite characters and is filled with the marvelous. In this never-never land humble heroes kill adversaries, succeed to kingdoms, and marry **princess**es" (Thompson, 8). This definition was published in 1946, but its basic elements are those that still surface in many discussions of the fairy tale: (1) The structure is episodic and constructed primarily on motifs; (2) the genre is unabashedly fictional, the setting indefinite, and the mode of reality in which the characters move is supernatural or fantastic; and (3) protagonists overcome obstacles to advance to rewards and a new level of existence (achieving wealth, power, **marriage**, and/or social status). To be sure, Thompson's description of the fairy-tale protagonist seems to exclude heroines, which at a minimum dates his definition; and the curious description of the genre as being "of some length" is not at all helpful.

Like Thompson's definition, most other definitions of the fairy tale tend to rely on a list of categories and perspectives to enumerate the defining qualities of the genre. Length is frequently used in defining the generic characteristics of the fairy tale. Whereas some definitions describe the fairy tale as short, others suggest it is a narrative of some greater length. Satu Apo improves a bit on Thompson's vague assertion that a märchen is "a tale of some length" when she writes that the fairy tale is "a long, fictitious narrative" (Apo, 16). Of course, in the context of folktale studies—where these two definitions occur—the fairy tale may be considered long when compared to forms such as the anecdote or joke. Relying on length, however, is problematic, especially outside the context of oral tales and **storytelling**. Is James **Thurber**'s "The Little Girl and the Wolf" (1940)—an adaptation of "Little Red Riding Hood" in a mere 182 words—a fairy tale, or is it too short? (Thurber himself included it in a volume entitled *Fables for Our Time.*) On the other hand, can a **novel**—such as Robin McKinley's 247-page *Beauty: A Retelling of the Story of Beauty and the Beast* (1978)—be a fairy tale, or is it too long? Clocking in at eighty-four minutes, is **Walt Disney**'s *Snow White and the Seven Dwarfs* (1937) too long, too short, or just right? Length, one could argue, misses the point and distracts us from considering the diversity of texts that are studied and should be studied by fairy-tale scholars.

Definitions of the fairy tale also have recourse to style as a defining characteristic. In his important work on the "form and nature" of the European folktale (by which he means wonder tale, according to his translator), Max **Lüthi** identified depthlessness and abstract style as a defining characteristic. These stylistic features have been applied repeatedly in definitions of the fairy tale, which point to the episodic nature of the narrative, its indefinite settings, bare-bones characterizations, repetitions, formulaic language, and so on. These qualities apply without question to the kinds of fairy tales published the Grimms' collection and to tales influenced by the Grimms. Nonetheless, it is useful to ask whether works that do not display these stylistic characteristics—literary, cinematic, and other forms, such as the **graphic novel** and **animation**—are disqualified from being fairy tales.

Definitions of the fairy tale also invoke its purpose. Apo's definition, for example, notes that the fairy-tale "narrative includes fantasy and . . . is told as a means of passing the time, as entertainment." While some definitions point to the genre's entertainment value as a defining feature, others single out the fairy tale's role in moral instruction and socialization. Still others stress its utopian purpose, its role in projecting a better society and modeling strategies for survival and empowerment. The genre seems clearly to have a variety of possible functions—not a single purpose—and these will hinge on the social, cultural, and historical contexts of a given fairy tale's production and reception, as well as its target audience. Openness to the diversity of the fairy tale once again gives us more insight into its nature than does the focus on a single function.

The fairy tale's proverbial happy ending and the obstacle-laden quest that the protagonist has successfully completed are staples in definitions of the fairy tale. Thompson includes these in his definition when he refers to the hero who kills his adversaries, gains a kingdom, and marries the princess. They are also evident in Vladimir **Propp**'s notion that fairy tales are narratives of **initiation**. This view suggests that the fairy tale models for its recipients a journey in which obstacles are overcome and problems are solved—a journey ending in integration, success, and happiness. From this perspective, the fairy tale is synonymous with the wonder tale and fulfills a sociocultural purpose, whether that is satisfying the audience's need to see its wishes realized or confirming a society's structure of status and power.

For most scholars, the mode of reality in which the action of the fairy tale takes place trumps all other categories when it comes to defining the genre. According to the sample definitions from Apo and Thompson, the world of the fairy tale is characterized by "fantasy," "unreality," or "the marvelous." Accordingly, Steven Swann Jones has written that "the incorporation of fantasy may be regarded as the most salient formal or stylistic feature of this genre" (Jones, 12). It is not the use of fantasy or the marvelous alone, however, that makes the fairy tale, for other genres also may utilize these. As Maria Tatar states, "the term *fairy tale* . . . is above all reserved for narratives set in a fictional world where preternatural events and supernatural interventions are taken wholly for granted" (Tatar, 33). In other words, whereas we understand the magical reality depicted in the fairy tale to be fiction, we and the characters in the fairy tale accept it without question. There is no "hesitation," no wavering in our belief as there is in fantastic fiction. From this perspective, "fairy tale" is again defined specifically in terms of the magic or wonder tale, which can appear either in oral or literary form. It might be simpler if the term "wonder tale" were to replace "fairy tale" altogether, but the history of the term and its popular usage make that unlikely.

Whatever future direction debates about the terms "märchen," "folktale," and "fairy tale" may take, it is important to recognize the diverse ways in which the terms have been used and the manifold forms that have clustered around them. It is also important to recognize that the focus on verbal art has allowed the oral-literary dichotomy to dominate discussions and definitions of terms that now need to be extended to new forms. *See also* Cautionary Tale; Didactic Tale; Fantasy; Magical Realism; Utopia.

Further Readings: Apo, Satu. *The Narrative World of Finnish Fairy Tales: Structure, Allegory, and Evaluation in Southwest Finnish Folktales.* Helsinki: Academia Scientiarum Fennica, 1995; Dundes, Alan.

"Fairy Tales from a Folkloristic Perspective." *Fairy Tales and Society: Illusion, Allusion, and Paradigm.* Edited by Ruth B. Bottigheimer. Philadelphia: University of Pennsylvania Press, 1986. 259–69; Harries, Elizabeth Wanning. "Once, Not Long Ago." *Twice upon a Time: Women Writers and the History of the Fairy Tale.* Princeton, NJ: Princeton University Press, 2001. 3–18; Jones, Steven Swann. *The Fairy Tale: The Magic Mirror of Imagination.* New York: Twayne, 1995; Lüthi, Max. *The European Folktale: Form and Nature.* Translated by John D. Miles. Philadelphia: Institute for the Study of Human Issues, 1982; Schenda, Rudolf. "Telling Tales—Spreading Tales: Change in the Communicative Forms of a Popular Genre." *Fairy Tales and Society: Illusion, Allusion, and Paradigm.* Edited by Ruth B. Bottigheimer. Philadelphia: University of Pennsylvania Press, 1986. 75–94; Tatar, Maria. *The Hard Fact of the Grimms' Fairy Tales.* 2nd edition. Princeton, NJ: Princeton University Press, 2003. 3–38; Thompson, Stith. *The Folktale.* 1946. Berkeley: University of California Press, 1977; Zipes, Jack. "Introduction: Towards a Definition of the Literary Fairy Tale." *The Oxford Companion to Fairy Tales.* Edited by Jack Zipes. Oxford: Oxford University Press, 2000. xv–xxxii.

Donald Haase

Fakelore

The neologism "fakelore," coined by Richard M. **Dorson** in 1950, designates any "spurious" and "synthetic" writings claiming to be genuine **folklore**. Dorson aimed to establish American folklore as an academic discipline and wanted to draw a distinction between oral folklore, directly collected from storytellers, and versions produced by writers using folkloric themes. The term "fakelore" has been applied to works such as James Macpherson's editions of Ossian (1760–63), Jacob and Wilhelm **Grimm**s' *Kinder- und Hausmärchen* (*Children's and Household Tales,* 1812–15), and Elias Lönnrot's edition of the Finnish national **epic**, the *Kalevala* (1849), all of which were presented as genuine folklore but might, to varying degrees, be considered products of editorial invention or intervention.

Clearly, the notion of "*fake*lore" presumes the **authenticity** of "*folk*lore." But both "**folk**" and "authenticity" are tricky terms. Folklore exists only through variation, which comes about in the creative acts of the folk. Given that the folk modify data in producing folklore, the assumption that tinkering with folklore yields fakelore presupposes a dichotomy between those who can produce legitimate **variant**s and those who cannot. So the question would be: Who are the folk?

Modern scholarship has emphasized the Romantic underpinning of "folk," and contemporary explorations of the continuum between expressive and popular culture have undermined its pertinence in today's world. Alan **Dundes**'s point that, among others, *we* are the folk reflects this dissolution, which necessarily affects the concept of fakelore. Because "fakelore" is the shadow image of the Romantic construct of "authentic" folklore, it is fading away alongside its master construct.

Further Readings: Bendix, Regina. *In Search of Authenticity: The Formation of Folklore Studies.* Madison: University of Wisconsin Press, 1997. 188–218; Dorson, Richard M. *Folklore and Fakelore: Essays Toward a Discipline of Folk Studies.* Cambridge, MA: Harvard University Press, 1976. 1–29; Dundes, Alan. "The Fabrication of Fakelore." *Folklore Matters.* Knoxville: University of Tennessee Press, 1989. 40–56; ———. "Who Are the Folk?" *Interpreting Folklore.* Bloomington: Indiana University Press, 1980. 1–19.

Francisco Vaz da Silva

False Bride

Stories of the false bride are of two main kinds: stories in which an intended bride is unwillingly displaced by another woman, usually of a lower social status, without the husband being aware of the deception; and "bedtrick" stories in which a bride arranges for a substitute to replace her on her wedding night (or first sexual encounter), usually to conceal that she has already lost her virginity. In the modern era, the latter story has appeared more in drama and farce than in folktale and focuses on the ramifications of the deception (the substitute's refusal to end the deception, for example, or the murder of the substitute). The former story has numerous folktale analogues found in **tale type**s such as The Black and White Bride (ATU 403), The Substituted Bride (ATU 403C), The Blinded Bride (ATU 404), The Three Oranges (ATU 408), The Animal as Bridegroom (ATU 425A), Little Brother and Little Sister (ATU 450), and The Speaking Horsehead (ATU 533). These types can be broadly divided into those focusing on the groom, as in The Three Oranges, and those focusing on the bride, as is the case in most of the other kinds.

Both types appear in Giambattista Basile's *Lo cunto de li cunti* (*The Tale of Tales*, 1634–36), where "Li tre cetra" ("The Three Citrons")—Basile's version of The Three Oranges—is used as a catalyst to resolve the **frame narrative**, which itself has elements belonging to The Speaking Horsehead tale type, best known in the variant published by the Brothers **Grimm** as "Die Gänsemagd" ("The Goose Girl"). All versions involve some form of magic either to sustain or disclose the deception, which is especially necessary in **variant**s in which the husband already knows what his wife should look like.

In The Three Oranges tale type, a **prince** sets out in search of a beautiful **princess** to become his wife. His is given, or finds, three oranges, each of which, when opened, contains a beautiful enchanted maiden. He succeeds in rescuing the third, who agrees to marry him, but he then leaves her while he goes to acquire suitable **clothing** for her. In his absence, a servant girl, gypsy, or **witch** takes the place of the maiden after enchanting her into animal form by sticking a pin into her head. The true bride is eventually disenchanted when the pin is removed and she is restored to her rightful place or, as in Basile, reappears from an orange picked by the prince from a tree that has miraculously grown upon her gravesite. The false bride is executed.

In other tale types, the narrative focus is on the heroine. Travelling to the realm of her future husband—as in Grimms' "The Goose Girl" and "Die weiße und die schwarze Braut" ("The White Bride and the Black Bride")—she is forced or tricked into changing places with her maidservant or stepsister and is reduced to servant or animal status. Her true identity is revealed when the bridegroom's **father** overhears the princess lamenting her change of state, and her restitution and the execution of the false bride follow. In other variants collected by the Brothers Grimm—"Brüderchen und Schwesterchen" ("Brother and Sister") and "Die drei Männlein im Walde" ("The Three Little Gnomes in the Forest")—the substitution takes place after the **queen** has given **birth** to her first child. In contrasting the beauty of the queen and the ugliness of the stepsister who temporarily replaces her, both tales draw on conventional symbolism for good and evil.

The pattern of inversion, restitution, and **punishment** in these tales is underpinned by a strong sense of social hierarchy, especially in their confirmation of a particular dynamic of **sex** and **gender**, power and identity. *See also* Marriage.

Further Readings: Tatar, Maria. *The Hard Facts of the Grimms' Fairy Tales*. 2nd edition. Princeton, NJ: Princeton University Press, 2003; Warner, Marina. *From Beast to the Blonde: On Fairy Tales and Their Tellers*. New York: Farrar, Straus and Giroux, 1994.

John Stephens

Family

Jacob and Wilhelm **Grimm** selected an appropriate title for their pioneering collection *Kinder- und Hausmärchen* (*Children's and Household Tales*, 1812–15). Not only do these stories exemplify those told in family circles, but typically their plots, often presented from a child's point of view, center on family life. This is true not only of the Grimms' famous anthology, but also of the numerous collections from around the world that follow their example.

Fiction typically evolves from conflict, and for fairy tales, family life has provided a seemingly inexhaustible source of tension-ridden situations around which stories can be built. Events experienced or observed by nearly everyone give rise to complications that call for "fairy-tale" solutions. The entire cycle of family life is represented: conception, **birth**, **childhood**, coming of age, leaving home for **marriage** or career, establishing one's own family, coping with old **age**, facing the **death** of loved ones, and dealing with one's own mortality. Throughout history and in all cultures, storytellers have used these events as settings for their tales, typically presenting everyday problems in exaggerated scale to achieve added drama.

Examples in fairy tales of these magnified conflicts are manifold. A child born with a defect or **disability** is not even human—possibly a fairy **changeling**, or even an animal (a common opening for tales about **animal bride**s and **animal groom**s, ATU 402 and 425–449). The birth of **twins** is depicted as an extraordinary—sometimes supernatural—event, but not always a positive one. In some **legend**s, multiple births give rise to suspicions about a mother's faithfulness to her husband, and dramatic consequences follow.

A belittled child, demeaned for his or her small size, is portrayed as being no larger than a thumb (ATU 700, Thumbling). Hungry children are threatened by their poverty-stricken parents with abandonment (ATU 327, The Children and the Ogre). The death of a **mother** (traumatic under any circumstance) brings an evil stepmother—often portrayed as a **witch**—into the household. Curiously, relatively few traditional fairy tales depict the family disruption caused by the death of a **father**. Sibling rivalry, especially between **sisters** and between **brothers**, often explodes into mortal conflict.

Coming-of-age issues are sharpened and focused, with the potentially disruptive years of puberty frequently compressed into a single encounter. A common formula for fairy tales briefly describes a character's childhood, then introduces a conflict that is resolved within (seemingly) a few days, at which time the heroine or hero marries.

If the negative aspects of family life are exaggerated in fairy tales, so are many of the benefits. Marriage is depicted as the supreme reward (see **Punishment and Reward**), both for young men and young women. Fairy-tale brides are beautiful beyond earthly human standards, and their regal bridegrooms excel in chivalry, charm, and wealth. Fairy-tale marriages bring power and wealth to both genders. A **Cinderella**-type heroine escapes from household drudgery through her marriage to a **prince**, and an ordinary **peasant**, **soldier**, or **tailor** can inherit a kingdom by marrying a **princess**. Furthermore, these will be successful marriages, for—at least in the English-language tradition—the storyteller assures us, after describing the wedding, that the bride and groom "lived happily ever after."

However, some tales suggest otherwise. **Jest**s from many lands show power struggles between husband and wife, with examples about evenly divided between tales depicting foolish wives and their husbands (ATU 1380–1404) and those featuring foolish husbands and their wives (ATU 1405–29). Tales of adultery are not unusual, and domestic disputes often result in physical **violence**, with children and wives as the most probable victims.

In addition to being the basic social group in traditional cultures, the family is also—for most individuals—the primary economic unit. Household tasks are assigned by custom—with **gender**, age, parentage, and marital status constituting the most important defining factors. Folktales and fairy tales often reflect conventional family work roles, sometimes defending them, but also allowing for miraculous exceptions.

The **fable** "Von dem Mäuschen, Vögelchen und der Bratwurst" ("The Mouse, the Bird, and the Sausage," ATU 85), as recorded by the Grimm brothers and others, depicts the perceived dangers of departing from customary roles. A mouse, a bird, and a sausage establish a family unit by setting up housekeeping together. The bird collects wood in the forest, the mouse carries water and tends the fire, and the sausage does the cooking. One day they decide to exchange tasks. The sausage goes into the forest to gather wood, but is eaten by a dog. The mouse falls into the stewpot and is scalded to death. The bird accidentally sets the house on fire, and then, while fetching water to put it out, falls into the well and drowns.

Another tale depicting the folly of violating traditional family work assignments is "Mannen som skulle stelle hjemme" ("The Man Who Was to Mind the House," ATU 1408) from *Norske Folkeeventyr* (*Norwegian Folktales*, 1841–44) by Peter Christen **Asbjørnsen** and Jørgen **Moe**. In this tale, a man complains that his wife has easier tasks than does he, so they exchange jobs for a day. Nothing is said of how the woman fares in the field, so one may assume that she experiences no serious problems. The man's day, however, is marked by a chain of catastrophes, all caused by his misguided attempts at efficiency. His final blunder is putting the cow on the sod roof to graze and then securing her there with a rope tied around her neck, dropped down the chimney and tied to his own leg. The cow falls off the roof and pulls him up the chimney.

A ribald version of this tale recorded by Aleksandr **Afanas'ev** in his *Russkie zavetnye skazki* (*Russian Secret Tales*, 1872), "A Man Does Woman's Work," takes a particularly nasty turn. The husband, while mismanaging his domestic duties, loses his clothes. He covers his nakedness with a bundle of hay, but a horse eats the hay, and, with one vicious bite, literally emasculates the househusband.

Fairy-tale families often transcend the traditional father-mother-children grouping. Foster children, servants, and apprentices are included in many tales, often as disadvantaged outsiders. However, in good fairy-tale tradition, they frequently succeed royally, thus reversing customary workaday roles. Live-in apprentices typically play important parts in the internationally distributed Strong John group of tales (ATU 650A), where a superhumanly strong hero proves himself superior to his master. Similarly, tales of types ATU 1000–29, also widely told, describe labor contracts between live-in farmhands and their masters—contracts that the servants, through feigned stupidity and other tricks, turn to their advantage.

Extended families of other types also find mention in folktales, often with ensuing conflicts that give the tales their plots. For example, "The Armless Maiden" from Afanas'ev's *Russkie narodnye skazki* (*Russian Folktales*, 1855–63) depicts a brother and a sister who live together happily until he marries. Jealous of her sister-in-law, the new wife slanders her relentlessly. In the end, the husband sides with his sister (who has now married) and kills his wife. The three survivors return to the new husband's parental home, where the mixed family of five adults all prosper and live together happily.

The plot of "The Magic Fiddle" (ATU 780, The Singing Bone), as published in *Indian Fairy Tales* (1892) by Joseph **Jacobs**, arises from the jealousy of the wives of seven brothers toward their unmarried sister-in-law, who does all the cooking for the seven-family group. Similarly, stories from cultures allowing polygamy often depict conflicts between jealous co-wives.

Finally, although the establishment of a new family through the marriage of hero and heroine is the stereotypical fairy-tale ending, there are notable exceptions. Again drawing on the Grimms' *Kinder- und Hausmärchen*, the tale "Das Lämmchen und Fischchen" ("The Little Lamb and the Little Fish"; ATU 450, Little Brother and Little Sister) depicts the life-threatening conflict between a brother and sister and their wicked stepmother. At the story's end, the brother and sister find refuge in a little house in the woods, where they live together by themselves, contented and happy.

Further Readings: Sparing, Margarethe Wilma. "The Family." *The Perception of Reality in the Volksmärchen of Schleswig-Holstein: A Study in Interpersonal Relationships and World View.* New York: University Press of America, 1984. 50–106; Tatar, Maria. "Victims and Seekers: The Family Romance of Fairy Tales." *The Hard Facts of the Grimms' Fairy Tales.* 2nd edition. Princeton, NJ: Princeton University Press, 2003. 58–82.

D. L. Ashliman

Fantasy

Fantasy and **wonder tale**s (or magic tales) are closely related generically, and they also share plots, character galleries, **motif**s, and partly settings. However, while wonder tales are products of **folklore** and go back many thousands of years, fantasy is a modern genre, tightly connected with the development of Modern Age philosophy, psychology, natural sciences, and general worldview. Although some important features of fantasy, such as imaginary countries, can be traced back to Jonathan Swift, fantasy literature owes its origins mostly to Romanticism with its interest in **folk** tradition, its rejection of the previous, rational-age view of the world, and its idealization of the innocent and therefore omnipotent child (see **Childhood and Children**). Fantasy stands close to the **literary fairy tale**, as it is created by a specific author, even though it may be based on a traditional narrative. Similar to literary fairy tales, fantasy is less rigid in plot structure and character types.

Brief History

Most scholars agree that E. T. A. **Hoffmann**'s *Nußknacker und Mausekönig* (*The Nutcracker and the Mouse King*, 1816) matches most definitions of fantasy and is therefore recognized as a pioneering work, even though many other **novel**s by the German Romantics might claim priority. Reflecting in part the influence of German Romantic writers such as Hoffmann, **Novalis**, and Ludwig **Tieck**, fantasy emerged as a significant tradition in Britain in the second half of the nineteenth century in the work of authors such as Lewis **Carroll**, Charles Kingsley, and George **MacDonald**. MacDonald stands closest to fairy tales proper, even though several of his major works have a firm anchor in reality and a strong sense of hesitation. At the turn of the twentieth century, E. **Nesbit**, responding to impulses from many predecessors, renewed and transformed the fantasy tradition, focusing on the clash between the magical and the ordinary, and on the unexpected consequences of magic when introduced in the everyday realistic life. Unlike fairy tales, fantasy is closely connected with the notion of modernity; for instance, the first time-shift fantasies by Nesbit are influenced by the contemporary ideas of the natural sciences and by the science fiction of writers such as H. G. Wells.

The golden age of English-language fantasy arrived in the 1950s and 1960s, with the work of writers such as J. R. R. **Tolkien**, C. S. **Lewis**, Ursula **Le Guin**, and Alan **Garner**. While these authors are clearly indebted to Nesbit, their fantasy reaches a higher level of sophistication. This tradition was affected by the tremendous changes that the modern world had undergone, including achievements in quantum physics and hypotheses about the origins of the universe, which allow nonlinear time and a multitude of alternative worlds.

Outside of the English-speaking world, fantasy as a genre has never enjoyed the same popularity or status; however, one should remember such famous works as Carlo **Collodi**'s *Pinocchio* (1883), Antoine de Saint-Exupéry's *Le petit prince* (*The Little Prince*, 1943), Astrid **Lindgren**'s *Bröderna lejonhjärta* (*The Brothers Lionheart*, 1973), and Michael **Ende**'s *Die unendliche Geschichte* (***The Neverending Story***, 1979). To be sure, Russia and Eastern Europe have a flourishing fantasy tradition that is hardly known in the West. Among the earliest, *Chernaya kuritsa, ili podzemnye zhiteli* (*The Black Hen, or The Underground People*, 1829) by the Russian Antony **Pogorels'ky**, marked by overt didacticism, bears a close resemblance to Hoffmann's *Nutcracker*. During the years of the Communist regime in the Soviet Union and the satellite states, fantasy was often a means of avoiding censorship while presenting the contradictions of society. Fantasy created a welcome counterbalance against the prescribed norms of social realism because of the genre's appeal to the child's imagination, playfulness, and curiosity about the world. The frequent motif of good and evil could be interpreted as an allegory of the oppressive authorities. Thus, fantasy became the main channel for subversive literature by mainstream writers, for instance *Korolevstvo krivykh zerkal* (*The Land of Crooked Mirrors*, 1951) by the Russian writer Vitaly Gubarev. Similar works appeared in Estonia, Lithuania, Hungary, Czechoslovakia, Yugoslavia, and Albania. Gradually fantasy became more philosophical and is today used not merely for didactic or entertaining purposes but as a metaphor for a young protagonist's inner world. Some contemporary writers venture into fantasy based on national mythology.

English-language fantasy in the West, sometimes referred to as postmodern, takes the developments of the 1950s and 1960s still further, reflecting the late twentieth- and twenty-first-century human being's ambivalent picture of the world. The boundaries between dream and reality, between the the "primary" and "secondary" world, become more elusive, and the passage often subtle, so that the hesitation is amplified. The protagonists' actions in a secondary world make an immediate and crucial impact on their own reality. Contemporary literature tends to view parallel worlds as equally real, thus accepting more than one reality and more than one truth. Many novels take place in a secondary world, while the reader's own reality appears in the periphery, as the "other." Uncertainty, indeterminacy, and ambiguity become typical features. Diana Wynne **Jones**, Philip **Pullman**, and Neil **Gaiman** are among the authors who consistently employ traits of **postmodernism**, including **metafiction**, **intertextuality**, and fluctuant subjectivity.

Definition and Generic Features

The definition of fantasy is often imprecise and ambiguous. In different sources, the concepts of fantasy, **fairy tale**, literary fairy tale, gothic tale, **utopia**, and science fiction may overlap and sometimes are used interchangeably, without further argument. Even in studies devoted wholly, to fantasy there is no consensus about the distinctive characteristics of this genre or about the scope of texts it encompasses. Moreover, there is no agreement about fantasy being a genre at all. It is treated as a style, a mode, or a narrative technique. Fantasy has been defined as a metaphoric mode, opposed to realism as metonymic.

Collectors of **folktale**s generally strive to preserve a story as close to its original version as possible, even though individual storytellers and **editors** may convey a personal touch, with each version reflecting its own time and society. Fantasy literature is a conscious creation, wherein authors choose the form that suits them best for their particular purposes. Fantasy is also an eclectic genre, borrowing traits from **myth**, **epic**, romance, picaresque, gothic tale, mystery, science fiction, and other genres, blending seemingly incompatible elements within one and the same narrative. Also, short tales and picture books can be categorized as fantasy.

The difference between fantasy and science fiction can be explained in terms of credibility: science fiction is based on the assumption that there are, or at least can be conceived in the future, technological means of transportation, communication, or artificial intelligence. The distinction between fantasy and horror, gothic, or **ghost story**, is that the latter usually has some rational explanation. Fantasy is also associated with nonsense; however, while nonsensical elements can be present in fantasy, as well as in other genres, nonsense is a stylistic rather than a generic feature.

Suspension of Disbelief

The most fruitful way to distinguish between fairy tales and fantasy is by probing into their epistemology, the matter of belief and the suspension of disbelief. The most profound difference between fantasy and fairy tales is the position of the reader/listener toward what is narrated. In traditional fairy tales, taking place "Once upon a time" and "East of the Sun, West of the Moon" (or some equal formulas), a clearly detached time-space, the reader is not supposed to believe in the story. The hero's task in a fairy tale is impossible for an ordinary human being. It is symbolic or allegorical. In fantasy, characters are ordinary, and writers often stress that the hero is "just like you."

There are at least two possible interpretations of events in fantasy. They can be treated at their face value, as actually having taken place, which means that as readers we accept magic as a part of the fictional world. On the other hand, magic adventures can also be accounted for in a rational way, as the protagonist's dreams, visions, or hallucinations. Tolkien was among the first to question the legitimacy of rational explanations. In his essay "On Fairy Stories" (written in 1938, but first published in 1947), he dismisses Carroll's *Alice's Adventures in Wonderland* (1865) because the heroine wakes up and her adventures turn out to have been a dream. Tolkien's concept of fantasy literature (although he calls it fairy stories) is based on the suspension of disbelief. Genuine and skillful fantasy creates a "secondary" belief (unlike the so-called "primary" belief of myth and religion), putting the reader in a temporary state of enchantment. As soon as suspension of disbelief is disturbed, the spell is broken and, Tolkien adds, art has failed.

The essence of fantasy literature is thus the confrontation of the ordinary and the fabulous. Tzvetan Todorov distinguishes among the uncanny, the marvelous, and the fantastic. According to Todorov, the fantastic is characterized by a strong sense of hesitation. Fairy tales, in this typology, fall under the category of the marvelous, and gothic tales under the uncanny, while the essence of fantasy lies in the hesitation of the protagonist (and the reader) as confronted with the supernatural—which can be anything that goes beyond natural laws. As soon as hesitation is dispersed, the reader has inscribed the text within either the uncanny or the marvelous. Todorov admits, however, the existence of marginal areas, such as the fantastic-uncanny and fantastic-marvelous. In the latter, such classics as L. Frank **Baum**'s *The Wonderful Wizard of Oz* (1900), C. S. Lewis's *The Lion, the Witch and the Wardrobe* (1950), J. K. **Rowling**'s Harry Potter series (1997–2007), and Philip Pullman's His Dark Materials trilogy (1995–2000) would be included.

Fairy Tale and Fantasy

Most fantasy novels demonstrate similarities to fairy tales. They have inherited the fairy-tale system of characters set up by Vladimir **Propp** and his followers: hero/subject, **princess**/object, sender, helper, giver, and antagonist. The essential difference between the fairy-tale hero and the fantasy protagonist is that the latter often lacks heroic features, can be scared and even reluctant to perform the task, and can sometimes fail. Unlike fairy tales, the final goal of fantasy is seldom **marriage** and enthronement; in contemporary philosophical and ethical fantasy, it is usually a matter of spiritual maturation.

Fantasy also has inherited many of the fairy tale's superficial attributes: wizards, **witch**es, genies, **dragon**s, talking animals, flying horses and flying carpets, invisibility mantles, magic wands, swords, **mirror**s, lanterns, and magic **food** and drink. However, the writers' imaginations enable them to transform and modernize these elements: a genie may live in a beer can rather than in a bottle, flying carpets may give way to flying rocking chairs, and supernatural characters without fairy-tale origins might be introduced, such as, for instance, an animated scarecrow.

Fantasy has also inherited the basic plot of fairy tales: the hero leaves home, meets helpers and opponents, goes through trials, performs a task, and returns home having gained some form of wealth. It has inherited some fundamental conflicts and patterns, such as the quest or combat between good and evil. While most **wonder tale**s have happy endings, fantasy can have an unhappy or ambivalent ending.

Secondary Worlds

The element essential to fantasy is the presence of magic in an otherwise realistic, recognizable world. This presence may be manifest in the form of magical beings, objects, or events; it may be unfolded into a whole universe or reduced to just one tiny magical bit. This element in itself is not different from fairy tales, but the anchoring in reality is. The most common denomination for the various representations of magic in fantasy literature is the concept of the secondary world. Thus, fantasy may be roughly defined as a narrative combining the presence of the primary and the secondary worlds, that is, our own real world and at least one magical or fantastic imagined world. The passage between worlds is often connected with patterns such as a door, a **magic object**, and a **magic helper** (messenger). All of these patterns have their origins in fairy tales. There are, however, fantasy stories that, at least superficially, take place in a magical secondary world without any contact with reality.

A specific **motif** in fantasy literature has caused some scholars to view the texts where this motif occurs as a subcategory: the motif of time distortion. It appears presumably first in Nesbit's *The Story of the Amulet* (1906) and, more than any other fantasy motif, is influenced by contemporary scientific thought, especially the theory of relativity. The scope of problems that fantasy authors encounter when they venture to the exploration of time patterns is irrelevant in fairy tales: the questions of predestination and free will, of the multitude of possible parallel times, of time going at a different pace or even in different directions in separate worlds, the mechanisms of time displacement, and the various time paradoxes.

The relationship between real and magic time in fantasy is the opposite of that in fairy tale. A common folktale motif is the land of immortality, where the hero spends what to him may seem like a day, or three days, or a week. When he returns to his own world, it many thousand years may have elapsed. By contrast, in fantasy, the characters may easily live a whole life in the imaginary world, while no time has passed in their own reality.

Subcategories

Like fairy tales, fantasy is not a heterogeneous genre, and several subcategories can be distinguished. To begin with, the distinction is made between narratives that build up a separate universe and take place exclusively within it. Tolkien's Lord of the Rings series (1954–55), with its several related volumes, is frequently used as an example, also referred to as high, or heroic, fantasy. It can further be illustrated by Lloyd **Alexander**'s series The Chronicles of Prydain (1964–68), Le Guin's Earthsea books (1968–2001), and a vast number of contemporary mass-market novels. It is also manifest in fantasy **film**s, such as *The Dark Crystal* (directed by Jim **Henson**, 1982) and *Willow* (directed by Ron Howard, 1988). On the other hand, C. S. Lewis' Narnia books (1950–56), Susan Cooper's *The Dark is Rising* (1965–77) and the Harry Potter books have also been categorized as heroic fantasy, although they show tangible connections to the primary world. The heroic patterns of quest and struggle against evil should be considered as motifs rather than generic traits.

In secondary world fantasy, the premise is the protagonist's transition between the worlds. The initial setting of most fantasy literature is reality that is anchored to a particular time: a riverbank in Oxford (*Alice's Adventures in Wonderland*), a farm in Kansas (*The Wonderful Wizard of Oz*), or a country house in central England during World War II (*The Lion, the Witch and the Wardrobe*). From this realistic setting, the characters are transported into a magical realm and typically (but not invariably) brought back safely. Alternatively, the magical realm itself may intervene into reality, in the form of magical beings (the Psammead, Peter Pan, and Mary Poppins), magical **transformation**s, or magical objects. Fantasy that takes place wholly in the primary world and introduces elements of magic into it has been called low fantasy. Since the appearance of fantastic features often produces humorous or even nonsensical effects, some scholars suggest the category of comic fantasy. Recently, the term "**magical realism**" has been proposed for this type of fantasy. It is, however, not always adequate, with its relationship to Latin American magical realism characterized by strong social criticism.

Animal fantasy features intelligent talking animals, either within realms of their own environments (Kenneth Grahame's *The Wind in the Willows*, 1908) or in contact with ordinary humans. Toy fantasy, portraying animated dolls and toys, has many similarities to animal fantasy. Frequently, the objective of the toys is to come alive or at least become independent, or else the toys are the human protagonists' secret companions. Apart from anthropomorphism, these characters do not possess any supernatural traits; thus, it might be argued whether such books belong to fantasy or constitute a genre of their own. The function of the fairy-tale magic helper can also be performed in humorous fantasy by miniature people, dragons, fairies, elves, genies, and other mythical creatures.

The contemporary enthusiasm for fantasy, underscored by the revival of Tolkien (much due to the recent film versions) and the unprecedented success of Harry Potter, has resulted in a vast wave of so-called sword-and-sorcery fantasy, a more or less mass-market literature following standard fairy-tale quest or struggle plots and often involving romance. Some famous authors in this category include Terry Brooks, David Eddings, Barbara Hambly, Robin Hobb, Tanith **Lee**, Ann McCauffrey, Michael Moorcock, and Tad Williams.

The Uses of Fantasy

Fantasy frequently is accused of being escapist in nature; however, this is equally true about romance, the crime novel, science fiction, and other popular genres. In fact, fantasy can be purely entertaining, but it can also be used for a vast variety of other purposes: educational, allegorical, religious, feminist, ethical, ideological, and philosophical. Moreover, these aspects can appear on different interpretive levels within the same text. Interestingly enough, fantasy has a different status in general literature, where it is considered a mass-market genre, and in **children's literature**, where it is one of the most important and respected genres. *See also* Time and Place; Young Adult Fiction.

Further Readings: Attebery, Brian. *The Fantasy Tradition in American Literature: From Irving to Le Guin.* Bloomington: Indiana University Press, 1980; Goldthwait, John. *Natural History of Make-Believe: Guide to the Principal Works of Britain, Europe and America.* New York: Oxford University Press, 1996; Hume, Kathryn. *Fantasy and Mimesis: Responses to Reality in Western Literature.* New York: Methuen, 1984; Hunt, Peter, and Millicent Lenz. *Alternative Worlds in Fantasy Fiction.* London: Continuum, 2001; Jackson, Rosemary. *Fantasy: The Literature of Subversion.* New York: Methuen, 1981; Le Guin, Ursula, and Susan Wood. *The Language of the Night: Essays on Fantasy and Science Fiction.* New York: Putman, 1979; Manlove, C. N. *Modern Fantasy: Five Studies.* Cambridge: Cambridge University Press, 1975; Nikolajeva, Maria. *The Magic Code: The Use of Magical Patterns in Fantasy for Children.* Stockholm: Almqvist & Wiksell International, 1988; Rabkin, Eric S. *The Fantastic in Literature.* Princeton, NJ: Princeton University Press, 1976; Sammons, Martha C. *"A Better Country": The Worlds of Religious Fantasy and Science Fiction.* New York: Greenwood, 1988; Swinfen, Ann. *In Defence of Fantasy: A Study of the Genre in English and American Literature since 1945.* London: Rutledge & Kegan Paul, 1984; Todorov, Tzvetan. *The Fantastic: A Structural Approach to a Literary Genre.* Translated by Richard Howard. Cleveland: Press of Case Western Reserve University, 1973; Tolkien, J. R. R. "On Fairy Stories." *Tree and Leaf.* London: Allen & Unwin, 1968. 11–70.

Maria Nikolajeva

Father

"What Father Does Is Always Right" ("Hvad Fatter gjør, det er altid det rigtige"), the title of a story by Hans Christian **Andersen**, could serve as a motto for thousands of folktales. Mainstream anthropologists see most traditional cultures as patriarchies, and the father-dominated **family** is a backdrop for **storytelling** around the world.

There are exceptions, but even these tend to support the general rule. Countless stories feature children abused by stepmothers, for example tales of type ATU 510A, **Cinderella**, told internationally in hundreds of versions. In stories about cruel stepmothers, the fathers typically are either negligent in allowing their wives to abuse the children, or they are absent altogether. In most instances, such fathers remain in the background throughout the tale, although sometimes they belatedly recognize the harm being inflicted on their own children and reclaim their authority. For example, in "Baba Yaga" (ATU 313, The Magic

Flight), as presented by Aleksandr **Afanas'ev**, when the father of a daughter abused by her stepmother discovers what is happening, he summarily shoots his wife. Then he and his daughter live happily together.

Folktale **mother**s and stepmothers who mistreat their children typically are spared no **punishment**. Folktale fathers can also be abusive, but unlike their female counterparts, they are seldom punished. "The Girl with No Hands," as recorded by Ruth Ann Musick in her *Green Hills of Magic: West Virginia Folktales from Europe* (1970), is typical of its many international counterparts. Combining types ATU 510B, Peau d'Asne, and ATU 706, The Maiden without Hands, this is the ultimate tale of patriarchal abuse, both sexual and physical. In the opening episode, the father (who is also **king**, redoubling his authority over the child) attempts to commit **incest** with his daughter and then has her hands cut off. The mutilated woman makes her way to another country where she marries a **prince**. Adding to her tribulation, a jealous stepmother attempts to have the young bride burned alive. In the end, the heroine's hands are miraculously restored, and the wicked stepmother is torn to pieces by four horses. However, the man who set the series of tragic events into motion, the heroine's father, apparently escapes all punishment. He is not mentioned after the story's opening episode.

A father's authority over his daughter plays a central role in another large body of folktales, wherein he uses his right to give her in **marriage** as a tool to reform or punish her. "König Drosselbart" ("King Thrushbeard," ATU 900) from Jacob and Wilhelm **Grimm**'s *Kinder- und Hausmärchen* (*Children's and Household Tales*, 1812–15) tells such a story. A **princess** refuses to accept any of her father's choices for a bridegroom, so he angrily marries her to a man he thinks is a beggar. However, the new husband is a king in disguise, one of the suitors previously rejected by the princess. He repeatedly humiliates his bride, ultimately bringing her to full submission, a process begun by the woman's father and then completed by her husband. Similar tales are known around the world, and the excesses practiced first by the father and then by the husband are almost never condemned by the storytellers.

Less cruel, but still demeaning, are the innumerable tales wherein a king offers his daughter to whatever man can cure her of some defect—for example, an illness, the unwillingness to laugh, or the tendency to dance with forbidden partners. The man who meets this challenge is often a **peasant**, **tailor**, **simpleton**, or **soldier**, but his low rank is less important than is his ability to carry out the father's will.

The Grimms' "Die zertanzten Schuhe" ("The Danced-Out Shoes," ATU 306) offers an example. A king locks his twelve daughters in their room every night, but they somehow escape and dance their **shoe**s to pieces. The father offers any man who can stop this activity one of the princesses for a wife. An old, wounded soldier discovers how they make their escape and with whom they are dancing. He thus succeeds as a guardian of their virtue where the father had failed, and is given one of them in marriage as a reward (see **Punishment and Reward**).

Another stereotypical father-daughter relationship in fairy tales is his unquestioned right to offer her as payment for services rendered. Examples are found around the world, for example "The Killing of the Rakhas" (ATU 300, The Dragon-Slayer) from India, recorded in *Folklore of the Santal Parganas* (1909) by Cecil Henry Bompas. A country is being ravaged by a *rakhas* (**ogre**), leading the raja to proclaim that anyone who can kill it will be rewarded with the hand of his daughter. A youth named Jhalka answers the call and prepares a box with a **mirror** inside. Confronting the *rakhas*, Jhalka shows it the box. Distracted by its image in the mirror, the *rakhas* lets down its guard, and Jhalka dispatches it with an ax. The raja's daughter is forthwith married to Jhalka.

The father-child relations discussed above deal with daughters. Father-son conflicts are also well represented, but are quite different in nature. Fathers do not offer their sons as prizes for tasks rendered, but there are quarrels about a son's presumed laziness or stupidity. The Grimms' "Märchen von einem, der auszog, das Fürchten zu lernen" ("A Tale about the Boy Who Went Forth to Learn What Fear Was"; ATU 326) offers a case in point. A boy who knows no fear is deemed by his father to be a simpleton and is therefore disowned. The father sends him away with instructions to tell no one who his father is. Once on his own, the boy's fearlessness serves him well, and he earns the hand of a princess. The conflict between the hero and his father is soon forgotten, for after the boy establishes his independence, he never looks back. *See also* Childhood and Children.

Further Reading: Warner, Marina. "The Silence of the Fathers." *From the Beast to the Blonde: On Fairy Tales and Their Tellers.* New York: Farrar, Straus, and Giroux, 1995. 335–52.

D. L. Ashliman

Feminism

Feminism has occupied itself with an interdisciplinary critique of patriarchal literary and cultural practices and looks at the conditions within society that restrict women's access to the public sphere and denigrate their activities in the private realm. Of special interest to feminists in folktale and fairy-tale studies are the processes of canon formation, the production and reception of folktales and fairy tales, and the representation of **women** in these traditions. The feminist critique has deeply influenced folktale and fairy-tale research and has led to a reevaluation of canonical traditions, disciplinary constructs, and a valorization of traditions by women writers. Feminists embrace women's contributions to scholarship and expressive culture.

Spurred by the feminist debates of the early 1970s, the modern feminist critique of the fairy-tale tradition began with the women's movement in the United States and Europe. Literary and social historians began to look at the negative stereotypes within the canonical tales and how those images conditioned female acculturation. Feminists viewed the most popular fairy tales as a primary site of contention within the civilizing process and argued that the most popular stories shaped the sexual, **gender**, and social **politics** of modern society and kept women subordinate to **men**. Addressing both literary production and reception, feminists studied the **collecting** and editorial practices in the **Grimm**s' *Kinder- und Hausmärchen* (*Children's and Household Tales*, 1812–15) and examined how editorial interventions shaped a message of those tales to create an increasingly restrictive image of womanhood. To counter those negative images of women, feminist scholars began anthologizing fairy tales—from both the canonical and other, relatively unknown traditions—with strong, independent, and brave females. The role of women as **informant**s and contributors to the canonical tradition also received much attention, while other scholars looked at female traditions that had preceded or paralleled male-authored collections but had been eclipsed by male contemporaries or had received no modern critical or scholarly attention. Within the canonical tales, feminists often focused on the female voices—of nubile heroines silenced through semantic shifts and careful **editing**, and of mature, powerful women endowed with the evil loquacity of **witch**es. In search of the genuine female voice in fairy tales, major recovery work was done on previously unstudied or ignored traditions of women that show a continuity of feminist concerns across national borders and over centuries. Anthologies of alternate or countertraditions, from the tales of the French *con-teuses* (female authors of the late seventeenth and early eighteenth centuries) to nineteenth-century contemporaries of the Grimms, also began to appear. With the new feminist wave, contemporary feminist writers rejected, rewrote, and responded to the canonical tradition and, as early female writers had done, used the subversive potential of the genre to criticize the patriarchy and its messages of female subordination.

Many of these same concerns have informed the feminist critique of folktale research. Feminist scholars argued that **folklore** studies were amazingly apolitical and unconcerned about gender issues, but three broad areas of feminist concern—the conditioning effects of negative images of women projected in verbal folklore, the female use of folklore, and the valorization of female folk performers and artists—closely parallel the critical agenda of their peers in fairy-tale studies. Since the late 1980s, feminist folklorists have been evaluating the genres of expressive culture that have received scholarly attention, as well as women's representation as informants and published scholars. A bibliography on women and folklore appeared as early as 1899 in the *Journal of American Folklore*, but a study of the 100-year publishing history of that journal indicates that topics on women had been limited to birthing, charms, quaint folk remedies, and the like, while superior-quality research by female scholars was often overshadowed by inferior scholarship of male colleagues through the editorial practices of the journal boards. Feminist research also has revealed a preference for **performance** contexts favoring genres of male expressive culture and has shown that field researchers sought materials from a female informant only when no male was available. Interesting studies have appeared that frame the male collector's recollection of his encounter with a female informant in terms of a tale of marvels in which the long-silent woman is awakened to the value of her stories and given a voice by the male field researcher and scholar.

An important aspect of feminist fairy-tale and folktale research has been the dismantling of their scholarly apparatus and disciplinary tools. Feminist critics have studied the entries in such seminal works as Antti **Aarne** and Stith **Thompson**'s *The Types of the Folktale* (2nd rev. ed., 1961) and Thompson's *Motif-Index of Folk-Literature* (rev. ed., 1955–58) and uncovered inherent gender biases. In folklore studies, feminist scholars have revealed the effects of the gender divide and how public versus private plays out in research agendas: since men's expressive culture is typically public and hence more accessible than women's more-private domains, it is often assumed to be the dominant or only area where expressive culture occurs. Feminist scholarship is beginning to create a space to evaluate the expressive culture of women.

For all its efforts to elevate the position of women in every aspect of society, the feminist critique itself has not been immune to criticism. There have been charges that white feminist scholars have used their privileged position in academies to press an agenda that does not represent women in non-Western contexts. Scholarly articles on traditions outside of the Western focus have recently attempted to redress such concerns. Feminism has broadened the interdisciplinary approaches to folktale and fairy-tale research and continues to expand the understanding of women's roles in these creative forms. *See also* Feminist Tales; Sex, Sexuality.

Further Readings: Haase, Donald, ed. *Fairy Tales and Feminism: New Approaches.* Detroit: Wayne State University Press, 2004; Hollis, Susan Tower, Linda Pershing, and M. Jane Young, eds. *Feminist Theory and the Study of Folklore.* Urbana: University of Illinois Press, 1993; Jarvis, Shawn C. "Feminism and

Fairy Tales." *The Oxford Companion to Fairy Tales.* Edited by Jack Zipes. Oxford: Oxford University Press, 2000. 155–59.

Shawn C. Jarvis

Feminist Tales

Depending on how they are defined, feminist tales can encompass either a vast corpus, quantitatively and historically, or a limited body of more-recent tales. In the latter case, feminist tales could be understood as a response to the rise of **feminism** in the 1960s and 1970s and, thus, as an explicit critique of both the patriarchal structures in many of the best-known Western fairy tales and the socialization of **gender** norms they perform. But in the former case, they might include a broad array of both folktales and fairy tales that are concerned with the diverse roles and challenges that face **women** across a variety of cultures. Whether or not such tales qualify as "feminist" is open for debate; but there is hardly a consensus about the meaning that label carries, and even some recent authors of what are commonly understood to be "feminist" tales reject it. To gain the broadest possible historical perspective on the phenomenon, "feminist tales" will refer here to those narratives that question the patriarchal oppression of women, either in subtle or explicit ways, before and after the rise of modern Western feminism.

From their beginnings, oral folklore and the **literary fairy tale** have been closely associated with women. How deeply the West has gendered such narratives can be demonstrated by the mythic origins attributed to the **storytelling** of old wives, **Mother Goose**, Ma Mère l'Oye, and other female **archetype**s. If it is true that women in preindustrial Europe told stories, some of which may have borne resemblance to modern fairy tales, and if it has been shown that nineteenth-century female storytellers constituted entire repertories of tales about and for women, it is nonetheless undeniable that the cultural work that went into feminizing the fairy tale and its reception went far beyond an acknowledgement of the historically demonstrable "roots" of the genre. A by-product of social efforts to domesticate girls and young women, the **myth** of the original female storyteller had as its impetus anything but a "liberation." Yet, long before the advent of feminism and the resulting feminist criticism of fairy tales, writers—mostly women—appropriated and reworked this myth so as to establish storylines that departed from the patriarchal plots of literature and **folklore**. The *conteuses* (the female authors of fairy tales) of late seventeenth-century and early eighteenth-century France were the first to seize on the opportunities presented by this myth and to revise some of the patriarchal plots from the literature and society of their day. Tales by Marie-Catherine d'**Aulnoy**, Catherine **Bernard**, Marie-Jeanne **Lhéritier de Villandon**, Henriette-Julie de Castelnau, Comtesse de **Murat**, Marie-Madeleine de **Lubert**, and Gabrielle-Suzanne de **Villeneuve**, among others, illustrated the growing importance of women in the literary fields of the day. Although there are numerous differences among them, the tales of the *conteuses* as a whole tend to glorify female power (especially through the figure of the **fairy**), defend women's right to education, celebrate women's language, modify or even reject **marriage** arrangements, and deflate grandiose conceptions of male heroism. Eighteenth- and nineteenth-century Germany witnessed the next growth in fairy tales by women that confronted both fictional and real patriarchal plots. Among other things, tales by Benedikte **Naubert**, Bettina von **Arnim**, Marie Ebner-Eschenbach, Isolde Kurz, and Ricarda Huch, for instance, offered critical perspectives on marriage, suggested new forms of female community, valorized women's voices, and, by the fin de siècle, directly challenged men's attempt to assimilate and silence a feminine tradition of fairy-tale writing. Victorian England also saw a significant number of female-authored fairy tales, many of which take up themes treated by contemporaneous German women writers and their French predecessors. Through an intertextual dialogue with men who wrote fairy tales at the time, Juliana Horatia **Ewing**, Jean **Ingelow**, Mary **De Morgan**, and Christina Georgina **Rossetti**, for example, resisted the nostalgic portrayal of femininity and asserted a stronger role for **mother**s.

The next great outpouring of feminist tales came in response to the feminist movement of the 1960s and 1970s, particularly in the United Kingdom and North America. It also occurred as feminists grappled with the meaning and effects of folktales and fairy tales (for example, the debate between Allison Lurie and Marcia Lieberman in the early 1970s). This production can be divided into two main groups: tales written expressly for children and tales written primarily for adults. Feminist tales for children perform numerous revisions of readers' expectations generated by many of the best-known fairy tales. Tales by Roald **Dahl**, Jeanne Desy, Barbara **Walker**, Jay Williams, and Jane **Yolen**, among many others, employ such techniques as reversal of gender roles, comic inversions, assertive female characters, and reconfiguration of the marriage plot. All of these writers play on the patriarchal expectations instilled by "classic" fairy tales and thereby prove the mutability of the genre.

Feminist tales for older readers are varied in both form and content. Some of the most widely hailed are found in the form of **poetry** rather than prose (for example, Anne **Sexton**, *Transformations*, 1971, and Olga **Broumas**, *Beginning with O*, 1977), creating a complex distancing effect from the familiarity of the prose formulas readily associated with the genre. More numerous by far are prose tales that play on the stylistic and structural conventions of the best-known fairy tales, some even translating the feminist critique of power into multiple narrative points of view (an example is Angela **Carter**, *The Bloody Chamber*, 1979). Central to a great number of these tales is an exploration of feminine **sexuality** that casts women as active desiring subjects, whether or not a happy outcome results. Notable in this regard are tales not only by Broumas, Carter, and Sexton, but also by Emma **Donoghue** (*Kissing the Witch*, 1997). Numerous also are tales that foreground the emotional and physical struggle women face at the hands of abusive **men** (for example, Margaret **Atwood**, "Bluebeard's Egg," 1983; Alison Lurie, *The War between the Tates*, 1974; Sylvia Plath, *The Bell Jar*, 1963; and Alix Kate Shulman, *Memoirs of an Ex-Prom Queen*, 1972). Whatever their thematic focus and whether celebratory or dark in tone, all of these tales depict women's self-consciousness of the reality and potentialities of their lives.

Anthologies of feminist folktales and fairy tales have flourished since the 1970s. These collections typically feature stories from many different cultures that spotlight active heroines and untraditional gender relations. Thereby, they aim to counter the negative effects of the restrictive gender norms promoted by many "classic" Western fairy tales. Among the numerous anthologies that have appeared are: Rosemary Minard, *Womenfolk and Fairy Tales* (1975); Ethel Johnston Phelps, *The Maid of the North: Feminist Folktales from Around the World* (1981); James Riordan, *The Woman in the Moon and Other Tales of Forgotten Heroines* (1984); Suzanne Barcher, *Wise Women: Folk and Fairy Tales from Around the World* (1990); Angela Carter, *Old Wives' Fairy Tale Book* (1990); Virginia **Hamilton**, *Her Stories: African American Folktales, Fairy Tales, and True Tales* (1995); Kathleen Ragan, *Fearless Girls, Wise Women, and Beloved Sisters: Heroines in Folktales from around the World* (1998); Jane Yolen, *Not One Damsel in Distress: World Folktales for Strong Girls*

(2000); and Jane Yolen and Heidi E. Y. Stemple, *Mirror, Mirror: Forty Folktales for Mothers and Daughters to Share* (2000).

The large number of feminist tales that have been published since the 1970s demonstrates just how important this subgenre has become within the larger corpus of folktales and fairy tales, especially in the English-speaking world. Still, in spite of the important work done by feminist folklorists and writers alike, several questions remain. How many women and girls today really are familiar with these stories, as opposed to more traditional versions (for example, in the variants by Walt **Disney** and the **Walt Disney Company**)? To what degree have revisionist feminist plots actually begun to eclipse traditional patriarchal plots? Are these stories read by men and boys, or have they been packaged and told in ways that keep male readers from becoming familiar with them? Even without definitive answers to these questions, one suspects that there is still much work to be done so that both genders become more familiar with feminist fairy-tale plots, but also so that these plots create nonpatriarchal norms of both masculinity and femininity. *See also* Intertextuality.

Further Readings: Bacchilega, Cristina. *Postmodern Fairy Tales: Gender and Narrative Strategies.* Philadelphia: University of Pennsylvania Press, 1997; Haase, Donald, ed. *Fairy Tales and Feminism: New Approaches.* Detroit: Wayne State University Press, 2004; Jack Zipes, ed. *Don't Bet on the Prince: Contemporary Feminist Fairy Tales in North America and England.* New York: Methuen, 1986.

Lewis C. Seifert

Fēngshén Yănyì

Translated as *The Investiture of the Gods* or *The Creation of the Gods*, *Fēngshén Yănyì* is one of the most-celebrated Chinese vernacular novels combining historical romance and popular mythological tales. With its numerous tales of deities and evil spirits, it serves as an important resource for research involving Chinese mythology and the Taoist pantheon.

Fēngshén Yănyì was first published in book form around 1567 to 1619, and its authorship is attributed to Xú Zhònglín or a Taoist Lù Xīxīng. The book tells of a legendary war led by King Wén of the Zhōu dynasty (1122–221 BCE) against the merciless ruler, King Zhòu, of the Shāng dynasty (1766–1121 BCE). Supernatural immortals and demonic spirits engage in the endless sequence of battles between the two sides, featuring the integration of human affairs and a celestial scheme. The story starts with King Zhòu's blasphemous poem to Goddess Nǚ Wā, who furiously summons a seductive vixen spirit to help overthrow Shāng. The magic warfare ends with the toppling of Shāng and the creation of the Zhōu feudal system. The deceased or slain spirits and mortals on both sides are canonized as deities in the Taoist pantheon under a celestial hierarchy.

Mythical figures, **motifs**, and tales in the novel correspond to those present in popular oral and written narratives that were in circulation at the time. These popularly disseminated tales of deities and demons had Taoist, Buddhist, and folkloric origins, and their popularity has continued into the present. *See also* Chinese Tales.

Further Readings: Kao, Karl S. Y. "Domains of Moral Discourse: Self, History, and Fantasy in *Fengshen yanyi*." *Chinese Literature: Essays, Articles, Reviews* 24 (December 2002): 75–97; Wan, Pin Pin. "Investiture of the Gods (*Fēngshén Yănyì*): Sources, Narrative Structure, and Mythical Significance." Dissertation. University of Washington, 1987.

Jing Li

Ferré, Rosario (1938–)

Rosario Ferré is a Puerto Rican author who frequently rewrites and subverts **myth**s and fairy tales. Ferré's works constitute an analysis and critique of repressive paternalistic traditions in the island's society and culture. In works such as the short stories of *Papeles de Pandora* (*The Youngest Doll*, 1976) and the poems of *Fábulas de la garza desangrada* (*Fables of the Wounded Heron*, 1982), Ferré incorporates elements of mythology, **fantasy**, and fairy tales, often reinterpreting well-known characters such as Antigone, Medea, and **Sleeping Beauty** from a contemporary feminist perspective. Ferré has also written books specifically for children, such as *El medio pollito* (*The Little Chicken*, 1978) and *La mona que le pisaron la cola* (*Someone Stepped on the Monkey's Tail*, 1981), which consist of **fable**s, and *Los cuentos de Juan Bobo* (*Tales of Juan Bobo*, 1981), which focuses on an uneducated but witty boy who is part of traditional Puerto Rican **folklore**. In 1989, Ferré compiled some of her children's tales in the volume *Sonatinas*. Although written for young people, those books also give new forms to traditional stories, relating them to social problems in contemporary Puerto Rico. *See also* Feminism; Feminist Tales.

Further Readings: Fernández Olmos, Margarite. "Constructing Heroines: Rosario Ferré's *cuentos infantiles* and Feminine Instruments of Change." *Lion and the Unicorn* 10 (1986): 83–94; Glenn, Kathleen M. "Text and Countertext in Rosario Ferré's 'Sleeping Beauty.'" *Studies in Short Fiction* 33 (1996): 207–18; Hintz, Suzanne. *Rosario Ferré: A Search for Identity.* New York: Peter Lang, 1995.

Víctor Figueroa

Fieldwork

In the social sciences, the term "fieldwork" describes research conducted within a specific group of people for a specific period to collect raw data. It can be contrasted with "armchair" research, which does not entail direct contact with a group in its environment. In the study of **folktale**s, fieldwork involves research aimed at **collecting** and understanding oral texts, either as verbal texts or as sociocultural events. This work is carried out by transcribing and/or recording the texts with reference to their **context**. The meaning and relevance of "context" depend on the fieldworker's methods, which in turn are determined by the discipline in which he or she is working and by the results the fieldwork is expected to produce.

Historically, the first attempts at fieldwork in Europe were folktale collections undertaken to preserve oral texts in written form. By capturing the oral texts in print, these collections enabled further study of the tales, especially as literary or linguistic phenomena. Those attempts, which contributed to the development of **folklore** studies in Europe, started in the early nineteenth century with Jacob and Wilhelm **Grimm** and focused on the text itself, paying little attention to the social, cultural, and artistic context of the narration. However, assumptions implicit in this early work anticipated the future relevance of considering important factors such as an **informant**'s precise repertoire, his or her level of literacy, or intercultural contacts and exchanges. Those first attempts revolved primarily around either the procedure for archiving, cataloguing, and classifying texts, or with publishing selections of local **oral tradition**s. They produced voluminous corpora of national and regional folktales.

In the twentieth century, polysemic approaches to the folktale went hand in hand with significantly enriched fieldwork methods and techniques. The **storytelling** event itself was brought to the foreground and became a distinct object of consideration. Anthropological methods, such as "participant observation"—first introduced by Bronisław Malinowski and by which the researcher gains knowledge of a culture through involvement in it and through relationships with informants—opened the way not only for an association with the community's social life, structure, and values, but also for important ethnolinguistic investigations. The shift of folklore perspectives in the 1960s from archival-oriented field research to "emic" considerations (that is, the insider's view) gave birth to **performance** theory and ethnopoetics (as in the work of Dell Hymes and Dennis Tedlock), which connected storytelling with competence, artistry, and the performer's social group.

The use of audiovisual technology in fieldwork has allowed oral narratives to be fixed in a format that is very close to the originals (oral texts and storytelling events) and made it possible to produce minutely detailed transcriptions, descriptions, and analyses. A recorded folktale, however, never corresponds exactly to its original because the ambient feeling, with all its sensory stimuli, remains elusive.

The fieldworker's interest in the oral text and the context in which it is produced also involves a responsibility toward the informant. The informant-ethnographer relationship requires the ethnographer to respect matters of ethics and copyright. *See also* Anthropological Approaches; Archives; Authenticity; Ethnographic Approaches; Linguistic Approaches.

Further Readings: Calame-Griaule, Geneviève. *Des cauris au marché: Essais sur des contes africains.* Paris: Société des Africanistes, 1987; Dégh, Linda. *Folktales and Society: Story-Telling in a Hungarian Peasant Community.* Translated by Emily M. Schossberger. Expanded edition. Bloomington: Indiana University Press, 1989; Hymes, Dell. *"In Vain I Tried To Tell You": Essays in Native American Ethnopoetics.* New edition. Lincoln: University of Nebraska Press, 2004.

Marilena Papachristophorou

Film and Video

The migration of fairy tales from oral **folklore** into literary and thence into dramatic and cinematic forms was always inevitable. An ancient, familiar, and powerful mode of **storytelling**, the fairy tale is ideally equipped to colonize developing cultural expressions. Its short, sparse, action-centered narratives have proved to be suited for dramatic and visual forms such as **theater**, **opera**, **dance**, the musical, and **pantomime**, and it has been associated with cinema from the earliest days of the medium. Fairy-tale narratives proliferate across both live-action cinema and **animation**, occupying every niche from serious avant-garde cinema to the most commercial of Hollywood productions, and spreading into the related worlds of video, DVD, and **television**, both in the new lease on life given to theatrical releases in DVD format and in the space such forums offer for lower-budget productions.

While the power of folkloric narratives makes such proliferation understandable, at the same time, **translation** into film and theater is in other ways an interesting and perhaps unlikely development. As a nonrealist and magical form, the fairy tale tends to be imbued with the structured third-person recitation of the oral form, functioning through description rather than dialogue and relying on a simplicity of expression, which requires the imaginative engagement of the listener in a more-or-less personal way. **Fantasy** writer J. R. R. **Tolkien** famously disliked even **illustration**s to fantastic narratives, arguing in his essay "On Fairy Stories" that such visual realization restricts the imagination of the reader to one version of the narrative and thus blunts its ability to operate through the personalized ramification of symbol. In the case of drama, and, even more so, film, the timeless ahistoricity of the fairy-tale narrative runs the risk of being fixed into ever more realist interpretations.

Tolkien's other problem with dramatic presentations of fairy tales is less compelling. His suggestion that the magical cannot be counterfeited well enough to be convincing tends to fall away under modern developments in special effects and CGI.

Despite such concerns, the proliferation and success of the fairy tale in the cinematic medium suggests that potential limitations on the form's functioning are equally matched by characteristics that empower it.

From left to right: Fiona (voiced by Cameron Diaz) and Shrek (Mike Myers) in the 2001 animated picture *Shrek*. [Dreamworks/Photofest]

Here, the operation of film as an essentially magical medium is key: like the fairy tale, film presents itself as the narrative of the master magician, a technological marvel that dazzles the senses and confounds reality with illusion and deception. While live-action cinema is the genre of absolute realist representation, by extension it lends to its magical visual trickery the equal status of the real, and thus fosters acceptance and wonder as a response to the magical. In another way, this sense in which film is technological magic is underlined by the ongoing affinity between the fairy-tale narrative and the playful unrealism of animation, which has also been notable from the early days of cinema.

Another reason for the association between fairy tales and film is perhaps simply in the shortness and simplicity of fairy-tale stories, whose characteristics are in some ways ideally suited to the embryonic technology of the early years of cinema. Both structured and recognizable, fairy-tale narratives are easily adaptable to lend shape and familiarity to short films; their elements of stylization and domesticity would have translated well into the set and acting requirements of the developing medium. As the cinema industry developed, fairy-tale narratives retained a place in short films, most notably in cartoon shorts (Betty Boop, Frederick "Tex" **Avery**, and the fairy-tale adventures of various **Walt Disney Company** cartoon characters). In more recent years, avant-garde fairy-tale shorts can be found on the independent film festival circuit, among them David Kaplan's sexy, provocative works *The Frog King* (1994) and *Little Red Riding Hood* (1997). However, it is in the full-length feature that the fairy tale has found its most successful and popular cinematic expressions.

The fairy tale in cinema occurs both explicitly and implicitly across a wide range of film types, from avant-garde experimentation that mines the form's inherent magic, to the most-commercial Hollywood productions. The strongly utopian thrust of many fairy-tale narratives meshes well with the functioning of mainstream commercial cinema, which creates consoling, upbeat narratives that are entertaining but undemanding to watch. The much-vaunted "Hollywood fairy-tale ending" represents a form of narrative that relies on structures similar to the quest of the fairy tale: conflict, moral testing, the overcoming of obstacles, and resolution, often in the form of **marriage** and wealth. There is considerable resonance not only between the fairy tale and the Hollywood romance, but also between the fairy tale and the American dream: both celebrate upward mobility and the accessibility of success through one's own efforts. Such correspondences tend, however, to exaggerate the implicit ideologies of the fairy tale, particularly with reference to **gender** roles. Certainly, in many film versions of fairy tales, as well as films that use fairy tales less explicitly to under-pin their more-contemporary popular narratives, the familiar tropes of passive **women**, active **men**, and of heterosexual marriage as the only desirable fate, are invoked and rein-forced. This tendency is particularly strong in early American film given the effect of the Hays Code, which deliberately precluded social commentary or overt sexuality or **violence**. The otherworldly simplicity of fairy-tale narratives could be easily made to fit the naïve ro-manticism and clear-cut moral outcomes of Hollywood cinema in the 1920s and 1930s. This tendency is still apparent in more contemporary cinematic fairy tales despite the gloss of contemporary awareness, particularly feminist consciousness, which is often laid over the re-actionary elements of the tale. Fairy-tale structures, in their frequent focus on wealth and beauty, mesh well with the goals of consumerism and highlight marketing tendencies to focus on a white, middle-class, male-dominated ideal.

In addition to the form's potential entrenchment of core middle-class values and racial or gender stereotypes, commercial fairy-tale film relies in many cases on the consumer's sense of nostalgia and ownership with reference to the familiar fairy tales. Critics such as Jack **Zipes** note the extent to which the problematical and reactionary ideologies of fairy-tale forms are mined and exaggerated by film's operation as a mass-market, commercial medium, which tends to entrench rather than question the status quo. In part, this tendency arises from the way in which film as a medium transforms the traditional functioning of narratives that are originally folkloric in nature. The fairy tale was transmuted by the capture of dynamic folkloric forms into the more static and fixed narratives of literature; cinema moves beyond the literate into the postliterate, into a form that has a far more popular, oral, and communal resonance than does the written word. Mainstream Hollywood cinema, in its strong market awareness, parodies and mimics the operation of a folkloric form, at least in the sense of ownership and investment it invokes in its audience. More importantly, however, in the enor-mous costs of the filmmaking process, cinema of all cultural texts moves most radically from the notion of communal generation of text into the top-down construction of cultural artifact by a privileged elite. In this sense, the development of the fairy tale in cinema throughout the twentieth century has not only reproduced and adapted the folkloric narratives of Western and other cultures but has to a certain extent usurped and replaced them. In many cases, the defining version of a tale, particularly in the minds of increasingly media-aware children, is the cinematic one. Given the power of the Hollywood marketing machine, this has tended to stamp fairy tales with a quality of specificity and authorship—or ownership—that operates strongly against the communal ownership of folklore. The Disney Company, with its fierce defense of trademark, is a particularly extreme example of this trend.

Fairy Tale Adaptations

Direct **adaptation** of the fairy tale as magical narrative is a recurring theme across cin-ema history. The long-term association between the magic of cinema and the marvels of fairy tales probably began with a pioneer of the form, the French theatrical illusionist and cinematographer Georges **Méliès**. His experiments with trick photography and special effects embodied the magic of fairy tales such as Charles **Perrault**'s *Cendrillon* (*Cinderella*, 1899) and *Barbe-bleue* (*Bluebeard*, 1901), which first demonstrated effects shots such as the dissolve. More importantly, it is possible that the strong narrative line of the fairy tale inspired his experiments with actual filmic narrative constructed from an edited series of shots, replacing the more common single, realistic slice-of-life shot used by his contemporaries. His efforts were paralleled in Britain by the work of George Albert Smith, who was similarly interested in trick photography. Like Méliès, he made numerous realist shorts but also produced a version of "Cinderella" (1898) and two of "**Aladdin**" (1898 and 1899). While both filmmakers produced black-and-white live-action silent films, the animated fairy tale was also developing in the work of Lotte **Reiniger**, whose work in both Germany and Britain resulted in fairy-tale films using her characteristic silhouette animation, among them *The Adventures of Prince Achmed* (1926), *The Frog Prince* (1954), and *Cinderella* (1955).

From the early days onward, live-action films have offered multiple versions of favorite fairy tales, mostly from Perrault and the Brothers **Grimm**, although the works of Hans Christian **Andersen** are also popular among filmmakers. Many of these cinematic fairy tales are rather flat, pedestrian adaptations. When changes are made, they are often additions to pad out the story with more detail and extra characters. These at times unimaginative adaptations often mine the form for its obvious moral content, familiar tropes, and encoded cultural clichés, and are as likely to be aimed at a child audience as at adults. Notably, fairy-tale films are a recurring theme in the comparatively low-budget, made-for-television market. Among feature fairy tales, **Cinderella films** seem particularly popular, possibly because of the story's strong parallels with Hollywood's fast-developing interests in beauty, success, and love as cinematic themes, as well as the appeal of the passive heroine rescued by her powerful **prince**. Early versions included James Kirkwood's *Cinderella* (1914), starring Mary Pickford, as well as numerous animated shorts and Disney's 1950 version; outside of Hollywood, numerous versions include Václav Vorlíček's Czech adaptation, *Tři oříšky pro Popelku* (*Three Nuts for Cinderella*, 1973), which features a strong, active heroine. Hollywood's *Ever After* (1998) is probably the most successful recent adaptation, and the theme can be found in the comic despised-younger-sister theme of *Ella Enchanted* (2004). Other popular types include **Snow White** movies and **Bluebeard films**, the latter most often invoked as an underlying structure to a more realistic investigation of marriage.

It is notable that earlier films tended toward stories that focused on human characters, the magic of the tale confined to the technically easier transformations of objects. It is only toward the end of the twentieth century that adaptations of tales such as "**Beauty and the Beast**" became widespread, reflecting the development in special effects. Early versions of "Beauty and the Beast" tended to be shorts, many of them animated. Jean Cocteau's 1946 *La Belle et la Bête* was an early example of a feature in which creative make-up and artistic, evocative visual effects deliberately and specifically translated the fairy tale's difficult magic to the screen; subsequent versions include Juraj Herz's darkly-toned Czech fantasy *Panna a netvor* (*Beauty and the Beast*, 1978) and Disney's popular animated feature (1991). The flying carpets, djinn, and enchanted horses of the *Arabian Nights* films also have a long history of successful Hollywood adaptations, notably in the various versions of *The Thief of Bagdad* (1924 and 1940), which heavily influenced Disney's later *Aladdin* (1992). Hans Christian Andersen films also form a substantial subset of cinematic fairy tale, with versions of Andersen's tales from Russia and Germany as well as Scandinavia and the United States.

The difficulty with representing the magical realistically was partially addressed in earlier films by combining live action with stop-motion animation, or, in the European cinematic tradition, with numerous fairy-tale versions using puppet animation. In Hollywood, stop-motion animation is most notably seen in the works of Ray Harryhausen and George Pal, who both produced films for Paramount. Harryhausen's most famous work is probably *The Seventh Voyage of Sinbad* (1958), loosely based on the **Arabian Nights**, but he also made films based on classical mythology. Hungarian-born George Pal is possibly better known for his science-fiction films, but his **Tom Thumb** (1958) is a comic and family-oriented version of the tale that incorporates other fairy-tale **motif**s into the main narrative, and which makes creative use of stop-motion in its inventive special effects. Pal is also notable for *The Wonderful World of the Brothers Grimm* (1962), which represents a recurring thread in fairy-tale film, namely the focus on storytellers as a framing device for embedded tales. Other examples include Charles Vidor's *Hans Christian Andersen* (1952) and Terry Gilliam's recent, somewhat problematical *The Brothers Grimm* (2005).

Mainstream live-action cinema tends toward fairy-tale films that stress the romance elements of the form, but more serious adaptations also explore the assumptions and structures of the fairy-tale tradition. Jean Cocteau's *La Belle et la Bête* offers the auteur's coherent artistic vision, exploring themes of beauty and worth; the folkloric films of Pier Paolo **Pasolini** likewise offer a distinctive political and literary vision. Neil Jordan's **The Company of Wolves** (1984) is a complex, exploratory film which uses the stories and screenplay by Angela **Carter** to investigate the social and cultural aspects of sexuality. Jordan's film also highlights the other possible interpretation of folkloric forms in its intersection with the traditional horror narrative, an effective combination that hearkens back to the more primitive and violent roots of oral folklore. Other horror versions of fairy tales are less intelligent: Michael Cohn's **Snow White: A Tale of Terror** (1997) touches on Freudian interpretations of the Snow White tale but is ultimately thin and overstated. The logical conclusion to the fairy tale/horror combination lies in such pseudofolkloric, mass-market horror films as *Leprechaun* (1993). Perhaps the most unlikely generic crossover is in the recent animated film *Hoodwinked* (2005), which rewrites **Little Red Riding Hood** as a multiple-viewpoint comic film noir, an uneasy meld that demonstrates a generally facile and unsophisticated use of fairy-tale motifs.

If horror and fairy tales are in some ways a logical combination, fairy tales and comedy are also surprisingly successful in the cinematic medium. This tendency strengthened toward the end of the twentieth century as the drift into postmodern awareness saw cinema audiences more appreciative of irony. Perhaps the most successful of recent fairy-tale films have been Dreamworks's **Shrek and Shrek II** (2001 and 2004). These animated films build on a tradition of fairy-tale **parody**, seen in earlier works such as Jerry Lewis's unabashedly ridiculous **Cinderfella** (1960), or Jim **Henson**'s Muppet version of the **Frog King** story (*The Frog Prince*, 1972). However, *Shrek* and its sequel offer a more sophisticated, subversive exploration of the form that self-consciously plays with fairy-tale convention even as it affectionately parodies it. A similar approach can be seen in *Ella Enchanted* or even, to a less-successful degree, in *Hoodwinked*. The ironic awareness demonstrated by these films is highly successful with contemporary audiences, far more so than the flatter, less-self-aware approach taken by Disney, although they perhaps approach this ironic awareness of form in *Chicken Little* (2005).

While commercial American cinema produces multiple adaptations of favorite tales within the mold of popular Hollywood genres, European versions are often linked to a strong folkloric awareness that celebrates the fairy tale through cinema as an act of cultural heritage. This partially accounts for the proliferation of the Brothers Grimm in film. Germany's strong tradition of fairy-tale films is expressed in the work of directors such as Fritz Genschow, who produced numerous fairy-tale films in the 1950s and 1960s, including *Frau Holle* (**Mother Holle**, 1954) and *Aschenputtel* (*Cinderella*, 1955). "Frau Holle" seems to be a favorite tale for German directors, and was made again, with a slightly surrealist visual feel, by Peter Podehl in 1961. A similar sense of folkloric heritage can be traced in other European and Scandinavian countries. A notable example is Norway's *Kvitebjorn kong valemon* (*The Polar Bear King*, 1991), directed by Ola Solum, is an effective children's film using the **animal-groom** motif.

The cinematic fairy tale does not escape the tendency first expressed in its eighteenth- and nineteenth-century literary versions, to appropriate the form for didactic rewriting aimed at children. This element is clearly visible in Disney fairy tales, which validate particularly conservative gender and class roles; but the tendency is seen most clearly in various socialist regimes, notably East Germany and Russia. In the German Democratic Republic, the Deutsche Film AG (German Film Company) demonstrated an interest in children's fairy-tale cinema with a bias toward socialist political education. Prominent directors included Gottfried Kolditz, who made versions of Grimm fairy tales including *Schneewittchen und die sieben Zwerge* (*Snow White and the Seven Dwarfs*, 1961) and *Frau Holle* (1963), and the prolific Walter Beck, among whose films were versions of *König Drosselbart* (*King Thrushbeard*, 1965) and *Froschkönig* (*The Frog King*, 1987). **Soviet fairy-tale films** are numerous, but are generally less overtly concerned with indoctrination, extolling universal virtues such as hard work but offering few fairy-tale films with an overbearing political message. As with European versions, many of the adaptations are motivated by a strong sense of folkloric heritage. In the years before the World War II, Aleksandr Ptushko produced a series of fairy-tale films using puppet animation. The war years saw some political control over filmmaking, but from the mid-1950s onward this relaxed somewhat, allowing the proliferation of folkloric cinema across Russia; Aleksadr Rou's Gorky Studios in particular produced numerous fairy-tale films aimed at children.

Musical Fairy-Tale Films

The fairy tale has always been a particularly good fit with the musical genre, perhaps because both narrative traditions rely on a degree of stylization and deliberate removal from realism. The willing suspension of disbelief of the audience can be applied as much to the taken-for-granted magic of the fairy tale as to the unlikelihood of characters breaking into song to express their feelings. This fit is underlined most strongly in the ongoing success of Disney's animated fairy-tale musicals, which dominated both animation and fairy-tale cinema throughout most of the twentieth century. As well as cinematic musicals, fairy-tale films have a fair degree of cross-pollination with musicals in the theater and, to a lesser extent, opera, with many successful screen adaptations of both musical forms, a fair proportion made specifically for television. Many of these film versions are not feature films designed for theatrical release, but are instead cast recordings of successful Broadway or operatic pieces, which find greater exposure through the medium of video and, particularly, DVD.

A few well-known fairy-tale musicals tend to dominate the cinematic niche, being continually remade, perhaps a testament to their enduring appeal. Richard Rodgers and Oscar Hammerstein's version of "Cinderella" occurs in three separate film versions (1957, 1964, and

1997), and the Broadway musical *Once upon a Mattress* exists as two separate cast recordings, from 1964 and 1972, as well as in the 2005 adaptation with Carol Burnett and Tracey Ullman. Another classic of fairy-tale musical is the Richard Chamberlain vehicle *The Slipper and the Rose* (1976), directed by Bryan Forbes, which also began as a theatrical musical. The Broadway hit *Into the Woods* is also available on DVD as the 1991 Broadway cast production, giving continued life to the self-conscious investigation and interrogation of the various familiar fairy tales embedded in its plot. Victor Herbert's nursery-rhyme operetta *Babes in Toyland* has been more extensively adapted for cinema, in both the 1934 version with Laurel and Hardy, and in Disney's 1961 version. The fairy-tale musical is also well represented in the 1980s by the Cannon Movietales, low-budget comedy musicals filmed in Israel, which have been rereleased on DVD in the last few years. Their wide range of adaptations include *Beauty and the Beast* (1987), *Red Riding Hood* (1989), *Snow White* (1987), and *Sleeping Beauty* (1987).

Outside of the European film tradition and Hollywood, the fairy-tale musical probably finds its strongest expression in the riotous glamour of Indian cinema's Bollywood productions, which boast both a strong song-and-dance tradition and the mythological subgenre rooted firmly in Indian **myth**, folklore, and **epic**, particularly the *Mahabharata* and the *Ramayana*. While explicitly magical cinema may feature the actions of gods, goddesses, and saints, the storylines of the epics are also present as an underlying thread in many contemporary Bollywood thrillers, dramas, and romantic comedies. The often carnivalesque feel of Indian cinema can also be linked to Indian folk theater. Like European fairy-tale films, Bollywood cinema offers a fantastic, vibrant celebration of folkloric heritage and a powerful expression of the classic fairy-tale's unquestioning acceptance of the magical.

Fantasy Film

Cinema's attraction to magical narrative is expressed not simply in straightforward adaptations of classic fairy tales, but in a number of offshoot Hollywood genres that rely in some sense on the motifs and expectations of the form, most notably magic itself, but also **transformation**s, **magic object**s, talking beasts, and **magic helper**s. Thus fairy-tale cinema includes film versions of literary or theatrical **fantasy**, a more extended and complex genre that nonetheless embodies fairy-tale notions of quest, magical landscape, and the demonstration of worth in the overcoming of obstacles. Early examples of these films in Western cinema include adaptations of texts such as Maurice **Maeterlinck**'s theatrical fairy tale *L'oiseau bleu* (*The Blue Bird*, 1908), which saw several silent-film adaptations as well as the 1940 movie starring Shirley Temple, and animated versions in the 1970s. Sir James Matthew **Barrie**'s *Peter Pan* (1904) has similarly been adapted to cinema in various incarnations, including the Disney animated version (1953) and the successful postmodern reinterpretation of Barrie's classic in Stephen Spielberg's *Hook* (1991). Other literary classics with fairy-tale resonance include Lewis **Carroll**'s *Alice's Adventures in Wonderland* (1865), often interpreted with visual surrealism in cinematic versions, and, famously, L. Frank **Baum**'s *The Wizard of Oz*, in its film version of 1939 and its sequel, *Return to Oz* (1985).

These fantasy films share with fairy tales not only the quest motif, but a continuing delight in the ability of cinema to visually embody the magical, culminating most powerfully in the recent blockbuster successes of *The Lord of the Rings* trilogy, the **Harry Potter films**, and the start of a new franchise based on C. S. **Lewis**'s Narnia series. Film adaptations of classic fantasy have become an almost-guaranteed success for cinema producers, exploiting not only the enchantments of cinematic magic, but the nostalgic familiarity of audiences with well-known fantasy texts, often those of childhood. The trend is not confined wholly to adaptation, however, and in some ways relies on the success of earlier, original fairy-tale scripts in the 1980s, which resulted in the fantastic landscapes of films such as *The Dark Crystal* (1982), *Labyrinth* (1986), and **Willow** (1988), or the heroic quests of *Legend* (1985) and **The Princess Bride** (1987). Perhaps closest to folkloric forms are the cursed, transformed lovers of *Ladyhawke* (1985), striving to break the spell that separates them. The overall success of fantasy cinema suggests an appetite for wonders among viewers that is possibly not unrelated to folklore's ability to reformulate real-life concerns and ideas in mythic, symbolic form. More subtle resonances can also be found in the contemporary obsession with superhero films, which operate as fantastic narratives with mythic resonance, particularly in the inherently magical transformation of the alter ego into a superhero and his or her predestined confrontation, aided by gadgets which parallel magic objects, with the often monstrous supervillain.

If Western cinema demonstrates a healthy subset of fantasy and fairy-tale films, the same is possibly even more true of Eastern cultures. In addition to the mythological musicals of the Bollywood tradition, the martial-arts film tradition of China and Japan has powerful folkloric resonances, both in its celebration of folk heroes and famous warrior figures and in the strong thread of the magical that runs through many of its films. Chinese kung-fu films are created with a calm acceptance of the supernatural and incredible woven into the wirework extravaganzas of its fight sequences, in which heroes fly, bound, and run up walls as though magically free of the constraints of gravity. Recent examples that have been successful with Western audiences include Ang Lee's *Wò hǔ cáng lóng* (*Crouching Tiger, Hidden Dragon*, 2000), and Yimou Zhang's *Yīng xióng* (*Hero*, 2002) and *Shí miàn mái fú* (*House of Flying Daggers*, 2004). These films feature magical swords, predestined fates, and supernatural fighting abilities; they also reflect a certain stylization of narrative that is closely related to the folkloric. An ongoing awareness of folklore and **legend** is also often represented in Chinese cinema, notably in many of the martial arts films starring Jet Li: examples include *Wong fei-hung* (*Once upon a Time in China*, 1991), which follows the adventures of a nineteenth-century Chinese folk hero, and *Hóng xīguān zhi Shàolín wǔ zǔ* (*Legends of Shaolin*, 1994), whose heroic warrior battles supernatural monsters.

If Chinese live-action cinema has folkloric resonances, in Japanese film it is the animated tradition that most strongly demonstrates a similar interest. The genre of anime has gained massive popularity in the West only recently, but was a strong and popular tradition in Japan throughout the twentieth century. Its adult fantastic narratives are often science fictional but also feature magical and folkloric motifs in which warrior heroes, magical artifacts, and animal companions predominate. Most familiar to Western audiences are the folkloric films of **Miyazaki** Hayao, among them *Mononoke-hime* (*Princess Mononoke*, 1997) and *Sen to Chihiro no kamikakushi* (*Spirited Away*, 2001); these explore Japanese animism, nature deities, and the magical otherworld of spirit creatures.

Contemporary Fairy Tales

While the magic of the fairy tale is a common feature of fairy-tale films, not all adaptations operate within the traditions of the marvelous. In some instances, the powerful, recognizable, and psychologically interesting narrative structures of fairy tales are used to strengthen contemporary films in the realist tradition, much as they are used in a literary context by writers such as Margaret **Atwood**. This has been a recurring thread in fairy-tale cinema from its earliest days: films such as Leni Reifenstahl's ***Das blaue Licht*** (*The Blue Light*, 1932), while tenuously connected to the Grimm fairy tale of the same name, is essentially a realist film with some echoes of folklore. Similarly, Edgar G. Ulmer's *Bluebeard* (1944) is a low-budget horror film about a tormented serial killer/artist who strangles his models. These films generally avoid the explicit fairy-tale characters of their more magical counterparts and instead function through allusion, suggestion, and parallel: the viewer's recognition of the fairy-tale structure lends depth and complexity to the film's operation.

In Hollywood cinema, the resonance and structures of fairy tales are most commonly used to infuse romantic comedy with a self-conscious staginess and to underline the comforting predictability of the well-known plot. Possibly the best example of this is the successful Cinderella-narrative of ***Pretty Woman*** (1990), which rewrites the kitchen drudge as a prostitute and her prince as a wealthy corporate figure. Mark Rosman's more recent *A Cinderella Story* (2004) refigures the tale as a standard teen romance, with an exploitative stepmother as the obstacle to the heroine's prom-night dreams. Ron Howard's ***Splash*** (1984) updates to contemporary Manhattan the tale of a **mermaid** who assumes human form for love of a man. While this film retains some magical elements, they tend to become the excuse for romantic comedy rather than the focus of exploration.

As for romances, the fairy tale is an effective underpinning for horror film, most notably in the proliferation of Bluebeard films that investigate issues of marriage, desire, and **transgression** in a variety of contexts, often with the intimate violence of film noir. "**Little Red Riding Hood**" seems particularly appropriate to the psychological thriller and likewise offers mythic underpinnings to Matthew Bright's ***Freeway*** (1996), exploring the sexualization of both child and **wolf** in a serial-killer film set in the seamier underside of America. The tale is also less-overtly referenced by films such as Nicole Kassell's *The Woodsman* (2004), exploring the conflict within a convicted pedophile, and *Hard Candy* (2005), in which the inversion of the child's victimhood is even more extreme than in *Freeway*. Such dark rereadings of fairy tales suggest that the form continues to provide relevant structural and psychological insight in twenty-first century films. *See also* Andersen, Hans Christian, in Biopics; Brothers Grimm in Biopics; Davenport, Tom; DEFA Fairy-Tale Films; Peter Pan Films; *Popeye the Sailor*; Puppet Theater; Silent Films and Fairy Tales; Thief of Bagdad Films.

Further Readings: Berger, Eberhard, and Joachim Giera. *77 Märchenfilme: Ein Filmführer für jung und alt*. Berlin: Henschel, 1990; Davenport, Tom. "Some Personal Notes on Adapting Folk-Fairy Tales to Film." *Children's Literature* 9 (1981): 107–15; deGraff, Amy. "From Glass Slipper to Glass Ceiling: 'Cinderella' and the Endurance of a Fairy Tale." *Marvels & Tales* 10 (1996): 69–85; Haase, Donald P. "Gold into Straw: Fairy Tale Movies for Children and the Culture Industry." *Lion and the Unicorn* 12.2 (1998): 193–207; Schechter, Harold. "The Bloody Chamber: Terror Films, Fairy Tales, and Taboo." *Forbidden Fruits: Taboos and Tabooism in Culture*. Edited by Ray B. Browne. Bowling Green: Bowling Green State University Popular Press, 1984. 67–82; Stephens, John and Robyn McCallum. "Utopia, Dystopia, and Cultural Controversy in *Ever After* and *The Grimm Brothers' Snow White*." *Marvels & Tales* 16 (2002): 201–13; Zipes, Jack. "The Cinematic Appropriation of Andersen's Heritage: Trivialization and Innovation" and "Film Bibliography." *Hans Christian Andersen: The Misunderstood Storyteller*. New York: Routledge, 2005. 103–42, 157–66; ———. *Happily Ever After: Fairy Tales, Children and the Culture Industry*. New York: Routledge, 1997.

Jessica Tiffin

Finnish Method. *See* Historic-Geographic Method

Finnish Tales

Finnish **folktale**s derive from two European traditions. Folktales arrived in western Finland from Scandinavia, primarily from Sweden, whereas the folktales of eastern Finland were shaped by traditions of northern Russia. Because Finland was the endpoint of two major streams of tradition, its volume of folktales surpassed those in many neighboring countries. Approximately 160 **animal tale** plots are known, as well as 140 tales of magic, 100 **novella**s (realistic tales), and some 560 humorous tales (jokes, **anecdote**s, and stories of the stupid **ogre**). Because these tales have been collected as several variants, the folklore **archives** of the Finnish Literature Society contain more than 90,000 folktale texts.

Research suggests that magic tales (see **Wonder Tale**) began to circulate in Finland in the 1500s and 1600s, whereas animal tales were probably told since medieval times. In the past, scholars agreed that Finnish folktales, like *Kalevala*-meter poems, represented an ancient tradition that was transmitted only orally. Present-day folklorists are of a different mind. Most of the folktales now housed in the archives were written down in the 1880s and 1890s and clearly evince their links to the written tradition. Folk narrators had access to cheap broadsheets and **chapbook**s since the late 1700s. What is more, newspapers published in the early 1800s also contained a wealth of entertainment, including folktales and **legend**s. Fairy-tale literature published in Sweden also was available in Finland. Thanks to the existence of bilingual folktale narrators, examples and elements derived from this source also came to enrich the folktale tradition among Finnish speakers.

Internationally, the best-known fairy-tale writers are Zacharias **Topelius** and Tove **Jansson**, both of whom wrote in Swedish. Finnish-speaking writers, such as Anni **Swan**, initially drew their influences from German and Nordic Romanticism and Finnish folktales, especially from the anthology edited by Eero **Salmelainen**, *Suomen kansan satuja ja tarinoita* (*The Märchen and Legends of the Finnish People*, 1852–66). After World War II, inspired by British classics of **children's literature** (for example, Lewis **Carroll**, Sir James Matthew **Barrie**, and A. A. Milne), Finnish writers also modernized their contributions to fairy-tale literature.

Tales of Magic

Finnish archival data suggests that the great majority of tellers (approximately 80 percent) of magic tales were **men**. It is also highly plausible that the men who were taking down folktale repertoires rarely had access to the more intimate and domestic sphere, where **women** were more likely to have been telling folktales. Male narrators tended to favor the so-called heroic tales, in which the main character, a poor boy, overcomes a monster (a **devil**, mountain troll, or **dragon**) and frees a **princess** from its clutches. The poor boy also marries into royalty by successfully carrying out tasks set by the princess's **father**. Of these types, the most popular are The Three Stolen Princesses (ATU 301), The Dragon-Slayer (ATU 300), and The Twins or Blood-Brothers (ATU 303). The heroes are assisted either by **magic object**s (such as the water of life and **death** or a magic sword) or marvelous helpers (powerful dogs, servants able to grant all wishes, or spouses with magic powers or extraordinary skills). The hero may also be born with supernatural strength (ATU 650A, Strong John). The folktale hero also can behave like a **trickster**: the lazy boy wins the princess's hand by making her pregnant using magical words (ATU 675).

Women's repertoires contain numerous folktales describing the vicissitudes of a slighted or betrayed maiden or young wife. Aided by her fiancé, son, or husband, or sometimes by her deceased **mother**, the heroine invariably overcomes all obstacles and marries the **prince** or regains his affections. The Black and the White Bride (ATU 403) and The Three Golden Children (ATU 707) typify the folktale about the maltreated heroine. The kind girl may also be rewarded with a great fortune (ATU 480, **The Kind and the Unkind Girls**). Nevertheless, women narrators were clearly most enchanted by the story of **Cinderella** (ATU 510), of which some 200 texts have been archived. In the western Finnish variants, Cinderella gets her gown by helping an old man out of a ditch; he gives the maiden a wooden staff enabling her to get all she needs from a stone at the edge of the royal garden.

Another common folktale theme involves children being rescued from an ogre's clutches. In Finnish folktales, the most popular ogre-figure is the devil; less common is the wicked **witch**. In tales of The Children and the Ogre (ATU 327), three **brothers** or a boy and his sister put an end to the monster and seize his treasure.

Western and Eastern Traditions

Western European magic tales that most often came to Finland via Sweden had spread throughout the entire country all the way to the eastern frontier. The northern Russian influence could be felt in Karelia and in the traditions of the people from eastern Finland in Savo, both areas found along the country's eastern border. Certain folktales—for example, "Cinderella"— have been set down according to the narrative styles of both eastern and western Finland.

So far, folktale researchers have made only some preliminary observations regarding the differences between eastern and western magic tales. Western narrators have presented definite and constant plots that are easily recognized as fixed **tale type**s. The plot progresses logically towards the final resolution. Karelian narrators, however, have constructed their folktales with less uniformity. For example, Karelian narrators would occasionally extend the basic narrative by adding more adventures. The most extensive recorded items constitute veritable folktale novels filling up to forty to sixty pages.

There are also differences in casting. The main character of an eastern folktale tends to come from the upper classes: a son or daughter of the tsar, a son of an aristocrat, or the son of a wealthy merchant. People of rank, however, rarely figure as main characters in western folktales. The most common protagonist is a poor boy or girl who undergoes a radical rise in society by the end of the narrative. While a female villain—the cruel ogress (*Syöjätär*) with magical powers—often appears in Karelian tales, she is unknown in western regions.

When it comes to the fantastical, Karelian folktales are far more colorful than their western counterparts. While western narrators showed a preference for rational fantasies (a ship for both land and water as a means of transport, a sword capable of vanquishing all enemies, or a bottomless moneybag as a source of wealth), Karelian narrators told tales of eggs containing princes turned into golden flies, princesses rising from tree stumps, and dragons riding horses. The presence of religion—icons, monasteries, and saints—is an integral part of Karelian folktales. The fantastical elements of western magic tales, however, are almost invariably profane.

Animal Tales and Realistic Tales/Novellas

Finnish animal tales take place in northern coniferous forests, country villages, and **peasant** farmhouses. The most common hero is a fox, a bear, or a **wolf**. Both farm animals—horses, rams, and **pig**s—and those found within the house—dogs, **cat**s, and mice—also appear in many **fable**s. The only animal that was alien to the habitat of Finnish folk narrators and their audiences was the lion. Nevertheless, it was a familiar figure from the **Bible** and the Finnish coat of arms.

Finnish folktale narrators, too, have used animal tales as a medium for speaking about human relations. It is easy to discern the life lessons encapsulated in these concise and concrete narratives. Above all, animal tales caution against stupidity—the fox's cunning is more useful than the brute strength of the bear or wolf. Many folktales are even cynical: sympathy, helpfulness, and naiveté often lead to defeat in the struggle for social existence.

Judging by the items recorded, the most widely told folktale was The Unjust Partner (ATU 9). Here the fox, the bear, and the wolf thresh grain, grind the seed, and cook porridge. Not only does the fox manage to walk off with all the grain and leave the chaff for the bear and the wolf, he also convinces them that the porridge made from the chaff is just as tasty as that made from grain. Another frequently told fable (ATU 70, More Cowardly Than the Hare) describes a hare who finds, to his great delight, animals even more cowardly than himself.

The earliest account of a Finnish animal tale can be found in a fifteenth-century legal manuscript, the so-called Codex Kalmar. One of its ornamental pictures depicts the ending of the folktale Fox and Crane Invite Each Other (ATU 60), in which the crane offers his guest the fox a meal of gruel from a tall churn. This vessel does not appear in the fable tradition of Finland's neighboring countries. The oldest animal tales told in Finnish were published in the 1700s, when fables were highly regarded as a means of educating the young.

The narrative world of the novella-genre is realistic, without supernatural actors, magic objects, or metamorphoses. Finnish folk narrators have told and retold their own versions of many familiar stories from Giovanni **Boccaccio**'s *Decameron* (1349–50), William **Shakespeare**'s plays, and the *Arabian Nights*. Narrators—and their audiences—were most enamored with tales about clever and verbally adept peasants able to outwit priests, aristocrats, and royals. The young pauper succeeds in silencing the princess with bawdy teasing and thus becomes the **king**'s son-in-law (ATU 853, The Hero Catches the Princess with Her Own Words). The peasant also may solve a **riddle** beyond the king's grasp (ATU 921, The King and the Farmer's Son). The folktale The Clever Farmgirl (ATU 875) pays tribute to the intelligence of women: time and time again, the heroine rescues her father or her betrothed or helps a group of generals whom the king has ordered to skin a stone.

Folktale Research

Finnish folktale **collecting** began in the 1810s. Among the first sources of inspiration were the writings of Johann Gottfried Herder. Further impetus was given by the Jacob and Wilhelm **Grimm**'s collection, *Kinder- und Hausmärchen* (*Children's and Household Tales,* 1812–15). Finnish folk-poetry enthusiasts also paid close attention to the collection and publication of Scandinavian **folklore**.

At the outset, researchers were most intrigued by folktales told in the east because the much-revered *Kalevala*-meter folk poetry had been found in Karelia. The first publication of folktales—Salmelainen's *The Märchen and Legends of the Finnish People*—is based almost entirely on the eastern folktale tradition. It was only later, in the 1880s and 1890s, that the first western folktales were written down.

Even at the early stages of collecting, researchers observed that Finnish folktales did not differ from the narrative traditions of neighboring countries. Scholars were sorely disappointed by this discovery. Unlike *Kalevala*-meter poems, folktales failed to provide materials for constructing a particular cultural identity. However, the knowledge that animal tales reminiscent of the fables of antiquity could be found in Finland—a poor and faraway country—provided some consolation. Yet folktales were clearly overshadowed by the *Kalevala* **epic**.

Significant developments in folktale research were initiated in the 1880s with Kaarle Krohn's investigation of the relationship of Finnish and other Nordic animal-tale traditions to other traditional European fables. The German translation of Krohn's dissertation, "Bär (Wolf) und Fuchs: Eine nordische Tiermärchenkette" ("The Bear [Wolf] and the Fox: A Nordic Animal-Tale Cycle"), was published in 1889. Krohn made a historic-geographic comparison of folktale texts from various countries. His disciple Antti **Aarne** developed the method and applied it in his studies of numerous international folktales also known in Finland. Martti Haavio also used what became known as the "Finnish method" in his studies of the tale types "What Should I Have Said (Done)?" (ATU 1696) and The Rooster and the Hen (ATU 2021). Haavio published his *Kettenmärchenstudien I-II* (*Studies of Chain Tales*) in 1929 and 1932.

With the arrival of the 1960s, the **historic-geographic method** began to lose its hold—even in Finnish folklore scholarship. Researchers started to approach the folktale with a new set of questions. In the 1970s, folktale narrators came into focus. It was still possible to interview Karelian folktale narrators. Finnish-language scholar Pertti Virtaranta not only collected a vast number of folktales but also recorded autobiographical information about his Russian-Karelian narrators. The result of his work was the anthology *Kultarengas korvaan* (*A Golden Earring for the Good Listener*, 1971). Drawing upon church records and oral history, Virtaranta published *Annastuuna aikanansa* (*Annastuuna during Her Time*, 1969), in which he created an ethnographic portrait of one of western Finland's finest folktale narrators, Anna-Christina Korkeemäki. In the 1970s, Juha Pentikäinen, a scholar of comparative religion, drew up an anthropological and biographical study of Marina Takalo, an émigré from Archangel Karelia. Takalo was also skilled in the oral narration of folktales. In *Oral Repertoire and World View* (1978), Pentikäinen investigated her repertoire. The research dedicated to narrators showed that nineteenth-century folktale narration for adults took place largely among the lower classes, rural and urban workers. In the 1900s, folktales were last told in logging camps in the wilderness where no other entertainment was available.

The 1980s saw a renewed interest in the old archival collections. Satu Apo's *The Narrative World of Finnish Fairy Tales* (1995) focused upon the central themes, structures, and meanings of western magic tales. She also examined the material from a sociohistorical perspective. The archived texts revealed a previously hushed-up aspect of the genre: folktale narrators may have colored their **performance**s with coarse renderings of sexual, scatological, and violent themes.

From 1972 to 2000, folklore archives researcher Pirkko-Liisa Rausmaa edited a six-volume anthology entitled *Suomalaiset kansansadut* (*Finnish Folktales*). The series contains samples of all of the known folktale types from Finland.

Literary Fairy Tales

It was not until the mid-1800s that the **literary fairy tale** gained ground in Finland. Writers such as Zacharias Topelius drew inspiration from Nordic Romanticism with its mountain trolls, water sprites, and images of Ultima Thule. Following the lead of the Grimms and

Hans Christian **Andersen**, writers cultivated a mode of expression that combined clarity, concreteness, and colloquial speech. Salmelainen's folktale collection enabled writers to seek influences from homegrown **oral tradition**s.

Anni Swan, a woman writing in Finnish, became a master of the Romantic literary fairy tale. A dark psychological undercurrent runs through her stories: instead of being threatened by a dangerous supernatural force, many of Swan's heroines discover that they are incapable of loving their betrotheds. Swan's fairy tales have been translated into many languages, including German and Japanese. The works of Aili Somersalo also entered the canon of Finnish children's literature. Her fairy-tale **novel** *Mestaritontun seikkailut* (*The Adventures of the Master Elf*, 1919) has been dramatized and adapted for both stage and radio productions.

The process of modernizing Finnish fairy-tale literature began in the 1950s. Writers were primarily influenced by children's literature from the Anglo-Saxon tradition. As early as 1906, Anni Swan translated Lewis Carroll's *Alice's Adventures in Wonderland*. In modern fairy tales, imprisoned princesses have been replaced by small-town girls who encounter marvelous characters and objects brought to life, as in the fairy-tale novels by Marjatta Kurenniemi. Author Hannu Mäkelä has created an antihero, a ghost named Herra Huu (Mr. Hoo), who is at first so timid that he even fears children.

Making use of both folklore and the literature of **feminism**, Kaarina Helakisa renewed the traditional fairy-tale **fantasy** in her children's fiction. While Helakisa's princess grows wings for herself, another heroine, Queen Thrushbreast, using her wit and creativity, overcomes Prince Milkbeard. The latter fairy tale was included in Helakisa's collection of short stories *Annan seitsemän elämää* (*The Seven Lives of Anna*, 1987). Helakisa's fiction has been translated into Swedish, Estonian, and German.

Male writers have generally favored fables, the other major folktale genre. Jukka Parkkinen has populated his series of fairy-tale novels with ravens and other wild creatures that end up coming face-to-face with life in postmodern Finland (see **Postmodernism**). Mauri Kunnas has fabricated a zany canine world. Exuberantly illustrated with dogs taking the leading roles, Kunnas's stories retell the *Kalevala* and Finnish history. Some of Kunnas's tales are also set amidst the world of Santa Claus and his elves. Humor—relying on **intertextuality** and **parody**—is an integral part of the fables told by Parkkinen and Kunnas. Kunnas's books have been translated into more than twenty languages, including English, French, and Japanese. *See also* Estonian Tales; Russian Tales; Scandinavian Tales.

Further Readings: Apo, Satu. "Die finnische Märchentradition." *Märchen und Märchenforschung in Europa: Ein Handbuch.* Edited by Diether Röth and Walter Kahn. Frankfurt a.M.: Haag & Herchen, 1993. 80–87; ———. *The Narrative World of Finnish Fairy Tales: Structure, Allegory, and Evaluation in Southwest Finnish Folktales.* Helsinki: Academia Scientiarum Fennica, 1995; Henderson, Helena, ed. *The Maiden Who Rose from the Sea and Other Finnish Folktales.* Enfield Lock: Hisarlik Press, 1992; Huhtala, Liisi, Karl Grünn, Ismo Loivamaa, and Maria Laukka, eds. *Pieni suuri maailma: suomalaisen lasten- ja nuortenkirjallisuuden historia.* Helsinki: Tammi, 2003; Lehtonen, Maija and Marita Rajalin, eds. *Barnboken i Finland förr och nu.* Stockholm: Rabén & Sjögren, 1984; Rausmaa, Pirkko-Liisa, and Ingrid Schellbach-Kopra, eds. *Finnische Volksmärchen.* München: Diederichs, 1993.

Satu Apo

Fisherman and His Wife

"Von dem Fischer un syner Fru"—"The Fisherman and His Wife"—was one of two tales in a Low German dialect (*Plattdeutsch)* that the artist Philipp Otto Runge sent the publisher of *Des Knaben Wunderhorn* (*The Boy's Magic Horn*) in 1806. The other tale was "Von dem Machandelboom," or "The Juniper Tree," published by the German Romantic author Achim von Arnim in his *Zeitschrift für Einsiedler* (*Journal for Hermits*) in 1808. In 1809, Arnim also sent the original copies to Jacob and Wilhelm **Grimm,** who included them in the first edition of the **Kinder- und Hausmärchen** (*Children's and Household Tales*) in 1812. Some believe that the poetic simplicity of Runge's versions deeply influenced the Grimms' treatment of all their tales.

In Runge's "Fisherman and His Wife," the husband and his wife live in a *Piesspott* (chamber pot) near the sea. One day, the husband catches a huge flounder, which pleads with him to let him go because he is an enchanted **prince**. After he releases the fish, however, his wife sends him back to the water to make a **wish** for a cottage to live in. He calls the fish with the following chanted quatrain, which he repeats each time he makes a wish:

Manikin, manikin, that is me:
Flounder, flounder in the sea
My wife whose name is Ilsebill
Has sent me here against my will.

The flounder grants her request, but she is only briefly satisfied with the cottage, and then proceeds to demand a stone castle, then to be **king**, emperor, pope, and finally "like God." Their life becomes grander and grander, and more and more luxurious; each time the husband returns to make a new request, however, the sea is darker and more ominous. When he returns for the last time, a huge storm has arisen, with thunder, lightning, and earthquakes. He makes his wife's last request to be "like God" in fear and trembling; but the fish has had enough: "Go home, she's sitting again in the chamber pot."

In their annotations to the tales, the Grimms mention other German versions that give different names and details, but follow the same cumulative structure and have similar endings. (In a version from Hesse, however, it is the husband Männchen Domine, sometimes called Hans Dudeldee, who wishes that he could become God "and my wife the Mother of God.") The Grimms also suggest that the beginning of the tale may go back to much older versions: to the story of "The Fisherman and the Genie" in the **Arabian Nights**, to a Welsh **saga** about Taliesin, and to a Finnish tale, though all develop differently. They claim that the tale depends on an ancient **motif**, the woman who urges her husband to climb higher and higher—like Eve, the legendary Etruscan Tanaquil, and Lady Macbeth—though actually Runge's fisherman's wife wants the honors for herself.

Critics have often noted that this story, unlike most of the Grimms' tales, does not end in a rise in fortune or in a **marriage**, but rather returns the protagonists to their starting point. The wife's "foolish wishes," like the wishes of the husband in Charles **Perrault**'s tale of the same name ("Les souhaits ridicules," 1697), ultimately do not change their situation at all. Achim von Arnim in fact objected that the story was really not for children because it did not have a utopian happy ending. Others have pointed out that the wife's bullying and desire for power mirrors many of the Grimms' misogynist portrayals of older **women**. There has also been a lot of disagreement about polite ways to translate *Piesspott*. Perhaps the most anodyne interpretation of the tale is William Bennett's in his *Book of Virtues* (1993). He claims that the story's moral is "enough is enough," as if it were simply a critique of excess and unnecessary luxury.

Aleksandr **Pushkin**'s poem "The Tale of the Fisherman and the Fish" (1835), sometimes called "The Golden Fish," follows the Grimms' cumulative pattern, with a few Russian substitutions. Many twentieth-century writers took up the tale, refashioned it, or used it as a leitmotif in their own work. In *To the Lighthouse* (1927), Virginia **Woolf**'s central character Mrs. Ramsay reads the story to her son James. The darkening storm in the tale underlines the unwelcome possibility of bad weather in the novel; the wife's accelerating demands are also echoed in Mr. Ramsay's own ambitions and Mrs. Ramsay's hopes for her eight children, as well as in their complex relationship. In his long novel *Der Butt* (*The Flounder*, 1977), the German Nobel-prize winner Gunter **Grass** invents a **legend** about the flounder's meddling in the war between the sexes from the Neolithic period onward. Grass mixes contemporary debates about **gender** relations with the husband's long-winded storytelling and several idiosyncratic versions of the tale. Maura Stanton plays on the fisherman's wishes in her poem "The Fisherman's Wife" (1975), narrated by a **mermaid** caught as his "third" and also "last" wish. Ingrid Wendt, in her 1993 poem also called "The Fisherman's Wife," gives the wife a new, more thoughtful voice. Several **film**s have been based on the tale, all called *The Fisherman and His Wife*, including a short film narrated by Jodie Foster in the fairy-tale series *Rabbit Ears* (1989); a Canadian short film written and directed by Jochen A. Schliesser (1998); and a full-length movie set in contemporary Japan and Germany, directed by Doris Dörrie (2005).

Further Readings: Neumann, Siegfried. "The Brothers Grimm as Collectors and Editors of German Folktales." *The Reception of Grimms' Fairy Tales: Responses, Reactions, Revisions.* Edited by Donald Haase. Detroit: Wayne State University Press, 1993. 24–40; Rölleke, Heinz. "Von dem Fischer un syner Fru: Die älteste schriftliche Überlieferung." *Fabula* 14 (1973): 112–23; Tatar, Maria. "The Fisherman and his Wife." *The Annotated Brothers Grimm.* New York: Norton, 2004. 86–99.

Elizabeth Wanning Harries

Folk

The word "folk" has more layers of meaning than its dictionary definition as the common or ordinary people. In the history of **folklore** research, the German poet and philosopher Johann Gottfried Herder gave the word *Volk* (folk) currency in the late eighteenth century when he referred to creative expressions from the **oral tradition** and coined terms such as *Volkslied* (folk song) and *Volkspoesie* (folk literature). In England, "folklore" was first used by William Thoms in 1846 to signify the lore of the people.

The term "folk" has a history of meanings that variously identify not only the characteristics of the people designated by the term but also the nature of their cultural expressions and the mode of transmitting them. In the Romantic terminology of the early nineteenth century, "folk" represented the rural and pastoral people and conjured up images of countryside and people with a childlike simplicity living in harmony with nature. Early folklorists considered folk to be "natural" poets, not dictated by preconceived literary structures. For this reason, the folk song in particular represented for Herder the very soul of the people. However, for Herder, "folk" was initially a universal category. Eventually, the early nineteenth-century Romantic-nationalist usage of the term lent a sense of cultural cohesion among a set of linguistically and geographically identifiable people. Folklore therefore gained the status of being the cultural core of any group. Over the course of the nineteenth century and in the context of nationalist **politics**, the folk and their lore gained political validity and became major symbols of the emerging modern states based on mass politics.

This folkloristic and nationalist evolution of the term "folk" continued into the twentieth century with different political affiliations. Its extreme was hit in the connections that the fascist state in Germany created among the folk, their lore, and the state's own cultural politics. In the first half of the twentieth century, the term "folk" had also gained political importance in the context of communist movements and socialist states, where folklore was understood as the expression of the economically deprived and exploited sectors of the feudal society. The Marxist discourse preferred the term "people" as a sociopolitical category, and its relationship with "folklore" has had many different aspects. The definitions of folklore offered by Vladimir **Propp** helped direct the growth of folkloristics in the latter half of the twentieth century. On the other hand, the socialist states made folklore a part of the state's cultural propaganda. In the first half of the twentieth century, folklore played an important role in the independence movements of the colonized people in Asia, Africa, and other continents. In this context, folklore became the symbol of "native" culture as distinct from the culture represented by the foreign colonizers' transplanted lore.

The political overtones of the term "folk" point to the political potential implicit in folklore as a subject of research, study, or preservation. Almost every political ideology in every part of the world has tapped into this potential. From this arises the question: Does folklore actually express the politics of the people? And if it does, then what is the politics of folk? The contemporary field of folkloristics realizes that there is no single answer because individual oral texts of folklore have emerged in different historical times and **context**s. Folklore has no one political view but in fact reflects innumerable shades of political consciousness.

In the second half of the twentieth century, the term "folk" coexisted with comparable terms such as "people" and "masses." The folk song revival movements of the 1960s reflected this difference, and "folk" became the symbol of an ethnic, non-capitalist, and non-urban way of life. While the term's Romantic association with the rural and pastoral still dominates in popular perception, in the discipline of folklore, the definition of the term has been evolving along with the times and the changes in the lives of the people. The word signifies the nonruling sections of society—be they rural, urban, individual (performer), group, or even a virtual community. Folklorist Alan **Dundes** has gone so far as to define "folk" as "*any group of people whatsoever* who share at least one common factor" (Dundes, 6), a definition that does not rely on national or ethnic affiliation and recognizes the different communities to which individuals may belong. Dispelling the notion of the "folk" as an undifferentiated category of people, folklorists also acknowledge the existence of folk narrators, folk painters, folk performers, folk dancers, and others. These are practitioners of arts that have been passed down orally, traditionally, and without copyrights, in certain cases requiring training since early childhood and being exclusively performed by one community. The common folk, often socially unprivileged, have kept alive the knowledge of highly structured and lengthy texts such as oral **epic**s. In the twenty-first century, this area of expressive culture—the oral lore of different folk—has come under the purview of intellectual property rights, and its logistics are currently being discussed internationally. *See also* Colonialism; Folktale; Nationalism.

Further Readings: Dundes, Alan. "Who Are the Folk?" *Interpreting Folklore*. Bloomington: Indiana University Press, 1980. 1–19; Propp, Vlaidmir. *Theory and History of Folklore*. Edited by Anatoly Liberman. Translated by Ariadna Y. Martin and Richard P. Martin. Minneapolis: University of Minnesota Press, 1984.

Sadhana Naithani

Folklore

"Folklore" refers to the academic study of folklore, also known as folkloristics, as well as to certain types of expressive culture. To date, there has been no consensus as to how "folklore" should be defined, thus making it difficult to articulate precisely what is and what is not folklore. The word itself was coined by William Thoms in his 1846 letter to the *Atheneum* wherein he suggested the "good Saxon compound, Folklore,—*the Lore of the People*" as an alternative to the then-common English terms "popular antiquities" and "popular literature." While the term "folklore," most likely Thoms's rough translation of the German *Volkskunde*, entered the English vernacular and spread around the world in various translated forms, the term itself does little to clarify what, specifically, constitutes the "lore of the people." Thoms himself attempted a definition by way of enumeration and included "the manners, customs, observances, superstitions, **ballads**, **proverbs**, etc., of the olden times." In his 1965 *Study of Folklore,* the American folklorist Alan **Dundes** followed suit with a much longer enumeration, beginning with "major forms, such as **myth** and **folktale**," winding through "curses, oaths, insults, retorts" as well as "folk costume, folk dance, folk drama … food recipes, quilt and embroidery designs, house, barn, and fence types," to finally bend back around to a different type of major forms, specifically holidays and festivals such as Christmas, Halloween, and birthdays. Others have tried to capture the underlying commonalities among almost-infinite possibilities. Dan Ben-Amos offered "artistic communication in small groups" in his article in the 1971 *Journal of American Folklore*; Jan Brunvand suggested "the unrecorded traditions of a people; it includes both the form and content of these traditions and their style or technique of communication from person to person" in his 1968 *The Study of American Folklore*; and the American Folklife Preservation Act of 1976 contended that the cultural forms encompassed by the related term "folklife" are "mainly learned orally, by imitation, or in performance, and are generally maintained without benefit of formal instruction or institutional direction."

In many cases, definitions slide into criteria for assessing whether any given cultural expression might be considered folklore. Dundes proposed "multiple existence and variation" as one set of such criteria, meaning that any given folklore text or practice exists in many different versions. For example, consider the many competing sets of rules that children have for even the simplest game, such as hide-and-seek; each set of rules constitutes a variation of the game, and there is no institutionalized set of rules to which all children must adhere (unlike in professional sports, such as football). The test of "multiple existence and variation" has been particularly relevant for the study of **fairy tale**s and folktales, especially for scholars interested in differentiating between **literary fairy tale**s and tales that circulate in **oral tradition** (though some do both, of course).

Folklore as an academic discipline most frequently traces its roots back to the late eighteenth century and Johann Gottfried Herder's Romantic ideas about *das Volk*—the **folk**. Herder believed that a people's language and expressive culture—particularly their oral culture—embodied and sustained their unique characteristics as a group, their national character as it were, and these ideas were fundamental to the growth of German Romantic **nationalism**. For Herder, the *Volksgeist*, or "spirit of the people," was best captured in the oral traditions of the peasant classes, whose cultural traditions were not mediated by education, industrialization, or the general trends toward modernity. Deeply inspired by Herder's ideas, Jacob and Wilhelm **Grimm** sought to create an authentically and uniquely German collection of folktales and fairy tales in ***Kinder- und Hausmärchen*** (*Children's and*

Household Tales, 1812–15). Although several of the storytellers from whom the Brothers Grimm recorded most of the tales in their *Kinder- und Hausmärchen* have since been revealed as middle class and, in certain cases, French speakers, and although the tales themselves have been scrutinized for the Grimms' editorial and moralizing changes, their collection was for a time presented and received as a reflection of an authentic and unique German culture. It set the stage for other national collections, such as those edited by Peter Christen **Asbjørnsen** and Jørgen **Moe** in Norway (1841–48) and Aleksandr **Afanas'ev** in Russia (1855–63). While the emergence of the discipline of folklore is most closely associated with nineteenth-century German Romantic nationalism, folklore has been enlisted in nationalizing projects around the world and in different historical periods.

In the United States, folklore developed as an interdisciplinary field of study situated between the disciplines of anthropology and literary studies. In her intellectual history of American folklore studies, *American Folklore Scholarship: A Dialogue of Dissent* (1988), Rosemary Lévy-Zumwalt identified the tension between anthropological and literary approaches as embedded in the very foundation of American folklore scholarship. In fact, in 1888, when the American Folklore Society was first established, Francis James Child, a literary folklorist with a particular interest in ballads, became the society's first president, and William Wells Newell, an anthropological folklorist interested in Native American mythology, was named the first executive secretary. This dual disciplinary heritage continues to shape folklore as an academic discipline even in the contemporary period and is important for contextualizing the wide range of methodological approaches and interpretive strategies that folklorists utilize in the study of fairy tales and folktales.

Folklorists have both helped to develop and drawn upon virtually all of the methodologies and modes of interpretation presented in this encyclopedia. In the nineteenth century, folklorists were interested in trying to locate and reconstruct the original version of individual tales (what they called the "**urform**"), and the Finnish folklorist Julius Krohn developed a method for comparing different versions of **tale type**s in the pursuit of such goals. His son, Kaarle Krohn, further refined his father's method of comparison, which became known first as the Finnish method and then as the **historic-geographic method**. As the name implies, the historic-geographic method was an attempt to map, literally, different **motif**s from a given tale type across space and time in the belief that such mapping might reveal patterns of dissemination that could be traced back to any given tale's urform. In a similar vein, and in keeping with the spirit of trait classification borrowed from the biological sciences of the time, Carl von Sydow argued that motifs could adapt to specific cultural-geographic areas through natural selection and isolation, thus producing **oicotype**s (tales unique to any given geographic or cultural area). Historic-geographic studies can help identify oicotypes and other patterns of tale movement and transformation, but they are excessively labor-intensive and, as a result, very few have been completed. Though most folklorists have long abandoned the search for urforms, many still turn to historic-geographic studies as tools to aid in interpretation. For instance, folklorists have drawn upon the mapping of specific motifs to investigate the cultural factors that influence the use of different motifs among different groups who share the same tale type.

These early **comparative method**s relied heavily upon published collections of folktales and fairy tales as well as upon folklore **archives** where multiple versions of tale types were housed, often together with data about the person from whom the tale was collected. Nineteenth-century folklorists in Scandinavia, Europe, and the British Isles were avid **collectors**.

Their work to find, document, and archive the oral traditions they believed to be disappearing with the transition to industrial society and the advent of modernity helped to establish the earliest national folklore archives and contributed to the first published collections. These rich collections also proved invaluable to the Finnish folklorist Antti **Aarne**, a student of both Julius Krohn and Kaarle Krohn. Aarne sought to further develop the historic-geographic method and is best known today for *The Types of the Folktale*, the most widely used tale-type classification system. First published in 1910, Aarne's classification system was translated into English and expanded in 1928 by the American folklorist Stith **Thompson**; the second edition of what is commonly referred to as the "tale-type index" (or the "AT index") was published in 1961. This edition also gave rise to the "AT" numbering system, the predominant classificatory system for all folktales and fairy tales (as well as for other sorts of tales like **fable**s, **animal tale**s, numskull jokes, etc.). In 2004, the German folklorist Hans-Jörg Uther further expanded the AT index; folklorists now refer to tale types by their ATU numbers. In addition to the ATU index, many folklorists around the world have compiled tale-type indexes for stories told in their own regions, correlating the tale types to the ATU index where relevant. There are so many individual tale-type indexes that American folklorist and library specialist David Azzolina published an annotated bibliography (*Tale Type and Motif-Indexes: An Annotated Bibliography*, 1987) of all of the tale-type indexes. In addition to translating and expanding Aarne's *The Types of the Folktale*, Stith Thompson also compiled the massive, six-volume *Motif-Index of Folk-Literature* (1932–36; revised and enlarged edition, 1955–58). As the title implies, the *Motif-Index* contains cross-referenced information for every motif contained in the tale-type index as well as for many other motifs found in other types of folk literature such as myth, **legend**, and **joke**s.

The indexing of motifs and tale types necessitated that folklorists break down tales into their constituent parts, This was also undertaken (though for different ends) by the Russian structuralist Vladimir **Propp** in his *Morfologiya skazki* (*Morphology of the Folktale*, 1928). Influenced by Russian formalism in literary studies, Propp analyzed Afanas'ev's collection of Russian folktales to identify their underlying narrative structure. By separating the tales into their smallest components, which he called "**function**s," Propp argued that a typology of the folktale consists of thirty-one functions occurring in a regular sequence. Folklorists have debated whether Propp's typology is unique to **Russian tales** or whether it applies more broadly to Indo-European tales or, perhaps, to all tales; and some have attempted structural analyses of non-European tale types for comparative purposes.

In keeping with folklore's hybrid literary and anthropological heritage, Propp's textual **structuralism** was paralleled by Claude Lévi-Strauss' structural anthropology in the 1970s. Lévi-Strauss's structural anthropology was based on the idea that all cultures are structured around binary oppositions that must be resolved through various cultural practices, including ritual, mythology, and folktales. Where Propp's textual structuralism and Lévi-Strauss' structural anthropology are concerned, folklorists have largely applied the paradigms to various texts, such as fairy tales and folktales. However, in an innovative extension of Propp's typology, Dundes used the idea of discrete **motifeme**s (adapting the terms "morphemes" and "narratemes" that literary formalists used to refer to narrative units) to suggest a way of interpreting symbols in a much broader cultural context than he believed possible from the interpretation of a single tale. In his essay "Symbolic Equivalence of Allomotifs in The Rabbit-Herd" (AT 570) (1982), Dundes argued that the allomotifs (anything that could fill a motifemic slot in a given text's structure) in different versions of a tale (or any folklore text) are symbolically equivalent. Thus, if the riddle **princess** trades her nightgown (or her ring, **hair**, or virginity) for the answer to the **riddle** she cannot solve (ATU 851), then her nightgown, ring, hair, and virginity are all symbolically equivalent. Dundes pushes this argument further, suggesting that symbolic equivalents also exist across texts in any given culture, and he uses two versions of the same joke (one involving a large nose in the punch-line, the other a penis) to suggest that symbolic equivalents established in the joke might then be applied to a symbolic reading of "The Rabbit-Herd" so long as the symbolic equiva-lents come from the same cultural group.

Dundes's interest in the relationship between structuralism and the symbolic interpretation of tales reflects his larger interest in the psychoanalytic interpretation of folklore (see **Psy-chological Approaches**). Beginning with Sigmund **Freud** and Carl Gustav **Jung**, psycho-analysts have frequently turned to fairy tales and folktales in support of their theories on subjects as diverse as psychosexual development, repression, projection, and universal **archetype**s. Psychologists (both theoretical and clinical), anthropologists, and literary schol-ars have continued to investigate the relationship between psychoanalytic theories and folk-lore. However, while many psychoanalysts and other scholars have drawn upon folktales and fairy tales, few folklorists besides Dundes have really worked deeply with psychoana-lytic theories in the interpretation of tales.

In the 1960s, folklore was influenced by Dell Hymes's "ethnography of speaking" models of communication as well as other trends toward performativity that placed an emphasis on the communicative **context** in which tales (and other cultural expressions) are performed, communicated, recounted, and used for a range of social as well as individual purposes. As a result, folklorists often turned their attention to the tellers of tales (for example, the story-teller's sex, race, age, class, sexual preference, marital status, etc.), the social situations that give rise to specific tellings of tales, and the ways in which the complexly layered identities of the tellers as constituted in any given telling affect everything from the choice of tale told to the details of the tale itself. In many cases, folklorists used such models of **storytell-ing** as performative communication to suggest that storytellers might use tales as coded dis-course to comment on various social and political situations in a culturally acceptable or socially safe manner.

Folklorists' interest in understanding the contexts, texts, and subtexts of specific storytell-ing sessions highlights the longstanding relationship between folklore studies and functional anthropology. In his 1954 article in the *Journal of American Folklore*, American folklorist and anthropologist William Bascom suggested that folklore has four functions in addition to that of entertainment: to validate culture, to educate, to maintain social control, and to pro-vide a socially acceptable means of escape. Bascom's "four functions of folklore" have been extremely influential in the interpretation of many different types of folklore, including fairy tales and folktales.

In the contemporary period, when studying fairy tales and folktales, folklorists seem to draw on virtually any combination of these methodologies and interpretive strategies, as well as others informed by historical methods, Marxist perspectives, literary criticism, and anthropological theory. Critical cultural studies (in particular, the Frankfurt School, the Bir-mingham School, and American cultural studies), **feminism** and feminist theory, and critical race studies (see **Race and Ethnicity**) have also offered theoretical groundings for folklor-ists, especially those interested in the ongoing publication and production of fairy tales and folktales in postmodern, revised, commercial, commodified, material, musical, and cinematic forms. The rich diversity of tales is matched only by the range of theoretical, methodological, and interpretive strategies folklorists bring to their study. *See also* Anthropological Approaches; Ethnographic Approaches.

Further Readings: Azzolina, David S. *Tale Type and Motif-Indexes: An Annotated Bibliography.* New York: Garland Publishing, 1987; Bascom, William. "The Four Functions of Folklore." *Journal of American Folklore* 67 (1954): 333–49; Bauman, Richard, ed. *Folklore, Cultural Performances, and Popular Entertainments: A Communications-Centered Handbook.* New York: Oxford University Press, 1992; Ben-Amos, Dan. "Toward a Definition of Folklore in Context." *Journal of American Folklore* 84 (1971): 3–15; Bendix, Regina. *In Search of Authenticity: The Formation of Folklore Studies.* Madison: University of Wisconsin Press, 1997; Brunvand, Jan Harold. *The Study of American Folklore: An Introduction.* New York: Norton, 1968; Dundes, Alan. *The Study of Folklore.* Englewood Cliffs: Prentice Hall, 1965; Zumwalt, Rosemary Lévy. *American Folklore Scholarship: A Dialogue of Dissent.* Bloomington: Indiana University Press, 1988.

Kimberly J. Lau

Folktale

The folktale is a form of traditional, fictional, prose narrative that is said to circulate orally. In both colloquial use and within folkloristics, the term "folktale" is often used interchangeably with "**fairy tale**," "**märchen**," and "**wonder tale**," their histories being interrelated and their meanings and applications somewhat overlapping. The confusion of terms reveals the instability of heuristic generic categories, especially those ideologically laden and historically insupportable genres that are rooted in the insistence that literary and oral tales, including the hybrid transcribed oral tale, can be held distinct (the prefix "folk-" attached to the latter two forms to clarify and maintain this distinction). Accordingly, the folktale was conceived of as oral, whereas—although fairy-tale themes exist in folktales—the "true" fairy tale was a literary genre, and the ambiguous märchen and wonder tale were deployed to reinforce the requirement of orality in the more general folktale.

The term "fairy tale" arose in the context of the seventeenth- and eighteenth-century aristocratic French **salon** writers and their elaborate, layered, discursive conversational creations that were eventually put into print. A handful of these were to eventually become the so-called fairy-tale canon. These tales derived some of their thematic cores from material long in popular circulation, both oral and written. For example, one of the most highly elaborate plots of this group, the animal spouse, can be traced historically to Lucius **Apuleius**'s first-century work, *The Golden Ass.* Shared thematic concerns coupled with the tangled history of transmission of this material thus make clear distinctions between oral and written forms very difficult. Folklorists attempted to adopt the German term "märchen" to refer to those oral tales that contained fairy-tale themes. Not only was this effort unsuccessful, but because "märchen" in fact could refer to both oral and literary tales, its use was somewhat ironic. It was also redundant: the term "folktale" is, in fact, a direct translation and an attempt to Anglicize the German term *Volksmärchen*, in much the same way as "folklore" itself was an appropriation of the concept of *Volkskunde* into the English language. Finally, the wonder tale has been suggested as an appropriate oral equivalent to the **literary fairy tale**, segregating out those stories that deal specifically with aspects of the marvelous or wonder, transformation and metamorphoses. All of these terms confusingly coexist, but all also originate out of the same convergence of ideas and events that was to constitute the origins of modernity in Europe.

The generic categorization of folk narratives is inextricable from the disciplinary history of the field of folkloristics. From the early nineteenth century, not only were these particularly European narrative traditions the object of the field's study, but these genres were also central to the field's own constitution. Early folklorists such as Wilhelm and Jacob **Grimm** set the generic parameters, contrasting the **legend**, **myth**, and folktale as discrete narrative forms. Their proclamations that folktales were the remnants of a greater mythological system, and that legends were more prosaic and "this-worldly," in contrast to the more poetic, fantastic folktales, would undergird the work of successive generations of folklorists. William Bascom's 1965 article "The Forms of Folklore: Prose Narrative," reiterated this three-part division into the genres of myth, legend, and folktale, with the categorical distinctions being based on issues of belief, historicity, and whether or not the stories take place in real space and time (see **Time and Place**). Bascom's article, standard in all introductory **folklore** classes to this day, takes the issue of orality as *given*, as it does the distinctions between genres, although they are derived from the highly localized and ideologically motivated material of the Grimms.

For the Grimms, the folktale was one of the most important genres to their simultaneous and interconnected nationalistic and folkloristic enterprises. The tales in the Grimms' various edited collections of ***Kinder- und Hausmärchen*** (*Children's and Household Tales*, 1812–15), were motivated by Johann Gottfried Herder's Romanticism, which sought out a pure, uncontaminated German spirit in the poetry of the illiterate peasantry. Folktales were, thus, said to be the unmediated, uncorrupted voice of the **folk,** written down by the Grimms with "minimal editorial changes" and in adherence to the sentiments of the folk. These written folktale collections of the nineteenth century served to standardize and canonize the highly varied mix-and-match nature of tales told orally, serving also to reduce the variety, but not the volume, of tales in written form. More importantly, the editorial processes involved in the collections reveal an ideological bent, which, as both Susan Stewart and Elizabeth Wanning Harries have pointed out, required the construction of the folk prior to the construction and collection of the category of folklore. The people unconsciously maintained tradition; their words and very being were seen as offering a palliative to the ills of encroaching modernity. But according to this logic, the same forces of modernity were seen as threatening the traditional ways of the folk. Folklorists and folklore collectors were to be rescue workers, collecting and archiving the expressions of the folk before they disappeared. The ideological work required to sustain a fiction of an uncontaminated, pure folk, was accomplished through a system of re-presentations and editorial adjustments. If the folk were identified as **peasant**, illiterate, rural, old, and increasingly female (the antithesis of modern, urban, literate, and male), then informants needed to come from this group. Depictions of informants were thus forced into this generic peasant mold, obfuscating the middle-class, literate backgrounds of many of them. Dorothea Viehmann, the Grimms' ideal **informant**, whose tales the Grimms praised for their "truth" and consistency, and whose likeness evolved over successive editions and translations from an individual to a generic "Gammer Grethel," an "honest, good humored farmer's wife," was, in fact, a middle-class, educated, French-speaking Huguenot, whose repertoire included many of the widely disseminated literary fairy tales from eighteenth-century France (Warner, 189, 190–93).

The consequences for folklore scholarship were deep, profound, and long lasting. The manifestation of the ideological category of the folk was an equally ideological "authentic" folklore, which was, by definition, resolutely oral. Folktales in particular, masquerading as the inscription of oral tales, were increasingly shaped by the conventions of "orality"—intentional "distressing" the written tales to ensure their apparent "**authenticity**." The signs of this authenticity were simplified language and sentence structure; the insertion of colloquial and dialogic speech; short, unembellished plots; opening and closing conventions; and folksy and "traditional" themes. These markers of orality were then stylistically replicated in written collections, cited as evidence of authenticity, contrasted with highly embellished literary tales, in particular fairy tales, and, in a circular and self-perpetuating move, used not only in subsequent field collecting to differentiate true folktales from those that had been "contaminated," but also served as the definitional requirements of the (oral) folktale. (One could, in this way, "recognize" the vestiges of an oral tale by the ironically literary convention "Once upon a time.") The articulated rupture between the literary and the oral—impossible to maintain, and unsupportable by historical records—resulted in a hardening of the genres of folklore. Thus, the cleavage between the fairy tale and the folktale, seen as the opposition between literary and oral forms, is an artificial aftereffect of the ideological trappings of the Romantic nationalists, a cleavage that is fundamental to the disciplinary niche of folkloristics.

Yet another legacy of the Grimms with regard to the folktale is organizational and methodological. As comparativists, the Grimms filled their editorial notes with references to similar tales found in other traditions. As nationalists, the Grimms constructed an imagined national community out of the remnants of traditional oral forms. As cosmopolitanists, however, they were interested not only in capturing a broad international audience for their *Kinder- und Hausmärchen*, but in positioning their work as the model on which other budding nations could base their own folklore collections. The similarities in folktales across Europe, are, thus, self replicating, as were the methods of analysis.

The most prevalent of these methods, until the mid-twentieth century, was the **historic-geographic method**. This was grounded in the Enlightenment notion that folklore could be systematized and rationalized, organized and indexed, and it gave rise to the first index of **tale type**s by Antti **Aarne** (*Verzeichnis der Märchentypen*, 1910), followed by the much expanded *The Types of the Folktale* (1961) by Aarne and Stith **Thompson**. While Stith Thompson, who favored a **motif**-based approach to tale analysis, acknowledged that tales were passed down both "in writing or by word of mouth" (Thompson, 4), his approach was eclipsed by Aarne's typological approach, the legacy of the Grimms, with its oral imperative, which was to become the dominant paradigm in folkloristics. Aarne's index organizes tales according to thematic types. Each tale type, defined as a plot composed of individual plot elements, or motifs, was seen to display a great deal of integrity across time and space, and each tale referenced under the specific tale type was considered to be cognate. Comparative analysis would thus occur within a type, with the specific intention of reconstructing the original or ur-**variant** of the type (see **Urform**). In 2004, the Aarne-Thompson index was modified by Hans-Jörg Uther in *The Types of International Folktales*. This work revised and expanded its predecessor, particularly in its attention to international variants, but did not abandon the traditional premises of the Aarne-Thompson classification system.

The Aarne-Thompson-Uther tale-type index organizes folktales in a numeric system from 1–2399. Aarne-Thompson-Uther (ATU) numbers 300–749, the so-called Tales of Magic, are also those tales often identified as fairy tales, although, again, separating the literary fairy tale from those tales found in oral circulation is impossible. Furthermore, tales involving the supernatural or the marvelous typically spill not only beyond this boundary of ATU 749, but also beyond the generic requirements of the folktale/fairy tale. Each tale type includes a synopsis, or basic plotline, but although the index is putatively an analytic tool for folktales (that is, oral tales), these synopses in many cases are outlines of the versions of the tales found in the semiliterary *Kinder- und Hausmärchen,* or in Charles **Perrault**'s *Histoires ou contes du temps passé (Stories or Tales of Times Past,* 1697). Additionally, aside from the obvious problems of differential collecting methods and intensity from country to country, and across time, the historical-geographic method serves to further complicate the insistently separate realms of the literary fairy tale and the (oral) folktale. The tale-type index itself lists literary renditions of tales along with versions from informants in collections and **archives**, many of which themselves are retellings from literary sources. A cluster of versions could thus represent not the age or point of origin of a particular tale but rather the success of its published version.

With the move away from the historic-geographic method and positivistic, diachronic approaches in general in the latter half of the twentieth century, folklore is said to have undergone a paradigmatic shift, with **structuralism** at the heart of this change. Developing the basis of a literary theory of narrative that was unmoored from the search for origins, structuralism instead focused on providing abstract models or structures in narrative. Structural approaches were not dependent on an articulated rift between oral and literary forms. However, as Stephen Benson has pointed out, not only did Vladimir **Propp**'s *Morfologiya skazki (Morphology of the Folktale,* 1928), the seminal text in narratology, develop out of earlier historical models, but Propp's data itself derives from material infused with the ideological premises and methodological imperatives of the previous century. Propp selected 100 tales from Aleksandr **Afanas'ev**'s *Russkie narodnye skazki (Russian Folktales,* 1855–63), itself a highly edited collection of tales compiled on the model of the Grimms' *Kinder- und Hausmärchen,* and the tales included are not only fit into a literary mold, their uncorrupted oral origins are again impossible to maintain. The model may thus be flawed by sleight-of-hand in which the data has been intentionally distressed to masquerade as being clearly derived from oral sources, but which is, in fact, the result of self-conscious literary techniques, the apparent naturalness of structural paradigms being based on contrivances.

The folktale and the fairy tale continue to coexist in an uneasy balance. In theory, the folktale has become the purview of folklorists and anthropologists, maintaining the conceit that privileges the spoken, immediate world, whereas the fairy tale is more the domain of literary theorists. Even between these articulated camps, however, there is slippage, with folklorists notoriously claiming to be working with oral sources, and yet defaulting to analyses that derive from a relatively narrow band of canonical material. This slippage speaks to the basic instability and inherent productiveness of all narrative forms. *See also* Collecting, Collectors; Editing, Editors; Frame Narrative; Jack Tales; Nonsense Tale; Oral Tradition; Religious Tale; Tall Tale; Unfinished Tale.

Further Readings: Bascom, William. "The Forms of Folklore: Prose Narratives." *Journal of American Folklore* 78 (1965): 3–20; Benson, Stephen. *Cycles of Influence: Fiction, Folktale, Theory.* Detroit: Wayne State University Press, 2003; Harries, Elizabeth Wanning. *Twice upon a Time: Women Writers and the History of the Fairy Tale.* Princeton, NJ: Princeton University Press, 2003; Stewart, Susan. "Notes on Distressed Genres." *Journal of American Folklore* 104 (1991): 5–31; Thompson, Stith. *The Folktale.* 1946. Berkeley: University of California Press, 1977; Warner, Marina. *From the Beast to the Blonde: On Fairy Tales and Their Tellers.* New York: Farrar, Straus and Giroux, 1994.

JoAnn Conrad

Food

Food and meals are abundant in folktales. Food is an indispensable part of the **initiation** rite, since it is closely connected to **death** and resurrection. Death as a rite of passage is often represented by the novice being eaten by a monster (Jonah and the whale is an example), which during the rite itself is staged by the novice entering a cave or a hut (for instance, the famous Russian hut on chicken legs, inhabited by **Baba Yaga**). Resurrection is represented by the novice being invited to participate in a meal in the otherworld, the realm of death. By accepting food from the otherworld, the hero gains passage into it (Holy Communion is a remnant of this archaic rite, as well as the Jewish Sabbath meal). The Russian folktale hero Ivan replies to Baba Yaga's threats to eat him: "What is the good of eating a tired traveler? Let me first have some food and drink and a bath." He pronounces himself ready to accept witch food and go through a symbolic purification.

Thus food in folktale is connected to the three elements in the chain of death-fertility-life. Some folktales feature a woman getting pregnant by eating a special kind of food (for example, "Rapunzel"), which comes from insufficient understanding of **sexuality** and procreation (see **Birth; Infertility**). Further, food is connected to sacrifice. The mythical sacrificial death means that the sacrifice ensures fertility and affluence, often also eternal life. In many **myth**s, food is featured in marginal situations, around the passage from one existence into another, yet unfamiliar. Festive meals appear around certain holidays like the New Year; food is important in connection with weddings and funerals. The sacrifice itself includes food. The sacrifice that was the killing of an animal or a human, or giving them away to be eaten by a monster, was later changed to something more symbolic, to an act such as breaking the bread. To eat the meat and drink the blood of a sacrificial animal means receiving new forces. Therefore, every meal is by definition a ritual act. According to Mircea Eliade, there are no profane actions in the archaic world (Eliade, 27). There are many parallels between an altar and a table, an altar curtain and a tablecloth, a sacrificial knife and a butcher's knife, and naturally between a priest and a cook. In Christian tradition, the prohibition of cooking meals on the altar came as late as the seventh century.

In archaic thought, both food and sacrifice emphasize a person's belonging to a totem, a **family**, or a tribe (consider idioms such as "my own flesh" when speaking about children). Many myths include details such as gods' food, for instance, nectar and ambrosia in Greek mythology. The word "ambrosia" means "the immortal," since it was the source of the gods' eternal youth and immortality. From this belief, we have all of the habits around everyday food and festive food, ordinary food and ritual food, which are also reflected in the way food appears in folktales and fairy tales.

The most important underlying role of food in folktale is to accentuate the contrast between nature and culture. The origin of food is in nature, but it is used within culture, and it is the result of the transition from nature to culture. Thus food neutralizes this basic contrast. In Claude Lévi-Strauss's anthropological study *The Raw and the Cooked*, a typology of cultures is built upon the attitude to food, based on oppositions: human flesh-animal flesh, raw-cooked, and animal food-vegetarian food. Many **etiologic tale**s, especially stories about the origins of fire, which makes cooked food possible (see James G. Frazer's *Myths of the Origins of Fire*, 1930), are based on these oppositions and regulate rules and prohibitions around food. These oppositions are also related to all of the other dichotomies within a given culture, such as own-alien, male-female, home-away, sacred-profane, and so on. In folktales, the notions of own and alien are often connected with food habits. One's own food is perceived as natural and genuine. When the folktale hero departs from home, food can serve as a link back home. Since food emphasizes affinity, "own" food, food from home is especially desired. It is also important that the **mother** packs the food and supplies it with her blessing. This security of home represented by food is found in many different types of tales. Since home cooking provides security, it can also function as a trial. The hero is supposed to share his food with strangers, who become friends and helpers, while the false hero keeps his food for himself and therefore receives no assistance. As with the acceptance of alien food, a shared meal becomes a sign of union. Food becomes a token of belonging together in a quest or struggle, or belonging to a particular group, whether good or evil.

On the other hand, all "alien" food is unnatural, unclean, and basically "non-food." Food can be a means of enchantment, whereupon eating or drinking something transforms the hero. For instance, by drinking water from a goat's hoofprint, a boy is transformed into a goat. Food can captivate, corrupt, and even destroy. We see remnants of these archaic notions in the prohibition against certain foods in Islam and Judaism and in Christian dietary rules around Lent. Not just human flesh, but all "alien" food, "non-food" was prohibited in archaic thought. Food in the realm of death (and this includes all foreign countries, real or imaginary) was prohibited for ordinary persons; if you eat, it you will never come back. In the fairy tale, this develops into depictions of various forms of enchanted food with which the hero is tempted in the otherworld, or food that the antagonist uses to disarm or kill the hero (for example, the apple in "**Snow White**").

The prohibition against eating human flesh was one of the first steps in the civilization of humanity. **Cannibalism** was universally accepted in the archaic world, but later started to be viewed as alien. Cannibalism is often connected with the Fall, that is the loss of immortality (see Mircea Eliade's *The Myth of the Eternal Return*, 1955). In myths, the so-called cultural hero ends cannibalism by defeating the cannibal enemy. This is reflected in folktales such as "**Tom Thumb**" or "**Hansel and Gretel**." The condemnation of cannibalism expels it to the otherworld, where it is associated with evil (such as a **dragon**, an **ogre**, or a **witch**). Many folktales describe a witch who eats human beings, often children. "Hansel and Gretel" is of these stories. But it is far from a unique example, as this phenomenon is represented in all cultures, for instance, in the Russian tale "The Magical Swan-Geese." In "The Wolf and the Seven Kids" or "**Little Red Riding Hood**," an animal (originally a **werewolf**, which is also a figure from the otherworld) replaced the witch. In most cases, the children emerge alive, that is, the act symbolizes death and resurrection. Being eaten is often presented as positive and necessary; the witch is not evil, but is on the contrary a wise guide. Behind it we most probably find initiation rites, which included sexual intercourse.

The meaning of cannibalism is that, by consuming your enemy, you inherit his powers. In "The Story of the Grandmother," an early version of "Little Red Riding Hood," the girl eats her grandmother's flesh and drinks her **blood**, which has an ambiguous purpose; she is accused of cannibalism, but a deeper implication is that she acquires the wisdom of the progenitrix, which helps her to trick the wolf/werewolf. Later this notion of eating up the elder changed into ritual meals. To eat a symbolical figure signified receiving magical power.

Cannibalism could also be a sign of extreme love: when a man (more rarely a woman) ate his beloved, he owned her completely. Here again there is a parallel between food and intercourse, oral and sexual gratification. In some myths, parents devour their children out of great love. The opposite, a child's love for the parent, expressed through a food metaphor, is found in the folktale (which, incidentally, lies behind the initial scene of William **Shakespeare**'s *King Lear*), in which a **father** asks his three daughters how much they love him and denounces the one who claims that she loves him as much as meat loves salt. By contrast, in a version of "**Cinderella**" known as "The Juniper Tree," the evil stepmother kills her stepson and serves his flesh to the unaware father. The sister is warned and rejects the meal, thus avoiding the sin of cannibalism.

Like most elements in folktales and fairy tales, rituals around food have their origins in the most basic aspects of human behavior, connected with archaic beliefs of life, death, and rebirth, and hence also sexuality, fertility, and procreation. According to most scholars, meals in myths and folktales are circumlocutions of sexual intercourse. There is a direct connection between food and sexuality, and between certain food restrictions and certain **marriage** restrictions, such as **incest**. To eat your totemic animal or to marry it (which equalled incest) was viewed as an equally serious crime.

A number of etiological tales describe the origins of various types of food. A common plot is the supreme deity punishing his children (or spouse) by cutting them into pieces and throwing them down from heaven to earth (or hiding them underground); from their mutilated bodies, good and nutritious plants grow. An important mythical figure is the progenitrix, the incarnation of Mother Earth, the origin of everything. In most myths, she teaches humans to sow and to bake bread. In folktale, this figure is transformed into the figure of benevolent mother or godmother.

One of the most common folktale **motif**s connected with food is "to eat or to be eaten." In "Three Little Pigs," the characters are threatened by the wolf, who eventually himself ends up in a cauldron of boiling water. In some versions, the pigs eat the wolf. Little Red Riding Hood is going to her grandmother's house with a supply of food but is eaten herself. Hansel and Gretel are sent away from home because of famine. They long for food, especially sweets, but immediately are under the threat of being eaten. To eat and be eaten are thus two interchangeable notions, which is seen in the Christian tradition's most important sacrament, the Holy Communion. Jesus prescribed that His "body" be eaten, symbolizing a union of those who eat and Him who is being eaten, which together signifies a victory over death and a promise of resurrection. There is a very old archaic rite at the source of this, reflected in the quick changes of eating or being eaten in folktales.

Thus, like all folktale elements, food is highly ambivalent: it can be good or evil, and it can easily change its meaning. Alien food can be dangerous, like the apple in "Snow White." Forbidden food is, like so many other elements in the folktale, a circumlocution of sexuality. Sacred food is a magical agent in folktales: bread, milk, honey, apple, beans, and so forth. Many folktales reflect the mythical cornucopia, described as a magical mill (such as Sampo of **Finnish tales**), tablecloth, or bag. (It is considered a symbol of food and abundance.) In these tales, such as "The Sweet Porridge" and many other tales, the hero is rewarded for his good deeds with a **magic object** that provides food.

Summing up, we can say that food in folktales and fairy tales can fulfill a variety of purposes. Food can be a magical agent allowing the hero to enter the magical world. It can be the central symbol of security by its connection to home. Further, it can be a symbol of community, of belonging to a certain group. By accepting or rejecting food, the hero is associated with a group of people.

When folktales were incorporated into children's and family reading, their motifs often changed to suit social and pedagogical restrictions, so that the original meaning became still more obscure. The most offending elements, such as cannibalism and overt sexuality, were purified; yet basically all folktale motifs connected with food are present in modern **literary fairy tale**s, sometimes in transformed and disguised variants. For instance, the clever animated folktale pancake can take a different shape in the Australian classic *The Magic Pudding* (1918) by Norman Lindsay. In Lewis **Carroll**'s *Alice's Adventures in Wonderland* (1865), the most obvious role of food is that it governs the protagonist's **transformation**s and finally functions as a passkey. Food is also featured in other situations: at the Mad Tea Party, in the nonsensical tale about the treacle well, in the many misunderstandings during Alice's conversations with Mock Turtle (in itself a food-inspired character), and so on. The young child's desire for food is reflected in Pooh's passion for honey in *Winnie-the Pooh* (1926) by A. A. Milne. Characteristically, the monstrous Heffalump represents the child's secret fear of hunger. Enid Blyton's popular series of Famous Five books feature many scrumptious picnics.

Food as a symbol of bonding as well as a means of enchantment appears in C. S. **Lewis**'s *The Lion, the Witch and the Wardrobe* (1950), in which Lucy has gorgeous tea with the faun, the four children are treated to a meal by the Beavers, while Edmund is spellbound by Turkish Delight offered by the wicked White Witch. The magic never-ending food reappears in Elvish bread in J. R. R. **Tolkien**'s *The Lord of the Rings* (1954–55), where food also signifies the security of home, the sharing of hardships and deprivations. The famous picture book by Maurice **Sendak**, *Where the Wild Things Are* (1963), is built around the dilemma of eating or being eaten, and it also shows the parent's power in giving or denying the child food. In *Charlotte's Web* (1952), by E. B. White, the plot revolves around saving the little pig Wilbur from becoming ham. All of Astrid **Lindgren**'s fairy tales abound in food with highly ritual meaning.

Schlaraffenland, or the Land of Cockayne, reappears in many contemporary fairy tales, most conspicuously in *Charlie and the Chocolate Factory* (1964) by Roald **Dahl**. The voluminous meals in J. K. **Rowling**'s Harry Potter books (1997–2007) continue the tradition. The relatives' treatment of Harry is contrasted to his cousin Dudley's gluttony, and the Weasley family's hospitality is mainly presented through hearty meals, which Mrs. Weasley cooks with the help of her magic wand. Of the most recent narratives, the role of the "alien" food is emphasized in the animated film *Spirited Away* (2001) by **Miyazaki** Hayao, in which the gluttonous parents are turned into pigs while the shared meal gains the protagonist a passkey into the magical realm. There is also a frightening scene in which the enigmatic Black Figure eats up everything and everybody in his way. Since food is one of the main premises of human existence, it is no wonder that it takes such a prominent place in traditional as well as modern stories.

Further Readings: Allen, Brigid, ed. *Food: An Oxford Anthology*. Oxford: Oxford University Press, 1994; Bergstrand, Ulla, and Maria Nikolajeva. *Läckergommarnas kungarike: Om matens roll i barnlitteraturen*. Stockholm: Centre for the Study of Childhood Culture, 1999; Eliade, Mircea. *The Myth of the Eternal Return*. London: Routledge & Kegan Paul, 1955; Forster, Robert, and Orest Ranom, eds. *Food and Drink in History*. Baltimore: Johns Hopkins University Press, 1979; Frazer, James G. *Myths of the Origins of Fire*. London: Macmillan, 1930; Kiell, Norman. *Food and Drink in Literature: A Selectively Annotated Bibliography*. Lanham, MD: Scarecrow, 1995; Lévi-Strauss, Claude. *The Raw and the Cooked: Introduction to a Science of Mythology*. Translated by John and Doreen Weightman. 1969. Chicago: University of Chicago Press, 1983; Marin, Louis. *Food for Thought*. Translated by Mette Hjort. Baltimore: Johns Hopkins University Press, 1989; Nikolajeva, Maria. *From Mythic to Linear: Time in Children's Literature*. Lanham, MD: Scarecrow, 2000.

Maria Nikolajeva

Fool. *See* Simpleton

Forbidden Room

The forbidden chamber is **Motif** C611 in Stith **Thompson**'s *Motif-Index of Folk-Literature*. It refers to the narrative situation in which not only is a person "allowed to enter all chambers of house except one," but that room is also specifically prohibited. This interdiction, inevitably broken, carries with it not only an implied **punishment** but also the promise to reveal secret wonders and knowledge. The motif is part of a cluster of prohibitions enumerated in the *Motif-Index*, including: The one forbidden place (C610); Forbidden door (C611.1); Forbidden road (C614); and, more thematically distant but perhaps both structurally and symbolically related, Forbidden tree (C621) and Tree of knowledge forbidden (C621.1).

The forbidden room has most famously been associated with **tale type** ATU 312— Maiden-Killer or **Bluebeard**—made famous by Charles **Perrault**, but the motif is worked into the plotlines of many other tale types: Rescue by the Sister (ATU 311); The Magic Flight (ATU 313); Goldener (ATU 314); The Wild Man (ATU 502); Our Lady's Child (ATU 710); and, more tenuously, The Maiden in a Tower (ATU 310) and The Robber Bridegroom (ATU 955).

Interpretations of the motif have inevitably derived from Perrault's canonical version and the subsequent versions that have used Perrault's Bluebeard as a model. Perrault's own interpretive and moralizing focus was on the dangers of female curiosity and disobedience (linking the heroine of Bluebeard to her predecessors Eve and Pandora), and this has been the dominant analytic strain ever since. A quick look at the related motifs, however, reveals that they are not gender-specific, and that females as well as males are forbidden entry into various chambers. Disentangling **gender** from this prohibition, some have commented on the lure of the forbidden, not only as a plot motivator (Vladimir **Propp**) but as an entry into the unknown as a (dangerous) site of wonder and a source of knowledge. The reiteration of the dominant analytic focus on innate (negative) female curiosity and disobedience remains tellingly silent not only on the husband's being a serial murderer but also on his (necessarily) arbitrary imposition of authority, thereby reinscribing the privilege of schematic masculinity in the metanarratives, while also revealing the dangers of commentary based on a single literary source.

Stephen Benson sees the forbidden room as the literal and metaphorical core of the cluster of stories linked to Bluebeard, and he reads in the motific heart of prohibition the related themes of curiosity, cunning, and confinement. The latter two themes, discounted in earlier interpretations, derive from a horizontal, motific reading of texts. The forbidden room here represents the symbolic locus of knowledge that threatens to destabilize authority. This knowledge is often sexual in nature, and always transgressive. Subsequent feminist authors, notably Angela **Carter** (*The Bloody Chamber*, 1979) and Jane Campion (*The Piano*, 1993), have used the forbidden room tale as central to their revisionist texts, making more complex the nature both of gender politics and of sexual self-determination. For both, the chamber serves as the locus of curiosity, fear, and containment, as well as the means of self-exploration and ultimate escape. ***See also*** Bluebeard Films; Feminism; Feminist Tales; Transgression.

Further Readings: Benson, Stephen. *Cycles of Influence: Fiction, Folktale, Theory.* Detroit: Wayne State University Press, 2003. 198–246; Tatar, Maria. *Secrets beyond the Door: The Story of Bluebeard and His Wives.* Princeton, NJ: Princeton University Press, 2004.

JoAnn Conrad

Formula Tale. *See* Chain Tale; Nonsense Tale; Unfinished Tale

Fouqué, Friedrich de la Motte (1777–1843)

A German author of French Huguenot descent, Friedrich de la Motte Fouqué popularized—and banalized—the **motif**s and ideas of German Romanticism. The Germanic past, heroic **legend**s of the north, and French romances of chivalry equally stirred Fouqué's imagination and merged into a fantastic fairy-tale world in his dramas, novels, and fairy tales. While he is well known for his dramatic Nibelungen trilogy, *Der Held des Nordens* (*The Hero of the North,* 1808–10), today his most influential work is the fairy tale "**Undine**" (1811). Blending the mystic animation of nature with a psychological focus, "Undine" is a Romantic-era tale about a water spirit who enters the human world and eventually returns to the sea. An influence on Hans Christian **Andersen**'s "Den lille havfrue" ("The Little **Mermaid**," 1837), Fouqué's fairy tale is a **myth** about psychological creation. As an in-between creature, Undine has an ambiguous nature that resists being univocally defined or categorized. Nonetheless, Fouqué's tale does not reach the psychological depths of Andersen's text in its analysis of human development.

In addition to its widespread literary influence, "Undine" also inspired **opera**s by E. T. A. **Hoffmann** (1816) and Albert Lortzing (1845). Whereas the style of "Undine" is delicately fresh and straightforward, Fouqué's late Romantic fairy tales and novels are characterized by a more mannered narrative mode, which caused the reading public to turn against his works. In his later years, Fouqué increasingly opposed the spirit of the modern age in conservative attacks that harked back to the feudal world. *See also* German Tales; Mermaid.

Further Readings: Lillyman, William J. "Fouqué's 'Undine.'" *Studies in Romanticism* 10 (1971): 94–104; Max, Frank Rainer. *Der "Wald der Welt": Das Werk Fouqués.* Bonn: Bouvier, 1980.

Helene Høyrup

Fractured Fairy Tales (1959–1964)

Fractured Fairy Tales was an integral segment of the animated **television** series commonly known as *The Rocky and Bullwinkle Show* (1959–64). Created by Jay Ward and coproduced with Bill Scott, the series—titled *Rocky and his Friends* when it originally aired on the ABC television network (1959–61) and renamed *The Bullwinkle Show* for its prime-time run on NBC (1961–64)—featured revisionist storytelling of genres such as the adventure serial, nursery rhyme, **fable**, and **fairy tale**. The show enjoyed, and continues to enjoy, popular and critical praise for several reasons: its use of clean, limited **animation**; a linguistic humor marked by puns and other wordplay; its self-reflexive, even self-referential, references; and a parodic impulse that often crosses over into social satire. Exemplary of these characteristics, *Fractured Fairy Tales* not only spoofs individual tales but collectively skewers contemporary American culture, the entertainment industry, and fairy-tale conventions.

Many of the ninety-one *Fractured Fairy Tales* cartoons, all approximately five minutes long, are based on stories by the Brothers **Grimm**, Hans Christian **Andersen**, and Charles **Perrault**. Several different parodies of well-known tales were produced, including multiple versions of "**Sleeping Beauty**," "**Beauty and the Beast**," and "The **Frog King**." In *Sleeping Beauty,* the handsome **prince** does not awaken the **princess** but instead builds a profitable theme park, Sleeping Beautyland, around her; the cartoon points out her objectification within the tale while suggesting Walt **Disney**'s further commodification. The first *Beauty and the Beast*, in which an ugly beast misrepresents himself as a handsome prince to convince beauties to kiss him, uses the tale's generic conventions to address gender and romantic expectations. A focus on economic exchange is present in *The Frog Prince*, where the overwhelming demand for frogs leads one oppressed, much-transformed frog to file a complaint with the local **witch**es' union. Given such examples, it is unsurprising that *Fractured Fairy Tales* was criticized by network executives as being too sophisticated for its audience and was even feared as subversive.

Fractured Fairy Tales was replaced, under pressure from sponsors and the network, with what was presumed to be the more audience-friendly ***Aesop and Sons***. These pun-laced retellings of fables lack *Tales'* satiric bite, and only thirty-nine fables were made before audience response resulted in the return of *Tales*. In part because it appeals to children and adult audience members alike, *Fractured Fairy Tales* remains one of *The Rocky and Bullwinkle Show*'s most popular features. In turn, its success complicates commonly held assumptions about animation and fairy tales as inherently kiddie fare and instead demonstrates both the medium's and the genre's potential to convey cultural critique. *See also* Parody.

Further Reading: Scott, Keith. *The Moose that Roared: The Story of Jay Ward, Bill Scott, a Flying Squirrel, and a Talking Moose.* New York: St. Martin's Press, 2000.

D. K. Peterson

Frame Narrative

The term "frame narrative" applies to a story within which one or more other stories are told. As the name suggests, this narrative has a dual identity: it is a story by itself, but like a frame that surrounds a picture, this tale surrounds another story or stories.

The basic function of a frame story is to provide a narrative context for other tales and to bind these together within that context. A frame story allows a wide variety of tales to be grouped together, which in the **oral tradition** would be important for a storyteller's individual repertoire. The frame narrative also enables the introduction of newer tales, whether into a storyteller's personal repertoire or into an anonymous text that is passed on and may, in its historical and geographical distribution, be represented by manuscripts or published versions whose contents vary considerably. It can be safely assumed that the tales contained within frame narratives were not all included at once. Therefore, a detailed analysis of the tales within a particular frame may also reveal different historical periods and may help us understand the growth of that particular **storytelling** tradition.

The most famous frame narrative is perhaps that of the ***Arabian Nights***, the story of the King Shahryar and the young woman **Sheherazade**, who told the tales of the "Thousand and One Nights" to the king to save her life. The oldest known frame narrative, however, is the Indian classic ***Panchtantra***, the story of the eighty-year-old teacher who related tales to educate three dumb **prince**s and turn them into wise men. The oldest known cycle of tales, **Jātaka**s—which are stories of Buddha's former lives—also utilized a frame narrative. In this case, the frame tale serves to explain the Jātakas and to bind together the large number of stories ideationally. There is, however, still another level of framing at work here, for each individual story within the overarching frame has its own frame narrative. Each story's frame is an account of the context in which the Buddha related that specific episode from one of his former lives. It ends with the Buddha making a connection between the event he has recounted and the present reality of his listeners.

Some frame narratives are developed far beyond their functional role. When this occurs, they narrate an independent and altogether new tale that lends a particular meaning to the tales contained within it. The frame narrative of the *Arabian Nights* is so strong that its characters have fully developed personalities, and the story of their own lives progresses and changes as the storytelling continues night after night. The development and transformation of characters in the frame story do not come about by virtue of any single tale, but by the acts of narrating and listening. When Sheherazade's stories finally end, her own situation has changed, and she has become the teacher instead of the helpless girl she was supposed to be. Yet the suspense that the teller of the frame tale had introduced in the beginning—that Sheherzade is to be murdered in the morning—hangs in the balance until the very end. The frame story of the *Arabian Nights* sizzles with this suspense and keeps the listener or reader in a state of anxious curiosity. The overall suspense and mystery add to the nature of the tales told by Sheherazade, and the recipient seeks a connecting thread that is not visible until Sheherazade herself offers her loyal listener an interpretation in the space of a few sentences: namely, the stories are about different aspects of being human and demonstrate that all people deserve compassion. The king, too, has changed in the course of the narration, which further hints at the power of narratives, narration, and narrators.

Frame tales have no specific genre or length. They may be short or long, they may be narrated at one go in the beginning, or they may begin before every other narrative in the cycle and be concluded after all others have been told. The prevalence and importance of frame tales in the ancient cycles of storytelling may also be related to the medium of narration, that is, the human voice and oral texts, which, unlike the book, do not have any tangible existence.

A frame tale might also be the oral storyteller's way of including and highlighting his or her own identity in the text, or it might serve to hide the storyteller's presence. The fictional narrator reflects on the real narrator, but the latter is not solely responsible for the stories. The frame tale transports readers and listeners into its context, and they must hear, see, and judge the tale in that scope. For any kind of a sociopolitical commentary, a frame tale is an effective tool to create distance between the contents of the tale and the real narrator.

Mimicking oral storytelling situations, frame narratives have been employed by many authors of **literary fairy tale**s, including Giovan Francsco **Straparola**, Giambattista **Basile**, and Ludwig **Tieck**. Framing devices were also a favorite technique of the *conteuses*, the prolific female authors of fairy tales in late seventeenth-century France. Countless writers since have used frame narratives as a context for presenting their tales. Storytelling scenarios have also been used as frames in fairy-tale **films** such as *The Princess Bride* (1987) and *Ever After* (1998). In *Ever After*, the central action of the story is framed by the visit of the Brothers **Grimm** to the queen of France, who tells them the "true" story of **Cinderella**. Framing the central action of the film in this way not only challenges the classic version of the tales but also demands that the story of Cinderella be experienced as a story told by and about **women**. Accordingly, the film serves as a good example of the important interplay between frame narratives and the tales told within them. *See also* Metafiction.

Further Readings: Belcher, Stephen. "Framed Tales in the Oral Tradition: An Exploration." *Fabula* 35 (1994): 1–19; Haring, Lee. "Framing in Oral Narrative." *Marvels & Tales* 18 (2004): 229–45; Harries, Elizabeth Wanning. "New Frames for Old Tales." *Twice upon a Time: Women Writers and the History of the Fairy Tale.* Princeton, NJ: Princeton University Press, 2001. 104–34; Naithani, Sadhana: "The Teacher and the Taught: Structures and Meaning in the *Arabian Nights* and the *Panchatantra*." *Marvels & Tales* 18 (2004): 272–85.

Sadhana Naithani

Franz, Marie-Louise von (1915–1998)

A leading disciple of Carl Gustav **Jung**, German-born Swiss analytical psychologist Marie-Louise von Franz was an expert on the significance of fairy tales. After 1961, she carried on her mentor's work at the Zurich-based C. G. Jung Institute while developing some of his insights into her own theories.

Once her worldwide study of fairy tales had revealed extensive similarities between narratives from different cultures, von Franz interpreted numerous tales in accordance with Jungian archetypal psychology. Based on her vast knowledge of **myth**s, fairy tales, and dreams, her interpretations centered on the narratives' recurrent archetypal images. By amplifying the narrative themes and characters, she emphasized the tales' symbolic meanings.

Von Franz published several influential books on fairy tales. *Interpretation of Fairy Tales* (1970) illustrates, with several European tales, the steps involved in a Jungian approach to interpreting narratives. *Problems of the Feminine in Fairytales* (1972) investigates images of **women** in various tales from a Jungian perspective. *Individuation in Fairytales* (1977) exemplifies the psychological process of finding one's self, in the Jungian sense, with tales featuring the bird **motif**. *The Psychological Meaning of Redemption Motifs in Fairytales* (1980) distinguishes the Christian concept of redemption from the psychological significance of such motifs in fairy tales. *Archetypal Patterns in Fairy Tales* (1997) examines cross-cultural motifs in European, African, and **Chinese tales**. Von Franz's work represents the most extensive Jungian investigation into fairy tales to date. *See also* Archetype; Psychological Approaches.

Further Reading: Robertson, Robin. "A Guide to the Writings of Marie-Louise von Franz." *Psychological Perspectives* 38 (Winter 1998–99): 61–85.

Harold Neemann

Freeman, Mary E. Wilkins (1852–1930)

New England "local-color" author Mary E. Wilkins Freeman was a prolific writer for children and adults. Beginning in children's periodicals such as *St. Nicholas* and *Wide Awake* and in various Harper & Brothers imprints, she gained popularity and acclaim in the United States and Great Britain. Once lauded as on par with Nathaniel **Hawthorne** and Mark **Twain**, she was obscure at the time of her death but was rediscovered by scholars who noted the strong feminist and protofeminist themes in her work.

She loved fairy tales, and many of her children's stories explore fairy-tale **motif**s. The influence of fairy tales is also evident in her work for adults, suggesting that Freeman is a predecessor to female writers of the late twentieth century who revised fairy tales in ways that gave female characters much stronger and more diverse roles. Among her best-known works invoking fairy tales are "A Church Mouse" (1891), which recalls "Rapunzel," and "Old Woman Magoun" (1905), which alludes especially to "**Little Red Riding Hood**." In "The Prism" (1901), she relates the story of a woman who sees **fairies** through a single teardrop prism but who learns to repress her fantasies upon her fiancé's demands. *See also* Feminism; Feminist Tales; North American Tales; Women.

Further Readings: Carter, James Bucky. "Princes, Beasts, or Royal Pains: Men and Masculinity in the Revisionist Fairy Tales of Mary E. Wilkins Freeman." *Marvels & Tales* 20 (2006): 30–46; Terryberry, Karl J. *Gender Instruction in the Tales for Children by Mary E. Wilkins Freeman.* Lewiston, NY: Edwin Mellen Press, 2002.

James Bucky Carter

Reese Witherspoon stars in the 1996 film *Freeway*. [Photofest]

Freeway and *Freeway II* (1996, 1999)

Directed by Matthew Bright, the films *Freeway* (1996) and *Freeway II* (1999) are dark, urban retellings of fairy tales, respectively "**Little Red Riding Hood**" and "**Hansel and Gretel.**" They have a violent, gritty, and highly sexualized B-movie feel. Fairy tales' threatening forests become a metaphor for the unpleasant underside of low-class American culture, in particular the justice system as experienced by the damaged and underprivileged children who are forced to navigate it. Bright's interests are both political and satirical, but he achieves most powerfully an exploration of the inherent sexuality and **violence** of fairy-tale forms: the young protagonists of the films embody a fascinating and edgy conflation of sexual awareness with the kind of naiveté engendered by ignorance and emotional starvation.

Freeway is a more successful film than its sequel, both because of the higher caliber of its actors and because its exploration of the Little Red Riding Hood narrative is more sustained and overt: the opening credits of the film establish a cartoon-sketch sexualization of Little Red Riding Hood, reducing the **wolf** to a bumbling shaggy dog. This is borne out by the film itself, in which the illiterate, street-wise Vanessa, complete with red-hooded jacket and frankly incredible basket, ultimately transcends her origins (a prostitute mother and molesting stepfather, both drug users) and the justice system to defeat the wolf, a freeway-stalking serial killer. Her background and sexualization render her experienced with devouring male sexuality, to an extent unavailable to the innocent child of Charles **Perrault**'s fairy tale; and from the moment she identifies him as a sexual pervert, he becomes a smaller and less-threatening figure. The child's gun-wielding confrontation of the monster inverts the tale's outcome, asserting both her own necessarily self-reliant power and her pragmatic familiarity with violence, and successfully marking him with the outward and visible signs of his own inner grotesqueness. She defeats him completely in the film's somewhat melodramatic denouement, where the devouring monster in Grandma's bed is dispatched without recourse to the forces of the law poised to intervene.

Bright to a large extent repeats himself in *Freeway II*, although the narrative is less thematically unified, invoking "Hansel and Gretel" only occasionally during its rampaging serial-killer jailbreak; it lacks the subtle play of innocence and cynicism which mark Vanessa in the earlier film. The lost children figures are over-drawn and over-sexualized, a bulimic girl with multiple convictions for solicitation and violent robbery, and a lesbian serial killer whose victims include her entire family: the film's attempts to set up their respective mental disorders as childlike vulnerability are less successful than in *Freeway*. Attention to the fairy tale is spasmodic at best, and only really sustained in the final sequences, where the wicked **witch** manifests as a transvestite, cannibal nun. Bright's preoccupation with adult figures who abuse children's trust is evident here. Like *Freeway*'s serial-killer child psychologist, the nun is a monstrous **mother**-figure offering sanctuary, understanding, and nurturing; but ultimately he/she conceals a devouring sexual perversion. Overall, while ultimately somewhat sensationalist, both films tend to remain true to the darker spirits of fairy tales, rather than to their overt structures and circumstances. *See also* Cross-Dressing; Film and Video; Sex, Sexuality.

Further Reading: Orenstein, Catherine. "*Freeway*: A Ride in the Hood." *Little Red Riding Hood Uncloaked: Sex, Morality and the Evolution of a Fairy Tale*. New York: Basic Books, 2002. 219–38.

Jessica Tiffin

French Canadian Tales

French-speaking Canada enjoys a rich history of oral folklore—specifically, **folktale**s, **legend**s, and songs—and these traditions flourished well into the beginning of the twentieth century, far longer than was the case in much of the neighboring United States or in European countries. This vitality can be explained first of all by the historical particularities of this population. After their defeat by the British in 1759, French Canadians were isolated from France and subjected to unfavorable economic, judicial, linguistic, and political policies. As a consequence, **oral tradition**s became an important means of preserving cultural identity for the French-speaking colonists. That these traditions were primarily oral is clear on several accounts. Well into the nineteenth century, access to print was difficult (even before British rule, France had forbidden the creation of a printing press in New France); formal schooling in French was scarce; and illiteracy rates were high. Socioeconomic and geographical factors no doubt also kept oral traditions alive. Until at least the late nineteenth century, economic activity in French-speaking Canada was dominated by farmers on one hand and trappers, traders, and lumberjacks (*trappeurs, coureurs de bois,* and *bûcherons*), on the other. Due to the often-remote locales inhabited by the former and vast expanses of territory covered by the latter, and due to the long winters endured by both groups, folktales, legends, and songs were a central part of life. In addition, trappers, traders, and lumberjacks are credited with spreading French **folklore** across much of North America, and well beyond the boundaries of the French-speaking areas of Canada and New England. Evidence of their influence was even found in stories told by Amerindians, who incorporated **motif**s and entire plots from French Canadian tales into their own. Although oral traditions became less prominent during the first half of the twentieth century in most regions of French Canada, the Acadians, French speakers in New Brunswick, Nova Scotia, and Prince Edward Island, with their own dialect and their own tragic history, kept oral traditions alive much longer. Their folklore is also noteworthy because, subsequent to the "Great Expulsion" by the British in 1755, it spread to other regions where Acadian refugees settled, principally Louisiana.

In French Canadian usage, the word "*conte*" (tale) designates several different genres that folklorists usually treat as independent: not only magic tales (or **wonder tale**s), **animal** tales, and **religious tale**s, but also supernatural, anecdotal, and historical legends. When nineteenth-century French Canadian writers with nationalistic sentiments became interested in contes, they turned to legends and not to folktales per se. Abbot Henri-Raymond Casgrain is credited with leading the way by publishing his *Légendes canadiennes* (1861). Other writers soon followed suit, among them Philippe Aubert de Gaspé with *Les anciens canadiens* (*Canadian Ancestors*, 1863), Joseph-Charles Taché with *Trois légendes de mon pays* (*Three Legends of My Country*, 1861) and *Forestiers et voyageurs* (*Lumberjacks and Travelers*, 1863), and, at the turn of the century, Honoré Beaugrand and Louis Fréchette. The legends recast by these writers and others are all set in French Canada and recount adventures of historical figures from momentous periods in Canadian history (historical and anecdotal legends) or characters such as the **devil**, demons, **witch**es, **werewolves**, and other fictitious beasts (supernatural legends). One of the best known of the first group, "The Legend of Cadieux," tells the heroic deeds of a trapper who single-handedly fought off an ambush by Amerindians and ultimately sacrificed himself to save his companions. Perhaps the most famous supernatural legend, "La Chasse-Galerie" ("The Flying Canoe"), concerns a pact with the devil made by a group of lumberjacks eager to find a supernatural means of travel so as to celebrate New Year's Eve with friends. Besides illustrating and mythologizing French Canadian culture, the literary versions of such legends also typically illustrate the profound allegiance to Catholicism that was long prevalent among this population.

Folktales, distinct from legends, did not find their way into print until the early twentieth century, when the ethnographer/folklorist Marius Barbeau began publishing the results of his **fieldwork** in the *Journal of American Folklore*. A noted specialist of Huron traditions, Barbeau became interested in French Canadian folktales only after recognizing how many of them had been assimilated into Amerindian folklore. Barbeau's work led to the founding of the **Archives** de Folklore at the Université Laval (Quebec City) by his student Luc Lacourcière, himself a noted folklorist responsible for much important fieldwork on popular songs and folklore among Acadians. In turn, Lacourcière trained an entire generation of folklorists who, besides teaching and pursuing fieldwork, began to publish collections at a time when French Canadians, and especially the Québécois, were experiencing renewed nationalistic sentiments in the wake of the *Révolution tranquille* (the economic, political, and cultural modernization of Quebec in the 1950s and 1960s). Among these collections are those by Carmen Roy, *Contes populaires gaspésiens* (*Gaspesian Popular Tales,* 1952); Jean-Claude Dupont, *Contes de bûcherons* (*Tales of Lumberjacks*, 1976); and Conrad Laforte, *Menteries drôles et merveilleuses* (*Magical and Funny **Tall Tales**, 1978). But by far the most extensive published collection of French Canadian folktales is Father Germain Lemieux's *Les vieux m'ont conté* (*The Old Folks Told Me*, 32 volumes, 1973–91), based on the repertoires of French-speaking storytellers in Ontario.

Although Lacourcière's **tale-type** index of North American folktales in French remains unpublished, his scholarship indicates that magic tales (ATU 300–749) are the most numerous, composing almost half of the entire corpus. Significantly, few of these correspond to fairy tales that are best known today. At the beginning of the twentieth century, Paul Sébillot speculated that French Canadian folktales may have preserved forms of oral narratives that had disappeared in France. But other scholars, such as Paul **Delarue**, noted that the French Canadian corpus is in fact not so monolithic due to the influence of Irish and Scottish traditions. Although francophone folkloric traditions in Canada are better studied than their Anglophone equivalents, it appears French-speaking Canadians have had more of a propensity for the folktale than their English-speaking compatriots, who have tended toward shorter forms such as **proverb**s and jokes. *See also* French Tales; Jest and Joke; Native American Tales; North American Tales; Storytelling.

Further Readings: Boivin, Aurélien. *Le conte fantastique québécois au XIXe siècle.* Montréal: Fides, 2004; Fowke, Edith. *Folktales of French Canada.* Toronto: NC Press, 1979; Lacourcière, Luc. *Le conte populaire français en Amérique du Nord.* Québec: Les Archives de Folklore, Université Laval, 1959.

Lewis C. Seifert

French Tales

Origins of the French Tale Tradition

The earliest indigenous form of literature in the geographical location that came to be known as France was the *chanson de geste* (song of heroic deeds), a form of **epic** poetry that celebrated the military prowess of Christian knights best represented by the *Chanson de Roland* (*Song of Roland*, c. 1090). As feudal society began to stabilize, the masculine world of *Roland* made way for romance and a marvelous element not directly tied to Christianity. Drawing from Celtic lore and Arthurian romance, writers such as **Marie de France** and Chrétien de Troyes celebrated courtly love, depicting gallant knights who carried out feats to please their lady, not their god.

Many of these stories were well known in the golden age of French fairy tales and provided models for classic plots. In her twelfth-century collection of *Lais,* for instance, Marie de France included "Yonec," a source for Marie-Catherine d'**Aulnoy**'s "L'oiseau bleu" ("The Blue Bird"). In the fourteenth century, the Arthurian romance *Perceforest* included the story of Troïlus and Zellandine, an early version of the tale of **Sleeping Beauty**. Anticipating Charles **Perrault**'s "Donkey Skin" ("Peau d'âne," 1694) with its incestuous **king**, verse and prose versions of the **legend** of Belle Hélène de Constantinople circulated in the fourteenth and fifteenth centuries. During this same period, Jean d'Arras composed his famous romance of the **fairy** Mélusine, relating the fairy origins of the Lusignan family line. Perhaps one of the earliest collections of French tales in which **peasant**s recount stories in a traditional setting is Noël du Fail's *Propos rustiques* (*Rustic Sayings*, 1547). Influenced by du Fail as well as by Giovanni **Boccaccio** and Giovan Francesco **Straparola**, Bonaventure des Périers composed his posthumous *Nouvelles récréations et joyeux devis* (*Novel Pastimes and Merry Tales*, 1557), in which appears a tale about a **king** who makes his daughter wear a donkey skin, whose plot also recalls that of "**Cinderella**." Although a tale tradition indeed existed in France during the **Middle Ages** and the Renaissance, it wasn't until the seventeenth century that fairies truly came into fashion.

Seventeenth and Eighteenth Centuries: The First Phase, 1690–1705

Salon Tales. The first evidence that adults in fashionable court circles spent part of their leisure time reciting to one another stories of supposedly popular origin dates from 1677. On August 6 of that year, the Marquise de Sévigné, writing to her daughter, described a tale-telling session at Versailles. Louis XIV himself was infatuated with fairy tales and often incorporated magical elements into his royal festivals. At the same time, the elite, who attended the **salon**s, social gatherings presided over by **women**, enhanced their conversational arts to include reading tales they composed for their privileged friends. In 1690, a prominent aristocrat, the countess Marie-Catherine d'**Aulnoy**, published the first **literary fairy tale**, "L'île de la félicité" ("The Island of Happiness"), in her novel *L'histoire d'Hypolite, comte de Duglas* (*The Story of Hypolite*). This most prolific of the era's fairy-tale writers was acclaimed by high society and enjoyed fame equal to that of Charles Perrault, who, in the course of the nineteenth century, eclipsed her popularity. Although Perrault, known for his *Histoires ou contes du temps passé* (*Stories or Tales of Times Past*, 1697), is synonymous with the genre for many present-day readers, d'Aulnoy and her women colleagues—Catherine **Bernard**; Marie-Jeanne **Lhéritier** de Villandon; Louise de Bossigny, Comtesse d'**Auneuil**; Charlotte-Rose de Caumont de **La Force**; and Henriette-Julie de Castelnau, Comtesse de **Murat**—monopolized the fairy-tale vogue by composing approximately two-thirds of the narratives published from 1690 to 1705. Moreover, d'Aulnoy and Murat are credited with naming the genre by including the newly coined term *conte de fées* (**fairy tale**) in the titles of their collections, *Les contes des fées* (1697–98) and *Nouveaux contes de fées* (1699) respectively. In addition to Perrault, men who participated in the salon vogue of tale writing include Eustache Le Noble, François Nodot, Jean de Préchac, and Jean, Chevalier de **Mailly**.

Fairy tales written in the last decade of the seventeenth century drew equally upon the interplay of oral and written sources. D'Aulnoy, Lhéritier, Murat, and Perrault cultivated their affiliation with **oral tradition**s through the frontispieces and prefaces introducing their tales. Numerous fairy-tale narratives of the period integrate but alter certain elements of recognizable **folktale**s. However, it was Perrault who artfully aligned his tales with the storytelling of common **folk**. In the frontispiece to his collection, Perrault, depicting a peasant woman recounting tales to children, implies his ideological position in the century's Quarrel of the Ancients and the Moderns. This momentous debate, which opposed Greek and Roman literary models to indigenous French ones, attracted passionate advocates on both sides, whether learned men or elite society figures. Through his stories, Perrault set out to prove the moral superiority of modern French tales over ancient fables, a position he clarified in a manifesto delivered to the French Academy. To this end, he developed the concise, dramatic stories that have seduced readers throughout the centuries.

On the other hand, d'Aulnoy, together with the refined socialites who circulated their tales among themselves, embraced an oral tradition of a different nature, which related to the art of conversation practiced in the salons. D'Aulnoy vaunted her own brand of modernity in **frame narrative**s whose sophisticated exchanges bring to mind not only elite social gatherings but also the framing conversations immortalized by Boccaccio and Marguerite de Navarre. In contrast to Perrault's peasant storyteller, d'Aulnoy's frontispiece to her second collection portrays a bespectacled, literary woman who reads tales to her charges. Despite their differences, d'Aulnoy, Perrault, and their colleagues wrote fairy tales with **moral**s for fashionable adults.

All of those who published narratives during the first phase of fairy-tale production were influenced by the literary tradition, including narratives by the Italians Ludovico Ariosto, Matteo Maria Boiardo, Straparola, and Giambattista **Basile**. In the preface to her 1699 tale collection, Murat acknowledged that women's fairy tales were indebted to Straparola's *Le piacevoli notti* (*The Pleasant Nights*, 1550–53), whose example is likewise apparent in Perrault's "Le maître chat ou le chat botté" ("**Puss in Boots**"). Perrault notwithstanding, aristocratic writers and their affiliates borrowed liberally from the era's best-selling long **novel**s, to attract readers and at the same time establish the modern credentials of the new genre they were creating. Romantic couples who triumph over a series of extraordinary obstacles, a staple of the period's novels, are prevalent in the century's fairy tales. Both d'Aulnoy and Lhéritier were at the forefront of promoting the "modern" fairy-tale aesthetic, for which they and their colleagues were taken to task in a 1699 publication by the learned abbé de Villiers, who dismissed women's tales as poorly written nonsense. For, unlike Perrault, whose classically structured stories led past critics to equate them with "authentic" folktales, d'Aulnoy and her friends advertised their lengthy, descriptive tales of **prince**s and **princess**es as antithetical to those of masses. To be sure, protagonists lacking royal pedigrees, such as folktale-like parvenus who surmount class barriers, are found uniquely in Perrault and Le Noble. D'Aulnoy, who presided over the vogue, positions her regal characters in a luxurious universe forged from folkloric, literary, operatic, and other elements.

Since the evolving society of the times challenged traditional noble privileges, the era's fairy tales perhaps created an imaginary, nostalgic world to compensate for devalued social status. Equally pertinent, numerous women's tales take an ambiguous yet potentially subversive stance both with regard to established authority and to women's roles. For example, women writers often challenged the prevalent heroic model and created instead feminist utopias in which passion and sentiment were highlighted. The ironic d'Aulnoy, probably to avert censors, flatters Louis XIV in her 1698 tale "La biche au bois" ("Doe in the Woods"). However, she indirectly but effectively criticizes him through a myriad array of weak or corrupt **king**s and princes, who pale in comparison to her assertive heroines. Although the century's tales largely extol aristocratic values, most do not unequivocally praise the king. Whether it be Perrault's misalliances between nobles and commoners or d'Aulnoy's trademark metamorphoses that symbolically protest forced **marriage**, disorder and change are rampant in their tales. And, although Perrault's accessible narratives have won critical acclaim throughout the centuries, it was the aesthetic created by d'Aulnoy and her group that inspired parodies by eighteenth-century writers such as Claude-Prosper de Crébillon.

Seventeenth and Eighteenth Centuries: The Second Phase, 1705–1730

Oriental Tales.   While it is true that a variety of tales were published without interruption for a period of roughly 100 years, from 1690 to 1778, Antoine **Galland**'s eighteenth-century translation and adaptation of the *Arabian Nights*—published as *Les mille et une nuits* (*Thousand and One Nights*, 1704–17)—ushers in the second phase of the fairy-tale vogue. This period features the Oriental tale, written by learned men, as opposed to the women socialites who led the first phase. Salons, such as that of the Duchesse du Maine, continued to produce fairy tales, but the focus shifted from collective efforts to independent endeavors. Although the romantic plots prevalent in the preceding century were always in demand, the eighteenth-century **wonder tale** broadened the scope. **Parody** and satire infused a variety of forms with Oriental, moral, licentious, and philosophical themes. In contrast to the first wave of tale writing, linked to the values of rationalism and the integration of literature and society, the second and third phases, influenced by Enlightenment philosophies, challenged those ideals. Plays and novels with Oriental themes, as well as exotic travel literature, were published in the latter half of the seventeenth century. Galland's *Thousand and One Nights* appeared at a time when interest in Oriental cultures gave rise to numerous translations from Turkish, Arabic, and Persian. Galland's Oriental tale is characterized by **frame narrative**s that generate a series of embedded tales, which are, in turn, integrated into the framing story and affect its outcome. Intercalated stories can possess life-saving properties, as seen in the *Arabian Nights'* protagonist **Sheherazade**. Still others illustrate debates on philosophical, moral, or political topics. The reader's involvement is elicited as frame-story characters comment on both the consecutive tales and the art of **storytelling**. Authors of Oriental tales, including Thomas-Simon Gueulette, l'abbé Bignon, Pétis de la Croix, and Jean-François Melon, annotate their texts with learned references and adhere to the narrative style initiated by Galland. In response to the predictable plots and magical elements of the first phase of French tales, this alternative model deemphasized marvelous components to concentrate on dramatic suspense and surprise. The remarkable success of Galland and his colleagues expresses the spirit of openness and the willingness to explore cultural differences associated with the century's philosophers and exemplified in Charles-Louis de Montesquieu's 1721 novel, *Lettres persanes* (*Persian Letters*).

Seventeenth and Eighteenth Centuries: The Third Phase, 1730–1756

Libertine Tales.   The third phase of French tale writing, 1730–56, less homogenous than the preceding two, is defined by three concurrent and intertwining strains: libertine, sentimental, and moral. Anthony **Hamilton**'s fairy tales, written between 1705 and 1715 but published only in 1730, set the stage for increasingly frequent satires of the genre. Hamilton's risqué parodies of fairy-tale conventions at once anticipated the libertine trend and exceeded the discrete mockery and irony notable in prior tales by both d'Aulnoy and Perrault. The libertine or licentious tale was founded by Crébillon's 1734 publication of "L'écumoire ou Tanzaï et Néandarné, histoire japonaise." "L'écumoire" ("The Skimmer") blends traditional fairy-tale elements with those drawn from the period's libertine novels, known for their critique of moral interdictions. In Crébillon's tale, magical elements are restricted to the hero's erotic life, which unfolds comically against the backdrop of one of the major religious and political controversies of the era. The novelty of this and other libertine tales resides in their propensity for evoking contemporary facts in a burlesque light, all the while restricting marvelous adventures to the domain of amorous physiology. In the 1740s and 1750s, writers including Jean Galli de Bibenia, Jacques **Cazotte,** Denis Diderot, Charles Duclos, Charles de la Morlière, Jean-Jacques Rousseau, and Claude-Henri de Voisenon used satire and parody to address various moral and philosophical issues of the Enlightenment. Libertine narratives tend to rob a story of its heroic dimension. Since discrepancies between the fairy-tale past and the real world are suppressed, protagonists, readers, and narrators share the same universe. In this world, obstacles are no longer surmounted and the adventure's conclusion does not bring progress. Moreover, although the reader witnesses a tableau of sexual licentiousness, the perverse practices depicted are not seductive. On the contrary, such tales as Bibiena's "La poupée" ("The Doll," 1747) often question the power of the imagination and force a critical perspective on portrayals of love. Other narratives, including Voisenon's "Le Sultan Misapouf" (1746) and La Morlière's "Angola" (1746), associate unrestrained liberty with compromised sexual identities. After 1734, licentious tales were written exclusively by men.

Sentimental Tales.   The second component of the third phase is the sentimental romance that brought fame to women fairy-tale writers of the preceding century. Although, in the course of the eighteenth century, women wrote far fewer tales than men and no longer formed a coherent group of authors, they continued to distinguish themselves by publishing narratives with novelistic developments. Despite the extravagant adventures that recall those of their celebrated predecessors, writers such as Marie-Antoinette Fagnan, Louise Levesque, Catherine de Lintot, Marie-Madeleine de **Lubert,** and Gabrielle-Suzanne Barbot de **Villeneuve** expanded on the inherited model to produce a distinctively different version. Many of their tales are notable for complicated romantic conflicts that can jeopardize narrative coherence. Neither social prohibitions nor magic spells threaten their protagonists, since the major obstacles in their path involve their own unpredictable affections. Lubert, who defines the tale as an object of pleasure, adopts a hedonist perspective, devoid of both didactic and licentious overtones. In her narrative "Le Prince Glacé et la Princesse Étincelante" ("The Icy Prince and the Fiery Princess," 1743), two parallel and alternating plots reflect the discord between lovers never united, while commenting on the enigma of desire. As seen in Villeneuve's version of "**Beauty and the Beast**" (1740), women's romance tales frequently include strange features that evoke a dreamlike atmosphere. In a preface written for Catherine de Lintot's 1735 story collection *Trois nouveaux contes de fées, avec une préface qui n'est pas moins sérieuse* (*Three New Fairy Tales, with a Preface That Is No Less Serious*), the eighteenth-century novelist abbé Prévost defends this predilection for reverie and sanctions the penchant for the bizarre. Such features foreshadow the fantastic elements in later literature.

Moral Tales. The third distinctive strain in fairy tales of the last phase involves stories with moral or didactic features. With a view toward legitimating the new form they created, writers of the first phase concluded their tales with a moral meant to instruct the reader. Although in stories by d'Aulnoy and Perraut such morals seem merely appended or even mocking, they were considered essential to the genre. Taking their cue from François Fénelon, whose tales were included in *Dialogues des morts* (*Dialogues of the Departed*, 1718), three representatives of the third phase—François Auguste de Moncrif, Anne-Claude de Caylus, and Jeanne-Marie **Leprince de Beaumont**—return to the moral preoccupations of the first phase. Fénelon's **fable**s, intended for the education of his pupil, the Duke of Burgundy, can be considered **anti-fairy tale**s: they warn against unfettered desire and ambition and advocate a static social hierarchy. Both in response to Fénelon and in reaction to the excesses of libertine tales, Caylus published his *Féeries nouvelles* (*New Fairy Tales*) in 1741. In these tales that meld parody with traditional elements of the genre, fairies ensure the education of their charges by inspiring a love of work and a distaste for frivolity. Finally, in 1756, the pioneering Beaumont published her *Magasin des enfants* (translated into English as *The Young Misses' Magazine* in 1759), a primer for her students, which includes her version of the earlier tale by Villeneuve, "Beauty and the Beast." A far cry from royal heroines of the first vogue, Beauty rises early, attends to housekeeping chores, and then relaxes through the solitary activities of reading or playing music. In the *Magazine*, educational conversations between a governess and her young charges replace the salon conversations integral to the first phase. The moral of merit through work and education takes the place of illusion and metamorphosis. The seriousness with which Beaumont's governess guides her charges to extract moral lessons from each story stands in stark contrast to the playful banter characterizing tale commentaries by d'Aulnoy's frame-narrative characters. Beaumont, the first to claim her stories were intended uniquely for **children**, invented a new form of fairy-tale writing that would influence the following century.

Around 1760, the "classical" fairy tale of the seventeenth and eighteenth centuries reached the term of its creative development. From 1785 to 1789, Charles Joseph, Chevalier de **Mayer** edited his forty-one-volume work, *Le cabinet des fées*, which inventoried the marvelous tales of the two centuries, but excluded the libertine narratives.

Nineteenth Century

The pedagogical tradition of tale telling finds a continuator in Sophie, Comtesse de **Ségur**, whose tales first appeared in the children's periodical, *La semaine des enfants* (*Children's Weekly*) and who later published her first collection, entitled *Nouveaux contes de fées* (*New Fairy Tales*, 1857), illustrated by Gustave **Doré**. However, the nineteenth-century French tale truly came into its own by the 1830s and was deeply influenced by the fantastic tales of the German writer E. T. A. **Hoffmann** and by the Romantic movement. To put into question the literary traditions of the Old Regime, French Romantic writers drew from Hoffmann as well as other German Romantics such as Johann Wolfgang von **Goethe** and Heinrich Heine. In fact, Heine had relocated to Paris by 1831 and was a close friend of Gérard de Nerval. Both men were part of the Bohemian circles that included Théophile **Gautier**, Charles **Nodier**, Arsène Houssaye, Alexandre Dumas *père*, and Alfred de Musset, all of whom were interested in things fantastic and Oriental.

Nodier actively engaged in the defense of Hoffmann and the fantastic in an 1830 piece that appeared in the *Revue de Paris* entitled "La littérature fantastique en France" ("Fantastic Literature in France"). Gautier also wrote pieces in defense of Hoffmann, including the 1836 article that appeared in the *Chronique de Paris* entitled "Contes d'Hoffmann" ("Tales of Hoffmann"). In this piece, Gautier characterizes the Hoffmannesque fantastic in terms of "occult sympathies and antipathies, singular follies, visions, magnetism, mysterious, and wicked influences of an evil principle that he only designates vaguely, such are the supernatural or extraordinary elements that Hoffmann regularly employs." Hoffmann became the poster boy for the Parisian literary vanguard.

Such notions of the fantastic defined the literary tale of the period. Indeed, Nodier's most famous piece, *La fée aux miettes* (*The Crumb Fairy*, 1832) centers on madness, a state that allows one to go beyond the realm of normality to access another world. Gautier's fantastic tales certainly drew on the intrusion of the extraordinary into the everyday, particularly evident in "La cafetière" ("The Coffeepot," 1831). In "La main enchantée" ("The Enchanted Hand"), first published in September 1832 in *Le cabinet de lecture* and later appearing in *Contes et facéties* (*Tales and Quips*, 1853), Nerval relates a fantastic story centering on the occult and drawing from a tragic story by the sixteenth-century writer François de Belleforest. Based on Hoffmann's text, Dumas *père* wrote his own version of the *Histoire d'un casse-noisette* (*Story of a Nutcracker*, 1844), and it was Dumas's version that Pyotr Il'ich **Tchaikovsky** later set to music. Houssaye drew from both the classic and the Oriental tale to compose *La pantoufle de Cendrillon* (*Cinderella's Slipper*, 1851) and *Les mille et une nuits parisiennes* (*A Thousand and One Parisian Nights*, 1876). Also influenced by Hoffmann, George **Sand** composed fantastic tales situated in pastoral settings for her grandchildren.

While the first group of fantastic-tale writers can be grouped around the Romantics of 1830, the second generation came together in the Parnassian movement, itself growing out of Gautier's notion of art for art's sake. Later many of these same writers moved into the symbolist camp. This group included Catulle Mendès, son-in-law of Gautier; Théodore de Banville; Charles Marie René Leconte de Lisle; Paul Verlaine; and Anatole France. Like their predecessors, the Parnassian writers used the fantastic tale to criticize bourgeois values, as in the case of Banville's *Contes féeriques* (*Fairy Tales*, 1882). Anatole France composed a defense of the fairy tale in "Dialogue sur les contes de fées" ("Dialogue on Fairy Tales"), which appeared in *Le livre de mon ami* (*The Book of My Friend*, 1885), in which he remarks: "These tales are absurd. If they weren't absurd, they wouldn't be charming." In 1886, Mendès published *Les oiseaux bleus* (*The Blue Birds*), containing several tales inspired by the classic tradition. In "Le miroir" ("The Mirror"), an extraordinarily ugly **queen** removes all the **mirror**s in the kingdom. "Les mots perdus" ("The Lost Words") concerns a kingdom in which the words "I love you" have been removed from memory by a cruel fairy, "pretty as flowers, mean as the serpents that hide beneath them." In "Les trois bonnes fées" ("The Three Good Fairies"), the title characters manage to carry on their quest to lift the human race out of its misery despite the attempts of an evil enchanter to take away their powers. Anatole France likewise plays with the traditional plot of classic tales in "Les sept femmes de Barbe bleue" ("The Seven Wives of Bluebeard," 1909), in which the narrator questions the veracity of the legend, and suggests that, like Macbeth, **Bluebeard** is the victim of a slanderous history.

The younger generation who haunted the circles of Mendès and Banville included Maurice **Maeterlinck** and Marcel Schwob, who were part of the symbolist movement. Schwob, whose father knew Gautier and Banville, published *Le roi au masque d'or* (1892), a collection of symbolist tales including "Le pays bleu" ("The Blue Country"), which he dedicated to his friend, Oscar **Wilde**. A highly successful playwright, Maeterlinck published several symbolist plays with fairy-tale **motif**s, including *Pelléas et Mélisande* (1892), which Claude Debussy adapted to **opera** in 1902; and *Ariane et Barbe-bleue* (1901), also adapted to opera by Paul Dukas in 1907. The century's fascination with the Orient culminated in Joseph Charles **Mardrus**'s celebrated translation of *Les milles et une nuits* (*A Thousand and One Nights*, 1899–1904), each volume of which was dedicated to writers of his circle, including Stéphane Mallarmé, Schwob, Maeterlinck, France, and André Gide. In this Orientalist vein, Maurice Ravel produced a *Sheherazade* overture (1898) and later set to music three Sheherazade poems (1904) that were part of a collection of 100 poems by symbolist poet Léon Leclère (aka Tristan Klingsor); the collection itself drew inspiration from Nikolai **Rimsky-Korsakov**'s *Sheherazade* (1888). Ravel also created five piano duets for children entitled *Ma mère l'oye* (**Mother Goose**, 1908–10) based on tales by Perrault, d'Aulnoy, and Beaumont.

Although the literary tale of the nineteenth century was dominated by the influence of Hoffmann and the avant-garde, folkloric tendencies also existed. Tales by Jacob and Wilhelm **Grimm** were being translated into French by the 1830s. However, in France, **folklore** took on regionalist, rather than nationalist, dimensions. From 1835 to 1837, Emile Souvestre published his four-volume *Derniers Bretons* (*The Last Bretons*). Focusing on his native Provence, Alphonse **Daudet** wrote *Lettres de mon moulin* (*Letters from My Mill*, 1866), while Charles **Deulin** put together collections based on folklore from northern France. Emmanuel Cosquin, a folklorist from Lorraine best known for his *Contes populaires de Lorraine* (*Popular Tales of Lorraine*, 1860), was the only French folklorist known to have had any direct correspondence with the Grimms. Generally speaking, these regionalist collections emerged within a political climate in which the centrality of Paris and the rise of industrialization threatened the traditional culture of the provinces. Writers of such collections often sought to reassert local identities against the homogenizing efforts of the centralized state.

The history of the fairy tale in nineteenth-century France would not be complete without mentioning the incredible proliferation of *féeries*, a theatrical genre born after the French

Revolution aimed at lower-class audiences. These popular plays drew from melodrama, with marvelous elements and fairy-tale plots. At the Théâtre de la Gaîté, the Théâtre des Variétés, or the Théâtre du Vaudeville, one could see Jean-Guillaume Cuvelier de Trie's *Le chat botté, ou les vingt-quatre heures d'Arlequin* (*Puss-in-Boots, or the Twenty-four Hours of Arlequin*, 1802) or his version of d'Aulnoy's *Le nain jaune, ou la fée du désert* (*The Yellow Dwarf, or the Fairy of the Desert*, 1804). Both separately and in collaboration, Antoine Jean-Baptiste Simonnin and Brazier produced theatrical versions of *La belle aux cheveux d'or* (*Beauty with the Golden **Hair***, 1806), *Gracieuse et Percinet* (1806), *Riquet à la houppe* (*Riquet with the Tuft*, 1811), and *Le petit chaperon rouge* (***Little Red Riding Hood***, 1818). Among the most famous producers of *féeries* were the Cogniard brothers, Hippolyte and Théodore, who adapted to the popular stage everything from *La biche au bois* (*The Deer in the Woods*, 1845) and *La chatte blanche* (*The White **Cat***, 1852) to ***Ali Baba*** *et les quarante voleurs* (*Ali Baba and the Forty **Thieves***, 1853). As suggested by this brief overview, the mainstay of *féerie* plots came from Perrault, d'Aulnoy, and the **Arabian Nights**. A practically unexplored terrain in fairy-tale studies, the *féerie* certainly merits further scholarly attention.

Twentieth Century

The new technology of **film** took the fairy tale to a new level. Considered to be the founding father of special effects, Georges **Méliès** drew heavily from the theatrical *féerie* and from the Cogniard brothers in particular to produce fairy films such as *Barbe-bleue* (*Bluebeard*, 1901), *Le royaume des fées* (*The Kingdom of the Fairies*, 1903), and *Le palais des mille et une nuits* (*The Palace of the Arabian Nights*, 1905). Large-scale producers for an international market, the Pathé Brothers' firm released a plethora of fairy films whose creators likewise drew from the *féerie* tradition. These include *La belle et la bête* (*Beauty and the Beast*, 1899); *La belle au bois dormant* (*Sleeping Beauty*, 1902); *Le chat botté* (*Puss in Boots*, 1903); *Peau d'âne* (*Donkey Skin*, 1904); *Cendrillon, ou la pantoufle merveilleuse* (*Cinderella, or the Marvelous Slipper*, 1907); *Le petit chaperon rouge* (*Little Red Riding Hood*, 1907); *Finette, ou l'adroite princesse* (*Finette, or the Clever Princess*, 1908); *Blanche neige* (***Snow White***, 1909); and *Griselidis* (1912).

Several celebrated directors also tried their hands at fairy films. Jean Renoir, for instance, directed his wife Catherine Hessling in the **silent film** *La petite marchande d'allumettes* (*The Little Match Girl*, 1928), an adaptation of the Hans Christian **Andersen** tale. A year later, Renoir and Hessling starred together in the Brazilian-born director Alberto Cavalcanti's *Le petit chaperon rouge* (*Little Red Riding Hood*, 1929). Perhaps the most famous among fairy-tale films is Jean Cocteau's ***La Belle et la Bête*** (*Beauty and the Beast*, 1946), starring Jean Marais, who later plays the incestuous father in Jacques Demy's classic ***Peau d'âne*** (*Donkey Skin*, 1970), also starring Catherine Deneuve. In 1950, the director André Raoul added jewels to Little Red Riding Hood's basket in *Une fille à croquer* (*A Girl Good Enough To Eat*), starring Serge Reggiani and Gaby Morlay. One of the most sought-after directors under the Nazi Occupation, Christian-Jaque produced one of the first French color films, *Barbe bleue* (*Bluebeard*, 1951), starring Pierre Brasseur and Cécile Aubry. The story of **Tom Thumb** made it to the screen in 1972 with *Le petit poucet*, directed by Michel Boisrond, who had previously worked under Cocteau and René Clair. Director of the critically acclaimed *La môme* (aka *La vie en rose*, 2007), Olivier Dahan also released a version of *Le petit poucet* (2001) set in a war-stricken region, with Catherine Deneuve returning to fairy-tale film in her appearance as the queen.

Despite the influence of the new technology of film on the genre of the fairy tale, the tradition of adapting and **collecting** folk tales did not die out and continued to play a role in the affirmation of regional identities. Two of the most important French folklorists, Paul **Delarue** and Marie-Louise **Tenèze**, collaborated on the most extensive catalogue of French and francophone tales to date: *Le conte populaire français: Catalogue raisonné des versions de France et des pays de langue française d'outre-mer* (*The French Folktale: Structured Catalog of Versions from France and French-Language Countries Overseas*, 4 vols., 1957–2000). Fascinated by the folklore of his native Auvergne, Henri **Pourrat** compiled the thirteen-volume *Le trésor des contes* (*The Treasury of Tales*, 1948–62). Best known for *Le cheval d'orgueil* (*The Horse of Pride*, 1975), the Breton writer Pierre-Jakez Hélias published several collections of tales, including *Contes bretons du pays bigouden* (*Breton Tales from Bigouden*, 1967), *Contes bretons de la Chantepleure* (*Breton Tales from Chantepleure*, 1971), and *Contes du vrai et du semblant* (*Tales of Truth and Appearance*, 1984).

Writers and folklorists from francophone countries also compiled important collections of folktales. The Haitian ethnologist, historian, and diplomat Jean Price-Mars wrote about his country's folk traditions, including voodoo. Among the founding members of the négritude movement, the Senegalese poet and diplomat Birago **Diop** collected traditional Wolof tales, which appeared in *Les contes d'Amadou Koumba* (*The Tales of Amadou Koumba*, 1947) and *Les nouveaux contes d'Amadou Koumba* (*The New Tales of Amadou Koumba*, 1958). The Ivorian writer Bernard Binlin **Dadié**, active in the anticolonial movement, also published story collections, the most famous being *Légendes africaines* (*African Legends*, 1954) and *Le pagne noir: Contes africains* (1955; translated as *The Black Cloth: A Collection of African Folktales*, 1987). Inspired by the rich oral tradition of Gaspésie, the Québécois playwright and novelist Jacques Ferron composed *Contes du pays incertain* (*Tales of an Uncertain Land*, 1962) and *Contes anglais et autres* (*English and Other Tales*, 1964). Most recently, the Martinican writer Patrick **Chamoiseau**, active in the créolité movement, published *Au temps de l'antan: contes martiniquais* (*Creole Folktales*, 1988). As with the French regionalist movements, many francophone writers draw from folklore to reassert the singularity of their cultures against the hegemonic forces of the metropole, be that France or Anglophone Canada.

Like his symbolist predecessors, the poet Guillaume Apollinaire demonstrated interest in the marvelous. His final work, "La suite de Cendrillon, ou le rat et les six lézards" ("Cinderella Continued, or the Rat and the Six Lizards," 1919), is a humorous sequel that follows the adventures of the coachman-rat and includes **cross-dressing** and wordplays. In 1930, Jean Giraudoux created *Ondine*, a play based on the tale "Undine" (1811) by German Romantic writer Friedrich de la Motte **Fouqué**. One of the most-read works of French literature, Antoine de Saint-Exupéry's *Le petit prince* (*The Little Prince*, 1943), reads like a marvelous philosophical tale and appeals to children and adults alike.

Several twentieth-century authors turn the tale tradition on its head. Between 1934 and 1946, the novelist Marcel Aymé published a series of animal tales eventually published together in *Les contes du chat perché* (*The Wonderful Farm*, 1969), which includes a revision of "Little Red Riding Hood" in which the **wolf** is rehabilitated. A prolific author of tales, Pierre **Gripari** likewise plays on classical fairy-tale conventions yet resists political correctness. Philippe **Dumas**'s best-known collection of tales, *Contes à l'envers* (*Upside Down*

Tales, 1977), contains a version of "Little Red Riding Hood" situated in Paris and, as the title suggests, turns the genre on its head. The celebrated novelist Michel **Tournier** draws from the fairy-tale genre to discuss the darker side of life and to question authoritarianism. In a similar vein, Pierrette Fleutiaux, who won the Prix Goncourt for her collection of tales inspired by Perrault and entitled *Métamorphoses de la reine* (*Metamorphoses of the Queen*, 1985), uses the genre to subvert **gender** norms in part by giving secondary characters a voice. For instance, "La femme de l'ogre" ("The **Ogre**'s Wife"), which opens the collections, begins with: "The ogre's wife didn't like to cook flesh, but she didn't know it. When the odor filled the house and there was no more fresh air to breathe, she became agitated." While Gripari and Dumas focus on the more parodical uses of the genre, Tournier and Fleutiaux draw on its dark side.

The tradition of graphic art (the *bande dessinée* or BD in French) has enjoyed great popularity in France, and some of its most talented artists have been inspired by the fairy-tale genre. One of the most celebrated French "BDists," Marcel Gotlib, began a five-volume series in 1968 entitled *Rubrique-à-brac* in which he parodies **animal tale**s, fairy tales, and detective stories. F'Murr (birth name Richard Peyzaret), best-known for his series *Le génie des alpages* (*The Genius of the Mountain Pastures*), produced a superb version of "Little Red Riding Hood" in 1974 entitled *Au loup!* (*Watch out for the Wolf!*). ***See also*** Erotic Tales; Feminism; Feminist Tales; French Canadian Tales; Négritude, Créolité, and Folktale.

Further Readings: Barchilon, Jacques. *Le conte merveilleux français de 1690 à 1790: Cent ans de féerie et de poésie ignorées de l'histoire littéraire.* Paris: Champion, 1975; Delarue, Paul. *The Borzoi Book of French Folk Tales.* Translated by Austin E. Fife. New York: Knopf, 1956; Duggan, Anne E., *Salonnières, Fairies, and Furies.* Newark: Delaware University Press, 2005; Hannon, Patricia. *Fabulous Identities: Women's Fairy Tales in Seventeenth-Century France.* Amsterdam: Rodopi, 1998; Hopkin, David. "Identity in a Divided Province: The Folklorists of Lorraine, 1860–1960." *French Historical Studies* 23 (2000): 639–82; Jomand-Baudry, Régine, and Jean-François Perrin, eds. *Le Conte merveilleux au XVIIIe siècle: Une poétique expérimentale.* Paris: Éditions Kimé, 2002; Perrin, Jean-François. "L'invention d'un genre littéraire au XVIIIe siècle: Le conte oriental." *Féeries* 2 (2004–05): 9–27; Ransom, Amy J. *The Feminine as Fantastic in the* Conte Fantastique: *Visions of the Other.* New York: Peter Lang, 1995; Raynard, Sophie. *La seconde préciosité: Floraison des conteuses de 1690 à 1756.* Tubingen: Narr, 2002; Robert, Raymonde. *Le conte de fées littéraire en France de la fin du XVIIe à la fin du XVIIIe siècle.* Paris: Champion, 2002; Seifert, Lewis C. *Fairy Tales, Sexuality, and Gender in France, 1690–1715: Nostalgic Utopias.* Cambridge: Cambridge University Press, 1996; Sermain, Jean-Paul. *Le conte de fées du classicisme aux lumières.* Paris: Desjonquères, 2005; Tucker, Holly. *Pregnant Fictions: Childbirth and the Fairy Tale in Early-Modern France.* Detroit: Wayne State University Press, 2003; Zipes, Jack, ed. *Beauties, Beasts, and Enchantments*: *Classic French Fairy Tales.* New York: New American Library, 1989.

Patricia Hannon and Anne E. Duggan

Freud, Sigmund (1856–1938)

As the founder of psychoanalysis, Sigmund Freud developed important theories that have been used to explain the symbolism and psychological significance of folktales and fairy tales. Born in Vienna, Freud's interest in folklore and his development of psychoanalytical concepts were mutually influential. One of Freud's main discoveries was the existence of infantile **sexuality**, which led to his formulation of the Oedipus complex—the notion that all boys desire to marry their mothers and kill their fathers. This idea itself referred to an ancient Greek version of the folktale typified in ATU 931, Oedipus. Freud's concept of the unconscious is also central to his contribution to folklore and fairy-tale studies. Since folktales and fairy tales—like **folklore** in general—incorporate many fantastic elements, they can serve as wish fulfillment for individuals and communities, perhaps even providing a safe outlet for taboo desires. The desire for wealth, power, or **sex** that is evident in folktales and fairy tales may be expressed through symbols that are intelligible for their references to sexual stages of development.

Freud's own involvement with actual fairy-tale material was limited to a few essays since he tended to focus on other narrative forms such as jokes. However, he produced several notable essays that demonstrate the relationship he perceived between psychoanalysis and fairy tales. One essay, "Märchenstoffe in Träumen" ("The Occurrence in Dreams of Material from Fairy Tales," 1913), utilizes fairy-tale motifs in the interpretation of clients' dreams. Freud also makes the intriguing suggestion that investigat-

Sigmund Freud. [Library of Congress]

ing how dreamers use fairy tales may shed light on the interpretation of fairy tales. In a paper co-written with David Ernst Oppenheim, titled "Träume im Folklore" ("Dreams in Folklore," 1911), Freud analyzed dreams occurring within folktales and found that their symbolism corresponded to his own ideas about human sexuality and sexual development. One such symbol was deciphered through the substitution of a ring for female genitalia.

Freud's followers have developed his theories in various directions, which has multiplied the ways in which psychoanalytic theory can be applied to fairy tales. Carl Gustav **Jung**, one of Freud's most influential disciples, is also known for his attention to fairy tales, although he rejected many of Freud's basic theories in favor of his own notion of universal **archetype**s. Freud's original ideas have been more faithfully applied by individuals such as psychologist Bruno **Bettelheim** and folklorist Alan **Dundes**, whose works make use of concepts such as the Oedipus complex and, in Bettelheim's case, penis envy. Bettelheim and Dundes also utilized Freud's notion of projection, which is valuable because it does not rely on sexist and dated ideas such as penis envy. *See also* Incest; Jest and Joke; Psychological Approaches; Róheim, Géza; Trauma and Therapy.

Further Readings: Betteleheim, Bruno. *The Uses of Enchantment: The Meaning and Importance of Fairy Tales.* New York: Knopf, 1976; Dundes, Alan. "The Psychoanalytic Study of the Grimms' Tales: 'The Maiden without Hands' (AT 706)." *Folklore Matters.* Knoxville: University of Tennessee Press, 1989. 112–50; Freud, Sigmund. "The Occurrence in Dreams of Material from Fairy Tales." *The Standard Edition of the Complete Psychological Works of Sigmund Freud.* Volume 12. London: Hogarth Press, 1958. 279–87; ———. "Symbolism in Dreams." *International Folkloristics: Classic Contributions by the Founders of Folklore.* Edited by Alan Dundes. Lanham, MD: Rowman & Littlefield Publishers, 1999. 177–95.

Jeana Jorgensen

Frobenius, Leo (1873–1938)

Leo Frobenius was a German ethnologist who edited a large collection of African folktales. With an entirely autodidactic background, he originated the cultural-historical concept of

Kulturkreise (cultural circles) and the theory of cultural morphology, which is based on comparing items of material and immaterial culture to understand regional cultures as well as universal culture. One of his key terms was *Paideuma*, the "cultural soul" of the peoples of the world, which could be interpreted from the expressive styles of the objects being studied.

Frobenius's work consists of more than 270 articles and books and combines precise ethnographical descriptions and illustrations, travel experiences, folktale texts, and sketch maps of tale **motif**s, all written in an idiosyncratic cultural-philosophical diction. His theory of narrative motif research and stylistic analysis is largely laid down in his books *Vom Kulturreich des Festlandes* (*On the Continental Empire of Culture*, 1923) and *Kulturgeschichte Afrikas* (*Africa's Culture History*, 1933). Through this work, Frobenius rehabilitated Africa as a continent having its own true history and exerted great impact upon the négritude movement.

After having started as a private archivist and freelance ethnologist and writer Frobenius became director of the municipal Museum of Ethnology of Frankfurt in 1932 and honorary professor of the University of Frankfurt in 1934. With his excellent relations to Emperor Wilhelm II, Frobenius organized twelve larger expeditions to major regions of Africa in between 1904 and 1932. On these expeditions, he collected material artifacts, **oral tradition**s, and rock-art images. The bulk of his folktale collection appeared in the series *Atlantis: Volksmärchen und Volksdichtungen Afrikas* (*Atlantis: Folktales and Folk Literature of Africa*), which came out in twelve volumes from 1921 to 1928 and which documents more than 620 tales, **fable**s, **legend**s, "chapters" of **epic**s, and other narrative genres from the Maghreb, Sahel, western and central Sudan, Kordofan, the Guinea Coast, Kongo-Kasai, and Zimbabwe. This corpus contains tales of animal and human characters, of heroes and hunters, of **trickster**s and demons, as well as erotic miniatures, creation **myth**s, and griot traditions. Scholars criticize Frobenius for his indirect method of recording texts by using interpreters and languages of wider communication instead of the specific vernaculars, which further detracts from the storytellers' authenticity through the subsequent **translation** into German. Nevertheless, specific narrative styles can be distinguished. A recent trend in contemporary African scholarship is to retranslate the volumes of the francophone countries into French since many of Frobenius's recordings retain unique significance and high value for contemporary societies.

A small volume of twenty-nine tales translated into English was published by Frobenius and Douglas Fox in 1937 under the title *African Genesis*. The *Atlantis* volumes have been integrated into the general **tale type** and motif indexes of Antti **Aarne** and Stith **Thompson**. The Frobenius-Institute at the University of Frankfurt houses the researcher's unpublished diaries and field notes. A project currently underway will make some 430 tales from Frobenius' southern African recordings available in English in the form of a tale-type, motif, and keyword index. *See also* African Tales; Colonialism; Négritude, Créolité, and Folktale.

Further Readings: Frobenius-Institute. http://www.frobenius-institut.de/index_en.htm; Niggemeyer, Hermann. "Das wissenschaftliche Schrifttum von Leo Frobenius." [Bibliography.] *Paideuma* 4 (1950): 377–418.

Thomas Geider

Frog King

In part because it is the first fairy tale in the ***Kinder- und Hausmärchen*** (*Children's and Household Tales*, 1812–15) by the Brothers Grimm, "The Frog King" belongs to one of the most popular **tale type**s (ATU 440, The Frog King or Iron Henry), whether it occurs as a

didactic tale for children or as an erotic tale for adults. As a tale of a **princess** who promises a frog that he may eat and sleep with her if he retrieves a golden ball from a well, it is a narrative that serves as a warning that promises must be kept no matter how repulsive their actual execution might be. In the German variant, the **king**'s daughter throws the ugly frog against the wall, thus breaking the spell of a **witch** who had previously changed a handsome **prince** into the frog. In most other versions, the princess actually kisses the frog, which changes into a prince. The connection of this tale to the **Beauty and the Beast** cycle of folk narratives is much more prevalent here, since it obviously takes courage and self-control for the princess to kiss the beastly frog. It was Wilhelm **Grimm** who intentionally deemphasized the sexual allusions of this fairy tale in his later editions of the *Children's and Household Tales,* where he modified the tale so that the German variant could serve as a moralistic story for children.

One interesting and often overlooked aspect of the Grimms' tale is signaled by the two-part title, "The Frog King or Iron Henry." Following the **transformation** of the frog into a prince and his **marriage** to the princess, there is yet another, concluding episode that is less well known and less frequently interpreted. During the royal couple's return to the young man's kingdom, they hear a loud noise three times. The source is the prince's faithful servant Henry, who, brokenhearted at the earlier spell that had been cast on the prince, had had iron bands forged around his heart. Once the prince is released from the spell, Henry is full of joy, causing the iron bands around his heart to snap. Coming as it does at the very end of the story, this episode seems to place considerable value on the strong bond between the servant and the prince. Nonetheless, it is the earlier "happy ending," the transformation and the resulting marriage of the prince and princess that has endured in popular consciousness.

The **motif** of a prince who is transformed into a frog by a spell has its origins in the Middle Ages, with the actual fairy tale itself having been collected by Wilhelm Grimm, most likely from Dortchen Wild. Although the story's major intent might well be didactic and not sexual, it should be noted that the princess clearly goes through a maturation process. She not only comprehends that promises must be kept but also realizes that she must take matters into her own hands. It is this process of liberation and accepting responsibility for one's own life that is stressed by psychologists like Bruno **Bettelheim** in their developmental interpretations of this fairy tale. Of course, the Anglo-American variants in which the frog's transformation is effected by a kiss expand this explanation considerably by implying a sexual development as well. The fact that the sexual component is presented rather indirectly is yet another indication of the symbolic meaning of fairy tales in particular and **folklore** as a process of indirection in general.

The erotic implications of "The Frog King" have led to numerous reinterpretations in **poetry** and prose by literary authors and in humorous, ironical, or satirical **cartoons and comics**. Anne **Sexton**'s long poem "The Frog Prince" (1971) is a grotesque sexual interpretation of the tale with such lines as "Frog is my father's genitals." There are also less-overt sexual poems by Sara Henderson **Hay**, Robert Graves, Hyacinthe Hill, Susan Mitchell, Phyllis Thompson, Elizabeth Brewster, Robert Pack, and Galway Kinnell, indicating that many well-known modern poets delight in poetic reworkings and interpretations of "The Frog King." Their innovative poetic reactions to the traditional fairy tale concern questions about love, marriage, identity, happiness, and basic human communication. Many of these poems deromanticize the happy ending of the fairy tale, sometimes by describing what life is like after the princess and the frog-turned-prince have married.

The popularity of this fairy tale can also be seen by its frequent appearance in the mass media and its commercial exploitation. In fact, the kiss scene has been summarized into the internationally disseminated proverb, "You have to kiss a lot of toads (frogs), before you meet your handsome prince." This proverbial slogan about the frustrations of modern relationships can be found on greeting cards, bathroom walls, T-shirts, bumper stickers, and posters. Artists and **advertising** agencies have also been inspired by the kissing scene to create effective cartoons, comic strips, caricatures, and advertisements, where the topics range from **politics**, economics, social issues to human relations, love, and, above all, **sex**. It is, of course, exactly the possibility of a sexual interpretation of this fairy tale, which has made it so popular in the adult world, notably in such magazines as *Playboy* and *Penthouse*, and in adult films of erotica. A few captions from cartoons can illustrate what is at stake in these visual representations of the kissing motif: "Perhaps you could break the spell if you'd kiss me somewhere other than the mouth"; "Marriage! Good heavens woman! Royalty marrying a bird who goes round kissing frogs?"; "I started out looking for a prince, but now I just like to kiss frogs"; "Frankly, now that I've found out the size of my kingdom's national debt, I'd rather remain a frog"; and "Kiss me–I'm really a handsome GOP Tax Bill." Clearly, there are unlimited verbal and visual possibilities of interpreting the kiss between something positive and negative, indicating the universal appeal of just this one fairy-tale motif.

In any case, the wishful thinking of the original fairy tale is placed in juxtaposition to the realities of life in these poetic or prosaic reactions. For the most part, these reinterpretations of the traditional "The Frog King" are pessimistic reactions to the social and psychological frustrations of people whose dreams and wishes clash with everyday reality. Yet, the fact that this fairy tale about promises and love continues to be dealt with in literature and the mass media is a clear indication that people still hope for the transforming kiss that will lead to a life of happiness. *See also* Erotic Tales; Proverbs.

Further Readings: Bettelheim, Bruno. *The Uses of Enchantment: The Meaning and Importance of Fairy Tales.* New York: Alfred A. Knopf, 1976; Blair, Walter. "The Funny Fondled Fairytale Frog." *Studies in American Humor* 1 (1982): 17–23; Ellis, John M. *One Fairy Story Too Many: The Brothers Grimm and Their Tales.* Chicago: University of Chicago Press, 1983. 113–34; Mieder, Wolfgang, ed. *Disenchantments: An Anthology of Modern Fairy Tale Poetry.* Hanover, NH: University Press of New England, 1985; ———. "Modern Anglo-American Variants of The Frog Prince (AT 440)." *New York Folklore* 6 (1980): 111–35; ———. *Tradition and Innovation in Folk Literature.* Hanover, NH: University Press of New England, 1987. 13–22; Röhrich, Lutz. "Der Froschkönig und seine Wandlungen." *Fabula* 20 (1979): 170–192; ———. *Wage es, den Frosch zu küssen! Das Grimmsche Märchen Nummer Eins in seinen Wandlungen.* Köln: Eugen Diederichs, 1987.

Wolfgang Mieder

Frog Prince. *See* Frog King.

Frost, Gregory (1951–)

Philadelphia author Gregory Frost has been publishing works grounded in **myth** and fairy tales for more than two decades. Alongside numerous short stories—"The Root of the Matter" (1993), a frequently taught retelling of the tale of Rapunzel that explores the abusive nature of the relationship between the **witch** and her ward that is perhaps the most influential of his fairy-tale retellings—he has written five **novel**s. His first **fantasy** novel, *Lyrec* (1984), is a fantasy with elements of science fiction; his next two, *Tain* (1986) and

Remscela (1988), retell the myths of Cuchulain. Frost produced a dystopian science fiction novel set in an alternate Philadelphia, *The Pure Cold Light* (1993) before returning to the material of the fairy tale in *Fitcher's Brides* (2002), the most recent volume in Terri **Windling**'s Fairy Tale series.

Fitcher's Brides is Frost's reimagining of a variant of the **tale type** of "**Bluebeard**," set in a utopian commune in upstate New York in 1843. His Bluebeard, a charismatic preacher by the name of Elias Fitcher, believes that the world is soon to end, and he does not wish to face the afterworld alone: to that end, he weds repeatedly, until each new bride disappoints him. However, the third of the Charter sisters succeeds in defeating his aims and revealing him to his believers as the person he truly is. Frost managed the Sycamore Hill Writing Workshop with Judith Berman and Richard Butner until 2000.

Further Reading: Swanwick, Michael. "Singular Interviews: Gregory Frost." *New York Review of Science Fiction* 17.11 (2005): 19.

Helen Pilinovsky

Froud, Brian (1947–)

An English illustrator, Brian Froud has frequently drawn on fairy tales for his artistic projects. He is well known for works that recontextualize Victorian- and Edwardian-era beliefs about the realm of **faerie and fairy lore**. Froud has collaborated with other creative individuals such as Jim **Henson** and produced a number of illustrated books that have fairies as their subject.

Although Froud has provided illustrations for books inspired by fairy tales, such as Mary Norton's *Are All the Giants Dead?* (1975), his most prominent works based on fairies are his paintings that reflect folk beliefs about fairies. For his three books *Fairies* (1978), *Good Faeries, Bad Faeries* (1998), and *Goblins!* (2004), Froud has created paintings that draw on both folk beliefs and images from popular media. Under the fictional name Lady Cottington, Froud has also released several humorous art books that play with the Cottingley fairy phenomenon (a hoax perpetrated in 1917 by two young girls who claimed to have taken photographs of actual fairies) and the Victorian hobby of flower pressing. These Lady Cottington books include illustrations of fairies pressed inside the pages of books like flowers.

Froud has participated in the creation of two divination tools inspired by folktale, *The Faerie's Oracle* (2000) with Jessica Macbeth and *The Runes of Elfland* (2003) with Ari Berk. *The Faerie's Oracle* includes, for example, a card entitled "Faery Godmother," based on the character from some versions of "**Cinderella**." The accompanying book to *The Runes of Elfland* is written in a folktale style, though it is primarily an original work. Both of these works demonstrate Froud's use of fairy tales as inspiration. ***See also*** Fairy, Fairies; Jones, Terry; Illustration.
Further Reading: *World of Froud.* http://www.worldoffroud.com/index.html.

B. Grantham Aldred

Function

The concept of "function," introduced by Vladimir **Propp** in 1928 in his *Morfologiya skazki* (*Morphology of the Folktale*), is the basic underlying concept in the morphological study of the folktale, which was based on linguistic-style analysis of fairy tales. Put simply, a function is one of a series of elements from which the action of a folktale is constructed. The sequential occurrence of each function advances the action of the folktale.

The concept of function comes initially from the examination of Russian fairy tales, specifically tales collected in Russia categorized in Antti **Aarne**'s *Verzeichnis der Märchentypen* (*Index of the Types of the Folktale*, 1910) between **tale type**s numbered 300 and 749. Through comparative study, Propp identified thirty-one discrete functions, beginning with "absentation" and ending with "wedding."

According to Propp, functions have three characteristics important to their study. First, functions are "stable, constant elements" independent of the specific details of the tale. In other words, events in a narrative can be examined based not on the specific narrative details of the event but on the event's place in the structure of the narrative. Second, the number of possible functions in the Russian fairy tale is limited. Propp identifies thirty-one possible functions in the Russian fairy tale. Third, the sequence of functions is always identical. Thus, "absentation" will always occur before "lack," which will always occur before "pursuit," which will always occur before "wedding." *See also* Linguistic Approaches; Motif; Motifeme; Russian Tales; Structuralism.

Further Reading: Propp, Vladimir. *Morphology of the Folktale.* Translated by Laurence Scott. Revised and edited by Louis A. Wagner. 2nd edition. 1968. Austin: University of Texas Press, 1996.

B. Grantham Aldred